"Alex Mekonnen has written a wide-ranging and ambitious survey of African realities, past and present. While frankly admitting the dangers and difficulties the continent faces, he also offers hope in the form of applying the Jewish and Christian prophetic tradition to a region that seems so ideally suited for it. A daring exploration of the idea of the Kingdom of God in the contemporary world."

—**Philip Jenkins**
Distinguished Professor of History, Institute for Studies of Religion, Baylor University

"Building on an African centrist appreciation of the historical perspectives, this study successfully analyzes Africa/West relations from every perspective. Readers will learn much about advanced civilizations in Africa and the tragedies of internal and external (no longer only Western, but now predominantly from China) forces that repeatedly have brought the continent's inhabitants unimaginable suffering. Above all, I appreciate the author's awareness that any solution is to be found in the realm of the human heart and the question of faith. Read this work to understand the geopolitics of the modern world and the critical role of Christianity."

—**Rick Hess**
Professor of Old Testament, Denver Seminary

"Alemayehu Mekonnen's outstanding book on Africa is informative, serious, convicting, and thought-provoking for anyone who cares about humanity. For centuries, psychological, economic, social, and cultural injustices have been heaped on Africans by internal and external powers. Mekonnen shows how, in the midst of chaos and turmoil, Africans have successfully contributed major innovations in the fields of economy, science, medicine, philosophy, architecture, mathematics, technology, literature, the arts, and theology. With sincere optimism, Mekonnen points to the real answer for Africans—"the crucified Christ [who] has power to transform despair into triumph." A must-read by all serious Christians."

—**Hélène Dallaire**
Professor of Old Testament, Denver Seminary

"Passionate and deeply personal, *The West and China in Africa* is a detailed treatise on Africa's sociopolitical and economic condition. Mekonnen works to dispel Western stereotypes, both secular and religious, of the continent. His is not the voice of victimization, as Mekonnen also points to African complicity in the centuries of sinful abuse. Succumbing neither to cynicism nor despair, he argues that any hope of justice for Africa's long-suffering peoples must be grounded in the cross of Jesus and the kingdom of God."

—**M. Daniel Carroll R.**
Distinguished Professor of Old Testament, Denver Seminary

"Expect Alex Mekonnen's newest book to open your eyes wide and cause your spirit to lament what the West has done and what China may now be preparing to do in Africa (though the jury is still out). Economically, socially, and politically, even through well-intentioned humanitarian aid, untold human suffering has been provoked from the centuries of the slave trade until the present, exacerbated by the consistent corruption of many African leaders themselves. But Mekonnen does not become embittered or leave you without hope. The cross-centered gospel unpacked in all its dimensions, still provides answers for those with ears to hear."

—**Craig L. Blomberg**
Distinguished Professor of New Testament, Denver Seminary

"*The West and China in Africa* by Dr. Mekonnen is an expansive exposition of the affects of Western and Chinese elements on the African people. There have been many who have attempted to lay open the wounds that Africa has suffered at the hands of its 'conquerors,' but none that I know of have done as thorough and as heart-felt job as Alex has. The emotion of one who has suffered, both personally and empathetically, the wrongs of modernity, capitalism, and imperialism from extra-continental influences empowers the message of this book in a way that a mere academic treatise never would. I would highly recommend this book to all of us who, by intention or by default, are part of the oppressive nature of Western presence abroad. Alex brings truth to us in a palatable form, but in a realistic way that drives itself home to the soul of whomever is truly ready to receive it. May this message reach the heart of many so that 'our sins and the sins of our fathers' will not be repeated by our children."

—**Les Hirst**
Program Director, Global Engagement Program, Global Mapping International

"Thoroughly researched and lucidly argued, *The West and China in Africa* is an authoritative and balanced statement on the major causes of Africa's perennial distress. Without ignoring internal factors, Mekonnen shows in a forthright yet irenic tone that the West's long history of exploitative engagement on the continent, along with its legacy of anthropological denigration of Blacks at home and abroad, has contributed in no small way to Africa's deplorable condition. But the book doesn't stop there. It goes on to challenge and empower Africans and people of African descent, to shed that paralyzing legacy and forge a hopeful future by recovering and reclaiming their glorious past, and more importantly by trusting firmly in the God of the future. For Africans at home and in the diaspora, this is a must-read."

—**Dieumeme Noelliste**
Professor of Theological Ethics, Director of the Grounds Institute of Public Ethics, Denver Seminary

"Alex Mekonnen speaks to this topic with passion and from experience. He successfully avoids the extremes of an uncritical dogmatism, and a disconnected analysis of the current situation in Africa. Rather, here is an informed, knowledgeable, and fair assessment of an important topic from one who speaks with firsthand experience. This is certainly bound to emerge as the standard treatment of this crucial issue. A must-read for anyone dealing specifically with the topic of China in Africa and the resulting political situation, but also for a penetrating analysis of culture and issues of social justice. At the same time it will challenge those of us in the West, and perhaps will make us somewhat uncomfortable! I recommend this book highly."

—David Mathewson
Associate Professor, Denver Seminary

THE WEST AND CHINA IN AFRICA

The West and China in Africa

Civilization without Justice

ALEMAYEHU MEKONNEN

Foreword by Tibebe Eshete

WIPF & STOCK · Eugene, Oregon

THE WEST AND CHINA IN AFRICA
Civilization without Justice

Copyright © 2015 Alemayehu Mekonnen. All rights reserved. Except for brief quotations in critical publications or reviews, no part of this book may be reproduced in any manner without prior written permission from the publisher. Write: Permissions, Wipf and Stock Publishers, 199 W. 8th Ave., Suite 3, Eugene, OR 97401.

Wipf & Stock
An Imprint of Wipf and Stock Publishers
199 W. 8th Ave., Suite 3
Eugene, OR 97401

www.wipfandstock.com

ISBN 13: 978-1-4982-2018-7

Manufactured in the U.S.A.   07/22/2016

Dedicated to
Benyam, Nardos, and Yoseph
With deep love and appreciation for making my life in exile a home away from home

Contents

Foreword by Tibebe Eshete | ix
Preface | xiii
Acknowledgments | xxi
Abbreviations | xxiii

Introduction | 1

Chapter 1
Civlization | 37

Chapter 2
African Personhood—Being Human | 75

Chapter 3
Suffering in a Continent Teeming With Riches | 122

Chapter 4
Banks in a Bankrupt Continent | 147

Chapter 5
Compendium of Energy Resources | 163

Chapter 6
Africa: The Prize of Western Civilization and Capitalism | 195

Chapter 7
China in Africa | 232

Chapter 8
Leadership Crisis in Africa | 264

Chapter 9
Leading in a Turbulent Cultural Contexts | 298

Chapter 10
Christ: The Wounded Healer in Africa | 317

Chapter 11
The Hope of Humankind in the Hopeless Continent | 358

Conclusion | 388

Bibliography | 393

Foreword

THERE IS NO MAJOR study that can come to my immediate memory that has addressed the formidable challenge of Africa comprehensively, historically, and diachronically as that of Alemayehu's recent book entitled *The West and China in Africa: Civilization without Justice*. Authored by one of the few Ethiopians from the Evangelical Christian scholarly circles, the book has tackled wide-ranging issues pertaining to Africa's past and contemporary experiences from multiple angles.

Drawing from the well of his matured Christian faith, long reflections, critical scholarly engagements, and intimate concerns for the peoples of Africa, the author has given us a kind of last-breath illumination, refreshing and challenging at the same time for all of us who are connected to the continent of Africa and its people. A work of monumental significance written in a thorough and empirical manner, it is definitely a culmination of years of empathic scholarly endeavor that has taken someone with this author's caliber, pastoral care, and sensitivity.

With this book Alemayehu tackles what is perhaps one of the most central concerns of contemporary Africa, namely, what are the strongholds impeding and arresting Africa's advance in a sustained manner and how can Africa move forward steadily? By interrogating wide arrays of narratives, discourses, and theories that seek to explain the root causes of Africa's problems, the author makes a prophetic plea for Africans to rise with vindictive spirit, not for vengeance, but anchored in a futuristic vision, summing up the resilience of the African peoples and the continent's surplus history. The book is a violently optimistic cry for a radical reimagination and Africa's authentic renaissance.

In this major contribution to our understanding of Africa, Alemayehu guides the reader through the variegated realms of the African experiences describing its unique history and bringing its peculiar heritages into stark relief. Alemayehu goes back to examine Africa's rich civilizational levels along multiple lines detailing the sophisticated cultural, artistic, and technological achievements of the African society, neither to be part of the Afro-centric choir that merely glorifies the past, nor to ring a new voice to it, but to debunk the notion widely held by the West that Africa is primitive. He invites the current generations of Africans to latch onto that legacy and establish new "pyramids" of Africa, which posterity will look back to with pride. He provocatively calls for a radical civilizational accountability.

Gathering from several experiences across Sub-Saharan Africa, the book engages the reader in a critical and lively conversation about African past, recent and cotemporary history, not only eruditely but presented from a heart burdened with the agony of history, the plight of Africans, and laced with an earnest and forward-looking yearning for a bright future. Alemayehu gives a thorough and engrossing account of the multiplicity and plurality of Africa's daunting challenges by locating them appropriately in their historical and diverse origins.

Based on extensive consultations of relevant sources across different disciplines, the overview of Africa's past, specially the painful legacies associated with the slave trade and colonialism, offers both new and authoritative accounts of history as a moral discourse to demonstrate the need for global and fresh rethinking of a wider restorative justice that brings the victims and the culprits into a new redemptive bond.

The book sheds light on the distinguishing mark of Western or European civilization from Enlightenment to the Industrial Revolution, then to the technological and information revolution, and explains how the momentum has been globalized.

The West and China in Africa does not just limit its considerations to an academic discourse but deals to a greater extent with the concrete life of the African people today—in a world of so-called modernity and at time of globalization characterized by Western thought and technology. Africa has in the past been a source of supply of slavery and raw materials—the demonization has not gone far enough, much to our chagrin—which can only be reversed when Africans are capable of playing new roles and assuming new positions by supplying the West with what it does not have from its own resources. What is the game changer? That is the big question Alemayehu's book raises and the challenges it poses.

Africa is in the grip of development, but its meaning or direction, however, remains obscure. Admittedly, as also convincingly stated in the book, Africa has been bedeviled not just by endless cycles of violence over the last decades—through the hypocrisy and marginalization of Western powers—but also by the bankruptcy of the state, rising political corruptions, and the betrayal of its own leaders. On top of that, Alemayehu is troubled by the vexing challenges contemporary Africa is facing in connection with China's growing presence and influence. This new encounter, which may be termed imperialism by invitation, for lack of a better term, puzzles the author to raise the baffling question why would Africa need an external redeemer? Is the machine eternally broken to require an external fixer?

The paradox of Africa's tragedy is captured in the Amharic proverb, *Yeabayen lij wuha temaw*—the child of *Abay* (Nile River) is thirsty of water—or, to cite its English moral equivalent, "Water, water, everywhere. Not any drop to drink" (from Samuel T. Coleridge's poem). The author uses another metaphor: "watering a garden with a leaky bucket while streams of Africa lie alongside."

Thematically, the book captures the following major areas:

- *Africa's rich civilization and its unacknowledged contribution to the West*
- *The dehumanization of Africans by the West*
- *The leadership crisis Africa is facing and its way out*
- *African Christology and the theology of the kingdom of God*

Through substantive data and compelling socioeconomic and political analysis, the book provides an indictment of the West not only for the moral turpitude of the past but mainly for its wanton neglect of serious commitment to end the existing power and wealth differential and to enhance Africa's development by asserting its economic, military, technological, and informational might. The West is still contributing to the continent's inhibited economic and sociocultural growth as it asks Africa to dance around the dependency orbit, but with little efforts to bridge the gaps of the great divergence the industrial revolution and resultant developments have privileged.

Alemayehu does not just bemoan the past; he offers a solution with prophetic insights, a new interpretive Christian framework, and a distinctly redemptive voice. In his prognosis, he includes diverse categories of agents as actors and facilitators of transformations, made up of the whole international community: the West, descendants of Africa, those across the US, Latin America and the Caribbean World, and children of the continent.

Alemayehu, who has seen three regime changes in his own lifetime in Ethiopia, squarely places his hope and faith in the transforming power of the gospel of Jesus Christ, not on secular humanistic philosophies, however attractive they may sound to the intellect. His call is not for a new social hermeneutics that seeks to invoke sophisticated political ideologies. Ideology is not the solution. In fact, without the necessary element of social memory, community values, and an in-depth soul-searching contemplative dimension, political ideologies create dislocations and impetuous putative solutions. As the experience in some African countries have palpably demonstrated secular ideologies have derailed and misled the African youth and the intellectual to commit social suicide by valorizing violence as a short-cut panacea for Africa's malaise. It has disabled the African elite from identifying the root causes of Africa's problems and from searching for strategic/creative solutions from within to rebalance and attain breakthroughs from the vicious circles of poverty and recurring civil strife.

The book opens our eyes to the immense possibilities that lie in Africa's complexity, multivocity, and its myriad of untapped cultural resources drawing from the vantage point of a distinctly biblical worldview. Alemayehu firmly believes that the veritable hope for Africa's transformation lies in the church and the community of faithful disciples who truly seek to apply the whole of the Word of God to the whole of life by taking the biblical mandate boldly into every sphere of life, from the private to the public. He has a firm conviction that the gospel has a redemptive power in all areas of life. Harnessing the power of the spirit for social and ethical change is an urgent concern of paramount importance. He is unafraid in charging the church for its conspicuous absence in playing an influential role in shaping the moral contours and the civic culture of the African society in view of the mounting challenges and plights of the African. His petition is grounded on distinctly Christian, God-ordained transformation, faith-based and continentally anchored solutions, the epicenter of which is the church. Alemayehu posits a ringing defense of existential Christology, a new theological and pedagogical discourse, consonant with the African experience, addressing issues of life in concrete situatedness and limitedness in contradistinction from the Christ of Christendom. It is the soul and substance of a genuine African theology of incarnation and redemption that is to be taken seriously.

The author seeks to engage all of us in the daunting task of Africa's reconfiguration in a positive direction. For the African leaders, he calls on them to be stewards and moral guardians—preserving space for the underprivileged and protecting their peoples and cultures from global hegemony; for the peoples of Africa, to rise with dignity and acute sense of civic engagements; for the youth, to be innovative and socially responsible thinkers imbued with optimistic faith that adds value to redynamize the future; for the African Diaspora, to search for a new key and agenda of reconnecting with the mother land; for the elite, to be public servants by getting away from their pedantic and parochial confinements; for the international community, to be part of the process of the reinvigorated Africa that is renarrativizing its history, at least by sharing their part in stamping out the homogenized image of Africa.

I want to end my foreword for this book by pointing out what it is and what it is not. The book is not about dooms and glooms. It does not call for a vicious circle of introspection. It is not a defensive discourse of the past, neither is if offensive in its plea for the future. It is not written from an intellectual stature with high-sounding phraseologies. It is a book that is meant to serve as a template for a radical dissent in the imagination of Africa with a call to actions leading to holistic transformations that will per force leave enduring marks. It is written from the spirit of humility that places the strength of the intellect at the foot of the cross. It is about a reformulation that calls for a new personhood, in harmony with the identity that the Jesus Christ guarantees. It is about a cultural renaissance: down the road it anticipates a new Africa flowing with the Pauline spirit—forgetting the past pressing forward. This book is one more among the symphony of voices uttered by eminent African scholars. It is reconciliatory in its tone but loud and persuasive enough to convict its readers to take positive action on the continent of Africa. It is a timely message for Africa at a Crossroads.

Tibebe Eshete
Michigan State University.

Preface

MUCH INK HAS BEEN spent in the diagnosis of the ailing Africa for the last five hundred years both by African and non-African scholars. Various prescriptions have also been written for each diagnosis. And yet, Africa is fatally ill, lying on the sick bed of the global economy. Trapped in the intrigue of world politics, being a bone of contention for the superpowers for its natural resources, betrayed by her own children who are supposed to protect her from poverty, insecurity, disease, and despair; Africa is crying for justice and for respite from an endless cycle of bloody war, conflict, hunger, and exploitation.

Some scholars studied Africa like flies on a wall, being mere spectators. With truths divorced from real-life experience, by looking at Africans as mere objects and subjects of their studies, they determined that the main cause of Africans' problem is Africans themselves. They say, Africans are uncivilized, less intelligent, backward, lazy, more prone to war than to peace, and are barbaric in the way they treat each other. Hence, the West, particularly the United States, treats Africa and its issues, as I will show in this book, as something to avoid. However, just for the sake of America's self-interest Washington cannot afford to totally abandon Africa.

Studies divorced from the reality of life, no matter how their theoretical depth and finesse impress us, often fail to give us the real history and the present accurate picture of Africa. The Western scholarship that encourages detachment from the subject matter we are studying, leads to an inaccurate analysis of Africa and wrong conclusions. Hence, several African studies talk a lot about dictatorship, backwardness, illiteracy, poverty, etc., in Africa and hardly one discuss the civilization of Africa, the famous university in the twelfth century in Timbuktu, the natural wealth of the continent, the politically, socially, and economically sophisticated Nubian, Axumite, and Zulu kingdoms, and many more. The textile industries in West Africa and Congo, the naval and astronomic science, and the fascinating buildings in north, south, west, east, and central Africa before the arrival of Europeans on the continent have been deliberately ignored for centuries to justify the superiority of the Western civilization mission on the dark continent. Even after some revisions in African scholarship are done here and there, it is not easy to change the mentality and attitude of the global community toward Africans. People hardly know that while the above-mentioned African kingdoms were at their epic historical time, Europe and America were crawling on the pages of world history. When Europeans were worshiping idols, Christianity had existed for ten generations in some parts of Africa. Such stories barely get proper publicity in the academic circles and Western media that are primarily geared to serve the Western audience, which has little knowledge about Africans. As Thomas C. Oden rightly said, "Africa cannot wait to discover its own rich history. The struggle for identity is urgent and mounting" (2007:37).

Western academic contribution on African studies, Western financial aid, development projects, etc., have become like watering a garden with a leaky bucket while streams of Africa lie alongside. It is critical for all who have an undying interest in the continent to pause and ask why Africa is languishing in poverty. How long should Africa unjustly suffer? What needs to be fundamentally changed? These questions need to be raised and answered not only on the political and economic platforms. African theologians and missiolgists have to wrestle with it too and equip the church to be light and salt. A prophetic voice is badly needed in Africa, the West, and China.

Academic studies divorced from the real life of Africans also lack empathy. Impressive literary and film works are done on African wars, drought and starvation, refugees, malnutrition and the HIV Aid victims, etc. On a cognitive level, the African who are wronged are well described but they are hardly listened to. Billions of dollars, food, and medicine are poured out to treat the effects of the African malady. But the cause of Africa's problems are dismally analyzed and treated from an African's perspective—especially for those at the grassroots level who are gnashed day in and out in the jaws of injustice. For example, with regard to South Africa's former apartheid context, a university professor from Oxford, Harvard, or University of Pretoria can give an impeccable lecture with deep academic knowledge on civil rights, justice, and freedom without emotionally identifying with the people in the context. To hear stories from those who have experienced segregation through the tone of the sufferer and oppressed is quite something. To listen to black Africans meet and have face-to-face conversation with those who experienced apartheid schools, jails, slums, and the like is different than sitting in a lecture hall and listening to experts who have no personal experience of injustice. To live among Africans whose hands and legs were amputated during the colonial power and civil war, to interact with those who were herded off to refugee camps because of social unrest, to listen to the life experience of African families whose father, husband, or brother is lynched to subdue Africans who resist degradation, enables one to see how far and wide Africans are deprived of justice. I say deprived because justice is an inherent right given to all humankind by God. And without empathy, it is almost impossible to get a true and complete picture of Africans' situation—both the past and the present. What made Martin Luther King Jr.'s "I Have a Dream" speech famous was not mere eloquence. It was an empathy communicated through the tone of his voice, teary eyes, and a face that speaks volume about anguish. If we know how to read them, the sufferers speak volumes.

Others who have immersed themselves in and studied African culture, both native and outsiders, have not done their work without an Achilles heel either. For example, David Livingstone, with good intention and Christian motive, pleaded in various platforms of his country to save Africa with the famous 3 C's: Christianity, Civilization, and Commerce. He could hardly have anticipated that the saviors would turn out to be oppressors and exploiters. One wonders how many times Livingstone turned in his grave as the British Empire did contrary to his appeal and prayer for Africa. The Europe that had recently come out of a blood bath of wars on its continent, that had barely recovered from devastating famines and epidemic diseases that wiped out many lives all of a sudden, became the undisputed physician of Africa's social, economic, and religious sickness. And most of Africa's "viruses" and "infections," discovered by Europeans and justified for treatment by their own civilized medicine and religion, are historically and scientifically unsubstantiated. The assumed absence of Christianity and civilization in Africa before Europe's encounter with the continent is a good example. "Most Western historians have not been willing to admit that there is an African history to be written about, and that this history predates the emergence of Europe by thousands of years. *It is not possible for the world to have waited in darkness for the Europeans to bring the light because, for most of the early history of man, the Europeans themselves were in darkness. When the light of culture came for the first time to the people who would later call themselves Europeans, it came from Africa and Middle Eastern Asia*" (Jackson 2001:3; emphasis added).

Some Africans scholars who have suffered and gone through unpleasant experiences at the hands of white people in their home countries or while they were students in Western universities have been impaired to objectively understand human nature and have interpreted most of Africa's experience merely in the light of racism. The tone of their writings and negative attitude and stereotypical views of the white people in general created a larger gap and indifference between Africans and the West, neglecting or undermining the internal problems of Africa, for Africa's past and present misery on the slave trade, colonialism, and Western policies. Half-baked truths cannot resolve the challenges the continent is facing or bring reconciliation and development. There is no question that these African scholars are hurt beyond hurt. When physical and psychological injuries embitter one's soul it alienates one from objective truth, and others. Living in a no-man's land, these scholars have been unable to make a positive impact on both sides of the Atlantic.

As the West and Africans are pointing the finger of blame at each other, China has come on Africa's scene with a voracious appetite for its natural resources. Despite the country's ill reputation for democratic governance at home—using soft power, such as building roads, bridges, hospitals, clinics, schools, giving scholarships, and the like—China is thriving and succeeding in controlling various natural resources in Africa and winning the hearts and minds of millions of Africans. African leaders who are known for corruption and have been dealing with the West and Russia in the past are excited with the recent emerging star from the East. Many are dancing with the new patrons to the tune of oriental music.

There is a voice of dissatisfaction and frustration, however, among African workers who are employed in Chinese projects and companies in various countries of Africa. So long as China gets hold of the natural resources she wants, violating the human rights of Africans does not concern her. And corrupt African leaders are not famous in standing for the rights and well-being of their people. In the modus operandi of the West and the East in Africa, even though both are involved in Africa's affairs in the garb of civilization to "shape" the African culture and society in their likeness, this author observes that both have one thing in common: the absence of justice. Based on research I shall demonstrate what I mean by the absence of justice and its implication for the daily lives of millions of Africans in the past, today, and in the future.

In the pursuit of freedom, equality, and justice, humanity is not alone. The God of the Bible, who is the defender of the poor, the orphans, the widows, the oppressed, and the exploited, has compassionately identified with the destitute and fought for them through his prophets, Jesus Christ, and the apostles. In the context of injustice, God was not politically correct in his statements through the Old Testament. Neither was he whispering in the ears of authoritarian evil kings and rulers who were blinded by luxury and neglect the pleas of the poor. As he did through the prophet Amos, God was roaring his oracles. Jesus also confronted the evil of his time face to face, to the point of paying with his life.

One of the highlights of my research is learning how compassionate, loving, and caring God is for those who are economically and politically paralyzed throughout human history. It is very encouraging to me to know that the God I worship and serve is actively engaged both in the Old and the New Testaments to heal the sick and broken hearts, to right wrongs, to accept the rejected, to defend the poor, to feed the hungry, and to give peace to those who are troubled. This God of the prophets and the apostles, so some Western theologians believe, has written and taught that Africans are cursed by him (the curse of Ham). He is not a stranger in Africans' journey. He has been there with and for Africans. And the positive evidences for his presence are plenty.

Limiting Africa's study to theological anthropology, global economy, politics, and trends cannot bring justice and hope, which are desperately needed in Africa more than bread and milk. And it doesn't also give meaning for existence that is a source of energy and purpose to have and pursue dreams. Hence, without restricting my research to the history of human beings, I have made an attempt to understand Africa's pilgrimage and destiny from a cosmic and eternal perspective. As the African church reflects on her past without being imprisoned by it, she can look forward to the beginning of the end with hope and triumphant spirit. She should do so not as a lonely traveler on this globe but with all the redeemed people of God. In their existence between the now and the not yet, the Africa Christians groan with all creation, not as victims but as suffering saints patiently waiting for God's full reign on this earth.

At the end of reading this book, it is my utmost intention and desire that African people will have so many sojourners from the global community to come alongside with them. Be willing to identify with their rejection, suffering, and despair, exploitation, and give them some consolation, encouragement and fight on their behalf to give them respite from the seemingly endless misery before their last breath on this earth.

As one who had been mistreated by his own people, was a refugee and lived in exile for the last thirty-foour plus years, seen the various slums in Kenya, interacted with African refugees from the Sudan, Liberia, Ethiopia, Eritrea, Uganda, Congo, Somalia and Rwanda to mention the few the reader of this book should not expect an ivory tower theory divorced from the reality of Africans' life. Even if this book is heavily based on research, I am also an eye witness of the atrocities in Africa and have personally experienced imprisonment, torture and hunger. Hence, my approach to this writing is not mere bookish but a reflection of real life experience and research.

Preface

My journey from Africa to America has been transformative in so many positive ways. And it is also an eye-opening experience. I was a one-time refugee in Kenya. Now I'm a U.S citizen teaching in an academically reputable seminary with scholarly refined and godly colleagues. This country has given me freedom and opportunity of which the country of my birth deprived me during the reign of the Marxist government. I am forever grateful for that. When I decided to be a U.S citizen, I made a resolution, and in this book you see me living up to it. I said, by being a U.S. citizen, I'm going to be part of the good, the bad, and the ugly history of this nation. And I said I have to read a lot about the United States; that I did. The United States is a country of immigrants and it has given freedom and opportunities of various kinds to all who came to her shores, except to the African slaves.

One of the most disturbing and puzzling findings I came across through this study and in my interaction with African refugees is the inconsistency of the U.S. Constitution with the foreign policy of the United States in relation to various African countries. The cluelessness of millions of good Americans about America's involvement in numerous countries in Africa, which often led to the demise of those black nations, is equally disconcerting. Western media and philanthropist are good at showing the starved and destitute Africans to win the sympathy of innocent and generous givers in their society. But they give blind eyes and deaf ears to the policy of their countries and the greed of Western companies that have ruined Africa. It is my hope that this book will create awareness among American citizens, Christians or non-Christians, which is badly needed to make our government revisit the foreign polciy of the U.S. and its modes of operation in the continennt of Africa.

The Western church and theology have missed or intentionally neglected to engage with the issue of justice biblically in relation to the majority world. Both the Old and the New Testaments have given it significant attention. If we want the Scripture to be relevant in African cultural contexts (which is closer to the Old Testament and the first-century Mediterranean culture), both Africans and Westerners need to give heed to the justice of God. Injustice toward humanity not only breaks God's law, it breaks his heart. African theology and missiology should focus both on saving Africans soul and restoring their dignity. The prime task of justice is to do the latter.

Africa has been economically and politically marginalized by the West. And yet, Africa is at the center of Western industrialization. You will find Africa's fingerprint on the Western nuclear technology, in the cars we drive, the airplanes we fly, in the cell phones and computers we use, in sugar and other sweets we enjoy, in the diamonds and gold, and the like. Africa has offered not only her natural resources but the sweat and blood of her children so that we can live the kind of comfortable life we all live in the Western world today. While Africa enriched the West and the East, it is a paradox that the continent has been treated as economically parasitic destined to master carrying a beggar's bowl rather than to be self-sufficient and self-reliant.

I have to confess the truth that for me writing this book was a very difficult exercise emotionally. Throughout my reading and writing I was elegiac and felt helpless to avert the demise of Africans. "In their immediate consequences decay and instability are a matter of lament. But in their longer term repercussions, they may be a matter of celebration . . . Before a seed germinates it must first decay. A mango tree grows out of a decaying mango seed. A new Africa may be germinating in the decay of the present one" (Mazrui 1986:21).

Africans have been waiting for so long to see life and vivacity spring out of decay. Where should the hope of Africa's destitute be anchored? Where should they look for meaning and purpose, to the West or to the East? Küng shares his wisdom:

> Suffering, doubting, despairing man finds his ultimate support in the forthright admission of his inability to solve the riddle of suffering and evil. He is in content to renounce any pretentions to be a neutral and presumably innocent censor passing judgment on God and his world. He decisively rejects even the slightest, inarticulate mistrust, any thought that the good is not really good to man. Positively he relies on that certainly insecure and yet liberating venture of *giving an absolute and unreserved trust* simply and forthrightly to the incomprehensible God: in doubt, suffering and sin, in all mental distress and all physical pain, in all fear, anxiety, weakness, temptation, in all emptiness, comfortlessness, indignation. He clings to God even when utterly empty and burnt out, even in the most desperate situation, when all prayer dies out and no words come to his lips. This is a basic confidence of the most radical character, which does not superficially appease but encompasses and embraces anger and indignation and which also endures God's perpetual incomprehensibility. (1968:299–300; emphasis original)

It is such a kind of trust and cleaving "to the incomprehensible God" that helps millions of African Christians to make meaning out of life in their meaningless situation.

As I have stated in this book, a step in the right direction of change in Africa has been prolonged for various reasons. But it has to start soon. I have hope in the sovereign God and in people who pursue righteousness, kindness, peace, and justice for all. I am not a politician. "From a political point of view, Black America especially is Africa's most important external human resource, precisely because it constitutes a large concentration of people of African ancestry lodged in the most powerful nation in the world, certainly a nation with immense capacity to do Africa harm or good. A re-Africanisation of Black American allegiance and sympathies could help to re-orient American foreign policy towards Africa and transform it in the direction of greater sensitivity and sympathy with African aspirations and values" (Mazrui 1986:302). If a positive and lasting change would emerge in Africa, my expectation is not from China but from the U.S.— not through the same lip service given in talks and exploitative foreign policy in the past 300 hundred years, but through genuine democracy, a win-win foreign policy, transparent communication, accountability to the American and African people, innovation, and Christian service.

The Western countries need to revise their foreign policy, trade agreements, relationships in the area of education, diplomacy, commerce, and the like with Africa. They need to do this not only for Africans' sake but for the sake of their nations. Empty materialism and consumerism are rapidly breeding a nihilistic generation that aimlessly run their lives without purpose and meaning. If too much of wealth and material things are not helping the West to have a decent and godly society why do they need to starve and impoverish Africa to enrich the already rich? "What happens if the present global economic system should prove to be humanity's ultimate suicide programme, which is what the threatening climate catastrophe could suggest? The individual social and political will to live can turn into death drives. Then everything one does no longer minsters to life but to self-destruction" (Moltmann 2010:76). Disobeying God's teaching and abusing nature and exploiting people mercilessly involves an unpleasant price and leads to undesirable destiny. As we several times have seen in Scripture and in human history, injustice, no matter how long it will take, has divine consequence. The West has to decide; they cannot serve two gods.

There is no everlasting human civilization. The East also is not living beyond this human predicament. Despite economic success that takes the front page of the news in China and the Western countries, there is a permanent crisis that socio-revolutionary humanism has not solved. "Man—as individual and society—remains incapable of mastering his world, because he tries to cope with everything except himself. As he seems to be gaining the whole world, he is threatened with the loss of his own soul: in routine, bustling activity, endless talk, in disorientation and futility. This has little to do with the wickedness of man or of particular individuals. It is the legal constraints of the technocratic society itself, as we have seen, which threaten to crush man's personal dignity, freedom and responsibility" (Küng 1968:58). Moltamnn rightly said, "We want to know more than we need to know in order to survive" (2010:190). The whole purpose of this book is to contribute additional constructive information that can build a healthy bridge of relationship with all those who are involved in Africa for one reason or another.

The reconstruction of Africa should be the primary responsibility and burden of Africans. The African diaspora in the last four to five decades is another great potential to restore Africa. While leading a comfortable life in the West, we should not forget the continent of our origin that is bleeding. We can engage beyond sending remittance to people who are depending on our support. In this regard, African diaspora has a lot to learn from the Jewish people.

> We must recognize one basic fact: Although analysis shows that the world is so organized that it cannot but produce underdevelopment, injustice and misery, this structure is radically incompatible with the plan of God as God. A society that condemns millions of children to malnutrition and sickness cannot possibly be a part of God's plan for Africa today. It is precisely the ugly face of "the sin of the world" that the Lamb of God has assumed and carried away. We must highlight the contradiction to the will of God, starting with our own economic and social condition, and including its effects—the illness endemic in our historical and cultural environment. As we do this, we will hear the appeal to participate in the transformation of the badly made world.
>
> Today that participation is a prerequisite for any conversation to a living relationship with God. From now on, we need a fresh hearing of the Word of God, starting with underdevelopment and its consequences, which clarifies the actual pattern of cause and effect that can no longer remain hidden. Passive acceptance of the injustice generated by a medical system that reflects present African socio-economic structures is incompatible with the true worship of God—just as is idolatry. Active resistance is an essential feature of the practice of our faith. It must begin with problems of human health and move to challenge the unjust organization of African society. (Ēla 1990:82)

Preface

After two decades and five years of Ēla's plea, Africa is in no better condition. In fact, the living situation of millions of Africans continues to worsen. Hoping against hope, I am making the same call through this book. My intellectual labor is not only for the good of Africans. It is also for the well-being of the global community. If you believe in the God of Abraham, Isaac, and Jacob, I humbly submit to you the truth in love about Africa. In the illustrious words of Dr. Vernon Grounds, the patriarch of Denver Seminary, "Here is no unanchored liberalism, freedom to think without commitment. Here is no encrusted dogmatism, commitment without freedom to think. Here is a vibrant evangelicalism, commitment with freedom to think within the limits laid down in Scripture."[1]

As you go through this book, somewhere, somehow I hope you will be able to see the "burning bush" and hear God say to you, "Look! The cry of Africans has reached me, and I have seen how harshly they have been treated . . . I want you to do something positive about it."

I strongly believe that if there is a will, the global community can live peacefully and happily without turning the sub-Saharan Africa into a mass grave of the poor and the helpless. This book is a plea on behalf of millions of Africa's destitute who die like a fly daily and whose life has become a living hell.

---

1. Cited in Blomberg, *Can We Still Believe in the Bible?*, x.

Acknowledgments

Let alone writing a second book of this size, I never seriously thought of myself producing books that would interest readers and meet their intellectual needs. A person who saw my potential and fanned the dormant amber within me into a flame is Dr. Tibebe Eshete. He was also willing to write the foreword. I'm eternally grateful to him for challenging me to get into writing.

The humbling and overwhelming feedback on my first book inspired me to work on a prolonged writing project and complete it. Readers are guests to the intellectual banquet of authors. I'm thrilled and encouraged to hear and read the expressions of many from near and far who enjoyed reading *Culture Change in Ethiopia*. Your feedback has given me inspiration and energy to produce this book; I can't fully express my gratitude in words.

I did most of my writing from my home office. The price that family members paid dealing with a physically present but mentally absent husband and father was enormous. I'm immensely grateful to my wife, Roman, and our son, Yoseph, for their understanding, forbearance, love, and encouragement. In addition to her full-time work, my daughter, Nardos, did an excellent job in proofreading the manuscript. Her comments in various sections makes me burst into laughter and affirms that I am laboring for a worthy cause. Our oldest son Ben's analytical questions about the content have given me good perspective to shape and develop this book. He made sure that the villain in Africa that I write about includes the black people so that there is no impartiality in my approach; that I did. I thank God for my family and I am grateful to them for standing with me even when they felt they were not my priority while I was undertaking this writing project.

The idea of this book was conceived in my mind initially by observing the paradoxical existence of Africans. Out of the wombs of their suffering I saw in them dignity in the face of degradation, hope, and aspiration in the most discouraging and disappointing circumstances. Africans' abundant generosity out of scarcity, their love for family and God even when the capacity to love looks nonexistent, has been an amazing human potential to observe. The questions of my African students and their love for the church of Jesus Christ and the continent not only inspired me to write this book. Their dedication and sacrificial service have shaped my life, values, and hopes.

The faculty development fund at Denver Seminary was my huge resource to get most of the books from Amazon that I used for my research. I'm indebted to the

Acknowledgments

generous provision of the administration and moral support of President Mark Young, and Provost/Dean Randy MacFarland.

Professor Daniel Carroll's friendship, his pertinent and challenging questions related to my research, checking my motive and purpose of writing this book, are caring and loving gestures that I will never forget. He is a true brother indeed.

Aaron Wolcott, an American MK who was born and raised in Africa and worked there for a number of years, went through the manuscript and gave me valuable input. With his keen knowledge of Africans and Africna history, he did excellent editing work. His passionate love for Africans and his concern and respect for them is a rare medicine to heal the soul of a wounded African or black person. I thank him for his help and for being a source of hope and a model for the many Africans he serves.

Abbreviations

ABC	American Broadcasting Company
ADB	African Development Bank
AIU	African International University
AGTS	Assemblies of God Theological Seminary
AU	African Union
AMCU	Association of Mineworkers and Construction Union
AMISOM	African Union Mission in Somalia
ANC	African National Congress
BAES	British Aerospace Electronic Systems
BAO	Banque de L'Afrique Occidentale
BBC	British Broadcasting Corporation
BCA	Banque Commerciale de L'Afrique
CAD	Computer-Aided Design
CAE	Computer-Aided Engineering
CAM	Computer-Aided Manufacturing
CANOE	Conscientiousness, Agreeableness, Neuroticism, Openness, Extraversion.
CAR	Central African Republic
CBS	American Broadcasting Television Network. The name is derived from the initials of the network's former name, Columbia Broadcasting System.
CCC	Cross-Cultural Communication
CEC	Commission of the European Communities
CEO	Chief Executive Officer
CIA	Central Intelligence Agency
CITA	Christ Is the Answer
CNPC	Chinese National Petroleum Company
COSTAU	Congress of South African Trade Union
CPA	Comprehensive Peace Agreement

Abbreviations

CPC	Communist Party of China
CSFAC	China State Farm Agribusiness Corporation
DCO	Dominion and Colonial
DPU	Diamond Protection Unit
DRC	Democratic Republic of Congo
ECA	Export Credit Agencies
ECOMOG	Economic Community of West Africa States Monitoring Group
EHM	Economic Hit Men
EIB	European Investment Bank
EO	Excutive Outcome
EU	European Union
FAO	Food and Agriculture Organization
FCAO	Forum on China-Africa Cooperation
FDI	Foreign Direct Investment
GDP	Gross Domestic Product
GFI	Global Financial Integrity
GNOPC	Greater Nile Operating Company
GPL	General Public License
GPT	Geothermal Power Tanzania
IBM	International Business Machines
ICC	International Criminal Court
IDMC	Internal Displacement Monitoring Center
IDPs	Internally Displaced Persons
IFAD	International Fund for Agricultural Development
IMF	International Monetary Fund
ITC	International Trust Company
IQ	Intelligent Quotient
LISCR	Liberian International Ship and Corporate Registry
LSE	London School of Economics
MDGs	Millenium Development Goals
MK	Missionary Kid
MPLA	Movement for the Libration of Angola
NARC	National Rainbow Coalition
NEGST	Nairobi Evangelical Graduate School of Theology
NDC	National Development Corporation
NGO	Non-governmental Organization
NPFL	National Patriotic Front Liberia
NUM	National Union of Mineworkers

ABBREVIATIONS

NUMSA	National Union of Metalworkers of South Africa
OAU	Organization of African Union
OCED	Office of Community and Economic Development
OECD	Organization of Economic Cooperation and Development
PDF	People's Defence Force
PRC	People's Republic of China
RSA	Republic of South Africa
RUF	Revolutionary United Front
SAVAK	Sāzemān-e Ettelā'āt va Amniyat-e Keshvar (Organization of Intelligence and National Security)
SEZs	Special Economic Zones
SINCP	Sudan Islamist Islamist's National Congres Party, also called NCP.
SKA	Square Kilometer Array
SLA	Sierra Leone Army
SPLAM	Sudan's People Liberation Army/Movement
UAC	United African Company
UN	United Nations
UNDP	United Nations Development Program
UNESCO	United Nations Organizations for Education, Science and Culture
UNHD	United Nations Human Development
UNHCR	United Nations Commissioner for Refugees
UNIT	National Union for the Total Independence of Angola
USAID	United States Agency for International Development
USD	United States Dollar
VIP	Very Important Person
WB	World Bank
WEA	World Evangelical Association
WFC	World Food Council
WNLA	Witwatersrand Native Labor Association
WTO	World Trade Organization
ZTE	Zhongxing Telecommunication Equipment

Introduction

Many readers will find this an unsettling book because the Africa of the 1980s is neither a happy nor a hopeful place. The colonialists designed the scenario for disaster, and the Africans seem to be trying their best to fulfill it. Calamity waits within the arms' reach, oblivious of Africa's potential strength. Across the whole continent, economies are collapsing, cities are deteriorating, food production is declining, and populations are growing like weed-seeds turned loose in a garden. Governments fall at the whim of illiterate sergeants and disgruntled despots, prisons are as overcrowded as the farm lands are empty, and at last count the number of refugees in Africa had reached the incredible figure of five million—people driven from their homelands by wars, tyrants and poverty.
As troubled as these early years of nationhood have been, Africa needs not to dwell forever in the uncertain twilight zone. Its dreams have been only mislaid, not lost. The morass has escape routes. Africa is a continent of surprises: nothing is ever quite as it seems and nothing ever happens quite as it is supposed to.[1]

They drink wine in bowls, and anoint themselves with the finest oils, but they are not grieved over the ruin of [Africa]. (Amos 6:6)

The world is overwhelmingly rich; the human mind is incapable of paying attention to all its aspects. The painter sees the world in color, the sculptor in form; the musician in sounds, and the economist in commodities. The prophet is a man who sees the world with the eyes of God, and in the sight of God even things beauty or acts of ritual are abomination when associated with injustice. The world is overwhelmingly rich, but the prophet perceives the whole world in terms of justice and injustice.[2]

---

1. Lamb, *Africans*, xv.
2. Heschel, *Prophets*, 270–71.

The West and China in Africa

Since Europe scrambled for Africa and altered the geographical and political map, history, culture, education, and economy of the continent, for the last five hundred years, the West has been on the continent for good or ill depending on the perspective of the observers and writers of Africa's history. The World Bank, International Monetary Fund (IMF), Western NGOs, many aid organizations, philanthropists, etc., have poured billions of dollars in Africa for various reasons we will look at in detail later. The presence and modus operandi of the West in Africa, until China emerged on the African scene with a voracious appetite for natural resources, with financial means to feed her hunger and creative strategy to grab it, had a free reign with no competition.

For not willing to share the African pie, for fear of losing influence and dominance in Africa and the world, the West did not welcome the involvement and dominating presence of the East/China in Africa. The Western press, authors, and politicians have become vocal in criticizing China's involvement in Africa to the point of calling it neo-colonialism. Presumably they did this on behalf of and their concern for Africans. Many Westerners who know very little about Africa, and had no interest in the affairs of Africa, have become absorbed and engaged in conversation and discussion about Africa. This is a good thing to do. However, their approach on the issue, as usual, is from their side of story. "As the debates unfolded in conference rooms, blogs, and media outlets in the West and in Africa, and as rumors of a huge new aid program created a mix of alarm and anticipation, it was obvious that debaters and bloggers, and journalists were drawing conclusions with only scant information."[3] China is accused of the following major issues:

- Chinese aid is a means to grab oil/minerals and land in Africa.
- China enabled Sudan to get away with murder in Darfur.
- China hurts efforts to strengthen democracy and human rights in Africa.
- Chinese support kept Robert Mugabe in power in Zimbabwe.
- China is making corruption worse.
- Chinese aid and loans are part of a system of "unfair subsidies."
- China gains business with low environmental and social standards.[4]

Despite the above-mentioned allegations of the West, three scholarly writings by Oxford graduates,[5] did not substantiate the out-of-proportion ill-painting of China in Africa by the West. With impeccable academic research, these two authors fairly demonstrate how Western political and economic monopoly in Africa is encountered by China's disarming soft power, financially domineering, and multidimensional purpose. The Harvard and Oxford graduate, Zambian international economist, Dambisa Moyo, explains: "[T]he fact is that the Chinese way to date has shown none of the trappings of

---

3. Brautigam, *Dragon's Gift*, 3.
4. Ibid., 273–306
5. Ibid.; Moyo, *Dead Aid*; Moyo, *Winner Take All*—Brautigam and Moyo being Western and African scholars respectively.

European colonialism such as religious conversion, use of military force, or handpicking the local political leadership."[6] She adds,

> It is hard to argue that a half-century of Western involvement in African affairs has done much to incentivize better government across the continent. Time and again the developed Western nations have chosen to treat the governments of poorer African nations with kid gloves, often giving them a free pass on egregious graft and theft of public resources while continuing to reward their government leaders with even more aid money despite worsening expectancies, seemingly intractable illiteracy, and erratic economic growth. The villain is this system, not China. And only its complete overhaul—from one that rewards bad behavior into one that incentivizes and supports improvements in economic and living conditions—will turn the situation around. For the moment China would seem to be the forces actively working to improve Africa and the prospects of its people—not just Africa but also the livelihoods of hundreds of millions of people across the emerging world and beyond.[7]

Not too long ago, *The Economist* did a cover story on Africa: "A Failed Continent." In this failed continent, the West has been extracting both minerals and human power, by closely working with corrupt African leaders. And as the West is treating Africa as something to avoid and keep at a long distance, the Chinese saw a great opportunity and are planning to invest $83 billion per year for the next twelve years. Compare that to the $5 billion per year investment plan of the World Bank. "China is now a powerful force in Africa, and the Chinese are not going away. Their embrace of the continent is strategic, planned, long-term, and still unfolding."[8] Brautigam's and Moyo's books help their readers correct a wrong perception of China in Africa and not to be swayed by media hype and populist and ill-conceived repartee. But, is China in Africa for the Africans' sake? Yes, China's engagement in Africa is different than the West's approach. Does that mean the end result will be different? Does China practice justice in her involvement with African governments better than the West?

Analyzing the global economic factors, China's geopolitical strategy, her trade agreements with various African countries, Africa's perception of China and the U.S., etc., I will show the significant influence of China in Africa and the world. History is in the making. This author investigates the past, the present, and the future impact of global powers' voracity for the natural resources of Africa at the cost of justice. My approach is not to give an assessment of noble and evil behavior of humankind in the light of skin color in African context. The major conflict in Africa is between light and darkness, righteousness and sin, peace and war, freedom and bondage, greed and generosity, justice and injustice, life and death. Before we attempt to cast out the demons in others, we need to recognize the demons within us and deal with them first. Neither the West nor the East, nor African leaders themselves for that matter, have a moral and ethical ground to claim a messianic mission to save Africa or to blame others for the demise of the continent. Standing before the Truth like one would before a mirror each participant

---

6. Moyo *Winner Take All*, 157.
7. Ibid., 171.
8. Brautigam, *Dragon's Gift*, 311.

in African affairs needs to look at themselves and answer these questions—did I do the right thing? Have I taken advantages of the African poor?

Despite all the bad news coverage Africa gets, any sensible member of the global community cannot afford to ignore Africa and put the things that happen within the continent on the back burner. Africa lies at the heart of history. It is the continent from which the distant ancestors of every one of us, no matter who we are today, originally came. Its people participated integrally in the great transformations of world history, from the rise of agricultural ways of life to the various inventions of metal working to the growth and spread of global networks of commerce. Bigger than the United States, China, India, and the continent of Australia combined, the African continent presents us with a historical panorama of surpassing richness and diversity.

Yet traditionally history books, ironically, have long treated Africa as if it were the exemplar of isolation and difference—all because recent centuries marked by the terrible events of the slave trade. As key agents of that trade, many Europeans and their offspring in the Americas in the eighteenth and nineteenth centuries comforted and absolved themselves by denying the full humanity of Africans, and their rich history. That sad heritage continues to shape the envisioning of Africa today, not just in the West, but all across the non-African world and sometimes in Africa as well.[9] "Africa is the most thoroughly abused and the least understood region of the planet," so penned John Perkins.[10] His observation is based both from his personal experience in Africa and a scholarly research. In the history of humankind I don't know of any racial group that went through an immense and multiple kinds of suffering, humiliation, and dereliction without respite for more than five hundred years like the black people.

Africa and African studies are inseparably linked to paradox.[11] "Africa is the first habitat of man but is the last to be made truly habitable. The crisis of habitability in recent history ranges from problems of tropical diseases to difficulties in physical communications and transportation, and from political instability in black Africa to the complexities of white-dominated South Africa. The resulting exodus of refugees from both black tyranny and white racism is part of the crisis of 'living conditions' in a political sense. If Africa was Adams birthplace, the Garden of Eden today is in serious disrepair. What is wrong?"[12] asks a prominent African scholar, Mazrui, about twenty-four years ago. Even after apartheid the conditions of black Africans in South Africa and the rest of the continent is bleak. Mazrui's question is yet to be answered.

Following the scholarly footsteps of African protagonists, without considering myself in their category, I have made an attempt to show why the African continent is a giant with a foot of clay. Why the contradiction? Is the cause internal/inherent or

---

9. Ehret, *Civilizations of Africa*, 3. For an in-depth understanding, see ibid. and Diop's works of *African Origin of Civilization* and *Civilization or Barbarism*; C. Williams, *Destruction of Civilization*; Bernal, *Black Athena*, vols. 1–3; and Jackson, *Introduction to African Civilization*.

10. *Secret History of American Empire*, 251.

11. Paradox is a mode of analysis. Platonists, Hegelians, and Marxists also use paradox as a tool for studying reality, but they call it the "dialectic." Qualities that are seemingly contradictory are reconciled. Reality is always a unit of opposites (Mazrui, *Africans*, 2).

12. Ibid., vii.

external? Why are the black race and black history misinterpreted and misunderstood? What is the impact of historical and cultural disconnection on the collective and individual personalities of Africans and blacks of African origin? Where are we now? What is the potential of Africa? What is the best way of interpreting the situation of Africans and black people in general? What role can biblical Christianity play? These and more questions are addressed in this book. I have found that clarifying the ambiguity and incongruity of the condition of the continent is a crucial step to rediscover Africa and Africans and to re-Africanize the forcibly and cunningly Westernized African history and culture.

Among African scholars, little agreement has been made between the externalist and the internalist on the causes of Africa's multiple miseries. "Externalist believes the causes are external in origin and include colonial legacies, Western imperialism, the slave trade, an unjust international economic system, and exploitation by oligopolistic multinational corporations, among others. Internalists, on the other hand, emphasize such internal causes as incompetent leadership and establishment of defective political and economic systems in postcolonial Africa—systems that bear little or no relationship to Africa's own indigenous systems."[13]

This book takes both the externalist and the internalist stance, arguing that the causes are intertwined, and they equally damage the African people. "It is true that Africa is not just a playing-field for the great powers. We must be aware of the responsibility of the African ruling classes for the ongoing impoverishment of the masses. Injustice and oppression are generated from outside, but a train of miseries also results from the relationships between the African states and their people. The benefits of programs of modernization and efforts at growth are coopted by the èlites in power."[14] Perkins concurs: "Countries in Asia, Latin America, and the Middle East are interwoven with common threads. Africa is a tangled knot. Its history, geography, cultures, religions, politics, crops and natural resources are discordant. This engenders a sense of separateness—even isolation—that in turn facilitates exploitation from within as well as from outside. In many countries the colonial masters of the past, the European elites, have simply been replaced by native African elites. They follow patterns established by their predecessors and openly collaborate with foreign executives who wantonly ravage the land and its people."[15]

Because of the size of the continent and the numerous issues in various African countries, I'm unable to give a detailed analysis of each country or region. But by providing sufficient research work on topics like civilization, African personhood, African natural resources and the fight over them, African contribution to Western capitalism, the current role of China in Africa, the role of African despots and the leadership crisis in Africa, and the role of Christianity, I have made my best attempt to explain the cultural, socioeconomic, and political context that requires the justice of God and the theology of the cross.

---

13. Ayittey, *Africa in Chaos*, 26.
14. Èla, *My Faith as an African*, 124.
15. *Secret History of the American Empire*, 251.

As I mentioned earlier, for the last five centuries or so Africa has been a continent of incongruity. As if he is inviting his readers to watch a horror movie, David Lamb had no choice but to put the paradoxical words of introduction about his book on Africa, which I have quoted above. I am afraid that my book will take you deeper into the abyss before you can see hope; not in Africans, white people or Chinese, Jews or Gentiles, but in God. "The twentieth century saw the European nations destroy themselves in two world wars. In the twenty-first century we have inherited both these eras: the spirit of the scientific and technological progress, and the potential for destruction which can plunge humanity and the earth into the abyss."[16] Mazrui adds:

> The most devastating tradition of combat is genocide. It is now globalized. It is what nuclear war is about. The defence of New York requires the destruction of at least 40 million Russians in the ultimate analysis. The defence of Moscow requires the devastation of half of the United States.
>
> The northern hemisphere has created a new form of genocide. It is partly masochistic since its primary targets are northerners themselves (Europeans, Americans, and Russians).
>
> But the new genocide is also a throwback to primeval murder, cool and premeditated. Only this is *homocide* rather than homicide. The destruction of the human race is at stake, rather than the destruction of "merely" a single human person.
>
> The struggle against the new homocide is not "merely" about saving lives. It is more fundamentally concerned with the saving life itself on this planet.[17]

After such impressive analysis of the global human condition, Mazrui's proposal for the problem of nuclear proliferation, among others is more nuclear proliferation in the majority world and he gives Pakistan's achievement of nuclear power as an example. In simple terms, it seems that he is suggesting eliminating cancer with cancer. When one lives on this kind of precarious historical ground, "Man must live on the summit to avoid the abyss. There is nothing to hold to except God," said Heschel.[18] More than any time before, the global community is living under a nuclear threat in our time. The UN and World Evangelical Alliance (WEA) are taking the matter seriously:

> The United Nations steps up the efforts to fight the proliferation of nuclear weapons. The General Assembly has designated September 26 as the yearly day to remember this worrying legacy. Nuclear disarmament was the subject of the U.N.'s very first resolution in 1946 and today the threat is as large as ever.
>
> WEA recently co-sponsored an event at the Human Rights Council to launch the yearly day to remember the task ahead. Speakers from all corners underlined the problem. Concerned states from Mexico to Indonesia, from Kazakhstan to Argentina and also high officials of the Interparlementarian Union, Majors for Peace and the U.N. itself. The Japanese ambassador received a statement from the Japanese parliament. Kazakhstan's ambassador explained that his country

---

16. Moltmann *Sun of Righteousness Arise!*, 37.
17. Mazrui, *Africans*, 132; emphasis original.
18. *Prophets*, 19.

did not get unsafe at all after disposing of its arsenal. The countries responsible for the current proliferation were absent.[19]

For anyone who does not see the history of humankind through racial lenses, this book can be eye opening and soul searching. "A book on Africa must cross racial, cultural, ideological, geographical, ethnic, religious and class lines."[20] That is exactly what I am attempting to do. Evil is embedded in the nature of humankind, not in the color of their skins. Unfortunately, the relationship between the West and Africa is based on unfounded theories and assumptions that are entangled around racial, black-and-white issues; always the whites being superior to the blacks; the blacks as victims to the whites. This author did not find any purely demonic or angelic race in his research. The history of humankind is marked by the greatness and wickedness of all the participants in world history. The African case is not exceptional. In fact, my surprising discovery in writing this book is that, from the time of slavery until now, what attracted the West like a magnet to Africa was not racial hatred. It is greed. This vice is a common denominator both for the black, the white, and all colors of people.

As you read this book, you will see the ugly face of wickedness that is found in human nature. In cruelty and crookedness we are all inseparably united. In the words of the apostle Paul, "There is no one righteous, not even one; there is no one who understands, no one who seeks God. All have turned away; they have become together worthless. There is no one who does good, not even one. Their throats are open graves; their tongues practice deceit. The poison of vipers is on their lips. Their mouth is full of cursing and bitterness. Their feet are swift to shed blood; ruin and misery mark their ways. And the way of peace they do not know. There is no fear of God before their eyes" (Rom 3:10–18).

The West and China in Africa: Civilization without Justice can be summarized in these verses. It is the journey of fallen humanity. When people turn away from God, they turn against each other. They violate the moral law and disobey God. Why and how it has been done in Africa to the black race for more than half a century is the focus of this book. The good thing is, not only in wretchedness but also in greatness, human beings have commonality. Because of my Christian belief and faith in the goodness of God, his unfailing love, his promises of restoration and redemption for the cosmos, and not only human history, my approach to this study is more optimistic than nihilistic.

In 1997, the genesis of my research for this work started when I joined the faculty of what was then called Nairobi Evangelical Graduate School of Theology (NEGST) now called African International University (AIU), to teach in the missions department. Before I developed the curriculum for the missions program, I decided to read about Africa. The situations of the missions department demanded broad knowledge of the continent more than putting courses together and writing a curriculum. Missions was one of seven programs the school was running. When I got to Nairobi, I found one missions student in my department. Even the one student I found was not African, he was Korean. The

---

19. WEA Co-Sponsors Event on Day for the Total Elimination of Nuclear Weapons, October 16, 2014.

20. Ayittey, *Africa in Chaos*, 24.

Kenyan missiologist Dr. Mutunga resigned one year after I joined the school. Without a single missions student or a colleague in the department, I was left alone. I felt that the Lord took me back to Africa from the U.S. for the funeral service of a department that was dying even before it was born. In 1997, since David Livingstone stepped on African soil in 1852, there was no graduate or under-graduate missions program for the whole of East and Central Africa—an African region bigger than Europe. I asked why? "The question is the beginning of all thinking. In knowing how to ask the right question lies the only hope of arriving at an answer," said Heschel.[21] The "why" question and other subsequent questions are the reasons for this book to be "born."

Before I developed the curriculum I decided to read volumes of books on Africa that speak about the slave trade, missionary work, economy, politics, arms trade, mercenaries, chemical weapons trade, the interest and functions of Western journalists in Africa, colonialism, postcolonial Africa, etc. Finding out what the continent had gone through in the past and learning about the current condition was both embarrassing and very disturbing to me. It was embarrassing because, despite being an African, it took me more than three decades of my life to know the history of the continent. Born and raised in Ethiopia, a country that had gone through many radical changes and has her own problems,[22] though sheltered from the dominance of Western powers, had made me clueless what the rest of Africa experienced through the tragedy of slave trade and colonialism. It disturbed me because the brutality of the colonizers, the African despots who followed their steps, the merciless exploitation and oppression of internal and external powers, are beyond my comprehension. Finally, I said, Africa is like an antelope in the jaw of a crocodile, half alive and half dead. This was in 1997, and the situation of Africans is not much different now. Unfortunately, it will not be any different for the foreseeable future. Emmanuel M. Katongole concurs: "Neither Africa's independence nor what has been dubbed the "second revolution" of the 1980s has brought any significant gains for the majority of African peoples, but increasing marginalization and dispossession . . . the picture of a distress and distressing Africa: wide spread poverty, political instability, the civic unrest, and ethnic tension/clashes in many countries. Add to these the tremendous health and infrastructure problems recently complicated by HIV-AIDS epidemic (and Ebola), then one sees how dire the situation is."[23]

Africa is extremely rich with natural resources and yet the majority of Africans are poor, and they are mainly known for their destitute lives. "Seeing the decay of the cities, many Western visitors are startled to learn how potentially prosperous Africa is. Like a closet millionaire, it hides the riches that future generations on distant continents will need to prosper, produce, even survive. It has 40 percent of the world's potential hydroelectric power supply, the bulk of the world's diamonds and chromium, 30 percent of the uranium in non-Communist world, and 50 percent of the world's gold, 90 percent of its cobalt, 50 percent of its phosphates, 40 percent of its platinum, 7.5 percent of its coal, 8 percent of its known petroleum reserves, 12 percent of its natural gas, 3 percent of

---

21. *Prophets*, 43.
22. Mekonnen, *Culture Change in Ethiopia*.
23. "Violence and Social Imagination," 24, 26.

its iron ores, and millions upon millions of acres of untilled farmland. There is no other continent blessed with such abundance and diversity."[24]

It is legitimate to ask, then, why Africa is poor. Why the paradox? We shall look at the factors that caused life to be unbearable for many Africans and made people prone to war and bloodshed rather than a peaceful coexistence and developing of their resources to have a better life than they have now.

The dog-eat-dog war clips of Africa that the Western media occasionally show us are often happening between Africans and mercenaries. The mercenaries in most cases are Africans who are desperate for jobs and are trained and led by white people who have political or economic interest in the continent. *My Friend the Mercenary* by James Brabazon is a classic story of intrigue, greed, and violence in West Africa, in Liberia and Sierra Leone in particular. Brabazon's detailed account of the war in Sierra Leone between the Executive Outcomes (EO)[25] and Revolutionary United Front (RUF) gives insight to the reader of his book regarding why Africa is still lagging behind the rest of the world in many things. EO was consisted of Angolan mercenaries trained and led by white South Africans.

Revolutionary United Front (RUF) was trained by American mercenaries, specifically

> a retired US Army General, Robert A. Yerks, and Fred Rindel, a former US military attaché who allegedly helped train members of the RUF. The retired US General "was involved with ITC [International Trust Company] and is currently a senior official in LISCR [Liberian International Ship and Corporate Registry]." LISCR is allegedly an American company, registered in Tyson's Corner, Virginia. Congressman Fran wolf of Virginia, a member of the House Armed Services Committee, has testified that this "US based Liberian flag registry has been implicated in contributing to the continued reign of Charles Taylor, the leader one of the most brutal murderous and dangerous regimes in the world. In short there is blood on the flag." These companies were also major traders in blood diamonds from the Sierra Leonean rebels and the major funders of the Liberian government.[26]

RUFs "rebels" trained by Americans were so brutal and Freetown was gripped by fear, terror, and death. EO was hired by the president of Sierra Leon to fight against his "enemies" and the enemies of Sierra Leoneans. Preferring the mercenaries to the RUFs, Brabazon says, "Painted on the rear bumpers of taxis in the capital had been legend: *In God We Trust, but EO is our savior.*"[27] In 2001, The United Nations (UN) deployed 18,000 troops for the cost of around $1 billion a year to bring normalcy in the country.[28]

24. Lamb, *Africans*, 20.

25. Executive Outcomes was originally conceived as a front-organization for South Africa's increasingly isolated regime—an apparently legitimate commercial company that, like many others, was set up as part of a sanctions-busting operation in the late 80s and early 90s. EO was then transformed in 1993 by a consortium of English entrepreneurs, including a rich businessman called Tony Buckingham and a wealthy ex-SAS officer called Simon Mann (Brabazon, *My Friend the Mercenary*, 154).

26. Roberts, *Glitter and Greed*, 3.

27. Brabazon, *My Friend the Mercenary*, 68; emphasis original.

28. Ibid., 69.

The bottom-line for the death of civilians and the national horror and the intervention of the UN was to control the large deposit of diamonds in Sierra Leone. Whether the war was conducted by the nationals or the mercenaries, ultimately it is an outside power that has the capital and technology that will end up owning the diamond mine. Africans are left with their begging bowls. They survive under the crushing burden of debt, from the loan taken by their leaders who came to power undemocratically. In most cases the loaners are the International Monetary Fund (IMF), the World Bank, and Western Capitalist countries. Roberts writes:

> In Sierra Leone, the civil war had come to an end. This should have meant that there were fewer conflict diamonds in the market . . . But then a major change was introduced into the "conflict" diamond campaign. Its target was extended by the UN and government negotiators to include the "illicit" diamonds as if they were "conflict" stones. In future most of the so-called "conflict diamonds" will be entirely innocent of any association with terrorism. This greatly extended ban was excellent news for De Beers[29] for it had eliminated much unwelcome competition. It meant effectively the removal of 14 percent of the international trade, rather than 4 percent.[30]

The story of Congo, Zimbabwe, Angola, Mozambique, South Africa, Sudan, and Central African Republic is not different than the West African countries. In Africa's blood diamond industry, the US, UK, Canada, Belgium, Switzerland, Netherlands, Russia, South Africa, Australia, Germany, Israel, India, China, pro-Hezbollah Lebanese merchants, and Al-Qaeda, are involved, to mention the few of those implicated. When it comes to the diamond and glitters of Africa the cats and the mice that fight in different world arenas operate with the same values and for a common interest in various African countries. Hence, death, pain, and suffering often occur on the continent in silence. However, it is a paradox that out of all places, in Africa, greed turns rivals and enemies into economic competitors. "In Zaire, the Lebanese firm Soziadis and Israeli firm Overseas Diamonds were allegedly "comptoirs," the name given to diamond dealers who buy from illegal diggers and smugglers."[31] "A major diamond enterprise in Sierra Leon run by Israeli intelligence,"[32] and Roberts adds, "Suddenly the US, De Beers, and the UK all discovered the international campaign against the sale of diamonds used to fund wars and seemingly adopted it with zest."[33] "Approximately 80 percent of the world diamond is sold to the U.S."[34] As he states the list of who is who in the melodrama of the diamond business in West Africa, Sierra Leone and Liberia in particular, Greg Campbell says, "The two 24 year old men—Ahmed Khalfan Ghailani, from Tanzania, and Fazul Abdullah Mohammed of Kenya—were members of Saudi billionaire Osama bin Laden's Al Qaeda terrorist network. According to the FBI, they'd been buying diamonds from

---

29. De Beers is a South African Company owned by the Oppenheimer family and they control 65% of the world diamond (Roberts, *Glitter and Greed*).

30. Ibid., 10.

31. Ibid., 217.

32. Ibid., 204.

33. Ibid., 226.

34. Campbell, *Blood Diamonds*, 198.

the RUF since 1998; the same year U.S. embassies were destroyed by Al Qaeda operatives in Dar-es-Salam and Nairobi. Ghailani is accused by the FBI of helping to buy the truck that destroyed the building in Dar-es-Salam."[35] When the U.S was attacked on 9/11, "many Lebanese in Kenema and Bo, the diamond trading centers [in Sierra Leone], celebrated in joy at the news of the attacks."[36]

African minerals make few rich and many impoverished; they are also the cause of bloodshed on both sides of the Atlantic, but more so in Africa. "If nothing else, the story of Sierra Leone's diamond war has proven unequivocally that the world ignores Africa and her problems at its peril. Just like global commerce and the widening reach of terrorism, events far from home often have very tangible impacts. Sierra Leone has shown the world that there is no longer any such thing as an 'isolated, regional conflict.' Perhaps there never was."[37]

Africa is also a continent of contradiction on the issue of civilization. As Chancellor Williams skillfully demonstrated in his book *The Destruction of Black Civilization: Great Issues of Race from 4500B.C–2000 A.D*, the Arabs who visited Africa between the seventh and fifteenth century reported in their respective countries what they saw in Africa: "The magnificent stone and brick palaces, temples, churches, cathedrals, wide avenues lined with palm trees, government buildings, public baths, water supply systems, beautiful gardens, countless crafts industries, huge farms with extensive pastures where camels, horses, oxen, cows, sheep, goats, and pigs could be seen grazing lazily—all these were reported as messages were reported as unwritten message: Such is this Black Paradise."[38] As I will explain later in this book, before the beginning of slave trade or Western colonialism, there was civilization in various parts of Africa equivalent to and in some cases more advanced to that of European countries. And yet, Western historians and anthropologists indoctrinated and taught the world that Africans are savages who need to be saved through religion, guns, Western education, and forced migration. They say Africans best buildings are grass and mud huts. In Africa and different parts of the world, the repercussions of outsiders' violent and selfish intervention in the continent is still manifesting itself in the lives of the black people globally.

The current state of Africa, economically, politically, and socially, as well as its historical context, cannot be understood and analyzed in isolation from the interests and involvement of Western and Eastern powers. The dynamics of Africans' family situations, their self-esteem, their image in the eyes of the world, the various civil wars, and the diaspora, cannot be acurately diagnosed without the violent intervention of the West and the brutal treatment of Africans by the tyrannical African leaders.

In this book, as I engrave the dire situation of Africans, I do not want the reader to think that I am attempting to portray Africans as victims of only the white race. Neither history nor facts make the blacks immune from being part of the cause for the demise, destruction, and impoverishment of their people. During the colonial expansion of Europeans, Africans were part of the colonial troops fighting Africans. Rodney observes:

35. Ibid., 186.
36. Ibid., 201.
37. Ibid., 226.
38. C. Williams, *Destruction of Black Civilization*, 148.

"Quite early in the East African campaign, the British brought in an expeditionary force of Punjabis and Sikhs, as well as regiments of West Africans. Some Sudanese and West Indians were also there. At first, a few white settlers joined the war, because they thought it was a picnic; but within a year the white residents of British East Africa were showing extreme reluctance to join the local fighting forces. In effect, therefore, Africans were fighting Africans to see which European power should rule over them. The Germans and the British had only to provide the officers. According to the history books, the 'British' won the campaign in East Africa."[39]

The psychological, economic, social, and cultural injuries the African despots inflicted on their own people is enormous. Ayittey concurs, "The economic exploitation and political repression of the African people continued unabated. More treacherous perhaps was the continued denigration and, in some cases, the destruction of indigenous African institutions and culture—by the very African nationalists and head of state who claimed to have liberated Africa. From what? Economically, politically, and culturally, Africa today is worse off than they were at the time of independence in the 1960s."[40]

Expressing his grief about this matter, a devout Christian black scholar, Chancellor Williams, stated, "Only largely united people can successfully confront oppressors and, without praying on bended knees, or even pleading, secure the removal of all shackling chains. The choice is between unity of action in calm, careful thinking and planning the course of action through one vast organization of millions—either this or ultimate damnation. If the race is incapable of unity, it is incapable of survival as free and equal people, and will deserve all the iniquities imposed upon it, for it will have proved beyond all question it is indeed unfit to survive as a people free and equal in every aspect whatsoever with the other people of the earth."[41] Highlighting the importance of Africans' unity Diop writes: "A continental federation is an urgently vital necessity for the totality of African peoples. In my opinion, it is the pre-condition for our collective survival. The more time goes by, the more it will be seen that we must either join in a continental federation or fall into a generalized and endemic state of anarchy. In fact, we have already arrived at that stage."[42] As I will explain in detail later, you will see how the war in Sierra Leone and in other African countries manifests lack of national unity, high historical and cultural consciousness, and how Africans are self-destructive and prone to anarchy.

Reflecting on the inhumanity of Africans toward Africans and justifying his mercenary role for killing Africans in Angola, Sierra Leon, and elsewhere, Cobus, the leader of Executive Outcome, adds: "At a certain point a human being becomes less of a human being, and more of an animal, and then he should be culled and get rid of as quickly as possible so that the rest of humanity can go on with their lives. There should just be total annihilation for animals like that."[43] Brabazon adds, "In Sierra Leone, their contingent of around 100 men had fought and defeated a rebel army of 3,000–4,000,

---

39. Rodney, *How Europe Underdeveloped Africa*, 187.
40. *Africa Betrayed*, 7–8.
41. C. Williams, *Destruction of Civilization*, 326.
42. *Black Africa*, 94.
43. *My Friend the Mercenary*, 150.

often psychopathic killers."[44] Cobus's zeal and commitment of annihilating "animals" did not emanate out of the passion of a white mercenary's heart to kill black Africans. It has philosophical and theoretical foundation. In 1871, in his book the *Descent of Man*, Charles Darwin, stated, "With the savages, the weak in body or mind are soon eliminated; and those that survive commonly exhibit a vigorous state of health. We civilized men, on the other hand, do our utmost to check the process of elimination."[45] But, is annihilation or elimination of the "savages" a solution? What is the standard and how reliable and dependable is Cobus's criteria to call Sierra Leonean rebels "animals?" What are the criteria of savagery? Who is establishing them?

Both in Sierra Leone and Liberia, Africans were cutting the heads off fighters they captured from the opposite side. They dismembered the bodies of dead fighters and ate their hearts. They raped women and girls, inserting sticks in their genitals, and killed parents in front of their children. They recruited fighters as young as age twelve and took them to the war front with AK47s and hand grenades given to them through illegal arms dealers. When the young soldiers cried at the war front out of fear, the rebel leaders whipped them. In certain aspects of their existence, Africans have been "tormenting devils and tormented souls."

Largely, their social behavior and inhumane actions are attributed to lack of self-esteem, lack of purpose to live, degradation, dehumanization, lack of proper family upbringing caused by the slave trade, colonialism, and the oppression and exploitation of African despots. The hopeless situation of Africans caused by Europeans still endures and has made Africans turn against each other. African dictators also have a significant role in the current miserable conditions in the continent. Often, these dictators are picked and supported by the West.

Throughout this book, I will be using the term "the West" and it is appropriate to give you the designation or characterization of the term here:

> The West . . . includes Europe, North America, plus other European settler countries such as Australia and New Zealand. The relation between the two major components of the West has, however changed over time. For much of their history, Americans defined their society in opposition to Europe. America was the land of freedom, equality, and opportunity, the future; Europe represented oppression, class conflict, hierarchy, backwardness. America, it was even argued, a distinct civilization. This positing of an opposition between American and Europe was, in considerable measure, a result of the fact that at least until the end of the nineteenth century America had only limited contacts with non-Western civilizations. Once the United States moved out on the world scene, however, the sense of a broader identity with Europe developed. While nineteenth-century America defined itself as different from the opposed to Europe, twentieth-century America defined itself as a part of and, indeed, the leader of a broader entity, the West, that includes Europe.
>
> The term "the West" is now universally used to refer to what used to be called Western Christendom. The West is thus the only civilization identified by a compass direction and not by the name of a particular people, religion, or

---

44. Ibid.
45. Cited in Moltmann, *Sun of Righteousness Arise!*, 212.

geographical area. This identification lifts the civilization out of its historical, geographical, and cultural context. Historically, Western civilization is European civilization. In the modern era, Western civilization is Euroamerican or North Atlantic civilization. Europe, America, and North Atlantic can be found on a map; the West cannot.[46]

So, in this book whenever I refer to "the West" I would like the reader to know that I am in consent with Huntington's position. Among other things, modernization and rationalism are marks of the Western people. They grade themselves and other people through these grids.

In general, the West is defined in "the Declaration of Independence of the United States of America of July 1776 and the Statement of Human and Civil Rights ratified by the French National Assembly in August 1789. Both retain a veneer of religion, but in many places it is worn so thin as to be almost non-existent. The French one speaks of the *Supreme Being* in its preamble, and the American ones make a passing acknowledgment of the Creator. But neither have much time for him. Both are concerned with man and with what seems to be so obviously right in itself."[47] It is so ironic that the West that put man at the center of the universe who treated him as one who has come of age, a rational being who has the right to judge and even reject God, is unable to see the same quality in other races, the black people in particular.

In this book, I am using the word "race" for a lack of a better term to describe the relationship between the black and white people. "The concept of race as the English language uses the term today did not develop into a consistently applied set of ideas until nineteenth century European thinkers made it so. Through the most of human history and in nearly all parts of the globe, the *only* group distinction people made were based on cultural and societal differences. People have always tended to be *ethnocentric*: human beings, in other words, commonly feel that the ideas and customs they grew up with and are familiar and comfortable with are better than the different and unfamiliar ways of societies other than their own. Competition, strife, and even hatred between different ethnic groups have often been present in human history. But racism as we understand it today—with its foolish, baseless, and evil claims of inborn and perpetual genetic differences among human beings—did not exist in earlier historical ages, in Africa or anywhere else. . .for all its historical salience, race can no longer be considered a valid scientific concept."[48] Bernal adds:

> "Race" is certainly not a useful biological category, and until the Assyrian and Persian invasions in the first millennium B.C.E., it was not an issue for the Ancient Egyptians. However, it is a crucially important *social* classification for Europeans and North Americans today.[49]

The West happened to be the white people. "Through the philosophical school of Romanticism, which was in reaction to as a consequence of the Enlightenment, . . .

---

46. Huntington, *Clash of Civilization*, 46–47.
47. C. Brown, *Philosophy and the Christian Faith*, 39.
48. Ehret, *Civilizations of Africa*, 8; emphasis added.
49. *Black Athena Writes Back*, 23; emphasis original.

virtually every white nation regarded itself as being chosen for a particular destiny and as having a unique charisma."[50] He continues: "The Puritans believed that Anglo-Saxon race was divinely mandated to guide history to its end and usher in the millennium."[51] Such feeling and perception was embedded in the white race; even the missionaries were not able to escape it. "There were more traces of racism in the high imperial era than there had been before."[52] (Walls 1982:162). Such sense of superiority was planted and enhanced in the West through Puritanism, not Marxism. Therefore, fundamentally racial issues between black and white are primarily theological. Through this theological/biblical perception "[b]lack peoples have been weighed on the scales of history by others and been found wanting."[53]

In the eyes of the West, Africans are considered to be uncivilized. "What does it mean to be 'uncivilized'?" asks Christopher Ehret. "If it means as its common colloquial implies, to behave in a violent, disorderly manner and to act without the restraint of law or custom, then Europeans of the twentieth century, with their recurrent descents into genocide and pogroms, and those southern white folk of the early decades of the century who lynched black folk are among the most uncivilized people of history. But it is foolishness to distinguish societies as a whole by such criterion."[54]

Despite skin color, the consequence of injustice on humanity is the same. This is true for all other societies who are deprived of freedom, prosperity, hope, and meaning for existence. The domination, oppression and exploitation of the West in Africa, have made Africans to be cruel and merciless toward each other. Such phenomena are not limited to the black race. For example, Stalin's brutality had turned Ukrainians into anthropophagi. Parents had eaten their children. A devastating famine deliberately engineered by Soviet leader Josef Stalin claimed at least five million lives in Ukraine and around two million in the North Caucasus and elsewhere. Famine was so widespread people had been reduced to eating grass, tree bark, roots, berries, frogs, birds, and even earthworms. Many instances of cannibalism were recorded, with people living off the remains of other starvation victims or in some instances resorting to murder. Most peasant families had five or six children, and some mothers killed their weakest children in order to feed the others.[55] Suffering and oppression, despite skin color, can reduce people to the lowest point of existence; it deprives them of their humanity.

Before the black slave trade, indentured servants from Europe were brought to the U.S. for labor work. Between 1654 and 1685, ten thousand sailed from Bristol alone, chiefly for the West Indies and Virginia. In 1683 white servants represented one-sixth of Virginia's population. Two-thirds of the immigrants to Pennsylvania during the eighteenth century were white servants; in four years 25,000 came to Philadelphia alone. It has been estimated that more than a quarter of a million persons were of this class

50. Bosch, *Transforming Mission*, 299.
51. Ibid., 300.
52. Walls, *Missionary Movement in Christian History*, 162.
53. Diop, *Black Africa*, 114.
54. *Civilizations of Africa*, 5.
55. Askold Krushelnycky, "Ukraine: Famine."

during the colonial period, and they probably constitute one-half of all English immigrants, the majority going to the middle colonies.

Convicts, girls who had been imprisoned as disorderly, vagrants, rogues, idlers, petty thieves, gypsies, and persons who frequented unlicensed brothels were shipped to the New Land. Some were kidnaped. The transportation of these white servants shows in its true light the horror of the Middle Passage—not as something unusual or inhuman, but as a part of the age. The emigrants were packed like herrings. The status of these white servants became progressively worse in the plantation colonies. Servitude turned them into things. In Maryland, servitude developed into an institution approaching in some respects chattel slavery. They were grinding at the mills and attending the furnaces, or digging in the scorching islands; having nothing to eat. They washed their faces in the tears of their own afflictions; attached as horses and beasts for the debt of their masters. They were whipped at the whipping posts for their master's pleasure. The servants were regarded as "white trash."[56] Such kinds of treatment had created in the indentured servants social and psychological malfunction behavior. Their self-worth was low; they had no aspiration for life, and their existence was meaningless. The "white trash" trashed themselves and their fellow human beings.

So, Cobus's observation of Africans inhumanity to their people is not far from the truth. The weak side of Cobus's assessment, however, that "human being becomes less of human being," according to him, is that it is limited only to the black race. He was blinded to the fact of the carnage inflicted on black Africans by the white race including by his own Afrikaans across the continent and in the world.

An example of Western carnage in Africa is Belgium's colonization of Congo. Without counting those whose legs and hands were amputated and those taken to Europe for slavery, the Belgians killed an estimated ten to twelve million Congolese. When Belgians conquered Congo the US navy gave them twenty-one gun salutes and celebrated the Belgian victory with them.[57] The magnitude of the massacres was similar to that of the holocaust. "Sifting such figures today is like sifting the ruins of an Auschwitz crematorium. They do no tell you precise death tolls, but they reek of mass murder."[58] The author asks, "Statistics about mass murder are often hard to prove. But if this murder turned out to be even half as high, I thought, the Congo would have been one of the major killing grounds of modern times. Why were these deaths not mentioned in the standard litany of our century's of horrors? And why had I never before heard of them?" Hochschild asks.[59] Why have the champions of democracy today, Western missionaries, and those who try African despots for crimes in The Hague not condemned the injustice and cruelty of Belgians in Congo? Abraham J. Heschel rightly said:

> Indeed, the sort of crimes and even the amount of delinquency that fill the prophets of Israel with dismay do not go beyond that which we regard as normal, as typical ingredients of social dynamics. To us a single act of injustice—cheating in business, exploitation of the poor—is slight; to the prophets, a disaster. To us

56. E. Williams, *Capitalism and Slavery*, 8–18.
57. Hochschild, *King Leopold's Ghost*.
58. Ibid., 230.
59. Ibid., 3.

> injustice in injurious to the welfare of the people; to the prophets it is a death-blow to existence; to us, an episode; to them, a catastrophe, a threat to the world.
>
> Their breathless impatience with injustice may strike us as hysteria. We ourselves witness continually acts of injustice, manifestations of hypocrisy, falsehood, outrage, misery, but rarely grow indignant or overly excited. To the prophets even a minor injustice assumes cosmic proportions.[60]

If all human life is sacred, I wonder why the mass killings of Africans is not publicized and taught in schools like the death of Jews in Germany and Ukrainians by Stalin. Why are Africans not teaching, building museums, having archives, or providing degree programs in their various universities for students who would like to specialize in the African slave trade, colonialism, and the like that would remind this generation and the one to come about the injustice the black race went through and is still going through? Why is there no indignation even among the biblical scholars and Christian leaders about the situation of Africa, past and present? "The niggardliness of our moral comprehensions, the incapacity to sense the depth of misery is caused by our own failures, is a fact which no subterfuge can elude. Our eyes are witness to the callousness and cruelty of man, but our heart tries to obliterate the memories, to calm the nerves, and to silence our conscience."[61] The Westerners were not only controlling Africans and their resources but also information about their encounter with Africans. Niall Ferguson, in his Foreword for *Dead Aid*, accurately observed: "The African discussion has been colonized as surely as the African continent was a century ago."[62] *King Leopold's Ghost* by Hochschild is one of the books I read in 1998 and it gave me several days of sleepless nights.

The world has recognized the holocaust and thousands of articles and books are written and museums have been established for six million Jews killed by the Nazis. Cobus never thought of annihilating either the Belgians or the Germans. Truth has to be like a two-edged sword. It has to cut the fallacy of humanity on both sides. Without that there is no justice. The origin of evil thoughts and action in people goes beyond the color of their skin. Killing a fellow human being is the problem of humankind; it is not a race issue. "The very emphasis of the commandment *Thou shalt not kill* makes it certain that we spring from an endless ancestry of murderers, with whom the lust for killing was in the blood, as possibly it is to this day with ourselves."[63] Even Freud, who considers religion an illusion of human beings, concurs to the commandment of God about the human nature. "We spring from an endless ancestry of murderers." Perkins rightly said, "History was a tapestry of conquest and brutality that *we humans* had muddle through."[64] Sin and evil reigned primarily in the individual heart, not in society. The "we" Freud and Perkins talked about includes every human race. Freud's biblical reflection was not a revelation from above. It was an assessment on his cultural and historical context here on earth. "Without any justified or even detectible reasons for the war, the great Christian powers in Europe . . . fell upon each other. It was a war of annihilation

60. *Prophets*, 4.
61. Ibid. pg.5
62. Foreword to Moyo, *Dead Aid*, ix.
63. Freud, *Character and Culture*, 129; emphasis original.
64. *Secret History of the American Empire*, 225; emphasis added.

without any victory aims. A true symbol for this was the battle of Verdun in 1916. The German idea was that it was to be 'a battle of attrition.' After six months, there were more than 600,000 dead and almost no gains or losses of territory. In Ypes, the Germans began the poison-gas war and profited nothing by it."[65]

In my opinion, white Europeans did not kill Africans because they hate black people and they are racist. If we launch from this presupposition as a primary cause of today's African misery, we'll end up in a wrong conclusion—that is, an endless cycle of bigotry and sadistic treatment of each other. Human beings kill each other because "[w]e spring from an endless ancestry of murderers." Timothy Keller elaborates Freud's assertion: "Sin entered the world to deface and mar everything that had been made. Because we became estranged from God, we also are alienated from our true selves, and from each other. Our primal self-absorption has led to profound social evil—to war, crime, family breakdown, oppression, and injustice. When we lost our relationship with God, the whole world stopped 'working right.' The world is filled with hunger, sickness, aging, and physical death. *Because our relationship with God has broken down, shalom is gone—spiritually, psychologically, socially, and physically.*"[66] My African Christian response to the West's and China's involvement in Africa springs from this fundamental biblical premise. Hence, as I pursue humble cooperation with all humankind to bring shalom in African and the rest of the world, I also gently provoke all reared in the school of tradition. If the West is open to listen to African scholars in the global arena, I strongly believe that Christian scholarship needs a major reorientation. Even if it is painful for a moment, it is good to face the true stories of Africa and deal with them biblically and missiologically. Remembering past wrongs is prevention of the present and future evil atrocities done to humankind in the name of civilization and religious propagation.

It is important that Africans recall the dark side of the slave trade and European colonial expansion that brought them where they are today. Tswambe, a Congolese, remembers the state official Lèon Fivèz, who was Belgian, this way:

> All black saw this man as the devil of the Equator . . . From all the bodies killed in the field, you had to cut off the hands. He wanted to see the number of hands cut off by each soldier, who had to bring them in baskets . . . A village which refused to provide rubber would be completely swept clean. As a young man, I saw [Fievez's] soldier Molili, then guarding the village of Boyeka, take a net, put ten arrested natives in it, attach big stones to the net, and make it stumble into the river . . . Rubber causes these torments; that's why we no longer want to hear its name spoken. [Belgian] soldiers made young men kill or rape their own mothers and sisters.[67]

Rubber, a natural resource that God has blessed them with, became a nemesis to the Congolese because of the Belgians mayhem. When you add centuries of wars and unrest because of fighting over diamonds, gold, uranium, rare minerals more valuable than gold such as coltan used for computer chips, etc., nemesis turns to hell. That is where the Congolese have been living since the Portuguese attempted to colonize them in 1488.

65. Moltmann, *Sun of Righteousness Arise!*, 14–15.
66. Keller, *Generous Justice*, 176–77; emphasis added.
67. Hochschild, *King Leopold's Ghost*, 166.

Their poverty, high illiteracy rate, inadequate medical facilities, diaspora, suffering, and humiliation cannot be explained and fully comprehended without their historical journey under the heavy hands of Western powers. Despite these realities, there are millions of Christians in the Congo. But when you look at the gap in income and lifestyle between them and us who are in the West who embrace the same Bible and the same Christ, one wonders if we all live on the same planet. The Christology and missiology of the West in Africa has not yet produced the emancipation and justice the gospel promises.

For black people, it is difficult if not impossible to understand their past and present without the intervention of people in the West, which creates a conflict of thoughts in their minds. Africans know that white people are champions of democracy. And yet, it is white people who made them drink the bitter test of injustice and degradation. On one side of history, even if some critics say he paved a way for slavery and exploitation, there is David Livingstone who came and died in Africa for Africans out of his love for Christ and the African people. The white people have invented medicines that cured many and eradicated some diseases. They have invented airplanes that shortened the distance between nations, even though the use of planes has not been limited to transportation. The white people have invented phones, electric power, cars and trains, boats and ships, computers, email, Skype, and Facebook. White people have put man on the moon and demonstrated the great potential of human beings. Armstrong was not only an American hero he was a hero of all humankind. The list is too long to cover the positive things white people have done for the good of humankind.

On the other side of human history, Africans know well that it is the white people who enslaved them, who colonized and exploited them, lynched black people in Africa and elsewhere. Europeans started the two major World Wars, they caused the holocaust, almost eliminated Native Americans, built the first hydrogen bomb and used it on Hiroshima and Nagasaki, and made the world we live in under a nuclear threat—and they are still one of the major causes for the misery of Africans. The white people have produced Hitler and Stalin on one side of history, Billy Graham and Mother Teresa on the other.

Even if hopelessness and despair conditions them to do so Africans cannot and should not stereotype white people. Undoubtedly, there are innumerable good white people. Unfortunately, the image of a white person in the minds of many Africans is tarnished by the inhumane relational and historical experiences they have had with white people in Africa and elsewhere. It is a historical tragedy that the foreign policy of the West in Africa by and large does not represent the goodness, genuine care, and love of white people in most parts of the Western world for Africans.

Because there are God's remnants in every culture and a potential for all of us to be redeemed by the grace of God, I don't think annihilation, as Cobus embraced and applied it with passion, is a solution to build an Africa that is free from oppression and exploitation of her own people or any Western nation. If Africa becomes a superpower a century from now and the West ends up where Africa is today, hardly would any sensible African enjoy revenge and elimination of the white people. We have a lot to learn from the crucified Christ who forgave his enemies. And the great statesman Mandela is a noble example of reconciliation instead of annihilation. Howard Thurman, the son of slave parents who went through segregation and discrimination and one who knows Christ the crucified, said, "hatred destroys finally the core of the life of the hater. While it lasts burning in white heat, its effect seems positive and dynamic. But at last it turns to ash, for it guarantees isolation from one's fellows. It blinds the individual to all values of worth, even as they apply to himself and to his fellows. Hatred bears deadly and bitter fruit. It is blind and nondiscriminating . . . The logic of the development of hatred is death to the spirit and disintegration of ethical and moral values."[68] Guinness concurs: "In the Christian perspective, nothing that any man will do to us in life will ever equal what we have done to God and yet he has forgiven us in Christ. This means that if we deal with other men on any other basis than the way God has dealt with us, we are double-dealing God and he will not stand for it. The God and Father of Jesus Christ is loving but not soft."[69] Heschel adds, "God is compassion, not compromise; justice, though not inclemency."[70]

Developing the personality of Africans and making them Christ-like in the face of the two opposing realities of the West is a huge theological and ministerial task. Genuine conversion includes reconciliation with God and fellow human beings. To be dismissive of historical realities and the present situation creates question about the credibility of a Christian witness. To take sides is ungodly and unbiblical. For example, because Italy used chemical weapons like mustard gas on Ethiopians in the 1935–36 war, I cannot totally condemn or hate Italians and be blind to the inhumanity of Ethiopians to their own people. Ian Smith and Robert Mugabe, are both evil leaders with different skin color. In good conscious, an African Christian leader cannot accept Mugabe and reject Ian Smith. Some might argue that because Mugabe was colonized and was put in jail for ten years, he is a product of Ian Smith. But so was Mandela. On the day of his sentence to twenty-seven years of imprisonment he read these words in the court: "During my lifetime I have dedicated myself to this struggle of the African people. I have fought against white domination, and I have fought against black domination. I have cherished the ideal of a democratic and free society in which all persons live together in harmony and with equal opportunities. It is an ideal which I hope to live for and to achieve. But if needs be, it is an ideal for which I am prepared to die."[71]

> Among Nelson Mandela's many achievements, two stand out. First, he was the world's most inspiring example of fortitude, magnanimity and dignity in the face of oppression, serving more than 27 years in prison for his belief that all men and women are created equal. During the bleak years of his imprisonment on Robben Island, thanks to his own patience, humour and capacity for forgiveness, he seemed freer behind bars than the men who kept him there, locked up as they were in their own self-demeaning prejudices. Indeed, his warders were those who came to admire him most.
>
> Second, and little short of miraculous, was the way in which he engineered and oversaw South Africa's transformation from a byword for nastiness and narrowness into, at least in intent, a rainbow nation in which people, no matter what their colour, were entitled to be treated with respect. . .For all the humiliation he suffered at the hands of white racist before he was released in 1990, he was

---

68. *Jesus and the Disinherited*, 76, 77.
69. *Dust of Death*, 188–89.
70. *Prophets*, 19.
71. Meredith, *Fate of Africa*, 127.

never animated by a desire for revenge. He was himself utterly without prejudice, which is why he became a symbol of tolerance and justice across the globe.[72]

The African continent lacks leaders with the vision and persona of Mandela, who understood human nature and handled his leadership role with fairness to all. In human history, his kind of breed are rare and few. Hence, cruelty, suffering, and injustice outweigh peace, prosperity, and justice in Africa.

In the relationship between the West and Africa, unfortunately, the scale of justice is not balanced and fair. In the blood diamond war, it is Charles Taylor of Liberia who is taken to The Hague not King Leopold II or Harry Oppenheimer. Roberts describes the insult to injury of Africans this way: "Despite the exploitation of black labor in the Oppenheimer mines, the Stellenbosch University, the top Afrikaner institution in the Cape, astonishingly saw fit to create a new chair called—The Harry Oppenheimer Chair for the Study of Human Rights."[73]

The European Union, which is trying African despots in the Hague, chose Brussels, a city that has the blood of millions of Africans on her hands, as a place for their headquarters. In the face of such injustice, as Shakespeare said in Macbeth, one can conclude: "Life is a tale told by an idiot, full of sound and fury signifying nothing." But, to be pessimistic and to give up on life is not the call of Christians. In the case of the dilemma of the African church, the only safe and righteous place is to ground ourselves on the truth of the Scripture and allow the word of God, like a double-edged sword, to cut both ways. In my opinion, through a slow and painful process, this is the theological and biblical position the prophets in the Old Testament and the apostles of Jesus Christ took. Without it, it is impossible to understand the nature of human beings and the mercy of God. Hence, the apostles equally loved and served the Romans who destroyed their temple, killed their people, and caused their diaspora and the Jews who were the catalyst for the crucifixion of Christ.

For our present challenge, such tasks demand global hermeneutical community that makes the church of Jesus Christ accountable to God and fellow believers answerable to each other. The unidirectional Western theology that is always ready to teach and has no room to learn has not been helpful to develop the theological identity of Africans.[74]

In light of the suffering they had gone through, why should the Bible matter to Africans? An answer to this question should not be limited to missiologists. Bible scholars, primarily from Africa, need to speak and write biblically to the minds and souls of Africans and affirm that the God of Ezekiel still can communicate through violence and trauma. "Reading Amos, for example, in rich, relatively safe Westchester County, New York, make it easy to underplay economic, political, and theological consequences of this prophet's fiery speech, of God's rejection of worship without justice, of God's scorn for those who trample the head of the poor into the dust of the earth. The context makes it necessary either to overlook or defend the violence of this God and easy to reduce the

---

72. *The Economist*, December 14, 2013, p. 15.
73. Roberts, *Glitter and Greed*, 43.
74. Bediako, *Theology and Identity*.

text to limp themes divine justice and idealized forms of theological thinking, devoid of concrete realities of the life of the homeless, deprivation, and ways we have trampled and been trampled upon."[75] Africans are not that interested to know the origin of the biblical texts, history of composition, oral traditions, questions of authorship and those abstract ivory-towerish ideas. What they want and search for is meaning, life, hope, freedom, justice, peace, dignity, and security for their community. M. Daniel Carroll R. concurs:

> The book of Amos has always held an attraction for approaches seeking theological warrant for significant sociopolitical, economic, and culture change. The ongoing harsh realities of oppression and exploitation—of whatever sort—all around the world continue to sustain in powerful ways the motivation to engage the book of Amos, even as they have over so many centuries. What often distinguishes this sort of readings is a self-conscious "reading *as*" or "reading *from*" more marginalized groups rather than from the perspective of more classical scholarship. This are intentionally situated approaches, which argue that the study of the biblical text cannot be a strictly academic exercise. The prophetic words must move outside its pages either to capture or perhaps to repel its readers, whether to inspire them or to make them cast doubts upon its voice. These important angels on reality of faith come to the text from the very difficult stuff of life, and it behooves the broader Christian community to listen to them in order to probe further the depths of the Bible's message and impact.[76]

Western biblical theology and Christology hardly speaks to "very difficult stuff of life." Since Western scholars are devoid of "these important angels on reality of faith," it is difficult for them to make the message of the Scripture relevant to the African or the majority world contexts. "Western preoccupation with dominance and power is no doubt linked to and derived from [the] 'imperial image of God.' Clearly when that discernment of God is challenged, the images which take public form are placed in deep jeopardy."[77]

The universal body of Christ can learn a lot from those who have gone through suffering and encounter Christ in a difficult situation of life. Jürgen Moltmann, who became one of the best theologians and scholars, was a war prisoner after the end of World War II. Reflecting on the process of his restoration, he writes:

> [A] group of Dutch students came and asked to speak to us officially. Again I was frightened, for I had fought in Holland, in the battle of the Arnhem Bridge. The Dutch students told us that Christ is the bridge on which they could cross to us and that without Christ they could not talk to us at all. They told us the Gestapo terror, the loss of their Jewish friends, and the destruction of their homes. We too could step on this bridge which Christ had built from them to us, and confess the guilt of our people and ask for reconciliation. At the end we all embraced. For me that was *an hour of liberation. I was able to breathe again, felt like a human being once more, and returned cheerfully to the camp behind the barbed wire.* The question of how long the captivity was going to last no longer bothered me. In some English circles, Norton Camp counted as a camp where young Germans were supposed to be "re-educated" for a better Germany. But in reality it was *a*

---

75. O'Connor, "Mystery of Meaning," 59.
76. *Amos*, 53; emphasis original.
77. Fretheim, *Suffering of God*, xiii.

generous gift of reconciliation offered to former enemies; and as such it was unique . . . We were given what we did not deserve and received the fullness of Christ "grace upon grace". . . What we experienced was for many of us the turn from God's "hidden face" to "the light of his countenance." We experienced with pain his hiddenness and remoteness, and we sensed that he looked upon us "with shining eyes," and felt the warmth of his eyes.[78]

In contrast to annihilation, love, forgiveness, and reconciliation have the power to make a one-time inhuman person to be human. Even if Moltmann was in a camp behind barbed wire, he experienced liberation. He was not only embraced by his former enemies but by God, who was so remote to him.

John Newton, an Englishman captained a specially designed slave frigate named, simply enough, a Slave Ship. She could carry up to 600 people, chained side to side and lined up like timber. The purpose was to pack in as many slaves as the ship could hold since an average of 20 percent died during the two-month-long middle passage to Cuba. In 1748, Newton loaded slave cargo in Sierra Leone and weighed anchor into a massive storm that lasted eleven days. Convinced that he would not survive, he had a religious conversion on the deck, in the raging storm, bellowing out to God "to save his wretched soul." The experience led to his writing the psalm "Amazing Grace" some twenty years later.[79] In every human race, God has his own Moltmann and John Newton. The black African race should not be exceptional. The 3,000–4,000 RUFs who were eliminated by EO under the leadership of Cobus never had this chance. Roberts comments, "In Sierra Leone diamonds were financing another bloody war and mercenaries were again involved. Executive Outcome held 40 percent share in Branch Energy/Diamond Works' Sierra Leone operation. Independent observers noted that these mostly white mercenaries seem to have scant concern about killing black Africans."[80]

In the eighteenth century, ships from the West were coming to Sierra Leone to load African slaves. Now the West is sending grenades to the country and taking diamonds from Sierra Leone. It is in this context that African theologians and missiologists try to understand Christ and God's mission. At least for me, it has never been an easy experience. It is not naturally acceptable for African Christians who are victimized by slavery, colonialism, exploitation, oppression, exile, poverty, and disease to pray, "Hallowed be thy Name!" Especially, when they know the nations who embrace Christianity and are sending missionaries to Africa are the cause of their misery then and now.

The English and the Dutch people, through a magnanimous human gesture, re-educated the young German war prisoners in order to build a better Germany. The African colonialist and mercenaries have neither the heart nor the logic for a better Angola, Sierra Leone, Liberia, Congo, and Guinea, etc. For example, Guinea-Bissau's key natural resources include phosphates, granite, clay, bauxite, unexploited deposits of petroleum, and limestone. In 2010, the mineral production in the country was restrained to small-scale production of granite, sand and gravel, clay, and limestone. Gold, bauxite, phosphate rock, diamond, and heavy minerals were the country's most prospective mineral

---

78. Moltmann, *Source of Life*, 6, 7, 8; emphasis added.
79. Campbell, *Blood Diamonds*, 29.
80. Roberts, *Glitter and Greed*, 227.

resources in 2010.⁸¹ Despite these natural resources the country is still in the rank and file of the poorest countries in the world. David Lamb explains the reason:

> Unlike two other former Portuguese colonies, Mozambique and Angola, Guinea-Bissau had not been a white-settler colony. The Portuguese came only to administer and to save enough money to retire on back home. Within a few weeks of independence, all but 350 of the 2,500 Portuguese in Guinea-Bissau hurried home. Most departed with no sorrows. And what they left as a legacy of three hundred years of colonial rule was pitifully little: fourteen university graduates, an illiteracy rate of 97 percent and only 265 miles of paved roads in an area twice the size of New Jersey. There was only one modern plant in Guinea-Bissau in 1974—it produced beer for the Portuguese troops—and as a final gesture before leaving, the Portuguese destroyed the national archive.⁸²

To this Lamb adds, "When Tanzania gained its independence in 1961, it only had 16 university graduates to run the country. Zambia was a little luckier: It had 100 university graduates, 1, 500 dropouts from secondary education, and 6,000 with two year at secondary schools in a country of 4 million."⁸³

Natural resources without intellectual and technological skills cannot be turned into dollars. For over three hundred years the people in Guinea Bissau lived with a lack of self-esteem and self-worth believing their life and destiny was in the hands of the Portuguese who ruled them. For the natives their own country was like a big prison without a fence and without a gate with padlock. Hence, they did not excel in education, economy, development, nation building, and global network. Postcolonialism did not make them free from indirect pressure, threat, dependency, and control. They are partakers of the fate of West African countries.

After Brabazon got an award and money for his war film in Liberia, with a sense of guilt he summarized his experience in these words: "To be able to sit through other people's horror and come out into the bar at the other end: that was what we all wanted—to have experienced, survival and been paid. Some of us did it for real; some of us did it by proxy."⁸⁴ There is no moral, ethical, or legal guide when mercenaries and Western governments overthrow an African government. There are no tears, compassion, or empathy when filmmakers tape as Africans cut off the heads of their fellow Africans and butcher them. No voice of justice and freedom is heard from the mouths and pens of many Western journalists as they walk through piles of African corpses in Sierra Leone and Liberia. In fact, in their own words they are "happy" when they get these kinds of opportunities to capture these scenes with their cameras. This kind of film, again, makes "good entertainment" in Europe and in the U.S., they say. If the opportunity is not there, they demand to see action.⁸⁵ How then can Africa have respite from war? How can we call this civilization? Where is justice?

81. Thomas, "Guinea-Bissau."
82. Lamb, *Africans*, 5.
83. Ibid.
84. *My Friend the Mercenary*, 225.
85. Ibid., 210.

For many African destitute the turning point of Moltmann is worth mentioning here. In the Scottish labor camp, along with many other war prisoners, for the first time in his life he was given a Bible. He read most of it without much understanding until he came to Psalm 39, which held him spellbound: "I was dumb with silence, I held my peace and my sorrow was stirred [Luther's German is much stronger—"I have to eat up my suffering within myself"] . . . my life time is as nothing in thy sight . . . Hear my prayer, O Lord, and give ear to my cry; hold not thou thy peace at my tears, for I am a stranger with thee, and a sojourner, all my fathers were." They were the words of my own heart and they called my soul to God.[86] Without a platform for justice, with no one standing on their side, with rare words of comfort, counseling or therapy, many Africans have eaten up their suffering within themselves. More than the Christ of Christendom, I believe the Christ of the cross is more appealing to them. Moltmann concurs: "Then I came to the story of the passion, and when I read Jesus's death cry, 'My God, why have your forsaken me?' I knew with certainty: this is someone who understands you. I began to understand the assailed Christ because I felt that he understood me: this was the divine brother in distress who takes the prisoners with him on his way to resurrection . . .Christ's God-forsakenness showed me *where* God is."[87]

If properly contextualized and if Africans can read the Bible in their mother tongues as Moltmann did in German, the crucified God can be an everlasting inheritance to disinherited Africans. The best way to set the African church to live with eschatological hope and enable her to reap the fruit of the resurrection is by deepening her roots in the theology of the cross. Teachers, pastors, evangelists, and Christian counselors need to present Christ to Africans in such a way that they can, like Moltmann, also say, "This is someone who understands you." In a vast and rich continent, Africans are living behind a "barbed wire" of poverty, ethnic and religious violence, disease, exploitation, oppression, and the like. Despite the disappointing results of many African governments, the church will remain the best alternative agent for positive social and economic change. To play her role effectively in society, the church needs the contribution of Christian scholars who can develop a relevant theology and missiology of the cross. The crucified Christ has power to transform despair into triumph.

The two major faces of Africa today are discouraging and paralyzing social and economic problems and the growth of Christianity. Even if the church is directly affected by its context, solace and solution is expected from the church because of the object of her faith—Jesus Christ. Jesus has said, "The kingdom of God is in your midst" (Luke 19:20) and he has come to give us abundant life (John 10:17). What do these words mean in today's Africa? The diagnosis on the introduction of the gospel in Africa is essential. Without understanding the past, we cannot rightly interpret the present and pave the way to the future.

Africa is a continent of contradiction not only in the area of natural resources. It is also a continent of contradiction in the area of religion, Christianity in particular. "European-American exploitation which was centered on the enslavement of Africans was initiated by the Catholic nations Portugal and Spain, but was later dominated by the

86. Moltmann, *Source of Life*, 4–5.
87. Ibid., 5; emphasis original.

Protestant British, who defeated the Dutch in a series wars... Protestant Dutch and the English made slavery a system of Big Business, setting the stage for the Industrial Revolution, which England initially dominated in the eighteenth and nineteenth centuries."[88] Bosch adds: "Spain and Portugal introduced slavery and were soon emulated by other remerging colonial powers (Protestant ones as well), who claimed a share in the lucrative trade in human bodies. In 1537, the pope authorized the opening of a slave market in Lisbon, where up to twelve thousand Africans were sold annually for transportation to the West Indies. By the eighteenth century, Britain had the lion's share of the slave market. In the ten years between 1883 and 1893 a total of 800 slave ships left Liverpool, carrying over three hundred thousand slaves to the Americas. It has been estimated that the number of slaves sold to European colonies amounted to between twenty and forty million. And all along the (assumed) superiority of Westerners over all others became more and more firmly entrenched and regarded axiomatic."[89]

German Chancellor von Caprivi stated publicly in 1890, "We should began establishing a few station in the interior, from which both the merchants and the missionary can operate; gun and Bible should go hand in hand."[90] Von Caprivi doesn't seem to know the God of the Bible and his message for mankind when he said, "gun and Bible should go hand in hand."[91] The Old Testament prophets "proclaimed that might is not supreme, that the sword is an abomination, that violence is obscene... Questioning man's infatuation with might insisted not only on the immorality but also on the futility and absurdity of war."[92] When the Romans and the Jews arrested Jesus, "one of Jesus' companion reached for his sword, drew it out and struck the servant of the high priest, cutting off his ear. Put your sword back in its place Jesus said to him, for all who draw sword will die by the sword" (Matt 26:51–52). Not only did the Scriptures say this, one of the world's best known generals, Napoleon, did not find prosperity and lasting peace in war. In his later life, to his minister of education, he said, "Do you know Fontanes, what astonishes me most in this world? The inability of force to create anything. In the long run, the sword is always beaten by the spirit."[93] Centuries before Napoleon, Isaiah declared that the sword shall be destroyed: "They shall beat their swords into plowshares, and their spears into pruning hooks; nation shall not lift up sword against nation, neither shall they learn war anymore" (2:4). Somehow, European Christianity thought to run gun and Bible hand in hand suits the plan of God in Africa and the rest of their colonized world.

> The Christian nations in Europe conquered their colonial empires in Africa and Asia and spread Europe's "Christian civilization' with messianic zeal. They all participated: Holland in Indonesia, Belgium in the Congo, Italy in Libya and Eritrea, and finally Germany too, in East Africa and 'the German Southwest'

---

88. Clarke, *Christopher Columbus*, 11–12.
89. Bosch, *Transforming Mission*, 227.
90. Ibid., 304.
91. "Just as Islam spread north of the Sahara through conquest, so did Christianity spread south of the Sahara by the same means. If north of the Sahara Islam spread by the sword, south of the Sahara Christianity spread by the gun" (Mazrui 1990:136).
92. Heschel, *Prophets*, 203–4.
93. Herold, *Mind of Napoleon*, 76.

[Namibia]. The rest already belonged to the British Empire, which stretched from Calcutta to Cape Town and Cairo, as Cecil Rhodes boasted. In the United States, the transcontinental railroad carried settlers west; in Russia the Trans-Siberian Railway took the Cossacks as far as Vladivostok. By 1900, the time was not far off when the great Christian powers would carve up China too among themselves.[94]

Chidester further comment:

During their fifteenth-century explorations of the West African coast, Portuguese navigators planted crosses or erected limestone pillars with crosses on top to indicate the southernmost point they had reached on each voyage. Serving as navigational markers, the pillars—or *padraos*—also asserted a Portuguese claim to land. Standing six to eight feet in height, each pillar featured a square stone on which the date, the name of the explorer, and the name of the Portuguese king were carved in Latin and Portuguese. By the time the Portuguese navigator Bartolomeo Dias had planted a *padrao* at the eastern Cape of southern Africa in 1488, the Portuguese monument appeared all along the west coast of Africa. Often accompanied by the Catholic Mass, the act of setting up *padrao* was another European "ceremony of possession" with religious, political, and economic significance.[95]

In Africa, the task of Christian Europe was not only to colonize and civilize. It was to make Africans "human" or "people." The French governor of Madagascar, referring to the role of the missionaries in colonialism, said, "What we want, is to prepare the indigenous population for manual labor; you turn them into *people*."[96] Let alone the mortal Western missionaries, Jesus Christ did not come to turn Africans "into people." But the European imperialism and Christianity played a role to turn Africans into "beings" and then "believers." I think it is observing such kind of arrogance and incongruity that made Friedrich Nietzsche say that for Christians to be redeemed and free people they "would have to look more redeemed."[97] Yes, Christ has come in the form of a servant to save sinners; not as a master to change half-animals into people. If we are allowed to interpret African history through the lenses of Africans, what we see and understand is that Christianity is misused and abused by Western powers. Without this history, the lack of theological education in African churches, the "inch-deep" African Christianity, lack of trained pastors, shortages of Scripture in vernacular languages in Africa, poverty, insatability, etc., cannot be understood. However, it is not the purview of this author to explore the history and modus operandi of Western mission and the spread of European Christianity in Africa.

When American journalist, George Washington Williams asked what the king expected in return for all the money he had spent developing the Congo, Leopold replied, "*[W]hat I do there is done as a Christian duty* to the poor Africans; and I do not wish to

---

94. Moltmann, *Sun of Righteousness Arise!*, 10.
95. Chidester, *Christianity*, 412.
96. Spindler, "Meaning and Prospect," 24; emphasis original.
97. Quoted in Küng, *The Church*, 150.

have one franc back of all the money I have expended."[98] Leopold's Christian duty, "the white man's burden—and avowed mission to end slavery in Africa and bring civilization to a supposedly dark continent" in the eyes of many observers, "was in truth one of history's greatest rapes. Farming was made a crime wherever African labor is needed for rubber cultivation, and men who did not produce enough had their hand chopped off. But instead of trailing shame and guilt through the ages, this rape has mostly bequeathed to us tales of Western heroism."[99] To Leopold, killing, slavery, looting, and stealing the natural resources of Congo was a "Christian duty." Even if the degrees of atrocities differ, Christian Europe and North America did the same in various African countries. What kind of hermeneutics can give biblical justification to the acts of the colonialist without contradicting the teachings of Christianity and the God of the Christians? To exploit and dehumanize Africans "Even the holy robes of priests in Angola not only covered their real mission as agents of empire, but covered their insatiable lusts for the black bodies of their helpless slave girls. She had been forced by the actualities of black-white relations to distrust all whites, along with their tricky treaties."[100] Williams continues, "What the Blacks did not know, however, was that while both Christianity and Islam were in themselves great and acceptable faiths, they were being used by men whose main purposes were conquest and enslavement in pursuit of economic and political power. The whole continent of Africa was taken over, its wealth exploited, and its people dehumanized through enslavement, all in the name of Jesus Christ, Allah, and Civilization."[101]

The contradiction is done without a mask. For example, the historians of modern mission, graphically and accurately describe West Africa as the white man's grave. If you are a student of etymology, the nickname is a result of a high mortality rate among the missionaries and colonist. "Either malaria or Yellow Fever was very likely to kill the Europeans who tried to live there."[102] However, the same Western mission societies who were sending missionaries to Africa to share the love of God at the cost of their lives had policies not to accept black Christians as missionaries. In the case of American Churches many evangelical Christians including clergy owned African slaves.[103]

In Africa and in places the African slaves were taken, Africans were lynched by the West with no sense of remorse or repentance and no judicial process. In the U.S., "Hundreds of Kodaks clicked all morning at the scene of the lynching. People in automobiles and carriages came from miles around to view the corpse dangling from the end of the rope . . . Picture card photographers installed a portable printing plant at the bridge and reaped a harvest in selling postcards showing a photograph of the lynched Negro. Women and children were there by the score. At a number of country schools, the day's routine was delayed until boy and girl pupils could get back viewing the lynched man."[104] What kind of education do pupils gain by watching a lynched Negro? Even if it is baffling

---

98. Hochschild, *King Leopold's Ghost*, 106; emphasis added.
99. French, *A Continent for the Taking*, 53.
100. C. Williams, *Destruction of Civilization*, 269.
101. Ibid., 334.
102. "The white man's graveyard," http://www.rainforesteducation.com/terrors/default.htm.
103. See Hall, *Slaves in the Family*.
104. Allen et al., *Without Sanctuary*, 11.

to understand the value of such an education, its importance was demonstrated by extending the school program. "State execution is a mighty weapon, and in the colonial context it has generally been used sparingly. Not so in the Mau Mau emergency. Kenya's hanging judges were kept busy . . . In total, approximately 3000 Kikuyu stood trial between 1952 and 1958 on capital charges to the Mau Mau movement. In all, over the course of the emergency, 1090 Kikuyu would go to the gallows for Mau Mau crimes. In no other place, and at no other time in the history of British imperialism, was state execution used on such a scale as this. This was more than double the number of executions carried out against convicted terrorists in Algeria, and many more than in all the other British colonial emergencies of the post-war period—in Palestine, Malaya, Cyprus and Aden."[105]

By having a black president, one can see how far the U.S. has come. Even if there are pockets of racial discrimination and injustice against blacks, the country is making positive steps forward to improve the treatment of black people in the U.S. In our present situation, as we have seen in major U.S cities like Chicago and South Central Los Angles, the worst enemies of blacks are blacks. They mercilessly kill each other.

> On June 25, 1996, Bill Griffin, age twenty-six, was ambushed in a drive-by shooting and became one of more than 350 young black men who are killed in a street violence each year in our nation's capital. Black-on-black murders in Washington, DC, have become so common that Griffin's death was newsworthy only because he was the last of his mother's four children to be murdered before the age of thirty.
>
> The day after Bill Griffin was killed, hundreds of miles away in a Milwaukee neighborhood two young girls, thirteen-year-old Lawanda Moore and her best friend, elven-year-old Sholanda Young, were playing on a front porch when two cars came roaring down the street filled with young black men with guns blazing away at one another. Stray bullets took Lawanda's life and left Sholanda in a coma. Before patrol cars arrived at the crime scene, someone picked up the bullet shell casings and threw them into a sewer to prevent the police from gathering the evidence needed to track down the killers. . . .
>
> These tragic killings are just a handful of the more than nine thousand black-on-black homicides that committed throughout the nation each year in a virtual reign of terror that has plagued the black community for more than a decade. These deaths are not caused by marauding bands of the Klan of lynching by a White Citizen Council. These victims were killed at the hands of their own people. . .The crisis now facing black America is more than the combined impact of slavery, racial discrimination, and drugs. For now the enemy is within.[106]

Homicide among blacks is not a unique factor in American society. The whites also kill each other:

> Do black people kill one another? Sure they do. Ninety percent of black murder victims are killed by black assailants.
>
> But guess what? White people kill one another, too. Eighty-three percent of white victims are killed by white assailants. See, the vast majority of violent

---

105. Anderson, *Histories of the Hanged*, 6–7. For further reading, see ibid., *passim*.
106. Woodson, *Triumphs of Joseph*, 1–2, 3.

crime is committed within—not between—racial groups. Crime is a matter of proximity and opportunity. People victimize their own rather than drive across town to victimize somebody else.[107]

This is good evidence that killing human beings has nothing to do with the color of our skin or our racial and cultural differences. Had it been so, the first death in human history recorded in the Bible would not have been between siblings. As many whites were killed by whites in Europe, many Africans also are dying by the bullets of African soldiers and bandits. Slavery, discrimination, oppression and poverty can make a contribution to homicides among black Americans and to the genocide in Africa. But the real reason behind the destruction from outside and the self-destruction from within among the black people, as far as I am concerned, is not race but sin. As Tennent has stated: "Sin distorts God's original plan and purpose for creation, and the effects of sin can be observed not only in individuals but also throughout all cultural systems."[108] The "cultural systems" include the world of all humankind living in this world. Launching from this premise, based on research, I have made my best attempt to tell the truth in love about the past, present, and future of Africans and African decsent.

However, Western Christianity played the role of emancipation and discrimination in the history of black people. Up until recently African-American believers were not allowed to worship in a white church with white Christians because of segregation. The nations who were sending missionaries to Africa to preach the Crucified God to all humankind were crucifying blacks in Africa and in the destinies of African slaves. It was unprovoked and unjustified attack. Hochschild aptly puts Africans' understanding and question of salvation to William Sheppard, a British missionary, this way:

> The missionaries had come to Congo eager to evangelize, to fight polygamy, and to impart to Africans a Victorian sense of sin. Before long however, the rubber terror meant that missionaries had trouble finding bodies to clothe or souls to save. Frightened villagers would disappear into the jungle for weeks when they saw the smoke of an approaching steamboat on the horizon. One British missionary was asked repeatedly by Africans, "has the Savior you tell us of any power to save us from rubber trouble?"[109]

Mazrui elaborates the Belgians' involvement in Congo this way: "Under colonial rule came *forced labour* without commercialsed sale of 'niggers.' Nowhere was this post-slavery forced labour more brutally realized than in the so-called Congo Free State under King Leopold II of the Belgians. The natives of Congo were compelled to produce rubber for the rubber monarch under ruthless conditions. King Leopold of the Belgians had elaborate form of punishment for those who did not deliver: unrelenting forced labour mutilated limbs, villages razed to the ground because of the 'offence' of a single individual. Populations were decimated. *When Leopold's ambition arrived in the Congo,*

---

107. Pitts Jr., "Let's Talk about Black-on-black Violence."
108. *Invitation to World Missions*, 177.
109. Hochschild, *King Leopold's Ghost*, 172.

it was not the natives who needed to be civilized; it was the newly arrived white man."[110] Like beauty, civilization is in the eyes of a beholder and it is a relative term.

When pain and suffering comes on nations with a respite, it refines people as fire is to gold. What make the African tragedy difficult are the perpetual oppression, exploitation and dehumanization. It is souring their soul, ruining their family and community. If they have a listening audience, freedom and a platform to speak, millions of Africans today will say, "My eyes are swollen with weeping, and I am but a shadow of my former self . . . My days are over. My hopes have disappeared. My heart's desire are broken . . . my hope will go down to the grave. We will rest together in the dust" (Job 17:7, 11, 16). If not resolution, at least consolation alleviates the pain of suffering. Empathy can make a world difference. In King Leopold's Congo, even "the missionaries found themselves acting as observers in a battle field."[111] About three decades ago, keen American journalist rightly observed the austere situation of Africa this way:

> I would be hardly pressed to name more than four non-oil-exporting countries—Kenya, Cameroon, the Ivory Coast and Malawi—where there has been meaningful economic development, political stability, and an emerging middle class. Elsewhere the portrait of Africa is a bleak one of chilling consequences, for the continent is not catching up with the rest of the world, it is falling further behind. Africa is no longer part of the Third World. It is the Fourth World.
>
> - According to the United Nations Council on Africa, the economics of thirty sub-Sahara Africa's forty-six countries have actually gone backward since independence. The real per capita income of the non-oil producers has increased less than 1 percent over the past decade, and 60 percent of the 370 million people in sub-Sahara Africa are malnourished. Seventeen black states and 150 million people entered 1980 facing what the United Nations Food and Agriculture Organization called "catastrophic" food shortages.
> - The per capita income in Africa is $365 a year, the lowest in the world. In real terms that income—and the standard of living in Africa—is falling, with peasant farmers at the mercy of price fluctuations on the world market for their crops. A decade ago a Zambian farmer needed to produce one bag of maize to buy three cotton shirts; today the bag of maize buys only one shirt. A Tanzanian farmer could buy a Timex watch with the proceeds from 7.7 pounds of coffee; today he needs to produce 15 pounds of coffee to buy the same watch.
> - The infant mortality rate in black Africa, 137 deaths per 1,000 live births, is the highest in the world. In Upper Volta, where life expectancy is thirty-three years, the mortality rate is 189 deaths per 1,000 births. (By comparison, the rate is 12 per 1,000 in the United States.) Europe has one doctor for every 580 persons; Kenya, one of Africa's most developed countries, has one for every 25,600 persons.
> - Only 11 percent of the age-eligible children in Africa are in school, compared to 35 percent in Asia and 45 percent in South America. In the twenty- to twenty-four-year-old age group, 1.4 percent of Africans are studying at a

---

110. *Africans*, 232; emphasis added.
111. Hochschild, *King Leopold's Ghost*, 172.

university. In Asia the figure is 5.7 percent, in Latin America 6.7 percent and in the United States 48 percent.

- The illiteracy rate in Africa is about 75 percent. That rate should continue to drop as more children attended school, but if Africa's population doubles by the year 2000, as expected, 60 percent of the continent will be illiterate people in the world.

- When the independence era began in 1960, Africa produced nearly 95 percent of its own food. Today every country except South Africa is an importer, and by the year 2000 one of every two Africans will be eating food imported from other continents.[112]

Affirming the unchanged trend in Africa and reflecting on the recent economic, political, and social condition of the continent, Katongole writes, "A very distressed and distressing picture of Africa which, perhaps not surprisingly, tends to generate an increasing mood of Afro-pessimism."[113] The African church is not immune from the disturbing picture of the continent. The church has no option but to travail in pain with African society and at the same time remain to be the herald of hope and emancipation.

In the U.S., "Instead of feeling guilty for having too much fun, one is inclined to feel ashamed of if one does not have enough."[114] Living and growing up in this kind of culture, it is not easy for the West to understand the social, economic, and psychological conditions of Africans. It requires both cognitive objective knowledge and empathy to grasp the dilemma of Africans. The disparities in income and lifestyle, don't make it impossible to have mutual understanding and appreciation of each other so long as those who are privileged extend the right hand of fellowship to Africans and treat them with dignity and respect. I sometimes wonder how much Christians in the West know the economic disparity between the West and Africa is imposed and conditioned by the Western governments and their foreign policies.

The West is the only civilization that has substantial interests in every other civilization or region and has the ability to affect the politics, economics, and security of every other civilization or region. Societies from other civilizations usually need Western help to achieve their goals and protect their interests. Western nations:

- Own and operate the international banking system.
- Control all hard currencies.
- Are the world's principal customer.
- Provide the majority of the world's finished goods.
- Dominate international capital markets.
- Exert considerable moral leadership.
- Are capable of massive military intervention.
- Control the sea lanes.
- Conduct most advanced technical research and development.

---

112. Lamb, *Africans*, 20–21.
113. "Violence and Social Imagination," 26.
114. Mead and Wolfenstein, *Childhood in Contemporary Cultures*, 168.

- Control leading edge technical education.
- Dominate access to space.
- Dominate the aerospace industry.
- Dominate international communications.
- Dominate the high-tech weapons industry.[115]

The West has an impressive resumé and profile. As you read through this book, you'll see what the above-mentioned superior "achievements" mean to the rest of the world and if these accomplishments are unshakable foundations to hold Western civilization.

In military and many other aspects, the United States is the leader of the West and has a wide spectrum of influence in the world. Noll writes, "The United States' cultural and economic clout has continued to expand and broaden, despite stiff new competition, into the twenty-first century. Although the rapidly expanding economies of China, India and other non-Western countries point to a different pecking order for the future, the global reach of the United States in the early years of the twenty-first century remains second to none."[116] He adds, "American missionaries, whether for good or for ill, have been the controlling, hegemonic or sovereign agents of change in the recent history of Christianity."[117] Newbigin concurs: "A century ago the Western nations so dominated the world that most of the rest of mankind stood in awe of the white man and accepted his claim to political, cultural, and religious leadership. Even when the movements for political emancipation began, the leaders of national movements accepted in large measure the cultural leadership of the West, using Western languages, political ideas, and forms of organization . . . 'development' was held out as the goal to which all efforts should be directed, and development was understood as the third-world people's movement in the direction taken by the peoples of Europe and North America."[118] To this Bosch adds, "[U]ntil very recently virtually all Westerners (and, in many cases, non-Westerners) took it for granted that the reshaping of the entire world in the image of the West was a forgone conclusion . . . this was a development all should applaud. Like all other Westerners in the Third World, missionaries were to be conscious propagandists of this culture."[119] It is, therefore, logical to analyze the role of the powerful and the superpower in the powerless African continent.

For good or for evil, the influence of the West in Africa encompasses both the secular and the sacred. If we need to understand the Africans past and present, we cannot ignore history. It is also important not to be intellectually and emotionally trapped by history. Ayitte gives both the wisdom and danger of studying history: "It is true that the past must be studied to provide guidance for the future. But a mind deeply obsessed with the past is captured by it. Such a captive mind is incapable of cogent analysis of

---

115. Huntington, *Clash of Civilization*, 82–83.
116. Noll, *New Shape of World Christianity*, 113.
117. Ibid., 107.
118. Newbigin, *Open Secret*, 6.
119. *Transforming Mission*, 292.

present and future issues. Nor can it take advantage of auspicious opportunities that are currently available. World conditions are certainly not what they were 50 or 100 years ago. There are new technologies, new commodities, new tastes, new attitudes, and new opportunities. But all these remain invisible to the mind that is deeply engrossed to colonialism. When a new market opportunity arises, many African presidents captured by the past analyzed it with woefully outmoded mental constructs."[120] The intention of this book is not to put readers in the prison of the past. But to use historical, cultural, economic, political, religious, etc., trends pertinent to Africa to help us interpret the present and forge a viable future for Africans.

To explore the realities about Africa and the West, it is crucial to start with the right and pertinent questions: Is Greece the distant mother of modern American technique and of Western civilization in its most refined and profound aspect? How did Africa, where civilization began, end up being controlled and influenced by the West? What role did Africans and their natural resources play then and now for the West to be where it is today? How did the current unbalanced wealth, education, technology, etc., affect Africans today?

Asserting Africans' contribution to the civilization of the West, Diop contends:

> The Black is clearly capable of creating technique. He is the very one who first created it at a time when all the white races, steeped in barbarism, were barely fit for civilization. When we say that the ancestors of the Blacks, who today live mainly in Black Africa, were the first to invent mathematics, astronomy, the calendar, sciences in general, arts, religion, agriculture, social organization, medicine, writing, technique, architecture; that they were first to erect buildings out of 6 million tons of stone (the Great Pyramid) as architects and engineers—not simply as unskilled laborers; that they built the immense temple of Karnak, that forest of columns with its famed hypostyle hall large enough to hold Notre-Dame and its towers; that they sculpted the first colossal statues (Colossi of Memnon, etc.)—when we say all that we are merely expressing the plain unvarnished truth that no one today can refute by arguments worthy of the of the name.[121]

Afro-centric views like Diop's and the Western scholars' understanding and interpretation differ in black civilization, particularly in Egypt. David Hume (d. 1776) wrote in his *Essay and Treatises*: "I am apt to suspect the Negroes...to be naturally inferior to the white. There never was a civilized nation of any other complexion than white, nor even any individual eminent either in action or speculation."[122] As one can see the gap between Afro-centric and Euro-centric view on African civilization is wide and seems irreconcilable. While I agree about the legitimate concern on academic integrity and validity of the conclusions on some of the works of Afro-centric scholars on African civilization, in the light of my research, I am more persuaded by my findings that there was African civilization in the continent of Africa created and developed by black people in different regions of the continent before Europeans came in contact with people in Africa. Stereotypical and racist assertions like David Hume's are not only false but raise

---

120. Ayitte, *Africa in Chaos*, 42.
121. *African Origin of Civilization*, 234–35.
122. Cited in Harris, *Africans and Their History*, 19.

questions on the methods, sources, motives, and integrity of books and papers written by Western scholars on Africans, their culture and history. Afro-centric scholars like Diop are not free from ethnocentrism either. In chapter 1, I present both views in detail.

Often, what we hear is the debt Africa owes the West. I've done my best attempt to show what the world and the West owe Africa. It is my hope that this book will enable you to see Africans with a different lens. "Any attempt to deal with the present without awareness of what has gone before can only lead to distorted vision and false judgment."[123] When you reflect on the facts and findings in this book, you will discover who owes who: "In the last 300 years Africa has helped substantially in building the West's industrial civilization. The phases of Afro-Western interaction are from the days of the trans-Atlantic slave trade to the coming of the nuclear age. At each stage, Africa helped to construct the wealth of Europe and North America."[124] As a person of African origin, I have found this research to be startling, eye-opening, disturbing and inspiring.

In Africa where Christianity is growing by leaps and bounds, Christians are still asking us if the Savior we tell them about has any power to save them from violence, war, hunger, disease, injustice, poverty, and exploitations of all kinds caused by internal and external powers whose value of life is based on greed and selfish motives. It is time for African Christians to know and teach that the *SAVIOR* has a lot in common with Africans while he was on this earth. He was born, raised, and died in a colony. He drank the bitterness of rejection, and experienced the life of a refugee. He went through betrayal, loneliness, homelessness, misunderstanding, insult, disrespect, hunger, injustice, suffering, and death. If we want him to be truly a Savior of Africans, the Christ of Africa should not be devoid of the crown of thorns and the cross. He is not only a Savior from grief, but he is a brother who understands suffering and who can understand Africans. To be known by the crucified Christ as we should be known is a beginning of restoration of lost identity, of renewal and being human. That can happen when we enable Africans to hear clearly Christ say, "Father, why have you forsaken me?" A forsaken God can be embraced by a forsaken people. This kind of Christology needs to be built in a re-Africanized cultural context. Christ has to be the Christ of Africans through a clear understanding of the gospel answering the questions of slavery, colonialism, diaspora, poverty, and the religious worldviews of Africans.

As Rahner rightly puts it: "The Christian life is the acceptance of human existence as radically threatened by suffering, as opposed to final protest against it."[125] There is a reason, why Christians' participation in the Eucharist is a remembrance of the death of Jesus Christ until he comes back. Starting from the birth of Jesus Christ, suffering is a part of the Christian faith. As a proof of his resurrection Christ showed to the disciples his scars, not the Star of David. This book explores the relevance of this aspect of Christology in a continent that desperately needs various facets of healing from the past and the present wounds. Mind you, Christ is not only a savior *from* he is also a savior *for*. Despite a staggering number of converts annually in the continent of Africa, the latter aspect of salvation is immensely lacking.

123. Newbigin, *Open Secret*, 3.
124. Mazrui, *Africans*, 159.
125. *Trinity*, 403.

Neither the Christology of Christendom nor the health and wealth gospel, which is transplanted from the West, is relevant to the African cultural context. The prosperity gospel, which has led African Christian leaders to have bodyguards and compete for the latest Mercedes and private airplanes in a poverty stricken continent, is not appealing to Africans. That kind of gospel is absurd and a contrast to the faith founded on the teachings of the prophets and the apostles. As Jenkins rightly observed:

> At its worst, a Faith Gospel of success and health can promote abuses and materialism, and it is easily mocked. Nigerian author Wole Soyinka presents a memorable satire of such a health-and-wealth sermon in his play. The trials of Brother Jero, in which the preacher promises: "I say who dey wala today, give them their own bicycles tomorrow . . . I say who dey push bicycle, big car tomorrow. Give them big car tomorrow." The doctrine also excuses corruption. If a pastor lives luxuriously, if he owns a very big car, he is simply living proof of the wealth that God has given him, while presumably someone who remains poor is just lacking adequate faith. The moral difficulties are all too obvious. Yet a doctrine promising glory in this world as well as the next has undoubted appeal.[126]

In contrast to the health and wealth gospel, Africans can identify with the Christ who suffered, was denied justice, and was crucified. Without neglecting the Christology from above, it is important for African theologians to help the African church understand the Christology from below. To do so, effective contextual analysis should take a preliminary task. The incarnation of Christ happened in human flesh within human culture. Human beings' cultural contexts are an unavoidable framework to understand and communicate the gospel effectively. In this book, I have attempted to do that in sequential order.

No matter how bleak and dark the history and the present situation of Africa looks like. In glory and suffering God is in the midst of it all. "In this presence of God in history, we find his future in his present and his present in his future."[127] In the words of George Eldon Ladd, "The historical is described in terms of the eschatological and the eschatological in terms of the historical."[128] As it happened in the beginning of human history so will it be in its consummation. God's future is not divorced from the present, and it is not something that will happen beyond yonder somewhere in the celestial sphere. In his own appointed time, his will in heaven will also be done on earth. Hence, the focus on anthropological, ecological, and historical issues in Africa should not be looked at only in terms of the present but in the light of God's future too. The purpose of this book is to show the hope of humankind in a seemingly hopeless continent.

---

126. *Next Christendom*, 78.
127. Moltmann, *Sun of Righteousness Arise!*, 165.
128. *Presence of the Future*, 323–24.

Chapter 1

Civlization

The racial arrogance of the West is old only as the power of the West is old, which has been for a mere moment of human time and a few centuries of registered history. Civilization is composite; an accretion of experience and ideas beyond race or region, and the term "Western civilization" is ultimately meaningless. Europe reads with the letters and counts in numbers that come from the crossroads of Africa and Asia. If in an area of the world commonly called the West, man first discovered how to split the atom, it was in the South that he probably first discovered how to make tools, and in the East that he probably first made fire. Newton's apple-tree was planted a great deal closer to the Congo than to London or New York.[1]

Black Civilization in Egypt

It is crucial to begin at the beginning point that would redefine, restore, invigorate, and reshape the self-image of Africans and the history of the black race, which is: civilization.

> The people of Africa have been brutally traumatized. European colonizers denigrated Africans for centuries as "subhumans" and denied them recognition of any meaningful intellectual, cultural, and historical accomplishment or experience. Called "savages," millions of Africans were carted off in bondage as slaves to Americas. Even when Charles Darwin speculated that it was Africa, not a Garden of Eden in the Near or Far East, where the evolution of the human race to be traced, intellectual prejudices of the time precipitated a spirited rejection of the notion that something good or new could originated from Africa. Allegedly its people had no history, no culture, no civilization, and nothing of value to contribute to the creation of the human being.[2]

---

1. Segal, *Race War*, 33.
2. Ayittey, *Africa Betrayed*, 3–4.

For centuries this myth about Africans has been made partly by simple tourists and partly in the name of academic research. Through the Western "scholarship" and media, the global community has been indoctrinated who Africans are—how backward, poor, illiterate, and uncivilized they are. Hence, the distorted perception about Africans and their culture is prevalent in the minds of the global community.

In this chapter we will see to what extent the labels and description given to black people by the West is erroneous, unfounded, misguided, and established by prejudices or how factual the academic research really was. To observe, validate, and propagate one's "findings" of other people who are outside of his/her culture, language and custom, only from an outsider's perspective, is, to say the least, ethnocentrism. "The imagined community of the nation contrast itself with the world outside. 'We' are special 'they' are inferior and do strange things. The sense of community in the modern world is developed and maintained by diverse means, including the reading of newspapers, editorial policies of which promote national identity most strongly by disparaging foreign people and nations."[3] The people of ancient Egypt themselves and their civilization, which became a bone of contention between Afrocentric and Western scholars, was not immune from one-sided interpretation of history.[4] Such an approach cannot stand and the whole claim of any party cannot be proven to be totally true in the bar of reason. "The history of interpretation warns us to be aware of biases, both our own and those of others, in interpreting history. There is clear evidence of a Eurocentric racist bias in certain interpretations that exalt whites and denigrate blacks."[5] The first stage of racist Western action is to disconnect Egypt from Africa. "The study of Egyptology developed in concurrence with the development of the slave trade and the colonial system. It was during this period that Egypt was literally taken out of Africa, academically, and made an extension of Europe. In many ways Egypt is the key to ancient African history. African history is out of kilter until ancient Egypt is looked upon as a distinct African nation."[6]

To do balanced research on a people and their culture, individuals who engage in such studies needs a meatacutural[7] framework to do justice to their findings. Other-

---

3. Kemp, *Ancient Egypt*, 21.
4. Ibid.
5. Yamauchi, *Africa and the Bible*, 211.
6. Jackson, *Introduction to African Civilization*, 12.

7. Metaculture is a versatile concept and may be defined and used in many different ways—all forms of human agriculture, horticulture, and food-gathering patterns may be referred to as instances of human metaculture. Human metaculture may refer as well to the characteristic style-patterning of a particular group in terms of its concrete manifestations, beliefs, ritual behaviors and customs, habits of dress, construction and organization of homes and communities, etc. Metaculture may also be used at a cross-cultural level to refer to systematic patterns of difference, sharing, contact, diffusion, change, and integration of human cultural patterning at many different levels and in many different areas in which this patterning becomes manifest.

Human Metaculture is the natural and rational consequence of human behavioral response to environments that is symbolically and cognitively mediated and socially shared and reinforced, primarily by means of human language. It can be expected to occur wherever and whenever human communities organize themselves for purposes of productive survival and reproductive success. The possibility and reality of human metacultural patterning, as the descriptive explanation of human systems, historically and sociologically, has been rooted in the natural history of human evolution, and cannot be divorced

wise, even the best of minds like Diop or Philo, and even the apostle Peter, could not escape the trap of ethnocentrism. "All societies have complex laws and rules of proper social behavior, whether written or oral, to which people are expected to conform, and a range of sanctions to be imposed on those who break the laws and rules. In that sense all societies throughout humanity's history have been civilized. Only during periods of breakdown of the social or political order does so-called uncivilized behavior predominate over civilized, and any society anywhere in time or place can potentially face such a breakdown."[8] It is in this light that we investigate African civilization.

There are two major kinds of approaches to African civilization. One comes out of a nervous aggressive intellectual reaction to the degrading remarks and labels of Western scholars of Africans' past and present. The other one is passive resistance to the Western civilization. Mazrui summarizes both in this manner:

> The massive cultural arrogance of Europeans was later to influence the indigenous personality of the continent, and create at times schizophrenia among the Westernised Africans. Defending themselves against the European contempt, one school of African thought emphasised Africa before the European had had its own complex civilizations of the kind of that Europeans regarded as valid and important—civilizations which produced great kings, impressive empires and elaborate technological skills. This particular school of African thought looked especially to ancient Egypt as an African civilization, and proceeded to emphasise Egypt's contribution to the cultures and innovations of ancient Greece. A particularly illustration of this attitude is the work of the Senegalese historian and scientist, Cheikh Anta Diop. Diop's effort to demonstrate that the civilization of ancient Egypt was not only African but Black, and that it provided the foundation of the intellectual miracle of ancient Greece, have been influential among Black people not only in Africa but also in the African Diaspora in the Americas.
>
> We may call this school of African assertion as school of *romantic gloriana*. It seeks to emphasise the glorious moments in Africa's history defined in part by European measurements of skill and performance, including the measurements of material monuments.
>
> In contrast to this tradition of romantic gloriana is what might be called *romantic primitivism*. In this the idea is not to emphasise past grandeur, but to validate simplicity and non-technical traditions. Romantic Primitivism does not encounter European cultural arrogance by asserting civilizations comparable to that of ancient Greece. On the contrary, this school takes pride in precisely those traditions which European arrogance would seem to despise.[9]

The proponents of romantic primitivism include people such as Aimé Cesaire who invented the word *négritude* and Leopold Senghor, former president of Senegal and the most distinguished advocate of négritude. Senghor believes that "the great genius of Africa lay not in European concepts of rationality, but in indigenous capacities for intuition; not in the principles of scientific method and objectivity, but in the wisdom

from these natural contexts of its origins or anthropogenesis—http://www.lewismicropublishing.com/AlternativeAnthropology/id111.htm.

8. Ehret, *Civilizations of Africa*, 5.
9. Mazrui, *Africans*, 72–73; emphasis original.

of custom and instinct; not in cold analytical reason but in warm responsive emotion. Hence, Senghor's controversial dictum; 'Emotion is Black . . . Reason is Greek.' To the French philosopher Descartes' assertion, 'I think therefore I am.' It is in this sense that Senghor has sometimes been accused of reducing the African genius to the poetic concept of the Noble Savage. Romantic primitivism is given the mind of the savage."[10]

This author's focus of study is in the romantic gloriana school of thought. "In African context proponents of this approach of African civilization looks to the pyramids as a validation of African's dignity, takes pride in the Great Zimbabwe ruins and adopts the mane for a newly independent country, and turns to the ancient empires of Ghana and Mali for official names of modern republics."[11] The leading thinker of this school of thought, until the three-volume works of Martin Bernal surfaced and caused a shock wave in Western Classical Civilization studies, as stated earlier, is Cheikh Anta Diop. Let us examine his work.

In his magnum opus work, *Civilization Or Barbarianism: An Authentic Anthropology*, Cheikh Anta Diop accurately observed: "The historical conscience, through the feeling of cohesion that it creates, constitutes the safest and the most solid shield of cultural security for a people. This is why every people seeks only to know and to live their true history well, to transmit its memory to their descendants. The essential thing, for a people, is to rediscover the thread that connects them to their most remote ancestral past. In the face of cultural aggression of all sorts, in the face of all disintegrating factors of the outside world, the most efficient cultural weapon with which a people can arm itself is the feeling of historical continuity. The erasing, the destruction of the historical conscience also has been since time began part of the techniques of colonization, enslavement, and debasement of peoples."[12]

Diop was the only Black African of his generation to have received training as an Egyptologist. He had acquired proficiency in such diverse disciplines as rationalism, dialectics, modern scientific techniques, prehistoric archeology, linguistics, cultural and physical anthropology, history, chemistry, and physics. Using these disciplines, "he forged new theoretical pathways and revealed new evidence in the quest to uncover the ancient origins and *unifying principles of classical African civilization*."[13]

Cheik Anta Diop was fully persuaded that the reconstruction of African's self-image should start at the beginning of African's destruction, which is their civilization, history, culture, and language. Diop lived through the African independence explosion that began with the independence of Ghana in March 1958. The aftermath of this event was bright and hopeful, but, unfortunately, short-lived. He lived to see Africa turn against itself, motivated in part by its former colonial masters, who were still behind the scenes controlling the destiny of the continent.

In 1967, the International Congress of Africanness had a meeting at the University of Dakar, in Dakar, Senegal. The office and laboratory of Diop was located in the campus of the University less than three hundred yards from the assembly where the congress

---

10. Ibid., 73–74.
11. Ibid., 73.
12. Diop, *Civilization or Barbarism*, 212.
13. Ibid., xiv; emphasis added.

was being held, yet he was not a participant at the conference, let alone a presenter. The sponsoring organization, the African Studies Association, was then dominated by white scholars, and to this day it has not recognized the scholarship of Cheik Anta Diop and his contribution to a new concept of African history. Neither his name nor his work was mentioned at the conference.[14] Even if he doesn't agree with some of Diop's assertions, Edwin M. Yamauchi recognizes the prominent role and place Diop has in the Afrocentric study. He writes "In the 1970s the works of a seminal scholar, Cheik Anta Diop of Senegal (1923–1986), who came from a Muslim background, was educated at the University of Paris. He was both a scientist, who became the director of a radiocarbon laboratory and a prolific author, who in numerous publications set forth his thesis that the Egyptian civilization was a black African one. When in 1967 the Congress of Africanness sponsored by the African Studies Association met in the home city of Dakar, Diop was not one of the participants. But his presentation in 1974 in Cairo became a chapter in UNESCO's General History of Africa. Though Diop was and still is ignored by mainstream scholars, he has gathered a devoted following among current Afro-centric scholars."[15] When Professor Diop as an African person is rejected despite his impressive portfolio, obviously his message/scholarship is rejected as well. In his writings, we often see him inviting debate of his assertions and conclusions on the original black civilization in Egypt. While the white scholars could have shut his mouth and killed his emerging academic work right on the platform of Dakar University by engaging with him in scholarly debate, they excluded him. Posthumously, as if Diop can rise up from the grave and defend himself or give explanation to his critics, we read statements such as this: "Cheik Anta Diop, whom Afrocentrists had adapted as their intellectual star, is not a trustworthy guide in linguistics or in history."[16] I wish those "distinguished experts" who held the conference on African studies in Dakar University a few yards from Diop's office would have said the same word to his face and given him a chance to respond. Anyone can play his/her card on the grave of a dead lion.

African studies have been predominately researched, discussed, and analyzed and the findings finalized and authorized mainly by white scholars. As Martin Bernal stated, these white scholars had racial bias toward blacks, and they deliberately fabricated the Ancient Greece Civilization theory.[17] Hence, in the circle of these white scholars, even Africans like Diop with distinguished various academic achievements were not worthy to participate at the conference in Dakar. "Imperialism, like a prehistoric hunter," said Diop, "first killed the being spiritually, before trying to eliminate it physically. The negation of the history and intellectual accomplishment of Black Africans was cultural, mental murder, which preceded and paved a way for the genocide here and there in the world."[18]

Based on research conducted in humanistic paleontology, particularly by Dr. Louis Leaky, and other scientific methods, Diop believes that the birth place of humanity is in

14. See ibid., xiii–xxi.
15. Yamauchi, *Africa and the Bible*, 208.
16. Ibid., 213.
17. Bernal, *Black Athena*, vol. 1.
18. Diop, *Civilization or Barbarism*, 1–2.

East Africa's Great Lakes region, around the Omo Valley. "All the other races drive from the Black race by a more or less direct affiliation, and the other continents were populated from Africa at the Homo erectus and Home sapiens stages, 150,000 years ago."[19] He continues, "If one bases one's judgment on morphology, the first White appeared only around 20,000 years ago: the Cro-Magnon Man. He is probably the result of a mutation from the Grimaldi Negroid due to an existence of 20,000 years in the excessively cold climate Europe at the end of last glaciation."[20] Ehret concurs:

> The species *Homo sapiens* had come fully into being entirely in Africa. Skulls found in African sites dating from 130,000 to 100,000 BCE were already almost fully modern in appearance. Except for a temporary advance of Homo sapiens into the far southwest corner of Asia between 100,000 and 70,000 years ago, it was not until after 60,000 years ago, and not until after 40,000 years ago in Europe, that any sites with modern human remains show up outside Africa. Instead, in both Europe and Asia, only more archaic species of Homo, such as the Neanderthal, are attested in the paleontological record of the period from 130,000 to 60,000.
>
> DNA gives us the same answer. Using both mitochondrial DNA a kind of genetic material passed from mother to daughter, and Y-chromosome evidence from males, scholars have demonstrated conclusively that the greatest genetic diversity of *Homo sapiens* lies in Africa. Greater human genetic diversity exists in Africa for the simple reason that fully evolved Homo sapiens have been present on that continent longer than they have been anywhere else . . . The evidence of tool making requires this conclusion as well."[21]

As Africa is studied, interpreted and analyzed by Western scholars, the history and civilization of the continent is not taken into consideration or looked at objectively and scientifically. Diop emphatically argues that Africans are robbed of their identity, history, and civilization and they are dehumanized. He made it his academic mission to demonstrate the significance of Black African civilization in the lives of Africans today. He writes, "The return to Egypt in all domains is the necessary condition for reconciling African civilizations with history, in order to be able to reconstruct a body of modern human sciences, in order to renovate African culture. Far from a reveling in the past, a look toward the Egypt of antiquity is the best way to conceive and build our cultural future. In reconceived and renewed African culture, Egypt will play the same role that Greco-Latin antiquity plays in Western culture."[22]

In three of Diop's books that I read, his meticulous academic research based on history, prehistory archeology, and field and library research combined with laboratory tests, demonstrated and elaborated Black civilization in Egypt. Diop firmly believes that for Africans, discovering their past and reconnecting with Black Civilization is an important step for meaningful existence in the continuity of history. He asserts:

19. Ibid., 11.
20. Ibid., 15–16.
21. Ehret, *Civilizations of Africa*, 21.
22. Diop, *Civilization or Barbarism*, 3.

Ancient Egypt was a Negro civilization. The history of Black Africa will remain suspended in air and cannot be written correctly until African historians dare to connect it with the history of Egypt. In particular the study of languages, institutions and so forth, cannot be treated properly; in a word, it will be impossible to treat African humanities, a body of African human sciences, so long as that relationship does not appear legitimate. The African historian who evades the problem of Egypt is neither modest nor objective, nor unruffled; he is ignorant, cowardly, or neurotic. Imagine, if you can, the uncomfortable position of a western historian who was to write the history of Europe without referring to Greco-Latin Antiquity and try to pass that off as a scientific approach.

The ancient Egyptians were Negroes. The moral fruit of their civilization is to be counted among the assets of the Black world. Instead of presenting itself to history as an insolvent debtor, the Black world is the very initiator of the "western" civilization flaunted before our eyes today. Pythagorean mathematics, the theory of the four elements of Thales of Miletus, Epicurean materialism, Platonic idealism, Judaism, Islam, and modern science are rooted in Egyptian cosmogony and science. One needs only to meditate on Osiris, the redeemer god, who sacrifices himself, dies and resurrected to have mankind, a figure essentially identifiable with Christ.[23]

Williams concurs: "There was no 'Egypt' before the black king from whose name it was indirectly derived. Before that the country was called Chem or Chemi, another name indicating its black inhabitants, and not the color of the soil, as some writers have needlessly strained themselves in asserting... Not knowing the racist twist that modern history was to take, those early historians, geographers and travelers reported what they found and described peoples in their own terms of speech. In doing so, they established beyond question that the Blacks were the first Egyptians and the builders of that ancient civilization."[24]

According to Diop, in Africa, there was monotheism and circumcision before Abraham. According to the eye witness of Herodotus, the father of history, when he visited the upper and lower chambers of the sepulchers of the kings' Labyrinth, he was allowed to see only the upper chambers and found them to excel all other human production. His description of the outer sepulchers matches the writing of Christiane Desrochess-Noblecourt about the recent excavations in Tanis.[25] "Herodotus' observation and explanation of the sepulchers and Nile's swelling in the summer, witnesses to the fact that Herodotus was not a man deprived of logic, unable to penetrate complex phenomena. It was him, who related his eye witness account informing us that the Egyptians were Blacks, then demonstrated, with rare honesty (for a Greek), that Greece borrowed from Egypt all the elements of her civilization. The civilization called in our period, developed for a long time in its early cradle; then it slowly descended the Nile Valley to spread out around the Mediterranean basin. This cycle of civilization, the longest in history, presumably lasted for 10,000 years. This is a reasonable compromise between the long

---

23. Diop, *African Origin of Civilization*, xiv.
24. C. Williams, *Destruction of Civilization*, 65.
25. Tanis is the Biblical Zoan, at the mouth of the eastern branch of the Nile Delta.

chronology (based on data provided by Egyptian priests, Herodotus and Manetho[26] place the beginning at 17,000 B.C.) and the short chronology of the moderns—for the latter are obliged to admit that by 4245 B.C. the Egyptians had already invented calendar (which necessarily requires the passage of thousands of years."[27]

In 1799, Bonaparte undertook his campaign in Egypt. Thanks to the Rosetta stone, hieroglyphics were deciphered in 1822 by Champollion the Younger, who died in 1832. He left as his "calling card" and Egyptian grammar and a series of letters written to his brother, Champollion-Figeac, during his visit to Egypt between (1828–1829). These were published in 1833 by Champollion-Figeac. From then on the wall of the hieroglyphic was breached, unveiling surprising riches in their most minute details. Egyptologists were dumbfounded with admiration for the past grandeur and perfection then discovered. They gradually recognized it as the most ancient civilization that had engendered all others. But, imperialism being what it is, it became increasingly "inadmissible" to continue to accept the theory—evident until then—of a Negro Egypt. The birth of Egyptology was thus marked by the need to destroy the memory of a Negro Egypt at any cost and in all minds.[28]

With convincing archeological evidence and historical and linguistic research, Diop aptly shows that several of the pyramids in Egypt were built by black engineers; the pharaohs of Egypt until the twelfth dynasty were blacks. And he strongly argues that until the fifteenth century, Black Africa never lost its civilization. Frobenius reports:

> Not that the first European navigators at the end of the Middle Ages failed to make some very remarkable observations. When they reached the Bay of Guinea and alighted at Vaida, the captains were astonished to find well-planned streets bordered for several leagues by two rows of tree; for days they traversed a countryside covered by magnificent fields, inhabited by men in colorful attire that they had woven themselves! More to the south, in the kingdom of the Congo, a teeming crowed clad in silk and velvet, large States, well ordered down to the smallest detail, powerful rulers, and prosperous industries. Civilized to the marrow of their bones! Entirely similar was the condition of the lands on the east coast, Mozambique, for example.
>
> The revelations of the navigators from the fifteenth to the eighteenth centuries provide positive proof that Black Africa, which extended south of the desert zone of the Sahara, was still in full bloom, in all the splendor of harmonious, well-organized civilizations. This flowering the European conquistadors destroyed as they advanced. For the new land of America needed slaves which Africa offered: hundreds, thousands, whole shipload of slaves! Nevertheless the black slave trade was never a safe business; it required justification; so they made the Negro half-animal, a piece of merchandise. Thus was invented the notion of the fetish, as a symbol of African religion. Made in Europe! As for me, I have never anywhere in Africa seen natives adoring fetishes.

---

26. Maanetho of Sebennytos, an Egyptian priest (third century BC), who wrote a chronicle on Egypt in Greek.
27. Diop, *African Origin of Civilization*, 22.
28. See ibid., 43–45.

> The idea of a barbaric Negro is a European invention that boomeranged and dominated Europe until the start of this century.[29]

Describing the negative impact of the "European invention of half-animal Negro" on African self-image, Williams write: "The incongruous attempt to replace his own values with those of the white man, the black man lost his own personality and, therefore, his manhood—almost absolutely. Nearly five hundred years have passed since the first Europeans landed on the coasts of West Africa and their phase of transforming blacks from men to half-men began. Yet even with this long background there are countless millions of frustrated Blacks, frustrated by the perpetual annoyance of the blurred vision and the blank wall as they struggle to see life through the blue eyes of Caucasians."[30] Diop's spectacular academic work is a medicine to the Africans' malady of identity crisis. I don't know of any African scholar who labored relentlessly in the face of rejection, criticism, and isolation to "define the image of a modern Africa and to reconcile it with its past and [prepare it] for its future"[31] with academic integrity and excellence like Diop. He always reminds us not to overlook the crucial starting point to discover the true identity and history of Africans. He writes:

> Once the perspectives accepted until now by official science have been reversed, the history of humanity will become clear and the history of Africa can be written. But any undertaking in this field that adopts compromise at its point of departure as if it were possible to split the difference, or the truth, in half, would run the risk of producing nothing but alienation. Only a loyal, determined struggle to destroy cultural aggression and bring out the truth, whatever it may be, is revolutionary and consonant with real progress; it is the only approach which opens on to the universal. Humanitarian declarations are not called for and add nothing real progress.
>
> Similarly, it is not a matter of looking for the Negro under a magnifying glass as one scans the past; a great people have nothing to do with petty history, nor with ethnographic reflections sorely in need of renovation. It matters little that some brilliant black individuals may have existed elsewhere. The essential factor is to retrace the history of the entire nation. The contrary is tantamount to thinking that to be or not to be depends on whether or not one is known in Europe. The effort is corrupted at the base by the presence of the very complex one hopes to eradicate.[32]

While using Africa as a vantage point and the basis for his theory, Diop does not neglect the wider aspects of history. He shows that history cannot be constrained by the limits of ethnic groups, nation or culture. Roman history is Greek as well as Roman, and both Greek and Roman history is Egyptian because the entire Mediterranean was civilized by Egypt; Egypt in turn borrowed from other parts of Africa, especially Ethiopia.[33]

---

29. Ibid., 161.
30. C. Williams, *Destruction of Civilization*, 250.
31. Diop, *African Origin of Civilization*, xvi.
32. Ibid.
33. Diop, *Civilization or Barbarism*.

Williams further affirms the blackness of the initial Egyptians: "For these early Blacks themselves a great people, excelling on many fronts from a line of builders so distant in the past it seems to have extended into the stone ages. It was a society of scientists, scholars, organized religions with organized priesthoods, mathematicians, scribes, architects, engineers, artists, sculptors, cloth makers, slaves, farmers, teachers, gold and silversmiths, blacksmiths, and so on, throughout the widest spectrum of an advanced society."[34] Diop summarizes:

> Nubia appears to be closely akin to Egypt and the rest of Black Africa. It seems to be the starting point of both civilizations. So we are not astonished today to find many civilizing features common to Nubia, whose kingdom lasted until the British Occupation, and the remainder of Black Africa. Right after the end of Egypto-Nubian Antiquity, the Empire of Ghana soared like a meteor from the mouth of Niger to the Senegal River, circa third century A.D. Viewed in this perspective, African history proceeded without interruption. The first Nubian dynasties were prolonged by the Egyptian dynasties until the occupation of Egypt by the Indo-Europeans, starting in fifth century B.C. Nubia remained the sole source of culture and civilization until about the sixth century A.D., and then Ghana seized the torch from sixth century until 1240, when its capital was destroyed by Sundiata Keita. This heralded the launching of the Mandingo Empire (capital: Mali) of which Delafosse would write: "Nevertheless, this little village is the Upper Niger was for several years the principal capital of the largest empire ever known in Black Africa, and one of the most important ever to exist in the universe." Next came the empire of Gao, the Empire of Yatenga (or Mossi, still in existence), the kingdoms of Djoloff and Cayor (in Senegal), destroyed by the Faidherbe[35] under Napoleon III. In listing this chronology, we have simply wanted to show that there was no interruption in African history. It is evident that, if starting from Nubia and Egypt, we had followed a continental geographical direction, such as Nubia-Gulf of Benin, Nubia-Congo, Nubia-Mozambique, the course of African history would still have appeared to be uninterrupted.
>
> This is the perspective in which the African past should be viewed. So long as it is avoided, the most learned speculations will be headed for lamentable failure, for there are no fruitful speculations outside of reality. Inversely, Egyptology will stand on solid ground only when it unequivocally officially recognizes its Negro-African foundation.[36]

However, Diop's, Ehert's, Williams's, Jackson's, and others' Afro-centric scholarly research and conclusions about Africa's civilization have never been free from counter-argument by Western scholars. In 1830, when the colonial partition of the African continent began, Georg Hegel, the famous German philosopher, dismissed Africans as insignificant to history.[37] Hegel wrote in his *Philosophy of History*: "It is manifest that want of self-control distinguishes the character of the Negroes. This condition is capable of no development or culture, and as we have seen them at this day, such has always been . . . At this point we leave Africa, not to mention it again. For it is no historical part

---

34. C. Williams, *Destruction of Civilization*, 71.
35. General Louis Faidherbe (1818–1889), France's most famous governor of Senegal.
36. Diop, *African Origin of Civilization*, 148–49.
37. B. Davidson (rev. ed.; New York: Macmillan, 1991) xxi.

of the world; it has no movement or development."[38] A century later, G. Seligman, who applied Darwinian to African ethnography, formulated the "Hamitic hypothesis," which held that Caucasian Hamites, including the Egyptians, created everything of value in Africa. He wrote in 1930: "Apart from relatively late Semitic influence . . . the civilization of Africa are the civilization of the Hamites. . .The incoming Hamites were pastoral "Europeans"—arriving wave after wave—better armed as well as quicker witted than the dark agricultural Negroes."[39]

Copleston states that "[t]he birth place of Greek philosophy was the sea-board of Asia Minor and the early Greek philosophers were Ionians. While Greece itself was in a state of comparative chaos or barbarism, consequent in the Dorian invasions of the eleventh century B.C., which submerged the old Aegean culture, Iona preserved the spirit of the older civilization, and it was the Ionian world that Homer belonged, even if the Homeric poems enjoyed the patronage of the new Achaean aristocracy" (1971:13). Furthermore, Western scholars and writers attribute the beginning of most of the modern science and math to the Greeks. Tenney writes:

> Geometry, literally the science of measuring land, had begun with the Babylonians and the *Egyptians*, and was brought to the Greek world by Thales of Miletus, if tradition be correct Euclid of *Alexandria* (c. 300 B.C.) developed plane geometry so completely that his propositions have been studied with little change to the modern day.
>
> Mechanics and physics had been investigated by Archimedes of Syracuse (287–212 B.C.), who developed the theory of the lever and discovered the principle of estimating the composition of bodies by the relation of their weight to the weight of the volume of water that they displaced. He found the formula for the ratio of the circumference of a circle to its diameter, and in doing so he discovered the basic approach to calculus. Several of his numerous mechanical devices were used in the wars of Syracuse against Rome.
>
> Astronomy made great advances in the pre-Christian world. The sphericity of the earth and its revolution on its own axis were known to some Greek scientist in the fourth century B.C. Hipparchus (c. 160 B.C) invented both plane and spherical trigonometry and calculated the size of the moon and its distance from the earth. . .Eratosthenes of *Alexandria* (217–192 B.C.) calculated the circumference of the earth to a surpassing degree of accuracy in spite of his crude instruments.
>
> The science which owed its greatest advance to its period including the first century was geography. Ptolemy of *Alexandria* (A.D. 127–151) wrote a work on astronomy which remained the standard until the rise of the Copernican theory in modern times. He created maps of the world which includes all regions known at that time. Medicine flourished in various centers of the world. The University of Tarsus had an affiliated hospital in the temple of Aesculapius where the sick went to be healed.[40]

---

38. Cited by Harris, *Africans and Their History*, 19.
39. Cited by Sanders, "The Hamitic Hypothesis."
40. Tenney, *New Testament Survey*, 55–56; emphasis added.

When we closely examine these inventions by the Greeks, the majority of them happened in Alexandria in Egypt. Three important questions need further investigations: 1) Why did the Greeks in Alexandria, a major city of Egypt, monopolize the science and math field? 2) If Greeks are the origin for geometry and other mentioned sciences, how were the pyramids that need accurate calculation and mechanical engineering built in Egypt and Sudan before the invention of math and science? Over many centuries, the ancient Egyptians developed a method of preserving bodies so they would remain lifelike. The process included embalming the bodies and wrapping them in strips of linen. Today we call this process mummification. 3) How could this be done without any medical or anatomical knowledge? I wonder if Diop's claim, that "the entire Mediterranean was civilized by Egypt and the Greek civilization emanated from the black Africans,"[41] was right. Jackson provides further proof giving credit to Africans' original contribution in the area of medicine, architecture, astronomy, philosophy, wisdom, and the like:

> Egypt gave the world some of the greatest personalities in the history of mankind. In this regard, Imhotep is singularly outstanding. In the ancient history of Egypt, no individual left a deeper impression than the commoner Imhotep. He was probably the world's first multi-genius. He was the real father of medicine . . . Imhotep, the Wise, as he was called, was the Grand Vizier and Court Physician to King Zoser and architect of the world's earliest stone building, after which the Pyramids were modeled. He became a deity and late a universal God of Medicine, whose image graced the first Temple of Imhotep, mankind's first hospital. To it came sufferers from all the world for prayer, peace, and healing.
>
> Imhotep lived and established his reputation as a healer at the court of King Sozer of the Third dynasty about 5345–5307 B.C. In addition to being the chief physician to the king, he was sage and scribe, Chief Lector Priest, architect, astronomer, and magician. He was a poet and philosopher. One of his best-known sayings, which is still being quoted, is "Eat, drink and be merry for tomorrow we shall die."
>
> Imhotep's fame increased after his death. He was worshiped as a medical demi-god from 2850 B.C., and as a full deity from 525 B.C. to 550 A.D. Kings and queens bowed at his shrine.
>
> When Egyptian civilization crossed the Mediterranean to become the foundation of what we think of as Greek culture, the teachings of Imhotep were absorbed along with the precepts of other great African teachers. When Greek civilization became predominant in the Mediterranean area, the Greeks wanted

---

41. On numerous occasions, reference has been made to the fact that the Greeks borrowed their gods from Egypt; here is the proof: "Almost all the names of the gods came into Greece from Egypt. My inquiries prove that they were all derived from a foreign source, and my opinion is that Egypt furnished the greater numbers."

Since the Egyptian origin of civilization and extensive borrowing of the Greeks from the Egyptians are historically evident, we may well wonder with Amélineau why, despite those facts, most people stress the role played by Greece while overlooking that of Egypt. The reason for this attitude can be detected merely by recalling the root of the question. As Egypt is a Negro country, with a civilization created by blacks, any thesis tending to prove the contrary would have no future. The protagonists of such theories are not unaware of this. So it is wiser and safer to strip Egypt, simply and most discreetly, of all its creations in favor of a really White nation (Greece). The false attribution of the values of a so-called White Egypt reveals a profound contradiction that is not the least important proof of Egypt's Negro origin. Diop, *Africa and the Origin of Civilization*, 234.

the world to think they were originators of everything. They stopped acknowledging their indebtedness to Imhotep and other great Africans. Imhotep was forgotten for thousands of years, and Hippocrates, a legendary figure of two thousand years later, became known as the father of medicine.[42]

As we go further exploring the African civilization in the Western, Eastern, Southern and Central region of the continent. We will unravel the factuality or fictitiousness of black civilization, which was developed independently from the Western influence. Then, we'll test Hegel's claim: "Africans are insignificant to history . . . it has no movement or development."

Having said that, we cannot underestimate the influence of the Greeks, particularly the Alexandrian Greeks, on Judaism and Christianity. The thinkers and theologians of both religions were heavily influenced by the Greek scholars. Regardless of this one-sided approach to history, as I will show in detail in chapter 10, the works of great African theologians, like Clement, Origen, Sabellius, etc., came from Egypt, particularly Alexandria. (Augustine of Hippo, one of the prominent theologians in Christian history, was also an African.) We will see how their patterns of thinking and reasoning was influenced by Greek philosophers—the root of such thinking can be traced back to balck Africa. The impact of Hellenism on Christianity goes back to Stephen and Paul of the early church.

Every civilization ends because of internal and external factors. "One of the worst and most fateful [internal] crises was during the Seventh, Eighth, Ninth, and Tenth dynasties, 2181–2040 B.C." in Egypt.[43] It was marked by civil war and power struggle. The external threat was equally remarkable and it brought the Egyptian civilization to end.

> In 332, Alexander the Great arrived and, having broken the imperial power of Persia elsewhere, had no trouble taking over Egypt. A Greek was crowned Pharaoh in 334 B.C., as Ptolemy I.
>
> The Greeks ruled Egypt for almost 300 years before the expansion of the Roman Empire into Egypt and ended that domination in 30 B.C. This was our flash back point of departure, but before returning to the Ethiopian churches, the significance of what we have been reviewing the last phase of the process of Caucasianization in Egypt that were so thoroughgoing that both the Blacks and their history were erased from memory: the Jewish ruled 500 years; the Assyrian interludes; the Persians, 185 years; the Greeks 274 years; the Romans 700 years; the Arabs 1,327 years—the long, long struggle to take from the Blacks whatever they

---

42. Jackson, *Introduction to African Civilization*, 14–15. Mazrui provides a sensible and more persuasive rationale about the role of Egypt's civilization. He asserts: "Egypt's proximity to other cultures provided additional stimulation, even though they were often weaker. The interaction between Egypt and her neighbours produced one of the greatest configurations of civilizations in history—the Mediterranean civilizations. The interaction between the Egyptians on one side and, on the other, Mesopotamians, Assyrians, Babylonians, Persians, Nubians, ancient Greeks and ancient Romans resulted in the explosion of one of the most dazzling galaxies of cultures in human history. Had it there been no Egyptian civilization would there have been Greek civilization in ancient times? Debates of this kind are probably eternal. For this author the balance of evidence would seem to suggest that ancient Egypt was a necessary condition though not a sufficient one for the flowering of the Greek intellectual miracle a little later" (*Africans*, 43).

43. C. Williams, *Destruction of Civilization*, 80.

had of human worth, their land all their wealth therein; their bodies, their souls, and their minds, was a process of steady depersonalization, dehumanization.[44]

"Ruined by all these successive invasions, Egypt, the cradle of civilization for 10,000 years while the rest of the world was steeped in barbarism, could no longer play a political role. Nevertheless, it would long continue to initiate the younger Mediterranean peoples (Greeks and Romans, among others) into the enlightenment of civilization. Throughout antiquity it would remain the classic land where the Mediterranean people went into pilgrimages to drink at the fount of scientific, religious, moral and social knowledge, the most ancient such knowledge that mankind had acquired."[45] The death of black civilization in Egypt made it impossible to penetrate to the interior of Africa and develop it as it did in Greece. African slave trade and colonialism also played a significant role in hampering the black civilization in Egypt.

The black civilization in Egypt studied from the Afro-centric view or Euro-centric view and their findings do not lead us to one absolutely error-free observation, interpretation, and conclusion. Hence, the research and the debate are ongoing.

While I strongly incline toward Diop's and Jackson's assessment of the ancient civilization of Egypt, which they credited the black people, I am open to the counter-claim of some Western scholars, which sounds credible but is very difficult to prove if they free themsleves of bias toward the black race. Unlike Diop, they disagree that the people of ancient Egypt are totally black. Yurco writes, "The ancient Egyptians, like their modern descendants, were of various complexions of color, from the light of Mediterranean type (like Nefertiti), to the brown of Middle Egypt, to the darker brown of Upper Egypt, to the darkest shade around Aswan and the First Cataract region, where even today the population shifts to Nubia."[46] Sasson adds, "There was no formal definition what constituted an Egyptian, and no concept of citizenship. In practice the Egyptians defined themselves by residence in the Nile Valley, by language, by religion, and by a culture... The capacity of Egyptian society to absorb people from a wide variety of ethnic backgrounds without prejudice was one of its characteristic features. The only requirement was a willingness to integrate. Signs of ethnic tension surface only rarely, when groups actively sought to retain their ethnic character by conspicuously adhering to un-Egyptian practices or by maintaining a high profile or physical separateness."[47] However, the works of Martin Bernal,[48] a white scholar, are breathtakingly informative and bold in conception and he convincingly writes that the Greek civilization is fabricated. In his three volumes and in his response to his critics, Bernal provides documentation to back up his thesis, as well as offering persuasive explanations why traditional scholarship on the subject of Classical Civilization remains inaccurate and why specific arguments lobbed against his theories are themselves faulty. In his first volume, Bernal convincingly asserts that the majority of Egypt's ancient civilization is an outcome of black Africans, and that the

---

44. Ibid., 138. Diop, *Africa and the Origin of Civilization*, 10.
45. Diop, *Africa and the Origin of Civilization*, 10.
46. Yurco, "Were the Ancient Egyptians Black or White?," 24.
47. Sasson, ed., *Civilization of the Ancient Near East*, 232, 233. See also Kemp, *Ancient Egypt*.
48. *Black Athena*, vols. 1–3; *Black Athena Writes Back*.

Renaissance is connected to Egypt as a place where ancient mysteries and initiations were first established.[49] To prove his theory of gravitation, Newton had "to retrieve the exact length of the original Egyptian cubit, from which he could calculate that of their stadium which, according to Classical authors, bore a relation to geographical degree."[50] He further explains, "Measurements of the Pyramids and surveys of Egypt on the basis of ancient sources that maintained that the Egyptian measures of length were based on a detailed knowledge of the world's circumference."[51] According to Bernal, "Egypt can be regarded as the mother of all theogonies and the source of all the fictions which the Greeks received and embellished, for it does not appear that they invented much."[52] Bernal also effectively demonstrate, "Jews like Josephus and the Church Fathers like Clement of Alexandria and Taitan . . . scored points against the Greeks by pointing out the lateness and shallowness of Greek civilization in comparison with those of the Egyptians, Phoenicians, Chaladeans, Persians and so on, and of course the Israelites."[53] "Before the fifth century B.C.E.," Bernal writes, "Egypt had a far greater impact on Greece than vice versa."[54] He adds, "Abundant Greek testimony specifies Egypt, rather than Mesopotamia, as the source of religion, justice, and knowledge."[55]

Responding to his critics who accused him stressing the "blackness" of the pharaohs, Bernal writes:

> I did it to counterbalance early-twentieth-century Egyptologists' emphasis on the image of Ancient Egyptians and the rulers as real or imagined northerners or "whites," and the continuing influence this image has in popular representation of Egyptians . . . Egyptologist . . . consistently portray Egyptians as made-up Europeans. Indeed, its striking cover and frontispiece is of a pharaoh with blue eyes and the features of the evangelist Billy Graham! The cover of the sophisticated board game *Civilization*, which was clearly developed in close consultation with archaeologists, features pyramids, a palm-fringed river with a felucca, the Acropolis, and Vesuvius. The center is dominated by the face of a bearded Greek Zeus/philosopher. Behind him to one side is a blond, blue-eyed Roman, and on the other side a gray-eyed, auburn-haired Cleopatra figure who makes Elizabeth Taylor look Mediterranean. In such a cultural environment, I believe it is useful to emphasize that the Ancient Egyptians were African."[56]

After I went through Bernal's work, I personally felt Diop was vindicated. The African scholar is no longer a lone voice in the wilderness on the issue of the blackness of ancient Egypt. In recent years, it is not only African scholars who are fighting for the authentic ancient black history and civilization to have its right place in academia. Honest and distinguished white scholars like Martin Bernal and Tom Oden have joined the

49. *Black Athena*, 1:153.
50. Ibid., 166.
51. Ibid., 184.
52. Ibid., 183.
53. Ibid., 193.
54. Bernal, *Black Athena Writes Back*, 21.
55. Ibid., 32.
56. Ibid., 29–30; emphasis original.

intellectual battle. On February 5, 2015 at 9:00 PM Colorado time, PBS presented the role of African blacks in Egypt. Around 800 BC, Kush, a little-known subject state of Egypt, rose up and conquered Egypt, enthroned its own Pharaohs and ruled for nearly 100 years. This unlikely chapter of history has been buried by the Egyptians and was belittled by early archaeologists, who refused to believe that dark-skinned Africans could have risen so high. Now, in the heart of Sudan, archeologists are finding indisputable evidence of an advanced African society with powerful armies, vast reach, and spiritually-driven imperial aspirations to rival the Egyptians.[57] The momentum to recover Africans' history and dignity has picked up. With all the internal and external dynamic changes in Africa and the global community, one wonders what impact this development would bring.

It is hard to show there were white people in a black continent from day one of the history of Egypt. Since this question is beyond the realm of my specialty, I leave the question to the Egyptologists. Many of us are anxious to learn more from future research. Regardless, one thing is true about the continent of Africa: "Africa is a cultural bazaar. A wide variety of ideas and values, drawn from different civilizations, competes for the attention of potential African buyers. The marketing of cultures has been going on for centuries but a particularly important impact has come from the 'Semites' (especially Arabs and Jews) and the 'Caucasians' (especially western Europeans)."[58] He adds, "Of the three ancient continents of Asia, Africa and Europe, Africa has again often played the role of a link, and sometimes mediator, between the Occident and the Orient. In history it has never been quite clear whether Africa was indeed part of the Orient or whether it should be included in the universe of the Occidentals."[59] Bernal rightly attests: "We should turn from the image of a civilization springing, like the conventional image of Athena from the head of Zeus, white virgin, and fully formed, to an image of a new civilization growing up at the intersection of Europe and the Middle East as a thoroughly mixed civilization in Antiquity, and the central role it played in the formation of all later European cultures, was not the result of isolation and cultural purity but of frequent contact and stimulus from the many surrounding peoples with the already heterogeneous native of the Aegean."[60]

Even if Diop's, Bernal's, and others' findings about the blackness of ancient Egypt are without error and black Africans are the ones who built the ancient civilization in that country, to totally or exclusively base Africans' dignity, freedom, equality, or superiority, ingenuity, and self-esteem on human civilization is like leaning on people who are thinking reeds and a vapor that vanishes and withers like a flower or grass under the heat of the sun. "All men are like grass, and their glories like the flower of the field; the grass withers and the flowers fall but the word of God stands for ever" (1 Pet 1:24). "Civilization may come to an end, and the human species disappear. This world, no matter shadow of ideas in an upper sphere, is real, but not absolute; *the world's reality is contingent upon compatibility with God*. While others are intoxicated with the here and

---

57. http://pw.myersinfosys.com/rmpbs/airlist/6.1/411390/detail?popup=true#sthash.pl7Qg2JC.
58. Mazrui, *Africans*, 97.
59. Mazrui, *African Condition*, ix.
60. *Black Athena Writes Back*, 11.

now, the prophets have a vision of an end."[61] I strongly believe that it is healthier and more lasting for Africans to not rely too much on their temporal historical and cultural background and be "intoxicated with the here and now." The fundamental and the ultimate should not be shrouded by the temporal.

In every civilization, past and present, we see the utter decay of society in all its phases, would lie open to gaze. Heschel rightly observed: "There was a moment when God looked at the universe made by Him and said: 'It is good.' But there was no moment in which God could have looked at history made by man and said: 'It is good.'"[62]

Therefore, there is no city or civilization that the black race can use or rely upon in absolute sense of the term as a source of their humanity or human dignity, a measure of their being, existence, and purpose in life. As Pascal did, Africans (the Black race) needs to go beyond the black civilization in Egypt and discover who they are—the greatness and wickedness of humankind in the gospel of Jesus Christ. This argument makes the case for Christianity by pointing out that any viable worldview must successfully explain the seemingly paradoxical nature of the human condition. The apparent irony is that human beings exhibit qualities of both greatness and wretchedness. Pascal argues that Christianity offers the best explanation for this condition based on its teachings that human beings are created in the image of God, yet original sin has tainted their nature.[63]

Diop had told us about the Egyptian god Osiris who can be seen as a type of Christ preceding the revelation of the New Testament. He argues that both Judaism and Christianity are indebted not only to the civilization of Egypt but also to the religion of black Egyptians/Africans. But Diop dares not to tell us that "[t]he Egyptian god Seth, conceived as Red Fiend, is power of darkness. He murders his brother Osiris, a nature god whose *original hostility to human beings* has been gradually transformed into beneficence; he had taught the Egyptian agriculture. The Thracian god Ares, worshiped in numerous places and in the later Greek system joined to Aphrodite, who nursed a strong passion for him, delights in the slaughter of men and the sacking of towns, and loves fighting for the fighting's sake."[64] Collingwood adds, "The power of Zeus is manifested in the thunderbolt, that of Poseidon in the earthquake, that of Apollo in pestilence, and that of Aphrodite in the passion that destroyed at once the pride of Phaedra and the chastity of Hippolytus."[65] Whether Egypt or Greece is the source of modern civilization, their religion is not something one desires. As oppressed and enslaved people, Africans have some commonality with Israel in Egypt. Like the Jews, Africans too can consider God's

61. Heschel, *Prophets*, 11; emphasis added.

62. Ibid., 214.

63. Velarde, "Greatness and Wretchedness." In the realm of philosophy, Blaise Pascal (1623–62) is perhaps best remembered for his wager argument. In his *Pensées* (*Thoughts*), however, Pascal offered several lines of apologetic reasoning, including what has been termed his anthropological argument. Pascal realized that it is sometimes necessary to shock a complacent skeptic into paying attention to the seriousness of his or her condition. Depending on the type of skeptic encountered, Pascal would use the anthropological argument to apply "existential shock" to either humble them or exalt them. This same approach is applicable today to belief systems such as humanism and New Age spirituality that exalt human beings or worldviews such as nihilism that ultimately lead to hopelessness and despair.

64. Heschel, *Prophets*, 312; emphasis added.

65. Collingwood, *Idea of History*, 22.

redemptive act as the central manifestation of his love and omnipotence in human history. The prophet Hosea was right when he said to Israel; "I am the Lord your God from the land of Egypt; *you know no God but me, and besides me there is no savior*" (13:4). This is true for Africans then and now.

Not only in the area of religion, ancient Egyptians were also not models to emulate in the area of worldview. They were ethnocentric or racist, a sin that the Western civilization and Westerners are accused of by Afro-centric scholars like Diop.

> Different myths of either national ancestry or the subculture of death were based on a conception of the world which did not distinguish the history of the human species from the history of the particular society. The village was the world; the nation was the universe. Even the ancient Egyptians, the first urban rather than village-based civilization in the African continent, still tended to equate their own destiny with the destiny of the human race. Like the Jews after them, the ancient Egyptians regarded themselves as the Chosen People. The Egyptians believed that gods had first manifested themselves in and through Egypt. It was in Egypt that the sun god ruled and fought as king. At their most arrogant, the ancient Egyptians saw only themselves as 'men' (*ronet*). The rest of the human species whether white or Black, were the equivalent of what Chinese have called 'barbarians,' and the Jews have called 'gentiles.' All these three ethnocentric traditions were variations of the image that the village is the world, the 'tribe' is the human race."[66]

As we study the history of humanity racial humility is essential for mutual respect, mutual understanding, reconciliation, and healing. Clinton A. Chisholm writes:

> There is need for pride in who we are, whomever and however we might perceive ourselves to be, but there is hardly a place for ethnocentric arrogance or racial intolerance. There is need for racial humility based on common-sense reasons and scientific reasons.
>
> From the stand point of common sense, one should realize that if humanity sprang from one common "ancestor"—whether primeval slime or primordial pair—then there is no defensible basis for ethnocentric arrogance or racial intolerance between and among "descendants," however distinct and diverse they might have or might be.
>
> From a scientific stand point, one brute fact should humble Eurocentrists especially and foster respect for Africa and Africans. C. Loring Brace et al say it quite succinctly, "Whether our assessments are based on biochemical or on fossil evidence, it is clear that all modern human populations can trace their ultimate roots to Africa."[67]

Even if we find the above statement debatable and we disagree on the fact that Africa is the place where Adam and Eve were created, at least we can agree that the origin of human beings goes back to them. Treat writes:

> Humanity as the pinnacle of God's creation further reveals the design of God's rule over the earth. Adam and Eve are, along with the rest of creation, under the

---

66. Mazrui, *Africans*, 97.
67. "Afrocentricity," 20.

rule of God; they are servants. Yet unlike the rest of creation, they are made in God's image and given the commission to "be fruitful and multiply and fill the earth and subdue it" (Gen. 1:28). They are servants of God, but rulers of the earth: servant-kings. God not only reigns *over* people; he also reigns *through* them.[68]

Crediting the ancient civilization in Egypt solely to the black race is problematic to the definition of Africa and Africans. Mazrui writes:

> The ambivalence has been so deep that in order to demonstrate that ancient Egypt was an African civilization, some have found it necessary to seek evidence that ancient Egypt was a *Black Civilization*. Skeletons and skulls of ancient Egyptians have been checked to see if there "Negroid." Noses in ancient Egyptian paintings have been examined to see if they were flat. The Sphinx has been scrutinized to see if it had Negroid features before wind and sand eroded its nose.
>
> My own feeling is that to insist that nothing is African unless it is Black is to fall into the white man's fallacy. No one insists that the Chinese, on the one hand, and Black Sinhalese or Tamils of Sri Lanka on the other hand, must be the same colour before they can all be regarded as "Asians" . . . Was Africa going to be as multi-coloured as Asia? Or was it going to be as uni-coloured as Europe?[69]

I think the answer is obvious. Africans are multi-colored. But the Eurocentric anthropology defines Africa as the black race and Hamitic. The Arabs in the north and the whites in southern Africa are the Semitic. We often forget that the Amharas, Tigres, and Oromos of Ethiopia are also Semitic.

West African Contributions to Science and Technology

When West Africa is mentioned in a historical context, it is usually presented as the traditional hunting ground for slaves. Very few writers have shown any interest in the contributions of West Africans to science and technology, and thus there has been very little research that challenges the perspective that all that West Africans have ever been historically is to be under the whip of other peoples.

Fortunately, the tide is beginning to change, a *National Geographic* article entitled *Reclaiming the Ancient Manuscripts of Timbuktu* mentioned that some scholars believe that 700,000 manuscripts, some dating to the twelfth century, have survived in the West African city of Timbuktu. They also say the manuscripts "covered an array of subjects: astronomy, medicine, mathematics, chemistry," etcetera.[70]

Jackson adds, "The Golden Age of West Africa has a special significance for the whole world. Europe was lingering in the Dark Ages at a time when western African is enjoying a Golden Age."[71]

---

68. Treat, *Crucified King*, 55; emphasis original.
69. Mazrui, *Africans*, 26; emphasis original.
70. Walker, *Blacks and Science*, 5.
71. *Introduction to African Civilization*, 18.

Robin Walker, in *Blacks and Science Volume Two: West and East African Contributions to Science and Technology and Intellectual Life and Legacy of Timbuktu*, presents a different side of West African historical achievement. Challenging all stereotypes, it is a general introduction to the exciting role played by early West Africans in the evolution of mathematics, astronomy and physics, metallurgy, medicine and surgery, boat building and navigation, architecture, crafts and industry.

In Walker's book, there are some interesting findings that appear somewhat unbelievable to the West who have perceived Africans as half-animals and to Africans who almost believed the label given to them by the West as people with no or low academic caliber. Here are some of the fascinating findings:

- The Bamoun Kingdom, now in today's Cameroon, has 7,000 surviving manuscripts in their own script.
- Timbuktu astronomers used cosine, tangent and cotangent, secant, and cosecant functions of trigonometry.
- The Dogon of Mali had an early and wholly indigenous notion of 'big bang' derived from a singularity.
- A number of iron and copper tools were excavated in Senegal that dated to 2800 BC.
- The total amount of gold mined in the desert regions of West Africa to the year 1500 AD was $35 billion at 1988 gold prices.
- A surviving sixteenth century Timbuktu manuscript has formulas for making toothpaste and adds that regular brushing of your teeth removes bad breath.
- The majority of enslaved Africans were inoculated against smallpox BEFORE they were deported from Africa.
- A 1342AD text published in Cairo mentions two royal Malian voyages sailing across the Atlantic involving hundreds of vessels.
- The royal palace of the Ashanti Empire contained a suite of apartments on its upper floor that reminded a visitor of the palace of Wardour Street in Central London.
- Glass was manufactured at the Yoruba capital of Ile-Ife in the sixth century AD.
- According to the *New Scientist*, there are surviving Timbuktu manuscripts that deal with climatology.[72]

"During the period in West African history from the early part of the fourteenth century to the time of the Moorish invasion in 1591, the city of Timbuktu and the University of Sankore in the Songhay Empire were the intellectual center of Africa. Black scholars were enjoying a renaissance that was known and respected throughout most of Africa and in parts of Europe. At this period in African history, the University of Sankore at Timbuktu was the educational capital of the western Sudan."[73] Ronald Segal was accurate when he said, "Newton's apple-tree was planted a great deal closer to

---

72. Walker, *Blacks and Science*.
73. Jackson, *Introduction to African Civilization*, 21.

Congo than to London or to New York."[74] Revealing the West's "rationale" to deny the intellectual, natural, cultural, and historical wealth of Africa, Segal writes: "Since Europe could not transport the American plantations to Africa's labour supply, it accordingly set out to transport the African labour supply to America's plantations. What followed was *a racial war, conducted for commercial profit, without precedent for human cost*. The doctrine of inherent Negro inferiority was developed to excuse conduct which the teachings of Christianity and twinges of traditional conscience alike disparaged, and a civilization which had barely emerged from the sick-bed pronounced itself the only one sound and capable of uplifting humanity."[75] Of course, the "uplifting of humanity" solely refers to the white people. In his books, *Profit over People: Neoliberalism and Global Order* and *Hegemony or Survival: America's Quest for Global Dominance*, the American critic Noam Chomsky, echoes the observation of Segal.

In the face of such evidences of civilization in Africa, supported and substantiated through historical and archaeological research, the West adamantly denied the products of African's intellectual labor to justify the slave trade, colonialism, and exploitation of African natural resources. The destruction of Africans' past disconnected them from their roots and robbed them of significant references that would contribute to their dignity and aspirations of higher achievements in academics and technology. For Africans, the chance of leading in innovation became a far-fetched or impossible dream. Their intellectual ability has been paralyzed by distorted history, poor self-perception and demeaning self-doubt, and lack of academic environment for research and innovation.

East African Contribution to Science and Technology

A couple of years ago, BBC 4 presented an interesting short film about multiplication in Ethiopia as part of a series about mathematics and numbers. Entitled *Go Forth and Multiply*, the film explained the millennial old system of multiplication used in Ethiopia by traders and merchants. One of the products the traders sold was coffee.

If an Ethiopian trader wanted to multiply 11 and 15, he would put the numbers in two columns. He would place the 11 in one column and he would place 15 in the other column.

In the first column he would continually halve the number ignoring the fractions. Thus 11 halved is 5 (i.e. ignoring the fractions), halved again is 2, and halved again is 1. In the other column he would double the numbers. Thus 15 doubled is 30, and doubled again 60, and doubled again is 120. The two columns might look like this:

Halving column	Doubling column
11	15
5	30
2	60
1	120

---

74. Segal, *Race War*, 33.

75. Ibid., 44; emphasis added.

There is a rule that one must IGNORE any even number(s) in the halving column AND the corresponding number(s) in the doubling column. Consequently, we shall ignore the 2 and the 60. Our table now looks like this:

Halving column	Doubling column
11	15
5	30
1	120

Finally we add up the numbers in the doubling column to produce our answer which is 15+30+60+= 165.

The narrator commented that: It seems unbelievable that a system can ignore fractions, even throw away parts of calculation and still come up with the right answer.

The underlying principle of this system is doubling which, as its core, is base 2 arithmetic. The narrator explained the significance of this: "It is a system that seems completely foreign to Western eyes but in fact we use it thousands of times a day because it's this system that powers today's computers."[76]

In the area of architecture East Africa also has a significant contribution to African civilization. Kerma, the capital city of the Early Empire of Kush, was a particularly distinguished center of architecture. The empire of Kush was located in the same place as modern Sudan and the southern portion of modern Egypt. Scholars divide the history of Kerma into the Ancient Period, the Middle Period, and the Classic Period. These periods take us from the same time period as Dynasty VI to Dynasty XVIII of Egypt. Robin Walker estimates c. 4200 BC to 1601 BC.

Kerma, at the peak of its power, was the largest city in Africa outside of Egyptian territory, covering sixty-five acres. Surrounding the central parts of the city was a wall of massive size with a ditch in front of it. The walls were thirty feet high and made of mud bricks. They had rectangular towers that projected and also had four fortified gates.

Archaeologists working in the city have detected a large audience hall probably dating from the Middle Period. This building was circular and may have been thatched. Also found were thousands of mud blanks that would have been used for making seals. This gives evidence that business transactions took place. There was also a great palace. It had an audience hall that included a throne on a raised platform. The king sat there and received delegations. Several large columns supported the roof and the building is believed to have been twenty-five feet high.

The empire of Kush flourished a second time between c. 860 BC and 350 AD. There was a later empire of Kush that also left behind a wealth of architectural evidence. There are at least 223 Kushites pyramids in the cities of Al Kurr, Nuri, Gebel, Barkal, and Meroë. They are generally twenty to thirty meters high with steep sides, sloping at around 70 degrees. They were made of smaller blocks than their Egyptian counterparts. The pyramids were used for royal burials and were entered by underground stairways on the eastern side. Meroë became the capital of the Kushite Empire from around 590 BC until about 350 AD, a period well attested by monuments. There are, for example,

---

76. Walker, *Blacks and Science*, 67–68.

eighty-four pyramids in this city alone, many built with their own miniature temple. Moreover there are ruins of a bath house sharing affinities with those of the Romans.

The same Kushite region flourished a third time between the fourth century AD and the fourteenth or fifteenth centuries AD. For most of this period, the region consisted of two great Christian states—the Empire of Makuria to the north, and the Kingdom of Alwa to the south (Christian Nubia). Some scholars, such as the great Howard University social scientist, Chancellor Williams, regard this as the best period in the whole of Black history.

Archaeologists have found in Makuria and Alwa evidence of forts, castles, churches, monasteries, cathedrals, palaces, toilets, and glass windows.

In Ethiopia, in the Tigre region, stands the ruined Temple of Almaqah. The pride of the city of Yeha, it is one of the oldest monuments in the country. Some think it was built before 500 BC. The temple is a two-story structure raised on a steeped plinth. It is twenty-five meters long and rectangular in plan. The walls are of huge limestone block, finely dressed and polished with two small windows.

In and around Axum, another great city, there are over fifty stelae, many of them undecorated. Some are believed to be very old, but firm dates have not been established. Near to some of these obelisks, one kilometer from Axum on the road to the city of Gondar, is a massive building containing a drainage system with "finely mortared stone walls, deep foundations and an impressive throne room."[77] Ethiopian tradition establishes this building as the place of Empress Makeda, the fabled Queen of Sheba (1005–955 BC). Tradition also establishes one of the obelisks, carved with four horizontal bands, each topped with a row of circles in relief, as the marker of the Queen's grave.

Axum itself has a series of seven giant stelae that date from perhaps 300 BC to 300 AD. They have details carved into them that represent windows and doorways of several stories. The largest obelisk now fallen, is in fact "the largest monolith ever made anywhere in the world."[78] It is 108 feet long, weighs a staggering 500 tons, and represents a thirteen-story building.

In the twelfth and thirteenth century AD, Roha became the new capital of the Ethiopians. Conceived as the New Jerusalem by its founder, Emperor Lalibela (c.1150–1230), it contains eleven churches, all carved out of the rock of the mountains by hammer and chisel. All of the temples were carved to a depth of eleven meters or so below ground level. The largest is the House (or Church) of the Redeemer, a staggering 33.7 meters long, 3.7 meters wide and 11.5 meters deep. It is one of four churches that give the illusion of being free-standing in Roha (also called Lalibela), connected only by their bases to the rock from which they were hewn.[79]

---

77. Quoted in ibid.
78. Quoted in ibid.
79. For more detail, see Walker, *Blacks and Science*, 70–82.

Southern Africa Metallurgy

In Southern Africa, there are at least 600 stone-built ruins in the regions of Zimbabwe, Mozambique, and South Africa. These ruins "show today an extraordinary cultural past." Most of them are said to date from the Middle Ages, but some authorities give much earlier dates for their construction. These structures are called Mazimbabwe in Shona, the Bantu language of the builders, and means great houses of stone. João de Barros, a Portuguese writer of the mid-sixteenth century, tells us "Symbaoe" (more correctly "Zimbabwe") in Shona "signifies court." Of the buildings themselves, they are almost cyclopean structures, with walls several meters thick; five at the base, three at the top, and nine meters in height. Edifices of all types can be found there from the royal palace, the temple, and the military fortification to the private villa of notable. The walls are of granite masonry.

The Great Zimbabwe was the largest of these ruins. It consists of twelve clusters of buildings spread over three square miles. Its outer walls were made from 100,000 tons of granite bricks. In the fourteenth century, the city housed 18,000 people (some give higher figures), comparable to the size of London of the same period. The building housed warehouses and shrines.[80] Again, like the black civilization in Egypt and elsewhere in Africa, Western scholars refused to give credit to black Africans' original contribution to the edifice in Zimbabwe. Yamauchi asserts, "In 1871 some extraordinary stone structures, including walls and towers called the Great Zimbabwe ruins, were discovered in southern Rhodesia by Karl Mauch, a German geologist, who ascribed them to Solomon. Still others attributed them to settlers from India. Under the influence of Hamitic hypothesis,[81] some scholars credited newcomers from the north rather than the indigenous Bantu peoples."[82] Here, again, we see the struggle of Western scholars to give credit to African ingenuity and creativity. "There has been a deliberate destruction of African culture and the records relating to that culture. This destruction started with the first invaders of Africa. It continued through the period of slavery and the colonial system. It continues today on a much higher and more dangerous level. There are now attempts on the highest academic levels to divide African history and culture within Africa in such a manner that the best of it can be claimed for the Europeans, or at the very least, Asians."[83]

Metallurgy

"In Swaziland, the men of the Upper Paleolithic Age mined iron 30,000 years ago in order to extract the red ore. It is the most ancient mine in the world."[84] To this Williams adds:

80. For further reading, see Walker, *Blacks and Science*, 83–84.

81. European interpreters of Gen 9:25 believe that the Africans' black skin and slavery is the result of the curse of Ham.

82. Yamauchi, *Africa and the Bible*, 29.

83. Jackson, *Introduction to African Civilization*, 29.

84. Diop, *Civilization or Barbarism*, 12.

Even as early as 300 B.C., when iron smelting was used for more useful purposes than ornaments, the royal monopoly still prevented widespread use. That they knew of the importance of iron is shown by the fact that kings and high priest were often heads of the guild, and the chief iron master would often gain the status of what a Prime Minster is today. Regardless of the delay, iron smelting and tool-making got underway on a vast scale in Ethiopia at a most crucial period for Africa. Its center was Meroe, and it appears that the biggest iron work were in and around this capital city. The development was at a crucial period because it was the period of increasing migrations from the heartland and the scattering of groups all over Africa. They carried their knowledge of this great technological revolution wherever they went and they began the use of iron and the development of iron industries wherever they had the opportunity to settle in iron ore areas and remain settled long enough to create a stable society.[85]

Thornton adds:

The peculiarities of African iron production that made European iron attractive come, perhaps, from its earliest years. According recent work on ancient African ironworking, the technology was developed by 600 B.C. or even earlier on the Sudanese fringe of the emerging Sahara desert, perhaps as a result of discoveries made in the copper-producing areas of the desert north of modern Nigeria. Because this was a fuel-poor environment, African iron workers developed methods to conserve fuel, of which the most important was devising a system to preheat the air blast that entered the furnace, which prefigured techniques used in Europe only in the nineteenth century. This not only saved fuel, but it allowed Africans to produce an amazingly good-quality steel—perhaps the best steel in the world of the time, and certainly equal to or even better than the steel produced in early modern Europe. Certainly research into the quality of metal produced by African countries in West Africa in modern times and recent archeology suggests that African steel was equal to that made anywhere in the fifteenth century.[86]

Such knowledge, in addition to the abundance of the natural resource of iron, highly developed technology, human skill, and capital, can enrich African nations. Unfortunately, because of social instability caused by external powers and internal African tyrants, those African countries with natural resources have not maximized their benefit yet. For example, Guinea has huge deposits of iron ore but the country is leasing it to a foreign company. *The Economist* states, "Buried beneath the mist-capped mountains of south-eastern Guinea is one of the world's biggest deposits of iron ore. Estimated at around 2.2 billion tonnes, the Simandou concession contains almost as much as the entire global iron-ore industry produced in 2013. Thanks to its size and unusually high quality, some experts say that whoever controls Simandou may dominate the world's iron-ore sector for a generation."[87] Sitting on such kind of wealth Guinea's economy is neither improving nor promising.[88]

---

85. C. Williams, *Destruction of Civilization*, 132–33.
86. Thornton, *Africa and Africans*, 48.
87. *Economist*, June 7, 2014, p. 57.
88. Guinea's economic freedom score is 53.5, making its economy the 133rd freest in the 2014

Metallurgy, astronomy, medicine and surgery, shipping and navigation, textile, etc., were not beyond the comprehension and implementation of the early Africa entrepreneurs and innovators. From what we see, these Africans were not all Semites. The Nubian kingdom and civilization and the West African civilization were built by Kushites and Hamites. Had these early stages of civilization and scientific and technological developments not been interrupted, with the natural resources the continent has, one can imagine what Africa would look like today.

According to a recent report in *The Economist*, Science in Africa is on the rise and it is very encouraging:

> Africa has a poor reputation for scientific innovation. But when South Africa jointly won a bid in 2012 to host the world's largest science project, for a radio telescope called the Square Kilometer Array (SKA), it hoped to foster a new image. "It is changing the way the world sees us, as somewhere for cutting-edge science and technology," says SKA's Burnie Fanaroff. "And also the way we see ourselves." . . . .
>
> African biomedical researchers are looking into diseases such as HIV/AIDS, tuberculosis and malaria, and tropical diseases often ignored by big pharmaceutical companies. . . .
>
> The number of scientific papers produced by Africans has tripled in the past decade, to cover 55,400 in 2013, according to Reed Elsevier, an Anglo-Dutch information company. That still only accounts for 2.4% of the world's total, but it is quite a jump. The quality is rising too. . . .
>
> International businesses are starting research programs in Africa. Last year IBM launched a laboratory in Nairobi, Kenya's capital. The firm wants to use its artificial intelligence technology to support health workers in areas where doctors are scarce. Philips, a Dutch electronics firm, is opening an innovation hub in Kenya to focus on health care and lighting.
>
> Most African countries are starting from a low base and still spend only a tiny proportion of GDP on scientific research. But programmes like IBM's and SKA's are luring talented African scientists back from across the world, reversing decades of brain drain. The next Einstein Institute at the South Africa-based African Institute for Mathematical sciences is now turning hundreds of top-notch scientist every year at five postgraduate centers across the continent, each specialising in an area related to African development. By 2023 it aims to have 15

Index. Its overall score is 2.3 points higher than last year, with notable improvement in half of the ten economic freedoms including investment freedom, labor freedom, and business freedom. Guinea is ranked 27th out of forty-six countries in the Sub-Saharan Africa region, and its overall score is below the world and regional averages.

Over the twenty-year history of the Index, Guinea's progress toward greater economic freedom has been uneven but generally downward. Overall, its economic freedom score has declined by 5.9 points, one of the twenty biggest drops in the history of the Index. Its scores for property rights, business freedom, monetary freedom, and financial freedom have deteriorated by more than ten points.

The overall entrepreneurial environment remains severely constrained. An overbearing regulatory framework, exacerbated by poor access to credit and high financing costs, stifles economic activity and hurts business expansion and the development of a vibrant private sector. Corruption, perceived as widespread, is a serious problem—http://www.heritage.org/index/country/guinea.

centers. Says the institute's Thierry Zomahoun, "We want to create a generation of scientists who will lead Africa's transformation."[89]

This kind of scientific progress cannot fully redeem the lost centuries of scientific stagnation but they can definitely change the image of Africans and alleviate their miseries. It is one of the promising hopes for Africa. When there is enough for the West and Africa to live by with a win-win political and economic agreement, the few should not control both the intellectual and natural resources of Africa. The true meaning of civilization and barbarism needs to be analyzed and discussed from the various angles of the realities of the world and humankind instead of limiting the description, definition, and understanding to the West. Without a more global approach to civilization, all of us will continue to live in a disillusioned human history. In forging a new era for Africa and building healthy relationship between the West and Africa, Western entrepreneurs can play a significant role. Some have already started. *The Economist* describes:

> Diplomats seeking to solve crises in Somalia, South Sudan and the Great Lakes region encompassing Rwanda and eastern Congo are based in Nairobi, which also hosts a plethora of UN regional headquarters from shifting their African headquarters from South Africa to Kenya, the fifth-biggest economy south of the Sahara. Kenya Airways is among the best in Africa.
>
> The country is also bidding to become a hub of IT. Its m-Pesa mobile-telephonic banking system, from which more than half of Kenya's people benefit, has proved a global model. The country has one of the highest rates of Facebook membership in Africa; more than half a million Kenyans are on Twitter. In the Kilimani suburb of Nairobi, a thriving outfit called the iHub, led by a red-bearded American called Erik Hersman, serves a burgeoning community of innovators, technology investors and researchers, spurred on by Google and Microsoft, among other companies."[90]

In the midst of a distorted self-image, and with all intellectual and emotional struggle that Africans go through, the death, resurrection, and the glorious coming of Jesus Christ beams like a sunrise in a world of human history darkened by greed and injustice.

> As the result of this hope in God's future, this present world becomes free in believing eyes from all attempts at self-redemption or self-production through labour, and it becomes open for loving, ministering self-expenditure in the interests of a humanizing of conditions and in the interests of the realization of justice in the light of the coming of justice of God. This means, however, that the hope of resurrection must bring about a new understanding of the world. This world is not the heaven of self-realization, as it was said to be in Idealism. This world is not the hell of self-estrangement, as it is said to be in romanticist and existentialist writing. The world is not yet finished, but is understood as engaged in a history. It is therefore the world of possibilities, the world in which we can serve the future, promised truth and righteousness and peace. This is an age of diaspora, of sowing in hope, of self-surrender and sacrifice, it is an age which stands within the horizon of a new future. Thus self-expenditure in this world, day-to-day love in hope, becomes possible and becomes human within that

---

89. *Economist*, August 9, 2014, p. 42.
90. *Economist*, March 15, 2014, p. 46.

horizon of expectation which transcends this world. The glory of self-realization and the misery of self-estrangement alike arise from hopelessness in a world of lost horizons. To disclose to it the horizon of the future the crucified Christ is the task of the Christian Church.[91]

Africans' Social and Political Organization

Before colonialism, the political system in Africa was highly democratic, was unsurpassed by any state anywhere in the world. The system was developed by Africans. The family was the smallest socio-economic political unit . . . The village council was the next political unit, with an elected headman and a Council of Elders. The elders were the representatives of the various family sections or wards that made up the village. The village council was the center of authority, subject to the will of the community. The districts were the next and large divisions, varying in size having many villages and towns. The district Naba (chief) was a very important official. Any number of districts made up of provinces and kingdoms which formed the nation. The great Nanamse (plural for Naba), were elected by their respective councils and subject to their will. This latter fact was generally well disguised by ceremonial phraseology, rituals and autocratic sounding decrees from the throne.[92]

Ibn Battuta visited the Sudan in 1352–1353 at the time of the Hundred Years' War. The people had the Madingo King, Suleyman Mansa. Among the admirable qualities of these people, the following are to be noted:

1. The small number of acts of injustice that one finds here; for the Negroes are of all peoples those who most abhor injustice. The sultan pardons no one who is guilty of it.

2. The complete and general safety one enjoys throughout the land. The traveler has no more reason to fear brigands, thieves, or ravishers than the man who stay at home.

3. The blacks do not confiscate the good of the white man [i.e., of North Africans] who die in their country, not even when these consist of big treasures. They deposit them, on the contrary, with a man of confidence among the whites until those who have a right to the goods present themselves and take possession.[93]

Diop adds: "The Empire of Ghana was probably founded about the third century A.D. and lasted until 1240. As we know, Charlemagne, founder of the first Western Empire, was crowned in 800. Ghana's magnificence was in every respect similar or superior to Mali's. Such then were the African States at the time they were about to enter into contact with the modern Western world."[94] To this William augments: "The Portuguese arrived at the mouth of the great Congo river West Africa in 1488. As ignorant of the African people as they had been about the shape of the earth, were not prepared to find

91. Moltmann, *Theology of Hope*, 321–22.
92. C. Williams, *Destruction of Civilization*, 213.
93. Cited in Diop, *African Origin of Civilization*, 162.
94. Ibid., 163.

highly advanced states there. The kingdom of the Kongo was their first great surprise, because its political structure and expertly organized administrative machinery equaled that of Portugal or any other European state known to them."[95]

It was not only the West, East, and Northern part of Africa that had civilization. South Africa had also had its contribution. The Zulu army was more than a fighting force. It was an educational institution for the young and an instrument for building loyalties that cut across clans and could be considered as national. Promotion came through merit and not through clan or regional origin. The enforced use of the Zulu branch of the family of Ngoni languages also worked in the direction of national consciousness. Over an area of twelve thousand square miles, citizens came to call themselves Ama-Zulu, and to relegate their clan names to second place. Over a much larger area still, Zulu influence was profoundly felt. Policies such as curbing the excesses of witchcraft diviners (*izanusi*) and the fact that Zululand became free of internal struggles led to an influx of population from outside its boundaries—a positive contribution to the resources of the Zulu state.[96] Chaka was a genius and far-sighted political and military leader and a king. Jackson attests:

> Southern Africa has furnished a more splendid array of warrior kings than any other part of Africa [obviously Ethiopians would dispute this]. Chaka, the Zulu king and war lord, is the most famous, the most maligned and the most misinterpreted of South African kings. By any fair measurement, he was one of the greatest natural warriors of all times. He fought to consolidate South Africa and to save it from European rule. When he died in 1828 he was winning that fight.
>
> For a period of more than a hundred years, African warrior nationalists, mostly kings, who had never worn a store-bought shoe or heard of a military school, outmaneuvered and outgeneraled some of the finest military minds of Europe. They planted the seed of African independence for another generation to harvest.[97]

Portugal's African enemies often possessed skilled and well-equipped armies and very often constructed strong fortifications. In 1659, Portugal had a particular campaign on one of the fortifications. They won and continued after taking the town, only to lose badly in another battle, with the result that virtually all its Portuguese members were killed.

Likewise, although the Portuguese played the role of a heavily armored infantry in many of the campaigns, their presence was not decisive, and in most respects their tactics were identical to those of their enemies. Portuguese soldiers could not win unsupported by Africans and were regularly massacred when they tried to do so. If Angola was a major participant in the Atlantic slave trade and the source of export for many thousands of people, it was not through the superiority of European arms.[98]

Robert B. Edgerton, in his book, *The Africa's Armies from Honor to Infamy: A History from 1791 to the Present*, traces the military history of sub-Saharan Africa from the

95. C. Williams, *Destruction of Civilization*, 245.
96. Rodney, *How Europe Underdeveloped Africa*, 131.
97. Jackson, *Introduction to African Civilization*, 34.
98. Thornton, *Africa and Africans*, 115–16.

precolonial era to contemporary Africa. He begins his sweeping chronicle by describing the role of African armies in precolonial times, when armed forces or militias were essential to the maintenance of and prosperity of their societies. During the colonial era, African soldiers fought with a death defying courage, earning high respect in the eyes of the Europeans. They were often recruited to the colonial armies not only to enforce the colonial power but to fight for the European homelands as well. During the Second World War, Meredith observes that, "Thousands of African troops were recruited for war service. From British territories, some 374,000 Africans served in the British army . . . African regiments were sent to India and fought with distinction in Burma. In India and Burma, African soldiers learned how nationalist movements there had forced promises of self-government from the British government even though their populations were mainly poor and illiterate."[99]

The West Africans had a well-developed specialized maritime culture that was fully capable of protecting its own waters. Although African vessels were not designed for high-seas navigation, they were capable of repelling attacks on the coast. They were specialized crafts, designed specifically for the navigational systems. From the Angolan coast up to Senegal, African military and commercial crafts tended to be built similarly. Generally, they were carved from single logs of tropical trees and only occasionally had their sides built up. Consequently, they tended to be long and very low in the water. They were almost always powered by oars or paddles and thus were maneuverable independent of the wind. They drew little water and could operate on the coast and in rivers creeks, and inland estuaries and lagoons. Crafts that were designed to carry soldiers could, according to contemporary witnesses, carry from fifty to one hundred men.

The presence of African naval crafts along most of the coast seems to have deterred a recurrence of a raid-and-trade pattern by most subsequent Portuguese voyages to Africa. In 1535 the Portuguese attempted to conquer the Bissagos islands, home of some of the most renowned sailors and raiders on the Guinea coast, but with disastrous results.[100]

In the thirteenth century the bulk of the Indian Ocean trading system passed into Muslim hands with the second great wave of Islamic expansionism, stretching down the coast of East Africa and reaching into India, Malaysia, and Indonesia. All along the sea board of Somalia, Kenya, and Tanganyika, Islamic communities took urban root, building in stone and rich enough to import porcelain from late Sung and early Ming China. At Kilwa (in present-day Tanzania), rich on the gold trade from the region of the Zambezi and the copper from Luba workings in Katanga, the sultans produced their own copper coinage in the earliest mint to be established south of the Sahara, placed governors over the old part of Sofala (in present-day Mozambique), and levied large duties on the ocean trade to and from the East. Malindi and Mombasa (in present-day Kenya) exported iron ore to India for the manufacture of steel swords and daggers, and from Mogadishu (in present-day Somalia) went cottons and camel-hair cloth for Egyptian market, while from most of the coastal settlements flowed steady streams of ivory and slaves. Neither the prosperity nor the cultural florescence along the coast were,

---

99. Meredith, *Fate of Africa*, 8.

100. Thornton, *Africa and Africans*, 37–39.

however, to last, for a new imperialism was rising and, for the first time since the fall of Rome a thousand years before, in Europe.[101]

Thornton further describes the coastal region this way:

> West central Africa was also oriented by its rivers, especially the Zaire and the Kwanza... These rivers bore substantial commerce. Not only was the Kwanza used by Portuguese in their conquest of Angola, but it was a major artery of commerce for Africans as well... the river commerce was connected to the costal commerce. For many Africans as well, the coast was like a river system that connected distant points; it nourished a trade that predated and often complemented that of the Europeans operating on the high seas... the role of coastal societies and navigation in West Africa... shows that maritime navigation provided coastwise communication between substantial regions, which has often been overlooked in earlier assessments. In Loango, Sengambia, Sierra Leone, and Liberia, coastal estuaries, creeks, and lagoons form an interconnected, protected system of waterways facilitating the large-scale movement of goods. Such coastal waterways also allow easy communication between the mouths of the Senegal and the Gambia. Likewise the coast of modern Ivory Coast possessed a system of lagoons and coastal lakes.[102]

As Williams described these coastal towns, cities and ports were gateways for the Europeans and Arabs to Africa. "It is the same old story of the same techniques of penetration and domination that had to be repeated over and over in these pages as we moved from a country to country. Ethiopia, Makuria, Alwa, Ghana, Mali, Songhay, the Mossi States of Kongo, Angola, and Kuba, were all destroyed as a direct result of the first trading post footholds established in their lands. And so it was for the other states of the continent, large and small."[103] What started as a route of trade, commerce, and communication between Europeans and Africans on equal terms turned into slave trade and colonialism to control African natural resources and to use Africans' labor to develop Western industrialization, commerce, and economy. We'll look at these subjects in detail in a different chapter.

In the seacoast commerce there were several African products that were sold and exported. One of them was African cloth. Early European travelers praised African cloth. For example, both Fernando and Pacheco Pereira had much to say about the Mandingo cloth they and their informants encountered. This cloth was widely traded in West Africa, and the Portuguese even carried Madinga weavers to the Cape Verde Islands, where they created the distinctive trade cloth that was a staple of West African commerce for the next several centuries.

This cloth was of very high quality, for Pacheco wrote in the early sixteenth century, "In this kingdom of Congo they make some cloths of palms, with a surface like velvet, and those with fancy work like velvetized satin, so beautiful that there is no better work done in Italy."[104]

---

101. See Segal, *Race War*, 42–43.
102. Thornton, *Africa and Africans*, 19–20.
103. C. Williams, *Destruction of Civilization*, 277. See also Davidson, *African Civilization Revisited*.
104. See statistics in Braudel, *Wheels of Commerce*, 347.

This cloth was also plentiful, for African cloth makers appear to have been efficient producers as well as skilled ones. The Portuguese purchased considerable cloth from eastern Kongo for export to the land to the east of Angola, and a memorandum on this trade in 1611 indicates that the eastern Kongo region was exporting over 100,000 meters of cloth to Angola alone per year. Such a level of export might indicate, when domestic consumption and exports to other parts of Africa are considered, total production perhaps twice as high. This level of exports, from a region whose total population probably did not exceed 150,000, places eastern Kongo on a par with the great Dutch textile-manufacturing centers of the same time—whose total annual production ran to the 100,000-meter range and whose total population (urban and rural) was also perhaps in the same range.

Various beads were long manufactured in Africa—akori beads, for example, have a respectable antiquity in the region of modern Nigeria. But even more than in the case of cloth, beads were valued for their prestige and foreigners were attracted to it. In the case of such commodities the idea of function must yield to consumer preferences.

Sengambe mats clearly went to the European market, and in large quantities. The trade is mentioned in the earliest sources, and such mats were often used in Europe as bedcovers. Not only that but they must have been manufactured and exported in considerable quantities, for in the early eighteenth century an English factory in Sierra Leone was instructed to acquire no less than one million of them, "if they could be got." Africans also manufactured other items for European customers. Most famous of these were the "Afro-Portuguese ivories," including mostly spoons but also horns and saltcellars. These goods were artistically wrought in a hybrid art style and were definitely for elite consumption, but they were sufficiently numerous to go beyond simple production.[105]

From what we have seen so far and from more discoveries we will have as we go through this book the mental agility, the dexterity of their architecture, the complexity of the political governance of Africans and their innovations in the area of science, technology, and math, doesn't fit the Western description and understanding of Africans. Obviously, the West is blinded by bias and the racial war. Commenting on the undermining of African civilization by the West, Diop said:

> Inflated by the recent technical superiority, the Europeans looked down on the Black world and condescended to touch nothing but its riches. Ignorance of the Black's ancient history, differences of mores and customs, ethnic prejudices between two races that believed themselves to be facing each other for the first time, combined with the economic necessity to exploit—so many factors predisposed the mind of the European to distort the moral personality of the Black and his intellectual aptitudes.
>
> Henceforth, "Negro" became a synonym for primitive being, "inferior," endowed with a pre-logical mentality. As the human being is always eager to justify his conduct, they went even further. The desire to legitimize colonization and the slave trade—in other words, the social condition of the Negro in the modern world—engendered an entire literature to describe the so-called inferior traits of the Black. The mind of several generations of Europeans would thus be gradually indoctrinated. Western opinion would crystallize and instinctively accept as

---

105. See Thornton, *Africa and Africans*, 48–53.

revealed truth the equation: Negro=inferior humanity. To crown this cynicism, colonization would be depicted as a duty of humanity. They invoked "the civilizing mission" of the West charged with the responsibility to raise the African to the level of other men [known to us as "the white man's burden"]. From then on, capitalism had clear sailing to practice the most ferocious exploitation under the cloak of moral pretext.[106]

African's ingenuity is not completely destroyed by slavery, hard labour, discrimination, lack of freedom, lack of education, and poverty. In his book, *Created Equal: The Lives and Ideas of Black American Innovators*, James Michael Brodie indisputably presents the creativity, hard work, discipline, and productivity of African descent in the United States. In a prejudiced world where black Americans had little promise of fame or fortune, with and without education; these blacks have shown powerful intellect, startling imaginations, and unbreakable will that endured the unbearable circumstances of their time.

In this wide-ranging, astonishing account of resourcefulness, one sees who is who among African-American inventors. To mention the few: Elijah McCoy (1843–1929) invented an oil-dripping cup for trains. Other inventors tried to copy McCoy's oil-dripping cup. But none of the other cups worked as well as his, so customers started asking for "the real McCoy." That's where the expression comes from. Lewis Latimer (1848–1928) invented an important part of the light bulb—the carbon filament. Latimer worked in the laboratories of both Thomas Edison and Alexander Graham Bell. Jan Ernst Matzeliger (1852–1889) invented a shoemaking machine that increased shoemaking speed by 900%. In 1992, the U.S. made a postage stamp in honor of Matzeliger. Granville T. Woods (1856–1910) invented a train-to-station communication system. Woods left school at age ten to work and support his family. George Washington Carver (1860–1943) developed peanut butter and 400 plant products! Carver was born a slave. He didn't go to college until he was thirty. Madam C. J. Walker (1867–1919) invented a hair-growing lotion. Walker grew up poor. But she became the first female African-American millionaire. Garrett Morgan (1877–1963) invented the gas mask. Morgan also invented the first traffic signal. Dr. Charles Drew was born on June 3, 1904. He invented the blood bank. During World War II, Britons turned to American doctor Charles Drew to provide and store blood for the wounded soldiers and civilians. Donated blood saved thousands of lives. Otis Boykin (1920–1982) invented the electronic control devices for guided missiles, IBM computers, and the pacemaker. Boykin invented twenty-eight different electronic devices. Dr. Patricia. E. Bath 1949 invented a method of eye surgery that has helped many blind people to see. Dr. Bath has been nominated to the National Inventors Hall of Fame. Lonnie G. Johnson (1949–) invented the world-famous watergun, the Supersoaker. Johnson's company just came out with a new Nerf ball toy gun.[107] Calderisi adds, "The accomplishments of Africans in free societies around the world are proof of their talent. Doctors, lawyers, scientists, engineers, and managers who emigrated have more than held their own in highly competitive environments; some have

---

106. Diop, *African Origin of Civilization*, 24–25.

107. Brodie, *Created Equal*; Schraff, *Dr. Charles Drew*. See also "The Top Ten African American Inventors," http://teacher.scholastic.com/activities/bhistory/inventors/bath.htm.

become pace-setters in their fields."[108] In the light of this incredible achievement of black intellectuals, Woodson challenges blacks of our time:

> Tragically, although our current generation is presented with opportunities that our forebears never dreamed of, it is enslaved in ways our ancestors never were. Today's youths have been indoctrinated with an ideology that has convinced them that their shortcomings are solely the result of racist oppression which has circumscribed their potential and has necessarily resulted in the rage, violence, and self-destruction that dominate their lives.
>
> The bondage of the hopelessness and dependency could be broken by giving voice to the black heritage that was marked by determination, self-sufficiency, and achievement. *The truth is that values such as strong families, religion, patriotism, and self-reliance are deeply rooted in authentic black history.*"[109]

The ingenuity of Africans both at home and in the land of slavery demonstrates that blacks like any human being are created equal. And like any human race, they have genius, average, and dumb people. All the derogatory, dehumanizing, and degrading labels are given to them to justify their exploitation by and the supremacy of the white people. Africans do not need to be "turned into people" to be Christians or scientists. They are already people created in the image of God. What they lack is opportunity. As I will demonstrate in a different chapter, the primary motive of the whites is not racism but economics. The "white trash" that were shipped from England for forced labor are a good example.

Without recognizing the rich history of civilization in Africa, without any sense of indebtedness to Africa's contribution to mathematics and science, the West came to Africa with a paternalistic mentality to civilize the "uncivilized." In the process, as some Western scholars think, "When a powerful, highly developed civilization comes into contact with a weaker, less developed civilization, the former tends to swamp the latter. This is what happened in Black Africa."[110] In the light of my research, I find it difficult to justify in the bar of reason Kane's comparative assessment of the two civilizations. True to his culture, world of opinion and school of thought, he cannot but describe African civilization as "a weaker, less developed." Others have said worse than that.

In my opinion, by not crossing the Atlantic to raid Europe and counterattacking the European raiders to defend their freedom and dignity, Africans demonstrate superior civilization and equal power. Hence, "the Europeans had little success in their seaborne attacks on the mainland. As a result, the Europeans had to abandon the time-honored tradition of trading and raiding and substitute a relationship based more or less completely *on peaceful regulated trade* . . . the Portuguese Crown eventually dispatched Diogo Gomes in 1456 to *negotiate treaties of peace and commerce with the African rulers of the coast. As a result, Portugal established and maintained diplomatic relations with a host of African states.*"[111]

---

108. Calderisi, *Trouble with Africa*, 85.
109. Woodson, *Triumphs of Joseph*, 55; emphasis added.
110. Kane, *Concise History of Christian World Mission*, 143.
111. Thornton, *Africa and Africans*, 37; emphasis added.

It was this diplomatic relationship with African states that turned to a slave trade and colonialism with all kinds of exploitation involved including the human body. Does breaking treaties, betraying the Africans' trust and hospitality, make Portugal more civilized? If the African states had no system of governance, organized bureaucracy, or political and economic system, how could they have had diplomatic relationship with Portugal? Can "half-animals" be asked political treaties, unless the one who asks has wrong and unsubstantiated truth about Africans?

Despite the false, biased, and unfounded writings and comments about Africans from Western observers who are blinded by greed and their hatred toward black people, Africans were as civilized—perhaps even more advanced—than some European countries at the start of their contact with them. "Not only did African naval power make it difficult, it also allowed Africans to conduct trade with the Europeans on their own terms, collecting customs and other duties as they liked. For example, Afonso I, king of Kongo, seized a French ship and its crew in 1525 because it was trading illegally on his coast. It was perhaps because of incidents like this that João Afonso, a Portuguese sailor in French service, writing at about the same time, advised potential travelers from France to Kongo to take care to conduct trade properly, explaining that when a ship enters the Zaire, it should wait until the officials on shore send one of their boats and do nothing without royal permission from the King of Kongo."[112] Well, as we will probe further, you shall discover that this was the Congo that the Belgians "civilized."

There were similarities between Europe and Africa, not only in civilization and development, but also in worldview and religion. The worldviews prevalent in Western Europe and in black Africa in about 1500 had a great deal in common: "No difference can be perceived between the practices of the Christians and those of the heathen . . . Religion was part of the continuum of life, not compartmentalized on its margins, and it was supernatural interventions that made rain fall, and determined the outcome of battle. The belief in whitchcraft and magic was as characteristic of Europe as of Africa, and a study seventeenth-century Brittany suggests that the majority of the inhabitants of medieval Europe were sunk in animist worship of trees, stones and springs and that Christianity was the thinnest of veneers on top of this. In Portugal, the dead were thought to return on All Souls Day and the statues of saints were mutilated if they failed to provide expected benefits."[113] Wessels gives similar picture of Europe's Christianity:

> The first questions which arise in connection with any talk of a re-evangelization or re-Christianization of Europe are: how Christian was Europe really? To what extent has it been de-Christianized today? If by Christianization, one understands the reception of Baptism and certain ritual practices—such as attendance at Mass on a certain day—then England, France, and much of Germany were Christianized by 750. The church's fight against pagan superstition continued afterwards . . . After the Christianization of the Saxons, of the Germanic tribes only the inhabitants of the Scandinavian countries had not been yet Christianized. The Danes, Norwegians, and Swedes held on to their "paganism" longer. In the

---

112. Ibid., 39
113. Isichei, *History of Christianity in Africa*, 54.

ninth and tenth centuries these "Vikings" made raids on Europe and founded cities there. At this time the old pagan religion still flourished.

However, one may ask how deeply this Christianization had really penetrated the so called Christianized areas . . . Medieval Christianity was only a thin veneer. Only in the time of the Reformation in the sixteenth century was the northern part of Europe was Christianized . . . Before the Reformation and Counter Reformation "early modern popular culture" in Europe had fundamentally remained "pagan animist." There are those who see little difference between the French the sixteenth century and, for example, their "unbelieving" Indian contemporaries. "The French may well have done their Easter duty and married and had their children baptized in church, but their religion was an outward veneer." Only the shadow of the Christian symbol had been cast on them. Hence talk of the "legend of the Christian Middle Ages." "Christendom around 1500 is almost a mission country!" Some believe that they cannot even speak of a medieval Christendom. They go so far as to see the mediaeval Christianization as a failure.[114]

Andrew Walls also makes a parallel observation: "Western Christendom was Christian territory, and it was natural to wish to expand the area of the world which acknowledged the King of kings. Further, the only extensive experience Europe had of interaction with non-Christians (if we except the Jews) was of crusade. The first contact of Western Christians with the New World, of which Africa was a part, was conceived in crusading zeal. When the Portuguese took Ceuta in Morocco from the Muslims in 1415, it was to bring it into Christendom, make it Christian territory."[115]

More than anything, the pagan—and animistic—veneer of Christianity of the European culture during their contact with Africa explains the un-Christian behavior and the barbaric acts of Europeans in Africa and the manner of their treatment of black people, during the slave trade and during colonialism. For that matter, European engagement with Africa during neocolonialism doesn't show the virtues of a Christian continent either. In the twentieth-century Christianity of Europe, "[t]he pious churchgoer is a thing of the past, and is now replaced by the responsible Christian as an independent citizen in the realm of morality and culture. *For in the progress of world history Christ himself is striding ahead.* He is in the process of relinquishing his provisional way of life in the form of the church, and of acquiring his final, moral and political kingdom."[116] With this understanding of the Christian faith, to missionize became to colonize and to colonize to missionize. Without independent and absolute measurement of Western behavior and actions, everything was interpreted as a mission to civilize the uncivilized. Modern Western missions became a part of Europeans' civilizing mission. Hence, European Christianity lacked a prophetic voice in the face of injustice in Africa.

What is the measurement of civilization? If it is affluence, materialism, comfort, security, and development, the Israel of Amos's time would be a model just like Western nations. Under the long and brilliant reign of Jeroboam II (ca. 786–746 BCE), the Northern Kingdom, also called the Kingdom of Israel, reached the summit of its material power and prosperity, expanding its territory northward at the expense of Hamath and

---

114. Wessels, *Europe*, 3–4.
115. Walls, *Missionary Movement in Christian Africa*, 92.
116. Moltmann, *Sun of Righteousness Arise!*, 14; emphasis added.

Damascus, and southward at the expense of Judah. During this entire period Assyria was weak, and Syria on the decline; Jeroboam took advantage of the weakness of both to extend his dominion, foster commerce, and accumulate wealth.

When Amos appeared in the North there was pride (6:13–14), plenty, and splendor in the land, elegance in the cities, and might in the palaces. The rich had their summer and winter palaces adorned with costly ivory (3:15), gorgeous couches with damask pillows (3:12), on which they reclined at their sumptuous feasts. They planted pleasant vineyards, anointed themselves with precious oils (6:4–6; 5:11); their women, compared by Amos to the fat cows of Bashan, were addicted to wine (4:1). At the same time there was no justice in the land (3:10), the poor were afflicted, exploited, even sold to slavery (2:6–8; 5:11), and the judges were corrupt (5:12).[117] Whether it is in Egypt or Israel, the West or Africa, there has never been civilization without contrast. Behind the glory and success of the few, there is always the sweat and blood of the masses. Beneath the throne of the powerful, there are the downtrodden, the powerless, and the helpless. The gain of the few is directly or indirectly related to the loss of the multitude. The unrestricted freedom of the rich exists with the enslavement of others. The hoarding of the few often results in the starvation of the many. In today's global economy, obesity in some parts of the world is causing emaciation on another part of the globe.

In the modern world, the success of the Northern Kingdom of Israel is something other nations would emulate. The kingdom's wealth and prosperity is a sign of prestige and a higher degree of achievement. Good and high GDP is not only the measurement of economic health and wealth; it is also a source of power. Wealthy countries or nations are not only tourist destinations but the dreamland of refugees and the destitute of the world. Historians and journalists write about their glamor and glory. They hardly mention the cry of the poor, the exploited, and the oppressed. Not only human beings but also God is expected to prosper and bless these kinds of human success. The rulers and priests of Israel believed they were right with God and they kept the rituals—they sacrificed the best lamb, built nice and impressive altars, Sabbath was not violated, tithes were given. They were "blessed" and they expected God to bless them more. Until they hear the voice of a prophet everything looks normal.

Through Amos, a former shepherd from Tekoa, a village southeast of Bethlehem in the Kingdom of Judah, instead of endorsing the deeds of the Jews in Northern Kingdom, "God roared from Zion" (1:2). Amos's message was not a "politically correct" sweet and small voice that mollifies the minds of those who were in control and running the political, economic, and religious machinery. Not at all! "Fallen is Virgin Israel, never to rise again, deserted in her own land, with no one to lift her up" (5:2), said the prophet. "What had provoked the anger of the Lord? What had happened to shatter His silence? The answer is given in an account of events that happened in the world of which Amos was a part. Two things stand out in the prophets' condemnations: the absence of loyalty and the absence of piety."[118] Whether we look at Western civilization or African civilization we have no better scale to measure but God's standard of justice and righteousness. If a Christian doesn't have the backbone to stand on justice and righteousness as he/she

---

117. Heschel, *Prophets*, 32–33.
118. Ibid., 35.

analyzes human history, one needs to examine his/her ultimate allegiance. Is it to Caesar or to Christ?

Chapter 2

African Personhood—Being Human

When Europeans began imagining Africans beyond the Sahara, the continent they pictured was a dreamscape, site for fantasies of a fearsome and the supernatural. Ranulf Higden, a Benedictine monk who mapped the world about 1350, claimed that Africa contained one eyed people who used their feet to cover their heads. A geographer in the next century announced that the continent held people with one leg, three faces, and the heads of lions. In 1459, an Italian monk, Era Mauro, declared Africa the home of the roc, a bird so large that could carry an elephant through the air.[1]

We have known sarcasm and insults, endured blows, morning, noon and night, because we were "niggers"—Patrice Lumumba.[2]

Conception of Human Personhood

Africans have been described by the West as half-animals, savages, backward, uncivilized, "one eyed people who used their feet to cover their heads." But how do Africans perceive themselves? What does human personhood mean to them? Western culture, European Christianity, and Islam have altered so many aspects of African culture and self-image. One aspect that has a significant impact on the identity and personality of Africans is the changing of African names to Christian, Islamic, or European ones.

> Personal names are inseparable from the issue of identity in human affairs. Through identity personal names also become enmeshed in matters such as ideology, ethnicity, religion, sexual differences and social mythology.

1. Hochschild, *King Leopold's Ghost*, 6.
2. Witte, *Assassination of Lumumba*, 2.

> Until Christianity and Islam came to Africa, personal names generally were part of the collective uniqueness of each ethnic group. Whatever Polonius may have deduced from his society, in Africa it was not the apparel which proclaimed the identity of the man. It was his name. That told you his ethnic and cultural background. There were Chagga names, Nyoro names, Yoruba names, Ndebele names, Pre-Islamic Somalia names, Zulu names and the like. The collective uniqueness of the particular society was partly reflected in the personal names of its individual members. At least this was the ideal model, though in practice some names were shared across tribes either accidentally or through cultural influence.
>
> More than any other forces in history, it has been Christianity and Islam which have eroded the link between personal names and the collective uniqueness of each people. By insisting that there are such things as "Christian" and "Muslim" names, Christianity and Islam have proceeded to make universal what were originally Semitic names (sometimes in their Europianised versions). Semitic names such as John, James, Ali, Musa, Peter, and Muhammad have been part of the identity of millions of Africans. Some non-Semitic European names have also been elevated to full Christian status.[3]

The changing of African names has introduced a new identity that is not fully reconciled with its origin. Without contextualization a foreign ideology cannot speak to the African context. Torn between the often-coerced change and tradition, mentally many Africans live in a no-man's land of identity. They live in constant tension to reconcile conflicting values of modernity and tradition. To appease their minds, they put their feet in two worlds. This leads to an incomplete sense of belonging. This leads in some cases to emotional, behavioral, and social problems.

African ontology manages to avoid two extremes: "On the one hand, the wisdom of the continent opposes a simple sort of metaphysical ontology which reduces all conceptions of personhood to change less common substance. On the other hand, it avoids a radical kind of relational ontology which takes the human to be totally relationally constituted or socially constructed. African ontology of personhood thus avoids the Scylla of metaphysics as well as the Charybdis of social ontology. It attempts to establish a sort of relational ontology on the basis of 'non-fixed' substance."[4] He adds, "The substance of human is synonymous with with human, but this is not human confined by his or her boundaries or the nature of her substance, rather one who has broken through his or her boundaries in a movement toward communion with others, the physical world and the spiritual realm."[5].

> In African ontology every being has a nature which is not rounded off and does not contain everything that the being could ever become. A being could be more complete, more perfect in its kind by giving and receiving inputs, qualities, and characteristics from its environment. Being is not a changeless substance (*ousia*) but as *it relates* to (that is, substance-in-relation). Being is an active and open form that is continually adjusting and improvising its relation to another being,

---

3. Mazrui, *Africans*, 253.
4. Wariboko, *Depth and Destiny of Work*, 97.
5. Ibid.

non-being, and to the world . . . Being is not regarded much as substance, but as actualization of substance. The substance is that which cannot be of its own self . . . Manhood, womanhood or personhood implies ek-stasis of being. It is not only by being itself that a person or a thing exists but by being-in-communion that he (she) is at all and he (she) is himself (herself). Indeed, existence, in a certain fundamental sense, is both *ek-stasis* and *eis-stasis*. Beings both stand out and stand-into relationship.[6]

Wariboko gives a good five step analysis of African relational ontology captured in the now famous phrase: "I am, because we are; and since we are, therefore I am"[7] in order to explicate the open ontology of Africa:

1. The phrase adequately conveys the notion of *ek-stasis* of communion which makes the individual unique, indispensable, and irreplaceable as part of the active and open relational existence and experience that is the African community. The statement also captures what it means to exist in the African society. Life or presence is emergence—emerging not only from "non-life," non-being, from a centered self, interiority and reaching into a process of giving and receiving, sharing and living together, but also emerging from destiny (potentiality, compelling givenness) into actualization, reality, self-realization, freedom).

2. The power of being or participating in the power of being (power of being which resists non-being: that infinite power which every being exercises in order to exist is grounded and sustained in human communion. The power in a being (power of being which enables it to uphold itself as a being and not to succumb to nonbeing, no-more-ness) before its end is suspended and cocooned in human relationships. Human and even gods uphold their power of being in human communion.

3. The assertion of "being there," particularly, when it relates to a person is an absoluteness of life, a cry for indestructibility (continuation) of life, not absoluteness of particularity of form. The being that is there, is believed, to continue long after the "I" that is addressed and dressed in beingness disintegrates or succumbs to nonbeing. The doctrine of reincarnation or ancestral life is an attempt to deal with the absoluteness of being, to elevate being beyond particularities and to attach fixity to its many forms.

4. In this understanding of origin of being and person we can see the contours of a relational ontology of personhood. We see the shape of relatedness with Creator and other created beings. From the notion of a God who created both human beings and the world we have the essential attribute of space between *Teme*[8] and humans (nature). God is not mixed up with her creation—yet she stands in the same *Teme* with all he creatures.

---

6. Ibid., 96–97.

7. Mbiti, *Philosophy of Religion*, 108–9, 117.

8. The Kalabari word for the underlying reality that serves as the ontological ground of all that exists is *teme, inyon* (breath, power of life, rhythmic and animating pulse of life). These can be translated as spirit, spiritual stuff, or force (strength of life). Wariboko, *Depth and Destiny of Work*, 68.

5. The final dimension of Wariboko's exegesis of Mbiti's phrase is about the conception of otherness.[9]

The question Wariboko asked is: Does the relatedness that is the essential aspect of African's understanding of personhood suffocate individuality? What is the exact nature of the connection between commonality and individuality? According to Wariboko's assessment the relatedness is not considered necessarily heteronomous or an offense to independence and freedom. The substratum that animates all life has movement and plurality at its core such that it does not remain the same in all manifestations and modifications. Human beings are not reduced to some abstract common qualities but are particularized and identified. Personhood is an expression of the superabundance of intra- and interpersonal lives. Life by its nature is above, overflowing beyond itself. Existence itself, as we have argued, is opaque and closed in on itself; each person participates in a structure of meaning: it gives and receives. Even the cycle of interpersonal relationships between any two persons is not closed in itself; it opens to others as vehicle of social practices.

"It is a commonplace that the sense of community is strong in Africa. A society is equilibrium when its customs are maintained, its goals attained and the spirit powers given regular and adequate recognition. Members of society are expected to live and act in such a way as to promote society's well-being; to do otherwise is to court disaster, not only for the actor bust also for society as a whole."[10] The African community includes the living and the dead, the visible human beings and the invisible spirits. And the well-being of African community is maintained and sustained through rituals. Without a community individuals can hardly have what it takes to be a being in the African sense of the word. "A person in traditional [African] society is organically linked in a series of associations that include the community and the ancestors. There was no such thing as an individual achievement because it was the community that conferred on one identity and rights, which one exercised for the good of the community. The point of reference for anything valuable was the community."[11]

Mazrui captures Africans self-perception of the past and the present most accurately:

> There was a time for many African societies, in some cases fairly recently, when the village was the world. The myth and the legends of the society focused on the immediate human community, and the people concerned sometimes visualized themselves as directly linked to the origins of humankind. The ancestry of the 'tribe' was often equated with the ancestry of human beings generally. There was a tendency to globalise the village or globalise the "tribe." What Africa has experienced, especially in the twentieth century, is the momentous transition from the village globalised ("my people are the world" to the world villagised ("the people of the world are my people"). A rude shock has occurred all over the continent and beyond—the shock that the village is not the world; on the contrary, the world is the village. The concept of the global village is at hand, and

---

9. Ibid., 99–109.
10. Dickson, *Theology in Africa*, 62.
11. Orji, "Religion, Violence, and Conflict," 90–91.

the idea that planet Earth is lonely island in the cosmos is competing with more ancient myth and legend in Africa.[12]

It takes another book to analyze anthropologically the impact of such radical change on the personality of Africans. As a Francophone wit has put it, "Africa has its feet in the Neolithic and its head in the thermonuclear age. Where is the body? It is managing at best it can."[13] The introduction of European Christianity, Islam, and the change from "globalized village" to "world villagized" has caused tension and conflict between traditional and modern values of understanding personhood as an African. Since cultural changes are not done through planning and are not implemented following principles of innovation, diffusion, adaption, and assimilation, both individual and social transformation has insignificant impact as far as bringing a desirable change in understanding African personhood. The "globalized village" was destroyed through slave trade, colonialism, and the introduction of Christianity and Islam. The "world villagized" is unfriendly, racist, and dehumanizing to the black race.

"The collective personality, the crucial identity of a people, centered on three components— linguistic, historical and psychic."[14] Only two could be comprehended scientifically, that is, the linguistic and historical factors. When people are cut off from these three components that are essential to build and sustain healthy personality, the negative consequence in their personal and social life is generational. In Africa, no foundational political sovereignty, economic sovereignty, or psychic autonomy can be made without an aggressive approach and restoration of the historical consciousness of the black race and African people.

> Once we awaken to the historical realities through a scientific approach to history, we find that the very people who were considered to be historical debtors were actually the historical creditors. From ancient Egypt, from the oldest world civilization, came the scientific and technological knowledge, the religious ideas and cultural, artistic contributions which shaped the European world. The day when Africans and blacks in general will impose that point of view, a view supported by scientific verifiable data, the self-images of blacks and the warped image of that others entertain about blacks will have to undergo a most profound revision. It will mean that an entire vision of the universe will have to be changed.[15]

In the light of African ontology, one can imagine the degree of devastation slavery and colonialism made on the personhood of Africans. Africans' hands and legs have been tied by the strong cord of isolation and the world is expecting them to walk. The roots of their existence have been cut off and we want them to live a decent life. In hopeless cultural, economic, social, and political situations, black people are expected to be hopeful. Despite mistreatment, they are expected to be civil.

---

12. Mazrui, *Africans*, 295.
13. Cited in ibid.
14. Diop, *Black Africa*, 119.
15. Ibid., 114.

"Traumatic violence typically takes away victims' abilities to speak about what happened to them. Violence so overwhelms their senses that they cannot take it in as it happens. Instead, violence imprints itself in the mind as fragments of the events. It shuts down speech and turns people mute even as violence keeps recurring. To survive, the victim needs to find ways to speak about the violence, to name it in ways that do not retraumatize them."[16] Küng concurs, "Suffering imposes a limit to all reasoning."[17] In the words of Buchanan, "Sorrow seeks to render us mute."[18] The African songs, the African proverbs, idioms, and arts reflect O'Connor's and others' observation on the impact of violence on people's life. Years of oppression and injustice have made Africans less verbal and vocal. In silence, they suffer.

Perceived Unequal

> In 1924, the convenor of the Church of Scotland Foreign Mission Committee wrote a book entitled *Our Empire's Debt to Missions*. The chapter most concerned with Africa is called "The Civilizing Work of Missions among the Child-Races of the Empire." The implication is clear: child races need a firm, patient tutor. Nothing could better indicate how far both missions and missionary language had traveled since the days of Buxton and Livingstone. Much as they believed in what they called "civilization," that generation never saw Africans as *children*.[19]

"China had not so much broken with the paternalism of the West that it so often decried, as replaced it with a new one of its own. Africans were not really brothers. Not at all. Behind the fraternal masks, Chinese officials thought of them as children, capable on of baby steps, to be brought along with sugary inducements and infantilizing speech."[20] In so many aspects of Western non-Westerners interaction with Africans, the explicit and implicit notion of the "child race" is expressed in the form of a tutor and a pupil. The Western perceptions of Africans and all the exaggerated mind-boggling stories they spread about Africans, their culture, and the society had affected negatively the rest of the world and millions of Africans, young and old. Katongole accurately capture the power of stories: "Stories not only shape how we view reality but also how we respond to life and indeed the very sort of person we become. In other words, we are how we imagine ourselves and how others imagine us . . . Who we are, and how we are capable of becoming, depends very much on the stories we tell, the stories we listen to, and the stories we live. Stories not only shape our values, aims, and goals; they define the range of what is desirable and what is possible. Stories, therefore, are not only fictional narratives meant for our entertainment; stories are part of our social ecology. They are embedded in us and form the very heart of our cultural, economic, religious, and political worlds."[21]

---

16. O'Connor, "Mystery of Meaning," 62–63.
17. *On Being a Christian*, 413.
18. *Spiritual Rhythm*, 33.
19. Walls, *Cross-Cultural Process*, 98; emphasis original.
20. French, *Continent for the Taking*, 221.
21. Katongole, *Sacrifice of Africa*, 2.

The distorted information about Africans has also affected the self-understanding and self-knowledge of Africans themselves. In 1996, when my wife and I decided to go back to Kenya as missionaries, our two American-born children were eight and six years old. When we broke the news of going back to Africa to them both of them were uncomfortable. The older, Ben, was more disturbed by the inevitable change of culture and geography than his younger sister, Nardos. His anxiousness was reflected by the comments and questions he addressed to his parents, particularly to me. He asked me a number of bizarre questions about Africa and Africans and I had a hard time understanding where the questions were coming from. After all, he is the son of two African parents. Before Ben made up his mind, he asked me, "Dad, Africans need you, not me, why do I have to go with you?" "Do Africans sleep on a tree?" "Can elephants and lions come at night and attack us?" Patiently and gently I answered his questions until one day he came to our bedroom at 6:00 am to wake me up from my sleep and said, "Do Africans wear clothes?" I was a bit upset and offended by his perception of Africans and also felt tickled by his innocent question. To give him shock therapy, I told him, "Africans do not wear clothes. Even your mom and I only started wearing clothes at the airport when we came to the U.S. When we go back we will start living according to our tradition." In bewilderment, he gave me a wide-eyed look and said, "Really?" and ran to his bedroom. I had to run after him to explain his question and calm him down. Fortunately, four years later at the age of twelve, when we were on furlough/leave in the U.S. he said, "Dad, thank you for raising me in Africa." Wanting to know that he was anchored in his African roots, those words gave me great relief.

The questions of my son and the struggle he went through to reconcile his perception of Africans with his own identity demonstrates the degree of degradation Africans went through as black people. "The great ecumenical challenge to Christian theology today is not the personhood of the people in the Frist world, who have become the 'determining subjects' of their own lives. It is the human dignity of the people in the Third World, who have been turned into non-persons."[22] Because Moltmann's life was "born" out of suffering, his keen theological intelligence is sandwiched between empathy and respect for human dignity. Initially, the term "Third World" and its connotation was used to describe the difference between Marxist countries in the Eastern bloc, the capitalist countries and the colonized African, and Latin American and Asian countries.[23] Later on the term Third World developed a derogatory connotation that disparages the

---

22. Moltmann, *Way of Jesus*, 65.

23. Franz Fanon is generally agreed to have been the first to talk about "three worlds." Fanon was a West Indian psychiatrist, an anti-imperialist nationalist who worked in Algeria during the struggle against French colonialism, and he developed the idea in his book *The Wretched of the Earth*. He saw the alignment of forces in the world differently from the view put forth by the "three worldists;" for Fanon the "first world" was the imperialists or "free world" as they preferred to call themselves; the "second world" consisted of all those countries that called themselves socialists—the U.S.S.R., China, Cuba, Korea, Vietnam, Albania, and the other people's democracies of Eastern Europe; and the "third world," the colonies and former colonies. For Fanon this "third world" had its own special goals and purposes. While he spoke often of socialism, he upheld this separateness, and wouldn't completely take the side of the socialist camp. See *Encyclopedia of Anti-Revisionism On-Line*, Red Dawn Committee (Marxist-Leninist), The Theory of Three Worlds, http://www.marxists.org/history/erol/ncm-1a/red-dawn.htm. See also Rapley, *Underdevelopment*.

self-image of people in the majority world. Even the sharp intellect and genuine empathy of Moltmann could not escape the use of the term.

Slavery and colonialism is as old as human history. What makes the situation in Africa different is perpetual dehumanization. Describing the superiority of the white race over the blacks, Henry E. Garrett, while he was on staff at the University of Virginia, Charlottesville, wrote this: "No matter how low (in a socioeconomic sense) and American white may be, his ancestors built the civilizations of Europe; and no matter how high (again in a socioeconomic sense) Negro may be, his ancestors were (and kinsmen still are) savages in an African jungle."[24] Chisholm is right when he says, "There is, among some white folk, the view that, once you think of ancient Africa (or modern Africa for people like Garret) you think of a monolithic primitive society and of 'savages.' Ignorance is commingled with ethnocentric or racist arrogance and each feeds on and fuels the other and together they provide a fertile setting for ethnocentric or racist myths or exaggerations."[25] "To set the process [of slavery] in motion," said Clarke, "the African was totally dehumanized in the minds of the Europeans. So far as most of them were concerned, the Africans were outside the grace of God; Africans became living commodities in a world trade system that laid the basis for modern capitalism."[26] Ayittey concurs: "By the 1840s the slave trade had been abolished, but it left blacks persistently stigmatized as 'inferior.' It was probably this, rather than the physical and economic damage of the slave trade, that wrenched the heart from inner psyche of blacks and assailed the very cultural soul of their existence. This helps to explain why the slave trade, which occurred centuries ago, continues to draw emotive reactions from blacks in general."[27] Mazrui adds, "The slave trade rapidly transformed Africans into *the most humiliated race in human hi*story. Cages, iron balls, whips, all became part of the totality of the Black experience."[28]

Anthropologists tell us that personality is made of heredity plus cultural environment. Even if one is born from two human parents, if the child is treated like an animal, raised in a cage without human interaction, tortured and humiliated, the chances of developing language and human behavior are none. "Man has not only got his origin from outside of himself, he is and exists only *with* others . . . No man can be man in isolation. We are people because we are talked to, carried, fed, and loved. It is the variety of relations which goes to make up a life. However, we are not only molded by relations with other people, but our home and the culture of our narrower surroundings shape our thinking and our emotions. The rationality of man is always very concrete. One does not live universally and in 'the everywhere' but at one definite place and among particular people. That emphasizes the variety of ways of life."[29] As I will explain in detail later, for Africans back at home or at the destiny of their enslavement, slave trade and colonialism

---

24. "Racial Differences," 982, 984.
25. Chisholm, "Afrocentricity Black Consciousness," 6.
26. Clarke, *Christopher Columbus*, 77.
27. Ayittey, *Africa Betrayed*, 5.
28. Mazrui, *Africans*, 231; emphasis added.
29. Yates, ed., *Mission and Invitation to God's Future*, 41; emphasis original.

did not create the necessary social and communal conditions to build their personality with emotional dignity and spiritual health.

Social scientists say, "Civilization has succeeded only to a limited extent in enforcing instinctual renunciation and endowing it with a sense of social purpose... Renunciation imposed by force cannot give satisfaction; it produces temporary compliance, and that is all. The proposition we are trying to establish is that deprivation of love on this scale should not be accepted as a fact of life as unalterable as natural law. On the contrary, the predominance of loveless force belongs rather to an environment in which a shortage of vital necessities prevails and the great majority live periodically or permanently in a state of material want. Poverty is the product of partial cultural development."[30] The "predominance of loveless force" and permanent "shortage of vital necessities" have negatively impacted Africans' self-image in the eyes of the world and themselves. Poverty, hunger, and malnutrition are the byproducts of cruel treatment by loveless Western powers and African tyrants. The Western oppression outweighs any kind of suffering that Africans had gone through in the past. That suffering has been sustained under the African tyrants who took over the positions of the colonial powers.

> The present day confused outlook of the African people is the result of centuries of Caucasian accumulation, a quite natural process wherever one people come under the economic, political and social domination of another people. The ideologies and value system of the oppressors quite unconsciously become those of the oppressed even when the result is demonstratively against themselves. But all other oppressed peoples, whether Indian, Chinese or Japanese, were able to hold doggedly to their own racial pride and cultural heritage as the last resources for survival as a people. Unlike the Blacks, they were never completely cut off from this sustaining life-line of every people.[31]

In the gigantic machinery wheel of slave trade and colonialism, Westerners found every kind of wrong in Africans and none in themselves. As Freud said, even "Science herself has lost her passionless impartiality; in their deep embitterment her servants seek for weapons from her with which to contribute towards the defeat of the enemy. The anthropologist is driven to declare the opponent inferior and degenerate; the psychiatrist to publish his diagnosis of the enemy's disease of mind or spirit."[32] One might think Freud is talking about or defending an oppressed or discriminated black or Asian race somewhere in the corner of the world outside of Europe. As scholars and his own autobiography tell us, Freud is reflecting on his own personal struggle of discrimination and prejudice that he faced as a Jew in Europe. Hans Küng explains:

> Freud considered himself a Jew and was proud of the fact. But he had to suffer for this, although he was quite clearly first in his class at secondary school and rarely had to fail tests there. As an outsider at primary and secondary school, his position was similar to that of Carl Marx: he had only a few non-Jewish friends; humiliations of all kinds at the hands of anti-Semitic "Christians" were his daily lot. He would have preferred, like his nephew John, to be educated in the more

30. Mitscherlich, *A Society without the Father*, 72–73.
31. C. Williams, *Destruction of Civilization*, 331.
32. Freud, *Character and Culture*, 107.

liberal atmosphere of England. But he lost much of his respect for his father when he learned at the age of twelve that Jacob Freud had simply swallowed the insult when a boy had thrown his new fur cap into the mud and shouted: "Get off the pavement, Jew." Such experience unleashed in Freud feelings of hatred and revenge at an early date and made the Christian faith completely incredible for him. It was no better at the university: "Above all, I found that I was expected to feel myself inferior and an alien because I was a Jew. I refused absolutely to do the first of these things." He was sixty nine when he recorded this in his *Autobiography*.[33]

Whether it is Jew or African, discrimination and the perception of being inferior and treated as such deeply hurts. The scar in the soul cannot be erased by the knowledge and expertise of a world-renowned psychologist like Freud, let alone for uneducated Africans. For Freud, his Jewishness was the problem for "Christians" in Europe. For Africans, it is their black skin color, their "thought" level, their "backwardness," etc., as perceived by Europeans. Barnett comments,

> Most Europeans and Americans, priding themselves upon the complexity of their civilization, are predisposed to belittle the intellectual accomplishments of vast numbers of people in other parts of the world. Impressed, and rightly so, by the enormous difference between their cultural inventories and those of the so-called primitive peoples, they are prompted to explain the disparity on biological grounds. Some have maintained that the mental equipment of the primitive is near the *animal level*. In their view the savage's perceptive powers are keener than those of civilized man, but his ability to remember the past, to imagine the absent, to envisage future possibilities, and to think abstractly are definitely limited. He is often pictured as being *naïve* and *childlike* in his emotional reactions, his lack of self-discipline, his simple tastes, and his gullibility. He said to be impulsive and unreflective, lacking in ability to free himself from the limitations of immediate and materialistic considerations."[34]

Bernal adds, "By 1680s there was in fact a widespread opinion that Negroes were only one link above apes."[35] The advocates of such thinking were philosophers John Locke, David Hume, and Georg Hegel. These kinds of rationalizations justified Europe's and America's forceful and negative involvement in the lives of Africans. Neither ethics nor commonsense, rule of law nor virtues of a civilized, knowledgeable, Christian person guided the thoughts and actions of Western slave traders and colonizers in Africa. "Racism certainly influenced slavery and the slave trade to a great extent, and converted Africans into commodities to be acquired and sold on the world market.[36] The comment of Lamin Sanneh about the African dictators applies here: "Freedom without accountability was a sentence of misrule and mass suffering."[37] That is the experience of Africans in the last five hundred years.

---

33. Küng, *Does God Exist?*, 266.
34. Barnett, *Innovation*, 21; emphasis added.
35. Bernal, *Black Athena*, 1:203.
36. Mazrui, *Africans*, 103.
37. Sanneh, *Summoned from the Margin*, 149.

The supposed superiority of the white race over the black was partly developed through etiology and environmental theory. Goldenberg writes:

> The ancient Greeks noticed that those who lived in the remote northern regions of the world were the lightest-skinned people and those in the remote south had the darkest skin, and they developed the theory that the extremes of weather and environment in the far distant areas caused the different ethnic traits, including skin color. The extreme cold and lack of sun in the north produced light skin while the extreme heat and rays of the sun in the south produced dark skin. The closer one came to the center of the world, i.e. Greece and Rome, the more balanced was the environment and thus the effects of the environment on people. In the center humans were the most beautiful physically, in complexion and features, and nonphysically, in temperament (e.g. courage), character (e.g. intelligence, morality), and culture.
>
> The environmental theory is the most common explanation found in classical sources accounting for human color variation, but the Greeks and Romans also recount the myth of Phaeton, who brought the sun chariot too close to the earth. As Ovid said, "It was then, as men think, that the peoples of Ethiopia became black-skinned."[38]

It was not only in science and anthropology; the inequality of race was also justified by theology and biblical teaching in many Western Christian circles. Edwin M. Yamauchi writes:

> No other verse in the Bible has been so distorted and disastrously used down through the centuries for the exploitation of Africans and African Americans as Genesis 9:25: "He [Noah] said 'cursed be Canaan!/ the lowest of slaves/ will be to his brothers'" (NIV). The earliest use of the curse of Ham to justify slavery in America dates to the 1670s.[39]

Referring to Gen 9:18–25, Goldenberg also states:

> THIS BIBLICAL STORY has been the single greatest justification for Black slavery for more than a thousand years. It is a strange justification indeed, for there is no reference in it to Blacks at all. And yet just about everyone, especially in the antebellum American south, understood that in this story God meant to curse black Africans with eternal slavery, the so-called Curse of Ham.[40]

Burton makes a similar observation:

> The basic teaching of an inclusive God abounds in Scripture, yet some have used God's Word to perpetuate the myth of a cursed race—the dark skinned sons of Ham. The myth have become so common that many have placed the text about "the curse of Ham" in their own imaginative Bibles next to verses like "cleanliness is next to godliness" or "God helps those who help themselves." Armed with a cadre of textual misinterpretations, allegations of a cursed race have been

---

38. Goldenberg, "Early Jewish and Christian Views of Blacks," 2.
39. Yamauchi, *Africa and the Bible*, 19, 28.
40. Goldenberg, *Curse of Ham*, 1. For an in-depth understanding, see ibid., passim. In addition to the Protestants' interpretation of Gen 9:25, you will learn about the Rabbinic, Arabic, and Mormon's view.

used to subjugate the people of Africa and other dark skinned people for over a millennia."[41]

Rodney asserts:

> The interpretation that underdevelopment is somehow ordained by God is emphasized because of the racist trend in European scholarship. It is in line with the racist prejudice to say openly or to imply that their countries are more developed because their people are innately superior, and that the responsibility for the economic backwardness of Africa lies in the generic backwardness of the race of black Africans. An even bigger problem is that the people of Africa and other parts of the colonized world have gone through a cultural and psychological crisis and have accepted, at least partially, the European version of things. That means that the African himself has doubts about his capacity to transform and develop his natural environment. With such doubts, he even challenges those of his brothers who say that Africa can and will develop through the efforts of its own people. If we can determine when underdevelopment came about, it would dismiss the lingering suspicion that it is racially or otherwise predetermined and that we can do little about it.[42]

Despite all the facts I mentioned in chapter 1 about the civilization in Africa before European encounter, despite the black Africans innovation and contribution in the area of science, math, philosophy, architecture, naval science, medicine, etc., the West dismissively labeled the "difference between their cultural inventories and those of the so-called primitive peoples . . . on *biological grounds*."[43] As if the biological ground is not enough, theological reasons were given for the inferiority of the black people. It was not only science and revelation that fabricated widespread reports giving Africans the image and behavior of animals.

Benjamin of Tudela, after his visit to Egypt, reported: "There is a people . . . who, like animals, eat of the herbs that grow on the banks of the Nile, and in the fields. They go about naked and have not the intelligence of ordinary men. They cohabit with their sisters and anyone they find . . . These sons of ham were black slaves."[44] If Africans were cohabiting with their sisters, colonizers should have not forced them to sleep with their sisters and mothers. As the British in Kenya and Belgians in the Congo forced Africans to do morally unthinkable things, as I indicated in this book, some Africans have committed suicide.

The interpretation or theology of the curse of Ham gained popularity with the development of the African slave trade in the fifteenth and sixteenth centuries. David Brion Davis comments:

> In 1676 Edmundson had felt it necessary to attack the assumption that Negro slavery was a fulfillment of the curse of Canaan. The great attention Coleman

---

41. Burton, *Blessings of Africa*, 11.
42. Rodney, *How Europe Underdeveloped Africa*, 21.
43. Barnett, *Innovation*, 21; emphasis added.
44. Cited by Hess "The Itinerary of Benjamin of Tudela," 17.

devoted to this question may have indicated an increasing tendency of Americans to identify Negroes with the children of Ham.[45]

Augustin Calmet wrote a four-volume of dictionary of the Bible (1722–28) in which he stated: "Noah having cursed Ham and Cain, the effect was, that not only their posterity became subject to their brethren, and was born, as we may say, in slavery, but likewise that the colour of their skin suddenly became black."[46]

The Genoveses remark: "Some southerners, including clergymen, tried to reconcile the biblical sanction of slavery with racism by arguing that the Canaanites and other non-Hebrew slaves of the Israelites had in fact been black Africans."[47] Yamauchi writes, "Between 1836 and 1846, ten thousand descendants of Dutch colonists called Boers or Afrikaners escaped British jurisdiction in the Cape colony by trekking into the interior of South Africa. There they defeated the Zulus in the battle of Blood River in 1838 and subjugated various tribes, such as the Khoikhoi and the Hottentots. According to George Fredrickson, the Trekboers invoked the curse of Ham to justify their expansion."[48] Even though Africans are proud of his scholarly theological work and claim him to be an African, Origen did a lot to contribute to the degradation of black Africans. And he set a precedent for all Western theologians who came after him to follow his line of interpretation about the curse of Ham. "Origen's biblical exegesis was enormously influential on the church fathers who followed. His interpretation of Song's maiden as an Ethiopian, and his use of this and other biblical Ethiopians as a metaphor for those in sin (i.e. the gentiles), became widespread in later patristic literature. It set the tone of all later exegesis. In sum, the patristic hermeneutic tradition saw the biblical Ethiopian as a metaphor to signify any person who, not having received a Christian baptism is black in spirit and without divine light. In a similar way "Ethiopia" came to symbolize the as yet unevangelized and spiritually unregenerated world of sin."[49]

What we understand from the theology of the curse of Ham is a biblical justification for the inferior nature of black people and the justification for African slave trade and later for colonization. Hence, not only are human beings but God is also dragged into the miserable conditions of the black people. The creator of peace, love, and harmony is pictured as the one who destined black people to be slaves and to the misery that comes along with it. The Scriptures clearly states that God created man in his own image. "Then God said, 'Let us make man in our image, in our likeness, and let them rule over the fish of the sea and the birds of the air, over the livestock, over all the earth, and over all the creatures that move along the ground'" (Gen 1:26). The purpose of God's creation of humanity is plainly explained: to make us rulers over all things except fellow human beings who are created in God's image. We are created to enjoy nature—to enjoy an abundant life of the celestial and terrestrial world. Because of sin we missed the mark and all of us have committed disobedience. We are all in need of the mercy of God. Because of

45. Davis, *Problem of Slavery in Western Culture*.
46. Cited in Peterson, *Ham and Japheth*, 44.
47. Genovese and Genovese, "The Divine Sanction of Social Order," 224.
48. Yamauchi, *Africa and the Bible*, 30.
49. Goldenberg, "Early Jewish and Christian Views of Blacks," 13.

his abundant grace, even after the fall God has not left humanity alone. Humanity was sought out by God for reconciliation. And God's search for reconciliation includes every human being. "God is not an enemy of unbelievers, nor is he the executioner of the godless. God has consigned all men to disobedience, that he may have mercy upon all (Rom. 11:32). So we must view and respect all human beings, whatever they believe or don't believe, as those on whom God has had mercy. Whoever they are, God loves them, Christ has died for them as well, and God's spirit works in their lives too."[50]

Unfortunately, for the advocates of the "Curse of Ham," Moltmann's type of theological anthropology is far from their thoughts and belief system. The apostle Paul, a Jew, correcting the worldview of Athenians, said: "The God who made the world and everything in it is the Lord of heaven and earth and does not live in temples built by hands . . . *From one man he made every nation of men*, that they should inhabit the whole earth; and he determined the times set for them and the exact places where they should live. God did this so that men would seek him and perhaps reach out for him and find him, though he is not far from each one of us. *'For in him we live and move and have our being.'* As some of your own poets have said, *'we are his offspring.'*" (Acts 17:24, 26–28; emphasis added). The very statements of Paul are good enough to discredit the thought of any arrogant person who would think otherwise about the origin of human beings.

The Bible also says, "The Lord saw that the wickedness of man was great in the earth, and that every imagination of the thoughts of his heart was only evil continually. And *the Lord was sorry that he had made man on the earth, and it grieved him to his heart*" (Gen 6:5–6). Sin spread throughout the earth, wherever it was inhabited by human beings, both among the descendants of Cain and Seth and among those who indeed now were mixed together and had become one people. They were "multiplied" as the word also signifies; they were both great in quality and great in quantity. The people were frequently committed to sin, and that everywhere; the degeneracy became universal. The heart of man is evil and wicked, desperately wicked. The wickedness of human beings itself, is a fountain of iniquity, out of which an abundance of evil flows. Evil thoughts are formed in the heart, and proceed from it; they are vain, foolish, and sinful, and abominable in the sight of God, by whom they are seen, known, and understood from afar. The corruption of human nature is inclusive of all humankind, and shows it to be universal; for this was not only true of those of the old world, but of all humankind; the same is said of humanity after the flood as before, and of all humanity in general without any exception (Gen 8:21; Ps 14:1–3; Rom 3:9–11).[51] Tennent elaborates sin's entrance into and impact on this world: "Genesis 3 depicts what is known as the Fall, the entrance of sin, and the brokenness of the human race apart from God. The subsequent chapters develop cycles of human wickedness and a rebellion that culminate in the narratives about Noah (Gen. 6–9) and the Tower of Babel (Gen. 11). The effect of human rebellion are shown to be both personal and systemic, not only separating individuals from God (e.g. Adam and Eve), but also fracturing all relationships (e.g., Cain and Abel) and society as

---

50. Moltmann, *Sun of Righteousness Arise!*, 144.

51. For further exposition on the verses, see Berkhof, *Systematic Theology*; Henry, *Commentary*; and Stott, *The Message of Romans*.

a whole (e.g., Noah's world)."[52] In the light of these verses, it was all humanity, not any particular race, that was wicked and made God grieve. It doesn't say it was black people. However, people who were racist could not see the depth of their own wretchedness and how much we all desperately need the mercy of God—the only one who can take us out of our human predicament. "Sin is not something evil about the human being who has been created good; it is an evil and godless *power* to which human beings have come to be subjected through their own fault. They are 'slaves of sin' (Rom. 6:17)."[53] "They" include both the Gentiles and the Jews—to be relevant to our topic, both whites and blacks. "Sinners are not loved because they are lovely; they are lovely because they are loved. Being loved really does make the ugly beautiful."[54] This kind of biblical truth needs to be taught in African churches, not only to heal the scar of racism between black and whites in the past and present but to avoid bloodshed that is often caused among Africans through tribal and ethnic conflicts.

In some research and writings, some anthropologist and philosophers even went further saying that Blacks are not decedent of Adam. John Locke, for example, "was particularly skeptical of the inconvenient category of 'man.'"[55] He adds, "It is certain that Locke and most 18th-century English—speaking thinkers like David Hume and Benjamin Franklin were racist: they openly expressed popular opinions that dark skin colour was linked to moral and mental inferiority."[56] However, "Man's nature is as present anthropologist like to say is 'eccentric,' i.e. man stems beyond himself. He does not get life by his own efforts. His center is outside of himself. Man does not rest within himself; he cannot create himself and cannot give himself his own character and shape. In other words: man lives and exists on foundations which he cannot lay for himself. In theological language: man is a creation bearing the image of God. However, man has to realize his being as creature. He does this with his life, his strength, his senses, and his feelings in grieving and in love. He is not autonomous but has to find his foundations and thus become sure of his identity."[57] Even if it is a hard pill to swallow for some, human beings are created in the image of God. This is true for the deformed, lepers, HIV victims, whites, blacks, and yellows.

In addition to Christian theology, etiology, and environmental theory, the symbol of black-and-white disseminated through Western literature, art, and media has damaged the self-image and personality of the black people. In 1837 the painter and theorist Jacques Nicolas Paillot de Montabert wrote:

> White is the symbol of Divinity or God;
> Black is the symbol of the evil spirit or the demon.
> White is the symbol of light . . .
> Black is the symbol of darkness and darkness expresses all evils.
> White is the emblem of harmony;

52. Tennent, *Invitation to World Missions*, 106.
53. Moltmann, *God in Creation*, 232; emphasis original.
54. Moltmann, *Sun of Righteousness Arise!*, 122.
55. Bernal, *Black Athena*, 1:203.
56. Ibid.
57. Yates, ed., *Mission*, 40.

> Black is the emblem of chaos.
> White signifies supreme beauty;
> Black ugliness.
> White signifies perfection;
> Black signifies vice.
> White is the symbol of innocence;
> Black that of guilt, sin, and moral degradation.
> White, a positive color, indicates happiness;
> Black, a negative color, indicates misfortune.
> The battle between good and evil is symbolically expressed
> By the opposition of white and black.[58]

These kinds of literatures and the theological perception of the West about black people have created racial differences, a different economic status, different levels of technological development, a different health care system and life expectancy, different education levels, and the like. Without stirring up hatred and irreconcilable division, the issue of African personhood and the history of Africans need to be addressed with *correct* biblical, theological, anthropological, and historical perspective. Without it, we cannot solve the current problem of Africa and Africans.

On Fox News's *O'Reilly Factor*, Jesse Watters presented a program called "Watters' World." In the program, Watters shows different kinds of interviews he made in different parts of the United States. If one judged Americans' intelligence by the knowledge of the interviewees, it would be easy to conclude Americans are dumb people.[59] To make the kinds of assertions that interviewees as scientific or theological fact, is not only foolishness but academic suicide. In my opinion, the seventeenth- and eighteenth-century Westerners who wrote many absurd things about Africans fall in this kind of category.

Philosophically speaking, "Life is something that visits my body, a transcendent loan; I have neither initiated nor conceived its worth and meaning. The essence of what I am is not mine. *I am what is not mine.* I am that I am not."[60] "Life is . . . transcendent loan"; "You are not your own," said the apostle Paul (1 Cor 6:19b). Unfortunately, everybody does not embrace this biblical conviction. And the so-called Christian nations have violated it the most. "The accident of what we have done or achieved, personally or ancestrally, can ground our pride but should be seen as secondary to the fact that all of us in the human family are alike human persons created by, and in the image of God. The recognition of our common God-connection, if taken seriously, can foster genuine respect for all peoples."[61]

Any person who is genuinely concerned to understand a human being, instead of rushing to analyze "others" and label them as "half-animal or "full human," needs to first ask "Who am I?"

---

58. Cited in Goldenberg, *Curse of Ham*, 2.

59. "Watters' World: X Games Edition," Fox News, http://video.foxnews.com/v/4013916317001/watters-world-x-games-edition/?playlist_id=1383651764001#sp=show-clips.

60. Heschel, *Man Is Not Alone*, 48; emphasis added.

61. Chisholm, "Afrocentricity Black Consciousness," 5.

> What is the direct content of the "I": the blooming of consciousness upon the impenetrable soil of the subconscious? The self-comprises no less unknown, subconscious, than known, conscious reality. This means that the self can be distinctly separated only at its branches; namely, from other individuals and other things but not at its roots.
>
> All we know of the self is its expression, but the self is never fully expressed. What we are, we cannot say; what we become, we cannot grasp. It is all a cryptic, suggestive abbreviation which the mind tries in vain to decipher. Like the burning bush, the self is aflame but it is never consumed. Carrying within itself more than reason, it is in travail with the ineffable. . .to exist implies to own time. But does a man own time? The fact that time, the moments through which I live, I cannot own, while the timeless in my own temporality is certainly not my private property. However, if life does not exclusively belong to me, what is my legal title to it?[62]

Great persons struggle with the fundamental question of *being human*, to understand themselves within the context of the cosmos. When they get it right, they realize that humanity is created for Sabbath as the crown of creatures not creation, to represent God in the world and the world before God. We are not meant to slaughter each other, dehumanize each other, and exploit each other.

For those who suffer from a superiority complex, especially we who claim to be Christians, who are discriminating the Jews, Gypsies, Latinos, the blacks, the Tutsis, Hutus, Amharas, Oromos, etc., the Scripture challenges us: "What is man that he can be clean? Or he that is born of a woman, that he can be righteous? Behold God puts no trust in His holy ones, the heavens are not clean in His sight; How much less one who is abominable and corrupt, a man who drinks iniquity like water!" (Job 15:14–16). "For there is no man who does not sin" (1 Kgs 8:46). "Surely there is not a righteous man on earth who does good and never sins" (Eccles 7:20). However, time and again, in human history we see one ethnic group or race overruling, dominating, oppressing, and shaping the destiny of the other by force. Küng was right when he said; "Man is free. But he is not free to be free."[63] Paul attests to this truth of bondage with a desperate cry, "What a wretched man I am! Who will rescue me from this body of death?" (Rom 7:24). To have a will without power and freedom to do good with it has caused two major World Wars in Europe. "Verdun and Stalingrad, Auschwitz and Gulag Archipelago are names typifying the unimaginable crimes against humanity which marked the twentieth century. In them *the progressive, modern, and Christian world destroyed itself.*"[64] Mind you, Moltmann did not say uncivilized, ignorant, backward, savage, and heathen people destroyed each other; quite the contrary.

Beginning with the Berlin conference (1884–1885) there was a growing support for white settlement and colonization of Africa, a continent that appeared as a safe haven for European emigrants rather than a dumping ground for unwanted blacks. Related to it is a belief that whites should rule blacks. In this game of racial oppression and exploitation,

---

62. Heschel, *Man Is Not Alone*, 46.
63. Küng, *Does God Exist?*, 438.
64. Moltmann, *Sun of Righteousness Arise!*, 14; emphasis added.

because it was biblically justified by some, even missionaries were also invited to join the supremacy of the whites over the blacks:

> While acquiring colonies, the United States also supported and encouraged colonization of Africa. Government officials, as well as American civilians, shared prevailing notions of a world divided between civilized and uncivilized parts; Europe and the United States constituted the civilized areas which had a right to colonise Asia, Africa and Latin America. The people of Asia and Africa were considered barbarians to be treated differently from other people. For instance, John Kasson believed that white military conquest of the Africans was beneficial to the world. Arthur Donaldson Smith, a Philadelphia physician, traveler and avid zoological collector, recommended white settlement in East Africa. Theodore Roosevelt, after leaving the White House in 1909, proposed that East Africa be turned into a white man's country by making every effort…to favor the growth of large and prosperous white population. He advised missionaries and government officials to work hand in hand to rule Africans with wisdom and firmness, and when necessary with severity.[65]

The history of the Horn of Africa, the past and present crisis of all kind, cannot be accurately analyzed and understood without the involvement of Britain, Italy, France, Germany, Russia, and the US, by physical presence and by proxy. As you proceed reading this book, I will show my argument.

Indeed, Africans were "treated differently" than white people in Africa. The dehumanization of Africans by the West happened in various ways. Here is one aspect of it:

> In 1897, when a world's fair took place in Brussels, the most talked-about exhibit was on the outskirts of the city, at Tervuren. More than a million visitors came to see this celebration of the Congo. Items on display ranged from that great instrument of civilization so praised by Stanley (who twice visited the fair), the maximum gun, to a large set of linen tapestries portraying Barbarism and Civilization, Fetishism and Christianity, Polygamy and Family Life, Slavery and Freedom. The most extraordinary tableau, however, was a living one: 267 black men, women, and children imported from the Congo.
>
> With great fanfare they were brought by train to Brussels's Gare du Nord and then marched across the center of the city to take the train for Tervuren. There, in a park, they were installed in three specially constructed villages: a river village, a forest village, and a "civilized" village. A pair of Pygmies rounded out the show. The "uncivilized" Africans of the first two villages used tools, drums, and cooking pots brought from home. They danced and paddled their dugout canoes around a pond. During the day they were on exhibit in "authentic" bamboo African huts with overhanging thatched roofs. European men hoping to see the fabled bare breasts of Africa went away disappointed, however, for the women were made to wear cotton dressing gowns while at the fair. Clothing, a local magazine observed, was after all, "the first sign of civilization"
>
> Leopold himself came to see the Congolese, his dream made flesh, and was introduced to one of their chiefs. Told that some of the Africans were suffering from indigestion because of the snacks and candy given them by the public, he ordered up the equivalent of a don't-feed the-animals sign. The placard said:

---

65. Munene, *Truman Administration*, 16–17.

THE BLACKS ARE FED BY THE ORGANIZING COMMITTEE. They were fed—and slept—in the royal stables.

The local press titillated its readers by speculating about whether the "uncivilized" Africans were dangerous. A reporter approached a circle of them. "At the center, sitting on a log, was the chief, motionless and sacrosanct. The voice of a singer was first heard alone; then a chorus picked up a refrain, accompanied by hand claps and the banging of sticks on metal objects, and by a swaying motion of these crouching bodies. And what were the soloist and chorus singing about? The magnificent deeds of [Force Publique Captain Hubert], Lothaire, the great warrior. All was well.

The Africans of the civilized village included ninety Force Publique soldiers, some of whom made up a military band. The soldiers marched, the band played, and, near the end of their stay were guests at a banquet. A black sergeant rose and proposed a toast to King Leopold II. When the Africans sailed for home, a newspaper rhapsodized, "The soul of Belgium follows them and, like shield of Jupiter, protects them. May we always thus show the world an example of humanity!"[66]

One wonders how a self-proclaimed civilized, superior, and Christian nation would treat Africans like animals in a zoo park and call it an "example of humanity!" When young Africans are gathered and forced to rape their mothers and sisters, when the hands of Africans are amputated and collected in a basket to be counted as if a farm product, when Africans are hunted for sport like animals in a game park, when Africans are imported to be shown on exhibition, when African women and girls are forced to sleep with white mercenaries and several catholic missionaries and the women see their family members and fellow Africans killed and enslaved by the same people, it makes them feel less of a human.[67] And the same oppressors describe Africans as people who have "the mental equipment of . . . near the animal level."[68] Hence, "White officers were shooting villagers, sometimes to capture their women, sometimes to intimidate their survivors into working as forced laborers, and sometimes for sport."[69] The impact of this kind of traumatic existence lasts for generations. Lack of respite from it has turned the existence of Africans into an undesirable situation. Endless conflict, malnutrition, disease, drought, and starvation are taking the lives of the young and old. There are not enough trauma centers for those who went through and are still going through unbearable and horrible ordeals. The medical system in most African countries is pathetic and the judicial system is utterly corrupt. The foreign policy of the West with African countries is not promising and the political systems of African governments in general are authoritarian and oppressive. From Cairo to Pretoria and from Lagos to Addis the pattern is the same.

In the past, Africans' historical places and rich archives were burned to the ground and Africans were told and taught by Westerners that they have no history but the Europeans' history in Africa. This has made Africans like withering trees without roots. Africans are told with a derogative tone that they do not know how to build anything

66. Hochschild, *King Leopold's Ghost*, 175–77.
67. Ibid.; Elkins, *Britain's Gulag*; Meredith, *Fate of Africa*; C. Williams, *Destruction of Civilization*.
68. Barnett, *Innovation*, 21.
69. Hochschild, *King Leopold's Ghost*, 111.

but mud huts, despite the undeniable civilizations with advanced architecture in Egypt, Axum, Mali, Congo, Ghana, Zimbabwe, etc., by Africans. Because of the high illiteracy rate in modern Africa, the ancient universities in Timbuktu, world-renowned scholars, black scientists, and innovators are often overlooked and seldom mentioned. In the introduction to his book: *The African Origin of Civilization: Myth or Reality*, Diop observes: "Our investigation have convinced us that the West has not been calm enough and objective enough to teach us our history correctly, without crude falsification."[70] Hence, for not wanting to give credit to black intelligence, the black African civilization in Egypt and in Ethiopia is not publicized with academic integrity. And African heroes like Dedan Kimathi, Patrice Lumumba, Nelson Mandela, Steve Biko, and Herbert Chitepo are mocked, imprisoned, tortured, and killed.

In addition to the obvious forces we observed so far, "the subtle weapons which have been more devastating in conquering the Blacks and reducing them to an inferior status. Caucasians victory was complete and seemingly permanent when the Blacks throughout the world joined the whites in glorifying all things white and condemning all things black, or even tinged with black, including themselves. Here we are the very heart of the race problem, this self-abnegation, self-effacement, the loss of self-identity by cutting their roots with the past and thereby losing the very links with their history from which a people draw strength and inspiration to move forward to even higher ground and, in fact, the reason for being."[71] Goldenberg, commenting on the symbol of white and black color, adds, "According to many anthropology reports, the phenomenon is common in black Africa. It appears that the symbolism of black-negative and white-positive is wide spread among people of all colors."[72] The English translation of some verses in the Bible such as "God is light and in him there is no darkness at all" (1 John 1:5), which is not the exact but the closest translation of the Greek text, gave a divine sanction to the "black-negative" perception.

When their dark skin is despised and they are looked down on because of it. It makes Africans develop low self-esteem and self-doubt, in one aspect, and in another aspect it creates black consciousness and determination to fight injustice, and also a hunger for liberation and freedom. When they saw such resolve in Africans, the colonizers did all they could to squash it. Caroline Elkins, in her book *Britain's Gulag: The Brutal End of Empire in Kenya* said:

> Virulent racism and European self-interest prejudiced the colonial justice system, punishment typically included floggings, stiff fines, and long prison term. Indeed Kenya had one of the notorious harsh penal systems in all of Britain's African colonies. When these repressive measures were not enough to thwart the growth of Mau Mau, the colonial government declared the State of Emergency, enacted dozens of draconian regulations, and began to employ terror as a means to subdue the suspected Mau Mau population.

---

70. *African Origin of Civilization*, xiv.
71. C. Williams, *Destruction of Civilization*, 250.
72. Goldenberg, *Curse of Ham*, 3.

> The British colonial government's works camps in Kenya were not wholly different from those in Nazi Germany or Stalinist Russia; they functioned on what Wolfgang Sofsky called "the economy of waste."[73]
>
> The world behind the barbed wire rendered utterly transparent, for the first time, the dark side of Britain's colonial project. The hypocrisies, the exploitations, the violence and the suffering were all laid bare in the Pipeline. It was there that Britain finally revealed the true nature of its civilizing mission.[74]

She adds, "Thus Mau Mau became for many whites in Kenya—what the Armenians had been to the Turks, the Hutu to the Tutsi, the Bengalis to the Pakistanis, and the Jews to the Nazis. As any recipient genocide, the logic was all too easy to follow. Mau Mau adherents did not belong to the human race; *they were diseased, filthy animals who could infect the rest of the colony, and whose very presence threatened to destroy Kenya's civilization. They had to be eliminated.*"[75] The key guerrilla leader of the Maua Mau was Field Marshal Dedan Kimathi. He was "captured, interrogated and eventually tried and hung."[76] Jomo Kenyatta, the first president of Kenya, who wanted to please the white settlers/colonizers, played down the heroic role the Mau Mau contributed for the independence of Kenya. As Obama says, "Kimathi became a name on the street sign, thoroughly tamed for the tourists."[77] Kimathi was not a hero that Kenyans and Africans should study and emulate; just a street name. What a missed opportunity to teach Africans about Kimathi to build the self-esteem of Kenyans and Africans.

Africans have a tendency to undermine their own history and heroes. When the current government of Ethiopia took power in 1990, one of their primary goals was to destroy the statue of emperor Menelik, who was the only black leader to defeat a European power on African soil. Had it not been for the struggle and determination of the then-young artist Tamagne Beyene and the patriotic Ethiopian people, the statue of Menelik—a great figure in the history of Ethiopia and a symbol of pride for the black — would not have remained intact. When the African Union (AU) wanted to build a statue of Haile Selassie alongside of Nkrumah on their fiftieth anniversary as a tribute to the founding fathers, the current government refused and even now Haile Selassie still has no statue. Despite all his weaknesses, Haile Selassie brought Ethiopia from her outdated feudal system to modernity and he made significant contributions for the independence of many African countries. In order to gain respect for and to bring a healthy cultural and historical restoration Africans need to stop mistreating and degrading each other. Reconciliation within the continent and with outsiders comes when truth is communicated in love, humility, forgiveness, and a sincere apology is included. All who are involved in the tragic history of Africa should show courage to promote and demonstrate this kind of healing process and civility.

The West has apologized to the Middle and Far East for the Crusades. And they say, "But when have Christians demonstrated this love to Muslims or Jews? We have gone

---

73. Sofsky, *Order of Terror*.
74. Elkins, *Britain's Gulag*, 152–53.
75. Ibid., 49; emphasis added.
76. Ibid., 55.
77. Obama, *Dreams from My Father*, 312.

to them with swords and guns. We have gone to them with racism and hatred. We have gone to them with feelings of cultural superiority and economic domination. We have gone to them with colonialism and exploitation. We have even gone to them with the Gospel cloaked in arguments of superiority. Only a few have ever gone with the message of Calvary . . . We must do more than carry the message, we must be the message."[78] Such kinds of gestures from the West toward Africans or toward the black race in general are yet to be seen. Sixty-three years later, the British, after a long and costly legal battle, compensated the Mau Mau survivors. *The Economist* titled it: "The Old Colonial Power has Apologized, sort of." And the occasion was described this way:

> Independence songs were sung, antique walking sticks were waved and Britain's representative in Kenya gamely ventured some words in Swahili to express his regret that Kenyans had been tortured during the Mau Mau uprising against the colonial rule in the 1950s. As Britain made carefully climbdown over colonial-era abuses on June 6th, none of those words was the Swahili for sorry. Britain has not formally admitted liability for torturing some of the 90,000 Kenyans detained during the rebellion. The compensation offered is modest compared with the payouts British citizens would expect for similar mistreatment back home.
>
> More than 5,000 Mau Mau veterans, some of whom gathered in Kenya's capital, Nairobi, for the formal announcement, will each get about $4,000.00. Wamatuwe Ngau, now 82, who never had children after being castrated by colonial officers, said the money was "nothing much" but that an apology was worth accepting.
>
> Britain opted to settle after the High Court in London ruled last year that there was enough evidence of torture for four old Kenyans to take their case to trial. It took a British law firm, Leigh Day, as well as a clutch of historians, ten years to win the argument. The settlement is worth $21m. The legal costs were around $9m.[79]

Meredith asserts the pattern of the colonialists across Africa saying, "Scores of African rulers who resisted colonial rule died in battle or were executed or sent into exile after defeat. Samori of Mandingo was captured and died in exile two years later; the Asantehene, King Agyeman Prempeh, was deposed and exiled for nearly thirty years; Lobengula of Ndebele, died in flight; Behazin of Dahomey and Cetshwayo of Zulu were banished from their homelands."[80] From the moment that the European powers stepped on African soil, Africans went through grinding poverty, oppression, imprisonment, torture, and death. Unemployment, poor content and irrelevant Western education, and lack of health care reduced their life expectancy on the cusp of the twenty-first century. Africans spoke of themselves as endangered species and as objects of dictatorial and mercenaries' genocide.

Some emerging African leaders saw that the restoration of Africans' self-esteem comes, among other things, through economic independence and political freedom. One of the early champions of such ideas was Patrice Lumumba of Congo. Instead of

---

78. Robinson, "Christian Apology for the Crusades"; emphasis original. http://www.religioustolerance.org/chr_cru1.htm.

79. "Drawing a Line under History," *Economist*, June 15, 2013, p. 52.

80. Meredith, *Fate of Africa*, 3.

being a hero and nation builder of his people, the West saw him as a big threat to their interest and a villain that needs to be nipped in the bud.

Innocent Victim

The trends in the global village are often impacted or influenced by major historical incidents. The Second World War had unplanned and unintended positive consequence on African colonialism.

> A strange thing had happened. Whereas the West's expanding technology of production had once resulted in the enslavement of Africans and the colonisation of their continent, the West's expanding technology of destruction in two World Wars helped to liberate Africa. The Second World War was especially critical. The war weakened the great imperial rulers irreversibly, as France, Belgium and Italy were humiliated; Britain was impoverished; and Portugal and Spain were morally bankrupt as a result of their association with fascism and Nazism. These imperialist countries still maintained their hold over their African colonies but the grip was weakening, in the aftermath of a masochistic European War which had become world-wide.
>
> Nationalism and anticolonial fervor erupted all over Africa almost as soon as the Second World War ended. Barely fifteen years after the end of this war the bulk of the African continent had attained formal political sovereignty. Never was a whole continent so swiftly subjugated, and then so rapidly emancipated. *Europe's pursuit of production in the industrial revolution had once resulted in the colonisation of Africa. Europe's pursuit of destruction in the Second world War had reversed the process and helped to initiate Africa's decolonization.*[81]

Patrice Lumumba was the first democratically elected and popular prime minster of Congo. He was a man of "considerable intelligence who believed, with much justification that Belgium had plundered his country and left it impoverished."[82] Like many emerging leaders of his time, Lumumba was convinced that the degradation the Congolese went through could be reversed through political freedom and economic independence. He thought Africans' dignity and personhood could be reinvigorated through freedom of speech, freedom of thought, freedom to control their natural resources, and freedom to pave their destiny.

Ludo de Witte captures the transition scene from colonialism to independence this way:

> On the independence day in the Congo, 30 June 1960, the Palis de la Nation in Lèopoldville is packed with Congolese and foreign dignitaries. The bronze statue of Lèopold II, founder of the independent state of the Congo, still dominates the front entrance by way of a welcome, as if the handover of the political power is going to change nothing. The newly elected Congolese politicians—members of parliament, senators and ministers—are gathered in a semicircle, as are the national and international press, and all the great and the good of Belgium. In a speech heavy with paternalism, King Baudouin paints a glowing picture of

81. Mazrui, *Africans*, 161; emphasis added.
82. Roberts, *Glitter and Greed*, 174.

colonialism and an equally promising neo-colonial future. "The independence of the Congo is the result of the undertaking conceived by the genius of King Lèopold II," he says later adding, "Do not compromise the future with hasty reforms, and don't replace the structures that Belgium hands over to you until you are sure you can do better . . . Don't be afraid to come to us. We will remain by your side, give you advice, train with you the technical experts and administrators you will need."[83]

It takes an extremely genius psychiatrist to comprehend the mental status and personality of King Baudouin, who could admire King Leopold II, and glamorize colonialism. The most difficult thing for Africans to understand about the West is this mentality and attitude toward Africans. How can a society that has written laws for animal rights justify mass murder, slavery, oppression, and exploitation of the Congolese? Unless all Europeans think of Africans as "filthy animals" who need to be "eliminated" like the British thought of the Mau Maus, why did Belgium not apologize instead of giving a paternalistic lecture on the day of the transition speech? This question is better answered by the intellect of the Western mind than by wounded Africans whose perception of the West is filtered through their psychological, physical, economic, political, and social scars.

After the Belgian king it was "the turn of Joseph Kasa-Vubu, the Congo's first president to speak. He gave a perfectly innocuous speech, confirming exactly what the former masters expect from the new African elite."[84] For some reason, Westerners like this kind of African leader. As one breaks a horse, there are Africans who are broken by the Western power and unable to speak the truth and face the truth.

After Kasa-Vubu, the first bombshell in their eighty years of ruling was thrown on Belgians in the form of words from the mouth of Patrice Lumumba. Witte writes the dramatic event this way:

> Immediately after Kasa Vubu's few words, the president of the House of Representatives, Joseph Kasongo, invites Prime Minster Patrice Lumumba to speak. Baudouin and the Belgian Prime Minister Gaston Eyskens are flabbergasted. The programme makes no mention of a third speech and Infor Congo has not provided them with an advance copy of Lumumba's text, although it has been circulated to the assembled press. The content of the speech makes their blood run cold. The Prime Minister does not address himself to his former masters, but to the Congolese men and women, fighters for independence, who are today victorious. Suddenly, the foreign dignitaries disappear from the center of the political stage and become spectators at the celebration of a nationalist movement and its first victory. They listen in astonishment as the nationalist leader addresses the Congolese people and responds to the king, who meanwhile has turned a deathly pale. Talking directly to the people looking over the head of the assembled diplomatic corps, he explains that the granting of independence is not a generous gift offered by Brussels, as King Baudouin maintains. Independence has been proclaimed in agreement with Belgium, but: "no Congolese worthy of the name can ever forget that it is by struggle that we have won [our

---

83. Witte, *Assassination of Lumumba*, 1.
84. Ibid.

independence], a struggle waged each and every day, a passionate idealistic struggle, a struggle in which no effort, privation, suffering, or drop of our blood was spared."

Lumumba describes in the frankest of terms the colonial system that Baudouin had glorified as his great-uncle's chef-d'oeuvre and condemns it as "the humiliating slavery that was imposed on us by force." He goes on:

We have known sarcasm and insults, endured blows morning, noon and night, because we were "niggers." Who will forget that a Black was addressed in the familiar *tu*, not as a friend, but because the polite *vous* was reserved for Whites only? We have seen our land despoiled under the terms of what was supposedly the law of the land but which only recognized the right of the strongest. We have seen that this law was quite different for a White than a Black: accommodating for the former, cruel and inhuman for the latter. We have the terrible suffering of those who banished to remote regions because of their political opinions or religious beliefs; exiled in their own country, their fate was truly worse than death itself. . .And finally, who can forget the volleys of gunfire in which so many of our brothers perished, the cells where the authorities threw those who would not submit to a rule where justice meant oppression and exploitation.

Lumumba puts the role played by Brussels in the process of decolonization into perspective: "Belgium, finally understanding the march of history, has not tried to oppose our independence."

Lumumba's speech is interrupted eight times by sustained applause from the Congolese present and honoured by a veritable ovation at the end. In no time, the thousands following the festivities on the radio have spread the news of the bombshell to the four corners of the Congo. Lumumba has spoken in a language the Congolese thought impossible in the presence of a European, and those few moments of truth feel like a reward for eighty years of domination. *For the first time in the history of the country, a Congolese has addressed the nation and set the stage for reconstruction of Congolese history. By this one act, Lumumba has reinforced the Congolese people's sense of dignity and self-confidence.*[85]

"For the first time in the history of the country" an African leader addressed his nation and "reinforced the Congolese people's dignity and self-confidence." His speech was not a street insult but was intelligently crafted and full of truth that could pierce the soul of the Belgians, maybe for the first time in their eighty years of iron-fist ruling of the Congolese. Instead of encouraging, admiring, mentoring, and assisting this young emerging African leader to restore law and order, build the infrastructure of his country, restore the dignity of his people, bring democracy and economic prosperity in Congo—the West was threatened by him and decided to cut him short. Describing the reaction of the Belgians, Roberts write:

The Belgians panicked. They feared they will lose their lucrative trade in Congolese resources, so immediately took action. Belgians troops invited themselves back into Congo. The Belgians claimed this was to protect the Syndicate diamond mining companies and the majority interest in their mines held by the Belgian government. Lumumba promptly denounced this invasion as a gross violation of his country's sovereignty, but on July 11th, 1960 when he saw the danger the European diamond mine staff really were in from locals bent on vengeance for

85. Ibid., 2–3; emphasis added.

the years of colonization, he pragmatically agreed to Belgian troops staying on to protect them.

But he had a shock the very next day when his plane was prevented from landing in Katanga by troops led by Belgian officers. The day before, the Congolese province of Katanga had declared its independence—so the action of these troops prevented him from quickly intervening to negotiate an end to this secession.

Société Génèrale[86] then gave the rebels vital financial support. Katanga province was producing a quarter of the world's copper and three-quarters of the world's cobalt. The company immediately paid the royalties due to the Congo, 1.25 million Belgian Francs, to Katanga instead.

Powerful businessmen also planned for the diamond rich Kassai province to join Katanga in secession. When, in august 9th, 1960, Albert Kalonji declared South Kasai independent, it was dubbed the "Republique de la Forminière—Forminière the diamond mining subsidiary of Société Génèrale. Thus, within a month of independence, the Congo was torn apart, with its richest parts detached and under the control of Belgium.[87]

Commenting on the volatile situation of the Southern Congo and how it was a bone of contention to regional and global powers, Brabazon said: "Katanga . . . the Congo's massive southern province, fabulously rich in minerals and diamonds, and the source of the uranium that powered the atomic bombs dropped on Japan at the end of the Second World War. It had been a magnet for mercenaries since the 1960s. From the outset of the Congo's independence from the Belgium, Katanga had striven, with hired guns for an army, to become a very rich, independent nation."[88] Diop adds, "Belgian-American interests, preparing for the political instability that would prevail in the colonies following World War II, working at maximum rate and beyond, mined all the uranium of the Belgian Congo in less than ten years and stockpiled it at Oolen in Belgium. The Shinrolowbe mines in Zaire today are emptied, having supplied the major part of the uranium that went into the Nagasaki and Hiroshima bombs. Until 1952, Zaire was the world's leading uranium producer, now it ranks sixteenth in reserves and has ceased to be counted among the producers."[89]

During the Second World War, London and Washington collaborated fully on the development of the atomic bomb[90] and shared control of Congo Uranium. This collaboration continued after the War, even with a growing sentiment in the United States for an

---

86. It is a French bank.
87. Roberts, *Glitter and Greed*, 174–75.
88. Brabazon, *My Friend the Mercenary*, 16.
89. Diop, *Black Africa*, x.

90. With the detonations of the American atomic bombs in Hiroshima and Nagasaki, it was clear that this bomb was the weapon of the future. The atomic bomb was superior to everything known hitherto and became "a symbol of great power and no state could risk being left without one." In addition, it was originally believed that the bomb would result in reduction of the defense costs because it would replace manpower and other conventional military resources. In this sense, the atomic bomb transformed the nature of war and consequently the defense policies of Britain and several other countries (Konzett, "McMahon Act," 1).

American atomic monopoly. However, when the August 1946 *McMahon Act*[91] effectively removed the British from access to American atomic information, London considered the act a breach of trust. On their part, in 1947, Washington pressured London to give up its role in the Anglo-American atomic project. After protracted negotiations, Britain relinquished its share of control over Congo uranium as well as its participation in the atomic program.

Belgian interest in the atomic program produced a different problem. While the British had participated fully in the production of the bomb and had shared control of atomic materials with the United States, the Belgians had sold the uranium and had relinquished any say in the matter to the Anglo-American. After the war, internal political pressure forced the Belgian Government to demand a share in the atomic program. This came at a time when the United States wanted to restrict the involvement of other countries in atomic projects and to maintain the utmost secrecy of such information.[92]

"The Belgian government [had] received substantial aid from the U.S.A. to implement a ten-year economic program in Congo from 1950–1959; and, as the price of the aid, United States monopolies established control over some companies in Congo. The U.S.A. took second place after Belgium in Congo's foreign trade, and United States capitalist had to be granted a range of privileges."[93] Hence, it was not only Belgium who was not pleased with the emerging of Patrice Lumumba. The U.S was also disappointed and angry. As a country that benefited from the natural resources of Congo, the United States should have made a grateful gesture to show that it had been on the side of the Congolese people. This is not too much to ask from a country that champions freedom and democracy and fought for its independence from British colonialism. Instead, Eisenhower "expressed his wish that Lumumba would fall into a river full of crocodiles."[94] When the US made its opinion clear, the strong extended arm of the superpower, the UN reinforced the US decision. "While Brussels strengthened Tshombe's in Katanga unhindered, the UN kept the legal Congolese government on a tight rein. Hammarskjold rejected all bilateral aid to Leopoldville from Moscow, Ghana, or any other country, stating that any aid to the Congo had to go through the United Nations."[95]

"Richard Bissell, the CIA's Deputy Director for Plans and its head of clandestine operations, said later: 'The Agency had put a top priority, probably, on a range of different methods of getting rid of Lumumba in the sense of either destroying him physically, incapacitating him, or eliminating his political influence.' At about this time, a CIA scientist named Sidney Gottlieb was order to collect biological material with the view to assassinating an unidentified African leader. US ambassador Timberlake sprang to action."[96] Before too long, Belgium and the United States decided to eliminate Lumumba.

---

91. The McMahon Bill was essentially an act dealing with the American atomic energy program, an Act for the development and control of atomic energy.
92. See Munene, *Truman Administration*, 81–85.
93. Rodney, *How Europe Underdeveloped Africa*, 195.
94. Roberts, *Glitter and Greed*, 179.
95. Witte, *Assassination of Lumumba*, 9.
96. Ibid., 17.

The young promising African leader fell into the jaws and intrigues of a Western trap and it cost him his dear life. Roberts narrates the saga in the following manner:

> The CIA and the Belgians joined forces and tried to get the support of the President of the Congo, Joseph Kasa-Vubu, for the elected Prime Minister Lumumba, but failed. Larry Devlin reported this to Langley, the CIA headquarters, on August 24, 1960.
>
> CIA drug expert, Dr. Sidney Gottlieb, was then instructed to seek advice from the Army Chemical Corps at Fort Detrick about a poison that could kill Lumumba without being traced back to the US, preferably a poison indigenous to Africa.
>
> The Americans and Belgians now backed Devlin's choice of the 29-year old Colonel Mobutu to replace Lumumba. The CIA, in order to make sure of Mobutu's loyalty, persuaded him that Lumumba was planning to kill him and only the CIA could guarantee his survival. On September 14th, ignoring the vote by the Congolese Senate endorsing Lumumba by 41 to 2 majority, Mobutu tried to stage a coup and to close the Soviet Embassy but was unsuccessful. Lumumba was prevented from immediately punishing Mobutu for this treachery by the troops the US had arrived and equipped for Mobutu . . .
>
> In the same month, CIA poisons expert Dr. Gottlieb arrived from the US with the virus chosen to kill Lumumba without creating any suspicion of foul play . . . When Justin O'Donnell, a Senior CIA Case Officer, also arrived to join Devlin in the assassination attempt, he was shown the "virus" in the station refrigerator and latter commented, "I knew it was not for someone to get his polio shot up to date."
>
> But Devlin could find no one on Lumumba's staff willing to put the virus into Lumumba's food or toothpaste so, in frustration, it was eventually dumped into the Congo River. Devlin there requested by cable a "HIGH POWER FOREIGN MADE RIFLE WITH TELESCOPIC SCOPE AND SILENCER" be sent to him via the diplomatic bag from the US. He also located a suitable place to ambush Lumumba. O'Donnel rented "an observation post overlooking Lumumba's palace," but no opportunity presented itself that would not have betrayed the hand of the CIA . . .
>
> Other CIA agents were recruited into the Devlin assassination team. One was code-named QI/WIN "a foreign citizen with criminal background. According to Richard Moloney, his real name was Mozes Maschkivitzan and he was a Belgian. It is possible that his appointment was a joint Belgian-American initiative since Belgium was conspiring with the US to assassinate Lumumba. The Belgian named this "Operation Barracuda."
>
> Another CIA agent was WI/Rogue, "a forger and former bank robber" who planned an "execution squad." The CIA provided WI/Rogue with plastic surgery and a toupee to hide his identity. CIA's African division recommended him as a man who "can rationalize all actions." His particular job was to neutralize Lumumba's supporters in the north of the Congo.
>
> It was not long after this that Lumumba was seized and thrown into prison by plotters. He was brutally tortured. The final act came on January 17th, 1961 when the Leopoldville authorities placed, Lumumba and two of his leading supporters aboard an aeroplane bound officially for Bakwana." Other supporters of Lumumba had been killed there in horrible a circumstance . . . the place was known as the 'slaughterhouse.'" . . . The plane took him to Katanga and, after

further torture; Lumumba was killed on January 17th 1961 with complicity of Belgian officials, of the president of Katanga, Moisé Tshombe, and of the CIA. A CIA officer drove around with Lumumba's body in his trunk until a way was found to dispose of it, according to the report of the Senate Intelligence Committee and John Stockwell, a former CIA chief in Angola.[97]

In contrast to the real story of Lumumba's death, *Time* magazine, in the 2006 cover story entitled "The Deadliest War in the World," stated bluntly that Congo's "first elected Prime Minster (Lumumba) had been killed by the Belgian-and U.S backed opponents because of his growing ties to the Soviet Union."[98] "Thirty years [after the assassination of Lumumba], Devlin would confide that he did not think Lumumba was a communist but that he 'naively thought he would use the commies.'"[99] In the sinful world we live in, right is wrong and wrong is right. Even if the theory of ethics and justice is developed through the pen and mind of intellectuals and often debated within the bar of reason in the West, in Africa those who live above the rule of law are the ones who define and implement ethics and justice. Therefore, social chaos in the continent is perpetual and the psychological and physical pain of the African people is neverending.

In his reflection on blacks' struggle for liberation and the oppression of the West, Segal writes,

> The truth is that it is not neutralism or socialism that the West distrusts, as much as independence. And there is a peculiar anger displayed by the West when an African state flexes its independence. In part it is the anger of disappointment, of and affronted service. The West knows what is best for Africa that is governed for so long, bringing peace and law and order and the ceaseless productive demands of the modern world; to reject its standards, its institutions, its continuing supervision is not just stupidity, it is ingratitude. And this anger is no less real for being lodged in less than half a truth. It has indeed all the force of guilt. But the anger is anger, too, of outrage, of affronted arrogance. The west needs African dependence—provided always that it does not cost too much, and proves on balance profitable—as an enduring sign of Western, and white, superiority. The rejection of such dependence is a challenge to the assumptions of the present no less than to the pride of the past.[100]

"When Guinea refused to enter into a continued 'cooperation' agreement with France on the eve of Independence, French officials stripped off the country everything they could, ripping even hospital equipment from sockets, to punish this 'ingratitude.' Even after formal colonialism had ended, French forces overthrew governments and installed puppet regimes almost at will. French companies cornered the market of the 13 countries that are "'Africa' to the French—those that speak their language. Pharmaceutical companies bilked rich and poor alike by blocking the importation of genetic

---

97. See Roberts, *Glitter and Greed*, 174–90; Witte, *Assassination of Lumumba*.
98. Cited in Perkins, *Secret History of the American Empire*, 256.
99. Roberts, *Glitter and Greed*, 180.
100. Segal, *Race War*, 117.

drugs. And as late as 2002, Air France was earning 60 percent of its overall profit from its African routes."[101]

Here is the underlying motive of the West to keep Africa underdeveloped and always in need of financial, technological, educational, political, and military assistance from Western powers that historically and intentionally controlled and exploited the continent. This planet can be habitable by sharing natural, intellectual, and technological resources. Human beings don't have to see and treat each other like cat and mouse. Anyone who can answer Rodney King's question, "Why don't we get along?" should deserve a Nobel Peace Prize.

Since Alfonzo, the last emperor of Kongo, was dethroned by the Belgians in the 1800s, the Congolese never had a political leader of their choice. Lumumba was the first and last Congolese leader who was democratically elected. At least on a small scale, Americans who were alive and went through the assassination of President John F. Kennedy can understand what the Congolese went through when they lost a bright and promising leader, Patrice Lumumba. For Americans, Kennedy was not their first president after independence from England; but for the Congolese Lumumba was their first democratically elected leader after eighty years of colonialism. Lumumba was their hope, their source of inspiration and self-confidence. As George Washington was to the American people, so was Lumumba to the Congolese. Without stealing or rigging votes like most African dictators do, without manipulation or bribery, out of their love and respect for Lumumba, the Congolese voted for him and they were proud of him. However, in the eyes of the United States and Belgium this was a crime that deserved death. The voice of the voiceless was silenced and the seed of democracy in Congo was buried with Lumumba. In the absence of the magnanimous gesture of the United States that lifted many European and Asian countries out of the dust, the Congo descended into her hopeless economic and political state. The ray of freedom faded into the sunset of anarchy and bloodshed before the Congolese saw the dawn of liberty.

Even if they had uranium, Congolese were nowhere near to building an atomic bomb. Their need was not to be a global superpower; their need was to put food on their plates and to have a roof over their heads and have respite from the oppression and degradation that dehumanized them. In more ways than one the life of the Congolese and millions of Africans has been violently robbed. Moltmann rightly said: "A country that uses torture cannot be a 'father land.' But if a country's glory radiates from its constitution, and if its value rests on the human dignity and human rights it guarantees, that country cannot permit torture, not even in extreme situations. Even if in some individual case, everything would seem to speak to its favor, here the foundation of the constitutional democratic state is infringed. A soldier or a policeman who tortures other people in the name of his country is destroying that country, not protecting it."[102]

Etienne Tshisekedi, a Congolese politician frustrated by the intervention of the West in his country's political and economic life, particularly the U.S. in the recent past, described the African chaos best: "It is America that has decided that Paul Kagame is a great leader, and that Yoweri Museveni is a great leader, now they want us to consider

101. Calderisi, *Trouble with Africa*, 25.
102. Moltmann, *Jesus Christ for Today's World*, 63.

Kabila as a great leader. What we want to know is why it is that was bad for the countries that lived under the Soviet influence should be good for the Congolese?"[103] The list of America's endorsement and support of despots in Africa and other parts of the world is too long to mention here. John Perkins describe the US involvement in Africa this way:

> The men and women [Americans] who have been so intimately involved in shaping the last four decades of world history seem absorbed by activities in [African] continent: the United States' role in the assassination of Patrice Lumumba in the Congo, our support of dictators like Jonas Savimbi in Angola, Mobutu Sese Seko and Laurent Kabila in the Congo, Abacha and Olusegun Obasanjo in Nigeria, and Samuel Doe in Liberia, as well as recent atrocities in Rwanda, the Sudan, and Liberia. Some were distressed by the Clinton administration's 'African Renaissance,' which most agreed was a not-so-subtle ploy to support one ruthless strongman after another. They talked at length about more recent attempts to forgive debt in many countries, of the Bush administration's determination to craft this seemingly generous act into the latest and most subtle EHM[104] trick to promote the rule of the corporatocracy."[105] [106]

John Perkins is not an enemy of the United States. He is an American who loves his country and loves Africans. He has sufficient personal experience in the continent of Africa to speak with authority about the situation of Africa and the foreign policy of the United States in Africa.

After the US put Mobutu in power and he left Congo in a miserable situation, America turned against him and said:

> "The mess you are in is not our mess," Richardson said. "You do not govern your country." Given the thick ropes of complicity that had tied Mobutu's Zaire to Washington's Cold War agenda in Africa, these were self-serving half-truths at best. Already the superpower was writing history, and Richardson had crafted a bluntly effective epitaph for America's longtime erstwhile ally.
>
> "You have got about a week," Richardson told Mobutu, handing him a letter from Clinton asking him to bow out quickly, gracefully.[107]

A dictator who was put in power by Americans undemocratically and shamefully was asked to step down gracefully. Mobutu was involved in ethnic cleansing in Kivu, one of many genocides in Africa. He had used divide-and-rule to plunder Congo like his predecessor King Leopold II.

> According to 1993 report in African Business, Mobutu and his associates smuggled abroad diamonds to the value of $300 million a year. Zaire declared its 1992 official diamond production as 13 million carats—but other industry source reported the real production to be 30 million carats. The omission 17 million

---

103. French, *A Continent for the Taking*, 242.

104. Economic Hit Man (EHM).

105. They run our largest corporations and, through them, our government. They cycle through the revolving door back and forth between business and government (Perkins, *Secret History of the American Empire*, 6).

106. Ibid., 249.

107. French, *A Continent for the Taking*, 208.

carats represented in volume nearly twice the production of all South African diamond mines.

Mobutu acquired a palace in Switzerland, villas, and chateaux in France, Belgium, Italy, and Portugal. He built a "new Versailles," complete with illuminated fountains, at his birth place of Ghadolite, 700 kilometers north of Kinshasa. But when any Zairians outside the privileged elite tried to acquire a diamond for themselves, the government did all in its power to prevent them. On one occasion, Mobutu's troops, policing the diamond fields in a helicopter gunship, massacred a party of picnicking school children mistaken for unlicensed diamond prospectors.[108]

Lamb adds, "Zaire's debt to foreign banks and governments soared to $4 billion in 1980, and shortages of food and parts became critical. The government's news agency closed down for lack of paper, 360 abandoned buses stood rusting near the airport, and the national airline, Air Zaire, could afford only enough fuel to operate one of every four domestic flights each day. Its Boeing 747 and Douglas DC-10 were repossessed. Through it all, Mobutu kept insisting that Zaire and its people were doing fine; the problems Western journalist wrote about, he said were illusionary ones that merely underscored the media's bias against Africa."[109] Ayittey rightly said: "The problem of corruption cannot be solved when the head of state is a chief bandit."[110]

In 1989, the external debt amounted to $9 billion. The country's creditors, alarmed by the decimal state of the economy and the disarray in public finances, were loath to lend more. Payments on past loans were overdue. To solve his financial worries, Mobutu visited his old time friend President George H. W. Bush in Washington, D.C. Mobutu was the first African leader to be received in the White House. President Bush lauded him as "one of our most valued friends" in the entire continent of Africa and announced that Zaire had taken "the constructive step of signing an economic policy reform agreement with the International Monetary Fund." The IMF came through with $187 million, in fresh lending. The World Bank chipped in $87 million more, lifting Zaire's cumulative debt to the Bank to more than $900 million.

Fresh loans from the IMF and the World Bank did not save the financial hemorrhage and the inevitable bitter end of Mobutu's dictatorship. Mobutu's relationship with his external backers had deteriorated after his 1989 visit to Washington. Calling for an end to US assistance to the regime in March 1991, US Congressman Stephen Solarz, a member of the house subcommittee on Africa, declared that Mobutu "has established a kleptocracy to end all kleptocracies, and has set a new standard by which all future international thieves will have to be measured."[111]

This was the leader the United States picked instead of Lumumba for the nation that was colonized for eighty years by Belgium. Describing the extent of the U.S. involvement in Congo after the assassination of Lumumba, Roberts said, "The U.S was still highly involved in the Congo. Alongside Belgium, it helped to arm a military operation against

---

108. Roberts, *Glitter and Greed*, 200.
109. Lamb, *Africans*, 47.
110. Ayittey, *Africa in Chaos*, 25.
111. See Ndikumana and James, *Africa's Odious Debts*, 1–8.

the Lumumba government, which in 1964 still controlled 40 percent of the Congo. The operation involved some 300 Belgian officers and many mercenaries. Its victory was very savage—some 200,000 lives were lost. After this further US funds were needed to support Adoula."[112]

> Fighting between non-Portuguese Angolans and the colonial government in Lisbon broke out in April 1966 and raged for nine years before independence was granted in 1975. Peace was short lived as civil war broke out between the Movement for the Liberation of Angola (MPLA) and the National Union for the Total Independence of Angola (UNITA). The former was heavily supported by the Russian and Cuban governments. In the late 1970s, approximately 37,000 Cuban 'technical assistants' were sent to assist the MPLA. UNITA was supported by the United States, South Africa, and, for a period of time, China. To complicate matters, UNITA obtained money to buy arms through both illicit aid from the United States and by transporting diamonds, while MPLA bought its arms through the revenue from its Cabinda oilfields, operated primarily by U.S. multinationals. To an extent, the United States, either directly or indirectly, provided both sides with the financial capability to wage the civil war, resulting in thousands of casualties.[113]

On the issue of Angola, even if the U.S. and China are on the opposite end of the political spectrum, their involvement makes them look like identical twins. Eisenman explains: "In Angola . . . at separate times—and sometimes at the same time—the CPC (Communist Party of China) supported the ruling Popular Movement for the Liberation of Angola, as well as its rivals, the National Liberation Front of Angola and the National Union for the Total Independence of Angola (UNITA). Beijing and UNITA leader Jonas Savimbi capitalized on the latter's ties to South Africa, even using that racist regime as a transit point for weapons supplies to UNITA fighters."[114] It was not only China; the United States also supported UNITA and had a charming relationship with Savimbi. "With all the praise heaped on him by the President Regan and other Western admirers, Savimbi was ruthless dictator with a messianic sense of destiny, insistence on total control and intolerant of dissent and criticism from anyone in his movement. He systematically purged Unita of rivals and critics, ordering death sentences not only for party dissidents but for members of their families as well . . . '[His] sexual practices went beyond most usual concepts of lust. He chose wives for his senior officers and slept with them in a bizarre rite of passage before they were married.' He had even seduced his own teenage niece, Raquel Matos, and made her one of his concubines. 'Raquel's parents protested and were executed,' said Bridgland."[115] Like in many parts of Africa, the Angola war was a war by proxy between global powers to control natural resources.[116] Time and

112. Roberts, *Glitter and Greed*, 187; emphasis added.
113. Lee and Shalmon, "China's Oil Strategies in Africa," 117–18.
114. Eisenman, "China's Political Outreach," 231.
115. Meredith, *Fate of Africa*, 604–5.
116. The oil and gas sectors account for 40 percent of Angola's GDP and have attracted many of the World's largest multinational corporations. Exxon, Mobil, BP, Eni, Agip, Total, and Chevron all have major investments in Angola, and all have historical relationships with the government of Jose Edwardo dos Santos, president since 1979. Angola's role in the world's oil market is significant because there

again, Africans are used like chess pawns. As one looks at the trend in various African countries, it looks like the morally corrupt and psychologically inept Africans like Savimbi suit the partnership model of Western powers. This kind of Western value gives a wrong understanding of good administration and leadership. Preferring immoral and inept African leaders by the West adds confusion to a clear understanding of the public leader. I wonder when this vicious, costly, and bloody cycle will end.

U.S. Congresswoman Cynthia McKinney (D-Georgia) exposed many aspects of the "Anglophone conspiracy" during a hearing she chaired on April 16, 2001. Her opening statement included the following indictment:

> Much of what you hear today has not been widely reported in the public media. Powerful forces have fought to suppress these stories from entering the public domain.
>
> The investigation into the activities of Western governments and Western businessmen in post-colonial Africa provide clear evidence of the West's longstanding propensity for cruelty, avarice, and treachery. The misconduct of Western nations in Africa is not due to momentary lapses, individual defects, or errors of common human frailty. Instead, they form part of long-term policy designed to access and plunder Africa's wealth at expense of its people . . . at the heart of African's suffering is the West's, and most notably the United States,' desire to access Africa's diamonds, oil, natural gas, and other precious resources . . . the West, and most notably the United States, has set in motion a policy of oppression, destabilization and tempered, not by moral principle, but by a ruthless desire to enrich itself on Africa's fabulous wealth . . . Western countries have incited rebellion against stable African governments . . . have even actively participated in the assassination of duly elected and legitimate African Heads of State and replaced them with corrupted and malleable officials.[117]

When the political honeymoon with Mobutu was over, America said, "This is not the mess we created." After so many lives were lost and economic and social damage done, the Clinton administration said, "We have no part in the mess Mobutu created." Not learning from their mistakes or because of being not willing to learn, the U.S. picked another dictator for Congo—Laurent Kabila.

---

are few countries in which oil reserve estimates are increasing rapidly and that produce light oil. Most companies understand the value of forging a relationship with the Angolan government and gaining access to its growing supply of crude oil. The competition is tense.

China's task was daunting. It had to create a relationship with a government that it had actively opposed, at least through the end of the Cold War. Between 1990 and 2004, China's involvement in Angola consisted of little more than isolated technical assistance projects, primarily focused on agriculture. Yet, two years later, Angola supplied 47 percent of the oil that China bought from African countries or about 15 percent of China's total imports. In addition, Angola has become China's second largest African trading partner. How did this situation turn around so rapidly? (Lee and Shalmon, "China's Oil Strategies in Africa," 118–19).

Note: According to the IMF, over $8.5 billion in public money was unaccounted for between 1997 and 2001. Angola ranks near the bottom of Transparency International's Corruption Index (ibid., 119).

117. Cited in Perkins, *Secret History of the American Empire*, 258.

When the Secretary of State, Madeleine Albright, visited Congo during Kabila's reign, one tough African journalist, Mwamba Wambumulamba, an editor from the Kinshasa newspaper *Le Potentiel*, asked her, "Ms. Albright, your government regrets having created and supported President Mobutu. During your visit to Kampala, you showered praise on the Ugandan president Yoweri Museveni. Some media reports even said that you presented him as the strongman in the subregion. Since Uganda is not an example of democracy and respect for human rights, is it possible that you are in the process of creating another Mobutu just to regret it later?"[118] Some Western journalists who love democracy, and would like to see an independent and free Africa smiled and were proud of their profession when this African journalist confronted Albright. As the U.S. planned, Kabila came to power with their endorsement and blessings, and before too long Kabila verified that he was "another Mobutu." It is only time, not logic or reason, which proves the Western powers wrong. From the eighteenth century to this day the Congolese people never had a democratically elected leader of their choice.

Don't rush to conclude that Americans' involvement in Congo is only through mercenaries for mere exploitation. In contrast to this chapter of history, there were American missionaries who sacrificially served the Congolese, loved them, and died for them. My own denomination, the Evangelical Free Church of America, has over seventy years of service in Congo. Because of their dedicated service, today, according to information I got from Rev. Selenga, there are 176,990 Christians, 996 local churches, and 866 pastors in the Evangelical Free church in Congo. Their great challenge is discipleship, that is, lack of theological education. This is the result of only one Western mission. Christianity cannot be comprehended out of context. The paradox of Western involvement in Africa is difficult to reconcile. While the white mercenaries killed millions of Africans, the white missionaries were God's instruments for the salvation of millions of Africans.

"Africa's dictators had been supported for decades by East and West, and were often handpicked by outside powers. Their misrule had placed the continent in the deep hole it now found itself."[119] Not having the right to vote, being extremely and negatively conditioned, and not being able to build one's country and nation dehumanizes people. These are major factors that make Africans turn against each other. And their wars are brutal and coldhearted and many atrocities are done by blacks to blacks. The condition of the continent demands us to ask:

> *But what is life?* Nietzsche, Whitehead and Albert Schweitzer believed that "life is robbery," because Darwin had impressed on them that the animal sphere is a "struggle for existence" which is about "the survival of the fittest." So life is a struggle, and the struggle for life heightens life—though of course only the life of the stronger one. Every life wants to live, in the midst of other life which wants to live too. That was not just an objective observation. It also offered the biological justification for the domination of the white man, who thinks he is the crown of creation. Life is robbery: that may reflect the experience of the combative male. Yet life is in origin a gift, as every mother and every child knows. Life is born in pain. It is only for the male "will to power" that life and death are one. But

---

118. French, *Continent for the Taking*, 246.
119. Ibid., 158.

love distinguishes clearly between life and death, and gives what further life the preference, over against what leads to death. But every time life is robbed, life is the presupposition. One can only kill what is alive. So birth is superior to any death.[120]

Contrary to this logic, when it comes to the life of Africans, in the eyes of the West and African dictators, death seems superior to birth.

Cyril Orji righty concluded: "The political, economic, social, and religious problems that have beleaguered Black Africa are not isolated issues. Their roots are in the checkered history of the slave trade, colonialism, and neocolonialism."[121] "Africa is the most thoroughly abused and the least understood region on the planet today . . . beyond any doubt that responsibility for the current endemic poverty lies at the feet of the post–World War II empire builders."[122] French concurs: "Leopold fondly describes his newly acquired territory, which he run brutally as his personal domain, as a '*magnificent African cake*,' and for Leopold and subsequently for Belgium and others, the Congo, as it was known then, became synonymous with a succession of cruel and shameless get-rich-quick schemes. For ivory, tropical hardwoods, rubber, and finally copper, cobalt and uranium, the country saw one European rush after another."[123] Belgium, many other Western countries and, as of recently, China are all still enjoying the "African cake." The question my African students were asking me was for how long? How long will the Congolese and many other African countries that are rich with mineral resources suffer in the midst of enormous wealth? What should the voice of Evangelicals be? What kind of Christology can enrich African Christianity and enable them to see life beyond suffering and death?

Since they suffer because of it, Africans hate their natural resources. Greg Campbell, in his well-written book *Blood Diamond*, quoting Sorious Samura, said: "Much of our wealth has come from things most people have little knowledge of. They should have been a blessing; instead they are a curse. They have torn Sierra Leone apart in a bloody civil war, because who control them controls the country. They are diamonds."[124] The diamond, which is glamorized in the West and used by young men as a symbol of expression of their ultimate love for the one they decide to marry, has caused millions of people misery and death in Africa. "In 1999, an estimated $75 million worth of gemstones had flowed from the RUF to the world market, a vast amount of capital for a bush army, moving completely undetected, untaxed, and unrecorded. In return, an army's worth of munitions, fuel, food, and medicine flowed back."[125] Campbell adds, "The diamond industry, [its] buying and selling policies had resulted in the death of some 3.7 million people in various Africans war zones and displaced 6 million."[126]

120. Yates, ed., *Mission*, 31; emphasis original.
121. Orji, "Religion, Violence, and Conflict," 90.
122. Perkins, *Secret History of the American Empire*, 251.
123. French, *Continent for the Taking*, 52; emphasis added.
124. Campbell, *Blood Diamond*, 79.
125. Ibid., 184.
126. Ibid., 200.

In these war-torn, mineral-rich African countries, Campbell adds, "who could once have been called a civilian had long since been recategorized. Now they were called refugees, war victims, prisoners of war, and child combatants. Kailahun was a depressing human collage of teenage soldiers nearly blind from lifelong bouts with malaria smirking dementedly at graffiti-spoiled walls; naked toddlers abandoned to the whims of luck, fear, grief, and hunger; and the vacant stares of drooling amputees who were no more than a few hours from death's welcome embrace."[127]

Christ in the Context of suffering

Suffering unjustly is the reality of life in Africa. What should the message of the gospel in the African context be? What is the biblical and moral obligation of the universal church? "If a being is revealed only in its opposite," said Moltmann,

> then the church which is the church of the crucified Christ cannot consist of an assembly like persons who mutually affirm each other, but must be constituted of unlike persons. "Like seeks after like," as Aristotle says in his discussion of friendship (*Ethics*, Book VIII). But for the crucified Christ, the principle of fellowship is fellowship with those who are different, and solidarity with those who have become alien and have been made different. Its power is not friendship, the love for what is similar and beautiful (*philia*), but creative love for what is different, alien and ugly (*agape*). Its principle of justification is not similarity, but the justification of the other (Hegel), the creative making of the righteous unrighteous and the attribution of rights to those who are without rights. Consequently, the church of the crucified Christ cannot be assimilated to what is different and alien to it. Nor can it shut itself away from what is alien in the social ghetto, but for the sake of its identity in the crucified Christ, must reveal him and itself, by following him, in what is different and alien. Otherwise, it does justice neither to the one to whom it appeals nor to those to whom he revealed himself. Only in the practical form of fellowship with others can bear witness to the crucified Christ and live out in life the justification of the godless in which it believes, and from which it derives its own life.[128]

The Christ of Christendom is different than the Christ of the gospel—he is a conqueror, uninvited guest, one who has no regard for Africans and their culture. His messengers, at their best are paternalistic—closer to the powers in their homelands and colony than to the alienated and rejected Africans. "The image of Christ . . . as the ideal and most relevant to the suffering Africans can be summarized as follows: [Africans] want Christ who is the liberator in all dimensions of life, Christ who is the healer par excellence of all their diseases and anxieties. They desire uncompromised Christ of the Bible who set His people free in the here and now. They want 'a sick Christ' amid the sick, 'a fighting Christ' with the fighting, and 'a deprived Christ' among those living in deplorable situations. In sum, the Christ identified is the tangible, functional, African

---

127. See ibid., 168.
128. Moltmann, *Crucified God*, 28.

and dynamic Christ with whom they can fully and at all times feel at home."[129] Moltmann adds: "We need an answer to our questions which we can live and die with. That means that every Christology is related to Christopraxis: what we know and what we do belong together. And practice is the touchstone against which a Christology's authenticity has to be tested. We believe in Christ with all our senses and with the lives we live, just as believing in God can only mean believing with all our hearts and all our senses."[130] Western theology and Christology are hardly concerned with the spiritual, psychological, social, emotional, and physical hunger of Africans. "Today the church and theology must turn to the crucified Christ in order to show the world the freedom he offers. This is essential if they wish to become what they assert they are: the church of Christ and Christian theology."[131]

Mark A. Noll, in his book *The New Shape of Christianity: How American Experience Reflects Global Faith,* gives excellent insight about the influence of Western Christianity in the past and the prospect of global Christianity in the future. With the lenses of a good historian, Noll explains the role American Christianity has played in the changes that are being seen in global Christianity today. Terms like "American experience," "American Christianity," "American Mission," "American power," etc., undoubtedly express the American role in the expansion of Christianity. As they attempted to spread the gospel, Americans, by and large, did not decontextualize either their theology or their understanding of missions. Hence, Noll rightly chooses for the subtitle of his book, "How American Experience Reflects Global Faith." Both American orthodoxy and orthopraxis were taught and reinforced as golden standards in various parts of the world.

Church buildings, musical instruments, ministers' attire, choir robes, hymns, names of converts, schools, and curricula had American religious, cultural, and economic trademarks. The Christianity that addressed issues of life in the American cultural context was transplanted in different parts of the world. Unlike the transition of the Hebraic-Christianity from the Jewish culture to the Gentile world in the first century, which developed its own unique theological, cultural, and leadership identity in a short period of time. The phenomenal growth of Christianity in the majority world has been largely influenced by the dominance of American Christianity. As a result, Christian faith in many parts of the world is not well anchored in local theology. And, to most of the churches in the majority world, up until recently, missions has been viewed as a Whiteman's burden. The centralized American Christianity has been in control of the thoughts and activities of Christians in the majority world. But now, the current decentralized global Christian movement is shaking up the foundations and assumptions of American Christianity itself.

"The New Shape of World Christianity" describes the changes that have evolved in the postcolonial and neocolonial era. The political freedom of African independence led to all kinds of emancipation from Western cultural captivity—one of which is the absence of missionaries dominating leadership in the indigenous churches. As nationals took more roles in teaching, pastoring, evangelizing, and leading, the power of the

---

129. Waliggo, "African Christology," 106–7.
130. Moltmann, *Crucified God,* 2.
131. Ibid., 1.

gospel began to change lives. In addition, Christian converts transformed culture like yeast in dough. The passive, nonviolent change by the majority-world Christians has had significant implications for our present and future situation. "The magnitude of recent change means that all believers, including those in the former Christian heartlands of Europe and North America, are faced with the prospect of reorientation. But the scale and pace of recent developments means that more than just history need to be reoriented; the awareness of where North American and European believers now fit with that history requires reassessment as well."[132] For all Christians, Noll's book can be an excellent tool for "reorientation" of the past, present, and future of global Christianity. It is my hope that this book will make good contribution towards that goal. Depending on the attitude, outlook, and personality of individual believers reading this book or Noll's work could give them a rude awakening, shock, frustration, or hope.

As the individualism, cultural dominance, interwoven beliefs and practices, and capitalistic attitude of American evangelicalism gives way to the cultural appropriations of Christianity by Asian, Latino, and African believers, global Christianity will be marked by a theology brewed in a pot of suffering, rejection, poverty, forgiveness, reconciliation, and love. Theology that has been developed rationally to address the issues of cognitive needs raised within the American cultural context will be broadened to encompass the effective, volitional, and evaluative aspect of people in their own culture. With full liberty, academic integrity, and accountability, Scripture will be read, interpreted, and applied as it is seen and understood through the eyes and experiences of people from the majority world. Obviously then, the Christ of America will have a different look than the Christ of Africa, Asia, and Latin America.

After centuries, missions will again be from the poor to the rich, the powerless to the powerful, from unidirectional to multidirectional. As it often does, Christianity will demonstrate its adaptability in cultures where it finds a home. Neither Americans nor the rest of the world will be able to claim a monopoly on the Christian faith or consider itself the custodian of the gospel. "The impression that Christianity in its essence is either European or American is, however, simply false. Christianity began as Jewish; before it was European, it was North African, Syrian, Egyptian and Indian. While in recent history it has indeed been American, it has also been Chilean, Albanian, Fijian and Chinese. The gospel belongs to every one in every culture; it belongs to no one in any one culture in particular."[133]

For ethnocentric Christians, who tend to believe their Christian lifestyle or expression of faith and theology is a norm, they will find the change a nemesis rather than enjoying it as the sovereign act of God who redeems people from different cultures, languages, and nationalities. Both to Americans and majority-world Christians, Noll's book challenges us to see our faith as a result of a revelation comprehended because of the sheer grace and mercy of God. No human being has become a follower of Christ because of their culture or IQ. "All have sinned . . ." and all need grace to be saved. Emphasizing this fundamental biblical truth, Noll urges Christians toward a worthwhile global partnership. Quoting Lamin Sanneh, Noll reminds us to make a wise choice, saying: "The

132. Noll, *New Shape of World Christianity*, 23.
133. Ibid., 191.

fact that disadvantaged peoples and their cultures are buoyed by new waves of conversion has created alignments of global scope at the margins of power and privilege. The paradigm nature of realignment compels a fundamental stocktaking of Christianity's frontier awakening, and an imperative of partnership with it. When opportunity knocks the wise will build bridges while the timorous build dams. It is a new day."[134] Time will tell which theological institutions, mission agencies, churches, or denominations will build bridges and which dams.

By providing numerous theological, missiological, and historical insights, Noll's book invites us to usher in a "new day." Whether we choose to be a "bridge" or "dam," Christianity will continue being a stranger and a permanent dweller in every culture it enters. It is a translatable revelation, not a closed dogma. Christianity was born under the Roman Empire among the Jewish society. Initially it was propagated in Aramaic then Greek, by Christ and the apostles whose mother tongue was Hebrew. The Great Commission encompasses the world, not just Jerusalem and Judea. Christianity cannot be chained down by cultural, linguistic, and geographical boundaries. It is a universal religion. It transcends every barrier it encounters. In his book, by affirming the inclusiveness and universality of our faith, Noll echoes the voice of the prophets and the apostles. Therefore, the "new day" is not really a new day. It is the fulfillment of God's promise leading to the culmination of redemptive history.

Ultimately the salvation of Africans comes from the "wounded healer, a striking modern parable which touches what the Gospel is all about."[135] "The Jesus who began by proclaiming the eschatological Reign of God ended by obediently accepting his role as the victim whose death and vindication would bring salvation . . . the violent death he now foresaw clearly he would have accepted not merely as the unavoidable consequence of his prophetic mission, but as the ultimate embodiment of his loving service, as the culmination and climax of his pro-existence: He would be, to the end, the 'man for others.'"[136] In his own time, Christ will bring holistic healing to Africans.

Unless Africa is fundamentally transformed and the policies of the West with regard to trade and diplomatic relationships with Africa are changed to a win-win siutation, the secular and Christian aids will remain like the bandaid of the Red-Cross in a war zone. The West has been concurrently inflicting wounds on Africans while writing prescriptions for the various psychological, physical, economic, etc., wounds and injuries. Yet, for centuries, the continent remains in the sickbed of civilization.

I'll further elaborate why Congo is still a bone of contention not only to the outside powers but also for African countries that are sharing the plunder. "The actors change, but the script seems to be unchanged. The recent fighting in eastern Congo, which has left 3.8 million dead and many more homeless, only indicates its escalation and democratization. Where once there was a state-sponsored violence and plunder, there is now any array of private militias, some with the backing of neighboring countries

---

134. Ibid., 197.

135. Yates, ed., *Mission*, 61.

136. Dupuis, *Who Do You Say I Am?*, 51, 52.

like Uganda and Rwanda, each fighting for control of a portion of mineral and natural resources of Congo."[137]

Fundamental Questions for Existence and Understanding Personhood

Africans deal with fear as a disease and with Europeans as a haunting ghost. I still remember my conversation with a middle-aged Kenyan professional about fifteen years ago. Sharing his experience with the British in colonial Kenya, he said, "British were brutal. To this day when I see a Brit, my whole emotion and body repulse them." Living in this kind of psychological and mental status, it is extremely difficult to engage with imaginative and innovative thoughts. Campbell concurs: "Those who live through so much death and suffering during the war and who still struggle to survive from day to day tend to think only in terms of their immediate needs. Planning for the future does not often enter the equation."[138] Thurman rightly said,

> In this world the socially disadvantaged man is constantly given a negative answer to the most important personal questions upon which mental health depends: "Who am I? What am I"?
>
> The first question has to do with a basic self-estimate, a profound sense of belonging, of a counting. If a man feels that he does not belong in the way in which it is perfectly normal for other people to belong, then he develops a deep sense of insecurity. When this happens to a person, it provides the basic material for what the psychologist calls an inferiority complex. It is quite possible for a man to have no sense of personal inferiority as such, but at the same time to be dogged by a sense of social inferiority. The awareness of being a child of God tends to stabilize the ego and results in a new courage, fearlessness, and power. I have seen it happen again and again . . .
>
> This established for them the ground of personal dignity, so that a profound sense of personal worth could absorb the fear reaction. This alone is not enough but without it, noting else is of value. The first task is to get the self-immunized from the most radical of the *threat* of violence . . . There are some things that are worth than death. To deny one's own integrity of personality in the presence of the human challenge is one of those things . . .
>
> "What am I?" This question has to do, not with the sense of innate belonging, but rather with personal achievement and ability. All of the inner conflict and frustrations growing out of limitations of opportunity become dramatically focused here.[139]

In response to the questions "Who am I and what am I?" African intellectuals who led the struggle for freedom have come up with two solutions: "Black consciousness calls for black realization of the humanity of black folk. It is a transcendence of racial self-hatred. It is also the realization that freedom is a standard much higher than equality,

---

137. Katongole, *Sacrifice of Africa*, 15. For detailed reading, see Stearns, *Dancing in the Glory of Monsters*.

138. Campbell, *Blood Diamonds*, 263.

139. Thurman, *Jesus and the Disinherited*, 39–43.

although equality is more than just than inequality . . . Black liberation, the project that emerges as a consequence of Black Consciousness, calls for changing both the material conditions of poverty and the concepts by which such poverty is structured."[140] To Biko, there was a fundamental disorder in a society where blacks outnumbered whites four to one, yet were subjected by the white minority South African government to the most extreme forms of social, political, and economic suppression with no hope of blacks escaping unjust regulations. The legal system, for instance, made it illegal for blacks to live in certain parts of South Africa, or to live together as husband and wife without special permission—social engineering backed up by the awesome military and police strength.

For generations, South African government suppression and subversion of basic human rights had blacks believing that their condition was hopeless. But it was clear to Biko that, while the government was very nearly overwhelming in concrete physical terms, the more damaging oppression was occurring psychologically. Biko was fully persuaded that the entire issue of black suppression, and in turn the future of black survival, hinged on the psychological battle for the minds of black people.

The task confronting Biko was formidable—to reverse years of negative self-image and replace it with a positive and dynamic identity that would permit blacks to move on to the next stage of their liberation. What was needed was an attitude of mind, a way of life that would liberate black aspiration and black people. The concept of Black Consciousness held that it was necessary to first effectuate mental emancipation as a precondition to political emancipation.

Biko's nonviolent, nonpolitical politics was to restore the self-image and dignity of the blacks. His struggle for freedom, at a very young age, like Lumumba, led him to jail and then to the grave. Biko's funeral was attended by 15,000 mourners, in spite of police action that kept thousands more away. Thirteen Western states sent senior diplomatic representatives to the funeral to pay respect.

Following his death, many, both in the press and in governmental circles, referred to Steve Biko as a "moderate." He was an extremely sensitive, compassionate man filled with a sense of humanity. His ethical and moral commitment to decency and dignity was total, a commitment that cost him his life.[141] "The main problem for us here is not our own world—what Bonhoeffer termed 'the world that has come of age.' Our main problem is the world that we have made incapable of coming of age. If liberty is the central theme of modern European theology and philosophy, then for people in the Third World this means 'liberation' from oppression and apathy. Without their liberation, there cannot be any true liberty in the First world either. For true liberty is not a peculiar privilege. It is universal and indivisible."[142]

Some African scholars argue that Pan-Africanism and Black consciousness are an outcome of Western imperialism. Mazrui explains his view this way:

> 1. It was primarily Europe which decided the boundaries of Africa as we know them today. Western Europeans did not invent the name 'Africa' but Europeans

---

140. Biko, *I Write What I Like*, xi.
141. For further reading, see Biko, *Steve Biko: Black Consciousness in South Africa*.
142. Moltmann, *Way of Jesus*, 65.

played a decisive role in applying it to the continental land mass that we recognise today.

2. The second process through which Europe Africanised Africa was the process of racism in history. This was particularly marked in the treatment of the Black population of the continent. The humiliation and degradation of the Black Africans across the centuries contributed to their mutual recognition of each other as 'fellow Africans.'

3. The third inter-related process through which Europe Africanised Africa was imperialism and colonialism. This generated a sufficient sense of shared identity for the movement of Pan-Africanism to be born.

4. A fourth process of Europe's Africanisation of Africa was truly dialectical. This was the fragmentation of Africa in terms of artificial state boundaries, in terms of reinforced ethnic nationalisms and in terms of new élite formation. By a curious identity, these criss-crossing boundaries of sectional identity have sometimes increased the value of a regional or continental African identity.[143]

This imposed new identity of Africans ironically has been dis-Africanized through forced diaspora and denied freedom and opportunity to develop on its own soil through enculturation of Western values, norms, and customs. Black consciousness comes by learning the history of Africa by Africans—and by studying science, politics, economy, etc., with a relevant curriculum that is free from Western bias and a sense of superiority. Also, education has to be done in total freedom, without the threat of being in jail or killed. However, both the Western powers and African dictators have not allowed this to happen in Africa's learning centers. Even seminaries are not free from this blame. Adopting a transplanted Western curriculum, the motto of African International University (AIU), where I taught, was "School in the heart of Africa with Africa in its heart," but none of the issues I address in this book were taught or freely discussed in that setting. It was taboo to talk about Steve Biko, Dedan Kimathi, the Mau Maus, the British Pipelines, Patrice Lumumba, about the past apartheid in South Africa, Nelson Mandela, and many others. When African students were sharing with me about Western intervention in their respective countries, it was almost as if they were whispering to me. Even though they came from mineral rich countries, they were almost totally relying on Western scholarships for their education and sustenance. In the process of being recipients, they ended up with a paralyzed will and self-esteem.

Decades after the so-called independence, the full emancipation of Africans' mind is still in the making. "The Europeans not only colonized history, they colonized information about history."[144] In every aspect of the academic field, if our commitment is strong, and our motive pure and genuine, to bring a transformational change in Africa, like Biko, "we must restore the historical consciousness of the African people and *reconquer a Promethean consciousness*."[145] Then and only then, "to his surprise and satisfaction, [an African] will discover that most of the ideas used today to domesticate, atrophy, dissolve, or steal his "soul," were conceived by his own ancestors. *To become conscious of that fact*

---

143. Mazrui, *Africans*, 101. I have made this quotation a numbered list.
144. Clarke, *Christopher Columbus and the African Holocaust*, 35.
145. Diop, *African Origin of Civilization*, xv; emphasis mine.

is perhaps the first step toward a genuine retrieval of himself; without it, intellectual sterility is the general rule, or else the creations bear I know not what imprint of subhuman."[146]

Western domination and Africa's economic dependency has paralyzed the aspirations of generations of Africans. Especially those who have come from countries affected by wars are living under the burden of various responsibilities. You see it on their faces deprived of a smile, and emotion that hardly expresses joy. Still millions of Africans struggle with the questions "Who am I and what am I?" Self-knowledge is a foundation upon which to build restoration and reformation of all kinds. Without questions, Africans need it more than all the material wants they may have.

The main area of struggle and soul searching question for African Christians is the latter question "What am I?" Christianity without means for intellectual and economic growth, without political stability, and cultural and social development has made African Christians like birds without wings. Lack of aspiration, creativity, lack of power to change their own lives and the society they live in emanates out of their hopeless circumstances and enforced limitations. Yes, African Christians are the children of God, and they are grateful to the Lord for it, but they live in suffering. Jesus has said, "Blessed are the meek, for they will inherit the earth" (Matt 5:6). Many African Christians wonder if Jesus meant they would inherit their graves. Jenkins comments on the unpleasant and critical social situation of African Christians this way:

> People want prosperity—or at least economic survival—but just as critical is the promise of health, and the desperate public health situation in the new cities go forward towards explaining the emphasis of the new churches on healing of mind and body. Apart from the general range of maladies that North Americans and Europeans, the Third World poor also suffer from the diseases associated with poverty, hunger, and pollution, in what has been termed a "Pathogenic society." Child mortality is appallingly high by Northern standards. The attacks of these "demons of poverty" are all the graver when people are living in tropical climates, with all the problems arising from the diseases and parasites found in those regions. As well as physical ailments, psychiatric and substance abuse problems drive desperate people to seek refuge in God. Talking all these threat together—disease, exploitation, drink, drugs, and violence—it is easy to see why people might easily accept the claim they are under siege from demonic forces, and that only divine intervention can save them.[147]

For Africans to blame their misery on "demons of poverty" and to seek solutions only "through divine intervention" is a wrong way of interpreting the gospel. When people grow and live fearfully in colonial and dictatorial governments that don't allow free thinking, it is safe and easy for Africans to put the blame for their wretchedness on the devil. However, when Jesus ushered in the kingdom of God on this earth and taught about it, he differentiated the demons from the Roman powers, the tax collectors, and the Pharisees.

---

146. Ibid.; emphasis mine.

147. Jenkins, *Next Christendom*, 77–78.

The emergence of charismatic religious leaders and exploitation of the desperate economic and psychological situations of the black race is not uncommon in African history. Williams asserts:

> The numerous movements, led by charismatic leaders with catchy slogans to shout, are roads many will take. The bigger crowd-drawing route will always be baited with some kind of "religion," led by some prophet or mystic. For religion, any kind of religion has been the means by which *hope was maintained by a people without any basis of hope*. And the search for real leaders has always been so desperate that the people flock to this or that promoter's movement, hoping that a true leader has been found at last.
>
> The personal wealth amassed by these leaders in a matter of pride for many of their followers—to the poor and ignorant who are being fleeced, even the palatial mansion with colorfully uniformed servants reflect the power and glory of their leader. Criticism is silenced. For the leaders are shrewd "natural" psychologists. They know exactly what appeals to the deprived masses, what will give them a feeling of being "somebody" and uplifted. Thousands continue to be exploited by the smarter ones who know all the tricks that stir the emotion and empty pocket.[148]

Twenty-seven years later, *The Economist* tells us that, in Africa, prophets and profits are still alive and well. Describing the affluence of Nigerian pastors and misappropriation of church funds, *The Economist* writes,

> Little wonder that many of Nigeria's super-pastors have been catapulted into the ranks of the super-rich. Followers make tithes and other offerings in hope of winning blessings from on high. Most churches do not have proper governing boards, so there is little financial accountability. Beyond donations, such "pastor-preneurs" also rake in cash by publishing and distributing devotionals, running hotels, renting private jets and investing in real estate. *Forbes* reckoned in 2011 that Mr. Joshua was Nigeria's third-richest pastor in a list headed by David Oyedepo (estimated to be worth $150m). Ayo Oritsejafor, who leads the Christian Association of Nigeria and is a close ally of President Goodluck Johnathan, was embroiled in a recent scandal when a private jet he had leased out was found to be carrying $9.3m in cash into South Africa, supposedly a payment for an arms deal on behalf of the Nigerian government.[149]

The African church is at the crossroads of establishing authentic and transformational Christianity or embracing the message of the false prophets of the faith. The African Christians are in desperate need of relevant African theology and Christology that will emancipate them to think freely and help them to answer the fundamental questions for existence: "Who am I and what am I?" "The separated Black churches," to express their psychological and social resistance to the domination of the whites, "preach an ideology of resignation, but their very separateness they generate consciousness of an alternative to absolute submission to the colonizer. Thus we see Ethiopianism and the Watchtower spread from the mining concentrations of southern Africa, and

---

148. C. Williams, *Destruction of Civilization*, 327–28.
149. *Economist*, Oct. 4, 2014, p. 58.

the independent churches being forbidden in the Rhodesian compounds."[150] To define their isolation Africans need to have a clear biblical understanding of who they are. "Who am I? What does it mean to 'be'? The answer is this: I am a child of God related to my heavenly Father. I must belong to him. Resting in that knowledge, I know what it is to be his. I should pursue doing God's will, then, and by his grace he will enable my will."[151] Whether black or white the essential unity of God's people is a precondition for a proper knowledge of God and his relationship and involvement with all people. This unity should transcend social class, culture, and race. In his paper for the Laverna Consultation of the Ecumenical Association of African Theologians on 15–17 September 1982 David Bosch wrote, "If the church is rooted in a defective ecclesiology and then finds itself in a specific context (like racist South Africa), it can easily become separatist or schismatic, denying the essential unity at the heart of the church's existence. This leads to Christian aberrations, indeed to heresy, because *a church which so willfully cuts itself off from community with other Christians is defective in its understanding of the Christian faith.*"[152] The African Independent churches should heed the words of Bosch. Regeneration in Christ sets a spiritual bond among believers that no issue under the sun can offer an excuse to isolate a local church from the universal body of Christ.

Salivation of the soul without authentic African identity is problematic. Western education and Western Christianity has made Africans like the shepherd David in Goliath's kingly attire. Bediako strongly suggests that if African Christians need to have the right self-definition we should wear our own theological robes:

> As it emerged in the post-missionary context of African Christianity in the 1950 and 1960s, the question of identity entailed not only confronting constantly the problem of how "old" and "new" in African religious consciousness could become integrated in a unified vision of what it meant to be a Christian and African. The issue also forced the theologian to become in himself or herself the point of intersection of his struggle for integration through an inner dialogue which became infinitely personal and intense, if it was to be authentic. African theology, therefore, by "becoming something of a dialogue between the African Christian scholar and the perennial religion and spiritualties of Africa" was thereby a struggle for an appropriate Christian discourse which would account for and hold together the total religious experiences of Africans in a coherent and meaningful pattern. *Identity itself thus became a theological category, so that development of theological concern and the formulation of theological questions were linked as inevitable by-product of a process of Christian self-definition.*"[153]

Despite the incredible growth of Christianity in Africa, in theological and missiological scholarly development, we are not yet where Bediako urges us to be. There is a reason. "In spite of that stunning change, surviving mental habits still locate Christianity's intellectual and political center of gravity in Europe and North America. The physical map of Christianity looks very different from the mental map of the religion, and since most people take their cue from their

---

150. Vidrovitch, *Africa*, 232.
151. Zacharias, *Grand Weaver*, 126.
152. Kritzinger and Saayman, *David J. Bosch*, 120; emphasis original.
153. Bediako, *Christianity in Africa*, 256; emphasis mine.

mental picture of the world, it is not surprising that Christianity's intercultural history is still so little understood."[154]

A theology brewed in an African pot will make a world of difference both for the church and society in Africa, as well as the global church. There is no better example to state here than the transition of Christianity from the Jews' influence to the Gentiles, and from the Middle East to Europe. A distinguished scholar and champion of African theology, Andrew Walls amplifies the role African theology would play in the continent in these words:

> The experiences, traditions, and agendas of Africa are reshaping Christianity. The continent has seen immense theological activity over a long period, and the activity seems likely to intensify. It has hitherto been mainly conducted, not by academics, but by thousands of people who never thought of themselves as theologians, some of them barely literate in English, who have been making Christian choices kinship obligations, ancestors, shrines, customary rites, healing, possession, divination, reconciliation. Their sources have been the Christian Scriptures (usually in the vernacular), the Christian tradition as they know it, and their understanding of local patterns of thought, action and relationship. The result of their work has already meant a substantial enlargement of Christian theology; for, as we have seen, they have had to relate the historic Christian tradition to the preexisting structures of African belief system and religious consciousness, affirming, denying, suppressing, reshaping, redirecting, and reinterpreting the various elements in the process. It will be in the task of African academic theology to explore and articulate the forms and formulations of Christianity already made in thousands of congregations. There will be alternative formulations; it is clear that diverse trends are already discernable. Africa is, in fact, a great theological laboratory, dealing with issues—literally—of life and death, of deformation and reformation, of fossilization and revival. It is also in the process of generational religious change, which, as Ogubu Kalu has shown, is critical and may be explosive. And understanding it will give scope for a whole lifetime of African Christianity projects.[155]

Even if Christianity is misused to subjugate, oppress, and exploit Africans, for all those who found solace in Christ, being a child of God has healed and boosted their self-identity. For Africans, whose longstanding sources of identity and systems of authority are disrupted by unintended and undesirable changes, the Christian faith has given them solace, renewed identity, and energy. For those who have moved from the countryside to an urban setting, becoming separated from their cultural roots, being exposed to various people in a multicultural context, has been a real challenge to which they had to adjust. Living without a job, going through civil wars, and ending up in a refugee camp with no hope in sight creates enormous social and psychological needs. Through the Christian faith and fellowship of the church, millions of Africans have found new sources of identity, new forms of stable community, and new forms of moral precepts to provide them with a sense of meaning and purpose. In many ways, Christianity has answered the "Who am I?" question of Africans. The question they struggle with is "What am I?

---

154. Sanneh, *Summoned from the Margin*, 231.
155. Walls, *Cross-Cultural Process in Christian History*, 133.

Chapter 3

Suffering in a Continent Teeming With Riches

Much of this terrible widespread lung disease epidemic among mineworkers, if correctly diagnosed, could have been prevented, albeit at some financial cost to the mining companies. It could be stopped by the effective removal of the dust at the point when it is created... De Beers' immoral failure to control the toxic dust in its mines has exposed its mineworkers to great dangers.

Yes, there really are blood diamonds. But only a very few them are traded to support wars. They are rather the millions of gems splattered by the blood coughed up by TB victims, by the bloodshed in lungs, by the blood of greed. It is now the production of these deeply tainted diamonds in South Africa that urgently needs to be cleansed.[1]

If you ever intend to have children, and want them to live prosperous lives, you damn well better make sure that we [Americans] control the African continent—George Rich.[2]

Pain behind the Glitter

FOR CENTURIES AFRICA HAS been dubbed a Dark Continent: underdeveloped, backward, and impoverished. The Western media footage of Africa is of people stricken with hunger, malnourished children with extended bellies, and piles of corpses, all the result of famine or civil war, and destitute refugees. Our eyes are familiar with Africans who are suffering because of HIV or Ebola, without medical care and hospital beds lying on a dirt floor in their mud huts. In the midst of these ugly and horrifying scenarios the

---

1. Roberts, *Glitter and Greed*, xxi. For an in-depth knowledge on diamond, see further ibid., *passim*. It is very comprehensive, detailed, and eye-opening research.

2. Perkins, *Secret History of the American Empire*, 41.

two good things we see in the Western media that are anesthetic to our minds and souls are: the Western philanthropy and African wild animals. Beyond this surface level of understanding, the majority of the West has no clue about the wealth of Africa that has made an unparalleled contribution to Western capitalism. I don't know of any Western evangelical scholar who has done academic research and written a book on African minerals, the exploitation of the West, and the economic input of these minerals in Europe, Canada, and North America. Without addressing these issues we cannot talk about justice. If we need to understand the Africans' past and present, and shape and reshape the fast growing Christian influence, the natural resources of the continent that are vital for economic, social, educational, and technological developmental and industrialization of Africa cannot be ignored. Hence, we look deep into this matter in this chapter.

> Africa's natural resources and mineral wealth are widely claimed as vast and diversified. It has 40 percent of the world potential hydroelectric power supply, the bulk of the world's diamonds and chromium, 30 percent of the uranium in noncommunist world, 50 percent of the world's gold, 90 percent of it phosphates, 40 percent of platinum, 7.5 percent of its coal, 8 percent of its known petroleum reserves, 12 percent of its natural gas, 3 percent of its iron ore, and millions of acres of untilled land. In addition, Africa has 64 percent of the world's manganese, 13 percent of its copper and vast bauxite, nickel, and lead resources. It also has strategic minerals as cobalt, critical in the manufacture of jet engines, rhodium, palladium, vanadium, and titanium. Without these essential minerals many industrial plants in the West would grind to a standstill.[3]

Time and scope will not allow me to cover in detail all these minerals. Because of its global demand and market, and the bloodshed, slave labor, and exploitation it has been causing within the continent, diamonds takes the priority. Here is the genesis of the blood diamond in Africa:

> In 1866, a 15-year old named Erasmus Jacobs found a pretty-looking rock on the banks of South Africa's Orange River, and he pocketed it to give to his little sister, who collected interesting stones. A short time later, while the children were playing pebbles on the street, the glittering one caught the eye of a passerby, a local politician. Suspecting that it may be a diamond, he liberated it from the children and passed it on to a local peddler, who in turn mailed it to the government mineralogist. The stone turned out to be a 2.25-carat diamond, and it was sold to the governor of Cape Colony for 500 pounds sterling. The following year, it was displayed at the Paris Exhibition, mainly as an oddity. At the time, no one knew of the wealth to be had in South Africa.
>
> Until diamond mining took permanent hold in South Africa in the 1870s, most diamonds were found in India and Brazil; in fact, the discovery of Jacobs's stone did little to change anyone's opinion that those two countries were the only places to find diamonds. The find in Africa was written off as a fluke initially—at least until more were plucked from the riverbank: The second find was a magnificent 85-carat white diamond. The discovery was so awe-inspiring that Cape Town's colonial secretary, Sir Richard Southey, laid it on the table at the South African Parliament and proclaimed proudly, "Gentlemen, this is the rock

---

3. Ayittey, *Africa Betrayed*, 2–3.

on which the future South Africa will be built." The diamond was named the Star of South Africa.[4]

The key instrumental person in the development of the international diamond industry was De Beers's founder, Cecil Rhodes. He "used an army of mercenaries in 1893 to beat down the Matabele people in what is now Zimbabwe; each soldier who volunteered was given nine square miles of land and two gold claims, an amount that equaled roughly 10,000 pounds sterling. Rhodes conquered the territory for the sake of his British South Africa Company, a gold-mining venture, and named the country Rhodesia, after himself."[5] Rhodes saw "creating artificial scarcity in diamonds, and therefore high prices, as a tool for paying for troops to extend the British Empire. He believed England was destined to rule Africa: 'I contend that we [the English] are the first race in the world and the more of the world we inhabit, the better it is for the human race.' An early version of his will left funds to regain North America for the British Empire."[6] Right from the outset, with strong conviction that English people are the first race, the diamond trade was used to fund illicit wars in Africa and beyond to expand the British Empire. From the time of Cecil Rhodes to this day, the conflict-diamond money has been used to hire mercenaries, supply weapons, and overthrow governments, which are the cause of enormous pain and bloodshed in Africa.

When Rhodes was at the peak of his power in May 1896, Ernest Oppenheimer was only just commencing work as a sixteen-year-old junior clerk in Dunkelshuhler Company, a member of London diamond syndicate that purchased De Beers's diamonds. It already employed his brothers Louis and Bernard and was owned by a relative through marriage. Ernest stayed with Louis in the inner London suburb of Camden Town. They were to work together for the rest of their lives and even to marry sisters. Family connections were all important. Their company also employed their cousin, Gustav Imroth (who later became Managing Director of Johannesburg Consolidated Investment, one of South Africa's leading finance houses). Two more brothers, Gustav and Ott, were to follow Ernest into the diamond trade.

Ernest had been born in Friedberg near Frankfurt as the eighth child and the fifth son of the cigar merchant Eduard Oppenheimer and his wife, Nanette. It was a time of unrest. There was much resentment in Germany over the million Jewish refugees given refuge by Emperor Franz Joseph in the 1880s when they fled racial intolerance in Russia and Eastern Europe. Ernest in his turn escaped the anti-Semitism spreading in Germany by moving to London. Through smart business maneuvering and discerning of the right timing to make a business deal, eventually De Beers was owned by the Oppenheimers. They created a syndicate that controls 65 percent of the world diamond today.[7]

As I stated earlier, Germany was one of the European countries involved in blood diamonds. "In South west Africa the Germans had claimed rights over thousands of diamonds that were literally lying sparkling in the moonlight. The Germans employed

4. Campbell, *Blood Diamonds*, 102–3.
5. Ibid., 75.
6. Roberts, *Glitter and Greed*, 84.
7. See ibid.

local blacks to crawl all night in a line over the dunes putting diamonds into tins hung from their necks. *Their mouths were gagged lest they try to keep a diamond by swallowing it.* In 1909 the Germans set up the Germans Colonial Company to mine its diamonds."[8] When we see the miserable pictures of Africans today, I wonder how often the image of muzzled/gagged Africans crawling at night, picking diamonds for European powers out of their own land for nothing, comes to our mind. This process involved multiple humiliations that left scars on Africans' souls for generations. The debilitating impact of exploitation of Africans on their economy, social stability, and development, still stands as a witness to all of us. Africa's diamonds were not supposed to be a stumbling block for progress and a cause of fear, poverty, and death for Africans.

In South Africa, more diamond mines were discovered in Kleinzee farm on the bleak Atlantic coast of Namaqualand, Buffer marine, Koingnass, Michells Bay, Orange Mund, Kimberly, Bellsbank, Lexton, Koffierfonteen, Frank Smith, etc.[9] However, "Blacks were not to be allowed to own diamond leases or to mine their own stones. The government restricted the number of black mineworkers a white man could employ in order to ensure even competition between the white diggers. It organized races to peg claims when new land was released for diamond mining. On August 20th 1926, 10,000 white people lining up for one of these races included several women and a man on crutches."[10] A Canadian company purchased the Frank Smith Mine and Bellsbank. "It reported that Frank Smith was producing fine gem quality stones, worth some $220 per carat, and this gave the mine a 'free cash flow' of some $3.3 million a year. Bellsbank's diamonds were reportedly not as good on average as Frank Smith's, but more in number. It was making declared profit $5 million a year."[11] According to Roberts's research, the racial discrimination among the mineworkers is still the same even after apartheid has officially become a thing of the past. The staggering profit of the Canadian company happened in the recent past. The astounding profits in dollars, the glittering diamonds that are used as a symbol of love and prestige in the West, have many kinds of dark and inhuman facets.

In the West, the value of a diamond is measured by the dollar price for it. For Africans, even if they are the legal owners who have a right for it, diamonds cost them their lives, their dignity as human beings, and the unity and emotional and financial health of their families.

In 2003, the Bushmen at Central Kalahari Game Reserve were dispossessed of their land when over 78,000 square kilometers of the land in Botswana—one-third of it in Kalahari—was leased to BHP-Billiton, the Australian mining giant. This meant that, between BHP-Billiton[12] and De Beers, virtually the entire Reserve was covered with

---

8. Ibid., 86; emphasis added.
9. Ibid.
10. Ibid., 94.
11. Ibid., 33.

12. This is the current identity of a much-expanded Australian mining company originally known as Broken Hill Propriety Ltd., that, from 2000, has mined diamonds in Canada and extracted them offshore in South Africa.

prospecting leases. They set up a company called Kalahari Diamonds Ltd. to explore these leases. The World Bank gave it $2 million toward the survey costs.

Botswana has a black government, but the degree of racism in their treatment of Bushmen is equal to anything whites have done. Botswana is today a country with widespread literacy and a free press. Its wealth derives 80 percent from diamonds mined in partnership with De Beers. But most of the wealth is in the hand of the government officials and their families, with the gap between the rich and the poor comparable to Brazil.[13]

Indeed, as Cape Town's colonial secretary, Sir Richard Southey, rightly said, diamonds are the rock on which South Africa was built. What Richard Southey did not realize then was the capacity the minerals in South Africa have to build Western capitalism. "For a long while," commented Rodney,

> South Africa was the most important raw material reservoir for the whole imperialism. Britain was the European power which had already been entrenched in South Africa for many years when gold and diamonds were discovered in the nineteenth century, on the eve of the Scramble . . . As capitalists of other nationalities entered into relations with South Africa through the investment and trade, those capitalists agreed to strengthen, and did, the racist/fascist social relations of South Africa . . . As time went on, the U.S.A. got an ever bigger slice of the unequal trade between the metropolis and colonial Africa. The share of the U.S.A. in Africa trade rose from just over 28 million dollars in 1913 to 150 million in 1932 and to 1,200 million dollars in 1948, at which figure it represented nearly 15 percent of Africa's foreign trade. The share of the U.S.A. in West Africa trade rose from 38 million dollars in 1938 to 163 million dollars in 1946 and to 517 million dollars by 1954. However, it was South Africa which was America's best trading partner in Africa, supplying her with gold, diamonds, manganese, and other minerals and buying heavy machinery in turn. Apart from direct U.S.A.-South African trade, most of south Africa's gold was resold in London to American buyers, just as most Gold coast and Nigerian coca was resold to the U.S.A.[14]

Meredith concurs:

> The assets South Africa possessed to help overcome [the economic problem] were considerable. They included one of the world's richest stores of minerals, with 44 percent of world diamond reserves, 82 per cent of manganese reserves and 64 per cent of platinum-group metal of world production. Its financial, banking and legal systems were well established and efficient; the Johannesburg stock exchange was the tenth largest in the world. Its manufacturing base, though overprotected and uncompetitive by world standards, was capable of major expansion. The infrastructure of roads, railways, ports and airports was well developed. Telephone and electricity services were reliable. Universities and technical colleges turned out a ready supply of competent graduates. In statistical

---

13. For details, see Roberts, *Glitter and Greed*, 73–81.
14. Rodney, *How Europe Underdeveloped Africa*, 191–92.

terms, South Africa, with a gross domestic product of $120 billion, ranked as one of the world's twenty-five largest economies. In Africa it stood out as a giant.[15]

As flowers attract bees, Europeans, Americans, Canadians, Australians, and Asians have always been attracted by the minerals in Africa. De Beers was not limited to the diamonds in South Africa. It expanded to Angola, Mozambique, Sierra Leone, and Liberia.

> Sierra Leone was founded by former North American slaves freed for fighting on behalf of England in the revolutionary war. At the end of the war, more than 15,000 former slaves who had accepted the offer made their way to the Great Britain. Although slavery was still legal there, in 1772 a court had ruled that once freed, a slave was free for life. Unaccustomed to making the life of their own, and aided little by the government they had fought for, many of the new residents suffered crushing poverty and unemployment.
>
> In 1787, a group of British philanthropist purchased 32 square miles of land near Bounce Island, a large landmass in the Sierra Leone River just north of the Freetown Peninsula, from local Temne leaders. Their idea was to create a "Province of Freedom" for the ex-slaves. Later that year, 100 European prostitutes and 300 former slaves arrived in what would become Freetown. Many of the freed slaves knew nothing of Africa, having being born in Europe and the Americas. Even if they had, very few of them—perhaps none of them—had ancestors from Sierra Leon. Although Sierra Leon have been plied for the slaves prior to that time, Ghana, Ivory Coast, Nigeria, and Cameroon were the main players in the trade. Of the original 400 settlers dropped at the peninsula's deep water harbor, only 48 survived the next three years, the rest succumbing to a gallery of deadly diseases, warfare with the local inhabitants, or the temptation to leave Sierra Leone in search of their original homelands.
>
> Undaunted, the philanthropists tried again in 1792, this time shipping some 1,200 former slaves from the United States who had fled to Nova Scotia, Canada; they later sent 500 more from Jamaica. It was during this period that Sierra Leone settlers first started profiting from the country's natural resources.[16]

Stephen Neil adds,

> Sierra Leone on the West coast, where the hills rise to 2,700 feet and break a coast-line which is low and monotonous almost everywhere until broken again by the splendid mountains of the Cameroons, had been picked on by the friends of the slaves as a home for those who had been freed, and a colony had been established. One of the early governors was the evangelical Zachary Macaulary, the silent father of the historian T.B. Macaulary, the greatest talker that the world has ever known. By 1846, 50,000 slaves had been brought in; it was reckoned that they spoke 117 different languages, and inevitably they developed among themselves as their lingua franca the peculiar form of Africanized English known as Creole. They could not be said to be promising material; they have been described (by the German historian of missions Gustav Warneck) as a confused mass, destitute of the slightest feeling of community, who lived in a state of constant conflict

---

15. Meredith, *Fate of Africa*, 649.
16. Campbell, *Blood Diamonds*, 27–28.

among themselves, and were dull, lazy, and in the last degree unchaste, besides being in bondage, without exception, to heathenish superstition.[17]

The political bondage of the so-called "free slaves" had complicated their personal and communal life, their language, their past, present, and future. "It has to be remembered that in the nineteenth century the alternatives for many peoples were not independent and enslavement, but total destruction (by unscrupulous exploiters or slave-trade) and the possibility of survival in a state of colonial dependence."[18] "It is a terrible and irresponsible thing to free slaves without providing for them," said Dorothy, a free slave in the U.S. "When freedom came, the white people realized that it was not an open door to success and happiness and safety. White people knew that there was going to be pandemonium, and it was. The Negroes were taken advantage of by unscrupulous strangers, and they were taken advantage of by each other. They were terribly dishonest and cruel to each other. To this day they are not accustomed to taking care of themselves."[19] The African slaves who were freed and sent to Sierra Leone ended up in the chains of colonialism. The change is like jumping from the fire into the frying pan. And they were slowly cooked to the point of destruction.

A city founded by former slaves and prostitutes one can hardly think would create interest in the hearts and minds of the West. But it did. Not because of its beautiful beaches but because of her natural resources, particularly diamond.

> A British geologist named J. D. Pollett made a discovery in 1930 and found diamonds on the bank of Gbobora River, not realizing at the time he had stumbled onto one of West Africa's most valuable diamond deposits that would, over the next 40 years, produce more than 50 million carats of diamonds, half of which were astounding gem quality. Pollett estimated that the diamond field he discovered extended over the Sewa River and extending east into Liberia. Towns within that area—Kenema, Yengema, Koidu, Tongo field, and BO—would be transformed within two decades from sleepy bush villages in the middle of a rain forest that few people would ever care to visit to centers of violent intrigue and international commerce, both legal and illegal. On that day in 1930 Sierra Leone officially became diamondiferous, a designation that has always been both a blessing and a curse for any nation with a similar geology; the promise of vast wealth invariably invites chaos. The discovery of the diamonds—which, until then, had been deemed to be just another worthless piece of gravel by the locals—placed Sierra Leone on a course that would effectively destroy the entire country by the end of the century.[20]

Greed is indiscriminate of skin color. Its venom sours the human soul and leads people to cut each other's throats for a gain that no one will carry beyond the grave. The discovery of diamonds in Sierra Leone caused political turmoil within the country and the state house became a revolving door for one president after another within a short period of time. Those who were unable to get the presidential position to exploit their

17. Neill, *History of Christian Missions*, 305–6.
18. Ibid., 249.
19. Ball, *Slaves in the Family*, 59.
20. Campbell, *Blood Diamonds*, 8.

people under the guise of leadership decided to be guerilla fighters. "Along with three other Sierra Leoneans in the 'art of revolution' by Libyan president Colonel Muammar Qaddafi, former Sierra Leone Army (SLA) Foday Sankoh trained about 100 men in northwestern Liberian camps run by Taylor's rebellion, the National Patriotic Front of Liberia (NPFL). In 1991, Sankoh's soldiers of the newly formed Revolutionary United Front marched into Sierra Leone and captured Kailahun District."[21] At first, the people in the district welcomed the RUF with joy and optimism like their heroes, thinking that "the best way to get the current government's attention, it seemed, was to capture some of the diamond mines, holding them for a ransom for a more democratic system and a bright future for the majority of the country's citizens, who lived much like their ancestors had in the provinces."[22] One common factor that I observed among Africans, including my birth place, Ethiopia, through my research is that Africans take war as an effortless and smart solution to build a nation. The short route to the highest leadership position for many aspiring African leaders is not a ballot but a bullet. Instead of engaging with their political opponents in civil dialogue or debate, fighting with ideas to win the minds of voters democratically, they rush for AK-47s and hand grenades to eliminate everybody that stands in their way. For war-mongering Africans there is always somebody waiting at the edge of their country to provide arms. It is a lucrative business. Campbell writes:

> The AK-47 assault rifle is the bread and butter of armed conflicts the world over. Now used by more than fifty armies, the weapon was invented in 1947 by Red Army soldier Mikhail Kalashnikov and adopted for regular use in the Soviet army in 1949. Its distinctive crescent-shaped magazine holds 30 pounds of 7.62x39 millimeter cartridges that can be fired at a rate of 400 rounds per minute, with a muzzle velocity of 2,240 feet per second. Loaded, the AK-47 weighs almost 11 pounds, light enough for a medium-sized child to carry with little difficulty, and because of the simple chamber/action design it is almost impossible to jam . . . AKs are cheap. Kalashnikov firearms are a guerilla's best friends and Sierra Leone is awash in them.
>
> Because of their diamond wealth, throughout most of the war the RUF was better armed than its adversaries. Diamonds bought Kalashnikovs by the hundreds, Browning 12.7-milimetre heavy machine guns by the tens of dozens, and ammunition in million-block orders. Light artillery included rocket-propelled grenades, mortars, and SA-7 shoulder-launched surface-to-air-missiles. The RUF bought helicopters for supply and, whenever they could, they stoles trucks, armored fighting vehicles, and armored personnel carriers from the Sierra Leone Army and ECOMOG[23]. The RUF funded this with proceeds from illegal diamond mining.[24]

Purchasing weapons is not leading to a bowl dance in a jovial state dinner party. The inevitable and enviable civil war started in Sierra Leone. The inexperienced Sierra Leonean army was not ready to handle the challenge of the RUF. "In fact," said Campbell, "other than participating in the odd coup once or twice in a decade, Sierra Leone Army

---

21. Ibid., 71.
22. Ibid. See also Meredith, *Fate of Africa*, 562–72.
23. Economic Community of West African States Monitoring Group
24. Campbell, *Blood Diamonds*, 62–63.

soldiers mostly called upon to carry the national flag during federal holidays and march in arms at Lungi Airport when important foreign diplomats paid a visit. And now they were getting slaughtered in their own jungles and not getting paid for it."[25]

Unpaid soldiers are ticking bombs, prone to be manipulated and used by dictators with evil intentions. "In 1992, 27-year old SLA Captain Valentine Strasser decided that enough is enough and marched a band of soldiers from the battlefield in the Kailahun District back to Freetown to demand their pay. When that failed within hours of arriving, he persuaded his followers to join him in overthrowing the government. The coup was popular in Freetown: Momoh had been promising a return to multiparty politics under mounting pressure from citizens who'd enough ineffective one-party leadership, but he'd used the war with RUF as an excuse to postpone elections. Strasser set up the national provisional Ruling Council, the NPRC, and was sworn in as youngest head of state in Sierra Leone's history."[26]

The historically and culturally rootless former slaves and prostitutes dumped by the British in Freetown about 100 years ago built a nation that sits on internationally demanded valuable natural resources but is languishing in poverty. The nation hardly has models that it can look up to as military, political, academic, athletic, and judicial icons. Sierra Leoneans lack values that enable them to transcend their ethnic and cultural boundaries to see the good in others and live with a win-win principle harmoniously. Youth that are deprived of good schools and good teachers, libraries, sports, and clubs, but provided AK-47s to fight a senseless war without pay, wearing rags—the lucky ones with flip flops, others in bare feet—turned Sierra Leone into a prison without a wall, a mass grave, and hell to run from to refugee camps. When the founders of a nation are people who have never experienced freedom as they grow up, like in the case of Sierra Leone, they cannot build a society and culture seasoned with civility, stability, and tranquility. As the saying goes, fruit does not fall far from the tree. I am not trying to use the slave trade as a scapegoat for the problem in Sierra Leone, but I wonder how any thinking mind could correctly interpret the effect without the cause?

To counter the skill and power of the RUF, the young Sierra Leonean President, Strasser, decided to hire mercenaries—not with cash from the national bank, but with the promise of leasing the diamond mines with a lucrative deal. Who would not jump for a diamond deal to shed the blood of Africans?

> The first company Strasser hired was Gurkha Security Guards, under the leadership of American Vietnam veteran Robert MacKenzie. Ironically, prior going to Sierra Leone, MacKenzie had served in Rhodesian Army.
>
> Mackenzie's efforts in Sierra Leone did not bear much fruit. After two weeks of training SLA and Kamjor fighters in the bush, he was killed in an RUF ambush near Port Loko, near the coast. Rumor has it that his remains were eaten by the RUF. The remainder of the Gurkha force refused to mount a counteroffensive and their contract was quickly canceled.
>
> Strasser turned next to the Executive Outcomes, a South African security company that is to private armies what De Beers is to diamonds. Founded in

---

25. Ibid., 73.
26. Ibid.

1989 by Eeben Barlow, a former South African special forces officer, EO is either the embodiment of all the worst things about mercenaries or a source of stability and security in a continent that has been effectively abandoned by Europe and America to fend for itself. It depends on whom you ask.

EO's operations are necessarily shady. It's known that the company has worked extensively in Angola against UNITA rebels, who also illegally mine and sell diamonds, in Papua New Guinea and Perhaps Colombia. The company is capable of rapidly mobilizing a battalion-strength force almost anywhere in the world with impressive asset support. EO owns a slew of armored fighting vehicles: two Boeing 727s and a C-47, attack aircraft such as Mi-24 gunships and two MiG-23/27 fighter planes, and all manner of light and medium artillery. According to its glossy brochures EO provides its clients (either directly or through affiliated companies) military training, VIP protection; gold, diamond, and oil exploration and mining; airline transport; civil engineering; even chartered accountancy and offshore financial management services. Finally, EO also provides its own Russian technicians, medical support, intelligence, and infrared photo reconnaissance, and before the company dissolved in 1999, was reportedly contracting with private firms to provide satellite imagery. With fourteen permanent staff at the time of its intervention in Sierra Leone, EO maintained a database of possible recruits numbering around 2,000.[27]

In 1999, an estimated $75 million worth of gemstones had flowed from the RUF to the world market, a vast amount of capital for a bush army, moving completely undetected, untaxed, and unrecorded. In return, an army's worth of munitions, fuel, food, and medicine flowed back. In the Sierra Leonean's tragedy of the 90s the list of who-is-who includes Sam Bkaire, better known as Major General Mosquito, an RUF battle-group commander who fell out of favor with an instrumental middleman in moving diamonds out of Sierra Leone. Also named was Victor Bout, the former KGB agent who owned and operated the complicated network of private planes that shipped munitions and weapons to the RUF from Eastern Europe. Wealthy Lebanese businessman Talal El-Ndine was named as well; he was the inner-circles paymaster. Ibrahim Bah was on the list, as was Nassour's cousin, Samiah Osailly, another Antwerp diamond broker.[28] When one closely investigates, it looks like both the mercenaries and RUF soldiers were using the same source for ammunition. Time and again, in Liberia, Angola, Congo, and in Sierra Leone, I have noticed that the same weapon traders and news agencies are working concurrently both on the government and the rebels side. It is greed not ethics that runs the African affair. So, what was the result of the military showdown between the mercenaries and RUF in Sierra Leone? Campbell writes:

> Freetown was filled with war-ravaged beggars and thieves. There were too many refugees and not enough humanitarian aid to go around. People crippled with polio staked out street corners, and tried to extort money from those passing within reach. Waiters would try to sell you diamonds or offer to rent their sisters to you for weeks at a time. Children with bloated bellies scratched at the windows of downtown restaurants.

---

27. Ibid., 75–76.
28. See ibid., 184–85; Roberts, *Glitter and Greed*, 13.

> Just when you thought you have found a safe corner to escape to—some dim tent of a street side restaurant where few people could see into the gloom and you could order out another beer and let your mind wander to something other than death, disease, and torture—in would stumble a multiple-amputee a man who'd had his arms, lips, and ears sawn off with a rusted ax. If it was really an unlucky day for you, the guy would also have polio and malaria and be partially retarded. There is no shortage of such people, and when they corner you in a restaurant whose walls are composed of stolen UNHCR rain-plastic, there are only two things to do: Stair stoically through him as if he doesn't exist, or reach for your wallet and hop a limp leone-note worth 50 cents penance enough. When giving money to the amputated, you must put it directly into their pockets.[29]

RUF soldiers did not only impoverish their people, they left people without hands that are unable to receive alms to put in their pockets, let alone to work and earn income—that is, if jobs could even be available. How low can a nation go? In my opinion, in Africa, it is not the ancestors who are the living dead, as some theologians say; it is the war-ravaged Africans, the amputees, the homeless, the beggars, the sick, and the refugees. "Between February 8 and February 12, 5,000 Sierra Leoneans and 6,000 Liberians seeking asylum straggled into the border towns. This was only a small portion of Sierra Leone refugees still stranded in neighboring countries, however. In all, UNHCR operated six camps in Liberia with approximately 35,000 refugees from Sierra Leone. Another 55,000 Sierra Leoneans were camped in Guinea, 8,000 more in The Gambia. The organization was only capable of moving about 1,200 people per week from the border of Liberia to temporary camps within Sierra Leone, another 500 per week from Guinea."[30]

As the Scripture says, "Jesus Christ is the same yesterday and today and forever" (Heb 13:8). But what kind of Christ would appeal to the minds and souls of the disinherited Africans? How can African theologians and pastors incarnate Christ both in word and deed to people like those in Sierra Leone? The author of Hebrews, just before verse eight, said, "Remember your leaders who spoke the word of God to you. *Consider the outcome of their way of life and imitate their faith*" (Heb 13:7). Whose outcome of way of life do African Christians need to consider? Whose faith should they imitate? What kind of church and Christian community gives the right spiritual and social atmosphere to restore the dignity of downtrodden Africans? What should be the content of the gospel message? What should be the message of African Christians' hymns and songs? In a different chapter we will wrestle with these questions.

Nevertheless, I don't want you to leave Sierra Leone with an unanswered question about the cause of the bloodshed. After the war ended what happened to the diamond? I strongly believe that whoever won the bone of contention is equally responsible for what the country went through. It takes two to fight. "More than anywhere in Sierra Leone, Koidu has proved worth kicking over the dirt at one's feet; diamonds can be found everywhere, which might explain why the roads have never been paved."[31] As

---

29. Campbell, *Blood Diamonds*, 26–27.
30. Ibid., 215.
31. Ibid., 231.

usual this delectable "African cake" did not end up in the hands of the nationals. "South Africa—based Koidu Holdings runs the largest operation, Koidu Kimberlite Project, and a conglomerate international investors runs a smaller site called the Thunderball Mine. Rumor has it that the best restaurant in the provinces is inside the Koidu Holdings compound, as is a state-of-the-art medical clinic and a well-stocked company store."[32] This is the happy ending of the war in Sierra Leone.

If nations that are rich in mineral resources have the right to own it and they properly utilize and manage them, they should live a better life, have good education, excellent medical facilities, efficient transportation systems, and advanced technology. Instead, for centuries, Africans remain the subjects and objects of poverty. The African minerals and natural resources have done what they are supposed to do for human beings, but not within the continent, in the West. Here are some examples:

- Ever since the fifteenth century, Europe had a strategic control of world trade and of the legal organizational aspects of the movement of goods between continents. Europe's power increased with imperialism, because imperialism meant that investment (with or without colonial rule) gave Europe control over production within each continent. The amount of benefits to capitalism increased accordingly, because Europe could determine the quantity of different raw material inputs that would need to be brought together in the interest of capitalism as a whole, and the bourgeois in particular. For instance, sugar production in the West Indies was joined in the colonial period by cocoa production within Africa, so that both merged into the chocolate industry of Europe and North America.

- In the metallurgical field, iron ore from Sierra Leone could be turned into different types of steel with the addition of manganese from the Gold coast or chrome from Southern Rhodesia. Iron ore was not one of Africa's major exports in the colonial days and it may therefore appear an irrelevant example. However, iron was very significant in the economy of Sierra Leone, Liberia, and North Africa. It can be used to illustrate the trend by which the international division of labor allowed technology and skills to grow in the metropoles. Furthermore, it must be recalled that Africa was an important source of the minerals that went into making steel alloys, notably manganese and chrome. Manganese was essential in the Bessemer process. It was mined in several places in Africa, with Nouta mine on the Gold Coast having the largest single Manganese deposit in the world. American companies owned the Gold Coast and North African mine and used the product in the steel industry of the U.S.A. Chrome from South Africa and Southern Rhodesia also played a similar role in steel metallurgy, being essential for the manufacture of stainless steel.

- Columbite was another of the African minerals valuable for the creation of steel alloys. Being highly heat-resistant, one of its principal uses was in making steel for jet engines. First of all, it was the rapid development of European industry and technology that caused columbite to assume value. It had been a discarded by-product of tin mining in Nigeria up to 1952. Then, once it was utilized, it gave

---

32. Ibid., 230.

further stimulus to European technology in the very sophisticated sphere of airplane engines.

- Copper was Africa's chief export. Being an excellent conductor for electricity, it became an indispensable part of the capitalist electrical industry. It is an essential component of generators, motors, electric locomotives, telephones, telegraphs, light and power lines, motorcars, buildings, ammunition, radios, refrigerators, and a host of other things. The vital copper export from Congo, Northern Rhodesia, and other parts of Africa contributed to the leading sector of European technology.

- African minerals played a decisive role both with regard to conventional weapons and with regard to the breakthrough in atomic and nuclear weapons. It was from the Belgian Congo during the Second World War that the U.S.A. began to get the Uranium that was a prerequisite to the making of the first atomic bomb. In any case, by the end of the colonial period, industry and the war machine in the colonizing nations had become so intertwined and inseparable that any contribution to one was a contribution to the other. Therefore, Africa's massive contribution to what initially appeared to be a peaceful pursuit, such as the making of copper wire and steel alloys, ultimately took the shape of explosive devices, aircraft carriers, and so on.

- In 1885, while Africa was being carved up at the conference table, one William H. Lever started making soap on the Merseyside near Liverpool in England. He called his soap "Sunlight" and, in the swamps where his factory stood, the township of Port Sunlight grew up. Within ten years the firm of Lever was selling 40,000 tons of soap per year in England alone and was building an export business and factories in other parts of Europe, America, and the British colonies. Then came Life buoy, Lux, Vim, and, within another ten years, Lever was selling 60,000 tons of soap in Britain, and in addition had factories producing and selling in Canada, the U.S.A., South Africa, Switzerland, Germany, and Belgium. However, soap ingredients did not grow in any of those countries. The basic item in the manufacture was stearin, obtained from oil and fats. Apart from animal tallow and whale oil, the desirable raw materials, namely, palm oil, palm-kernel oil, groundnut oil, and copra, all came from the tropics. West Africa happened to be the world's great palm produce zone and was also a major grower of groundnuts.

- In 1887, the Austrian firm of Schicht, which was later to be incorporated in the Unilever combine, built the first palm-kernel crushing mill in Austria, supplied with raw materials by the Liverpool firm of oil merchants. In 1910, Lever purchased W. B. McIver, a small Liverpool firm in Nigeria. That was followed by acquisitions of two small companies in Sierra Leone and Liberia. Indeed, Lever (at that time called Lever Bros.) got a foothold in every colony in West Africa. The first breakthrough occurred when Lever bought the Niger Company in 1920 for 8 million pounds. Then, in 1929, the African and Eastern, the last big rival trading concern, was brought into partnership, and the result of the merger was called the United Africa Company (UAC). During the 1914–18 War, Lever had begun making margarine, which required the same raw materials as soap, namely, oils and fats. The subsequent years were ones in which such enterprises in Europe were constantly getting bigger through takeovers and mergers. The big names in soap and margarine manufacture on the European continent were two Dutch firms, Jurgens and Van der Bergh, and the Austrian firms of Schicht and Centra. The Dutch companies first achieved a dominant position; and then in 1929 there was a grand merger between their combine and Lever's, who in the meantime had been busy buying off virtually all other competitors. The 1929 merger created Unilever as a single monopoly, divided for the sake of convenience into Unilever Ltd. (registered in Britain) and Unilever N.V. (registered in Holland).

- The main investment in Liberia was undertaken by Firestone Rubber Company. Firestone made such a huge profit from Liberian rubber that it was the subject of a book sponsored by American capitalists to show how well American business flourished overseas. Between 1940 and 1965, Firestone took 160 million dollars' worth of rubber from Liberia, while in return the Liberian government received 8 million dollars. In the earlier years, the percentage of the value that went to the Liberian government was much smaller, but, at the best of times, the average net profit made by Firestone was three times the Liberian revenue. In Liberia, the United States rubber industry obtained a source that was reliable in peace and war—one that was cheap and entirely under American control. One of rubber's most immediate connections was with the automobile industry, and so it is not surprising that Harvey Firestone was a great friend and business colleague of Henry Ford. Liberian rubber turned the town of Akron, Ohio into a powerful rubber tire manufacturing center, and the tires then went over to the even bigger automobile works of Ford in Detroit. "Firestone's Liberian holdings instantly became world's largest rubber plantation, and it had cost the company only six cents an acre, barely a third of what the British had paid for their competing plantations in Malaysia. Despite the huge cost advantage over his British competitors, firestone imposed an aggressive drive to cut corners, and for years afterward the plantation was dogged with charges of employing slave labor and coercive recruitment of laborers, eventually provoking a suspension of relations with Liberia by the Hoover administration and an investigation of the plantation by the League of Nations."[33]

- The complex of southern African mining concerns operated not just in South Africa itself but also in southwest Africa: Angola, Mozambique, Northern Rhodesia, and Southern Rhodesia.

- Congo has consistently been a source of wealth for Europe and the United States.

- In North Africa, foreign capital exploited natural resources of phosphates, oil, lead, zinc, manganese, and iron ore.

- In Guinea, Sierra Leone, and Liberia, there were important workings of gold, diamonds, iron ore, and bauxite.

- The oil in Nigeria, the gold and manganese in Ghana, the copper and diamond in Tanzania, the copper of Uganda, are a few among many to mention.

33. French, *Continent for the Taking*, 96.

- In the mid-1950s, British investments in South Africa were estimated at 860 million pounds and yielded a stable profit of 15 percent, or 129 million pounds every year. Most mining companies had returns well above that average. De Beers Consolidated Mines made a profit that was both phenomenal and consistently high—between $26 million and $29 million throughout the 1950s.[34]

At the cost of the impoverishment of the majority of South African blacks, the country gave a huge economic boost to the European countries and the United States.

> In the years that Nelson Mandela spent in prison on Roben Island, South Africa became a fortress of white power and prosperity. Throughout the 1960s it experienced one of the highest rates of economic growth in the world, second to Japan. Its mines produced record amount of gold and other minerals; factories proliferated as never before. Foreign trade with Western countries rose in leaps and bounds. Foreign investors from the United States, Britain, France and Germany competed vigorously for positions in new industries. The annual net flow of foreign capital into the country in 1970 rose a level six times above the pre-Sharpeville era. The economic boom also brought to South Africa a flood of white immigrants, mainly from Europe; between 1960 and 1970 there was a net gain of some 250,000. All this gave white South Africans a growing sense of confidence about the future. Black resistance had been crushed; the security apparatus seemed capable of meeting any contingency. A vast bureaucracy existed to ensure government control. Above all, the government had the resources to make white supremacy a success.[35]

The South Africa-based De Beers is in control of diamond mines in the Central African Republic, Congo, Angola, Mozambique, Liberia, and many other countries. As we observed in Sierra Leone, "In Angola, the brutal diamond-funded war between the Government and the UNITA rebels also came to an end in 2002, after the death of the UNITA's leader Jonas Savimbi. Initially CIA had sustained UNITA's war to undermine Angola's socialist. After CIA support was withdrawn. UNITA continued to fight, using revenue from captured mines. Hundreds and thousands died, then came a peace deal and an internationally supervised election. But when UNITA lost this election, it did not accept the result launching the 1993 'War of the Cities,' which caused in five months 182,000 casualties. Between 1992 and 1998 UNITA made over $ 4 billion from stolen diamonds—enough to import military aircraft and very sophisticated weaponry."[36]

The Scum of the Earth in African Mines

In a world where animal rights are protected and those who violate them are prosecuted, fined, and sentenced, African mineworkers have been living in degrading situations for centuries, robbed of their human rights and dignity in multiple ways. Except for the writings of a few Western journalists, African mineworkers have no voice in the global

---

34. For detailed reading, see Rodney, *How Europe Underdeveloped Africa*.
35. Meredith, *Fate of Africa*, 412.
36. Roberts, *Glitter and Greed*, 4.

arena of the political and judicial system in their country. Behind the glamor of diamonds there is shame and atrocity beyond comprehension.

> In 1879 a Cornish mine engineer, T. C. Kitto, advocated adopting the methods used with black slaves in Brazilian diamond mines. He wrote: "The blacks are housed in barracks built in the form of a square, . . . an overseer looks them in every night . . . I believe the natives of South Africa, under European supervision, are capable of being made almost—if note quite—as good as the blacks of Brazil, providing they are dealt with the same manner. The mine owners thought this an excellent suggestion that would keep down wages and stop theft. In 1882, Cecil Rhodes advocated that all De Beers' black workers (but not white) should be confined to barracks when not at work. He calculated that selling food to the captive workers would pay half his labor costs. In July 1886 De Beers confined its 1,500-strong black work force in a barracks. By 1889 all 10,000 miners in Kimberly were in these prison-like compounds.
>
> This system allowed De Beers to mix convicts with blacks to further minimize labor costs. From 1884 to 1932 De Beers used hundreds of convicts in its mines, paying a minimal to the government instead of paying wages. Ironically, or perhaps deliberately, many of these were only imprisoned because they went to the diamond mines to seek paid work despite the government not giving them travel passes. The workers could not bring their wives or children with them into the compounds. When they wanted to leave the compound, they were dosed with mild laxatives and locked naked into cells for five to ten days with their hands fastened into leather bags. Every part of their body and excrement was inspected for diamonds. Eventually a machine was invented to inspect human stool for excreted diamonds.
>
> Many of these diamond mine practices became enshrined in South African legislation. In 1889 it was decreed that: "No native shall work or be allowed to work in any mine, whether in open or underground mining, excepting under the responsible charge of some particular white man as his master or 'baas.' Apartheid was now effectively established."[37]

De Beers guarded the local diamonds so jealously, Roberts was told by mine workers, that, whenever an ostrich was killed or injured by a car, the miners called security. They also called the abattoir. They have to come and slaughter it and cut out its crop. Ostriches eat small stones to help with digestion, so their crop might contain diamonds. The crop is delivered to the "DPU" or "Diamond Protection Unit." The ostrich meat would go to the bosses.[38] Thank God for the laxatives! The African miners didn't have to be slaughtered, but were locked in a cell naked from five to ten days and had all parts of their body, including their excrement, checked, which is instead a psychological death. As I said earlier, in my opinion, the living dead are not the African ancestors. It is the downtrodden, despised, humiliated, exploited, impoverished, and diseased millions of Africans.

> In 1893, the first color bar was created, on the insistence of the White workers; in 1987, a wave of discontent followed reductions in salaries; and in 1907 the White laborers called a strike against the employment of Blacks for skilled labor.

37. Ibid., 21.
38. Ibid., 37.

Again in 1913 and 1914 large-scale strikes were held by white workers. Each time, workers and management clashed violently, and shots were fired, but the white miners finally succeeded in having their unions recognized. This helped to validate the color bar. Most important, the Mines, and Works Act of 1911 gave only Whites the right to perform skilled labor and made striking a crime for Black workers under contract (including piece-workers and day laborers). This law henceforth dominated the social history of South Africa. Meanwhile, the influx of African immigrant labor form nearby territories reduced the cost of replacing "native" workers from one-half to one-sixth of the proletarianized Whites and encouraged employers simply to dismiss disobedient workers.[39]

Many of the diamond mines are sitting on asbestos. African miners go underground ill-protected with inadequate masks. Since the ventilators break down quite often the miners are exposed to asbestos—and quite a number of them end up in a lingering death.

African miners who work for De Beers do not have health insurance. Most mineworkers only get diagnosed with TB when it is too late, within a few months of their death, so they get no treatment at all. Many are not diagnosed even then; their TB is only discovered at autopsy. Retired mineworkers are rarely monitored, even though it is well know that silicosis or TB might take fifteen years or more to develop. It is simply presumed that, as these diseases are fatal and have no cure, there is no value in monitoring their potential victims. South Africa has "1000% more TB cases than the USA. It has 4 cases of TB per 100,000. [They] have 500 cases per 100,000-minimum-probably more like 750 new cases per 100,000 every year. Among [their] mineworkers it is far worse. They have from 4,000–5,000 cases every year. When a group of mineworkers are returning to Lesotho were tested, 60% had TB, There are 330,000 new cases of TB a year [in South Africa] with some 7 million active cases."[40] Roberts adds, "White workers with damaged lungs get 49,000 to 51,000 Rand. Colored workers get over 30,000 Rand. But 2,800 Rand is the maximum for black worker."[41] And Rodney concurs about the situation of African mineworkers elsewhere: "It is exploitation without redress. In 1934, forty-one Africans were killed in a gold mine disaster in the Gold Coast, and the capitalist company offered only 3 pounds to the dependents of each of these men as compensation."[42]

The luxury gem diamonds rich people enjoy are extracted by African miners whose life and health are in danger. During her research, the miners at Koffiefontein told Roberts, "De Beers treats [them] as tools to be thrown away when worn out."[43] Richard Spoor, one of Roberts's informants, said employers "have paid no regard to this fundamental obligation to [look after] their workers and as a result thousands of their employees have been killed and maimed after contracting preventable occupational lung diseases. The wives and children of these mineworkers have themselves been plunged

39. Vidrovitch, *Africa*, 237.
40. Roberts, *Glitter and Greed*, xv.
41. Ibid., 25.
42. Rodney, *How Europe Underdeveloped Africa*, 151.
43. Roberts, *Glitter and Greed*, xix.

into poverty and unrelenting hardship by the loss of the support of their husbands and fathers."[44]

He continued: "The apartheid system made it possible for the gold mining industry, quite literally, to use, consume and discard black workers as if they were just another commodity."[45] Roberts said that what Spoor said of the gold mine in South Africa can equally be said of diamond mining today. As far as my reading and research indicate, the condition of mineworkers of the De Beers Company in South Africa has not improved after apartheid. Roberts asserts: "The truth is that diamond mining, as practiced by De Beers, is not harmless but uniquely dangerous."[46]

Mineworkers could not go home for family sickness or family emergencies. They were frequently humiliated by being publicly stripped naked for medical examinations. It was a form of slavery. The miners also complained of poor pay and poor food and the lack of privacy in hostels where ten men shared a prison-like room with closed windows at ceiling height. They could not stay up at night for the lights were switched on and off at fixed times from the administration block. They didn't have dining halls. There were no partitions, cubicles, or doors in the lavatories so people had to defecate in public. These conditions are not only in diamond mines but also in the Oppenheimers' gold mines.

If a woman mineworker got pregnant she had to leave for three months and not return with her child—if she wished to keep her job. A black husband could make a booking for one of the houses made available for conjugal visits—but the waiting list was very long as there were between 2000 and 3000 black workers at Kleinzee. In all mining places, white miners were allowed to bring their wives and houses are provided for them. But blacks who were married were not allowed to bring their wives. All black mineworkers felt that De Beers's diamonds were a symbol of love in the West but it is destroying their families in Africa. If a black employee died he will be buried there for fear that he might have diamond in his body. His family will never see him again.[47] In addition, "The Afrikaner working class benefited in particular from the government's policy of white job protection. Almost every skilled trade and craft was reserved for white workers. The English-speakers congregated, were said to have the greatest concentration of swimming pools outside of Beverly Hills. But the main beneficiaries were Afrikaners. In 1946 Afrikaner incomes on per capita basis were just under half that of English speaker incomes. By 1970 they had passed the two-thirds mark."[48] This is what the excruciating physical and psychological pain behind the glitter looks like. The conditions of South African black mineworkers are still the same.

In the midst of spiritual and political darkness in South Africa, there was a prophetic voice:

> It was during the 1970s that Bosch came to the fore as an outspoken critic of the *status quo* in South Africa. His overarching diagnosis of South African society

---

44. Richard Spoor, quoted in ibid.
45. Ibid.
46. Ibid., xx.
47. See ibid., 21–40.
48. Meredith, *Fate of Africa*, 413.

was that "the society [he lived in] is a sick society. The sickness is not presented only in the racist ordering of South African society, but also in the high rate of crime, of divorce, of alcoholism, etc." But "our sad failure," he said, was in the field of race relations. The failure presented itself, amongst other things, in the low wages paid to the black labourers, the system of black migrant labour which was even then diagnosed as a "cancer" in our society, and the way in which white South Africans unthinkingly humiliated black South Africans in everyday life. The reaction among whites to all these symptoms of sickness was mainly apathy and withdrawal from the problems by pretending they did not exist. The reaction among especially young black South Africans was growing impatience and even hatred and talk of violent reaction.

But then Bosch made a startling accusation: the South African church, he said, was an integral part of this sick society, part of the problem rather than part of the solution. For that reason he referred to both the Old and New Testaments to indicate God's warnings to his people in such situations.[49]

Low-earning income was for the black workers a common pattern in the colonized African countries, not only in South Africa. On the discrepancies of wages for the African employees during colonialism, Rodney comments:

> Wages paid to workers in Europe and North America was much higher than the wages to African worker in comparable categories. The Nigerian coal miner at Engu earned one shilling per day for working underground and nine pence per day for jobs on the surface. Such a miserable wage would be beyond comprehension of a Scottish or German coal miner, who could virtually earn in an hour what the Enugu miner was paid for six-day week. The same disparity existed with port workers. The records of the large American shipping company, Farell Lines, show that in 1955, of the total amount spent on loading and discharging cargo moving between Africa and America, five-sixths went to American workers and one-sixth to Africans. Yet, it was the same amount of cargo loaded and unloaded at both ends. The wages paid to the American stevedore and the European coal miners were still such as to insure that the capitalists made a profit. The point here is merely to illustrate how much greater was the rate of African exploitation.

He continues:

> Where European settlers were found in considerable numbers, the wage differential is readily perceived. In North Africa the wages of Moroccans and Algerians differential were from 16 percent to 25 percent those of Europeans. In East Africa the position was much worse, notably in Kenya and Tankanyika. A comparison with white settler earning and standard brings out by sharp contrast how incredibly the African wages were. While Lord Delamere controlled 100,000 acres of Kenyan's land, the Kenyan had to carry a *kipande* pass in his own country to beg for a wage of 15 or 20 shillings per month. The absolute limit of brutal exploitation was found in the southern parts of the continent; in southern Rhodesia, for example, agricultural laborers rarely received more than 15 shillings per month. Worker in mines get a little more if they were semi-skilled, but they also had more intolerable working conditions. Unskilled laborers in the

---

49. Kritzinger and Saayman, *David J. Bosch*, 89.

mines of northern Rhodesia often got a little as 7 shillings per month. A truck driver on the famous copper belt was in a semi-skilled grade. In one mine, Europeans performed that job for 30 pounds per month, while in another, Africans did it 3 pounds per month.[50]

To this Catherine C. Vidrovitch adds:

> Mining had played early in colonial history. Diamonds were discovered in South Africa in 1867, and gold in Rand in 1886; in Rhodesia, gold had been mined since 1893. The first mines in Namibia (southwest Africa) date from the same period. In the Belgian Congo, mining of copper at Shaba (Katanga) and of diamonds at Kasai began in the first decades of the twentieth century. In Northern Rhodesia (Zambia), the copperbelt started production in 1920s, and diamonds were discovered in Angola in 1912 and in Sierra Leone in the early 1930s. The mines, although great consumers of manpower, were often situated in underpopulated areas. The chronic shortage of labor led to a systematic organization of migrations, and compounds were established that housed large concentrations of migrations of workers. In Southern Africa, first Indians were brought to work in the sugar cane plantations of Natal. Next, Chinese were recruited. By 1905, 27 percent of the workers in the gold mines were Orientals. This proved to aggravate the racial problem, however, and soon mines ceased to employ Chinese.
>
> Thus in the interior of the continent there arose the scourge of recruiters, who at an early stage organized the first great labor migrations. South Africa obtained workers chiefly from Nyasaland (Malawi) and Mozambique; in 1929–1930, 10 to 12 percent of the budget of Mozambique derived from the 50,000 emigration permits officially negotiated with Transvaal via the Witwatersrand Native Labour Association (WNLA), created by the Chamber of Mines. These 250 recruiters had the right to engage up to 80,000 Mozambicans a year. Between 1913 and 1930, 900, 000 workers left for the mines, and of these a third returned with injuries. By the 1930s the WNLA had exhausted the local supply of manpower and was forced to broaden the scope of its recruitment. Of 31,000 miners recruited abroad in 1952, nearly half came from Portuguese territories, compared to 23 percent from Malawi, 16 percent from Tanzania, 10 percent from Namibia, and 6 percent, from Zambia. Of 371,000 miners in 1969, foreigners constituted 68 percent, of whom 27 percent were form Mozambique and 18 percent came from the Cape Province. Most of these were worker-peasants who had come to obtain a little ready money to supplement subsistence agriculture; the employers found maintain salaries at the lowest possible level.[51]

Meredith adds, "In 1970 it was estimated that more than 2 million men spent their lives circulating as migrants between their homes and urban employment. Many of them were deprived of all normal urban family life, confined for months on end to a bleak and barren existence in overcrowded barracks notorious for high rates of drunkenness and violence. Others spent hours each day travelling long distances and work in packed buses and trains, rising before dawn and returning home late into the night."[52] The migration of these African mineworkers was not like pulling work forces from different parts of the

---

50. Rodney, *How Europe Underdeveloped Africa*, 150, 151.
51. Vidrovitch, *Africa*, 226.
52. Meredith, *Fate of Africa*, 415.

United States. Africans, even though the majority have the same color skin, they speak many different dialects and languages. They have different religions and customs. They uphold different cultural values and norms. Adding to their cross-cultural tension, low wages, separation from the family, hard labor, and oppression, the helplessness of their situation often manifested through signs of maladjustment, such as "[t]heft, alcoholism, suicide, and magical and religious practices. These are symptoms of psychological resistance not necessarily objective manifestations of social resistance as practiced by the proletariat in the Russia. They are just as much means of accommodation to the system. Moreover, *each of these practices carries within it the power of Self-destruction.* Because in a coercive framework these indirect forms of resistance cannot express still vague grievances, they remain equivocal and can be manipulated or neutralized by the authorities."[53]

The power of self-destruction was not limited to men who were recruited and exported to work at different mines in Africa. It had poisonous ramifications on their families too. Hence, the self-destruction was not only psychological but was also social. It ruined families that are the core to African community.

> One of the strange ironies of the Western impact on the issue of polygamy in Africa is that instead of ending it altogether it has begun the process of making it more symmetrical. Far from the Western impact terminating situations where men have more than one wife, the Western impact in parts of Africa has sometimes resulted in women having more than one husband. This is particularly acute in those societies which export a lot of migrant labour to work in mines or cities either in those same countries or neighboring more prosperous societies. Southern Africa has been particularly affected by the consequence of large scale-separation of families as men trek to jobs distant from the places where their wives live, and wives in turn take *de facto* additional husbands while they wait. What has already emerged is the strange paradox of a Western world which once aspired to stop African men having more than one wife, and yet created conditions where African women are forced to have more than one husband.[54]

It is no wonder that social stability is far from reached in Africa. When the family is fragmented, society can hardly live in cohesiveness. When children grow up without a male figure, when wives are forced to marry another husband for biological, economic, and social needs, norms and values turn upside-down. Perverted family environments breed perverted generations who kill each other without mercy. Savagery is not genetic; it is a social problem created and enhanced through imbalanced global political and economic powers.

In February 2014, there were a number of huge demonstrations of the Anglo-American Company mineworkers in South Africa. Representing some 80,000 mineworkers who were on strike, the Association of Mineworkers and Construction Union (AMCU) said it would meet with employers on Tuesday, February 11. More than 80,000 mineworkers at Amplats, Impala Platinum (Implats) and Lonmin went on strike on January 23.

53. Vidrovitch, *Africa*, 232; emphasis mine.
54. Mazrui, *Africans*, 252.

The strikers were demanding a minimum monthly wage of 12,500 rand (about USD $1,200) for entry-level workers, an amount that was more than double the previous level. The mining companies said that the wage demands were unaffordable and unrealistic. Roger Baxter, the chief operations officer with the South African Chamber of Mines, said ongoing strikes in the country's platinum mines were costing South Africa around 400 million rand (about USD $36 million) a day. South Africa's mining sector was paralyzed by strikes and violent protests since August 2012. Dozens of people have been killed in strike-related violence ever since.[55]

> In other unrest, an Anglo American employee was in critical but stable condition after being assaulted by strikers while on his way to work at the Khuseleka mine near Rustenberg city earlier in the week, the company said. It said protesters have damaged at least 14 vehicles and it noted a "significant increase" in violence and intimidation.
>
> In 2012, South African police shot and killed several dozen miners during labour unrest at a Lonmin platinum mine. South Africa is the world's leading producer of platinum, which is used in medical, electronic and other industries.
>
> Separately, the death toll following an underground fire at a gold mine rose to nine after searchers found the body of the last miner who had been missing, the Harmony mining company said Friday. The miners were killed after an earthquake triggered a rock fall and a fire deep inside Harmony's Doornkop mine, west of Johannesburg. Two other Harmony miners died in accidents at other mines in recent days.
>
> Six of the nine miners killed at Doornkop were South African, and the three others came from Lesotho, Swaziland and Mozambique, according to union officials.[56]

The endless cycle of African poverty cannot be understood unless we see it through the eyes of history and we objectively analyze their past and present condition. It is a paradox if not a tragedy that millions of Africans are under the mercy of Western donors and Western philanthropists while the West is enriching itself through the minerals and natural resources of Africa. Living in this kind of disparity that is unjustifiable, legally and ethically indefensible, for more than four centuries, what kind of credibility and integrity does the West think that it has to teach Africans about democracy? And what explanation can evangelicals in the West provide to Africans for their silence?

> Jesus' attitude to justice and poverty goes beyond the message of the Old Testament prophets on the subject. The prophets had spoken in favor of the poor and the oppressed and in defense of their rights. Their prophetic discourse was clearly indicative of God's mind on their behalf: God's predilection for the poor and divine wrath at the injustice inflicted upon them. Jesus, however, does not manifest a preferential option for the poor; he is not merely "in their favor." He identifies with them personally and associates with them preferentially. He is not only *for* the poor; he belongs *to* and *with* them. In this belonging and association

---

55. See "Mining Employers, Workers to Hold Talks in South Africa," PressTV, February 10, 2014, http://www.presstv.ir/detail/2014/02/10/350036/talks-planned-over-south-africa-strikes/.

56 See "Markikana Massacre 16 August 2012," South African History Online, http://www.sahistory.org.za/article/marikana-massacre-16-august-2012 (accessed October 1, 2015).

of Jesus with the poor, God's preferential love for them comes to a climax. Jesus' attitude is not only indicative of God's mind for the poor; it embodies God's commitment to and involvement with them.[57]

This is where the missing link of Christian theology and missiology are evidently exposed in Africa. Charitable Western acts done in the midst of exploitation and injustice, in silence and indifferent to the situations of the African poor, are nowhere near the teachings of Jesus Christ about the poor, nor his identification and embodiment with the poor. "In the absence of all hope ambition dies, and the very self is weakened, corroded. There remains only the elemental will to live and to accept life on the terms that are available. There is a profound measure of resourcefulness in all life, a resourcefulness that is guaranteed by the underlying aliveness of life itself. The crucial question, then, is this: Is there any help to be found in the religion of Jesus that can be of value?"[58] What kind of development and church can be built on the "weakened, corroded" self? What kind of engineer would tell you first to destroy a foundation and then to build a castle? Practically, the Western "civilization" in Africa has been doing that. As of now, Western Christianity has not answered Thurman's question on Africa. From its inception to todays' expansion, Western Christianity in Africa, in the words of Katongole, is "[v]isible invisibility." He comments, "If Christianity is to be about the business of shaping a new future in Africa, it was becoming clear to me, Christianity itself would have to find a way of overcoming this Western heritage, to move beyond the narrow spiritual and pastoral areas to which it is consigned and claim full competence in the social material, and political realities of life in Africa."[59]

This is exactly the same question Thurman was asked by the Congolese more than a century and a half ago: "Has the savior you tell us of any power to save us from the rubber trouble?"[60] If I may amplify their question, they are saying, if our body is the temple of the Holy Spirit, why are the Belgian "Christians" destroying it? In the place of "rubber" add all the African minerals I mentioned in this book and the ones omitted. The messenger of the good news will have hundreds if not thousands of questions like this on their table to answer for Africans.

The sad thing is that the question of the Congolese was not a deep soteriological question like election, regeneration, justification, sanctification, or about the kingdom of God and the glorious hope and promise believers are given. Their question was one of survival. Africans are not bodiless souls who only need a salvation ticket for the paradise in the *not yet*. They need food, a decent place to live, health care, security, freedom, ownership, etc., in the *now*. To ask about the power and bondage of sin, about the control and influence of demonic spirits, and about the healing power of God from diseases is one thing—but asking to be saved from Belgians who came to their country under the guise of philanthropic and missionary work but then were cutting off their hands and legs is perplexing and disturbing. And it is the wrong way of starting the Christian pilgrimage.

57. Dupuis, *Who Do You Say I Am?*, 48; emphasis original.
58. Thurman, *Jesus and the Disinherited*, 36.
59. Katongole, *Sacrifice of Africa*, 10.
60. Hochschild, *King Leopold's Ghost*, 172.

How can the Congolese objectively see the love of God who gave his only begotten son as a sacrificed lamb for them? Jesus came to make them whole and give them an abundant life, not to cut them alive.

With their question unanswered, before the eyes of Western missionaries, in full awareness of Europe and the U.S., who claim to be the watchdogs of democracy and ombudsmen of human rights, Congolese were enslaved, amputated, killed, and plundered. A keen Western journalist rightly observed:

> I was reminded that the roots of Africa's dilemma were far deeper than the mere fact that its democratic revolution was happening simultaneously with Europe's. Indeed, Africa's misfortune, where the West is concerned, has always been deeper. How else to explain the ability of Europeans to rationalize the centuries-long slave trade, decades of forced labor for rubber and cotton, colonization on the fly and finally their abandonment of the continent to the very tyrants Africans were struggling to throw off? The answer lies partly in the fact that for the Europeans, Africa has always been an irresistible "other." This may sound like a tautology, but that does nothing to diminish its truth. Like the indelible taint of original sin, the problem of Africa in the minds of Westerners is that is Africa.[61]

The handpicked tyrant loyalists, like Mobutu, who got to the top leadership of African countries through the support and endorsement of Western powers, have dashed the hope of Africans who were eagerly waiting for their political emancipation from colonial powers. Katangole writes:

> It is quite true that the most damaging impact of colonialism in Africa was psychological: the freezing of Africa's history, and the erosion of her self-confidence. But to the extent that this same story is embodied and perpetuated within the nation-state, the latter has indeed become a burden—"the black man's burden" and even an "enemy"—whose constraining grip and violence the "masses" would constantly have to survive in attempt to advance their social struggles. In the final analysis, the critical issue arising out of this discussion is really not about the failures of the nation-state in Africa. The question is not so much one of what the nation-state had failed to do *for* Africans, but what it is doing *to* Africans—how it is narrating, defining and structuring their lives in terms of helplessness, disempowerment and violence.
>
> In terms of *telos*, this means that everyday practices cease to have any meaningful *telos* to energize them into forms of commitment, precisely because they are defined or narrated by the overriding story in such a way that denies of them being capable of any *telos*. This is indeed dis-empowering and points to the need for alternative narratives which can radically challenge and even provide an alternative definition of everyday social struggles in view of energizing those activities within a hopeful *telos*. Without any such alternative, the majority of Africans will feel condemned to a wobbly existence where "survival" becomes their chief and perhaps only project.[62]

Without a purposeful life and a ray of hope, living under dictatorial oppression in grinding cyclical poverty, survival and shaky existence have become the only options for

---

61. French, *Continent for the Taking*, 159.
62. Katongole, "Violence and Social Imagination," 41–42.

Africans. Even if Africans have the IQ of Albert Einstein or Steve Jobs, they die without altering the circumstances of their lives. *Telos* is an engine to pursue noble goals and to achieve them. It also gives a firm foundation and meaning for human existence. Without *telos* life is in disarray and Africans have been aimlessly floating from one yoke of burden to another.

To ensure that Africans would live in social, economic, and political predicaments created for them, the West left no stone unturned. And the Western diagnosis and treatment of African maladies always deals with and is limited to the symptoms or effects, not the causes. To make things worse, on Africa's social and economic scene, the West becomes both the victimizer and the Good Samaritan. Hence, Africans not only remain in their sick beds with confusion but they live and interact with the West with irreconcilable perceptions and values of the Western people. How can an African reconcile the godliness and humble service of Billy Graham on the continent with explorers like "Henry Morton Stanley who are still celebrated with stories about their great exploits, while the details of how he made Leopold's conquest possible, by driving long columns of heavily chained Africans to their death as they bore his boats and guns and supplies through the great forests of the Congo River basin? Stanley was, in fact, something of a sadist, and was known for shooting Africans on a whim, simply because he did not like the way they looked at him. Westerners have forgotten these truths, basking instead in the comforting myth of our civilizing mission, but unsentimental memories of Stanley live on with the Congolese."[63] "Exploration was followed, or accompanied by exploitation. The white man still came to trade, but he nearly always stayed to rule."[64] How can an African reconcile the work of Compassion International, a Christian organization that is committed to impoverished children and works with African churches to restore and give hope to African families with that of De Beers, which is driven by greed and literally destroying thousands if not millions of African families? The contradiction of the West is also evident in the financial system that is supposed to be neutral, scientific, ethical, and transparent.

63. French, *Continent for the Taking*, 53.
64. Neill, *History of Christian Missions*, 247.

Chapter 4

Banks in a Bankrupt Continent

The core problem with Africa is not an absence of cash, but rather that its financial markets are acutely inefficient—borrowers cannot borrow and lenders do not lend, despite the billions washing about.[1]

ECONOMY IS AN ESSENTIAL part of social and political life in any given society. In highly advanced countries, it is considered the lifeline of a nation and is handled in a sophisticated, organized, and operational system. Some countries have economic espionage and economic hit men. And these kinds of operations are funded well.[2]

Mismanagement of capital, capital outflow, and corruption in the banking system are rampant in Africa. The focus of this chapter is to explore this endemic problem, which is one of the major causes of poverty in Africa.

Banking system

The root history of banking in Africa goes beyond the geographical boundaries of the continent. Africa made major contributions to the establishment of European banks that turned around to haunt the financial life of the continent. Many of the eighteenth-century banks established in Liverpool and Manchester, the slaving metropolis and the cotton capital respectively, were directly associated with the triangular trade. The triangular trade included the mercantile system, production, and the slave trade. In 1718 William Wood said that the slave trade was "the spring and parent whence the others flow."[3]

The Heywood Bank was founded in Liverpool in 1773 and endured as a private bank until 1883, when it was purchased by the Bank of Liverpool. Its founders appear in the list of merchants trading to Africa in 1752 and their African interest survived up

---

1. Moyo, *Dead Aid*, 137.
2. Fialka, *War by other Means*; Fink, *Sticky Fingers*.
3. William Wood, *A Survey of Trade*, 193.

to 1807. The senior partner of one of the branches of the firm was Thomas Parke (of the banking firm of William Gregson, Sons, Parke and Morland), whose grandfather was a successful captain in the West Indian trade. In 1788, the firm set up a branch in Manchester at the suggestion of some of the leading merchants. The Manchester branch, called the "Manchester Bank," was well known for many years. Eleven of the fourteen Heywood descendants up to 1815 became merchants or bankers.

Thomas Leyland, one of active slave traders in Liverpool, became senior partner in the banking firm of Clarkes and Roscoe in 1802. Leyland struck off on his own in 1807, in a more consistent partnership with his slave-trade partner, Bullins, and the title of Leyland and Bullins was borne proudly and unstained for ninety-four years until the amalgamation of the bank, in 1901, with the North and South Wales Bank Limited. William Gregson, the founder of Hanly's bank, as well as Captain Richard Hanly, Robert Fairweather, Jonas Bold, Thomas Fletcher, etc., who founded the banks or became bankers, were mainly slave traders and were involved in the triangular trade.

What has been said of Liverpool is equally true of Bristol, London, and Glasgow. The famous Barclay from London, the founder of Barclay Bank, had two members of his Quaker family, David and Alexander, who were engaged in the slave trade in 1756. David was not only a slave trader; he owned a great plantation in Jamaica. His father's house in Cheapside was one of the finest in the city of London, and was often visited by royalty.

The rise of banking in Glasgow was intimately connected with the triangular trade. The first regular bank began business in 1750. Known as a ship bank, one of the original partners was Andrew Buchanan, a tobacco lord of the city. William Macdowall, Alexander Houston, and Andrew Cochrane were merchants who had big lucrative businesses in the West Indies. The Thistle Bank followed in 1761, an aristocratic bank, whose business lay largely among the rich West Indian merchants.[4]

In brief, what we can see in an indisputable way is that Africans' labor, their natural resources, and their own bodies and souls played a significant role in the banking system established in the UK.

Banks in Africa

One thing that I discovered during this research is that academic sources on certain topics during the colonial period in Africa are hard to find. For example, I looked for a book on the history of banks in Africa in my local libraries and at Amazon. I could not find one so, because of my limitations, I refer you again to the meticulous work of Walter Rodney:

> In the background of the colonial scene hovered the banks, insurance companies, maritime underwriters, and other financial houses. One can say "in the background" because the peasant never dealt directly with such institutions, and was generally ignorant of their exploiting functions. The peasant or worker had no access to the bank loans because he had no "securities" or "collateral." African banks and financial houses during colonialism mainly dealt with other

---

4. See E. Williams, *Capitalism and Slavery*, 98–102.

capitalists who could prove to the bankers that whatever happened the bank would recover its money and make a profit.

In the earliest years of colonialism, the banks of Africa were small and relatively independent. This applied to the *Banque de Senegal*, started in early 1853, and to the Bank of British West Africa which began as an offshoot of the shipping firm of elder Dempster. However, the great banking houses of Europe, which had carried or remote control of developments ever since the 1880s, soon moved in directly on the colonial banking scene when the volume of capitalist transactions made this worthwhile. The *Banque de Senegal* merged into the *Banque deL'Afrique Occidentale* (BAO) in 1901, acquiring links with the powerful Bank of Indochina, which in turn was a special creation of several powerful metropolitan French bankers. In 1924, the *Banque Commerciale de l'Afrique* (BCA) emerged in French territories, linked with *Credit Lyonnais* and the BNCI in France. By that time the Bank of British West Africa had its finance backed by Lloyds Bank, Westminster Bank, the Standard Bank, and the National Provincial Bank—all in England. The other great English banking firm, Barclays, moved directly into Africa. It purchased the Colonial Bank and set it up as Barclays DCO (i.e., Dominion and Colonial).

The Bank of British West Africa (which became the Bank of West Africa in 1957) and Barclays held between them the lion's share of the banking business of British West Africa, just as French West and Equatorial Africa were shared out between the BAO and the BCA. There was also a union of French and British banking capital in West Africa in 1949 with the formation of the British and French West Africa Bank. French and Belgian exploitation also overlapped in the financial sphere, since the *Socêtê Gênêrale* had both Belgian and capital. It supported banks in French Africa and the Congo. Other weaker colonial powers were served by the international banks such as Barclays, and also used their colonial territories as grazing ground for their own national banks. In Libya, the *Banco di Roma* and the *Banco di Napoli* operated; while in Portuguese territories the most familiar name was that of the *Banco Ultramarino*.

In Southern Africa, the outstanding banking firm was the Standard Bank of South Africa Ltd., started in 1862 in the Cape Colony by the heads of business houses having close connections with London. Its headquarters were placed in London, and it made a fortune out of financing gold and diamonds strikes, and through handling the loot of Cecil Rhodes and De Beers. By 1895, the Standard Bank spread into Bechuanaland, Rhodesia, and Mozambique, and it was the second British bank to be established in British East Africa. The actual scale of profits was quite formidable.

In 1960, the Standard Bank produced a net profit of 1,281,000 pounds and paid a 14 percent dividend to its shareholders. Most of the latter were in Europe or else were whites in South Africa, while the profit was produced mainly by the black people of South and East Africa. Furthermore, these European banks transferred the reserves of their African branches to the London head office to be invested in the London money market. This was the way in which most rapidly expatriated African surplus to the metropolis.[5]

Banks are financial institutions that are involved in borrowing and lending money. They take customers' deposits in return for paying customers an annual interest payment.

---

5. Rodney, *How Europe Underdeveloped Africa*, 162–63.

Banks play an important role in the economy for offering a service for people wishing to save. Banks also play an important role in offering finance to businesses that wish to invest and expand. These loans and business investments are important for enabling economic growth. Such institutions in colonial Africa are not meant to serve African customers. As Rodney observed, banks were "handling to the loot of Cecil Rhodes and De Beers." Banks were "making profits and paid a 14 percent dividend to its shareholders—white Europeans and South Africans."

This brings us to see the sword hanging on the necks of African countries—debt. Africa's external debt in the mid-80s was estimated at about $150 billion. This might seem insignificant when compared to the corresponding figure for other Third-World regions, particularly Latin America. It was, however, a very heavy burden for the fragile economies of Africa to bear. By the reckoning of the World Bank, Africa's debt represented about 36 per cent of its total GDP. Conclusions reached by the IMF are even more alarming. According to the 1985 data provided by the IMF for non-oil-exporting countries, debt represents up to 55 per cent of GDP, so that its relative weight is greater than that in all other developing areas. In fact, debt service for non-oil-exporting countries was estimated by the IMF to have raised exports of goods and services 27 percent during that year. This puts Africa second only to Latin America. In fact, in some countries—notably the Sudan, Zaire, and Côte d'Ivoire—debt has become a crushing burden on the balance payments, practically choking off growth.

The rapid accumulation of external debt is in itself due to the disequilibrium between resource needs and resources domestically available. In other words, external debt has been used to supplement declining domestic savings, augment foreign exchange receipts, and smooth the consumption path over time. Particularly, the growth of the fiscal deficit in many African countries has made a significant contribution to the debt problem.

In addition to these endogenous factors, there were even more exogenous factors that have contributed to the debt crisis. These include the slow growth in world demand for primary commodities, the aggressiveness of foreign banks in their lending behavior to African countries considered credit-worthy, structural changes in the flow of financial resources to Africa, the hardening of terms of external borrowing, and the appreciation of the currencies in which external debt is contracted and serviced.

The emergence of the external debt crisis has contributed in large measure to a lack of growth of the GDP in Africa. The instability of the countries stemmed the inflow of new resources or at best has led to higher borrowing costs and more stringent conditions for import payments.[6]

"Between 1970 and 1990, Africa lost half of its share of the world markets to other developing countries . . . This represented a loss of income for Africa about $70 billion per year. There was not enough money in the world—let alone in the World Bank—to fill this gap. It exceeded the amount of foreign aid being spent in all of Africa, Asia, and Latin America combined."[7] In addition to this subsidy for farmers in the West made Africa's economic woes more lamentable: "The members of the Organization of Economic

6. Senghor, *Towards a Dynamic African Economy*, 23–25.
7. Calderisi, *Trouble with Africa*, 18.

Cooperation and Development (OECD)—a club of rich nations—spend almost US $300 billion on agricultural subsidies (based on 2005 estimates). This is almost three times the total aid from OECD countries to all developing nations (of course, some aid advocates suggest compensating Africa for this imbalance with more aid). Estimates suggest that the Africa loses around US$500 billion each year because of restrictive trade embargoes—largely in the form of subsidies by Western governments to Western farmers."[8] To maintain income and investment, "African governments borrowed heavily in the 1970s. Total African debt had risen 24-fold since 1970 to a staggering $400 billion in 1996, which was equal to its yearly GNP, making the region the most heavily indebted in the world. (Latin America's debt amounted to approximately 60 percent of its GDP.) Currently debt service obligations absorb about 40 percent of export revenue, but only about half of the outstanding debts are actually being paid. On the other half, arrearages are continually being rescheduled."[9] "In the international trade game, African nations were caught in the forces they could not control. Crippled by foreign debt, they became net contributors to, not gainers from the Western economies. Foreign diagnosis (physician heal thyself) sagely recommended to the ailing economies remedies that could be enforced only by harsh repression and widespread suffering."[10]

Léonce Ndikumana and James K. Boyce, in their book *Africa's Odious Debts: How Foreign Loans and Capital Flight Bled a Continent* have superbly written about the role of international banks and corrupt African leaders in impoverishing Africans. "The capital flight from sub-Saharan countries over 1970–2008 period (in 2008 US dollars) amounted to $735 billion. This is equivalent to roughly 80 per cent of the combined GDP of these countries in 2008. This indicates that the capital flight from African countries is not a transitory product of unusual circumstances, but rather an outcome of persistent underlying causes. If the funds that left African countries this period were invested in assets that earned the interest rate on short-term US Treasury bills, the cumulative stock of flight capital with imputed interest earnings in 2008 would amount to $944 billion."[11] This huge amount of money could partly pay the debt of these countries and could be invested in infrastructure, education, technology, and development to improve the income and living standard of Africans. "In loans to Africa and other developing nations, the people were the principals and top government officials were the agents. Officials borrowed in the name of the government, lined their own pockets and those of their cronies, and left the people with the debts."[12]

In his book *The Secret History of the American Empire: Economic Hit Men, Jackals, and the Truth about Global Corruption,* John Perkins lucidly explains the identity and role of the World Bank this way: "The World Bank (WB) is not really a world bank at all; it is, rather, a U.S. bank. Ditto its closest sibling, the IMF. Of the twenty-four directors on their boards, eight represent individual countries: the United States, Japan, Germany, France, the United Kingdom, Saudi Arabia, China, and Russia. The rest of the

---

8. Moyo, *Dead Aid*, 115.
9. Ayittey, *Africa in Chaos*, 11.
10. Walls, *Cross-Cultural Process*, 109.
11. Ndikumana and Boyce, *Africa's Odious Debts*, 46.
12. Ibid., 28.

184 member countries share other sixteen directors. The United States controls nearly 17 percent of the vote in the IMF and 16 percent in the World Bank; Japan is second with about 6 percent in the IMF and 8 percent in the World Bank, followed by Germany, the United Kingdom, and France, each with around 5 percent. The United States holds veto power over major decisions and the president of the United States appoints the World Bank president."[13] The World Bank has consistently supported ill-conceived aid projects that do terrible harm both to the poor and the environment. Out of 189 projects recently audited, 106 were found to have serious shortcomings or to be a "complete failure."[14]

The role of this bank in Africa's economic misery is enormous. To cite one example, during Mobutu's last breath, when the financial hemorrhage drained the national bank and he was unable to pay salaries, it was the World Bank that played the role of the Red Cross. But it did not avert the inevitable—Mobutu was overthrown through another dictator assisted by the U.S.

Country	Year	Amount	Lead and manager banks
Zaire	1974	$22,264,043	American Express International Banking Cooperation Crèdit Commercial de France
Sudan	1974	$200,000,000	Crèdit Commercial De France Banque National de Paris Banque Arabe et International d'Investment
Gabon	1976	$20,000,000	American Express International Banking Corporation Citicorp International Bank Ltd Wells Fargo International
Cóte D'Ivorie	1976	$50,000,000	Citicorp International Bank Ltd Brandts Ltd Chase Manhattan Ltd Amex Bank Ltd Bank of Montreal First Chicago Ltd Merrill Lynch International Bank Ltd
Kenya	1976	$200,000,000	National Westminster Bank Group Bank of Montreal Bank of Tokyo Ltd Barclays International Group Chase Manhattan Banking Group Citicorp International Group Deutsche Bank Compagnie Financière Luxembourge First Chicago Ltd Fuji Bank Ltd Manufacturers Hanover Ltd Royal Bank of Canada Standard Chartered Bank

13. Perkins, *Secret History of the American Empire*, 3.
14. See Hancock, *Lords of Poverty*, Part 4.

Nigeria	1981	$308,000,000	Midland Bank Ltd, BankAmerica Int. Group, Barclays Bank Group, Croker National Bank, Fuji Bank Ltd, Mitusi Trust & Banking Company Ltd Orion Royal Bank Ltd[480]

The lending agencies knew that their loans were not used for bona fide purposes and, invested in projects whose returns would enable borrowing countries to pay them back with interest. These lenders did not lack competence to screen borrowers with due diligence or make borrowers accountable for every penny they take. However, for the same negative result they kept on lending and accumulating the debt on these poor nations until the burden of loans breaks their back. According to the studies done by the World Bank, African Development Bank, and Inter-American Development Bank, "securing loan approvals was a more powerful motivator for staff than working to ensure project success or larger development goals."[16]

A further motive for lending by official creditors—a motive that again is independent of the loan's productive impact in the borrowing country—is export promotion. In the case of Export Credit Agencies (ECAs) such as the US Export-Import Bank, this is, in fact, the explicit primary objective. But it has also been a significant motive in bilateral official development assistance, the importance of which is reflected in correlations between the aid disbursements and donor exports. Multilateral creditors are also aware of the political salience of export contracts: the World Bank, for example, maintains state-level procurement records in the USA in order to facilitate lobbying of congress corporations winning bank contracts.

More immediate gratification came upfront in the form of loan origination fees. These could be looked at as profits in the same financial quarter that the loan was issued. A 1.5 per cent fee on a $100 million loan would amount to $1.5 million, a tidy sum. This was taken off the top from the money disbursed to the borrower.[17]

Greed is indiscriminate of people's skin color. African dictators who are blinded by the love of money have made the lives of Africans unbearable. High infant mortality, lack of sanitation, high illiteracy, food shortages, malnutrition, rampant crime and violence in various African cities, are because of the few who are hoarding while the majority are starving. "As of 2008, Congo-Brazzaville's external debt stood at almost $5.5 billion. In a nation of 3.6 million people, this amounted to more than $1,500 per person. The same year, according to World Bank data, 74 per cent of the country's population lived on less than $2 per day. In Libreville, the capital of Gabon, elegant glass marble palaces line Omar Bongo Triumphal Boulevard. These edifices were constructed at a cost of $500 million by President Omar Bongo, who ruled the country for four decades until his death in Barcelona in 2009. [He] forsake roads, schools and hospitals for the

---

15. Adopted from Ndikumana and Boyce, *Africa's Odious Debts*, 26.

16. Ibid., 24.

17. For further details, see Ndikumana and Boyce, *Africa's Odious Debts*, 22–25; and Moyo, *Dead Aid*.

sake of Bongo's 66 bank accounts, 183 cars, 39 luxury properties in France and grandiose government constructions in Libreville."[18]

Williams rightly observes:

> The medium of exchange, which in relatively recent times became money, was expanded to facilitate the spread of necessities of life for the common welfare. But somewhere back through the years the whole upward trend was reversed as aggression inspired by greed led to the easy acquisition of both wealth and political power by the daring few at the expense of the many. Mass poverty, and the ignorance and disease which are its inseparable companies, spread as the wealth belonging to all the people came to be owned or controlled by the few in every country, no matter what system or ideology is claimed. This is no the direction civilization is supposed to take. We have what should be of reflection: advances in science, technology, great skyscraper cities, skies filled with aircrafts, moon flights—improvements in everything *but man himself, his murderous, greedy soul being still ages back there in the caves of his ancestors.*[19]

Both the lenders and borrowers physically live in luxurious houses, drive the best and most expensive cars, and have millions in their accounts. But mentally and psychologically, they are "still ages back in the caves of [their] ancestors." President Mobutu Sese Seko of Zaire, the eccentric dictator, owned fifty-one Mercedes Benz motor cars, while at the same time he dismissed 7,000 school teachers in the late 80s from the Zairean education system on the grounds that there was no money to pay their salaries. Despite such outrages, his government remained one of the most favored recipients of Western aid in Africa.

Foreign Aid

Aid to developing countries became an institution as World War II was ending. In July 1944 a group of forty-four nations (including twenty-four from Latin America and the Caribbean, Africa, and Asia) met in the high-ceilinged, wood-paneled buildings of the Mount Washington Hotel in the New Hampshire resort of Bretton Woods to design a multilateral postwar financial architecture. British economist John Maynard Keynes laid a plan to construct a system that would provide a lender of last resort, a kind of group insurance against another Great Depression. As the result of that meeting, the International Monetary Fund (IMF) and International Bank of Reconstruction or World Bank were created. Though the wealthy countries stack decision making to ensure that the more money a member country provided, the more votes it had, these new institutions were expressly constructed to foster trade capital flows, growth, and economic development.[20] It was clear that the post-world war Europe needed a massive financial injection to rebuild its infrastructure, reduce unemployment and poverty, and reopen several factories that became unproductive because of the war. Moyo writes: "Post war aid can be broken down into seven broad categories: its birth at Bretton Woods in the

---

18. Ndikumana and Boyce, *Africa's Odious Debts*, 18.
19. C. Williams, *Destruction of Civilization*, 330; emphasis added.
20. Brautigam, *Dragon's Gift*, 26; and Moyo, *Dead Aid*, 10–11.

1940s; the era of the Marshall Plan in the 1950; the decade of industrialization of the 1960s; the shift towards aid as an answer to poverty in the 1970s; aid as the buttress of democracy and governance in the 1990s; culminating in the present-day obsession with aid as the only solution to Africa's myriad of problems."[21]

This author's concern is the current Western obsession with aid for Africa. "In 2000, Africa became the focus of orchestrated world-wide pity . . . Thus the way was paved for the army of moral campaigners—the pop stars, the movie stars, the new philanthropists and even Pope John Paul II—to carve out niches for themselves, as they took on the fight for more, not less, aid to be sent to Africa, even after the billions of dollars in debt were cancelled—in essence, cancelling debt on the one hand, and replacing it with a swath of new aid, and the prospect of fresh debt all over again, with the other. The aid campaigners capitalized on the success of raising cash for the aid; something entirely different . . . One disastrous consequence of this has been that honest, critical and serious dialogue and debate on the merits and demerits of aid have atrophied."[22]

When we look at the foreign aid poured from the West to the Mobutu's of Congo, Barre's of Somalia, and al-Bashir's of the Sudan, regimes with proven dictators and human right abuses, it raises ethical and value questions on the motives and modus operandi of the Western governments' involvement in Africa after the so called "independence." "In trying to correct Africa's problems, no one was satisfied or vindicated" said, Robert Calderisi who worked for the World Bank in Africa for many years and worked for the UN. "Donors saw themselves offering a safety net to someone in free fall; Africans thought they were being hounded all the way to the ground. Hoping to stabilize the situation, aid agencies sometimes felt they were pouring concrete into quicksand. Meanwhile, Africans believed they were undergoing painful procedures without anesthetics and being asked to stop wriggling and whining on the operating table. It was a colossal misunderstanding."[23] Moyo summarizes the effect of Western aid in Africa in these mind-captivating words:

> Has more than US$1 trillion in development assistance over the last decades made African people better off? No. In fact, across the globe the recipients of this aid are worse off; much worse off. Aid has helped make the poor poorer, and growth slower. Yet aid remains a centerpiece of today's development policy and one of the biggest ideas of our time.
>
> The notion that aid can alleviate systemic poverty, and has done so, is a myth. Millions in Africa are poorer today because of aid; misery and poverty have not ended but have increased. Aid has been, and continues to be, an unmitigated political, economic, and humanitarian disaster for most parts of the developing world.[24]

For example, "97 percent of the government budget of Ethiopia and The Gambia is attributed to foreign aid."[25] The higher foreign aid the African country receives

---

21. See Moyo, *Dead Aid*, 10–28.
22. Ibid., 27.
23. Calderisi, *Trouble with Africa*, 150.
24. Moyo, *Dead Aid*, xix.
25. Ibid., 72.

the lazier the people become and the higher innovation and creativity are hampered and the greater the degree of corruption. "More than $2 trillion foreign aid has been transferred from rich countries to the poor for the past fifty years—Africa the biggest recipient, by far. Yet regardless of the motivation for aid-giving—economic, political or moral—aid has failed to deliver the promise of sustainable economic growth and poverty reduction."[26] "Since independence Africa has received far more foreign aid than any other region in the world. More than $300 billion of Western aid has been sunk into Africa, but with little discernible result."[27] The top ten poorest countries in the world are in sub-Saharan Africa. Paradoxically, Congo is the poorest of the poor (see table 1 below). These countries are rich in minerals and have been receiving foreign aid since their independence.

The West gives aid to African countries regardless of the recipient country's human rights, corruption, or democratic election record. "Oil-rich Cameroon ruled by the dictator Paul Biya since 1982 and ranked by the BGO Freedom House as one of the fourteen worst countries in Africa for political and civil liberties, received aid worth almost $1.5 billion in 2006. Freedom House gave to Ethiopia, another donor favorite, a dismal five out of seven on both civil and political liberties (with one being best). Between 2004 and 2006, donors gave Ethiopia $5.6 billion in aid. When we move from the rhetoric to the reality of aid, it seems that in the less publicized cases the Chinese and the traditional donor community are not so far apart."[28]

Moyo provides not only the negative effect of Western aid in Africa but also why it is not effective and why the West keeps on injecting aid money into the continent despite its disastrous consequences on social, economic, political, and developmental aspects of the recipient nations. Her scholarly and brazen work is a homemade medicine for a continent that has not been able to stand and climb the world economic ladder for the last five hundred years. However, aid is not an economic disease that one can easily cure. It is addiction. "Like the challenges someone addicted to drugs might face, the withdrawal is bound to be painful. Drug taker, or drug-pusher, in the end someone has to have the courage to say no."[29]

As of now neither Africa nor the West is willing to be free of this addiction that is ruining societies on both ends of the Atlantic. The emergence of China as an investor and economic power might turn things around in Africa. It is a big "might." With the corrupt African leaders and corrupt African elites that jointly rob African wealth, neither the West nor the East can bring a fundamental change in Africa. Despite this unpromising scenario, China is involved in Africa. "In an effort to help fast-track Africa's development, China has in recent years pledged to train, 15,000 African professionals, build thirty hospitals and 100 rural schools, and increase the number of Chinese government scholarships to African students from the current 2,000 per year to 4,000 per year by 2009. In 2000 China wrote off US 1.2 billion in African debt. In 2003 it forgave another US$750 million. In 2002, China gave US$ 1.8 billion in development aid to African

---

26. Ibid., 28.
27. Meredith, *Fate of Africa*, 683.
28. Brautigam, *Dragon's Gift*, 285.
29. Moyo, *Dead Aid*, 75.

countries. In 2006 alone, China signed trade deals almost US$ 60 billion. The Chinese are moving in, and they move in a big way."[30] We'll look at this issue in depth later.

If foreign aid is not working, why does the West keep on injecting itself in African countries? Is aid the only economic prescription the West thinks works for Africa? Moyo answers these questions: "By the mid-1950s Africa was undergoing profound changes—with Western powers loosening the chains of colonialism, many countries were gaining their independence. Countries such as Ghana in 1957, Kenya in 1963, and Malawi and Zambia in 1964 broke from the colonial fold to become independent states between 1956 and 1966; in all, thirty-one African countries did so. Independent they may have been on paper, but independence dependent in the technical largesse of their former colonial masters was the reality. For the West, aid became a means by which Britain and France combined their new-found altruism with a heft dollop of self-interest—maintaining geopolitical holds. For the U.S aid became the tool of another political contest—the cold war."[31]

Moyo outlines the following points to show how the Western aid affected Africa:

1. With aids help, corruption fosters corruption; nations quickly descend into a vicious cycle of aid. Foreign aid props up corrupt governments—providing them with freely usable cash. These corrupt governments intervene with the rule of law, the establishments of transparent civil institutions and the protection of civil liberties, making both domestic and foreign investment in poor countries unattractive.

2. In a context of high degrees of corruption and uncertainty, fewer entrepreneurs (domestic or foreign) will risk their money in business ventures where corrupt officials can lay claim to its proceeds, so investment stagnates, and falling investment kills growth.

3. Unfortunately, unfettered money (the prospect of sizable ill-gotten gains) is exceptionally corrosive, and misallocates talent. In an aid-dependent environment, the talented—the better-educated and more-principled, who should be building the foundations of economic prosperity—become unprincipled and are drawn from productive work towards nefarious activities that undermine the country's growth prospects. Those who remained principled are driven away, either to the private sector or abroad, leaving the posts that remain to be filled by the relatively less-educated, and potentially more vulnerable to graft.

4. Endemic corruption also targets public contracts. In these environments, contracts which should be awarded to those who can deliver on the best terms, in the best time, are given to those whose principal aim is to divert as much as possible to their own pockets. What ensue are lower-quality infrastructure projects, and enfeebled public services, to the detriment of growth.

5. The allocation of government spending suffers as corrupt officials are likely to choose projects on the basis of public welfare and more on the opportunities for extorting bribes and diverting funds. The bigger the project the bigger the opportunity.

30. Ibid., 104.
31. Ibid.

6. Aid increases the risk of conflict. In the past five decades, an estimated 40 million Africans have died in civil wars scattered across the continent; equivalent to the population of South Africa (and twice the Russian lives lost in the Second World War).

7. Aid engenders laziness on the part of the African policymakers. This may in part explain why, among many African leaders, there prevails a kind of insouciance, a lack of urgency, in remedying Africa's critical woes. Because aid flows are viewed (rightly so) as permanent income, policymakers have no incentive to look for other, better ways of financing their country's longer-term development.[32]

The ultimate indictment of foreign aid and the role of NGOs in Africa comes from the pen of John Perkins:

> NGOs enforce Western cultural, social, and economic standards that create a gap between aid workers and the people they're trying to serve—a gap that Africans are constantly striving to narrow by emulating the foreigners. Western values overturn cultural beliefs and send local economic systems into upheaval . . .
>
> Aid organizations are like a fig leaf that Western governments hide behind when they don't have—or want—a diplomatic or political solution. In any conflict, any crisis, Aid organizations go in first. So the West can say "look, we're doing something," even if they don't really want to solve the real problems in the end.
>
> Ultimately, it's not just that the West is apathetic or has no motivation to solve conflicts; it is that the West has a real stake in keeping Africa poor. People in Western countries have sincere feelings of charity and they have faith that aid works—but Western governments and multi-national corporations reap enormous benefits from the continued instability and destitution of African countries. The successful manipulation of the cheap labor and agricultural products, smuggled resources, and arms trading relies on corrupt politicians, prolonged warfare, and an underdeveloped civil society that lacks the capacity to stand up for its rights. If there were peace and transparency in the Congo, it would be much more difficult to exploit the mineral resources; if there were no rebel groups or tribal conflicts, there would be no market for small arms. . .if the West truly wanted to see a stable, developed Africa; the continent would be well on its way. Instead, the situation is worse after decades of Western involvement and billions of dollars of aid money.[33]

The metaphor I used in the introduction, "Africa is like an antelope in the jaw of a crocodile, half alive half dead," is not far from the truth and the real situation and existence of many African states. The irony of dependency further elaborates the enigma of foreign aid:

> All the evidence seems to suggest that post-colonial Africa has to try to walk a tightrope between the abyss of decay and the sea of dependency. When an African countrytry to break out of dependency, it finds itself and its institutions

---

32. Ibid., 49–66. I have made this quotation a numbered list.
33. Perkins, *Secret History of the American Empire*, 254–55.

in the process of decay. Nkrumah's Ghana and Nyerere's Tanzania put up a fight against dependency—and found their economies condemned to decomposition.

On the other hand, Francophone African countries such as the Ivory Coast have so far averted too rapid a pace of economic decay but only at the expense of considerable dependence upon the former colonial power.

Post-colonial Africa is finding it hard to walk that tightrope. Virtually all African countries have fallen into either the abyss of decay or the ocean of dependency. Some countries are desperately swinging between the two.[34]

In a different chapter, we shall closely examine how such desperate conditions set the stage for China and enabled her to run her affair in Africa with minimal contest from the West.

Top 10 Poorest African Countries- 2013 List[35]

Rank	Name of Country	Per capital income
1	Congo	$364.48
2	Liberia	$490.41
3	Zimbabwe	$516.47
4	Burundi	$639.51
5	Eritrea	$776.98
6	Central African Republic	$789.21
7	Niger	$863.46
8	Malawi	$882.67
9	Togo	$926.67
10	Madagascar	$948.86

Source: Global Finance Magazine.

It is so absurd that Congo (formerly known as Zaire) is listed as Africa's poorest country. In various sections of this book, I've stated the natural wealth of this country. To make you understand how all of us who benefited from the natural resources of Congo impoverished her, let me give you more information about the paradoxical existence of the Congolese.

In area it can swallow up France completely.[36] In mineral resources it could buy France if France is for sale . . .

34. Mazrui, *Africans*, 213.

35. See http://answersafrica.com/top-10-poorest-countries-in-africa.html.

36. Those who speak of the Zaire Republic often forge that this is an immense territory, ten times the size of Great Britain, five times that of France, three times that of Nigeria, eleven times the size of Ghana and eight times that of Belgium. Superimposed on a map of Western Europe, the Republic of Zaire would cover Belgium, France, Holland, Denmark, Sweden, Norway, Luxemburg, Spain, West Germany, Portugal, and Switzerland. Thus, the size of Zaire is a permanent feature that must be taken into account when any interpretations of political events in Zaire are made or when the country is compared to other African states.

The Republic of Zaire is also rich. The potential wealth of the country is enormous, whether one

> Without the minerals that Zaire exports[37] to the outside world, it is estimated that up to a third of the airpower of the North Atlantic Treaty Organization would be in a serious trouble. Defence budgets would have to increase or perhaps aeroplanes would be in short supply or perhaps both difficulties would be encountered. International civil aviation might also be affected very seriously. Aircraft could be so expensive that some of the major international airlines would shut down all together. And yet the same country which is in a position to hold international air traffic to ransom cannot even maintain its own modest fleet of aircraft. The national airline periodically lays off staff, or runs short of spare parts for its antiquated aeroplanes, and seeks either Israel or Western investors to bail it out for another few years. Zaire is a tragic illustration of how Africa's resources help to industrialise the Western world, while Africa itself remains pitifully stagnant.[38]

The values, principles, strategies, motives and goals of the West as they intervene and are involved in Africa to grab natural resources are baffling to a logical mind. And it is difficult if not impossible to get a satisfactory rationale and justification for it. One thing, however, is true of the West: as they are good in building capitalism at home they are also effective and efficient in creating systemic poverty and disaster in Africa.[39]

But, what does the Bible say about ownership and utilizing natural resources? Wright comments:

> Since the earth is given to all human kind, its resources were meant to be shared and be available to all. Access to, and use of, the resources of the whole planet constitute the legacy bequeathed to the whole human race. The creation narratives cannot be used to justify privatized, individually exclusive claims of ownership, since it is to humanity as a whole that the earth is entrusted. This is *not* to say that there can be no legitimate private ownership of material goods . . . It *is* to say that such individual property rights, even when legitimate, always remain subordinate to the prior right of all people to have access to, and use of, the resources of the earth. In other words, the claim "I (or we) own it" is never a final answer in the economic moral argument. For, ultimately, God owns all things and I (or we) hold them only in trust. And God holds us answerable to himself for others who might have greater need of that which is in our possession. Ownership of land and resources does not entail an absolute right of disposal, but rather responsibility for administration and distribution. The right of all to *use*

---

considers agricultural possibilities, or the mineral, which have yet to be accurately estimated, or the potential resources of energy. See Kanza, "Zaire's Foreign Policy," 235.

37. In reality it is the Western companies that own different mines that export minerals from Zaire and other African countries. "In addition to being the main consumer of Africa's mineral wealth, the West is the main manager of that wealth. A few Western firms control the processing, manufacturing, and marketing of most of Africa's mineral resources. Anglo-American, DeBeers, Roan Selection Trust, the old Union Miniere are only a few of the names that have shaped this phase of Africa's contribution to Western industrialisation. This is quite apart from the oil giants—Shell, British Petroleum (BP), Gulf, Exxon, Mobil, Chevron, Texaco and smaller independent firms. Even the smaller ones often have capital value which is greater than the Gross National Product of most African states," Mazrui, *Africans*, 164.

38. Ibid., 308.

39. For an in-depth study, see Valentine, *Culture and Poverty*; and Lewis, "The Culture of Poverty," 19–25.

the resources of the earth seems to be morally prior to right of any to *own* them for exclusive enjoyment.[40]

Donald Kraybill, in his book, *The Upside-Down Kingdom*, states that within God's redemptive plan lies the scoioeconomic essence of the kingdom of God. More than that, the Jubilee demonstrates God's prevailing principle of justice, equality, and his concern for the poor. The Jubilee occurs every seventh sabbatical year, and it shook up the Hebrew society in three primary ways. Land was left fallow and was returned to the family that owned it at the beginning of the fifty-year period. Slaves were released from bondage, and debts were cancelled. These three—land, slaves, and debts were elements of the economic fabric of the Israelites and the Jubilee covers them all. In doing so, God prevented the oppression of the poor and downtrodden by providing reliable and systemic means of redistribution and safeguards against rampant greed and merciless exploitation.

The Lord sought to instill in the minds of his people the concepts of divine ownership, divine liberation, compassion, mercy, rest from labor, and grace. Reverberating throughout the concept of Jubilee is the message of God's ownership of natural and human resources. It is for this reason that slaves can be released, debts erased, and land redistributed. It is entirely all the Lord's to do with as he pleases.

The driving motivation for the Jubilee was Israel's liberation from Egypt by the Lord's redemptive hand. This episode of Hebrew history was etched on the hearts of every person residing within the context of Jewish culture, and as such would have proven a prevalent inspiration for providing for their own poor and marginalized in a way that mirrors their own liberation.

The New Testament has no less concern for the poor. "What line ought Christianity to take in economics, and what trend ought it to pursue with the means at its disposal?" asked Moltmann. And he answered: "The Old Testament always recognized the earth as 'the Lord's property.' The earth is the Lord's and the fullness thereof, the world and those who dwell therein' (Ps. 24:1). Rabbinical exegesis used the word *oikonomos* at this point, and explained: 'God is the Lord of the house, because the whole world is his property, and Moses is his oikonomos.' When in the New Testament Christ is acknowledged as the Lord of God's kingdom, it means nothing less than this. The 'house' of which Jesus is Lord and which is to be kept in order according to his will, is called *oikumene*, the world, and 'those who dwell therein' are called *katoikunets*. In this sense economics cannot be excluded from the liberating lordship of Christ."[41] The kingdom of God is the rule or reign of God. According to the Gospels, the kingdom of God is dynamic, always becoming, spreading, and growing like yeast in dough. When God's rule impacts our horizontal or social and vertical or class relationship the kingdom of God is actualized in the midst of society. "Mercy, love and compassion are the new yardsticks of God's inverted kingdom."[42] And "the kingdom is something people enter, not something that enters them. It is a state of affairs, not a state of mind."[43]

40. Wright, *Old Testament Ethics*, 147–48; emphasis his.
41. Moltmann, *Church in the Power of the Spirit*, 173; emphasis original.
42. Kraybill, *Upside-Down Kingdom*, 108.
43. Ibid., 18.

Despite this biblical truth, human history is marred by wars over natural resources, exploitation, oppression and the dehumanization of people. It doesn't seem that we have taken a lesson from history. Philips observes:

> Human nature has hardly ben remolded. Prehistoric societies were often at blows over natural resources, food water, and wood for fire and shelter. Modern history has been only slightly subtle. Natural resources caused or aggravated sixteenth, seventeenth, and eighteenth-century wars to secure Baltic timber and naval stores, North Atlantic fisheries, East Indies spices, Caribbean sugar and salt, as well as New world gold and silver. After the industrial revolution, fossil fuels such as coal and oil moved into great-power gun sights.
>
> Many resource grabs have succeeded. The broad dilemma for the twenty-first century United States unfortunately has a financial twist. Past leading powers have eventually suffered from imperial hubris—a misplace cocksureness that leads them into a strategic they can no longer afford. The result has often been a humble hegemon, left with crippling debt burdens, lost trade advantages, a stricken currency, and increasing vulnerability as rivals increase their stature as creditor nations, financial centers, and technological innovators.[44]

The West might preach and teach democracy to the Africans but they cannot model it to them. African despots might occupy the highest political seat in their countries, but they cannot lead. Since the words of the powerful are not backed by action, they could not win the hearts of the observers and influence them to do well. Social, economic, historical, and cultural progress in Africa is hampered by the greed of external powers and their African loyalist political leaders who are driven by insatiable hunger for power, money, and luxury in the midst of misery.

---

44. Philips, *America's Theocracy*, 5–6.

Chapter 5

Compendium of Energy Resources

The earth can exist without human beings and did so for millions of years, but the human race cannot exist without the earth and other living things. So human beings are dependent on the earth, but the earth is not dependent on human beings. The simple conclusion for this realization is that human civilization has to be integrated into the ecosystem of the earth, not, conversely, that the earth must be subjugated to the human system of domination.[1]

ENERGY IS VITAL FOR basic needs and better lives, yet half the world's population lacks adequate energy access. As many as 1.2 billion of those lacking energy are children. Energy is essential . . . like food and water. It's the key to a better life for half the world's population, improving health, education and longevity. The world's strongest economies continue to turn to coal as the sustainable go-to fuel and the catalyst that enables people to live longer and better.[2] "[For] 600 million [people] in sub-Saharan Africa, life as it is known in the rich world stops after dark. Vietnam consumes as much power as all of sub-Saharan Africa outside South Africa . . . Without reliable power, business and economies cannot develop; factories cannot meet orders; vital connections to markets cannot be maintained. More than half of African business leaders identify a lack of power as a large constraint on growth. No surprise that when it comes to pressing development needs, many of Africa's most dynamic leaders say that power is more important than anything else."[3]

In Africa, power is inaccessible, unaffordable, and unreliable for most people. This traps people in poverty—students find it difficult to read after dark, clinics cannot refrigerate vaccines, and businesses have shorter operating hours.

---

1. Moltmann, *Sun of Righteousness Arise!*, 34.

2. https://www.advancedenergyforlife.com/?utm_source=GOOGLE&utm_medium=cpc&utm_term=energy%252520sources&utm_campaign=Energy%257cUS#.

3. Elliot, "Lighting up Africa," 76.

Today, 25 African countries face an energy crisis. The African continent is well endowed with energy resources but most remain untapped. Solutions to this problem include: boosting cross-border power trade, improving existing utility companies, improving access to electricity on a large scale, while helping countries chart low-carbon growth paths.[4]

In a continent known for multiple crises, it is not surprising that an energy crisis is one of them. In his book, *Black Africa: The Economic and Cultural Basis for Federated State*, Cheik Anta Diop has brilliantly and scientifically written about the opulent energy resources in Africa. For Africans to be "trapped in poverty" because of an energy crisis is like the children of a fabulous restaurant owner dying of hunger. Let me elaborate my observations as follows.

Hydraulic energy

World reserves of hydraulic energy are estimated at 50 billion kilowatt-hours per year, of which almost 90 percent are concentrated in underdeveloped regions; Europe has only 3 percent, the United States 4 percent, and the (then USSR) 3.5 percent.

Black Africa leads the entire world in hydraulic energy with its reserves of thousands of billions of kilowatt-hours representing about half of the total world resources. The Zaire[5] River, the second largest in volume of flow (30,000 to 60,000 cubic meters per second), by itself holds more than 600 billion kilowatt-hours of annual reserves or two-thirds of the entire production of the world at the present time, the Sanaga Ogooué half as much. Engineers have calculated that the Sanaga (Cameroon), having its source at 1,400 meters altitude and a flow three times that of the Rhône at the Génissiat hydroelectric plant, could deliver as much energy as all of the waterways of the French Alps combined.[6]

Water is an essential element for the existence of life. Food production, animals, and humans depend on it to survive. In various parts of the world today, there is a shortage or lack of water. For example,

> although at first glance China looks like it has reasonably sizable "home" access to renewable water sources, in practice many of its water resources are contaminated and not safe for human uses. Thus a large part of China's rush relates to efforts to secure access to water for its population. In 2030 China's water demand is expected to reach 216 trillion gallons, but its current supply amounts to just over 165 trillion. The numbers are large and hence can be hard to grasp, but the imbalance between supply and demand is stark . . . Between 1850 and 1980, . . . 543 medium—and large-sized Chinese lakes (roughly one-third of estimates of China's total lake count) disappeared due to irrigation projects. Sixty percent of

---

4. Energy in Africa, The World Bank, 2013, http://web.worldbank.org/WBSITE/EXTERNAL/COUNTRIES/AFRICAEXT/EXTAFRREGTOPENERGY/0,,contentMDK:21460357~pagePK:34004173~piPK:34003707~theSitePK:717306,00.html.

5. The current name of the former Zaire is Democratic Republic of Congo (DRC). It is now called the "Congo River."

6. For detailed information, see Diop, *Black Africa*, 38–39.

China's 669 cities suffered water shortages in 2005, and groundwater overdraft or overuse (when water removal exceeds water replacement) is more than 25 percent in China and continues to rise."[7]

According to the observation of hydrologists, water like oil will be one of the natural resources that countries will eventually fight over to control. "Forecasts suggest that in forty years the global demand for water could exhaust the world's available supply. Already there are indications enough to cause alarm. In 1990, twenty-eight countries with a combined population of 335 million faced chronic water stress or scarcity; a situation in which the demand for Portable water exceeds its supply."[8] Water shortage or lack of rain can lead to drought, disease, starvation, and death. The number of famines in Africa and the lives of humans and animals that have been lost are still fresh memories to most Africans. As I write this book, many people in different parts of the world are living through it.

In Africa, it is not only shortage of water that is a problem, it is lack of knowledge on how to use what is currently available that is killing Africans. For example, the "Nile River has an average daily discharge of about three hundred million cubic meters a day."[9] And yet, millions of Ethiopians, Sudanese, Eritreans, Ugandans, and Kenyans have died from famine. The loss of cattle, forced migration, and human crisis because of drought is never ending in the Horn of Africa. Because of lack of power, medical service in hospitals and clinics are extremely difficult to provide at night. Pregnant mothers and babies die in delivery rooms in the presence of helpless doctors and nurses. Students cannot study at night. In most African countries, full-time night jobs are limited to security guards.

China's involvement in the development of hydropower in Africa is another major environmental concern: "Hydro dams are the center of much of the social and environmental critique of China's role in Africa. China's Eximbank has financed a small number of hydropower projects since the turn of the millennium: on the border between Benin and Togo (Adjarala Dam), in Congo (Imboulou), Ethiopia (Tekeze), Ghana (Bui), and Sudan (Merowe). Many others are under discussion. Sudan's Merowe Dam across the Nile is a bitter, and so far extreme, example of a problem project. In 2006, Sudanese police shot and killed several farmers during protest over forced resettlement in arid conditions far from the lush bank of the Nile."[10] China, a country that has a poor record of conserving her own surface and underground water and lakes, both environmentally and quantity-wise, is entrusted to handle and manage the African water for Africans. It is like handing over your sick child to a physician who has a reputation of patients dying under his/her watch. China's primary motivation of involvement in African water

---

7. Moyo, *Winner Take All*, 34, 41.

8. Ibid., 36–37. "In theory water should never be lacking. Water covers approximately 71 percent of the earth's surface; however 97 percent of it is too salty for productive use. Of the 2.5 percent that is usable fresh water; 70 percent is ice caps, and much of the rest is in the ground. This leaves just 0.007 percent of the earth's water supply in the form of readily accessible fresh water, and like arable land, that freshwater is not evenly distributed," ibid., 34.

9. Ibid., 36.

10. Brautigam, *Dragon's Gift*, 302.

is to meet the demand and need for water of her own people not Africans. In spite of this, African leaders put the safety and security of their own people over to the outside donors.

Diop reminds us of the kind of hydraulic power with which we are blessed. Instead of utilizing and maximizing its usage, African leaders are too busy with internal fights, siphoning money, and widening the exit door to exile for African intelligentsia who can transform the continent through their gifted minds and skills.

Solar energy

On average the sun daily sends to earth 1015 kwh (one quadrillion kilowatt-hours) of energy, that is to say, a quality of energy comparable to the sum total of the energy resources in oil, coal, uranium, and the natural gas presently known to exist on our planet. Each square kilometer on which the sun shines each day gets a quantity of energy equivalent to that of an ordinary atomic bomb. However much atomic energy there may be, scientists agree that solar energy is that of the future, since it will exist as long as there is a sun.

Present expectations are that future installations for harvesting solar energy will not be on the equator itself, because of the permanent cloud cover there, but territories on either side of the tropics might be ideal for solar installations: the Sahara, Libya, all of the Sudanese zone as far as Ethiopia, and a large part of the southern African region.[11]

"The solar industry had gone from laboratory hobby of rocket scientists to off-grid hippie diversions to a mainstream investment, supported by feed in tariffs in more than 60 countries. But, in 2012, Africa was not a player in solar demand." Mark Hankins asks "Why?" and provides the following reasons:

1. Africa has been slow to invest in all renewables. According to Bloomberg New Energy Finance, of $268.7 billion invested worldwide in renewable energy last year, only about $4.3 billion was made in Africa—and most of this went to South Africa and north Africa. But it has been particularly slow to join the solar PV party.

2. The inability to connect and market solar "on to the grid" has kept major solar companies out of Africa and has made solar a tool with limited markets, an expensive choice for rural people without cash, often peddled with missionary zeal by aid agencies and NGOs.

3. The first major blockage to the development of African's solar sector has been political. As is still the case in much of the developed world, actors who think "big" manage electricity sectors from Capetown to Cairo. Centralized power from large coal, hydro and petroleum plants has been the order of the day for decades among African power companies, and they are always planning large projects to overcome many obstacles they must deal with. Small, decentralized PV power projects do not easily fit into their programs. In developing big fixes to solve short-term problems, solar PV is overlooked in favor of crisis management. When the hundred million dollar focus is on expanding the grid

---

11. See Diop, *Black Africa*, 39–41.

to the whole country, off-grid solar does not play well among bureaucrats or politicians.

4. Africa's policy makers have been among the last in the world to adopt the message of decentralized power.

5. It is impossible to ignore the entrenched interests that actively seek to maintain the status quo. In much of East and West Africa, electricity sector power is increasingly produced by diesel-powered thermal generators. Diesel generation is extremely expensive for consumers, but it is lucrative business for the well-connected moguls that have the supply contracts. Even if solar were cheaper (and it is lower cost that diesel generation from $100/barrel petroleum!), what business interest would the powerful elite have in replacing their generators with customer-owned solar?

6. Finance is another key problem. Unlike Germany, there is a comparative lack of middle class to invest in solar PV systems (though commercial classes invest heavily in generators). Banks and financiers are uneducated about renewables and they tend to be ultra-conservative. The long payback periods, small size and the lack of established business models make solar PV a foreign language to the finance community. Instead, they chase more lucrative large-scale power projects. High interest rates mitigate heavily against solar PV—when banks want upwards of 20 percent interest on home loans, no math anywhere can make a loan for a PV system a smart move.[12]

Environmental think-tanks recently wrote:

"Sub-Saharan Africa's lack of electricity is hindering development but this can be reversed if countries turn to ambitious, large-scale renewable energy projects. The region—home to 41% of the world's energy-poor people, with 65% of primary schools and 30% of health centers having no access to electricity—faces an energy crisis that development models are not addressing. Even with robust economic growth, [the region's] existing energy infrastructure is a brake on progress. With population growth continuing to outstrip electrification, the number of people without energy access is only projected to grow," say the authors. "This has significant implications for development, with impacts on health, education and household economy. Disproportionate amounts of time and income are spent securing energy by other means, such as gathering wood, which also has detrimental impacts on the natural environment."[13] The impact of deforestation in Ethiopia is a good example. "In Ethiopia, forests play a considerable role in the maintenance of environmental stability (soil erosion control, soil fertility maintenance, catchment protection, and micro-climate amelioration), provision of fuel wood, saw logs, building, and construction materials, etc. As the result of the loss of vegetation, an estimated one billion cubic meters of top soil is being lost on annual basis resulting in a massive land and environmental degradation."[14]

---

12. Hankins, "Why Africa is Missing the Solar Power Boat?" I have changed the quotation to a numbered list.
13. Vidal, "Solar Power to the People."
14. Tesema, "Tackling Deforestation."

Atomic Energy

Controlled fission of uranium and thorium is at the basis of atomic energy. A chain reaction is created, giving off enormous heat. Two thousand metric tons of uranium 235 is the energy equivalent of all the world's reserves of petroleum.

Until 1952, the then Belgian Congo supplied 50 percent of the world's production of uranium. Today, Africa in all likelihood comes immediately after Canada and the United States with nearly five thousand metric tons of uranium metal in marketable concentrations (Congo and South Africa combined).

There is uranium in Ethiopia, Cameroon, Nigeria, the Sahara, [Congo], Ghana, Zambia, Mozambique, Uganda, and the Union of South Africa, where a thorium mine has also been found. A good deal of vigilance must be exercised in the exploitation of nuclear energy.[15]

> Uranium is, of course, as indigenous to Africa as the "flame trees of Thika" or the baobab tree of Senegal. Africa in the 1930s and 1940s helped to provide the uranium which launched the Western world into the nuclear orbit. It was in part Africa's uranium from Zaire which helped to set in motion the first nuclear reactor in North America. And for better or for worse, Africa's uranium may have gone into those atomic bombs which were dropped on Hiroshima and Nagasaki in August 1945. But, of course, Africa had no say on the matter. An African resources had simply been pirated by others, and once again played a major role in a significant shift in Western industrialism.
>
> The second service (after uranium supply) which Africa rendered to the nuclear age was also symbolic. Africa provided the desert for French nuclear tests in the early 1960s. In this case Africa's nuclear involvement had slightly shifted from a purely indigenous resource (uranium) to a partially Islamic context (the Sahara).
>
> The third African point of entry into the nuclear age has been through the Republic of South Africa. South Africa is either already a nuclear power or is close to it, indirectly as a result of those earlier nuclear tests in Algeria. A circle of influence developed. The progress of the French nuclear programme and its tests in the Sahara probably helped the Israel nuclear programme. This was a period when France was quite close to Israel in terms of economic and technological collaboration. The French helped the Israelis build a nuclear reactor Demona and seemed at times to be closer to the Israelis in sharing nuclear secrets than even the Americans were. The evidence is clear—the French nuclear programme in the late 1950s and 1960s served as midwife to the Israelis nuclear programme. And French tests in the Sahara were part of France's nuclear infrastructure in that period.
>
> By a curious twist of destiny, the Israeli nuclear programme in turn came to serve as a midwife to the nuclear efforts of the Republic of South Africa in the 1970s and 1980s.[16]

The Western powers have been amassing uranium from Africa for centuries. China is in Africa for no less than nuclear power. "China, though seems hardly to have noticed

---

15. Diop, *Black Africa*, 41–42.
16. Mazrui, *Africans*, 166–68.

the bad news for nuclear of recent years. In fact, its nuclear expansion plans are nothing short of awesome. The country plans to increase its nuclear power generation to around 200GW by 2050, twice the amount currently produced by the United States. China is planning to construct twenty nuclear power plants and roll out thirty-six nuclear reactors over the next decade, a plan that, if accomplished would be the fastest nuclear roll-out program in the world's history... China will have to meet an increased demand for uranium, a commodity that is a key component of nuclear production."[17] Currently China has made a multi-billion-dollar agreement with Kazakhstan, which produces roughly 30 percent of the world's uranium. China's eyes are also on many African countries, like Central African Republic and the above-mentioned African countries that have uranium.

Thermonuclear Energy

Atomic, more properly nuclear, energy is a first step in the creation of thermonuclear energy. A mass of uranium, disintegrating within a confine containing a certain variety of hydrogen (deuterium or tritium) in a millionth of a second creates heat on the scale of 16 million degrees Centigrade (or 29 million degrees Fahrenheit) comparable to that inside of hot stars, especially the sun (26,000,0000C, 36,000,0000F). Unlike atomic energy, thermonuclear energy is not yet available for industrial use.

Once thermonuclear reactions are adapted for industry, humankind will, without a doubt, as scientists foresee, have an abundant new source of energy. Electrolysis of seawater would become a direct source of the indispensable raw material, heavy hydrogen or deuteron present in seawater to the extent of .02 percent. This tiny percentage is not to be scoffed at, considering the enormous temperature reached by fusion. Production and processing centers would necessarily have to be near the sea in Africa.[18]

Energy is in high demand; according to the World Bank, only about 24 percent of the population of sub-Saharan Africa currently has access to electricity. South Africa is the only sub-Saharan African country with active nuclear power plants. However, research-oriented nuclear reactors have been tested in a few other countries—including Kenya, Ghana, and the Democratic Republic of the Congo—and it is clear that there is widespread interest in a nuclear-powered future all across the continent. Uganda, Nigeria, Senegal, Niger, and others have expressed interest in building up nuclear expertise within their borders. But Shaukat Abdulrazak, head of Kenya's National Council for Science and Technology, argued that "[c]ountries such as Namibia, Niger and South Africa have uranium minerals and ore that can be processed as fuel for nuclear power plants. Africa has sufficient water and land for nuclear plant construction and, compared with other regions, it is relatively unaffected by earthquakes." "The advantages of nuclear include a reduced and stable energy price, national energy self-reliance and the reduction of greenhouse gas emissions, as well as industrial growth and development," he added.[19]

---

17. Moyo, *Winner Take All*, 188, 189.
18. Ibid., 42–45.
19. Abdulrazak, "Can Africa Go Nuclear?"

"South Africa has approved 64 renewable-energy projects ranging from fields of wind turbines and solar cells to generators that burn sugar cane."[20]

Wind Energy

It has been discovered that, thanks to trade winds, the entire West Coast of Africa could be equipped with huge windmills, as could the Cape region. The Canaries and Kerguelens are already so equipped. It would be wrong to minimize this source of energy, since in Denmark, for instance, wind energy supplies 15 percent of national requirements. Wind-motors or windmills would work wonderfully for initially irrigating the soil and supplying water to cattle in the impoverished regions of Senegal, such as the Ferlo, Cayor, part of Baol, and Djambour.[21]

With over half a billion people on the continent lacking access to electricity, Africa is faced with the challenge of generating more power to meet existing and future demand. For many countries, an opportunity exists to do so in a clean and sustainable manner. The continent is well endowed with renewable energy resources that constitute plausible solutions to address existing power shortages. Indeed, Africa's reserves of renewable energy resources are the highest in the world, and the continent has enough renewable energy potential to meet its future energy needs. It is estimated that eighteen of the top thirty-five developing countries ranked highest in renewable energy reserves, normalized by annual domestic energy consumption, are located in Africa. Similarly, at least eight African countries are among the developing world's most endowed in terms of wind energy potential. *The Economist* concurs: "Africa has some of the world's best potential sites for wind, solar and hydropower. Investors are proving readier to test the market by putting up a few windmills than by committing to big power stations. Wind farms solar parks can also provide decentralized or 'off-grid' power directly to customers, reducing the load on congested transmission lines. Given the high cost of power from diesel generators in Africa, renewable energy can be an attractive alternative."[22]

While global wind-based electricity generation is still underdeveloped relative to exploitation of other renewable fuels such as hydro, it has grown at an average annual rate of about 30 percent between 1996 and 2008, making wind one of the world's fastest growing energy resources in terms of both coverage and technological innovations. Using a technical feasibility method based on technologies available in 2005, Byrnes and other scholars found that eight African countries, namely, Somalia, Sudan, Libya, Mauritania, Egypt, Madagascar, Kenya, and Chad, had large on-shore wind energy potential. Mauritania's potential, for example, is about four times its annual energy consumption in tons of oil equivalent, while Sudan's is equivalent to 90 percent of its annual energy needs. Yet, there is variability in terms of geographic location of wind potential across countries. In particular, the study finds that five additional African countries—Mozambique,

---

20. Ibid., 46.
21. Ibid., 45.
22. Ibid., 47.

Tanzania, Angola, South Africa, and Namibia—have potentially large off-shore wind energy resources.[23]

Africans do not lack the intelligence to exploit the natural resources that God has given them. What they lack is opportunity and technical and educational resources to develop their knowledge and skill to capitalize the raw material that sits underneath and around them. *The Boy Who Harnessed the Wind* is a remarkable true story about human inventiveness and its power to overcome crippling adversity. It will inspire anyone who doubts the power of one individual's ability to change his community and better the lives of those around him. The book changes outsiders' perception of Africans and Africans' perception of themselves. The scientific innovation has a direct implication of social and psychological transformation. "William Kamkwamba was born in Malawi, a country where magic ruled and modern science was mystery. It was also a land withered by drought and hunger. But William had read about windmills, and he dreamed of building one that would bring to his small village a set of amenities that only 2 percent of Malawians could enjoy: electricity and running water. His neighbors called him misala—crazy—but William refused to let go of his dreams. With a small pile of once-forgotten science textbooks; some scrap metal, tractor parts, and bicycle halves; and an armory of curiosity and determination, he embarked on a daring plan to forge an unlikely contraption and small miracle that would change the lives around him."[24]

Instead of flooding Africa's jobless and desperate African youth with AK-47s to destroy each other, the West and African tyrants can improve the education sectors so that innovators like Kamkwamba can flourish in the continent. A brilliant young man like him should not be limited to outdated science textbooks, insufficient library resources, and no lab. The story of Kamkwamba, which became a source of inspiration for many Western readers, can do the same for many young Africans. This is a book that needs to be in every high school and college in Africa.

Thermal Energy of the Sea

Carnot's formula[25] can be used to power a plant through the temperature differential at the sea's bottom and its surface. The method is that of George-Claude Boucherot. It was applied in Abidjan between the coastal lagoon and a ditch known as a "bottomless pit," five hundred meters deep. The temperature differential is 22 degrees Centigrade (70 degrees Fahrenheit), enough to make a 7500-kilowatt powerhouse practicable, according to du Jonchay.[26]

---

23. Byrne et al., "Evaluating the Potential." For a fascinating study of this topic, read Mukasa et al., "Development of Wind Energy in Africa."

24. Quoted from the back cover of Kamkwamba and Mealer, *The Boy Who Harnessed the Wind*.

25. Carnot's theorem, developed in 1824 by Nicolas Léonard Sadi Carnot, also called Carnot's rule, is a principle that specifies limits on the maximum efficiency any heat engine can obtain, which thus solely depends on the difference between the hot and cold temperature reservoirs. See also Steven Holzner, "Measuring Heat Efficiency Using the Carnot Principle," For Dummies, 2015, http://www.dummies.com/how-to/content/measuring-heat-efficiency-using-carnots-principle.html.

26. Diop, *Black Africa*, 45–46.

General Public License (GPL) currently holds six Prospecting Licenses in Tanzania through its subsidiary Geothermal Power (Tanzania) Limited (GPT) and is actively inspecting potential in neighboring countries.

Extensive geothermal investigation has been undertaken by European agencies in Tanzania resulting in the identification of an area near the city of Mbeya as having the greatest potential. This geotechnically well-defined area exhibits both conventional geothermal and hot water potential.

GPL has identified Tanzania as having the right commercial and political environment to launch GPT's operations based in Dar es Salaam. GPL holds 70% equity interest and is providing strong geothermal potential power and the management. The remaining 30% of equity is held by the Tanzanian Government's "National Development Corporation" (NDC) and local company "Interstate Mining & Minerals Ltd."

Geotechnical results from GPT lease areas incorporating extensive hot springs (80 °C) along the Mbaka fault regions indicate thermal water of more than 160 °C at a relatively shallow depth (less than 800m), located to the north of Lake Nyasa in southwest Tanzania. At Lake Ngozi, a conventional geothermal resource has been identified at less than 2,500m depth with temperatures in excess of 220 °C and capable of supporting a 100 MW geothermal power station.[27] "Kenya is drilling holes deep into the Rift Valley in Hell's Gate National Park to build what will ultimately be the world's largest single geothermal plant. At Lake Turkana, a particularly windy spot farther north in the Rift Valley, private investors are building Africa's biggest wind farm."[28]

Egyptologists might find Diop wrong in his battle for ancient black civilization in Egypt. Leading German and American geothermal consultants have proven him right in thermal energy. He is also on target with atomic, solar, and wind energy in Africa. On social, scientific, historical, and political platforms, Diop had championed the cause of Africa but he was a prophet without a listening audience. Time, the global political situation, and Africa were not harmoniously suitable for him to make the desired change for humankind, and for Africans in particular, that he fought for.

Tidal Energy

Making use of the movements of the tides, one can harness an appropriate estuary and create reservoirs, some of which, being relatively high up, might be filled by siphoning at high tide. The reservoirs thus created would act exactly as do the holding lakes behind dams. At low tide, the water would flow from these reservoirs toward the turbines to keep them working.[29] "Wave power is the most promising source of ocean energy for South Africa and a very conservative estimate is that some 8,000 to 10,000 megawatts of electricity could be generated from the Cape's west and south coasts," says marine engineer Professor Deon Retief.

---

27. "Geothermal Energy in Africa," Geothermal Power, http://www.geo-t.de/downloads/gpl_informationsheet-v4.pdf.

28. Abdulrazak, "Can Africa Go Nuclear?," 47.

29. Diop *Black Africa*, 46–47.

He says Eskom has identified the top ten methods of generating oceanic energy and will be installing technology to monitor wave patterns and conduct a geographical survey of the ocean floor. Saldanha Bay with a coastline of 40 km has been identified as a suitable site for a 770 MW installation that could produce electricity for 60 to 75 cents per kw/h.

Tidal energy has important economic benefits because it does not require fuel. The rise and fall of tides afford a reliable consistency with an expected plant production life span of 75 to 100 years. This massive economic scale compares favorably with the thirty-five-year output of a fossil fuel plant.[30]

"In South Africa, on November 19th, Eskom was forced to ask its biggest industrial customers to cut their consumption by 10% at peak time. The curb was meant to last for ten days, so Eskom could be sure to avoid 'load-shedding,' the polite term for scheduled power cuts for all users. It ended after only two days; Eskom said its spare capacity was much improved. But bitter complaints from industry about lost production owning to the curbs on electricity may also have influenced the decision . . . It is strange that a country whose exports depends heavily on energy-intensive industries, such as car making and mining, has been so careless about power. Fitful electricity may now be as much a turn-off to much-needed investment by foreign companies as red tape and strikes."[31] For a country that is in desperate need of energy, the innovation in tidal and wind energy is good news for the African nations' economy and wellbeing.

Global Heat

Carnot's principle can be applied, as well, to the temperature differential between the earth's surface and a hot subterranean source reached by drilling. The differential could boil water and produce steam under a vacuum at well below 1000 Centigrade (2120 Fahrenheit). Research and a start toward application have already been out in (Congo).[32]

Even if there is a great potential scientific possibility to turn Global Heat for the well-being of human beings, lack of financial resources, human skill, suitable political systems, and governance, has not allowed for the convertion of the global heat into energy. Instead drought and famine is taking its toll on the lives of millions of Africans. Describing the drought and famine of 2002, Meron Tesfa Michael writes:

> A devastating famine, provoked by drought, is steadily moving north from Southern Africa, where it has affected more than 13 million lives. Two years of alternating droughts and floods, mismanagement of land and food supplies, political instability, and regional conflicts are being blamed.
>
> Emergency warnings and appeals for aid are coming in from East, West, and Central Africa. In Eritrea, because of the lack of seasonal rains and the aftermath of war with Ethiopia, 1 million of the country's 3.7 million people face drought and starvation. Farmers in Gambia are despairing as a shortage of rain is

30. "The Turning Tide of Renewable Energy," Essential Publishing, October 20, 2010, http://www.essentialmag.co.za/index.php?pg=art&bk=177&sq=3515.
31. "Energy to South Africa."
32. Abdulrazak, "Can Africa Go Nuclear?," 47.

causing new seedlings to wilt and die off. The International Institute of Tropical Agriculture in Nigeria has estimated that by 2010 around 300 million people in sub-Saharan Africa—nearly a third of the population—will be malnourished.[33]

The cause of hunger in Africa is not limited to climate change or lack of rain. It is political, economic, and global. I'll address this issue under a different topic. However, the global heat that could be converted to energy has been the cause of drought and death both for humans and animals.

Volcanic thermal energy and geothermal energy

Volcanic thermal energy can be employed on the spot by thermal generators that send a great mass of water into pipes buried in lava, which, as it evaporates, delivers steam to turbines. Generally speaking, all of East Africa (Ethiopia, Kenya, Uganda, Tanzania, and the entire Rift Valley region) would be eminently suited for the installation of plants powered by geothermal energy.[34] Moderately intense volcanic and geothermal activity occurs along the two continental rifts in East Africa, each almost 2000 km. long.

> Volcanism and rifting started in the Eastern Rift (Eritrea/Djibouti to Northern Tanzania) at least 15 Mill. yrs. ago. Over 30 major hydrothermal systems occur along this branch (almost half have steaming ground) together with at least 10 volcanic-geothermal and 10 volcanic systems which have been active during the last 2000 yr. The hydrothermal systems discharge heat at a rate of at least 4000 MW.
>
> Volcanism and rifting began c. 10 Mill. years ago in the Western Rift (Northern Uganda to Southern Malawi). However, there are only 3 major high temperature systems in this rift together with 4 active volcanic systems. A few concealed advective geothermal systems occur at the margin and probably at the bottom of deep rift lakes. The total anomalous heat discharged by the Western Rift is an order-of-magnitude less than that discharged by the Eastern Rift. There appears to be an overall inverse relation between the energy released by crustal earthquakes and that transferred by geothermal systems.[35]

Industrialization of Black Africa

If Africa has such astounding natural and energy resources, why hasn't sub-Saharan Africa been industrialized? Why is the continent that can boast the oldest civilization in the world centuries behind the West in terms of industrialization? Why is sub-Saharan Africa the poorest in the world with the majority of the population living on less than a dollar a day? An answer to these questions could make another book. As you read this book, it doesn't require a rocket scientist to deduct why Africa is not industrialized. Here, I would like to give the following two brief reasons:

33. Karanja, "Corruption Scandal."
34. Abdulrazak, "Can Africa Go Nuclear?," 48.
35. For a good comprehension of this topic, see Hochstein, "Heat Transfer by Hydrothermal."

One reason is the limited degree of social coherence in most African populations. Quite simply, industrialization depends on large numbers of cooperative people with extensive economic connections and a low level of disruption due to violence or warfare. Sub-Saharan Africa, while having a large enough population for industrialization, doesn't develop large cooperative groups and even when it does not for long enough periods to support the specializations needed for industrialization. As I showed earlier and will elaborate on further in another chapter, the social coherence before and after the intervention of imperialism in Africa stand in stark contrast to one another. The black civilization and its destruction is a good example.

A second reason in the eyes of many Africans and Westerners is economic. If the purpose of industrialization is efficient production and distribution of resources, having a competitor that does it better and faster really limits your success. Once Africa collides with European and Asian cultures, industrialization is less competitive except (possibly) in the short term. I'll explain later how this is an inadequate reason.

Backed with historical facts, Mazrui gives more convincing reasons why Africa was not industrialized:

> First, the trans-Atlantic trade disrupted west Africa the most; and west Africa was the region which held the greatest promise of independent industrial take off. It had made the most progress in local textiles and in taming and using metals before European penetration.
>
> Second, alongside the slave trade, the importation of European cloth *before* colonial rule dealt a severe blow to local textile industries. Traditional iron melting declined in most parts of Africa as a result of the European impact. The slave trade took potentially creative and productive youth.
>
> Third, some African rulers sought to be taught Western technology rather than import Western goods. In Ethiopia, Lbena Dengel in the seventeenth century and Theodros in the eighteenth century wrote to European rulers for asstance in industrialization. In the eighteenth century King Agaja Trudo of Dahomey thought the best way of stopping the slave trade was to industrialise west Africa with European help. Opoku Ware of Asante in the nineteenth century also tried to innovate industrially. In each case, Europe refused to help.
>
> Fourth, Colonial rule helped to build an infrastructure of roads, electricity, railways, postal services and rudimentary telephone systems. Colonial rule also encouraged importation of Western industrial products such as motor cars, Lorries and locomotives, and luxury goods such as perambulators, radios and gramophones. But colonial rule did little to transfer technological skills to Africans. At the time of independence many African countries could not even make their own bulbs and plugs.
>
> Fifth, cultural Westernization was promoted more vigorously than genuine technological modernisation. The French policy of cultural assimilation helped to keep the so-called "modern" sector under French control even after independence. Colonial schools were transmitters of Western culture rather than transmitters of Western technical skills. Brilliant graduates were at best potential Shakespeares but almost never potential Einsteins or potential Edisons or Graham Bells.
>
> Sixth, colonial conditions encouraged the importation of Western equipment without transfer of Western technology. In post-colonial Africa governments

continue to import inappropriate Western equipment at great expense and do little to promote effective technology transfer and effective technical training for their people. Many industrial projects are for prestige rather than production. Below-capacity production is the norm rather than the exception.

Seventh, imported Western tools of destruction have been more potent than imported Western tools of production. Political power in Africa often resides among those who control the means of destruction rather than the means of production.[36]

Despite her enrichment with natural resources and minerals that are suitable for industry, these are the major reasons why Africa is not industrialized. Since instability is the major concern of Africans, I'll further elaborate the last point later.

For now, let us look at the proposals of Diop to industrialize Africa:

The (Congo) River

With its 650 billion kilowatt-hours of annual reserves of hydraulic energy (almost two-thirds of world production) the Zaire River Basin is destined to become the leading industrial region of Africa, the principal center of our heavy industry. In the final stage, hydraulic energy will supply all the electricity needed for the various branches of industry using the resources of raw materials in neighboring territories—including the cooking coal of south Africa Zimbabwe, the iron of Angola and even Zaire, cobalt (65 percent of world production), chromium (one third of the world production), tantalum, manganese, tin, copper (overlapping from Upper Shaba into Zambia), diamonds, gold, and uranium (the Shinkrolobwe mines, the top exporter in the world, 60 to 70 percent of total mined).[37]

The Gulf of Benin region

Its hydraulic reserves total 250 billion kilowatt-hours (200 in maritime Sanga, 50 in Nigeria). Moreover oil (had) been discovered in Gabon (appropriated the Kuwait of Africa); all existing indication point to oil becoming a significant factor among the various sources of energy that will industrialize the country. There the possibility still exists of seeing the growth of a powerful wood chemical industry: distillation, pulp, man-made fabrics.[38]

Ghana and the Ivory Coast

These two countries jointly have 25 billion annual kilowatt-hours in energy reserves, once harnessing the Upper Volta, Bandama, and Comoe rivers is complete. Ghana's suitability for the development of an aluminothermal industry is obvious: bauxite is

---

36. Mazrui, *African Condition*, 164–66.
37. For further details, see Diop, *Black Africa*, 52–56.
38. Ibid., 57.

abundant, close to hydraulic energy. Ghana entered the era of aluminothermy in 1970, producing 157,200 metric tons of aluminum in 1974. The Akosombo Dam produced 3,304,400 kilowatt-hours of hydroelectric power in 1972.

Manganese, on which Ghana has a virtual African monopoly, might find appropriate local use in electroplating if systemic exploration by plane or other methods were to reveal the presence of iron and nonferrous metals in Ghana and the Ivory Coast.[39]

Guinea, Sierra Leone, Liberia

This is a metallurgical region par excellence, ideal for the installation of a powerful combine. It has more than 25 billion kilowatt-hours of hydraulic energy reserves. The Konkouré Dam in lower Guinea is expected to deliver 200,000 kilowatts of power.

The iron ore of the Kalum peninsula has a yield of 50 percent. It is estimated to reach 2 billion metric tons. The bauxite of the Loos Islands in Guinea is estimated at 10 million metric tons. Bauxite is also found, disseminated here and there, in other regions as far as Upper Guinea. To these ores we should add the iron of Liberia (Boni Hills). There are also industrial diamonds and uranium in the Macenta. This whole region, from Liberia to Guinea, is good for raising hevea.[40]

Tropical zone (Senegal, Mali, Niger)

Oil exploration, being carried out more and more systematically in the South Sahara, will in all likelihood totally change the energy picture in these heretofore seemingly energyless tropical regions. Petroleum would supply both the indispensable energy source for the establishment of thermal power plants and the necessary raw materials for a petrochemical industry. The two tropical zones of Africa can turn into production of textiles, dyes, oil seeds, fishing, wood chemistry, rice, reforestation, cattle, etc.[41]

Nilotic Sudan, Great Lakes, Ethiopia

This region, several times as large as Europe, has its principal energy source in the reserves of the Nile and its tributaries: potentially more than 60 billion kilowatt-hours per year. The port of Mombasa in Kenya on the Indian Ocean is due to become a great naval-construction center.

---

39. See ibid., 58–59.

40. Ibid., 60. The genus Hevea is a member of the family Euphorbiaceae. Only three species of the genus yield usable rubber, Hevea brasiliensis, Hevea guianensis and Hevea benthamiana. Other species have too high a ratio of resin to rubber in their latex. Hevea brasiliensis is the only species planted commercially and is the primary source of natural rubber. "*Hevea brasiliensis* (rubber tree)," Kew Royal Botanical Gardens, http://www.kew.org/science-conservation/plants-fungi/hevea-brasiliensis-rubber-tree.

41. See ibid., 61–75.

Growing cotton, sugar cane, hemp, sisal, oil palms, and cocoanut trees (in the coastal plain) calls for setting up corresponding industries. On the other hand, maize and other cereals, coffee and tea, are grown for consumption and export.[42]

Zambezi River Basin

The energy potential here, according to figures published by du Jonchay, is 45 billion kilowatt-hours annually. Again, there are uranium deposits.[43]

Union of South Africa

This country has already been industrialized by its European-minority inhabitants. It has gold, diamonds, cooking coal (in Transvaal, Natal), uranium, thorium (at the Cape), and wool of international quality from merino sheep.

There is prosperous sugar cane rising on the Indian Ocean coast, and it would appear that Kalahari Desert at its northern border is as oil-rich as the Sahara.[44]

Diop also accurately observed the importance of surface, air, and sea transportation that facilitates travel across the continent to connect countries and people. These enhance trade and multicultural knowledge for Africans. To this he adds the importance of professionally- and technically-trained Africans, and high academic level scientific researchers. African universities should play a significant role in producing the needed trained personnel and the advancement of research.

China is effectively engaged to connect the continent through railways and highways. "While the Tanzania line links Zambia to the east coast, the Benguela line links the Copperbelt—Zambia and the Democratic Republic of Congo (the DRC)—to the west coast. Starting at Lauanshya in Zambia and ending at the Angola port of Lobito, that rail line is also being reconstructed by Chinese firms accessing preferential financing from China's banks. Together, the Tanzam and Benguela lines bisect sub-Saharan Africa. The strategic intent of the construction of these transportation corridors is to reduce supply side risk to Chinese mining firms engaging in resource extraction. The rehabilitation of these two railway lines will—for the first time—create a functioning of east-west infrastructural corridor across the subcontinent."[45]

What the African Diop researched and envisioned to be primarily used for the development of Africans is successfully implemented by the West and East for the ultimate well-being of their nations. In recent years, this endless tragedy and paradox of African existence is precipitated and perpetuated by African tyrants and corrupt African elites. I have devoted one chapter for this issue and we will closely examine it later.

---

42. Ibid., 76.
43. Ibid., 77.
44. Ibid., 78.
45. Davies, "Special Economic Zones," 150.

Investment funds

Here are the five suggestions Diop gave as a solution to economic problem to industrialize Africa:

1. Companies would have to be jointly owned and operated with the State's share constantly increasing.
2. For hard currency and machinery, exchange precious metals, gold, silver, and platinum.
3. Sell excess strategic raw materials as long as African industry could not absorb them.
4. The establishment of a collective public manpower pull to serve their countries.
5. Loans could then be made against international investment funds, but they must never get so high as to risk becoming a delusion.[46]

Social Instability—a Major Stumbling Block

All Diop's great ideas of African industrialization cannot be accomplished without social stability and unity among the nations. Toward that goal he put forth fifteen proposals for consideration.[47] However the current condition of African states does not indicate desire from leaders to entertain Diop's ideas, let alone implement them. The West African war, the war in Sudan, the seventeen-year civil war in Ethiopia, the war in Angola, and the war in Congo that involved Rwanda, Uganda, Zimbabwe, and the Congolese, were anarchy that led to untold bloodshed and destruction of nations. Ayittey observes:

> Since the beginning of the 1980s—described by most analysts as 'the lost decade'—one African country after another has collapsed, scattering refugees in all directions: Ethiopia (1985), Angola, (1986), Mozambique (1987), Sudan (1999), Liberia (1992) Somalia (1993), and Rwanda (1994). In March 1994 the United Nations Development Program (UNDP) grimly predicted that nine more African countries were on the brink of complete social disintegration: Angola, Burundi, Egypt, Liberia, Mozambique, Nigeria, Sierra Leone, Sudan, and Zaire. In November 1996 the threat of imminent starvation of 1.2 million Hutu refugees in eastern Zaire compelled the international community to prepare a military intervention force to be led by Canada. Its objectives were twofold: to feed the starving refugees and to establish an 'aid corridor' to facilitate the return of Hutu refugees to Rwanda.[48]

If not all, the majority of these African wars were instigated and fueled by outside powers that had either geopolitical interests or an insatiable hunger for natural resources. Meredith adds, "The United States . . . despite the repression Numeiri unleashed in the southern Sudan, invested heavily in his regime to bolster him as a counter-weight to

---

46. Diop, *Black Africa*, 83–86.
47. Ibid., 88–89.
48. Ayittey, *Africa in Chaos*, 13.

Gaddafi and Mengistu, both of whom it regarded pro-Soviet activists; US assistance to Numeiri totaled $1.5 billion."[49] "The Soviet Union had, an average $300 million a year to Africa (58 percent went to Ethiopia)."[50]

So long as a country serves the U.S.'s interest it is considered a "friendly" country. Hence, the undemocratic and radical Islamic state of Sudan became a base for those on a mission to accomplish the U.S. agenda in the region. "In the Sudan Lieutenant-General Omar el-Bashir proclaimed an 'Islamic Revolution' that would deliver Sudanese from abject poverty and squalor by tapping the country's oil and mineral riches to create a model economy. But Sudanese complain of rampant inflation (about 70 percent), high unemployment, corruption, and endless conflicts . . . The civil war rages, the secret police operate without restriction, the press is censored, the military reigns, and political opponents languish in ghost houses when they are not simply killed. Like so many would be reformers in other places and other times, the professors [of Islamic revolution] proposed enlightenment but delivered a nightmare."[51]

Working with the Sudanese government, and launching its mission out of Khartoum, the U.S. decided to destabilize Ethiopia and led the country to seventeen years of war, the death of millions in every corner of the country, and an unprecedented diaspora that resulted among other things in a huge brain-drain. The major blow was the Eritrean secession, which made Ethiopia a landlocked country. Ethiopia lost her people, rich cultural religious, and historical connections and geopolitically and economically strategic parts of the country. "The Cold War [was] one cause of Africa's problems that stands up to analysis—within limits. The main charge is that the superpowers protected their shipping lanes and military bases, as well as their access to vital minerals and energy supplies in Africa, by shoring up dictatorships across the continent. But the number of countries affected by such tensions (Angola, Ethiopia, Mozambique, and Zaire) was rather small [small in his eyes]. . . *Foreign interventions were actually intended to dismember countries rather than keep dictators in power*; France supported Katanga's unsuccessful secession from Zaire in 1960 and Biafra's attempted separation from Nigeria in 1967."[52] "Each [Katanga & Biafra] had one economic resource and each might have made a viable state; but each failed, and failed in blood."[53] For African despots "foreign recognition and support is a crown jewel and actively sought. This support comes in the form of diplomatic recognition, military and development assistance or aid. The leader may use weapons supplied and military assistance to suppress the opposition and to strengthen his grip on power. He may use development aid to fund projects for his supporters or his tribal region and thereby buy loyalty or political support. In competing for influence in Africa, *especially during the Cold War, external patrons, wittingly or unwittingly, helped prop up African dictators and buttered their repressive capacity. In the process, foreign governments promoted governmental irresponsibility, oppressiveness, and venality in Africa.*"[54]

49. Meredith, *Fate of Africa*, 358.
50. Moyo, *Dead Aid*, 24.
51. Ayittey, *Africa in Chaos*, 20–21.
52. Calderisi, *Trouble with Africa*, 26; emphasis added.
53. Walls, *Cross-Cultural Process*, 109.
54. Ayittey, *Africa in Chaos*, 166; emphasis added.

Mengistu of Ethiopia, Bare of Somalia, Numeri of Sudan, the "rebels" in Sudan, Eritrea, and Ethiopia, and many others in the Horn of Africa were chess pawns for Russian and American leaders during the Cold War. "Africa's strategic location has provided other areas of linkage. For example, the politics of who controls the Red Sea have bedeviled diplomacy and politics in the Horn of Africa. Competition between the West and the Soviet Union in influencing Somalia and Ethiopia has in part been a debate about how ideologically "red" the Red Sea should be."[55] Another bone of contention between the East and the West in the Red Sea region is the Suez Canal. "Linking Europe with the Middle East oilfields and with Asia, the canal was the world's most important international waterway, used by 12,000 ships a year from forty-five nations, the main artery of oil for Europe, carrying more than 20 million tons of oil a year for Britain alone, half of its supplies."[56] Nasser wanted to nationalize and have full control of the canal. "Britain could not tolerate having Nasser's 'thumb on her windpipe' . . . The Americans favored a system of international control over the canal."[57]

The intensity of American and Russian involvement in Africa is different now, but the trend of outsider's participation in the affairs of Africa is still the same. In politics, economics, and location Africa is central, yet in terms of global influence and power the continent is marginal and African countries in most UN votes and global affairs are a rubber stamps for their patrons.

Eritrean secession succeeded, but what did Eritreans gain at the cost of Ethiopia's loss? In short and by large, misery: "In Eritrea, you turn eighteen and go into the Army, and you stay in the Army for many years, sometimes for the rest of your life. You work for a few dollars a day—in construction, farming, [and] mining. Those who refuse are sent to prison. There is no other choice."[58] To avoid a life of forced labor determined by the government Eritreans can manage to leave the country to seek asylum at the risk of their own lives. The recent tragedy in Lampedusa is a good example of how dangerous, painful, and degrading the lives of the escapees can be. A few of the Eritrean survivors told the story this way:

> We wanted a better life, a free and normal life . . . We walked west, into Sudan to Khartoum, then into the Sahara and into Libya. There were hundred and thirty one of us . . . One day in Libya, a band of armed Somalis came upon us. They forced us into vans and brought us to the town of Sabha, where they locked us up in a house. They made us stand for hours. They tied us upside down and beat the soles of our feet. They held weapons to our head and fired bullets into the floor. They drove two of our young women into the desert, raped them, and returned with only one. They poured water over the floor and tried to shock us with a live wire, but they succeeded only in burning out the lights.
>
> The Somalis wanted thirty-three hundred dollars a head. Two weeks later, most of our families had paid, so they drove us to Tripoli. They took us to a smuggler Ermias. He was dark-skinned, around thirty, well fed. He took sixteen hundred dollars from each of us to arrange a boat to Lampedusa. It is an Italian

55. Mazrui, *Africans*, xv.
56. Meredith, *Fate of Africa*, 40–41.
57. Ibid., 41.
58. Schwartz, "Letter from Lampedusa," 77.

island about a day off the Libyan coast. Many of us had never seen the sea and did not know how to swim. We asked if we could pay extra for life jackets; Ermias refused. His men locked us in a ware house with many others, where we waited through the month of September, 2013. On October 2nd, hours before dawn, they drove us to the shore and ferried us out to a boat, sixty-five feet long. They packed more than five hundred of us into the bridge and the deck and down in the cabins. The smuggler did not like the look of the boat, so heave and low in the water, and so old. But they said, "God willing we will be lucky."

The boat set off. We sent the women and the children belowdecks, where they would be more comfortable. Some of us wrote the phone numbers of our families on our clothes. One woman, pinned in a crowded cabin, wrote a number on the wall. It belonged to a catholic priest, Abba Mussie Zerai—Father Moses. His number is written in the walls of prison in Libya. We believed that he could make a rescue boat appear in the middle of the sea.

The captain was a Tunisian man who did not speak our language. He ran the engine through the sunset. At three in the morning of October 3rd, the engine stopped. We were close enough to see the lights on shore. Lampedusa. We waited for the engine to start again. We began to take on water. The captain picked up something and ripped it—was it a bedsheet, a piece of clothing, a blanket? He dipped it in fuel and set it on fire to signal for help. Some people panicked when they saw it burning, and everybody pushed towards the bow. It sank beneath our shifting weight, and the boat turned over and dumped us into the sea.

We said, "Let's us try our luck." We started swimming. Hands reached out to drag us down. We shook them off. Through the portholes, we could see inside the cabins. Some saw their sons and daughters and wives and chose to drown; some drowned trying to save them. Some called out their names of their villages, so that news of their deaths might be carried to shore . . .

Coast Guard drivers spent the next week pulling bodies from the hull. Among them, under a hundred and fifty feet water, was a newborn baby attached by the umbilical cord to mother, who had drowned while giving birth.[59]

This tragic day was remembered not in Asmara but somewhere else—Italy:

A day of national mourning was held on October 4th after as many as 300 people drowned in the Mediterranean's worst recent shipwreck, just off Lampedusa. Candles were lit and a flag flew at half-mast. But this was not in Eritrea, where most of the dead came from, but in Italy, the country they lost their lives trying to reach.

Some 30,000 people reached Italy illegally in boats in the first nine months of 2013, three times as many as in the whole of 2012, according to Frontex, the European Union's border agency. Many hail from Syria, Afghanistan and Somalia, three countries in varying stages of civil strife. But the largest batch came from Eritrea, a country that has supposedly been at peace for the past 13 years . . . Most make their way overland. Some 40,000 have sought refuge in Israel, 87,000 in Ethiopia and 125,000 in Sudan . . . The main reason for the mass flight is that the a growing number of Eritreans feel they are living in a prison camp, rivalled—some say—only by North Korea.[60]

---

59. Ibid., 77–79.
60. "Uganda and Its President," 60.

For the Regan administration it sounded so casual to say, "let us destabilize Ethiopia." The consequence for one of the poorest nations in the world has been enormous and extremely costly in more ways than one. In the history of our nation, Ethiopians/Eritreans have never been degraded at the hands of the Arabs and Somalis like in the last five decades or so. Partly, these two nations brought this misery on themselves. Knowingly and unknowingly, many Ethiopians and Eritreans turn themselves into tools in the hands of the West, Russians, and the Arabs. Not willing to live under the same flag, they fought one of the worst civil wars in Africa for over seventeen years—just to live as refugees side by side in Sudan, Kenya, and many other parts of the world. A self-destructive people are prone to the violation and abuse of outside powers. Before their own eyes, and witnessed by their own children and the world, they see their dignity trampled on. Being trapped between a rock and hard place, they find out that it is too late to make a reverse in the course of history. As a result, they suffer miserably and hopelessly.

The current Ethiopian government that the United States helped bring to power has been ruling the country for the last twenty-four years. I have described the strengths and weaknesses of this government in my book *Culture Change in Ethiopia: An Evangelical Perspective*. The U.S. has been giving enormous financial aid to the current government as the American government did in the past to the archaic monarchy in the fifties and sixties. And yet, "Ethiopia is Africa's second-worst jailer of journalists, ahead only of its ultra-repressive neighbor and bitter enemy, Eritrea. Cementing its lamentable reputation, on August 4th Ethiopia briefly resumed the trial of ten journalists and bloggers, nine of whom it has kept in prison since April; one is being tried in absentia."[61] In addition to this, Ethiopians are still lacking global communication. The government controls the masses and social media and other means of communications. For example, there are limitations on mobile phones and internet access. *The Economist* writes:

> Ethiopia has Africa's last big telecoms monopoly. The absence of competition has seen a country of more than 80m lag badly behind the rest of the continent in an industry that has generally burgeoned alongside economic growth. Mobile-phone penetration, which averages 70% of the population elsewhere in Africa, is closer to 25% in Ethiopia. A paltry 2.5 percent of Ethiopians have access to the internet, compared with 40% in neighboring Kenya.
>
> Ethiopia's authoritarian leaders are as keen as any on the economic benefits of modern telecoms but fear the political ramifications; pesky dissidents become even more irritating when wire. That explains a $1.6 billion agreement with China's two leading telecoms-equipment companies to upgrade its network. The deal with Huwawei and [Zhong Xing Telecommunication Equipment] ZTE[62] will preserve Ethiopia's state dominance and further put off the opening up of

---

61. "Ethiopia and Its Press," 42.

62. ZTE Corporation is a Chinese multinational telecommunications equipment and systems company headquartered in Shenzhen, China. ZTE operates in three business units—Carrier Networks-Terminals-Telecommunication. ZTE's core products are wireless, exchange, access, optical transmission, and data telecommunications gear; mobile phones; and telecommunications software. It also offers products that provide value-added services, such as video on demand and streaming media. ZTE primarily sells products under its own name but it is also an OEM. ZTE is one of the top five largest smartphone manufacturers in its home market, and in the top ten, worldwide, http://www.abbreviations.com/ZTE.

one of Africa's largest economies ... What the government want from China are cheap loans and more control over its citizens.⁶³

Describing the root causes of the war in Sudan and the change of regimes in the region through the involvement of the U.S., Johnson writes: "The Sudan entered the twenty-first century mired in not one, but many civil wars. What had been seen in the 1980's as a war between North and South, Muslim against Christian, 'Arab' against 'African,' has, after nearly *two decades of hostilities*, broken the bounds of any North-South conflict. Fighting has spread into theaters outside the Southern Sudan and beyond the Sudan's borders. A war has been described as being fought over scarce resources is now being waged for *the total control of abundant oil reserves*."⁶⁴ Johnson continues:

> Chevron's exploration for oil created a stronger US interest in the Sudanese economy, and after 1980 the US became increasingly involved in development schemes, in funding the infrastructure for regionalization, and in servicing the growing Sudanese national debt. But a succession of international events, beginning with the overthrow of Haile Selassie in 1974, the subsequent alliance between Ethiopia and the Soviet Union, the Camp David Accord brokered by the US, Libya's growing hostility to Egypt, and the election of a Republican government in the US in 1980 all combined to influence the Sudan's role in international politics.
>
> The Sudan became important to the US as a regional counter weight to Soviet-backed Ethiopia. The Regan administration's high profile hostility towards Libya, which justified a US naval build up in the Mediterranean, drew the US and the Sudan into a closer military alliance. The Sudan became part of the Rapid Deployment force, allowing US forces to carry out joint manoeuvers with the Sudanese army on Sudanese soil. Alleged Libyan military threats to the Sudan enabled the US to deploy its ships off the Libyan coast in February 1983.⁶⁵

"Chevron USA began exploring oil in 1974 in the Mugald Basin. But when civil war broke out for the second time in the mid-1980s, Chevron abandoned more than $1 billion of private investment and sold its interest to a Canadian firm, which formed the Greater Nile Operating Company (GNPOC). In 1997, GNPOC sold a 40 percent share to China's largest oil company, [Chinese National Petroleum Company] CNPC. The goal of the newly formed company was to develop the Sudan's oil fields in the south-central part of the country and build a 1,500-kilometer (about 930-mile) pipeline to a coastal port facility at Marsa al-Bashir, near Port Sudan."⁶⁶ China's justification to engage in oil exploration with Sudan was that European companies had left the region, oil exploration is at an early stage, and China has the money, skill, and power and has an enormous need for oil.

In addition to oil exploration,

---

63. "Telecoms in Ethiopia: Out of Reach," *Economist*, August 24, 2013, p. 46.
64. Johnson, *Root Causes of Sudan's Civil Wars*, xi; emphasis added. See also Meredith, *Fate of Africa*, 594–95.
65. Johnson, *Root Causes of Sudan's Civil Wars*, 57.
66. Lee and Shalmon, "China's Oil Strategies," 125.

China has engaged in extensive arms sales to the Sudanese government, selling it some $100 million in arms between 1996 and 2003 alone. These weapons include jets and helicopter gunships, reportedly used for the repression of civilians in the South as part of the now terminated North-South conflict. The weaponry, which China sold to the Sudan throughout the 1990s, helped the government target villages in the South during the long running conflict with the Sudan's People Liberation Army. In particular, such targeting resulted in massive casualties and forced displacement. The depopulation of certain areas such as Unity State was not incidental; the government removed population for the areas target for oil exploration by CNPC. Violence has arisen since 2005 North-South peace agreement in parts of South where Petrodar, a consortium, involving Chinese and Malaysian companies, is conducting exploration. There has been significant displacement of the civilian populations (particularly Dinka) and environmental damage, with tensions leading to civilians killing the Petrodar team leader in January 2006"[67]

Hence, millions of Christians in Southern Sudan were killed under the watch of the EU, the UN, the United States and the Organization of African Union (OAU). "By the time the civil war ended, more than 2 million people had died and 4 million were displaced."[68] So long as oil, minerals, and geopolitical strategies are secured by the West or the East, the lives of blacks are not even worth the lives of animals. Like the carcasses of wild and domestic animals, vultures feasted from the corpses of the Southern Sudanese. If you want the proof, you can watch it in various YouTube videos. Sadly, some posted them as a pleasant thing to watch. To my horror, some people watch it with their children with laughter. It is totally incomprehensible to me how one can get joy out of watching a You Tube video of a corpse eaten by a vulture. Sub-Saharan Africa is a region of the world where many people are conditioned to die prematurely because of war, disease, and hunger.

> The powers of death make themselves felt in *social life* through rejection, isolation, and growing loneliness. If the social resonance withdrawn from us, if we are not only mentally hurt and injured in our sense of self-worth, then bodily disturbances are the result as well. Psychogenic death is not infrequently followed by suicide, into which people are driven through isolation. Social life too is a struggle against death, a fight for recognition against possible and fear rejections, a waiting for respect instead of defeat because of social coldness.
>
> Through exploitation, oppression and alienation, the powers of death reach deep into *political life*. Major decisions are incalculable consequences for the little lives of millions, even if this does not appear. They make life difficult if not impossible. The weak, the poor, and the sick struggle literally for survival every day. Before our very eyes the failure to render help on the political level contributes to mass death in Cambodia, Rwanda, Darfur, and other places where death is life.[69]

---

67. Brown and Siriam "China's Role," 256. See also Brautigam, *Dragon's Gift*, 281–84.
68. Lee and Shalmon, "China's Oil Strategies," 126.
69. Moltmann, *Sun of Righteousness Arise!*, 75–76; emphasis original.

Obviously, in the case of South Sudan there is a "failure to render help." Through Western support, Bashir formed his own militia, the People's Defence Force (PDF), modelling it on Iran's Revolutionary Guards. PDF numbers eventually reached 150,000. They were used to suppress civilian demonstration in northern towns and sent to the south as part of the war effort against rebel forces. The war itself officially became a jihad, a sacred duty for all Muslims to support. Pan Islamic activists like Turabi and al-Qaida founder Bin Laden were promoting their radical agenda through conferences and expanding construction businesses in the north while Christians were massacred in the south. Had it not been for the voice of conservative American Christians who opposed the war in Southern Sudan, according to Bashir's plan he could have wiped out the Christians in the south.[70]

"There are a vast number of metallic minerals spread all over the South Sudan: gold, copper, zinc, lead, manganese, iron, silver, tin, etc. Also industrial minerals exist: marble, limestone, dolomite, kaolin, clay, asbestos, etc. Apart from gold at Kapoeta and Luri; copper at Hofrat Ennahas, bauxite/iron ore at Wau area and marble at Kapoeta no other mineral has been prospected to an appreciable level."[71] With all these natural resources available in the country, I'll not be surprised if South Sudan will turn out to be another Congo or Angola in East Africa. The Horn of Africa is a volatile place for internal and global conflict because of its rich natural resources. "Recent massive gas discoveries in the east coast of Africa—Mozambique, Tanzania, and Kenya—mean this region could emerge as a major producer. But in a world of energy scarcity, the massive find also leaves the region vulnerable to incursions from military stronger actors as well as domestic turmoil as competing factions attempt to get their hand on the spoils."[72] The history of other African countries rich with natural resources is a good reminder of the potential problem in East Africa. "Four million people have been killed in what is euphemistically called Democratic Republic of the Congo (formerly Zaire) since 1998. They have died so the wealthier people can buy inexpensive computers and cell phones. Although the country won its independence from Belgium in 1960, it soon fell under Washington's influence."[73] "Each of these creature comforts requires commodity inputs—such as metals like copper, gold, lead, nickel, palladium, and circuit boards of computers or mobile phones. To place this demand in context as of 2010 an estimated 5.3 billion mobile phones were in use worldwide accounting for approximately 77 percent of the world's population and fast approaching one cell phone for every man, woman, or child on the planet today."[74] Then and now, Africa has made a significant contribution to the West. The return is neither gratitude nor financial gain, but poverty, disease, and death.[75]

70. See Meredith, *Fate of Africa*, 588–96.
71. Adde, "Geology and Mineral Investment."
72. Moyo, *Winner Take All*, 205.
73. Perkins, *Secret History of the American Empire*, 256.
74. Moyo, *Winner Take All*, 20.
75. July 2006 fact sheet titled "Recycle Cell Phone a Treasure Trove of Valuable Metals," compiled by the U.S Geological Survey, is revealing. It provided separate breakdown for 180 million cell phones then in use in the United States, another 130 million expected to be retired that year, and the 500 million

With the premature death of Dr. John Garang,[76] an educated and experienced leader who fought for the liberation of Southerners and yet was very much liked by the Sudanese, North and South, the pattern of oppression and exploitation of the West and the East had already begun. Every Southern Sudanese I interviewed told me Garang was killed by Americans. It is hard to verify these stories. But, if it is true, when the classified becomes unclassified—maybe fifty years from now—the generation at that time will find out, as we much later learned about the manner of death of Patrice Lumumba of Congo. The decent thing is, unlike African tyrants, America is good at recording her own sins.

As I stated in the footnote, Garang was closely working with the Chinese Communist Party more than the United States, not based on preference but for a lack of a better global partner. As China did in Angola, the Communist party is following the same pattern in Sudan—dealing with the government in power and the freedom fighters concurrently. Because the U.S. was closely working with the Bashir government to destabilize Libya and Ethiopia to counter the Russian influence in the region, it seems the American government was not interested in supporting two opposing factions at the same time in the Sudan—even if they had done so already in Angola. "The perception in many circles within SPLA/M[77] is that the United States may promise assistance and investments, but the Chinese actually deliver; this is a far different attitude than would have been found in the South two years ago. But what is more interesting is that the Chinese are working with the Kenya pipeline connecting the oilfields in Unity province with the port of Lamu in Kenya, which the Chinese likewise hope to develop. At the moment, the only way to export oil from the Sudan is through the port of Marsa al Bashir in the North."[78]

Recently, as I wrote this book, there was a huge ethnic clash in South Sudan. The International Crisis Group said [on April, 2, 2014] that the number of dead from the conflict was close to 10,000 people, a major increase from earlier estimates by the United Nations.

"Given the intensity of fighting in over 30 different locations in the past three weeks, we are looking at a death toll approaching 10,000," said Cassie Copeland, an analyst at

---

obsolete cell phones sitting in drawers and closets awaiting disposal. In the aggregate, . . . those 810 million cell phones contained over three thousand metric tons of metals, with a collective net worth of more than half a billion US dollars. To put it more graphically, the sum total of all phones in use, retired, and out of circulation in the United States in 2005, was equivalent to the amount of metal contained in fifty 747 jumbo jets. And this is just the United States in just one year at a time when cell phones were in their relative infancy. Ibid.

76. Since 2002 the Communist Party of China (CPC) has developed a close party-to-party relationship with the Sudan's Islamist National Congress Party (NCP), and until 2005 it had no contact with the opposition political parties, including the Sudanese Communist Party. After the signing of Comprehensive Peace Agreement (CPA) between the NCP and the opposition Sudan People's Liberation Movement (SPLM) in 2005, the two have joined to form a tenuous government of national unity. The CPA legitimized the SPLM and opened the door for the gradual expansion of SPLM-CPC political relations. The first outreach took place in March 2005, when then SPLM chief commander John Garang to head a SPLM delegation to China to hold talks on economic cooperation between the two parties. After the untimely death of Garang in July 2005, the CPC and SPLM party-to-party relations did not hold meeting in 2006. Eisenman, "China's Political Outreach," 238..

77. Sudan People's Liberation Army (SPLA) or Sudan People's Liberation Movement (SPLM).

78. Lee and Shalmon, "China's Oil Strategies," 130.

the International Crisis Group, a research and advocacy institution.[79] Fighting broke out at the same barracks in mid-December, 2013, triggering months of conflict that has claimed thousands of lives and displaced around 900,000 people across the young country that barely and recently got a respite from over forty years of war. The UN, which has more than 7,500 troops on the ground and has requested reinforcements, has promised it will not abandon civilians but experts say its forces will not be able to prevent violence across such a vast territory. Hence, "Both South Sudanese and the international community were ill-prepared to prevent or halt the conflict: the nation's closest allies did little to mediate leadership divisions within the Sudan Peoples' Liberation Movement (SPLM)."[80] As we have seen in Sierra Leone, Congo, Angola, and other African countries, one wonders if the mission of the UN soldiers is to protect civilians or secure potential mining places.

As I stated in this book, the Sudan region is one of the birthplaces of African civilization. However, since its creation, Southern Sudan did not have a paved road until 2012. The 192-kilometer-long Juba-Nimule Road was the largest infrastructure project ever built in South Sudan and the young nation's first paved highway. "This road literally paves the way to South Sudan's future," said the U.S. Ambassador's webpage. "The road has integrated South Sudan into East African transportation and trade corridors, bringing to the people of South Sudan ordinary goods they need day to day, humanitarian assistance for those in need, as well as equipment and materials for those who are investing and building in South Sudan."[81] The road was built with funding that came through the USAID (United States Agency for International Development). It is ironic that the economic and developmental injuries and sicknesses of Southern Sudan are treated by the USAID. Before the civil war ended, the U.S. was supporting Bashir and his regime indirectly attacking and killing Southerners. After the Cold War, mainly after 9/11, the U.S. switched its position. Now the U.S. is in South Sudan with the flag of a philanthropist.

As usual, changes and developments are introduced into African countries without the input of insiders, studies of cultural norms and values, and economic and social structures—the results of dreams and aspirations of the local people are as such

---

79. On 15 December 2013 the world's newest state descended into civil war. Continuing fighting has displaced more than 1,000,000 and killed over 10,000 while a humanitarian crisis threatens many more. Both South Sudanese and the international community were ill-prepared to prevent or halt the conflict: the nation's closest allies did little to mediate leadership divisions within the Sudan Peoples' Liberation Movement's (SPLM). The SPLM and its army (SPLA) quickly split along divisions largely unaddressed from the independence war. Were it not for the intervention of Uganda and allied rebel and militia groups, the SPLA would likely not have been able to hold Juba or recapture lost territory. The war risks tearing the country further apart and are pulling in regional states. Resolving the conflict requires not a quick fix but sustained domestic and international commitment. Governance, including SPLM and SPLA reform and communal relations, must be on the table. Religious and community leaders, civil society and women are critical to this process and must not be excluded (Copland, "South Sudan: A Civil War by Any Other Name").

80. "South Sudan: A Civil War by Any Other Name," *Africa Report* 217, April 10, 2014. See also Gouel, "Conflict in South Sudan"; "Back with a Vengeance," *Economist*, March 1, 2014; "South Sudan: Destroying Itself from within," *Economist*, January 4, 2014, p. 36.

81. "First Paved Highway in South Sudan Constructed by US Aid Officially Opened," USAID: From the American People, September 13, 2012, http://www.usaid.gov/news-information/press-releases/first-paved-highway-south-sudan-constructed-usaid-officially-opened.

irrelevant to the well-being of the people. "With only one paved overland road, south Sudan is not an obvious place for car lovers. Yet locals harbor intense feelings of devotion for certain Japanese vehicles. 'One day my son will drive a v8,' says a man making a living by renting out sockets to recharge mobile phones on a street corner in the capital ... The Dinka, the most powerful tribe in the new country, have long revered cattle to the point where they would rather go hungry than slaughter them. Cattle have been a status symbol, a store of value in a land without banks, the only way to pay dowries until now. With independence and modernity, a cream of v8 has become as desirable as a white bull. The first substitute for cattle may have arrived."[82] In a country that has more cattle than cars one wonders if the paved road is for the Southern Sudanese or a conduit to export oil and minerals.

"Modernity" not only whet the appetite of the African poor for outside commodities, it also drove Western powers for natural resources in Africa. George Rich, a venerable engineer who used to work for USAID once said, "I've spent a life time studying geology and I can tell you that during your life Africa will become a battleground over oil."[83] Depending on the U.S. position to get control or not, oil can save or destroy African countries. During the European scramble for Africa, the British wanted to detach the Ogaden from Ethiopia and sought to create Greater Somaliland, but also began to include the Ogaden in maps of Somalia. The U.S. blocked the strategy and the British plan did not materialize. It was not because the U.S. foreign policy was in favor of the well-being of Ethiopians or that they cared for the political and economic conditions of Ethiopians. Sadly, it was because Sinclair Oil Company had found oil in the Ogaden and British occupation would be an injury to the American commercial interest. Although Sinclair had received oil concessions from Ethiopia in 1945, it refused to engage in oil exploration until the political picture in the Ogaden was cleared.[84]

Like in Sudan and many other African countries, the US often plays both the role of a soldier who is wounding or inflicting injuries on others and a physician of the injured concurrently without conflict of conscience or values. The continent has been and will remain partly wounded, partly vigorous. What a dilemma!

With all of the good virtues I have seen in Americans during my stay in the United States for more than three decades, with all of their ingenuity, amazing organizational skills, magnanimous spirit, and abundant resources, if they will genuinely and sincerely engage to transform Africa as they did in Japan, Israel, and Europe, there will be a huge change in the continent. With a win-win relationship, true democracy, accountability, and transparency on both sides, Africa would be free of debt, starvation, malnutrition, conflicts, and wars.

> The world has lately been making extraordinary progress in lifting people out of extreme poverty. [Through the Millennium Development Goals (MDGs)], between 1990 and 2010, their number fell by half as a share of the total population in developing countries, from 43% to 21%—a reduction of almost 1 billion people.

82. "Vroom-Vroom in the Bush," *Economist*, July 13, 2013, p. 44.
83. Perkins, *Secret History of the American Empire*, 192.
84. Munene, *Truman Administration*, 68.

> Of the 7 billion people alive on the planet, 1.1 billion subsist below the internationally accepted extreme-poverty line of $1.25 a day . . . Nobody in the developed world comes remotely close to the poverty level that $1.25 a day represents. America's poverty line is $63 a day for a family of four. In the richer parts of the emerging world $4 a day is the poverty barrier. But poverty's scourge is fiercest below $1.25 (the average of the 15 poorest countries' own poverty lines, measured in 2005 dollars and adjusted for differences for purchasing power): *people below that level live lives that are poor, nasty, brutish and short. They lack not just education, health care, proper clothing and shelter—which most people in most of the world take for granted—but even enough food for physical and mental health. Raising people above that level of wretchedness is not a sufficient ambition for a prosperous planet, but it is a necessary one* . . .
>
> China (which has never shown any interest in MDGs) is responsible for the three-quarter of the achievement. Its economy has been growing so fast that, even though inequality is rising fast, extreme poverty is disappearing. China pulled 680m people out of misery in 1981–2010, and reduced its extreme-poverty rate from 84% in 1980 to 10% now . . . Poorer governance in India and Africa the next two targets, means that China's experience is unlikely to be swiftly replicated there.[85]

As *The Economist* stated above, unfortunately, the African continent has not had a respite from instability to convert natural resources and energy into industrialization. Not only that, Africans don't even own, in the true sense of the word, most of their natural resources that the West has been utilizing to enrich its capitalistic system. Now China is gobbling up resources with a voracious appetite—and African leaders are nowhere near bringing about healthy, effective, and holistic development. Neither the external nor internal factors are functioning for the good of African people and for the progress of the continent.

Founded on an enviable constitution, having a democracy that lies in the hearts and minds of Americans, I strongly believe the U.S. should have no part in the African political mud or participate in the injustice and exploitation of the African people. As I know them, Americans are freedom-loving people; they love and adore life, nature, and animals, especially dogs. And they are very caring people. They are patriotic: to protect their country and secure the freedom of their people, millions have shed their blood. They love justice, fair treatment, and equality. In all aspects of their lives they are fierce competitors. In over three decades of life experience in the U.S. and as a citizen of this country, there are many qualities and virtues of this nation that I can attest to and yet they have not been reflected and represented in the foreign policy of the U.S. in Africa and in their treatment of the black people in general.

The major weak point of Americans that I have noticed is that they have limited or no knowledge about the world, sometimes even to the point of being embarrassing to me. Like the question where is Ethiopia? When I was in the fifth grade in my social studies class, on a blank map of the U.S., I could fill in all of the states. When many American adults ask me where Ethiopia is, I don't know what to make of them. These are people who have a world of information at their fingertips. Paul Borthwick concurs that

---

85. "Towards the End of Poverty," 11; emphasis mine.

Americans are ignorant of global matters: "American citizens may be among the world's most prosperous, but according to a recent National Geographic study conducted by the Gallup Poll, their geographical knowledge is hardly world-class. In the nine-nation survey of 10,820 adults, U.S. respondents finished third from the bottom... Among the American respondents 75 percent failed to locate the Persian Gulf on a map. At the same time, fewer than half could find the United Kingdom, France, South Africa, or Japan. Using blank maps, the average American could identify only four of the twelve European nations, and fewer than six of ten U.S. States. Perhaps most humiliating, one in seven U.S. adults could not identify the United States on the map."[86]

Because of such limited knowledge, the majority of Americans do not have information about various cultures of the world, global politics, or economic affairs. Hence, the government is less accountable to the people for much of the uncalled-for U.S. involvement in different nations. Had they fully known, whether they are Christians or non-Christians, I don't think Americans would justify or condone the modus operandi of the U.S. in Africa for more than four centuries. The answer to my question—Why are Americans not standing for the rights of Africans as they did for Kosovo, the Jews in Europe, the Vietnamese, and Cambodians?—is because they don't know, not because they don't care. They don't care because they don't know. "Since Africa is the least understood continent, it is also the one most easily ignored and therefore vulnerable to plunder... Nigeria is the fifth largest supplier of U.S. oil, Angola is sixth, and Gabon tenth. Nigeria has the ninth-largest population in the world—just before Japan (tenth) and Mexico (eleventh). U.S. ignorance about Africa is ingrained in our educational systems, including the mainstream media. It is calculated. Because we do not know, we do not care. Because we do not care, these countries are open territory for mistreatment, even more than those that fall within our radar."[87] Calderisi adds, "Few international newspapers still have correspondents in Africa, the continent is generally absent from economic and financial news and hardly appears even in brief digest of world events. If not for their colorful national dress at international conferences, Africans would scarcely be noticed on the world stage."[88] Howard W. French, a prominent American journalist, concurs: "Africa occupied a relatively blank space in the minds of most Americans, and when they stopped to think about it, aided by old and deeply ingrained habits of press coverage, all they could imagine was violence, corruption, disease, and horror."[89] I often wonder what makes the CBS and ABC evening news, *world* news—the large part of coverage focuses on the United States. Unless we call the small bubble that we live in a world one can hardly find world news that justifies the title of the program. But, despite my disappointment, I watch it almost every day. That is one aspect of my being American, I guess.

It does not mean that the West lacks information or news about Africa. Mazrui states: "Africa has been swallowed by the global system of dissemination of information. What Africa knows about itself, what different parts of Africa know about each other, have been profoundly influenced by the West. Even in the field of the mass media, Africa

---

86. Borthwick, *How to Be a World Class Christian*, 48.
87. Perkins, *Secret History of the American Empire*, 48.
88. Calderisi, *Trouble with Africa*, 5.
89. French, *China's Second Continent*, 154.

is overwhelmingly dependent on the wire services of the Western world for information about itself. What Nigerians know about Kenya, or Zambians know about Ghana, is heavily derived from the wire services of the Western world transmitting information across the globe. African newspapers and radios subscribe to these wire services and receive data for their news bulletins from Western sources."[90]

My daily struggle as an Ethiopian-American is to reconcile the irreconcilable and contradicting values and norms of American foreign policy, democracy, norms, and transparency at home with that of dictatorial and imperialistic involvement in Africa. I'm neither a student of the American constitution nor a politician, but simple commonsense and keen observation tells me that most of the U.S. involvement in Africa impoverishes people, violates their human rights, and endangers the well-being and existence of millions of Africans. John Perkins puts the indictment on the U.S. and calls Americans to wake up in these words that will pierce your heart and soul:

> Every story about Africa hinges on deception. From Egypt to Mali to Diego Garcia, subterfuge and denial are the keys to the American Empire's policies. It is as ruthless as any in history. It has enslaved more people and its policies and actions have resulted in more deaths than those under the imperial regime of Rome, Spain, Portugal, France, and England, and Holland or at the hands of Joseph Stalin and Adolf Hitler, and yet its crimes go almost unnoticed, disguised in the robes of eloquent rhetoric. Our educational systems and media actively participate of IMF and World Bank policies. Latin America lights the way towards democracy and the Middle East exposes the extent to which neocolonialism has failed. Africa serves up what might turn out to be the most important lesson of all. Facing west towards America, Africa cups her hands around her mouth—where the Niger Delta joins the Bay of Guinea—and shouts out: Be Aware! Be alert and diligent. Take action....
>
> More than anywhere else, Africa highlights the urgency. She is the dead canary in the mine. The mine is a deathtrap. We need to save ourselves and we need to pave a way for our children to survive in a sustainable and stable world. To do so, we must listen to Africa. It is imperative that we open our ears to that voice screaming at us from across the Atlantic. *You live on a small planet, it says, in a tiny community. To save your kids, you must also help me save mine; they are one and the same; we are family.*[91]

According to Howard W. French, who has written two books on Africa, crisscrossed the continent, interviewed Western and Asian diplomats and prominent African scholars, has seen a number of civil wars in action, and knows Africans very well, said:

> In the eyes of so many . . . the West with its countless rules and procedural demands, its frequent if inconsistent insistence on good form in areas like democracy and human rights and corruption, had promised but never seemed to get around to.
>
> Countless conversations with Africans suggested to me that they saw the United States as the epitome of all of these disappointments. The idealism of its rhetoric far surpassed that of the world and knowing Europeans, who had

---

90. Mazrui, *Africans*, 13–14.
91. Perkins, *Secret History of the American Empire*, 266; emphasis his.

colonized Africa and never completely extracted themselves. But this only contributed to the Africans sense of being let down by the United States; Americans made beautiful, principled speeches and imposed countless conditions on all manner of things. But in the end, in Africa they seemed to move the ball very slowly. They regarded Africa not as a terrain of opportunity or even as a morally compelling challenge to humanity, but as a burden, and largely as one to be evaded as much as possible.[92]

In extracting mineral resources and using African labor to be where the country is today, the U.S. had taken more advantage of Africa than the colonizers Europe. It is hard to understand how Africa can be a burden to the United States. It should be vice versa.

The United States have had sincere and godly Christian presidents and currently has a black president whose father is a Kenyan.

> But when Barak Obama sets foot in Africa in June 26, [2013] . . . Warship accompanied the first African-American commander-in-chief, equipped with state-of-the-art- hospitals should he fall ill, fighter jets patrol sky non-stop, and three Lorries carry bulletproof glass for hotels where he beds down . . .
>
> Mr. Obama's election in 2008 was celebrated across the continent. The Nigerian foreign minister wept, Kenya declared a national holiday and Nelson Mandela said Mr. Obama proved "Africans should dare to dream." Soon after his inauguration, he repaid the compliment by showering the continent with public affection. "I have the blood of Africa within me," he declared on a 20-hour stopover in Ghana in 2009, raising hopes he would be Africa's global champion. But he has not visited since. Some Africans resent his long absence, suggesting he neglected them.[93]

Despite one democratic election after another by freedom- and justice-loving Americans, the foreign policy of the U.S. in Africa has not been improved to promote economic and political health in the continent. The mystery lies here: "The corporatocracy makes a show of promoting democracy and transparency among the nations of the world, yet its corporations are imperialistic dictatorship where a very few make all the decisions and reap most of the profits. In our electoral process—the very heart of democracy—most of us get to vote only for candidates whose campaign chest are full; therefore, we must select from among those who are beholden to the corporations and the men who own them. Contrary to our ideals, this empire is built on foundations of greed, secrecy, and excessive materialism."[94] Wrong, unethical, and unrighteous foundations cannot hold the empire for too long. Let us not be deceived by the "success" of the last two hundred years or so. We may be able to outsmart the global political and economic system; however, in human history, there is no superpower nation that out-smarted the righteous judge—the God of Isiah, Amos, and Hosea. "The prophets' preoccupation with justice and righteousness has its roots in a powerful awareness of injustice. That justice is a good thing, a fine goal, even a supreme ideal, is commonly accepted. What is lacking is a sense of monstrosity of injustice. Moralists of all ages

---

92. French, *China's Second Continent*, 152.
93. "Late But Not Empty-Handed," *Economist*, June 22, 2013, pp. 53–54.
94. Perkins, *Secret History of the American Empire*, 7.

have been eloquent in singing the praise of virtue. The distinction of the prophet was in their remorseless unveiling of injustice and oppression, in their comprehension of social, political, and religious evils. They were not concerned with the definition, but with the predicament, of justice, with the fact that those called upon to apply it defied it."[95]

---

95. Heschel, *Prophets*, 260.

Chapter 6

Africa

The Prize of Western Civilization and Capitalism

For every civilization has its reverse side, which is a barbarism; every victorious history has its underside, which is the misery of the defeated, and all progress has its price. This other side is generally neither seen nor heard.[1]

Woe to him who heaps up what is not his own . . . woe to him who get evil gain for his house, . . . the stone cries out from the wall, and the beam from the woodwork responds. Woe to him who builds a town with blood, and founds a city on iniquity. (Hab 2:6, 9, 11–12)

The Role of Christianity in Western Capitalism

IN MEDIEVAL EUROPE, FAITH dominated reason, the church's power superseded the state, and the influence of the clergy was more powerful than that of politicians. "With the aid of the Platonic idea of an immutable, static order of things, an all-embracing interpretation of the world emerged in the light of the Christian faith and at the same time a complete interpretation of the faith in the light of the geocentric world view. The Bible is understood cosmically and the cosmos biblically; Christian faith guarantees the world picture and the world picture guarantees Christian faith. Theology and cosmology, the order of salvation and the order of the world, appear to be in perfect harmony."[2] Until this worldview was broken down by the Copernican revolution, medieval theology was

---

1. Moltmann, *Way of Jesus*, 64.
2. Küng, *Does God Exist?*, 36.

determined by the Greco-medieval worldview down to the last detail. This worldview had enormously influenced the economic trend in Europe as it did the other aspects of the society, such as education, innovation, and gender relations.

In his widely-acclaimed book, *Religion and the Rise of Capitalism*, R. H. Tawney, has superbly described how Christianity in the West immensely suffered from the same disease it purported to cure. Tawney's object was to study how the medieval conception of social order, which had regarded it as a highly articulated organism of members contributing in their different ways to a spiritual purpose, was shattered. What emerged was—the "creed of the individual" as a "master of his own, with no obligation to postpone his own profit to the well-being of his neighbors."[3] Max Weber, in his seminal work *The Protestant Ethic and the Spirit of Capitalism* has brilliantly addressed the psychological conditions that made possible the development of capitalist civilization. The book analyzes the connection between the spread of Calvinism and a new attitude toward the pursuit of wealth in post-Reformation Europe and England, an attitude that permitted, encouraged—even sanctified—the human quest for prosperity. At its initial stage, the spirit of capitalism was not greed, love of money, and material things as we know it today. Weber write: "Unlimited greed for gain is not in the least identical with capitalism, and is still less its spirit. Capitalism *may* even be identical with the restraint, or at least a rational tempering, of this irrational impulse. But capitalism is identical with the pursuit of profit, and forever *renewed* profit, by means of continuous, rational, capitalistic enterprise."[4]

When economic science was in its first flush dogmatic youth during the medieval time, the religious opinion, Christianity in particular, adopted four main attitudes toward the world of social institutions and economic relations:

1. It may stand on one side in ascetic aloofness and regard them as in their very nature the sphere of unrighteousness, from which men *may* escape—from which, if they consider their souls, they *will* escape—but which they can conquer only by flight.

2. It may take them for granted and ignore them, as matters of indifference belonging to a world with which religion has no concern; in all ages the prudence of looking problems boldly in the face and passing on has seemed too self-evident to require justification.

3. It may throw itself into an agitation for some particular reform, for the removal of some crying scandal, for the promotion of some final revolution, which will inaugurate the reign of righteousness on earth.

4. It may at once accept and criticize, tolerate and amend, welcome the gross world of human appetites, as squalid scaffolding from amid which the life of the spirit must rise, and insist that this also is the material of the Kingdom of God.

5. To such a temper, all activities divorced from religion are brutal or dead, but none are too mean to be beneath or too great to be above it, since all, in their different degrees, are touched with the spirit which permeates the whole. . .Of

---

3. Tawney, *Religion and the Rise of Capitalism*, xx.
4. Weber, *Protestant Ethic*, 17; emphasis original.

the four attitudes suggested above, it is the last which is most characteristic. The first fundamental assumption which is taken over by the sixteenth century is that the ultimate standard of human institutions and activities is religion.[5]

The mercantilist thought of the later centuries owed a considerable debt to scholastic discussions of money, prices, and interest. But the specific contributions of medieval writers to the technique of economic theory were less significant than their premises. Their fundamental assumptions, both of which were to leave a deep imprint on the social thought of the sixteenth and seventeenth centuries, were two: that economic interests are subordinate to the real business of life, which is salvation, and that economic conduct is one aspect of personal conduct, upon which, as on other parts of it, the rules of morality are binding. Material riches are necessary; they have a secondary importance, since without them persons cannot support themselves and help one another.[6]

Usurers and the sin of avarice were not tolerated in the medieval West. "An archbishop of Canterbury is reminded that usury is perilous, not only for the clergy, but for all men whatever, and is warned to use ecclesiastical censures to secure the restoration, without the deduction of interest, of property which has been pawned."[7] Without this restrictive religious, economic, and social background the sumptuous shrine of Western civilization and the individualistic capitalistic economy of the West could not be fully understood. The tension between the teaching of the church and social institutions, particularly those who were engaged with business, trade, and commerce, was high. The conflict between wants and needs, the appetite to have more, and the discipline of frugality and contentment, the values and norms of the church and the aspiration of innovators and entrepreneurs were not easy exercises to reconcile.

The two reformers Luther and Calvin took an opposite view on the issue. For Luther, "The exploitation of the Church by Papacy, and the exploitation of the peasant and the craftsmen by the capitalists, are thus two horns of the beast which sits on the seven hills. Both are essentially pagan, and the sword which will slay both the same. It is the religion of the gospel. The church must cease to be an empire, and become a congregation of believers. Renouncing the prizes and struggles which make the heart sick, society must be converted into a band of brothers, performing in patient cheerfulness the round of simple toil which is the common lot of the descendants of Adam."[8] Calvin had a different theological approach. By developing the theology of work and ethics, sin and virtue, gaining and giving, Calvin made a huge contribution to the success of Western industrialization and the emergence of Western capitalism.

Tawney writes:

> Calvin did for the bourgeoisie of the sixteenth century what Marx did for the proletariat of the nineteenth century, or that the doctrine of predestination satisfied the same hunger for an assurance that the force of the same universe are on the side of the elect as was to be assuaged in a different age by the theory

---

5. Tawney, *Religion and the Rise of Capitalism*, 17, 19. I have made the original into a numbered list.

6. Ibid., 31.

7. Ibid., 47.

8. Ibid., 90.

of historical materialism. He set their virtues at their best in sharp antithesis with the vices of the established order at its worst, taught them to feel that they were a chosen people, made them conscious of their great destiny in the Providential plan and resolute to realize it. The new law was graven on the tablets of flesh; is not merely rehearsed a lesson, but fashioned a soul. Compared with the quarrelsome, self-indulgent nobility of most European countries, or with the extravagant and half-bankrupt monarchies, the middle classes, in whom Calvinism took root most deeply, were a race of iron. It was not surprising that they made several revolutions, and imprinted their conceptions of political and social expediency on the public life of half a dozen different States in the Old world and the New.[9]

In the assault on pauperism, moral and economic motives were not distinguished. The idleness of the mendicant was both a sin against God and a social evil; the enterprise of the thriving tradesman was at once a Christian virtue and a benefit to the community. The same combinations of religious zeal and practical shrewdness prompted the attacks on gambling, searing, excess in apparel, and self-indulgence in eating and drinking. The essence of the system was not preaching or propaganda, though it was as prolific of both, but the attempt to crystalize a moral ideal in the daily life of a visible society, which should be at once a church and state.

It was in that spirit that he made Geneva a city of glass, in which every household lived its life under the supervision of a spiritual police, and that for a generation Consistory and Council worked hand in hand, the former excommunicating drunkards, dancers, and contemners of religion, the latter punishing the dissolute with fines and imprisonment and the heretic with death.[10]

Like early Christianity and modern socialism, Calvinism was largely an urban movement. Like them, in its earlier days, it was carried from country to country partly by emigrant traders and workmen, and its stronghold was those social groups to which the traditional scheme of social ethics, with its treatment of economic interests as a quite minor aspect of human affairs, must have seemed irrelevant or artificial. As was to be expected among exponents of the faith, which had its headquarters in Geneva—and later its most influential adherents in great business centers, like Antwerp with its industrial hinterland, London, and Amsterdam—its leaders addressed their teaching, not of course exclusively but nonetheless primarily, to the classes engaged in trade and industry, who formed the most modern and progressive elements in the life of the age.[11]

The triumph of economic virtues was taken both by the church and the Western states as the new medicine to their poverty. Initially, peaceful sea route commerce trades, and discoveries of new lands took unprecedented growth. The need for human labor and raw materials with unbridled greed led to the African slave trade and a scramble for the continent. "The new resources commanded by Europe during the first half of the sixteenth century might have done something to exorcise the specters of pestilence and famine, and to raise the material fabric of civilization to undreamed-of heights . . . The

---

9. Ibid., 112.
10. Ibid. See ibid., 102–32.
11. Ibid., 104.

sluice which they opened to drain away each new accession of superfluous wealth was war."[12]

African Slave Trade

> I go back to Africa to try to make an open path for commerce and Christianity. Do you carry on the work which I have begun, I leave it with you. Was Livingstone, then in reality a colonialist, a forerunner of those colonialist exploiters who have made life in so many parts of Africa a horror and a nightmare? His words have been understood in that sense by some critics, but not by anyone who has taken the trouble to read what he said and to consider what he meant. The guilt of the white men on the west coast, and still more perhaps of the Arabs on the east coast, in carrying on the slave trade, has been beyond all reckoning. But Livingstone had realized that the slave trade could not have been carried on at all apart from the African's own participation in it. When slave-raiding is the easiest, indeed the only, way of making oneself rich, the temptation was ever present to engage in those raids on weaker neighbors which made life perilous for the weak and defenseless over so much of the continent. Only if the Africans could be persuaded to engage in legitimate commerce exchanging the products of their own fields and forests for those desirable things which the white man could supply, would the evil and destructive commerce be brought to an end.[13]

Paradoxically, the Christianity and commerce that Livingstone hoped would end the slave trade, maximized the African slave market and led to colonialism.

Who started the African slave trade, the West or Africans? Were the African slaves shipped to Arab countries, Europe, and the Americas sold and betrayed by their own people? Were Africans coerced to engage in slave trade by the Western powers? What was the understanding of Africans and the West about slaves? How did both treat African slaves? Before we indulge in the effect of the African slave trade in the West, it is crucial to answer these questions.

In his excellent academic work, *Africa and Africans in the Making of the Atlantic World 1400–1800*, John Thornton, after analyzing various views of scholars on the issue of slaves, concluded that "[t]he significance of African slavery can be understood by comparing it briefly with slavery in Europe. Both societies possessed the institution, and both tended to define slave in the same way—as subordinate family members, in some ways equivalent to permanent children. This is precisely how slaves are dealt with in *Siete partidas*, following a precedent that goes all the way back to Aristotle, if not before. Modern research clearly reveals that this is also how Africans defined slavery in the late precolonial and early colonial period."[14] What we see here is that the history of slavery is much older than the practice of Europe and Africa, and the institution existed in both continents before they even came into contact with each other. The fundamental difference between Europe and Africa is the way they viewed and treated their slaves. In

---

12. Ibid., 76. For an in-depth reading on the development of Western capitalism, see Smith, *The Wealth of Nations*.

13. Neill, *History of Christian Missions*, 315–16.

14. Thornton, *Africa and Africans*, 86; emphasis his.

Kongo, "where the remarkable documentation allows glimpses of underlying ideology, the term for a slave, *neke*, was the same as for a child, suggesting family idiom prevailed there."[15] "The prior existence of slavery in Africa is undeniable fact, but there can be little comparison between the age-old institution of African slavery, in which captives were typically absorbed and assimilated into the culture that captured them, and the industrial scale of Europe's triangular trade, and even less with its dehumanizing impact and brutality."[16] Perkins adds, "I had visited the slums of America, Asia, and the Middle East, had recoiled in shock at the Museum of the Inquisition in Lima and photos of Apache warriors shackled to U.S. Army dungeon walls; I knew about the violence of Suharto's military and the shah's secret police, the SAVAK; yet in my opinion, nothing compared to Africa. What I had seen I visualized and my visions included innocent men, women, and children snared in nets, hauled screaming aboard slave ships, piled one on top of another, purking, shitting, dying, while back home in Africa their lands, their people, animals, and jungles were ravaged by 'civilized' Europeans. All of it so my ancestors could strut in their cotton gowns."[17]

> It was in places such as the dungeons beneath Cape Coast Castle and the Elmina cells in Ghana that the captives waited for the slave ships that would take the aboard. They were often packed in close together, sweating on each other, sometimes lying in their own urine and in their own filth. If cholera broke out a whole cell could be wiped out almost overnight. And yet they were supervised by the same Westerners who very often proved supremely skillful in protecting their cattle or their sheep and yet here they were so appallingly inefficient in protecting the lives of their captives. Yes, I know, we have had slavery, too, domestic slavery not alien to African traditions. But this scale of callousness, this scale of indifference, was totally foreign to African societies.[18]

According to Wickins, "Enslaving and slave trading in East Africa were peculiarly savage in traffic notable for its barbarity. Villagers were burned, the unfit villagers massacred. The enslaved were yoked together, several hundred in a caravan (for) a journey to the coast which could be as long as 1280 kilometers . . . It is estimated that only one in five of those captured in the interior reached Zanzibar. The slave trade seems to have been more catastrophic in East Africa than in West Africa."[19] In general, the slave trade had a debilitating effect in Africa.

Thornton gives us further detailed reflection in comparison terms on how Europe and Africa handled their slaves as follows:

> Where the difference can be found is not in the legal technicalities but in the way slaves are used. In theory, there might have been no differences in this respect either, but in practice, African slaves served in a much wider variety of ways than did European or Euro-American slaves. In Europe [and] the New World as well

---

15. Ibid., 86–87; emphasis original.
16. French, *Continent for the Taking*, 21.
17. Perkins, *Secret History of the American Empire*, 226.
18. Mazrui, *Africans*, 230–31.
19. Wickins, *Economic History of East Africa*, 184.

> ... slaves typically had difficult, demanding and degrading work, and they were often mistreated by exploitative masters who were anxious to maximize profits.
>
> This is not the case in Africa, however. People wishing to invest wealth in reproducing form could not buy land, for there was no land property. Hence, their only recourse was to purchase slaves, which as their personal property could be inherited and could generate wealth for them. They would have no trouble in obtaining land to put these slaves into agricultural production, for African law made land available to whoever would cultivate it, free or slave, as long as no previous cultivator was actively using it.
>
> African slaves were often treated no differently from peasant cultivators, as indeed they were the functional equivalent of free tenants and hired workers in Europe. This situation, the result of the institutional differences between Europe and Africa, has given rise to the idea that African slave were well treated, or at least better treated than European slaves ... slaves in central Africa [were] "slaves in name only" by virtue of their relative freedom and the wide variety of employments to which they were put. Likewise ... slaves were often employed as administrators, soldiers, and even royal advisors, thus enjoying great freedom of movement and elite life-style.[20]

Thornton also sheds light to the higher status of Joseph in Egypt who was twice sold as a slave, once by his brothers to the merchants and again by the merchants to Potiphar's husband. In Egypt, according to many scholars' views, blacks were dominating and leading both the political and economic sphere of the country at his time.[21]

The dehumanization of African slaves and the dreadful experience of it started in the process of the transfer from Africa to the Americas and Europe. Thornton explains:

> The complex process of shifting people from Africa to the Americas was full of horrors and might well last several months, during which most slaves would witness the maximum inhuman degradation, while suffering themselves. Vomit, urine, feces, and perspiration made the holds of the ships intolerable by the end of the voyage, even on such ships that took precautions to clean them. Indeed it was the foul smell that wafted over New Amsterdam in 1655 that announced to the inhabitants that a slave ship had arrived and the Caretenga Jesuits believed that spending even an hour in the holds would make a person sick.
>
> Therefore, while enduring these conditions, they would be driven to the brink of death, see others die, often horribly, and at all times live under conditions of extreme deprivation. No doubt many were driven insane, and others suffered severe psychological shock ... If it were not enough that they had just been advised to forget their homes and former lives. Upon departure, slaves from Luanda were told that upon their arrival they would be killed and made oil and eaten.[22]

As Africans were dealing with slave trade with Europeans in the already existing market in Africa, the underlying perception and understanding of the transaction was that Europeans would be treating African slaves the same way the African masters used to handle their own slaves. Before too long, the West saw the lucrative business in the

---

20. Thornton, *Africa and Africans*, 87.
21. C. Williams, *Destruction of Civilization*; Ehret, *Civilizations of Africa*; Diop, *African Origin of Civilization*; Diop, *Black Africa*.
22. Thornton, *Africa and Africans*, 160–61.

African slave trade and engaged it with zest, treating African slaves as mere merchandise. Mintz concurs: "Slaves were treated ... as commodities. To obtain them, products were shipped to Africa; by their labor power, wealth was created in the Americas. The wealth they created mostly turned to Britain; the products they made were consumed in Britain; and the products made by Britons—cloth, tools, torture instruments—were consumed by slaves who were themselves consumed in the creation of wealth."[23] Britain also came up with two words that distinguished the status of slaves—"Chattels" and "freehold slavery." Edward Hall explains, "A freehold slave is a worker, bound to a piece of land, who could not be transferred or sold away from the estate. The master of a freehold slave claimed possession of the individual's labor, not his or her person. Freehold slaves included those in bondage to the Spanish in South America and in some parts of Africa ... A chattel slave was the equivalent of a property and could be sold away like a horse. Also the children of chattel slaves automatically assumed the slave identity of their mother, not always the case among freehold workers."[24]

The indentured slaves who came to the Americas to work on farms and sugar plantations were too weak to endure the heat and the hard labor. When they did not produce the expected results and racism was heightened against black people, both through theology and behavioral sciences, Africa turned into an open market for the slave trade. The underlying motive of Europeans to bring African slaves to the West was economic, not mere hatred of Africans. Of course, as I stated, Africans were not shipped to the West with no clue of civilization, education, and intelligence. They had emotion, will, self-esteem, family, and home. To subdue them, the slave owners used every dehumanizing means to break African slaves.

For the Iberian powers the Atlantic slave trade was a crucial connection with Africa that was to dominate the relations of Africa with the West for centuries to come. Africa was drawn into the commercial world of Europe and the Americas. On the basis of African labor, the economies of the Americas were reconstructed. Even Bartolomé de Las Casas, justly celebrated for his defense of the Amerindians, for a time approved the African slave trade because he believed the stronger, more robust Africans would survive the rigorous who were killing the native peoples under the new economy produced by the European conquest of the New World.[25]

About 1730 in Bristol it was estimated that on a fortune voyage the profit on a cargo of about 270 slaves reached 7,000 or 8,000 pounds, exclusive of the return from ivory. An eighteenth-century writer has estimated sterling value of 303,737 slaves, carried on 878 Liverpool ships between 1783 and 1793 at over fifteen million pounds. Deducting commission and other charges and the cost of the outfit of the ships and maintenance of slaves, he concluded that the average annual profit was over 30 percent.

The development of the triangular trade and shipbuilding led to the growth of the great seaport towns. Bristol, Liverpool, and Glasgow occupied, as seaports and trading centers, the position in the age of trade that Manchester, Birmingham, and Sheffield

---

23. Mintz, *Sweetness and Power*, 43.
24. Hall *Slaves in the Family*, 38.
25. Walls, *Cross-Cultural Process*, 93.

occupied later in the age of industry. It was the slave and sugar trade that made Bristol the second city of England for the first three-quarters of the eighteenth century.

The shipping entering Liverpool increased four and half times between 1709 and 1771; the outward tonnage increased six and a half times during same period, the tonnage and sailors over six times. Customs receipts soared from an average of 51,000 for the years 1750 to 1757 to 648,000 in 1785. Dock duties increased two and a half times between 1752 and 1771. The population rose 5,000 in 1700 to 34,000 in 1773. By 1770 Liverpool had become too famous a town in the trading world.

As a result of African slave labor, the English industry grew phenomenally. Astonishing results were made in the area of wool, cotton manufacture, sugar refining, rum distillation, pacotille, metallurgical industries, and the like.[26]

"From 1562 British seamen took part in the slave trade that supplied the Spanish colonies. Africans slaves were first offered for sale to the British colony in Virginia in 1619. In 1644 Boston merchants organized an expedition to import slaves from Africa. The slave traffic to the British colony expanded rapidly in the latter half of the seventeenth century. Between 1680 and 1700 more than 300,000 African slaves were imported into the British colonies."[27] Segal sheds light on this with another figure: some 900,000 Africans were actually landed in the Americas during the sixteenth century; at least 2,750,000 during the seventeenth; 7,000,000 during the eighteenth; and 4,000,000 during the nineteenth—a total of 15,000,000 slaves. These figures, of course, take no account of the numbers lost during the transatlantic crossing or "middle passage," when overcrowding and ill-treatment, disease and despair took a toll of seldom less than one in five. Of the numbers lost, it was the able-bodied men and women who were taken, leaving the unproductive young and old behind.

The increase of wealth for the few whites was phenomenal as was the increase of misery for the many blacks. The Barbados crops in 1650, over a twenty-month period, were worth over three million pounds, a sum that would be worth more than ten times today. The British Empire was, as contemporary sources described it, a magnificent superstructure of American commerce, a naval power built on African foundations.[28] In 1788 the sugar planters in the West Indies valued their holdings at £70,000 and in 1798 Pitt assessed the annual income from the West Indian plantation at £4,000,000 compared with £1,000,000 from the rest of the world.

The slave trade was more than the hinge of colonial exploitation, however; it was the basis of British—as well as French and American—mercantile prosperity and the source of industrial expansion. The technological achievements that were to give the West political and economic dominance over so wide an area of the world were made possible by the miseries of the middle passage.

The slave trade enriched—and sometimes ennobled—persons to the upper reaches of social acceptability and political influence. Some of the English merchants were widely renowned for their good works in establishing schools for the poor, homes for the aged, libraries and associations for the learned. Like their moral kinsmen in the slave

---

26. See E. Williams, *Capitalism and Slavery*, 37–84.
27. Yamauchi, *Africa and the Bible*, 28.
28. Polstlethwayt, *African Trade*, 4, 6.

states of America, or their twentieth-century descendants, with mining and industrial interest in Southern Africa, they saw charity as beginning—and ending—at home, with whitewashed walls.[29]

> Bryan Blundell of Liverpool, one of the Liverpool's most prosperous merchants, engaged in both slave trade and West Indian trades, was for many years trustee, treasurer, chief patron and most active supporter of a charity school, the Blue Coat Hospital, founded in 1709. To this charity, another Liverpool slave trader, Foster Cunliffe, his two sons are listed as members of the Liverpool Committee of merchants trading to Africa in 1752. Together they had four ships capable of holding 1,120 slaves, the profits from journey with sugar and rum. An inscription to Foster Cunliffe in St. Peter's church describes him thus: "a Christian devout and exemplary in the exercise of every private and publick duty, friend to mercy, patron to distress, an enemy only to vice, and sloth, he lived esteemed by all who knew him...and died lamented by the wise and good..." Thomas Leyland one of the largest slave traders of the same port, had, as mayor, no mercy for the engrosser, the forestaller, the greater, and was a terror to evil doers. The Heywoods were slave traders and the first to import the slave-grown cotton of the United States. Arthur Heywood was treasurer of the Manchester Academy where his sons were educated. One son, Benjamin, was elected member of the Literary and Philosophical society of Manchester, and was admitted to the Billiard Club, the most *recherché* club Manchester has ever possessed, which admitted the very best men as regard manners, position and attainments. To be admitted to the charmed circle of the forty meant unimpeachable recognition as a gentleman... the slave traders held high offices in England.[30]

As the church was applauding slave traders and the "Christians" were sharing the benefits of the trade, how could the biblical concept of justice prevail? Where is the saltiness and light of the church witnessing to the goodness of God and his righteousness in a corrupt and bankrupt world? We operate in contrast to the foundation of our faith, which is the message of the prophets:

> We and the prophets have no language in common. To us the moral state of society, for all its stains and sports, seems fair and trim; to the prophets it is dreadful. So many deeds of charity are done, so much decency radiates day and night; yet to the prophet satiety of the conscience is prudery and flight from responsibility. Our standards are modest; our sense of injustice tolerable, timid; our moral indignation impermanent; yet human violence is interminable, unbearable, permanent. To us life is often serene, in the prophet's eye the world reels in confusion. The prophet makes no concession to man's capacity. Exhibiting little understanding for human weakness, he seems unable to extenuate the culpability of man.
>
> Who could bear living in a state of disgust day and night? The conscience builds its own confines, is subject to fatigue, longs for comfort, lulling, soothing. Yet those who are hurt, and He who inhabits eternity, neither slumber nor sleep.

---

29. For detailed reading, see Segal, *Race War*, 31–132.
30. E. Williams, *Capitalism and Slavery*, 47–48.

> The prophet is sleepless and grave. The frankincense of charity fails to sweeten cruelties. Pomp, the scent of piety, mixed with ruthlessness, is sickening to him who is sleepless and grave.[31]

Today, it is the posterity of the slave traders and European colonizers who established the International Criminal Court (ICC) in The Hague and are trying and sentencing African leaders for the "injustices" they have done to their people. The West heaps insult to injury upon Africans in the double standard of justice and the contradiction of values and truth that still manifest in subtle and open ways to dehumanize Africans. The ICC should have visited the Oppenheimer mines and many other mines owned by Western capitalists in Africa and compensated African mineworkers who have been treated like slave for centuries. Instead, "The International Criminal Court (ICC) may have to wait to try its first sitting head of state. The prosecution of Uhuru Kenyatta, Kenya's president remains in the balance less than a month before his trial is due to start in The Hague. A resolution passed on October 12th at a meeting of African leaders at the headquarters of the African Union (AU) in Addis Ababa demanded immunity for the continent's leaders while in office. This has raised pressure on the court and its backers."[32]

The Economist adds:

> Heads of state from across the continent gathered in Addis Ababa, the Ethiopian capital, on May 27th to celebrate the 50th anniversary of the African Union and its forerunner, the Organization of African Unity. They congratulated themselves how well they had supposedly cooperated in decades past, and then spiced things up a little by firing off broadsides at the International Criminal Court in The Hague. Led by the Ethiopian Prime Minister, Hailemariam Desalegn, who chairs the union at the moment, they variously accused the court of racism and "hunting" Africans.
>
> It is true that, since it began to operate 11 years ago the court has paid Africa more attention than any other continent. But because the continent has experienced a glut of horrendous civil wars and because it's legal systems are, on the whole, the least solid. Two of the presidents at jamboree are in the court's cross hairs. Sudan's Omar al-Bashir is wanted for crimes against humanity, and Uhuru Kenyatta, Kenya's recently elected president, is set to stand trial on similar charges later this year.[33]

With the psalmist, the African church needs to pray out loud not only in churches and chapels but in the hills, mountains, valleys, prisons, courts, universities, mining places, oil refineries, coffee and rubber plantations, villages and cities, and the suburbs and slums of Africa saying: "Rise up, O God, judge the earth, for all the nations are your inheritance" (Ps 82:8). Without understanding God's redemptive plan not only for humans but for the cosmos, life in Africa is meaningless and senseless. "The groaning of creation as in the pains of child birth" (Rom 8:22) is more audible and visible in Africa. Despite the high rate of conversion and the manifestations of God's power in Africa,

---

31. Heschel, *Prophets*, 10–11.
32. "Kenya and the International Court."
33. Ibid.

the church cannot and should not ignore the groaning of creation and the suffering of Africans. Apocalyptic Scriptures can teach us a lot about suffering, rejection, endurance, hope, and ultimate victory.

Even if Jesus Christ started his ministry by preaching about the reign of God and demonstrated it through sign and wonders, paradoxically his calling is to the way of suffering, rejection, and death—to the way of the cross. He bears witness to the presence of the reign of God not by overpowering the force of evil, but by taking their full weight upon himself. Yet it is in that seeming defeat that victory is won. The resurrection is more than the manifestation of a victory. It is this, but it is more. It is the "firstfruits" (1 Cor 15:23) of a harvest that is still to come and that is the end of all God's works, the putting of all things into subjection of God's works, the putting of all things under God's reign. Proclaiming the reign of God over all events and things must involve some kind of interpretation of what is happening in the world, however provisional, modest, and tentative it may be.[34]

It is not only the secular court in Europe that insults Africans, the church in England, like St. Peter's church, described Foster Cunliffe, a former slave trader, as "a Christian devout and exemplary in the exercise of every private and public duty, friend to mercy, patron to distress, an enemy only to vice, and sloth, he lived esteemed by all who knew him . . . and died lamented by the wise and good . . . ," and in so doing has failed the African people in representing them before God and the world in a righteous way. For the church of Christ, such practices cannot be counted as fulfilling God's mission. "In the community of the incarnated God and the exalted man Jesus Christ there can be no division here. The church will always have to present itself both in the forum of God and in the forum of the world. For it stands for God to the world, and it stand for the world before God. It confronts the world in critical liberty and is bound to give it the authentic revelation of the new life. At the same time it stands before God in fellowship and solidarity with all men and is bound to send up to him out of the depths the common cry for life and liberty."[35] Tawney adds: "The Church in its wider sense is the Christian Commonwealth, within which that end is to be realized; in its narrower sense it is the hierarchy divinely commissioned for its interpretation; in both it embraces the whole of life, and its authority is final. Though practice is perpetually at variance with theory, there is no absolute division between the inner and personal life, which is 'the sphere of religion,' and the practical interests, the external order, the impersonal mechanism."[36] While having high levels of authority and influence, instead of being the voice of the voiceless, the enslaved and the oppressed, the church lauds the living and dead slave traders in the UK. "Justice dies when dehumanized, no matter how exactly it may be exercised. Justice dies when defied, for beyond all justice is God's compassion. The logic of justice may seem impersonal, yet the concern for justice is an act of love."[37]

---

34. See Newbigin, *Open Secret*, 81–84.
35. Moltmann, *Source of Life*, 1.
36. Tawney, *Religion and the Rise of Capitalism*, 20.
37. Heschel, *Prophets*, 257.

The secular world—formerly regarded as "this" world, the wicked world *par excellence*, a neopagan world—today is not only taken into account in Christendom, but largely and consciously approved and assisted in its development. There is indeed scarcely a larger church or as serious theology which does not claim to be "modern" in some sense, to recognize the signs of the times, to share the needs and hopes of modern man and actively to collaborate in solving the urgent problems of the world. At least in theory, the Churches today no longer want to be backward subcultures, organizations out of touch with the *prevailing mentality*, institutions proscribing advances in knowledge and productive curiosity: they want to break out of their self-imposed seclusion. The theologians want to leave traditional orthodoxy behind them and to make a more serious attempt to bring scholarly integrity to near even on dogmas and the Bible. The faithful are expected to display something of this new freedom regard to doctrine, morality, and Church order.[38]

In the case of African slave trade both Western theology and the Western church embraced "the prevailing mentality" of the time. The church's theology at home and philosophy of mission shaped and influenced both the slave trade and colonialism in Africa. "The missionaries in Kenya, like elsewhere in Britain's empire, were dependent upon the colonial government's goodwill, and never more so than during Emergency, when the governor could use his wide-ranging powers to remove missionaries from the colony or greatly circumscribe their activities. The colony's relationship with the churches was, nonetheless, one of mutual dependence as the colonial government relied on the missions to underwrite many of the social costs of Britain's *civilizing role*. . .*Christian missionaries . . . wanted above all else to continue God's work in upholding Britain's civilizing mission*."[39]

It was within this kind of social, political, and religious framework in Europe that the African slave trade and colonialism happened. All the while Christians claimed to believe, preach, and teach that Exodus is a divine intervention to free slaves and that the message of the prophets about justice, righteousness, holiness, and peace is inspired. When those who learned about the kingdom of God, which is incarnated in the person of Jesus Christ, do contrary to the message of the gospel and Christians who uphold the teachings of the apostles are seeing slavery and colonialism as a "civilizing mission," what better things can Africans expect to come from those who don't use the Scripture as their moral guide? To believe in *imago Dei* is one thing but to practice all people are equal seems something different to European Christians. If we apply it in earnest, "Christianity is designed to be the healing beginning of the healed creation in the midst of a disrupted and sick world."[40]

The Scripture is clear when it comes to God's righteous desire and compassion toward the poor and the oppressed: "God presides in the great assembly; he gives judgments among the gods: How long will you defend the unjust and show partiality to the wicked? Defend the cause of the weak and fatherless; maintain the right of the poor and the oppressed. Rescue the wick and the needy; deliver them from the hand of the

---

38. Küng, *On Being a Christian*, 28; emphasis added.
39. Elkins, *Britain's Gulag*, 94; emphasis added.
40. Moltmann, *Sun of Righteousness Arise!*, 69.

wicked ... Rise up, O God, judge the earth, for all the nations are your inheritance" (Ps 82:1–4, 8). The Bible is unique among the sacred books of the world's religions in that it is structurally a history of the cosmos. It claims to show us the shape, structure, origin, and goal not merely of human history but of cosmic history.

Newbigin writes:

> The biblical story is not a separate story. It is not a special history ("salvation history") apart from human history as a whole. The whole history of humankind is one single fabric of interconnected events, and the story of the Bible tells us part of it. The story of the Old Testament runs out into and draws upon the work of archaeologists and historians working on the early civilizations of Mesopotamia, Palestine and Egypt. The study of the New Testament cannot be done in isolation from the world of secular historians of first-century religion, politics, and culture in the eastern Roman Empire and from such discoveries as have been made through from the findings of the Dead Sea Scrolls. No fence can be erected around the biblical story; it is part of the human story ("The Word was made flesh"). Therefore it is and must be open to all the critical probing of the historian. The scholar must be and is free to test every part of the ground and to use all the skills that the modern study of history has developed. If, in the supposed interest of faith, we try to keep the critic out, we are in effect denying the historicity story and turning the gospel into a myth. The historical scholar must come in with all the tools of the trade."[41]

As Newbigin rightly said; "The whole history of humankind is one single fabric of interconnected events."[42] It is in this light that we investigate the African slave trade and examine, evaluate, and critique it through the eternal word of God instead of through Western civilization, which is used as justification for slave trade and colonialism in Africa. Because of this "one single fabric of interconnected events" the slave owner/traders and the enslaved, the colonizers and the colonies, the oppressors and the oppressed, the exploiters and the exploited exist inseparably in human history. The wealth of Western nations and the impoverishment of the black race and the misery of Africans cannot be adequately explained without the African slave trade.

The contributions of black slaves to Western capitalism are too broad to cover in this chapter. "In the eighteenth century technological change in the West resulted in even great 'need' for African labour. The new factories of Europe needed more labour-intensive crops such as cotton and indigo. And the new prosperity created new tastes in the West—which resulted in the growth of such additional labour-intensives crops as rice, coffee and tobacco in the South America, the Caribbean and the southern states of the United States."[43] Because of its global demand and lucrative trade, which came at the cost of the sweat, blood, and ingenuity of African slaves, I focus on the role the sugar industry had in contributing to the wealth of Western nations.

---

41. Newbigin, *The Open Secret*, 87–88. For further insight and reading, see ibid., *passim*..
42. Ibid., 87.
43. Mazrui, *Africans*, 159.

The Contribution of Sugar to Western Capitalism

"After the Crusades Europeans learned about sugarcane from the Muslims. Since the civilization of sugarcane is labor intensive, slaves were used to lower the cost of production. The cultivation of sugar spread westward from the Near East to Sicily, Spain, and then to the Maderia Islands (ca 1432) and the Canaries (ca 1480)."[44] Sidney W. Mintz, in his book *Sweetness and Power: The Place of Sugar in Modern History*, has done an excellent academic work with well-measured words. It is an eye-opening study that shows how Europeans and Americans transformed sugar from a rare foreign luxury to a commonplace necessity of modern life, and how it changed the history of capitalism and industry. He discusses the production and consumption of sugar, and reveals how closely interwoven are sugar's origins as a "slave" crop grown in Europe's tropical colonies with its use first as an extravagant luxury for the aristocracy, then as a staple of the diet of the new industrial proletariat. Finally, he considers how sugar has altered work patterns, eating habits, and our diet in modern times.

Lewis suggests that as the cultivation of sugar and cotton, and black slaves to harvest them, spread from Spain and the Atlantic Islands to the Americas, the myth of the curse of Ham was adopted by Christian defenders of slavery.[45] The myth was deeply entrenched in the minds of the British people, so much so that those who opposed William Wilberforce's struggle to abolish slavery were saying that "to abolish the slave trade was to shut the gates of mercy on mankind."[46] In the United States, "Not only did southern Christians see slavery as acceptable and even commendable, but many owned slaves themselves. In fact in the year before the Methodist split, 25,000 members owned 208,000 slaves; 1,200 Methodist clergy were slaveholders. From 1846 until the Civil War, every man who achieved the rank of bishop within the Methodist Episcopal Church, south, was a slaveholder. Other southern denominations had similar profiles. Slavery was clearly part of the southern vision for an orderly and virtuous Christian America with limited central government. In their eyes, slavery was part of a Christian society purer than aggressive and economically and socially oppressive North."[47]

Mintz observes:

> One could look around and see sugar-cane plantations and coffee, cacao, and tobacco haciendas, and so too, one could imagine those Europeans who had thought it promising to create them, to invest in their creation, and to import vast numbers of people in chains from elsewhere to work them. These last would be, if not slaves, then men who sold their labor because they had nothing else to sell; who would probably produce things of which they were not the principal consumers; who would consume things they had not produced, and in the process earn profit for others elsewhere.
>
> It seemed to me that the mysteriousness that accompanied my seeing, at one and the same time, came growing in the fields and white sugar in my cup, should also accompany the sight of molten metal or, better, raw iron ore, on the one

---

44. Yamauchi, *Africa and the Bible*, 27.
45. Lewis, *Race and Slavery in the Middle East*, 125.
46. E. Williams, *Capitalism and Slavery*, 49.
47. Emerson and Smith, *Divided by Faith*, 36.

hand, and a perfectly wrought pair of manacles or leg irons, on the other. The mystery was not simply one of technical transformation, impressive as that is, but also the mystery of people unknown to one another being linked through space and time—and not just by politics and economics, but along a particular chain of connection maintained by their production.

. . . Of all these substances, sugar has always been the most important. It is the epitome of a historical process at least as old as Europe's thrustings outside itself in search of new world . . .

A single source of satisfaction—sucrose extracted, perhaps even universal, human liking for sweetness became established in European taste preferences at a time when European power, military might, and economic initiative were transforming the world. That source linked Europe and many colonial areas from the fifteenth century onward, the passage of centuries only underlining its importance even while politics changed. And, conversely, what metropolises produced the colonies consumed. The desire for sweet substances spread and increased steadily; many different products were employed to satisfy it, and cane sugar's importance therefore varied from time to time.[48]

Highlighting the place of sugar in Western capitalism, Mazrui comments: "Just as European voyages to Asia (during the fifteenth and sixteenth centuries) were once greatly influenced by Europe's interest in spices, so were European slaving expeditions to Africa (during the sixteenth to nineteenth centuries) once influenced by the growing European taste for sugar. In the history of the slave trade, Europe's sweet tooth has much to answer for. Expanding demand for sugar in Europe resulted in expanding demand for slave labour in South America and the West Indies from the seventeenth century onwards."[49]

To this Williams adds:

The process of colonial raw materials gave rise to new industries in England, provided to a greater extension of the world market and international trade. Of these raw materials sugar was preeminent, and its manufacture gave birth to the sugar refining industry. The refining process transformed the crude brown sugar manufactured on the plantations into white sugar, which was durable and capable of preservation, and could be easily handled and distributed all over the world.

The earliest reference to sugar refining in England is an order of the Privy Council in 1615 prohibiting aliens from erecting sugar houses or practicing the art of refining sugar. The importance of the industry increased in proportion to its production on the plantations, and as sugar became, with the spread of tea and coffee, one of the necessities of life instead of the luxury of kings.

About the middle of the nineteenth century there were 120 refineries in England. Each refinery was estimated to provide employment for about nine men. In addition to the distribution of the refined into existence a number of subsidiary trades and required ships and wagons for the coastal inland trade.[50]

48. Mintz, *Sweetness and Power*, xxiv–xxv.
49. Mazrui, *Africans*, 159.
50. E. Williams, *Capitalism and Slavery*, 73.

Sugar cane was first carried to the New World by Columbus on his second voyage, in 1493; he brought it there from the Spanish Canary islands. Cane was first grown in the New World in Spanish Santo Domingo; it was from that point that sugar was first shipped back to Europe, beginning around 1516. Santo Domingo's pristine sugar industry was worked by enslaved Africans, the first slave having been imported there soon after the sugar cane. Here it was Spain that pioneered sugar cane, sugar making, African slave labor, and the plantation from within the Americas. Some scholars agree with Fernando Ortiz that these plantations were "the favored child of capitalism," and even Spain's achievement in sugar production did not rival those of the Portuguese until centuries later—their pioneering nature has never been in doubt.[51]

By 1526, Brazil was shipping sugar to Lisbon in commercial quantities, and soon the sixteenth century was the Brazilian century for sugar. In another Greater Antilles—Cuba, Puerto Rico, and Jamaica—Spanish settlers eventually brought in sugar cane, the methods for its cultivation, the technology of water- and animal-powered mills, enslaved labor, and the process for grinding and fabricating sugars and molasses from extracted juices, as well as for distilling rum from the molasses . . . within only a century, the French, and even more the British (though the Dutch helped from the outset), became the Western world's greater sugar makers and exporters.

The turning point for British sugar was the settlement of Barbados in 1627, an island Britain claimed after Captain John Powell's landing there in 1625, while returning to Europe from Brazil. It was not until around 1655—the same year the British invasion of Jamaica[52] was launched as part of the Western Design—that Barbadian sugar began to affect the home market, however. In that year, 283 tons of "clayed" sugars and 6,667 tons of "muscovado" sugars were produced in Barbados; meanwhile, other Caribbean acquisitions also began to contribute to homeland consumption, and to make of sugar and imperial source of profit. After 1655 and until the mid-nineteenth century, the sugar supply of the English people would be provided substantially with the skein of the empire. From the establishment of the first British colonies that succeeded by exporting unfinished products—particularly sugar—to the metropolis, imperial laws were passed to control the flow of such goods, and of the goods for which they were exchanged.

England fought the most, conquered the most colonies, imported the most slaves (to her own colonies and, in absolute numbers, in her own bottoms), and went further and fastest in creating a plantation system.

The success of slavery in pioneering islands like Barbados and Martinique marked the beginning of the Africanization of the British and French Caribbean. From 1701 to 1810 Barbados, a mere 166 square miles in area, received 252,500 African slaves.

---

51. Ortiz, *Cuban Counterpart*.

52. French sugar was invading the European markets and selling at half the price it was sold in England. Acquisition of such islands would have meant the eclipse of the older English planters. The latter, therefore, demanded their destruction rather than their acquisition. The governor of Jamaica wrote in 1748 that unless French Saint Domingue was destroyed during the war, it would, on the return of peace, ruin the British sugar colonies by the quality and the cheapness of its production. During the Seven Year's War, Britain captured Cuba from Spain and Guadeloupe from France. Both islands were restored to their owners in 1763, Britain taking in return Florida and Canada. E. Williams, *Capitalism and Slavery*, 114.

Jamaica, which in 1655 had been invaded by the British, followed the same pattern of "economic development"; in the same 108 years, it received 662,400 slaves. The eighteenth century was the apogee of the British and French slave-based sugar plantations.

The exclusion of non-whites from the temperate wages and consumption markets was the clear consequence of racist policies in such countries as Australia, New Zealand, Canada, and the United States. It is not merely ironical to point out that the white migrants would soon be eating more sugar produced by the nonwhite migrants at lower wages, and producing finished goods at higher wages, to be consumed by the non-white migrants.[53] "It was the Negro slaves who made these sugar colonies the most precious colonies recorded in the whole annals of imperialism."[54]

Slave and proletarian together powered the imperial economic system in that one kept the other supplied with manacles and the other with sugar and rum.

> For over 300 years, enslaved Africans were forced to work for Europeans. In the Caribbean, many laboured on sugar, coffee and cocoa plantations owned by North East Scots.
>
> Generations were born into this slavery. Millions died young because of poor diet, cruelty and relentless hard labour. The survivors lacked the most basic freedoms, such as the right to care for and protect family members.
>
> Many sugar labourers were women. A girl began work around age four, collecting grass to feed the mules and oxen. By ten she was weeding the cane fields, and by 18 she was planting and harvesting the canes.
>
> By 40 she was worn out, and was sent back to feeding the livestock. If she survived a few years more, she became a nurse to the babies on the plantation—a new generation of workers that probably included her own grandchildren. This was the life lived by a slave with a relatively mild owner, such as Thomas Gordon of Buthlaw and Cairness.
>
> It was in the planters' financial interests to look after their slaves, but nonetheless many inflicted high levels of violence on their workers. Slaves were routinely beaten for minor faults, such as failing to dig enough cane holes or collect enough grass. Slaves, who left the plantation without permission, even just to visit family members elsewhere, were confined in stocks, shackled or weighted down with iron. Those who repeatedly broke plantation rules or challenged the slave owner's authority were flogged mercilessly with a long cart whip that tore the skin from their back and buttocks. These punishments were inflicted on both men and women, including pregnant women. There are many accounts of enslaved women miscarrying after being beaten.[55]

The income from sugar industry was so lucrative that black slaves deliberately were used as a means to that end. Heschel rightly said, "How marvelous is the world that God has created! And how horrible is the world that man has made."[56] In this horrible world that humanity has made, the profit of one is a loss of the other. The luxurious life of the few is at the cost of misery for many. The joy of the oppressors is rooted in the bitter cry

---

53. For details, see Mintz, *Sweetness and Power*, 19–74.

54. E. Williams, *Capitalism and Slavery*, 52.

55. "A Northeast story—Africa, Scotland, and the Caribbean," University of Aberdeen, http://www.abdn.ac.uk/slavery/pdf/plantationslavery.pdf.

56. Heschel, *Prophets*, 98.

and tears of the oppressed. The gain of the few is inseparably linked to the economic damage of the impoverished masses. "The assessment of the 1798 annual income from West Indian plantations was four million pounds as compared with one million from the rest of the world. The profits of sugar plantation in any West Indian colonies are generally much greater than those of any other cultivation that is known either in Europe or America."[57]

The lives of slaves in Hispanic-speaking plantations was not that much different than that of slaves owned by the British or Americans. Thornton describes the misery of black slaves in Carategna: "Domestics were frequently beaten. Even short absences might brutally be punished, and sometimes such slaves were even killed as a result of them. Many were fed little and dressed in such poor clothing as to be almost naked. Some had to work on days off or festival days to earn money to purchase clothing that a master refused to provide. Sometimes, sick slaves were freed when gravely ill, so that the master would not have to pay the cost of their burial, and the street became their grave, even those who were good in Spanish and long serving.[58]"

Such was the life and labor of African slaves in the Caribbean. Ill-treatment, suffering, limited freedom, malnutrition, impoverishment, and illiteracy was not common among African slaves in the African continent. However, in the Americas and other destinies of African slaves, suffering was the reality of their unpleasant life.

Despite these kinds of hardships it was a black inventor that revolutionized the sugar industry for the United States.

> Norbert Rillieux, 1806–1894 developed a sugar-refining process. The lack of recognition he received, however, troubled him his whole life long. In 1843 Rillieux developed a method for refining sugar. It consisted of a series of vacuum pans combined in a step by step process to make heated evaporated sugar into crystallized granules.
>
> The significance of Rillieux's process to the American sugar-making industry cannot be overstated. At the time the method was introduced, American sugarcane planters lagged far behind Brazil and Haiti, which were still using cheap slave labor, making their production much cheaper. Rillieux made it possible for the United States to dominate the market. The basic concept of his evaporation process is still used for things like freeze-drying food, pigments, and other industrial products.[59]

The lack of recognition of Rillieux's contribution is not limited to one individual. Several black inventors had gone through the same experience. Some still do. The innovation and labor of Africans in various occupations have made significant contributions to the civilization and wealth of the West. This is without counting the natural resources that have been extracted out of Africa for the last five hundred years. As Moltmann said, "This other side is generally neither seen nor heard."[60] African slaves and African natural resources are the price of Western civilization recorded in the balance sheet of human

---

57. E. Williams, *Capitalism and Slavery*, 53.
58. Mintz, *Sweetness and Power*, 179.
59. Brodie, *Created Equal*, 42–44.
60. Moltmann, *Way of Jesus*, 64.

history. However, the story does not have a wide publicity like the slavery of the Jews in Egypt, their genocide in Germany, their oppression by their colonizers, their Diasporas and persecution from Russia. Africa is Africa. Neither the West, nor African leaders and the elites who replaced them, deeply care for the continent. In some cases obsession with the past oppression has become a way of escaping the present reality and finding a working and lasting solution to it. "Everyone recognizes the repugnance of the slave trade, colonialism, and racism. But obsession of many black leaders and intellectuals, as well as whites in the West, with these past travesties invariably distorts their perceptions of current black problems so that they are incapable of making a dispassionate, objective analysis."[61]

The sugar enterprise, which the West built through the labor and ingenuity of black slaves, is currently used to ruin the economy of the continent of their origin—Africa:

> The U.S sugar industry receives US$ 1.3 billion of support per year. European Union producers receive US$2.7 billion, and in the two years between 1999 and 2001 the OECD supported its sugar farmers to the tune of $6.4 billion, an amount more than the total value of sugar exports from developing countries, and 55% of the US$ 11.6 billion annual world sugar trade.
>
> Like cotton, sugar subsidies hurt Africa. The charity Oxfam estimated the regime has deprived Ethiopia, Mozambique and Malawi of potential export earnings of US$238 million since 2001. The cost of Mozambique sugar losses equaled one third of its development aid from the EU and its government's spending on agriculture and rural development. The EU also supports its producers by blocking the entry of developing-country imports into its markets with tariffs of more than 300 per cent. Oxfam estimated that Malawi could have significantly increased exports to the Union in 2004 but the market restriction deprived it of a potential UD$32 million in foreign exchange earnings, equivalent to around half the country's public-healthcare budget.[62]

The West leaves no stone unturned to keep Africa poor and dependent. There is neither a Christian nor a humanitarian voice that would say no to this never ending exploitation, political, economic, and psychological oppression. The few Africans who made an attempt to oppose the modus operandi of imperialism in Africa were assassinated and others died of mysterious diseases.

Colonialism

The death toll, economic and identity crisis, the deep psychological scars and disorientation of life that slavery caused for Africans are enormous.

> Africa barley recovered from the trauma of slavery before it was hit by another type of cultural adversity. The European scramble for Africa began in earnest in the 1880s, propelled by three forces that drew their impetus from Europe's

---

61. Ayittey, *Africa Betrayed*, 6.

62. Moyo, *Dead Aid*, 117. It is not just developed countries that are guilty of distorting trade markets. China is reported to support its cotton sector by estimated US$1.5 billion annually. Turkey, Brazil, Mexico, Egypt and India put US$.6 billion into their cotton sectors during 2001/2002. Ibid.

Industrial Revolution. The first was the need for new markets for surplus manufactured goods. As industrial activity expanded beyond England to France, Russia, Germany and Italy during the second half of the nineteenth century, far more good were produced than could be absorbed locally, and new colonial markets were needed. Second, increasing industrial competitions for such new materials as cotton, rubber, and minerals added further impetus to the desire to control or own the sources of the supply. The third factor is the race for colonies was the investment of surplus capital. As more and more profit was accumulated in European countries an outlet was needed for their investment . . . By July 1884, France, Britain, Germany, and Portugal were all actively staking out colonial claims on Africa. To lay down rules to govern this race and to avoid the possibility of open conflicts, an international conference was held in Berlin from Nov. 15, 1884 to Jan 30, 1885, under the chairmanship of Otto von Bismarck. On Feb. 26, 1885, the Berlin Act, which promulgated the "rules" for partition was, signed. One rule was that any power that wanted the claim of any African territory should notify the other signatory powers. Another was that to be valid, any such annexations should be followed by effective occupation. In this way Africa was carved up into colonies and transformed into economic appendages of European colonial powers. Boundaries were artificially drawn up with little regard to demographic configurations.[63]

Segal adds, "British, French, and German expeditions, financed by private associations and governments, set out to establish the direction in which a river flowed the source of a legend, or simply the character of a region where no white had been. The specific purposes varied according to sponsor and participant, but the general impetus was an association of the philanthropic, the pious and the profitable. Africa was to be introduced to the market-place of human progress, where ideas and goods were so usefully exchanged; its peoples would be converted to an industrious Christianity, their hunger by improved civilization, and their needs by the manufactures of Europe. That there was greed and self-righteousness at work does not cancel the existence, too, of generosity and self-sacrifice. But the era of penetration and philanthropy soon gave place to the era of colonization."[64] Pakenham succinctly described the genesis and motive of European Scramble for Africa this way:

> Livingstone sounded a call for a worldwide crusade to open up Africa. A new slave trade, organized by Swahili and Arabs in East Africa, was eating out the heart of the continent. Livingstone's answer was the "3 Cs"; Commerce, Christianity and Civilization, a triple alliance of Mammon, God, and social progress. Trade, not the gun, would liberate Africa . . . To imperialism—a kind of "race patriotism"—they brought a missionary zeal. Not only would they save Africa from itself. Africa would be saving of their own countries. At first European governments were reluctant to intervene. But to most people in their electorates, there seemed a real chance of missing something. Africa was a lottery and a winning ticket might earn glittering prizes . . . And it was in the Protestant Britain, where God and Mammon seemed made for each other, that Livingstone's words struck the deepest chord. The "3 Cs" would redeem Africa. That was not the way

63. Ayittey, *Africa Betrayed*, 6–7.
64. Segal, *Race War*, 51.

Africans perceived the Scramble. There was a fourth "c"—conquest . . . Europe had imposed its will on Africa at the point of a gun. It was a lesson that would be remembered, fifty year later, when Africa came to win its independence.[65]

Heschel comments: "We check manslaughter and isolated murders; we wage wars and slaughter whole peoples. Ferocity appears natural; generosity superimposed. Since the natural often seems sacred, we seldom dare suppress or try to remake what has been called 'all that fine belligerence within us.' We measure manhood by the sword and are convinced that history is ultimately determined on the fields of battle."[66]

In most African countries, to mention the few, Angola, Congo, South Africa, and Uganda, European penetration to the continent was initially done through trade agreements, philanthropy, and mission works. In most cases, the pioneer humanitarian and missionary workers found out to be spies preparing the ground for invasion or they were firm believers of European colonialism seeing it as the main or only means of civilization and economic recovery for Europe.

> As the haggling in Europe over African territory continued, land and peoples became little more than pieces on a chessboard. "We have been giving away mountains and rivers and lakes to each other, only hindered by the small impediment that we never knew exactly where they were," Britain's prime minister, Lord Salisbury, remarked sardonically, to a London audience. Britain traded the North Sea island of Heligoland with the Germans for Zanzibar, and parts of Northern Nigeria with the French for fishing rights off Newfoundland. France exchanged parts of Cameroon with Germany in return for German recognition of the French protectorate over Morocco. By the time the scramble for Africa was over, some 10,000 African polities had been amalgamated into forty European colonies and protectorates.[67]

The new map of Africa has been a divisive hindrance for peace, political stability, and economic development in many countries. And it has caused bloodshed in Nigeria, Rwanda, Uganda, and the like. The so-called African independence, for some African countries, turned out to be fuel on the ember of ethnic, regional, economic, and political conflict of the African people who were unwillingly unified by the colonial powers. Geographical boundaries could not fill the chasm of cultural, linguistic, religious, and political differences among Africans. Andrew Walls further captures the colonial situation this way:

> In the course of the nineteenth century, both the traditional and the Islamic state gave way to a new creation, the Western colonial state. In 1800, Europe knew little about Africa, and careless; by 1880, Europe cared intensely, and by 1910, the entire continent, except for Ethiopia[68] and Liberia (and they, too, had their

---

65. Pakenham, *Scramble for Africa*, xxii–xxiii. For an in-depth study on colonialism, see ibid., *passim*. Taking the entire continent as his canvas, with judicious poise, Pakenham has written the gold rush, the horror, and suffering, stripping the cloth imperialism was wearing.

66. Heschel, *Prophets*, 204.

67. Meredith, *Fate of Africa*, 2.

68. Mussolini attacked Ethiopia to avenge the Italian defeat in 1896 at Adowa. He wanted to teach Ethiopians to respect white men and to stop what he considered an offensive annual Ethiopian celebration

predators) was divided by agreement between Britain, France, Germany, Belgium, Portugal, Italy, and Spain. The process can be traced through the volumes of Sir Edward Hertslet's *The Map of Africa by Treaty*. The title is eloquent; the boundaries of African states were determined outside of Africa, but its creation of new type of state is a landmark in that history. The map of Africa is still in essentials the final draft of that 'map of Africa by treaty' produced between about 1880 and the First World War by the jostling of a handful of European powers enforced locally by the possession of technologically based firepower."[69]

"For the Africans the situation was unprecedented and absolutely chaotic. Centuries of European struggles for domination had left them with fabricated countries, borders that suited foreign powers rather than cultural differences. Their colonial rulers had done nothing to help them institutionalize governmental and commercial sectors. They were ill-prepared to accept responsibilities of independence and ripe for exploitation by anyone who could move swiftly to fill the vacuums."[70] French equally observes: "Nigeria had been created by the British as a colonial entity in 1914 and bequeathed to its people as an independent state in 1960. From the very beginning the prize of independence was booby trap, an eagerly awaited gift that would explode just as it was being unwrapped. The colony's masters in London had done little to prepare the population for the task of running a European-style nation-state. The truly explosive element, however, was the country's very composition. Nigeria was a creation of European imperialist and mapmakers, and it pulled together an amalgam of diverse regions and peoples who spoke mutually unintelligible languages."[71] It is not only Nigeria all African countries are the creation of Europeans. Meredith concurs: "Nearly one half of the frontiers imposed on Africa were geometric lines, lines of latitude and longitude, other straight lines or arcs of circles. In some cases, African societies were rent apart: the Bankongo were partitioned between French Congo, Belgian Congo and Portuguese Angola; Somaliland was carved up between Britain, Italy and France. In all, the new boundaries cut through some 190 culture groups. In other cases, Europe's new colonial territories enclosed hundreds of diverse and independent groups, with no common history, culture, language, or religion."[72] "What is Africa? It is what Europeans decided it was," said Mazrui.[73] A society that was living through mutual understanding and cooperation with each other cohesively turned out to be a mini-Babylon.

---

of Adowa as a national holiday. Secondly, he intended to turn Ethiopia into a colony under Italian control. Ethiopian independence, he believed, was a bad example to neighboring territories, which were still under European colonial rule. Using mustard gas on the Ethiopian army and people who disadvantaged by the embargo of the European countries not to sell modern weapons to Ethiopia. Italy won and occupied for five years. Because of the damage the Ethiopian resistance fighters were doing, Mussolini soon found out that the Ethiopian people were more difficult to conquer than the Ethiopian armies. Munene, *Truman Administration*, 34. See also Coffey, *Lion by the Tail*.

69. Walls, *Cross-Cultural Process*, 102.
70. Perkins, *Secret History of the American Empire*, 233.
71. French, *Continent for the Taking*, 33.
72. Meredith, *Fate of Africa*, 1–2.
73. Mazrui, *Africans*, 102.

"Nigeria, for example, contained as many as 250 ethno-linguistic groups."[74] To this day the tension between the north and south, the feeling of neglect by those who do not have political representatives at higher levels of government office, the misuse and abuse of natural resources like oil and many other minerals, is prevalent in Nigeria.

> Northerners habitually complain that politicians have made personal fortunes from the booming oil industry in the south, while failing to share its benefits. Mutterings of a north-south divide have grown louder with the prospect of President Goodluck Jonathan, a southern Christian, running for a second term in 2015. Northerners resent what they see as a violation of unwritten rule that the presidency should rotate every two terms between the largely Muslim north and the mostly Christian south. A southerner has held the post for 11 past 14 years.
>
> Nigeria's finance minister, Ngozi Konjo-Iweala, insist that government recognizes the North's need. Nigeria has courted $20 billion of foreign direct investment in the past three years, 10% of the African total. Yet most investors set up shops in Lagos. "When we advise investors coming to Nigeria, they don't even talk about the north," says a South African banker in the plush Hilton Hotel in Abuja, the capital, which lies between north and south. "It simply is not a consideration. It's the sad truth and it isn't about to change."[75]

Nigeria is one example among many in West Africa of the neverending tension within African nations because of the legacy of colonialism. When you go to East Africa,

> The problem of church and state conflicts in Uganda have been more serious and destructive than in other countries of Africa, with the exceptions of North Nigeria and Sudan, where more than two million Christians have been killed by the Arab Muslims. These tragic religio-political conflicts in Uganda led to the rise of President Idi Amin. The [conflict] also tragically resulted in the brutal murder of the Anglican Archbishop Janani Luwum of Uganda on the evening of February 16, 1977. In the case of Uganda, these tragic conflicts between Church and State can be traced back to the British Anglican missionary strategies and ideals in the founding of Christianity in Uganda. This process took place in the last quarter of the nineteenth century. The Christian establishment in Uganda and the hostile rivalry of the Anglicans and Catholics led to confusion among the Ugandans, including the kings of Uganda, who were all Anglicans. The oppressive Anglican hegemony is the root cause of political instability in Uganda, since the Roman Catholics and Muslims outnumber the Anglicans, and yet, political power has been traditionally monopolized by the Anglican political elites, kings and most chiefs."[76]

Per the invitation of Livingstone, Christianity and commerce from Europe entered into Africa side by side, complimenting and supporting each other with little manifestation of philosophical and ethical conflict between them. The big framework within which the two functioned in Africa was colonialism.

> The Anglican church establishment structure in the Baganda Kingdom became the normative paradigm for the other kingdoms and districts of Uganda. The

---

74. Meredith, *Fate of Africa*, 2.
75. "Energy South Africa," 47.
76. Twesinge, "Church and State Conflicts in Uganda," 148–49.

Anglican hegemony was established over the rest of Uganda by the British colonial policy of indirect rule[77] through the Baganda Anglican chiefs. The Anglican Baganda chiefs were considered to be the appropriate local agents of the British imperial and colonial government in Uganda. The Baganda Anglican converts went out as Christian missionaries and educators. The combined team of Baganda the Anglican missionaries and British colonial rule, effectively converted and transformed Uganda's traditional political structures and religion into those of national and local Anglican establishment, elitism and hegemony.[78]

When we think of African dictators the first picture that often comes to our mind is Idi Amin. *The Last King of Scotland* is a 2006 British drama film based on Giles Foden's novel of the same name. *The Last King of Scotland* tells the fictional story of Dr. Nicholas Garrigan (James McAvoy), a young Scottish doctor who travels to Uganda and becomes the personal physician to the dictator Idi Amin (Forest Whitaker). The film is based on factual events of Amin's rule and the title comes from a reporter in a press conference who wishes to verify whether Amin declared himself the King of Scotland. Amin was known to invent and adopt fanciful imperial titles for himself.[79] But how had Idi Amin come to power? Uganda had been one of the most peaceful territories—because it was a protectorate, not a colony, most land was still in African hands. Only a handful of settlers were allowed, so there was no bitter anticolonial struggle for land as there was in neighboring Kenya. But its politics was typical of post-independence Africa, an example of how innocently, ignorantly but inevitably, the seeds of catastrophe were planted by imperial rule. The country's name came from Buganda; the powerful and sophisticated lakeside kingdom founded around 1500 and ruled by a hereditary kingship, the Kabaka. At the end of the nineteenth century the British made Buganda the core of a bigger state, Uganda, extending the protectorate north, east and west to include other ethnic groups, some of whom had been at war with the Buganda kingdom before the British arrived. Britain's policy of indirect rule co-opted the local kings and chiefs to carry out their orders but left the execution of the orders to traditional local systems.

At independence in 1962, Britain attempted to leave behind a Westminster style democracy in the tropics with a President and a Prime Minister. An election gave victory to a northerner, Milton Obote. He became Prime Minister. The counter-balancing presidency, a ceremonial post like British monarchy, was given to the Baganda king, the Kabaka, Fredrick Mutesa. The Democratic Party was left in the wilderness. The British walked away. Disaster was only a matter of time.

The election in Uganda opened up seams and split the country along ethnic and religious lines. The system wobbled along for four years, then in 1966, Obote lost patience with Baganda attempts to gain greater autonomy and drove out President Mutesa in a coup, making himself Executive President. He gathered all power to himself, made Uganda a one-party state and planned radical socialism.

But in using the army to overthrow the constitution, he had involved the soldiers in politics. Idi Amin was the army chief and had led the attack on the king's palace. Obote

---

77. Lord Lugard is the architect of Britain's policy of indirect rule. See Mazrui, *Africans*, 265–66.
78. Twesinge, "Church and State Conflicts in Uganda," 158.
79. Masters, "Based on True Events," 200.

knew the army, and Amin in particular, were a threat. Obote tried to get rid of him, but Amin was canny and dangerous when threatened. He cultivated the rank and file soldiers and recruited many from his own area. After a minor mutiny several soldiers were sacked, but Amin quietly re-recruited them, making them beholden to him. As Obote went off to the Commonwealth conference in Singapore in January 1971, he left orders that Amin be arrested.

It has always been assumed that the British had a hand in the coup that brought Idi Amin to power. The British Foreign Office papers suggests that it was Israel, not Britain, that put Idi Amin in power.[80]

African leadership is a revolving door caused by coup d'état and counter-coup d'état, making personal and national plans hardly predictable. Obote was overthrown by Idi Amin, Idi Amin was overthrown by Obote, and Obote was overthrown by Museveni. "By 1986, after 15 years of dictatorship and disorder, Uganda, too, had had enough. The new president, Yoweri Museveni, cleaned house from top to bottom and ushered in a period of steady reform and economic growth. By the end of the century, Uganda had become the first African country to wrestle its way back to the per capita income it enjoyed in 1970. Upset by the deaths of many military comrades, Museveni was the first African head of state to become personally involved in fighting HIV/AIDS. As a result, by the year 2000, Uganda was also the first country to have reduced infection levels in some districts."[81]

Museveni has been one of the most admired and favorite leaders of the West, particularly the United States. However, in practice and ideology he falls in the category of African despots. Among other things transfer of power is not in his leadership vocabulary. He has been leading the country for the last twenty-eight years by manipulating elections. *The Economist* concurs:

> In the 1990s Mr. Museveni was hailed across Africa as a new kind of leader, empowering rather than impoverishing his people. He restored stability after decades of bloody upheaval. He boosted economic growth after long years of ruin. He beat back a dreadful HIV/AIDS epidemic. He was hailed in the West as an exemplar of a new breed of dynamic and democratic African leader who deserved generous aid for development. He remains popular at home and might win a fair election. But the coterie of loyalists who surround him dare not take that risk. Democracy in Uganda has been badly eroded . . .
>
> Mr. Museveni is virtually the only decision-maker in the government. Almost nothing gets done without his nod. Officials must travel down to his farm from Kampala to seek his blessings for their plans. But while the president's signature on a policy paper is necessary, it is not sufficient to move the sluggish state machine into action.
>
> The auditor-general recently reported $100m was diverted last year from government coffers. No sector of the economy has been as badly handled as oil, which was discovered seven years ago . . . Decades of presidential dominance have driven away the best officials, who have gone abroad or into private business-anywhere away from Uganda's shambolic government.

80. For further details, see Dowden, *Africa*, 11–50.
81. Calderisi, *Trouble with Africa*, 161.

Thus bereft of talent, the Museveni court is in disarray. Insiders fight among themselves. The prime minister, parliamentary speaker and other senior members of the National Resistance Movement, the ruling party, are building competing power bases in readiness for the president's eventual departure.[82]

In his well-researched book, *Histories of the Hanged: Britain's Dirty War in Kenya and the End of the Empire*, David Anderson has brilliantly told the shocking true story of Britain's first war in terror—a story of mass killings, of collective punishments, property seizures, human rights abuses, and a brutal battle conducted under the banner of an assumed superiority. Portrayed at the time as a conflict between whites and blacks, civilization and savagery, it was in fact a thoroughly bureaucratized conflict that pitted Kenya against itself and from which few emerged with credit. "British justice in 1950s Kenya was a blunt, brutal and unsophisticated instrument of oppression."[83] The acts of torture included castration and sexual assaults, which, in many cases, entailed the insertion of broken bottles into the vaginas of female detainees. At the order of the colonial power, camp guards beat many detainees to death. During interrogation, the guards would hang certain detainees upside-down and insert sand and water into their anuses. In 1957, the Colonial Administration decided to subject the detainees who still refused to cooperate and comply with orders to a torture technique known as "the dilution technique."[84] The technique involved the systemic use of brute force to overpower the Mau Mau adherents, using fists, clubs, truncheons, and whips. This brutality would continue until the detainees cooperated with orders and ultimately confessed and repented of their alleged Mau Mau allegiance.

Some aspects of the torture by the Colonial officers were intentional attacks on the core of their being—the cultural values, norms, and psyche that constitute the personality of the Kikuyus. The goal was to physically, mentally, and socially destroy them. The scar and its impact have not completely healed to this day. One woman from Nyeri District told Elkins:

> *At one point the villagers were ordered to remove every article of clothing and remain stark naked. You cannot start to imagine the shame and embarrassment we felt when, without any consideration for the small children, we were told to arrange ourselves in two rows, one for the men and the other for the women, old and young alike. To everyone's horror we were ordered at gunpoint to embrace each other, man with a woman, regardless of whether the man happened to be your father, father-in-law, or brother. It was all so humiliating that one woman hanged herself later, as she felt that she could not continue to live with the humiliating experience of having been forced to embrace her son-in-law while both of them were naked. In our custom that is a curse.*[85]

Britain's "civilization" and Christianity were introduced in Kenya, and for that matter in most parts of Africa, with this kind of injustice—injustice that contradicts the whole concept of civilization and the teachings of Jesus Christ. It is hard to believe that

---

82. "A Leader Who Cannot Bear to Retire," *Economist*, October 12, 2013, p. 59.
83. Anderson, *Histories of the Hanged*, 7.
84. Elkins, *Britain's Gulag*, 319.
85. Ibid., 249; emphasis added.

the British in colonial Africa were from the same culture and geography of John and Charles Wesley, William Carey, and Charles Spurgeon. "The entire cultural education of your countries is surely this," said Plato.

> You oblige your poets to say that the good man, because he is temperate and just, enjoys good fortune and is happy, no matter whether he is big and strong, or small and weak, or rich or poor; that even if he is richer than "Midas or Cinyras," and has not justice he is a wretch, and lives a life of misery . . . It is commonly said that health comes first, beauty second, and wealth third. The list goes on indefinitely: keen insight and hearing, and acute perception of all the objects of sensation; being a dictator and doing whatever you like; and the seventh heaven is supposed to be reached when one has achieved all this and is made immortal without further ado . . . all these things are possessions of great value to the just and pious, but that to the unjust they are a curse, every one of them all the way down the list."[86]

To fully understand Plato's analysis one needs to examine postmodern Western society and social problems such as drug addiction, obesity, high divorce rates, abortion, the increasing number of children out of wedlock, teen age pregnancy, and homicides. In the West, "[t]here is the brutal nihilism of some forms of art and cinema. Life is meaningless: so what? The failure and emptiness of so much of the promise inherent in the mythology of modernity have led to a great deal of pessimism in Western life, as well as a very shallow attitude of 'get what you can from the present: there isn't much future to look forward to.'"[87] To end up with this kind of worldview in a culture of affluence, with so many choices and opportunities is a misery. And it is no less than a "curse."

"Because freedom is a duty as well as a right, an obligation and not only an entitlement, all citizens in a free society are responsible for the right of others just as others are responsible for theirs. Unless rights are exercised freely, and unless responsibilities are protected vigilantly, freedom, becoming empty, will be eroded."[88] European powers have utterly failed in fulfilling this responsibility. "The colonial state had suppressed autonomous African capitalism; the predatory politics of independent African state ensured that African entrepreneurs remained paralyzed."[89]

Not only the maps but also the colonial roads were built to suit the agenda of the colonial powers, that is, to transport raw materials—to the port, not to connect African countries and the people.

French comments:

> The important roads were drawn like veins, in bold crimson with black borders, and what was most striking about them was their paucity. Most of them had been laid down under European rule. Studying them, one quickly understood Europe's goal was extracting as much value as possible from Africa's lands and from its peoples, and especially of making imperialism self-financing. There

---

86. Saunders, trans., *Plato: The Laws*, 97–98.
87. Wright, "Christ and the Mosaic Pluralism," 74.
88. Guinness, *Case for Civility*, 45.
89. Rupp, "Africa and China," 80.

was little variation in direct mine-to-port-routing for almost all the terrestrial infrastructure.

Expressions of narrow, national self-interest on the part of the colonizers were evident in lots of other small details, too, like the narrow gauge of the railways. But nothing jumps out at the map reader more than the disinterest shown by the empire builders in connecting African peoples across the borders imposed upon them, especially when the country next door "belonged" to a European rival.[90]

Anderson further describes the heavy-handed of British ruling of Kenya and the kind of white settlers who grabbed the land, 300–500 acres in the fertile region of the country:

Colonialism everywhere in Africa depended upon the threat of coercive power to sustain its authority, but in Kenya this had a particular sharpness... By 1920s the vast majority of those Africans convicted by all Kenya's colonial courts were flogged, this in addition to other punishments handed down, such as imprisonment or fines. Flogging was a far commoner punishment for African Kenya than in neighboring Uganda or Tanganyika... Happy Valley, as some liked to call the White Highlands, was always a violent place if you were African.

Race was what set the white settlers apart from the African masses, and from rival immigrants, the Hindus and Muslims from southern Asia. Race gave Kenya's white settlers a clear, visible superiority, and generated a solidarity that transcended difference in class and social attitude. Whatever his background, and no matter whether he came to East Africa directly from Europe, or via the Natal or Transvaal, every white man who disembarked from the boat at Mombasa became an instant aristocrat. They exploited Kenya to attain a quality of life that few could have aspired to elsewhere.[91]

Michela Wrong adds, "Much has been written about the antics of the dissolute aristocrats who made up the Happy Valley expatriate set. But most of the land-hungry British arrivals in 'Keenya,' as they pronounced were from decidedly modest backgrounds, grabbing the chance for a new start. In 1903 there were only around a 100 settlers; by the late 1940s the number had risen to 29,000, boosted by demobilized British soldiers. It would peak 80,000 in the 1950s. And as the new arrivals marked up their farms, everything began to change for more than forty local tribes."[92] When one reads the history of colonialism in Kenya and observes the current economic, education, underdevelopment, injustice, insecurity, crime, and corruption situation in the country, Wrong's observation, "everything began to change for more than forty local tribes," is either an understatement or vague.

In Kenya, colonialism manifested not only the greed and brutality of the whites in Africa. The cruelty of the blacks to their own people is a real historical fact of the nation. Often, it is the heroic, patriotic, and nationalistic struggle of the Mau Mau that many Kenyans heard and know. However, these Kikuyu guerrilla fighters were brutal to the Kikuyus who aligned with the white colonizers. Their violence was primarily directed to

---

90. French, *China's Second Continent*, 162.
91. Anderson, *Histories of the Hanged*, 78.
92. Wrong, *It's Our Time to Eat*, 47.

the people of their own, whom it butchered, man, woman, and child. They would burn their houses, villages, and farms and they raided and pillaged the Kikuyu community without a drop of mercy. Of course these unpleasant, inhuman, bloody, treacherous betrayals, and the suffering of the human drama in Kenya was orchestrated and planned by the colonial power. They believed that it was when the colonies hate and kill each other that they could prolong their rule.

The first president of Kenya, Jomo Kenyatta and his successor Daniel Arap Moi, intentionally ignored or played down the role of the Mau Mau to gain independence without threatening the security and property of the British colonialist. Barack Obama concurs: "Kenyatta had been released from prison and inaugurated Kenya's first president. He had immediately assured whites who were busy packing their bags that business would not be nationalized; the landholdings would be kept intact, so long as the black man controlled the apparatus of the government. Kenya became the West's most stalwart people in Africa, a model of stability, a useful contrast to the chaos of Uganda, the failed socialism of Tanzania. Former freedom fighters returned to their villages or joined the civil service or ran for a seat in Parliament."[93] Up until recently, some of the first settlers, a majority of their posterity, and many other British citizens lead a comfortable life in Kenya without any criticism from the people of Kenya, the press or the government. Most of the dark pages of the British government in Africa are exposed through the research of British scholars who love the truth more than their own race.

The deal for Kenya's independence from the British was in favor of the colonial power both for the short and long term. Through Kenyatta, who studied at University College London, and from 1934–1935 studied social anthropology under Bronisław Malinowski at the London School of Economics (LSE), the British knew their interests, freedom, and economic, social, and political power would be guarded. Kenyatta was not radical like the Mau Mau who wanted to expel the white settlers out of Kenya. To this day 60 percent of the steel company, the Delmonte plantation, and the trade market through Mombasa, immensely benefit the British government.

Mombasa is a lifeline port for Kenya and its landlocked neighbors, handling about 20 million tons of cargo currently. This is expected to rise 400 percent by 2030. The modernization of the port is not just timely but vital toward unlocking the economic potential of the region. The UK government gave $53 million toward port modernization and to improve efficiency at the Port of Mombasa. The donors believe the financial support represents the strong partnership between the UK and Kenya. The package will support short-term efficiency improvements as well as planning for the longer term, including:

- Improving rail linkages and space rationalization within existing port land;
- Improving port access through expansion of Gate 18;
- Improving yard facilities and stacking areas at berths 1–10 (Kilindini) and berths 11–14 (Kipevu);
- Institutional and legal Reforms—including Review of the KPA Act to give effect to new regulations (harbor, terminal, and port).[94]

93. Obama, *Dreams from My Father*, 312.

94. British High Commission, Nairobi: "UK Injects $53 Million into Mombasa Port Mordenisation,"

Today's Kenya's economy, politics, education, corruption, inadequate health care, poverty, and insecurity could not be fully comprehended without the colonial background of the nation and the scar and stigma it left in the minds and souls of the people.

Kenya's stalwartness to the people in the West in various ways, particularly economically and psychologically was costly. By and large Kenyans remained poor and ended up working for the white-owned farms and businesses for a minimum wage not even equivalent to a dollar an hour. The minimum wage was associated with an image of a menial worker. In restaurants and upper- middle-class hotels, Kenyans were discriminated against by Kenyan waiters, waitresses, and managers. The current president of the United States and his sister, Auma, had faced the discrimination at the famous Stanley Hotel where Western tourists enjoy first-class treatment, just because of the color of their skin, despite their social or economic status at home.

Obama narrates his experience this way:

> I took the opportunity to study these tourists as Auma and I sat down for lunch in the outdoor café of the New Stanley Hotel. They were everywhere—Germans, Japanese, British, Americans—taking pictures, hailing taxis, fending off street peddlers, many of them dressed in safari suits like extras in movie set . . . they were expressing a freedom that neither Auma nor I could ever experience, a bedrock confidence in their own parochialism, a confidence reserved for those born into imperial cultures.
>
> Just then I noticed an American family sit down a few tables away from us. Two of the African waiters immediately sprang into action, both of them smiling from one side to the other. Since Auma and I had not yet been served, I began to wave at the two waiters who remained standing by the kitchen, thinking they must have somehow failed to see us. For some time they managed to avoid my glance, but eventually an older man with sleepy eyes relented brought us over two menus. His manner was resentful, though, and after several more minutes, he showed no signs of ever coming back. Auma's face began to pinch with anger; again I waved to our waiter, who continued in his silence as he wrote down our orders. At this point the Americans had already received their food and we still had no place settings. I overheard a young girl with a blond ponytail complain that there was not any ketchup. Auma stood up.
>
> "Let us go."
>
> She started heading for the exit, then suddenly returned and walked back to the waiter, who was watching us with an impassive stare. "You should be ashamed of yourself," Auma said to him, her voice shaking. "You should be ashamed."[95]

This author had similar experiences in Kenya, which amounted to unforgettable culture shock. Africans' discrimination by Africans in Kenya was not limited to hotels and restaurants. I saw and experienced it in Christian institutions. For most of the 80s the ministry of major churches in Nairobi, such as Nairobi Baptist, Christ is the Answer (CITA), Anglican and Presbyterian, was handled by white pastors and white choirs. It was a weird feeling for me to see blacks passively receiving Western preaching and songs

---

21 June 2013, gov.uk, https://www.gov.uk/government/world-location-news/uk-injects-53-million-into-mombasa-port-mordenisation (accessed October 1, 2015).

95. Obama, *Dreams from My Father*, 312.

accompanied by Western musical instruments, played by Western musicians, week after week. The most costly price of slavery and colonialism for the black race is lack of self-esteem, resulting in mistreatment and disrespect for one another, which became an incubator for eventual self-degradation and conflict.

It is a paradox of life for Barack Obama to be ignored and underserved in a hotel in his father-land, only to become a two-term president in his mother's country that has an unclean and tarnished record in its treatment of black people. One wonders, despite the historical background of human rights in Kenya and the United States, which country is marching forward on the path of civilization and equality.

Among many social and economic challenges Kenya is facing today, one is health care:

> By 2016 the market for health care in sub-Saharan Africa will be worth $35 billion, according to a report by McKinsey, a consultancy. But a skills shortage is constraining it, since the continent is reckoned to host a quarter of the world's disease burden but has only 3 % of its medical workers. The World Bank reckons an additional 90,000 doctors and 500,000 nurses will be needed in the next few years.
>
> It is even harder to see how people can pay for health insurance, especially since few Kenyans work in the formal sector, where they might build up a fund. So far some 600,000 Kenyans out of 43m are estimated to have bought policies or been given workplace insurance.[96]

In Rwanda, the Great Lake region, and in other former African colonies, the root causes of refugees, Internally Displaced Persons (IDPs), war and genocide, in the eyes of many Western observers, is the "usual" African tribal conflict. "However, tribalism alone cannot account for the unstable political situation in Rwanda after independence in 1961. One must consider how the colonialists exploited socio-economic differences of ethnic groups for their own advantage. The scrambles for political power in the 1990's between minority Tutsis, and majority Hutus are closely linked to colonial legacy in Rwanda."[97]

Those who argue tribalism was the cause of conflict in Rwanda, say that the dominant aristocratic Hamitic Tutsi cattle owners were governed by the leadership of a king and that they made up 14 percent of the population. Some scholars and Tutsis themselves think they migrated from Ethiopia.[98] The Bantu Hutu majority farmers were 85 percent of the population and migrated from the northeast of Africa. Both Tutsis and Hutus were migrants many decades ago and settled in both Rwanda and Burundi. The tall Tutsis are pastoralists; Hutus are smaller in stature and mostly farmers. The minority Twa tribe, 1 percent of the population, was the earliest indigenous group whose main occupation was hunting and pottery. "The Tutsis enforced overlord-ship and segregation through wealth measured in cattle, superior military organization, and control over the allocation of land. The Hutu peasantry was held to an inferior status and force to labor

---

96. "A Middle Way?," *Economist*, Nov. 16, 2013, pg. 54.
97. Msoka, *Basic Human Rights*, 7.
98. Ayittey, *Africa in Chaos*, 55.

for the Tutsis as servants and tillers."⁹⁹ "Ethnologically, tribes are known to have distinct cultures involving languages, customs, and traditions. The Hutus, Tutsis, and Twa however, speak one language and practice similar customs and traditions in Rwanda. Furthermore they are not separated by distinct geographical boundaries. It is argued that during the pre-colonial era, these groups were one people known as Banyarwanda and spoke one language, Kinyarwanda. Over time, the Tutsis, the Hutus, and the Twa became increasingly distinguishable socially and politically, not on the basis of tribe, clans, language, customs and tradition, but rather on the basis of occupations."¹⁰⁰

During precolonial times, these three ethnic groups were peacefully coexisting and very few conflicts or civil wars occurred among them.

> The master-client relationship was accentuated at first by German colonialist (1890–1916) and then by Belgian administrators 1916–1962). The Tutsis were accorded authority and power over the country, given administrative jobs and a monopoly in the educational system set up by Catholic missionaries. The Hutu peasantry, held in centuries of resentful during colonial rule. On July 25, 1959, they rose in rebellion and overthrow their Tutsi overlords, killing an estimated 100,000 Tutsis. A shocked Belgian colonial government hurriedly and belatedly introduced political reform. A 1961 U.N. supervised referendum adopted a republican constitution, and parliamentary elections brought the Hutu majority party, *Pramehutu* to power. Independence was attained on 1 July 1962, but there after the Tutsis have launched sporadic guerrilla operations to regain their old hegemony. One such expedition in 1963 by Tutsi guerrillas, unwisely backed by China, resulted in the massacre of more than 200,000 Hutus.¹⁰¹

The colonial administration highly favored the Tutsis and provided education, job opportunities, and economic and political power to the minority Tutsis over the majority Hutus. The Belgians used "divide and rule" to have indirect control over their colonies in the Great Lake regions. "The majority Hutus were on the margin of the society economically, socially, and politically, and they were totally excluded from the colonial administration. Due to the scio-economic inequalities between the two tribes, the Hutus were deliberately subjugated to degrading and humiliating treatment both at the hands of the colonialist and their Tutsi masters."¹⁰² Yamauchi concurs: "The Hamitic thesis even influenced the Belgians to favor the fairer and taller Tutsi over the darker Hutu, which contributes the deadly enmity between these two tribes."¹⁰³

The dominance of the colonialists and the Tutsis over the Hutu caused war, death, and internal displacement of persons both in Burundi and Rwanda. The number of orphans and refugees multiplied. Economic and political crisis has been the pattern of these two countries since the eve of independence in 1961. In Burundi

> a brutal purge of Hutus from the army and the bureaucracy followed, leading to a Hutu uprising in April 1972 it resulted in the death of about 1,000 Tutsis.

99. Ibid.
100. Msoka, *Basic Human Rights*, 8.
101. Ayittey, *Africa in Chaos*, 55; emphasis original. Msoka, *Basic Human Rights*, 9.
102. Msoka, *Basic Human Rights*, 10.
103. Yamauchi, *Africa and the Bible*, 29–30.

> The ruling Tutsi autocracy decided to eliminate the 'Hutu threat' by killing every Hutu with education, a government job, or money. Within three months, more than 200,000 Hutus had been slain ... Then in August 1988, following an abortive coup attempt, the Tutsi-run military government under Piere Buyoya massacred an estimated 20,000 Hutus. U.N. officials at refugee camps near the border with Rwanda told of soldiers chasing, machine-gunning, and bayoneting fleeing Hutus. The scale and barbarity of the atrocities shocked many western aid officials. The carnage was repeated in 1993, following Burundi's first parliamentary elections, which were won by the Hutus ... Tutsi dominated military overthrew the civilian government and bayoneted its president to death, instigating a horrific tribal massacre that claimed over 100,000 lives and sent more than 500,000 refugees streaming into Rwanda, Tanzania, and Zaire ... In 1994 over 700,000 [some estimate 800,000] Tutsis were slain in Rwanda.[104]

"The Rwandan debacle is landmark event in the history of the Great Lake Region of the Sub-Saharan Africa."[105]

It is not only the heavy colonial hands of Germany and Belgium that have led to chaos in the region, the intervention of France and the indifference of the United States after independence have contributed to the turmoil in the Great Lake Region. "France has had an appalling record of supporting and coddling brutal African dictators. In the case of Rwanda, France was sending arms, helicopters, even 700 of its own soldiers between 1990 and 1993 to help the Hutu government of Juvenal Habyarimana fight off the Tutsi rebels of the Rwanda Patriotic Front. And when the Hutu government soldiers were routed France created a 'safety zone' for murderers—not for the victims of genocide—because French were more interested in maintaining their cultural dominance in Rwanda. The Tutsi rebels were invading from Uganda—an English speaking country, where they lost their French-language skills after decades in exile."[106] That was not the only reason. The Tutsi rebels were supported by the U.S., and France knew that the new Tutsi government in Rwanda would work closely with the United States keeping their interest in the Great Lake Region and particularly in Congo.

Paul Kagame, born 23 October 1957, is the sixth and current President of Rwanda, having taken office in 2000 when his predecessor, Pasteur Bizimungu, resigned. Kagame previously commanded the rebel force that ended the 1994 Rwandan Genocide, and was considered Rwanda's de facto leader when he served as Vice President and Minister of Defense from 1994 to 2000. Even if he has been one of the U.S.'s most favored African leaders and has been supported by the U.S. since he was leading the guerrilla army, he has hardly been democratic and fully transparent in his governance of a country that needs reconciliation, healing, justice, equality, freedom, peace, and lasting stability. Describing the most recent election in Rwanda, *The Economist* writes: "Many things were in doubt when Rwanda held parliamentary elections on September 16th, but not the outcome. Paul Kagame, the president, said before votes were counted that he had 'no reason to believe' in anything but overwhelming victory. His Rwandan Patriotic Front (RPF) won with 76%. Political election has been allowed only where it does not question

104. Ayittey, *Africa in Chaos*, 56–57.
105. Msoka, *Basic Human Rights*, 13.
106. Ibid., 23.

the RPF's role as the country's savior. Victoire Ingabire, the last important politician to challenge the view, sought to unseat Mr. Kagame at the last election and ended up in prison, accused of links to a Hutu rebel group led by a suspected mass killer."[107]

We can argue, debate, reason, and even agree to blame colonialism as the root cause of the internal displacement of persons and the bloodshed stated above in the Great Lake region, but to exclude Hutus and Tutsis from the responsibility to grow out of the colonial political and social structure and come up with a constitution that gives equal platform to the Burundians and Rwandese, is a huge failure of Africans. Africans are prone to slaughter each other with a butchering knife and then blame outside powers for their demise. We will look at this matter in detail later.

To have a good comprehension of human nature and its potential for murder, oppression, and exploitation let us look at the crisis in Liberia, one of the two countries in Africa that claim not to have been colonized. The other one is Ethiopia. Here is a good case study to prove that evil doesn't exist in the skin color of humankind: "Ever since Liberia was founded in 1847 by freed U.S. slaves, its history has been characterized by truculent perfidy. The freed U.S. slaves, known as Americo-Liberians, established an overlord-ship over the indigent that was similar to white settler colonialism in other parts of Africa. They even imposed force labor, akin to slavery, on the indigenous peoples. The sale of African slaves to Spanish colonialist on the Atlantic Ocean to the island of Fernando Po in 1930, so outraged Britain and the United States as to cause them to sever diplomatic relations with Liberia for five years. America-Liberians rarely mixed or shared power with the local population. Resentment boiled."[108] When the former slaves gained their freedom, they enslaved people of their own color. Britain and America, who were heavily involved in African slave trade with no conflict of their Christian conscious, became outraged when their former slaves imitated their masters. One wonders in whose court of law the African slaves could get justice. When criminals become prosecutors and judge and victim, slaves turn out to be victimizing masters. It clearly shows that, even at the zenith of human civilization, the world we live in is far from perfect and just. The imperfection inevitably makes you look for a perfect world beyond our realm of existence. In the face of such paradoxical and meaningless human history, our Lord's Prayer "thy/your kingdom come," makes real sense to those who hope for complete emancipation—to live in a world full of righteousness and justice.

The simmering antipathy in Liberia led to a number of coup d'etats and bloody civil wars. The chief among many of those who destroyed Liberia and caused havoc in Sierra Leone is Charles Taylor. "Thirty percent of Taylor's estimated 10,000 soldiers were child warriors under the age of 15. They were inducted by the mixture of coercion and enticement . . . The human and economic toll of Liberia's seven-year civil war was enormous. More than 150,000 people perished and over a third of Liberia's 2.3 million people fled to neighboring countries. The war also spilled over into neighboring Sierra Leone, eventually toppling the regime of General Joseph Momoh."[109] French also observes: "The dirty war fought in [Liberia] in the 1990s and early 2000s had wiped out people in huge

---

107. "Rwandan Elections Safe and Sorry," *Economist*, September 21, 2013, p. 52.
108. Ayittey, *Africa in Chaos*, 57–58.
109. Ibid., 59.

numbers relative to the size of these countries (Sierra Leon, Guinea, and Liberia). In Liberia, the toll has been estimated as a quarter of a million people, a figure approaching 10 percent of the population."[110] And Liberia proved to be an example of horror in Africa emanating mainly from internal factors. For some Africans who think the sole problem of Africa is the white race, slavery, and colonialism, the atrocities of Taylor, Doe, Sankoh, and their soldiers screams at them not to be blinded by reverse racism.

> When on 12 April 1980 a group of enlisted men under the command of Sergeant Samuel Doe, a member of the Krahn tribe, stormed Liberia's executive mansion and overthrew the regime of William Tolbert, native Liberians roared with euphoria. But it quickly evaporated. Liberians who are initially welcomed the coup recoiled in horror when Doe, an illiterate, proceeded to institute a brutal reign of terror and his own brand of tribal apartheid. All top positions in his governments, the army, and his presidential guards were filled with members of his own tribe.
>
> The coup itself was accompanied by acts of savage brutality. Tolbert was murdered as he lay in bed. The soldiers disemboweled the dead leader and gouged out one of his eyes with a bayonet. His mutilated body was displayed for two days at the John F. Kennedy Hospital morgue and then buried with 27 others in a mass grave. The soldiers then went on with an orgy of massacre and barbaric reprisals, killing an estimated 200 people. In a chilling spectacle that was televised nationwide, high government officials of the deposed regime were summarily tried and executed by drunken firing squad. Their half-naked corpses were then dangled from a row of telephone poles on the beach.[111]

To disagree with one's government, being frustrated and disappointed by its modus operandi, is one thing, but to go this far in barbaric acts is insane, savage, and inhuman. What lesson did Doe and his soldiers teach younger generations of Liberians? As a free black nation, what model were they setting for other African countries? I remember watching with great interest the whole public funeral service of Richard Nixon, the 37th president of the United States. Despite the Watergate scandal that made him step down from leadership and leave the White House before the end of his term, America gave him a moving and well-deserved tribute. Some young Americans who were interviewed after the service said that "this service made me proud that I am an American." Americans, as a nation, also demonstrated their utmost civility that transcends a party line to the whole world. African leaders like Doe, Mengistu, Idi Amin, and Bokassa, to mention a few, are a disgrace to the black people.

The United States, historically did not participate with Europeans in the scramble for Africa.

> America's political involvement with most African countries has been both recent and sporadic. Liberia, though, is a screaming exception to the pattern. The Firestone plantation served as America's strategic reserve of rubber supplies in World War II. Robertsfield was Africa's largest airport, a huge, air-conditioned, brushed aluminum structure that sat strangely out of place in the middle of a fetid swamp, before it was destroyed in the country's civil war. The airport was

110. French, *China's Second Continent*, 92.
111. Ibid., 58.

built with the Department of Defense funds, but the project had nothing to do with Liberian passenger traffic. The "gift" of an outsized airport, was meant to accommodate the largest planes, and Washington used the facility for years as a refueling point for large arms shipments to the anti-communist Angolan rebel movement, UNITA, sent by the CIA and the Pentagon.

Liberia was home, too, to Omega, a forest of soaring antennas maintained by secretive American technicians on the edge of Monrovia. Officially, this vast farm of steel towers that crackled with more electricity than all of downtown Monrovia was part of a maritime emergency navigational system. It also served as the regional rebroadcast center for the Voice of America. Liberians in the know, however, whispered that it had a less innocent function as well: transmitting coded American diplomatic and intelligence communications traffic around a large slice of the planet.[112]

The country is rich with minerals and natural resources and has been a bone of contention for outside powers and Africa despots. The civil war in Liberia was one of the worst on the continent and caused millions to end up in refugee camps in neighboring African countries and thousands more died. "The tenth anniversary of the end of a civil war that once made Liberia a byword for barbarity is celebrated," *The Economist* stated. But the country is still wobbling to stand on its feet; all sectors of society are not near to restoration yet. For example, "None of the 25,000 university applicants passed this year's entrance exams after administrators switched to a fair admission system based on real marks rather than bribes and family connections. Education in Liberia is a mess . . . Formal economy still relies heavily on the export of unprocessed rubber, palm oil, and timber and iron ore by foreign companies with concessions for half the country's land. Too few lucky Liberians are becoming very rich. The poor still bemoan lousy government services. Resentment and anger are rising."[113]

Liberia doesn't seem too far from another civil war. Incompetent leaders, 80 percent unemployment, inadequate food, three-quarters of the people eating one meal a day, poor infrastructure, and the ravages of Ebola lead to nowhere but civil unrest. The cycle of poverty, war, displacement, oppression, imprisonment, death, coup d'etats and counter coup d'etats in Africa seem inescapable and add up to an unavoidable social humdrum. But it is not unsolvable.

112. French, *Continent for the Taking*, 106.
113. "Liberia: Skin-Deep Success."

Chapter 7

China in Africa

Modern globalization's first great wave has now crested, and is being overtaken by a newer and potentially even more consequential tide. In this new phase, China has gone from being a vessel to becoming an increasingly transformative actor in its own right. Indeed, it is rapidly emerging as the most important agent of economic change in broad swaths of the world.[1]

> Africa attracted China as early as the T'ang dynasty (A.D. 618–907). Ninth-century reports of the meat-eating, ivory-exporting people of Po-pu-li in the "southwestern sea" may refer to the inhabitants of what is now modern Kenya or Tanzania. During the Sung dynasty (A.D. 1127–1279), Chinese shipping was common throughout the Western reaches of the Indian Ocean. Chinese objects of various kinds from this period, have been found from today's Somalia to Mozambique... Between 1417 and 1431, the Ming emperors dispatched three large expeditions to eastern Africa to collect walking proof of the celestial approval of their virtuous and harmonious reigns...China and Africa have enriched each other intellectually, culturally, and commercially ever since. But direct contact and interactive influence have been episodic. During the middle years of the twentieth century Maoist China funded and educated sub-Saharan African anti-colonial liberation movements and leaders.[2]

To most Westerners the emergence of China as a superpower is a recent historical episode. Some are caught by surprise and others ill-informed and have distorted knowledge of China's civilization. As we try to understand China, "[i]t should be realized that during the Middle Ages oriental technology was far more advanced than European technology, and that until the thirteenth century Europe, technologically was but an appendage of Asia. While the Greeks and Romans were weaving subtle philosophies, the

---

1. French, *China's Second Continent*, 3.
2. Rotberg, "China into Africa," vii–viii.

Chinese were busy inventing gunpowder, paper, alchemy, vaccinations, plastic surgery, paint, and even the pocket handkerchiefs, which was unknown to the fastidious Greeks."[3]

China is now in the third era of her engagement with Africa. In the eyes of many observers, "This one is much more transformative than the earlier iterations."[4] Ever since the world was divided between the Eastern (communist) and Western (capitalist) block after the Second World War, Russia and China and other Marxist/communist countries had history and influence in the continent of Africa. Throughout the Cold War, the East and the West fought to influence Africans and control their resources. Mazrui explains the conditions in Africa and the place of socialism from the 60s through the 80s as follows:

> The intellectual climate for socialism in Africa is quite good, but the sociological and material soil is not fertile enough for socialism. The favoring conditions are:
>
> 1. The reasons why the intellectual climate for socialism in Africa is good include basic historical continuities and discontinuities. For one thing, many Africans both north and south of the Sahara have conceptually come to associate capitalism with imperialism.
>
> 2. The accumulation of frustration over efforts to develop Africa through Western patterns of economic growth. Many Africans are seeking alternative strategies of social and economic improvement out of a sheer sense of desperation at the inadequacies of the first decades of independence.
>
> 3. The rampant corruption among the immediate post-colonial rulers of the continent.
>
> 4. The widespread belief that traditional African culture was basically collectivist, and "therefore" socialist.
>
> Because of this broadly favourable intellectual climate, most African leaders immediately after independence did seem to be congenial with socialism. Nasser, Nkrumah, Sékou Touré, Julius Nyerere and Boumedienne were seen as architects of a new socialist Africa. What then went wrong?
>
> 1. One obstinate sociological factor was simply the primary of ethnicity in Africa as against class consciousness. Most Africans are members of their ethnic group first and members of a particular social class second.
>
> 2. A second related factor is the strength of élites rather than social classes. The new élites especially have emerged out of the womb of Western imperial acculturation. It has not been the possession of wealth necessarily which opened the doors to influence and power, but initially the possession of Western education and verbal skills.
>
> 3. A third factor of this barreness of the soil concerns Africa's organizational capabilities in the present historical phase. Many hastily assume that a tradition of collective efforts in a modern setting. Unfortunately, much of the evidence points the other way. Collective effort based on custom and tradition and kinship ties leaves Africa unprepared for the kind of organized

---

3. Jackson, *Introduction to African Civilization*, 18.
4. Rotberg, "China into Africa," viii.

collectivism which need to be based on command rather than custom, on efficiency rather than empathy, on rationality rather than ritual.

4. Most African economies have already been deeply integrated into a world economy dominated by the West. African countries which become socialist domestically find that they are still integrated in the world capitalist system. The rules of that system overwhelmingly derived from principles evolved in the history of capitalism. In international trade countries seek to maximise their return and acquire profit. The rules of business and exchange at the international level, the banking system which underpins those exchanges, the actual currencies used in money markets and in meeting balances of payments, are all products of capitalist experience.[5]

As Mazuri aptly summarized above, for Russia and China to have the same level of inroads like the West in Africa during the Cold War, was a promising intellectual climate; the sociological soil was forbidding. China's current "success" in Africa, in terms of trade, economic, diplomatic, and industrial relationships with many African countries did not emanate from the ideological womb of the East. It came through the recently-developed economic muscle China.

China has a long history and like every nation in the world has her own comedies and tragedies of life. Not too long ago, from 1958 to 1961, the Great Chinese Famine ravished the country and is still the worst famine on record. While statistics of the loss of life are disputed, as few as 15 million and as many as 43 million were killed as a result.[6] Evolving from a tumultuous social and historical background, surviving the Maoist ideology that didn't give room for democracy and capitalistic entrepreneurship, and despite her marred global image on human rights, China has made an inroads to the heart and souls of Africans. "Growing rapidly and busting out of its long underdeveloped cocoon to become a major world power and global economic source, China needs sources of energy and the raw materials—copper, cobalt, cadmium, manganese, platinum, nickel, zinc, tantalum, uranium, and so on—that African nations can supply."[7] Furthermore, "China is attempting to quadruple its economy again by 2020, a goal that will require substantial energy and resources supplied from abroad."[8] China cannot find a better "abroad" than Africa for the resources she needs. Hence, China is in Africa in a big way.

If China's modus operandi in Africa continues uninterrupted, China will shape the history of the world and the direction of the global community. Brautigam describes the alluring start to China's recent relationship with African leaders this way: "For three days in November 2006, China's capital city was host to delegations from forty-eight African states gathered for the Beijing Summit of the Forum on China-Africa Cooperation (FCAO). As the African leaders strode up the red carpet of the Great Hall of the People to shake hands with China's President Hu Jintao, the streets outside were filled with billboards saluting 'Amazing Africa.' Hu's opening speech brought waves of applause as the Chinese leader outlined a plan for a new 'strategic partnership' a deepening of

---

5. Mazrui, *Africans*, 188–91.
6. *The Great Famine in China, 1958–1962: A Documentary History*, edited by Zhou Xun, 2012.
7. Rotberg, "China into Africa," 4.
8. Jiang, "China's Emerging Partnership in Africa," 56.

'economic cooperation' with African countries."⁹ The presence of forty-eight African delegates at the 2006 FCAO meeting in Beijing was a historic watershed in Chinese-African relationships. This meeting also shattered the long held perception of the West about China. "There is a view in the West that China is an insular country that has traditionally embraced a posture of isolationism. This view stem largely from images of China from the nineteenth century and the first half of the twentieth century. However, on a longer time scale, China can be seen as one of the greatest trading nations in the world. The Mongol Empire stretched halfway around the globe, and the Silk Road was one of the great trading routes. In the early fifteenth century, Emperor Zhu Di ordered the construction of what might have been the most impressive shipping fleet in the world. Commanded by Zheng He, Chinese ships reached Africa and established trading posts on the continent, decades before the Portuguese. For much of the last millennium China was a major global trader."¹⁰ Huang augments: "China's expansive political, economic, and military engagement in Africa reflects an increasing dynamic and accommodating approach toward the continent. Launched at the November 2006 Forum on China-Africa Cooperation (FOCAC) summit, China's renewed partnership with Africa marks a historic watershed in Chinese African relations. Chinese activity in Africa promises future gains that benefit Africa in significant, constructive ways, at the same time, challenges are fast emerging as Beijing seeks to translates its vision of a strategic partnership with Africa into a sustainable reality."¹¹ Hence, in this chapter, we focus on the implication of China's trade with Africa and her Foreign Direct Investment (FDI), and on the response of Africans and the West.

Timing

"When China launched its historic opening toward the end of the 1970s, the country and its people not only became the fortunate beneficiaries of astute new policies, but also—crucially—of magnificent timing."¹² It is important to analyze the "timing" from different angles in order to understand the rapid growth, influence, and large presence of China in Africa. The first angle to look at is the modern situation of Africa.

> Modern Africa, by contrast is the abode of the elites, the parasitic minority group. This sector is meretricious burlesque, operating by an assortment of imported or borrowed institutions. The end product is an internally contradictory system that bears no affinity to either the indigenous system or the colonial state. It is a monstrosity that was created by the ruling elites themselves after independence by copying and grafting here and there from foreign systems they little understood. Over time it evolved into the present-day bizarre politico-economic system that admits of no rule of law, no accountability, no democracy of any form, and even no sanity. Here common sense has been murdered and arrogant idiocy rampages with impunity. All key institutions of government—the

9. Brautigam, *Dragon's Gift*, 1.
10. Lee and Shalmon, "China's Oil Strategies in Africa," 116.
11. Huang, "China's Renewal Partnership," 296.
12. French, *China's Second Continent*, 1.

military, judiciary, civil service, banking and the government itself—have been debauched. For example, government as understood by Most Western analysts does not exist in many African countries.[13]

In the light of Ayittey's observation, one can imagine the precarious economic political, social, and judicial conditions of the continent. The dismal state of African governance created high unemployment, low production, shortages of all kinds of things, from food in the grocery stores to medicine in the pharmacies. This also led to the migration of thousands of educated Africans every year to places outside of the continent, wherever they can find jobs and support their families back home. Hence, the major means of survival for most African families is remittance. "Remittance flows to and within Africa approach US$40 billion. Countries in Northern Africa (for example, Morocco, Algeria and Egypt) are the major receivers in the continent. Eastern African countries depend heavily on these flows, with Somalia standing out as particularly remittance dependent. For the entire region, annual average remittances per migrant reach almost US$1,200 and on a country-by-country average represent 5 per cent of GDP and 27 per cent of exports."[14] Moyo also comments: "Although the actual remittance sums taken individually are relatively small, taken collectively the remittance amounts flowing into African nations' coffers (banks, buildings societies, etc.) are enormous. The US$565 million that flowed to Mozambique and the US$642 million that went to Uganda in 2006 most certainly contributed to bolstering their economies."[15]

On top of these predicaments, "Africa had been cast aside by the West in the wake of the Cold War."[16] The sidelining of Africa by the West and Japan was a gradual development:

> From the early 1980s to the end mid-1990s, Africa experienced a process of marginalization, expressed as a decrease in investment and increase in debts. From 1980 to 1990, although Africa was undergoing structural adjustments due to Western pressure, 43 of 139 British companies withdrew from Africa. Japan also held a pessimistic view of Africa, and the number of its companies in Kenya dropped from fifteen to two in the 1980s. The total debt of sub-Saharan Africa was $60 Billion in 1970; that figure grew to $84.3 billion in 1980. After the Cold War and dismemberment of the Soviet Union, the importance of Africa's strategic position greatly decreased, contributing to its further marginalization. African debt reached $200.4 billion in 1993 and 210.7 billion in 1994, equal to 82.8 percent of its GNP in 1994, as well as 24.5 percent of its export earnings. According to a 1995 World Bank report, the debt-export ratio of 28 African countries was over 200 to 1 at the end of 1994.[17]

Stephanie Rupp further explains how the African situation was conducive to the involvement and influence of China in Africa:

13. Ayittey, *Africa in Chaos*, 16.

14. The International Fund for Agricultural Development (IFAD): http://www.ifad.org/remittances/maps/africa.htm.

15. Moyo, *Dead Aid*, 134. For further reading, see ibid., 134–36.

16. French, *China's Second Continent*, 4.

17. Anshan, "China's New Policy toward Africa," 32.

Political and social upheaval, in the midst of economic ruin, characterized many regions of Africa in the 1990s. Many Africans distrusted their own governments at the same time they were disillusioned by the failure of structural "fixes" imposed by the United States, former European colonial powers, and lending institutions . . . Rather than replicating a colonial model in creating in its partnerships with African nations, however, China is successfully making use of structural similarities that it shares with postcolonial, independent Africa states. The irony is that the structures of political and economic domination that are most amenable to China's exploitation of Africa's natural resources are the very same structures that African governments inherited from European colonial powers and subsequently nurtured and deepened in their quest to maintain power during the decades after independence.[18]

Through centuries of discrimination, exploitation, oppression, and greed, Western antagonisms and huge debt led Africa to desperately welcome China with open arms.[19] The ramification of Africa's current economic, cultural, educational, and political relationship with China will be significant, globally and historically. For good or for evil, Africa had no choice but to go along with the new "redeemer."

Richard Behar succinctly captures the African situation:

[Life expectancy in sub-Saharan countries is] age 47, the statistical end of the line for the 770 million people who live in sub-Saharan Africa. An unfathomably vast terrain comprising of 49 nations, the sub-Sahara represents nearly one-fifth of the earth's landmass. Yet its total economy is tinier than Florida's. Here, 300 million people get by on less than $1 a day. Until they don't: It is the planet's biggest tomb, where compared to the 1960s, twice as many children under the age of 5 are now dying each day from disease; a bottomless badland where $500 billion of Western aid[20] since World War II (more than four Marshall Plans) has barely made a dent in the poverty; a region whose market share of world trade is shrinking by the hour as it gets left behind, perhaps permanently, in the dust of globalization; a place so desperate for everything—cash, trade, investment, infrastructure—and so powerless to negotiate strategically, that it's pretty much up for sale to the highest bidder. The sub-Sahara is now the scene of one of the most bare-knuckled resource grabs the world has ever seen.[21]

To these poverty-stricken regions, "from 2002 to 2005, Russia provided 25 percent of all armed delivered to sub-Saharan Africa, while China was in second place at 15 percent. From 2002 to 2005 Germany delivered the most arms ($600 million) to

---

18. Rupp, "Africa and China," 80, 81.

19. "In late 1995 . . . Vice Premier Zhu and Vice Premier Li visited thirteen African countries during that year to explain China's new foreign policy. A year later, China signed agreements to give low-interest loans to sixteen African countries. The new form of aid was gradually accepted. In 2000, the FOCAC implemented a new stage of bilateral relations; in response, China promised to relieve African debt. In 2002, China signed agreement with 31 African countries to relieve 156 debts, the sum reaching RMB 1.05 billion ($145 million). As of the end of 2007, the figure had increased to RMB 10.9 billion. According to PRC's ministry of Commerce, as of March 2008 China had forgiven the debt of thirty-two African countries, honoring pledges made at the FOCAC Beijing summit in 2006" (Anshan, "China's New Policy toward Africa," 33).

20. Take a note of the subtopic in this book: why aid doesn't work in Africa.

21. "Special Report: China Storms Africa" *LEADERSHP*, June 1, 2008

sub-Saharan Africa at 22 percent, while Russia and China tied at 18 percent or $500 million each. During this period, China delivered $100 million in arms to Algeria and $400 million in arms to Egypt. By comparison, the United States delivered $5.8 billion in arms to Egypt from 2002 to 2005."[22] These imported arms are used by tyrant governments and rebels alike, to fight over natural resources and suppress the exploited nations.

Paradoxically, it is in the area of natural resources that Africa is enormously rich. In the scramble for natural resources, the hungry China and starved Africans are attempting to feed each other's insatiable appetites. "The origin of China's fascination with Africa is easy to see. Between the Sahara and the Kalahari deserts lie many of the raw materials desired by its industries. China recently overtook America as the world's largest net importer of oil. Almost 80% of Chinese imports from Africa are mineral products. China is Africa's top business partner, with trade exceeding $166 billion. But it is not all minerals. Exports to Africa are a mixed bag. . . Machinery makes up 29%."[23] French adds, "China's trade with Africa zoomed to an estimated $200 billion in 2012, a more than twenty-fold increase since the turn of the century."[24] Africa is open to trade with the highest bidder. And the West is not in a position to compete with China. "EU countries have neither the power nor the will to continue to claim Africa as their backyard, and that is an important reason for the rapid rise of Chinese influence on the continent. The high-profile China-Africa summit indicates that Beijing sees Africa as available. There are few contrasting forces that could stop China from its influence."[25]

> In a world where cash is king, China's much-noted cash stock pile—over US$ 3 trillion in foreign currency reserves in 2012—affords it the ability to do what other countries can't do and go where other countries can't go. Simply put, the Chinese are on a global[26] shopping spree. And its voracious commodity appetite is unlikely to abate significantly even if China's economic growth rates were to cool . . . Meanwhile heavily indebted industrialized countries that need to raise revenues also capitulate, borrowing significant sums from China. In 2011, for example, China was the largest single holder of US government debt, with 26 percent of total US public debt). Increasingly, countries like Japan, South Korea, and others across the Middle East have embarked on their own commodity campaigns—particularly with regards to Africa's arable land—but China's size, cash

---

22. Shinn, "Military and Security Relations," 162–63.
23. Polgreen and French, "New Power in Africa."
24. French, *China's Second Continent*, 4.
25. Jiang, "China's Emerging Partnership in Africa," 59.
26. Just to give you two examples, "In the summer of 2007 a Chinese company bought a mountain in Peru. More specifically, it bought the mineral rights to mine the resources contained in it. At fifteen thousand feet (forty-six hundred meters), Mount Toromocho is an imposing landmass—more than half of the height of Mount Everest. It contains two billion tons of copper, one of the largest single copper deposits in the world. For a hefty fee US$3 billion, Mount Toromocho's title is transferred from the Peruvian people to the hands of the Chinese" (Moyo, "Beijing a Boon for Africa," 1). "In 2008 the Chinese struck a deal with the Greek government to manage two piers and container terminals in the Greek port of Piraeus—the main port of Greece, the largest port in Europe, and the third-largest port in the world. For Euro 4.3 billion (roughly US$5.6 billion), Cosco Pacific, China's state-owned shipping company, pledged to increase the capacity of the port by up to 250 percent over thirty-five years" (ibid., 80).

(i.e., its ability to outbid the competition), and unyielding determination mean, for now, it's mostly about China.[27]

She adds, "Rather than conquer Africa through the barrel of a gun, it is using the muscle of money. According to its own statistics, China invested US$900 million in Africa in 2004, out of the US$15 billion in the continent received, up from US$20 million in 1975. Roads in Ethiopia, pipelines in Sudan, railways in Nigeria, power in Gahanna—these are just a few of the torrent of billion-dollar projects that China has flooded Africa with in the last five years, each one part of a well-orchestrated plan for China to be the dominant foreign force in twenty-first century in Africa."[28] *After centuries of exploitation by the West, starved Africans are now dealing with China, who is hungry and has a voracious appetite for African natural resources. The question is who is making the banquet for whom?*

The internal factors in Africa and the global economic and political situation have offered the perfect timing for China to show up on the African scene in a big way. After the Cold War, Europe was deeply engaged with people of their own kind who were former communist countries. The economic and social issues of the former Eastern Bloc preoccupied Western Europe. To stabilize and address the pertinent economic and political issues that were affecting the region, European leaders and the United States were deeply engaged to ensure a smooth and lasting transition in Europe, thus neglecting the problematic Africa. The U.S. was also was caught off guard by the Al-Qaida attacks of the 90s and early 2000s. The country then immersed itself in the resource-draining Afghanistan and Iraq wars and the 2008 economic crisis, which resulted in high unemployment rates and housing and manufacturing crises. Without a competitor, China had full access to Africa.

Soft Power

In total contrast to the Western approach to Africa, China is applying a method that wins the minds and the support of Africans. Using soft power, China is disarming African people, allowing her to do as she wishes throughout the continent. China started at the storehouse of Africa's economic and political influence—the Organization of African Union (OAU). Kingsley Ighobor writes: "The new headquarters of the African Union, a towering 20-storey building in Addis Ababa, Ethiopia, is so called because China picked up the $200 million tab for the state-of-the-art complex. Ethiopia's tallest building, completed in December 2011 in time for an AU summit the following month, includes a 2,500-seat conference hall. The gift prompted Ethiopia's late Prime Minister Meles Zenawi to refer to Africa's current economic boom as a 'renaissance,' due partly to China's "amazing re-emergence and its commitments to a win-win partnership with Africa."[29]

The African Union headquarters is one among many soft powers China is using in Africa:

27. Ibid., 5.
28. Moyo, *Dead Aid*, 103.
29. Ighobor, Kingsley "China in the heart of Africa" *Africa Renewal*, January 2013 pg. 6

> The railroads more than anything else that enabled European colonialists to exploit Kenya's people and extract its wealth during the first half of the 20th century . . . The Chinese are the new game in town. Beijing has signed off on rail projects across the continent, from Angola in the South, Ethiopia in the East and Nigeria in the West, heralding an infrastructure-expansion boom on a scale never seen in Africa.
>
> On Nov. 28, presidents of four African nations gathered in Mombasa for the inauguration of what was billed as the largest single project in the region's history: a $13.8 billion standard gauge rail line that is expected to link five East African countries and replace the line built by the British. The massive rail networks, almost all of them leading to the sea, will doubtless reinforce the image of a resource-hungry China eager to extract as much as possible from the continent.[30]

In all that she does in Africa, China is determined to outshine the West, to make a political statement, and to reveal the greed and motives of the West in the past and present engagements on the continent. "Investments in the projects that (re)construct basic infrastructure is also essential to transport African resources to ports of exit efficiently. In this respect, Chinese (re)development of roads, railroads, ports, and airports *mirrors the self-interested construction* of these facilities during the European colonial era. For example, the cartography of colonial railroads along the West African coast illustrates that, *rather than serving the purpose of connecting African markets and communities within the continent, the rail lines were constructed to transport resources from the interior of the continent to coastal port cities, where European-owned vessels brought them directly to European industries and markets.*"[31]

> China's largess to Africa is not new. Previously China either donated or assisted in building a hospital in Luanda, Angola; a road from Lusaka, Zambia's capital, to Chirundu in the southeast; stadiums in Sierra Leone and Benin; a sugar mill and a sugarcane farm in Mali; and a water supply project in Mauritania, among other projects. At the fifth Forum on China-Africa Cooperation, held in Beijing in July 2012, Chinese President Hu Jintao listed yet more, including 100 schools, thirty hospitals, thirty anti-malaria centers, and twenty agricultural technology demonstration centers.[32] In addition to these magnanimous philanthropic gestures, China added the following: "Last summer, the then Chinese president Hu Jintao announced an expansive aid programme that will offer 18,000 government scholarships and train 30,000 Africans 'in various sectors' by 2015 . . . China advertises these programmes as a kind-hearted diplomatic gesture—the terms 'equality,' 'all-round co-operation' and 'mutual gain' pepper its state media reports and programme descriptions. Experts say they're a calculated, long-term investment to win the hearts and minds of Africa's future leaders, many of whom fear China's investment in the continent may come with invisible strings attached.[33]

30. Mutiga, "Africa and the Chinese Way."
31. Rupp, "Africa and China," 75; emphasis added.
32. Ighobor, "China in the Heart of Africa"; see also French, *China's Second Continent*.
33. Kaiman "Africa's Future Leaders." The doubts aren't coming from any soured feelings from African leaders themselves, most of whom still welcome (and profit from) China's embrace. The new

Improving the infrastructure in Africa not only benefits Africans but also puts China in historical contrast with the West and places her on the right side of the "civilizing" mission of the past in the continent. Stephanie Rupp asserts: "Aid package that target the refurbishment, reconstruction, or outright development of infrastructure such as roads, ports, and airports benefit local African communities for whom these axes of transportation are often insufficient. China's efforts to rebuild African infrastructure is a centrally important contribution and extension of infrastructure were sorely neglected throughout the continent during the final decades of the twentieth century, when trade and aid to Africa were dominated by Euro-American partners."[34]

Education is one of the major transformative methods that China is using as she deals with various African countries.

> Between 1949 and 1977, China sent volunteer teachers to nine African countries, including Algeria, Egypt, Togo, Congo (Brazzaville), Guinea Bissau, Mali, Somali, Tanzania, and Tunisia, with the first group sent to Egypt in 1954. The period 1978–1995 witnessed an increase, with teachers sent to twenty one countries. In 2003, there were 238 teachers in more than 30 African countries. Until recently, Chinese teachers in Africa have taught at the undergraduate through Ph.D. levels. Since the late 1980s, China has tried through various means to help Africa ... The number of African students in China has increased greatly since the 1950s. In 2000, at the time of the first FOCAC in Beijing, there were 1,388 African students in China; in 2005 the number was 2,757. Aside from the enrollment of African university students, China has held seminars, training courses, and symposia that concentrated on fields such as management capabilities, engineering skills, and school administration. By the end of 2003, China had established forty-three educational and research programs in areas such as agriculture, Chinese medicine, long-distance education, and computer technology, in addition to setting up twenty-one research laboratories.[35]

The Chinese do a variety of developmental projects, without causing major qualms for the majority of Africans. In Mali, they built a hospital and did more.

> In 1970, at the height of the Cold War, the Americans had built their big bridge over [the Niger] river, several hundred miles downstream, in Niamey, the capital of Niger, and named it after John F. Kennedy. Twenty-two years later, the Saudis had built their bridge, they named it King Fahd. In the last few years, Gaddafi's Libya had built an administrative city and two large hotels at the northern foot of the Fahd Bridge, naming it after their dictator and signaling their big push for influence in the Sahel. In the end, Gaddafi was killed before the new government complex could be occupied ... his name was ripped down that very day. Here was China's bid for soft power. There were no huge billboards or ostentatious

---

skepticism has even less to do with the hectoring of Western governments, the traditional source of Africa's foreign aid and investment (and interference). In a 2012 speech in Senegal, Hillary Rodham Clinton, then Secretary of State, implicitly warned Africa about China. The continent needs "a model of sustainable partnership that adds value, rather than extracts it," she said, adding that unlike other countries, "America will stand up for democracy and universal human rights even when it might be easier to look the other way and keep the resources flowing."

34. Rupp, "Africa and China," 73.
35. Anshan, "China's New Policy toward Africa," 28, 29.

language or grand names. It was simply called the Friendship Bridge, and it would soon be carrying perhaps a third of the people who crossed the river each day, taking them past the biggest and newest hospital in the country. And if people remembered one thing about it, for now, it would be that it was free.[36]

China has recently declared a twelve-year investment plan. This financial plan makes Western investments in Africa dwarf in comparison:

> China has pledged to provide $1 trillion in financing (paywall) to countries in Africa over the next 12 years. Speaking at a summit in Hong Kong, Zhao Changhui of China's state-owned Export-Import (Exim) Bank said the money will go toward helping the region build highways, railways, airports and other infrastructure.
>
> It's a big number, equal to the total amount of gross domestic product the continent is expected add between now and 2020. Here's another comparison: In 2011, World Bank spending was just $5.6 billion on the continent. If Zhao's promise can be believed, China will fund the region with about $83 billion a year, with about 80% of the money coming from Exim Bank in the form of direct investment and loans.[37]

Is China investing this amount of money in Africa because the Chinese love Africans more that Americans do? Or does China have undisclosed hunger that she desperately needs to feed in the coming twelve years? As various studies on China indicate, rapid urbanization and modernization in China are driving an unprecedented increase in demand for energy that puts China on a course to require more power than the United States and Europe combined by 2035. The growth of a middle class demands better houses, transportation systems, and heating and cooling systems in residential building and offices. The demand for electricity increases the megawatts, linking cities by rail and expressways requires material, and the need for more water and food forces China to invest in Africa and to control all the natural resources the Chinese can grab.

The foresight to make a strategic economic and energy plan twelve to fifteen years in advance is unheard of in Africa where leaders fail to make effective four-year government plans. In a continent with failed leadership, it is utterly foolish for Africans to buy the idea of a win-win economic relationship with China. From what we see, China is going to be in Africa for a long time. With China's current and projected consumption capability, coupled with the lack of long-term planning on the part of African leaders, the natural resources of Africa will be depleted sooner than one can imagine. As Boly, a keen Malian observer said, "China has a means of advancing which is different from that of the West. They are like a boa: it observes its prey quietly, taking its time. In the same way, the Chinese are waiting for a long-term return. They are waiting for a maximal result."[38] By the time they get to that point, the Chinese maximal result will be Africa's demise. African leaders' win-win strategy plan needs to be laid out now, not later when China has already constricted all the wealth from the continent. "Neither the African Union nor subregional organizations like the Southern African Development community have

---

36. French, *China's Second Continent*, 183–84.
37. Kuo, "China Promises Africa $1 Trillion."
38. French, *China's Second Continent*, 176.

an articulated policy regarding China and Chinese influence. Each of the forty-eight sub-Saharan countries goes in its own way, responding to China and Chinese entreaties (or Taiwanese in four cases)."[39] For example, "A new developmental model is in the process of being rolled out in key African countries—Special Economic Zones (SEZs). They provide liberalized investments focused on strategic industries to attract foreign companies . . . Kenya, Egypt, and Mauritius are the most proactive on the continent in establishing such zones. *What makes this new development model unique is that it has been initiated on the African continent by the government of the People's Republic of China (PRC). Rather than being initiators of this process, African governments are the recipients. China is carving out designated SEZs across the continent.* These zones are positioned to become Africa's new economic growth nodes."[40]

In the game of global economics and political relationships, those who are ahead of the curve are those who are proactive: who think and plan not only for the society they currently lead but also for the generation to come. African leaders are bad bosses at home and loyal and often passive followers on the global scene. Unless they change their patterns of thinking and leadership styles, and become leaders in all spheres of their engagements, nationally and internationally, they cannot negotiate on win-win terms.

The following strategic methods for the next generation are something that African leaders in all capacities ought to consider:

- The first statesmanship issue today is *technology*—automation. Automation means, specifically, information and communications technology, space exploration, nuclear energy, robotics, computer-assisted functions such as CAD, CAM, and CAE, biotechnology (Such as antibody engineering), and so forth.

- The second issue of statesmen, in politics and business as well as in science, the arts, and the professions, is *globalization*. Globalization means increasing interdependence of political, social, economic (labor, capital, energy, management) intellectual (world views, religion, mythology, political theory) currents.

- The third task with which the transition to the next millennium must cope is *acceleration of change*. Change alone is difficult enough, but acceleration is even more threatening. Organizations today are fast-paced; to reflect, regroup, and consolidate often means to be left behind . . . Here is where our creativity and imagination, our capacity for strategic thinking, our leadership competency are tested to the limit.

- Such chaos demands *cooperation*, the fourth task. Cooperation means overcoming alienation, learning to work and live together, taking the initiative to support one another. Cooperation is the task of creating dialogues among

---

39. Rotberg, "China's Quest," 18. China's African foreign policy can be divided into three periods: a period of normal development (1949–1977), a transitional period (1978–1994), and a period of rapid development. With the end of the Cultural Revolution and the change of the Chinese leadership, there was a gradual shift in China's policy toward economic development. The relation between diplomacy and economy was reversed, for example, "economy serving diplomacy" was changed to "diplomacy serving economy." This shift was followed by new foreign policy of independence, peace, and development (Anshan, "China's New Policy toward Africa," 22).

40. Davies, "Special Economic Zones," 137; emphasis added.

- people and taking a strong position on eliminating violence. It means to work through people and with people.

- The fifth task for the forthcoming millennium is to increase *freedom* in the world—to enhance our understanding of it and to mount a crash program to protect it . . . Freedom centrally entails responsibility—that is, autonomy, the ability and willingness to take care of oneself, to assume stewardship over one's own life and over the destiny of one's people. The development and preservation of the individual, in depersonalizing world of increasing population and ever more powerful corporations, international conglomerates, and national alliances, becomes the humane task for the Third Millennium . . . Freedom expresses itself politically, economically, and spiritually.[41]

"The timeline for resource depletion in many African countries is running in tandem with the timeline for the continent's unprecedented demographic explosion. At current rates, in the next forty years, most African states will have twice the number of people they count now. By that time, their presently known reserves of minerals like iron, bauxite, copper, cobalt, uranium, gold, and more, will be largely depleted. Those who have diversified their economies and invested in their citizens, particularly in education and health, will have a shot at prosperity. Those that haven't, stand to become hellish places, barely viable, if viable at all."[42] While being preoccupied with the temporal and peripheral, African leaders should not ignore the fundamental and long-term impact of China's policy in Africa.

> China's Africa policy is more complex, multidimensional, ambitious, and ultimately higher risk. China's increasing economic engagement is tied to conspicuously strategic goals, centered on access to energy and other scarce high-value commodities. On the diplomatic front, Beijing has shown a new determination to eliminate any bilateral ties between Taiwan and a dwindling number of African capitals, and to use its accelerating entry into Africa to consolidate global allegiances and Beijing has also taken on a more active role in the security sphere. China's contribution of soldiers and police to UN peace operations, especially in Africa have increased tenfold since 2001, albeit from a low base. As of early 2008, China provided more than 1,900 troops, military worldwide. Nearly three-fourths of Chinese peacekeeping forces are supporting UN missions in Africa (primarily Liberia, the Sudan, and the Democratic Republic of the Congo).[43]

Chinese Migrants in Africa

China's trade agreements and diplomatic, cultural, and educational relationship with Africa is often labeled as "win-win" or "mutual gain." In other words, the assertion is made that China is not only there to extract the natural resources of Africa and leave the continent as a skeleton to be fleshed with financial aid and NGO projects but is

---

41. Koestenbaum, *Leadership*, 305–10; emphasis original. I have made the original quotation into a bulleted list.

42. French, *China's Second Continent*, 93.

43. Huang, "China's Renewal Partnership with Africa," 300.

also investing in Africa to enable Africans to have their own bread and to make them givers. The rhetoric is great and it effectively plays as a counter-politics to the previous Western involvement in Africa. However, a keen observer reminds us to look at the things that Africans have overlooked: "One of the most important and unpredictable factors in China's relationship with Africa, however, has been oddly omitted from most of these discussions: China's export, in effect, of large numbers of its own people who are settling in as migrants and long-term residents in far-flung and hitherto unfamiliar parts of the continent. By common estimate, Africa has received a million or so of these Chinese newcomers in the space of a mere decade, during which time they have rapidly penetrated every conceivable walk of life: farmers, entrepreneurs building small and medium-sized factories, and practitioners of full range of trades, doctors, smugglers, prostitutes."[44]

If one thinks of it, Egypt did not become an Arab country overnight. The dominance of Greek culture in Alexandria did not happen by accident. The Portuguese in West Africa, Angola in particular, started penetrating into Africa primarily through trade agreements. Three to four hundred years later, they became the colonial power—and a brutal one at that. African leaders and elites, while welcoming the positive and the alternative approach of China, should refine and implement African policy in light of the continent's past history, the current crises and opportunities, and the potential for the future.

Even if the Chinese didn't come to Africa with the malice of a slave trader, as a conqueror who wishes to colonize, or as a guru of all disciplines to educate Africans, China is in Africa for the same reason and motive as Europeans—to be rich and to be a boss.

> In December 1999, a 24-year-old Chinese man called Zhang Hao left behind the freezing winter of his native Shenyang city to fly to Uganda. Zhang was nervous. He spoke no English. The journey was not even his idea, but that of his father, who had worked in Uganda a few years before on a fishing project involving the Chinese government.
>
> "If you want to start something—and be the boss—Africa is the place to do it," Zhang's father had told him when he asked for business advice.
>
> Zhang had quit university to travel to east Africa, but he did not need a degree to spot easy money-making opportunities as soon as he set foot in Kampala: goods that were available cheaply in every city in China were either expensive here, or unavailable. He started by importing shoes. Then schoolbags. Then fishing nets, nails, and bicycles.
>
> "I imported everything. At that time they needed everything!" recalls Zhang, an affable man with rimless glasses.
>
> His business grew quickly; he made money and local friends. But after a few years he grew weary of the long buying trips to China. So he and his wife bought a large plot of land in Kampala. On it they constructed a spectacular Chinese-Korean restaurant, with private dining areas, karaoke rooms and a giant 500-seat dining hall. To the side of the restaurant they built a bedroom, which became

---

44. French, *China's Second Continent*, 5.

their home. The business prospered, and soon he started additional enterprises including a bakery, a firm selling flat-screen televisions and a security company.[45]

French concurs that "a desire for better economic opportunities was the biggest driver behind their exodus. Still, contributing to the decision for many to take a great leap into the unknown and move to Africa was weariness with omnipresent official corruption back home, fear of the impact of a badly polluted environment on their health, and a variety of constraints on freedoms, including religion and speech. Many migrants also invoked a sheer lack of space."[46] While you read his recent book, *China's Second Continent: How a Million Migrants Are Building a New Empire in Africa*, time and again you come across the same kinds of stories like Zhang Hao. You will find Chinese with no farming background like Hao Shengeli, in Mozambique, "for a relative pittance he had won control of roughly five thousand acres. The land has been part of a large, abandoned colonial-era Portuguese plantation. A river flowed nearby, and irrigation canals cut back and forth, gridlike, across a fertile plain."[47] Hundreds and thousands of Chinese traders, mine workers, restaurant owners, and entertainers are roaming the continent of Africa in Senegal, Mali, Liberia, Zambia, Ethiopia, Nigeria, Ghana, Dakar, etc.

The euphemistic name for prostitutes is entertainers. Chen Rui, who ran a karaoke establishment, the Dynasty Bar, in Senegal has a strong resemblance to the stories of many thousand Chinese women trafficked both inside their country and overseas. In one country after another, they worked in restaurants and in the "entertainment" business, where they have effectively become indentured servants. In Maputo, [Howard French] met a twenty-four-year-old masseuse whose working name was Wang Fei. She had been in the country for two years, and claimed never to have had a meal outside the parlor where she lived and worked. Her boss, who feared seeing her disappear and losing his investment in her, would not allow it.[48]

> Like European migration into Africa and the lands of new settlement, Asian migration overseas has a long history. Chinese economic migrants populated many of the countries of Southeast Asia beginning in the fifteenth century. Singapore is almost entirely Chinese, of course, while ethnic Chinese make up 26 percent of the population in Malaysia and about 14 percent in Thailand. In Africa Chinese migration began in the nineteenth century with Chinese miners, plantation workers, and traders who settled in Mauritius, Madagascar, and South Africa as early as 1821. By the 1950s, the thousands of Chinese living in Madagascar had established more than 1,600 Chinese shops. More than 20,000 Chinese were living in Mauritius by then, nearly 3 percent of the population and more than 4,000 in South Africa. In the late 1980s…the isolated apartheid government also invited a number of wealthy Taiwanese families to invest and settle in designated regions of South Africa.[49]

---

45. Rice "China's Economic Invasion of Africa."
46. French, *China's Second Continent*, 14.
47. French, *Continent for the Taking*, 20.
48. Ibid., 76–78.
49. Brautigam, *Dragon's Gift*, 266–67.

The Chinese are not new to the African continent. However, instead of opening the door for a mass exodus for the Chinese migrants, the African leaders need to think about the short- and long-term consequences of allowing the Chinese to come in and own properties in various African countries. A good thinking and planning family would not attempt to adopt children when they can't feed their own.

The African continent, which "evolved into the present-day bizarre politico-economic system that admits of no rule of law, no accountability, no democracy of any form, and even no sanity," has become a den for the Chinese human traffickers, human rights violators, and abusers. In the midst of all kinds of trades and investment the Chinese and African poor are the losers. In Mozambique, the "farmer" "Hao was employing eight [African] men on the site for nine hours at just under $10 a day total."[50]

Why is Hunger a Threat in Sub-Saharan Africa?

Despite of the wealth of natural resources we discussed, the "[l]atest estimates show that thirty of the hungriest nations of the world are in Africa. The World Food Council (WFC) estimates that population in the African continent may be growing at three or four times the rate of growth in food production. The threat of famine in Africa will persist well into the twenty-first century."[51] "Of the billion people who go hungry every day, the highest concentration, around four hundred million, are in sub-Saharan Africa."[52] And yet Africa has ample arable land and plenty of rivers and underground water.

"The estimated one billion people on earth who go without food every day are almost perfectly offset by the one billion people medically deem to be obese, a disease attributed at least in part to overeating."[53] Why the never-ending paradox in Africa? "To the Chinese, Africa appears to be vastly underused."[54] If this is the case, then we must ask, why are Africans not engaged in farming to have enough food for themselves with excess for export to the world market? The answer to this question is more complicated than one might think.

First, there is an internal problem. "Food production, at its most basic level, depends on the quality of physical infrastructure—roads, machinery, and irrigation tools—on the legal enforceability of property rights and land titles. Many African nations blessed with arable land are also burdened by unreliable governments and ever-changing regimes, making for ineffective and sporadic enforcement of legal rights. No reasonable long-term investor is willing to invest in a place that lacks necessary infrastructure or enforceable property."[55] Instead of working out these internal challenges, facilitating for and encouraging African agronomist and entrepreneurs to produce more food, African leaders are waiting until famine hits their people to beg for wheat and corn from Canada, the U.S.,

50. French, *China's Second Continent*, 38.
51. Mazrui, *Africans*, 201.
52. Moyo, "Beijing, a Boon for Africa," 183.
53. Ibid., 179–80.
54. Brautigam, *Dragon's Gift*, 253.
55. Moyo, "Beijing, a Boon for Africa," 186.

and the European Union. "Agriculture, which employs the bulk of Africa's population, has performed abysmally. Since 1970 agricultural output has been growing at less than 1.5 percent—less than the rate of population growth. Consequently, food production per capita declined by 7 percent in the 1960s, by 15 percent in the 1970s, and by 8 percent in the 1980s. Over the postcolonial period 1961 to 1995, 'per capita food production in Africa dropped by 12 percent, whereas it advanced by leaps and bound in developing countries in Asia."[56] Zaire, now the Democratic Republic of the Congo, exported food when it was the Belgian Congo. Today, it cannot feed itself, nor can postcolonial Zambia, Sierra Leone, and Tanzania. In 1990, about 40 percent of the black Africa's food was imported, despite the assertion by the Food and Agricultural Organization (FAO) of the United Nations that the Congo Basin alone could produce enough food to feed all of black Africa. The situation has deteriorated so rapidly in Nigeria that many people eat only once a day.[57] Mazrui comments: "The most serious problem of production in Africa concerns agriculture. Part of the problem has arisen because of inadequate returns for farmers and disproportionate use of resources by bureaucracies of marketing boards. In a country such as Nigeria agriculture was, in a sense, murdered by oil wealth. The brief honeymoon of petro-power diverted skill away from cultivation to wheeling and dealing in the temporarily oil-rich Nigeria. In spite of slogans such as the 'green revolution,' under President Shehu Shagari Nigerian agriculture was mortally wounded by the petro-bonanza."[58]

Second, there is an external systemic problem. This is more dangerous and difficult to overcome and it has starved millions of Africans and led them to death—for many Africans death is a better option than suffering alive. Here is how the system of enforcing and multiplying hunger works:

> The US Farm Bill and the European Common Agricultural Policy each pump hundreds of billions of dollars toward artificially bolstering their farmers and domestic agricultural sectors. By covering much of the cost of production at home, these subsidies price other countries out of their food market. Not only these government policies discourage food production elsewhere; they actually encourage overproduction of food at home. The resulting trend distortion tends to disproportionately disadvantage the world's poorest agricultural producing countries, such as those in Africa and South America.
>
> The United States and France are two of the worst offenders. Fearful of relying on other nations for their food in the event of a global war and keen to protect their agricultural markets and win the backing of their powerful farming lobbies, these countries have pursued trade restrictions, subsidy packages, and barriers to keep out foreign produce. In the United States alone the total annual amount of farm subsidies stands at around US$15 billion. The 2002 US Farm Security and Rural Investment Act has rewarded US farmers with nearly $200 billion in subsidies in the subsequent ten years. US$70 billion more than previous programs and representing as much as an 80 percent increase in certain subsidies.

---

56. *Economist*, September 7, 1996, cited in Ayittey, *Africa in Chaos*, 10.
57. Ayittey, *Africa in Chaos*, 10–11.
58. Mazrui, *Africans*, 204.

The US subsidy programs have the greatest effects on grain, including wheat, corn, sorghum, barley, rice, and oats, but they also include peanuts, tobacco, soybeans, cotton, sugar, and milk. Excess food production is often wasted[59] or, in a nastily ironic twist, sent as food aid to regions where agricultural production has been decimated by the very government policies that have discouraged these poorer regions from growing crops....

The members of the Organization of Economic Cooperation and Development spend almost US$300 million on agricultural subsidies every year. Across Europe the Common Agricultural Policy (CAP) represents around half the European Union's budget of 122 billion Euros (US160 billion), with direct farm subsidies alone accounting for nearly 40 billion Euros (US$50 billion). The effect of these policies on poor would-be commodity exporter nations includes huge hits to national treasuries.[60]

To this Meredith adds,

Determined to protect their own producers, industrialized countries operate a system of subsidies and tariff barriers that have a *crippling effect on African producers*. The total values of their agricultural subsidies amounts to 1 billion dollars a day—$370 billion a year—a sum higher that the gross domestic product of the whole of sub-Saharan Africa. The European Union subsidy for each of its cows is about $900 a year—more than the average African income; the Japanese subsidy is $2,700 per cow. Western surpluses produced at a fraction of their real cost are then dumped on African markets, undermining domestic producers. Simultaneously, African producers face tariff barriers imposed by industrialized countries, effectively shutting them out of the Western markets.[61]

This system is effective to shut out African producers from the Western market so much so that the former cotton and sugar producing and exporting African countries no longer engage in this kind of commercial farming. "In similar fashion, African farmers have struggled to compete against a wide range of other subsidised agricultural products—European sugar, Asian rice, Italian tomatoes, Dutch onions; many have been forced out of business."[62]

So with China's involvement in Africa, what is happening to the vast arable land on the continent? "Chinese interest in land overseas is very real. They have a fifth of the world's population, and only 9 percent of its arable land."[63] "Between 1997 and 2008 the area of arable farmland in China fell by 12.3 million hectares—that is, a loss of around

---

59. Americans waste at least US$75 billion in edible foods each year, in part due to the 14 percent of food that the average American family goes to waste. That is an amazing US$600 a year per household—a decent chunk out of the annual grocery bill—including meat, fruit, vegetables, and grain products that never make it to a plate.
Not far behind, the UK wastes roughly 30 percent of its food. That amounts to about 6.7 million tons of purchased, edible food that is thrown out each year, or £10.2 billion worth per year (roughly US$15 billion). On an annual per household basis, that's between US$375 to US$600 of squandered food (Moyo, "Beijing, a Boon for Africa," 178).

60. Ibid., 180–81.
61. Meredith, *Fate of Africa*, 684.
62. Ibid., 685.
63. Brautigam, *Dragon's Gift*, 253.

1 million hectares per year—much attributed to the growth in urban centers."[64] As the Chinese do with other natural resources their insatiable appetite is equally unleashed to grab farmlands throughout the continent. They have entered into agriculture without restrictions from African governments but with much competition from Middle Eastern and other Asian countries. The Rhodesia-born tycoon "Tiny" Rowland bought 200,000 hectares of productive land across Africa. China State Farm Agribusiness Corporation purchased 3,573 hectares of land to set up the China Zambia Friendship Farm in Zambia in 1990. CSFAC invested $600,000 to buy the farm and then another $1.6 million to develop it. It is now worth $6 million. In Uganda, Mozambique, and other African countries, China is purchasing or leasing thousands of hectares for farming. The Chinese government has encouraged overseas agricultural investment under its general "going global" policies.[65]

While Africans are starving to death, nations outside of the continent are feeding and overfeeding themselves from the resources of the continent they invested in. "The Sudanese government for instance, has leased 1.5 million hectares of prime farmland to the Gulf States, Egypt, and south Korea for ninety-nine years. Egypt plans to grow wheat and corn on 840,000 hectares in Uganda. And beyond Africa Kuwait has leased 130,000 hectares of rice fields in Cambodia. In a similar vein the South Korean conglomerate Daewoo struck a deal with the government of Madagascar, and island off the east coast of Africa, that would have granted Daewoo full access and ninety-nine year lease to a tract of underdeveloped land half the size of Belgium."[66] In his article, *The Man Who Stole the Nile: An Ethiopian Billionaire's Outrageous Land Grab*, Frederick Kaufman writes,

> Forget about diamond heists, bank robberies, and drilling into the golden intestines of Fort Knox. In this precarious world-historic moment, food has become the most valuable asset of them all—and a billionaire from Ethiopia named Mohammed Hussein Al Amoudi is getting his hands on as much of it as possible, flying it over the heads of his starving countrymen, and selling the treasure to Saudi Arabia. Last year, Al Amoudi, whom most Ethiopians call the Sheikh, exported a million tons of rice, about seventy pounds for every Saudi citizen. The scene of the grain robbery was Gambella, a bog the size of Belgium in Ethiopia's southwest whose rivers feed the Nile . . . The government owns all the land in Ethiopia. They cannot sell it, but they can lease as much of it as they want. By leasing to the Sheikh, the directorate had given Al Amoudi's food grab the federal stamp of approval. Though the terms of the deal have never been released, the annual price per hectare has been estimated at no more than seven dollars [for 10,000 hectare tract]. In Zambia, by comparison, the average hectare leases for about $1,250 a year . . . Ethiopia, where 30 million of 90 million people are undernourished, would soon feed Saudi Arabia, where there was no particular lack of food.[67]

---

64. Moyo, "Beijing, a Boon for Africa," 29.

65. For further reading on China's food insecurity and her global farming plan, see Brautigam, *Dragon's Gift*, 252–72.

66. Moyo, "Beijing, a Boon for Africa."

67. Kaufman, "The Man Who Stole the Nile," 36, 37.

The business of palm oil is another factor that encourages foreign companies for a land lease in Africa. *The Economist* states:

> The oil palm is native to west Africa, but most of today's production is small-scale; exports barely exist. Yet restrictions on logging and the acquisition of land in Malaysia and Indonesia are pushing investors into Africa, where concessions for new plantations are more freely available. In the past decade, politicians in west Africa and countries of the Congo basin have leased out around 1.8m hectares of land for palm-oil plantations, according to Hardman, a London-based research company. Another 1.4m hectare is being sought. Foreign companies sniffing around include groups such as Wilmer, Olam, Sime Darby, Golden Veroleum and Equatorial Palm Oil.
>
> Demand for palm oil, whose annual global production is valued at around $50 billion, is soaring; consumption may triple between 2000 and 2050. The oil is taken from the oil palm's red fruit is used in roughly half of the packaged supermarket products, from margarine and ice cream to shampoo and cosmetics. It is increasingly used as biodiesel, too.
>
> But Africans are fast learning that it is a controversial business. Malaysia and Indonesia have been castigated for the environmental damage caused by palm oil. Deforestation has increased carbon emissions and destroyed the habitat of rare breeds of animals such as orangutans.[68]

In a continent where the population is expected to double in a decade or so, I wonder about the wisdom of leasing huge hectares of land for ninety-nine years here and there in Africa. One who owns a four-bedroom house can hardly sign a lease to rent three extra bedrooms for twenty years and plan to have seven children in ten years, especially if he/she has no financial means to buy another house. The affair of African governments defeats logic and commonsense.

Africans are not only leasing lands for farming but for corporations too. In Mauritius, "The $500 million manufacturing zone will host up to 40 Chinese companies, with a forecast of 5,000 jobs for locals and 8,000 for Chinese contractors. Construction on the 210-hectare zone's infrastructure began in 2007 and is slated for completion within 5 years. Key infrastructural projects include the construction of a fishing port, a dam, a road project from Verdun to Terre Rogue near Port Louis, as well as a new town development at Highlands."[69]

Labor Standard and Worker's Right

"The Chinese are notoriously lax about labor standards. . . .Hydropower dams, concessions for tropical hardwood and large rainforest plantations, roads, and large-scale mining all pose risk for the environment in Africa. They also require that people by the project be consulted, compensated, and properly resettled . . . Chinese investors are way behind the curve on all of this. So are many African governments."[70] This is a double

---

68. "Palm Oil in West Africa."
69. Davies, "Special Economic Zones," 145.
70. Brautigam, *Dragon's Gift*, 299–300.

jeopardy for Africans. When the long-term well-being of the people is forfeited for short-term gain, it makes the majority of the continent uninhabitable and the future state of Africa is put in great peril. "The earth can exist without human beings and is for millions of years, but the human race cannot exist without the earth and the other living things. So human beings are dependent on the earth, but the earth is not dependent on human beings. The simple realization is that the human civilization has to be integrated into the ecosystem of the earth, not conversely, that the earth must be subjugated to the human system of dominion."[71] China's shortage of water and arable land at home, and the way they feed their voracious appetite in their own land and abroad do not reflect Moltmann's wise observation about the integration of civilization with ecosystems. It would be foolishness to expect the Chinese to act any differently on other continents when their track record at home is tainted.

Kasonde, a Zambian mine worker, reported to French: "The Chinese are no good. But because we are in Zambia, where there is a big unemployment problem, we don't have any choice. But they don't treat us like people. They work us too hard and their jobs and their money are both no good . . . In seven months he had risen to a shift supervisor . . . We work very hard but they don't give good money . . . If you work one week they would pay you 50,000 kwacha [about $10], but you cannot survive in Zambia with 50,000. The safety, it is very dangerous. And then there was the food, which was not good. Every day cabbage and little tiny fish."[72]

Performance assessments of some Chinese investors have not been stellar. The managers of Chinese-run mines in Zambia have been accused of not taking adequate safety measures for their local workers. A Chinese oil firm is exploring in a Gabonese national park, angering environmentalists.[73] A continent known for high illiteracy and unemployment, injustice, anarchy, and poverty can hardly deal with China in a win-win relationship. "Out of desperation, much of the continent is selling itself into a new era of corruption and virtual slavery as China seeks to buy up all the metals, minerals and oil she can lay her hands on: copper for electric and telephone cables, cobalt for mobile phones and jet engines—the basic raw materials of modern life. It is crude rapacity, but to Africans and many of their leaders it is better than the alternative, which is slow starvation."[74]

There is also tension and frustration for Africans because of Chinese laborers. "By employing Chinese labor, Chinese companies side step African regulations of labor conditions and wages even as they maintain tight reins over their workers with implicit and actual threat of deportation for poor performance or resistance to company policies."[75] Henry and Shalmon write about this issue elaborating the resentment of Africans and the double standard of China—

71. *Sun of Righteousness Arise!*, 34.
72. French, *China's Second Continent*, 58.
73. Ighobor, "China in the Heart of Africa," 6.
74. Hitchens: "How China Has Created a New Slave Empire in Africa."
75. Rupp, "Africa and China," 72.

China is reluctant to hire local workers, both for management and for unskilled jobs. Therefore most of the people, who work in Chinese enterprises in Angola, as well as in other parts of Africa, are Chinese nationals. They live in their own enclaves, do not learn the local language, go to Chinese schools, and stand apart from the native population. The Chinese defend these practices by arguing that they allow them to ensure discipline within their labor force, increase productivity through better communication, improve morale within the workforce, and ensure quality control. It is not surprising that these practices also led to resentment in the local populations, as witnessed by the demonstrations against the Chinese in Zambia and Namibia. It is ironic that China, a country insistent on local content requirements and the hiring of local labor in contrast with foreign firms doing business in China, ignores this outside of its borders.[76]

This is where the African leader's role is expected to stand up to the discrepancies and fight for a win-win deal. When a foreign country is running businesses on its own terms in a sovereign country without judicial challenge or respect of law and human rights, it says there is something rotten. Jiang gives us food for thought in the form of good questions:

> When the ruthless competition for profits is very much the rule of the game in China's current development stage, how can one expect Chinese enterprises to operate differently abroad? Chinese firms pay their labor forces very little and have them work long hours; how can one expect them to behave differently overseas? With 6,700 Chinese coal miners dying from accident every year (17 a day) since 2001, how can one expect Chinese ventures to do better in other parts of the world? When corruption is rampant in China, how can Chinese firm do better in term of governance and transparency in Africa? China has severely damaged its own ecological system during its rapid modernization process; how can one expect it consciously to implement Western-style environmentally friendly measures elsewhere? When china has difficulties reforming its own political system, how can it possibly require democratic reforms in other countries? The Chinese central government has difficulties controlling market-oriented misbehaviors at home; how can one expect it to effectively moderate Chinese firms operating in other parts of the world?[77]

The Economist adds,

> The Communist Party has not habitually encouraged public pressure on local officials as a means of implementing its policies in enforcing environmental regulations have caused a flutter. Under the new rules that took effect in January 1st the environment ministry has called on 15,000 firms to make real-time public disclosures of emissions of air pollutants, wastewater and heavy metals. Environmentalists ate applauding, but the implementation is all.
>
> The companies were already required to install monitoring equipment and report the results to environmental regulators. But enforcement has been weak because most local officials are more concerned with economic growth than with preventing pollution. Leaders hope public disclosure can change that....

---

76. Lee and Shalmon, "China's Oil Strategies in Africa," 122.
77. Jiang, "China's Emerging Partnership in Africa," 61.

> A study by the Lancet, a British journal, in 2012 estimated that 1.2m premature deaths in China in 2010 could be attributed to the effects of pollution. Another study, published last year by China's environment ministry, said that direct economic losses in 2010 amounted to 2.5% of China's GDP, double the proportion in 2004. Perhaps more significant for the party, pollution is a leading cause of popular discontent.[78]

Before rushing to break a deal with China, African policy makers and leaders need to earnestly face the pros and cons of China's involvement in their countries. Unfortunately, as far as principle, the prevalence of corruption, poor ethics, lack of democracy, and transparency are concerned, China is dealing with people of its kind. The only difference is language and skin color. With all China's current investment and the friendly relationship between Africa and China that was previously established and enhanced through various kinds of legal and illegal deals, I am afraid it is too late to change the course of action between China and Africa. Neither Africa nor the Chinese governments allow their people to have a voice of dissent. With their intolerance to anything that stands in their way, the Africans who were mistreated in the mines of Cecil Rhodes, the Oppenheimers, the Belgian, French, British, German, and American companies in Africa, will face the same challenges with the new Chinese bosses.

That said, some African economists and analysts have a different perspective on the issue of China's exploitation of African minerals and labor:

> Despite all the scaremongering, China's motives for investing in Africa are actually quite pure. To satisfy China's population and prevent a crisis of legitimacy for their rule, leaders in Beijing need to keep economic growth rates high and continue to bring hundreds of millions of people out of poverty. And to do so, China needs arable land, oil and minerals. Pursuing imperial or colonial ambitions with masses of impoverished people at home would be wholly irrational and out of sync with China's current strategic thinking.
>
> Moreover, the evidence does not support a claim that Africans themselves feel exploited. To the contrary, China's role is broadly welcomed across the continent. A 2007 Pew Research Center survey of 10 sub-Saharan African countries found that Africans overwhelmingly viewed Chinese economic growth as beneficial. In virtually all countries surveyed, China's involvement was viewed in a much more positive light than America's; in Senegal, 86 percent said China's role in their country helped make things better, compared with 56 percent who felt that way about America's role. In Kenya, 91 percent of respondents said they believed China's influence was positive, versus only 74 percent for the United States.[79]

Western Response to China's Presence in Africa

China's involvement in Africa has gone unnoticed by Western powers, particularly the United States. "Western countries have found China's entry into the world economy disconcerting, if not threatening. This reaction is magnified when China pursues strategies

78. "Environmental Accountability."
79. Moyo, "Beijing, a Boon for Africa."

and arrangements different from those followed by Western governments and corporations. Nowhere has this been truer than in China's efforts to obtain access to raw materials—especially oil."[80] Dambisa Moyo, a Zambian economist writes, "Since China began seriously investing in Africa in 2005, it has been routinely cast as a stealthy imperialist with a voracious appetite for commodities and no qualms about exploiting Africans to get them. It is no wonder that the American government is lashing out at its new competitor—while China has made huge investments in Africa, the United States has stood on the sidelines and watched its influence on the continent fade."[81] She thinks that the labor hurdles and environmental issues, as well as the manner in which China runs her investments in Africa (which the West describes negatively), have been unrealistically portrayed and exaggerated by unsubstantiated facts. Moyo considers Western reports on these issues to have created predilections. "As the result of the lack of nuance in this and other noted criticisms of China's actions, a strange schism has developed between mostly Western foreigners and reporters, who seem to prefer to paint China's incursions as unanimously bad, and the presumed victims of this abuse, the locals who often view Chinese presence in generally positive terms."[82] It is not only the Western reporters who complain about China's engagement in Africa. "The European Investment Bank (EIB) has expressed concern that he world's development bank may have to water down the social and environmental conditions they attach to loans in Africa and elsewhere because they are being undercut by Chinese lenders."[83]

It is not only the African voice; some Western observers also see Chinese involvement in Africa in a positive light. Rotberg objectively and pragmatically assesses China's strategy this way: "China's goals are ideological as well as material. In addition to gaining sovereign control over stable supplies of primary goods, China wants to marginalize Taiwan's engagement with Africa . . . Admittedly, China has always preferred to acquire loyal friends in Africa—friends who supported its application on the permanent seat on the Security Council, its entrance into the World Trade Organization (WTO), and its desire to host the 2008 Olympics. China has wanted friends who would now and in the future back it in international fora everywhere and always."[84] "Ideology and political strategy were the primary thrusts behind China's extensive program."[85] Brautigam concurs. The urgent and main concern of many Africans is to feed their children, send them to school, and provide health care and security. According to Maslow's hierarchies of need these are fundamental and basic needs. In the light of the present pressing and life-threatening challenges the Western ideals are irrelevant to millions of Africans. "The four horses of Africa's apocalypse—corruption, disease, poverty, and war—can easily ride across international borders, putting Westerners at just as Africans . . . The West can choose to ignore all of this, but, like it or not. The Chinese are coming. And it is in Africa that their campaign for global dominance will be solidified. Economics comes first, and

80. Lee and Shalmon, "China's Oil Strategies in Africa," 116.
81. Moyo, "Beijing, a Boon for Africa."
82. Ibid., 163.
83. Moyo, *Dead Aid*, 106.
84. Rotberg, "China's Quest," 2.
85. 2009:18

when they own the banks, the land and the resources across Africa, their crusade will be over. They will have won."⁸⁶

Instead of playing the blame game or spreading misinformation about China, Brautigam suggests giving the issues an abstemious look and engaging with China in Africa and the global context. She writes: "China's rise in Africa is cause for some concern, but it need not evoke the level of fear and alarm raised by some who have condemned China's aid and engagement as destabilizing, bad for governance, and unlikely to help Africa to end poverty. Many of the fears about Chinese aid and engagement are misinformed, the alarm out of proportion."⁸⁷

However, as some critics comment about the U.S. "standing on the sidelines" that doesn't mean inactive engagement on a global level to encounter the potential threats of China to the United States and her allies.

> For Obama, there is a more pressing cause—China. Africa is China's success story. While the Americans bring drones, the Chinese build roads, bridges and dams. What the Chinese want is resources, especially fossil fuels. [NATO's] bombing of Libya drove out 30,000 Chinese oil industry workers. More than jihadism or Iran, China is Washington's obsession in Africa and beyond. This is a "policy" known as the "pivot to Asia," whose threat of world war may be as great as any in the modern era.
>
> Meeting in Tokyo between John Kerry, the US secretary of state, Chuck Hagel, the defence secretary, and their Japanese counterparts accelerated the prospect of war. Sixty per cent of US naval forces are to be based in Asia by 2020, aimed at China. Japan is re-arming rapidly under the rightwing government of Shinzo Abe, who came to power in December with a pledge to build a "new, strong military" and circumvent the "peace constitution."
>
> A US-Japanese anti-ballistic-missile system near Kyoto is directed at China. Using long-range Global Hawk drones the US has sharply increased its provocations in the East China and South China seas, where Japan and China dispute the ownership of the Senkaku/Diaoyu islands. Both countries now deploy advanced vertical take-off aircraft in Japan in preparation for a blitzkrieg.
>
> On the Pacific island of Guam, from where B-52s attacked Vietnam, the biggest military buildup since the Indochina wars includes 9,000 US marines. In Australia this week an arms fair and military jamboree that diverted much of Sydney is in keeping with a government propaganda campaign to justify an unprecedented US military build-up from Perth to Darwin, aimed at China. The vast US base at Pine Gap near Alice Springs is, as Edward Snowden disclosed, a hub of US spying in the region and beyond; it is also critical to Obama's worldwide assassinations by drone.
>
> "We have to inform the British to keep them on side," McGeorge Bundy, an assistant US secretary of state, once said. "You in Australia are with us, come what may." Australian forces have long played a mercenary role for Washington. However, China is Australia's biggest trading partner and largely responsible for its evasion of the 2008 recession. Without China, there would be no minerals boom: no weekly mining return of up to a billion dollars.⁸⁸

86. Moyo, *Dead Aid*, 151–52.
87. Brautigam, *Dragon's Gift*, 307.
88. Pilger, "More than Jihadism or Iran."

One can see the global economic and political repercussions because of China's involvement in Africa. During the Second World War, Africa's minerals, uranium and diamonds in particular have played a significant role for the Western alliance to win the war. One of the major reasons for Germany's fall was the shortage of diamond from Africa.[89] The building of the hydrogen bomb with uranium from Congo also put the United States in a leading role as a superpower. African armies have also played an important role. Without a doubt, the country that will have a lasting impact and influence in Africa in the next three or four decades will be the leading power in the world. That is, if we survive the environmental crisis and the rapid population growth in Africa. "The best way for the United States and other rich countries that have economic and political interests in Africa to respond is not by warning Africans about the advance of China—but rather, helping to strengthen African civil society and, thereby, governance. Washington should also encourage China and other up-and-coming players in the international economy, from Brazil to Turkey to Vietnam, to abide by higher transparency standards—and to rigorously abide by them, too."[90]

China is equally concerned about the Western military strategy and has her own plans. Shinn writes,

> Chinese military and security relations with Africa have progressed from support for independence and revolutionary movements in the 1960s and 1970s to a more pragmatic relationship in the 1990s and the first decade of the twenty-first century. China's national security interest focus overwhelmingly on its periphery: South Asia, Southeast Asia, Central Asia, West Asia (including the Middle East), Russia, Japan, Mongolia, and the Koreas. China is also much concerned about the ability of the United States and Europe to project military and economy power into Asia. Africa and Latin America, however, are not critical parts of China's security policy. Africa is a security issue only in terms of China's effort to secure the energy, mineral, and timber resources used to fuel its economy. These needs translate into a strategy that encourages a desire to strengthen stability in African countries that sell or have potential to sell China significant qualities of raw materials. Looking to the future, China may conclude that it needs a bluewater navy that no longer relies on the United States to protect the sea lanes from Africa and the Middle East that are used to transport essential imports.[91]

89. Roberts, *Glitter and Greed*.

90. French, "Into Africa: China's Wild Rush."

91. Shinn, "Military and Security Relations," 155. According to the U.S. Arms Control and Disarmament Agency, Africa acquired only $42 million worth of Chinese arms from 1961 to 1971. From 1967 to 1976, China transferred $142 million in arms to Africa. China's share of the African arms market was about 2.8 percent. Congo Brazzaville ($10 million), Tanzania ($57 million), and Zaire ($21 million) were the major recipients of Chinese arms transfer during this period. Cameroon, Guinea, Egypt, the Sudan, Tunisia, and Zambia each obtained an estimated $5 million in arms while Burundi, the Gambia, Malawi, Mozambique, and Rwanda each received about $1 million in arms. Between 1955 and 1976, an estimated 2,675 African military personnel were trained in China. Tanzania headed the list with 1,025, followed by Congo Brazzaville with 425; Guinea, 350; the Sudan, 200; Sierra Leone, 50 each; and Algeria and Somalia, 25 each.

The Congressional Research Service reported that, on a worldwide basis, China was the number six arms supplier from 1998 through 2001. Although China is a relatively small-scale arms provider compared to the top five, 83 percent of its transfers went to the developing world. China remained sixth

Western Democracy in Question

In the 20 years since the Cold War's end, free-market, multiparty democracy has been held forth as the ideal form of government (and a key to obtaining support from Washington). But now, drawn to the example set by the fast-growing economies of Asia like China, Singapore and Malaysia—all of which achieved phenomenal growth under modernizing authoritarian governments—a group of African leaders has emerged that openly declares its admiration for this mode of government.

Meles Zenawi, the Ethiopian leader from 1995 until his death in 2012, was perhaps the most forthright advocate of a system that emphasizes economic advancement over democracy. Speaking at the opening of the African Union headquarters in Addis Ababa in January 2012, Mr. Meles was effusive in his praise of China. Lauding Beijing for its aid in building the center, he declared that "the people of China and Africa share similar backgrounds that helped them to stand for one goal today, which is economic development."

Other African leaders, from Rwanda's Paul Kagame to Ali Bongo in Gabon, now speak in similar terms. Yet the growing appeal of the statist model has not drawn nearly enough attention in the West. In a talk in June sponsored by TED, the nonprofit organization that holds conferences on ideas, the Zambian economist Dambisa Moyo warned that Western powers need to pay attention to the growing admiration for the Chinese economic miracle.

Pointing to Beijing's success in moving millions of people out of poverty, she added: "It's not just in economics, but also in terms of living standards. We see that in China 28 percent of people had secondary school access. Today it's closer to 82 percent."

Critics note that while the leaders of Rwanda and Ethiopia have delivered considerable improvements in their people's livelihoods, neither Mr. Kagame nor Mr. Meles brooked any dissent and the repression in both lands is notorious.[92]

As I indicated earlier, people like Meles, Kigame, Museveni, Mobutu, and other African leaders came to power through the assistance and endorsement of Western powers, the United States in particular. They stay in political leadership through the financial aid that the U.S. has been pouring into each respective country despite their bad record of human rights violations.

In the game of politics, money plays a more dominant role than ethics and justice. Hence, recently, the same African leaders who were befriended by Washington when they were in African forest fighting as guerrilla leaders have begun admiring the "modernizing authoritarian governments... of China, Singapore and Malaysia." Moyo further explains why African leaders are attracted to and influenced by the Chinese government: "The proper extent of government involvement in an economy has been debated for centuries... China's celebrated economic success and America's ongoing economic woes have brought the debate back in vogue. Here we are: two different economic slants—one

---

for the period 2002–2005, but the percentage of its arms going to the developing world jumped to 94 percent. China was the fifth largest supplier of arms to the developing world from 1998 to 2005, well behind the United States, Russia, France, and the United Kingdom (for broader understanding, see ibid., 155–96).

92. Mutiga, "Africa and the Chinese Way."

largely state led, the other private-sector driven—involving two countries that could not be politically further apart. But both models are proof positive that sustained economic growth can arise from different economic paradigms and different political frameworks."[93] In China, "The government makes its financial muscle felt, so the line between public and private can appear deliberately obfuscated: for example, the Chinese state retains sizeable equity stakes in many publicly traded companies (in some cases upward of 70 percent of these companies are government owned) and virtually all of the top thirty Chinese enterprises investing in strategic sectors such as oil, minerals, or infrastructure are state owned, and thus, in a sense, they act as extensions of the party state. This structure has been central to China's global resource drive. For instance, the three leading investors in Africa state-owned oil companies: China Petrochemical Corporation, China National Petroleum Corporation, and China National offshore Oil Corporation."[94] The Chinese political framework, a one-party and centralized government, fits the dream of African tyrants.

For many Africans who underwent European domination and exploitation, Western democracy is a sham anyway. "More generally, many Africans scoff at the notion that Westerners should be outraged by Chinese implicit support of Africa's corrupt rogue leaders. It is, after all, under the auspices of Western aid, goodwill and transparency that Africa's most notorious plunderers and despots have risen and thrived—Zaire's President Mobutu, Uganda's President, Idi Amin and the Central African Republic's 'Emperor' Bokassa (who kept his victims heads in a fridge), to name just three."[95] Rupp gives us the distinction of Chinese approach to African leaders compared to the colonial powers: "China engages with African nations on a fundamentally different level, and in a substantially distinct manner, from the way European powers behaved toward their African colonies. African colonial states remained peripheral players on the international stage, participating as junior partners at best. In contrast, China actively cultivates and strengthen its diplomatic relationships with African states in bilateral as well as multilateral relations, taking great care to emphasize that African nations are political equals."[96] The main reason African leaders align with the West is for the dollar. When they found an alternative financial source in China, African leaders turned out to be missionaries of "a system that emphasizes economic advancement over democracy." To be treated as "political equals" is another major incentive.

The Chinese political modus operandi is closely allied with that of many African despots. Instead of turning off the oriental, political, and economic music, African leaders are dancing with their Chinese patrons. Some of them did it at the cost of their lives. What the African leaders have not fully realized yet is that they cannot eat from the plates of China and the West simultaneously with no conflict of interest, and without offending their hosts. In the clash of civilizations, the current trends indicate that African leaders will be more inclined toward China for the following four main reasons: 1) China's soft power is very appealing to African leaders; 2) China is not challenging

93. Moyo, "Beijing, a Boon for Africa," 91.
94. Ibid., 7.
95. Moyo, *Dead Aid*, 68.
96. "Africa and China," 68

corrupt African governments—instead, through bribery, it is giving fuel to them; 3) The West does not have the economic power that China has; 4) The West has no moral or ethical ground and historical backing to tell African leaders to be more democratic. "The European Union constantly criticizes China's human rights record, yet Britain, France, and Germany are trying to promote trade with China. The United States and China have issued human rights reports criticizing each other for several years, yet such criticism by no means hinders the exchange of goods and ideas, and both sides endeavor to increase their economic trade. With state behavior based on Western ideals, China does not necessarily accept the naming and shaming of certain African regimes as corrupt."[97] If actions betray what we say, words become cheap and meaningless. Western democracy to the ears of millions of Africans is just a "resounding gong or clanging cymbal." Words without justice, and centuries of promise without delivery, can't do magic in today's Africa.

The Zambian economist Dambisa Moyo was right when she said,

> If anything, the bulk of responsibility for abuses lies with African leaders themselves. The 2011 Human Rights Watch Report "You'll Be Fired If You Refuse," which described a series of alleged labor and human rights abuses in Chinese-owned Zambian copper mines, missed a fundamental point: the onus of policing social policy and protecting the environment is on local governments, and it is local policy makers who should ultimately be held accountable and responsible if and when egregious failures occur.
>
> China's critics ignore the root cause of why many African leaders are corrupt and unaccountable to their populations. For decades, many African governments have abdicated their responsibilities at home in return for the vast sums of money they receive from courting international donors and catering to them. Even well-intentioned aid undermines accountability. Aid severs the link between Africans and their governments, because citizens generally have no say in how the aid dollars are spent and governments too often respond to the needs of donors, rather than those of their citizens.[98]

The doyen African reporter Howard French, during his travels through Mali and Senegal for the research of his recent book, observed the extent of corruption in these countries. He writes, "It was the last of dozens of customs stops on this road, one final fleecing point by corrupt inspectors and police of truck and bus drivers and passengers before reaching Bamako, or alternately, the first of many who are heading toward Dakar . . . *The scene of law enforcement agents in a variety uniforms extorting money, which is reproduced daily across most of the continent, was a sad and vivid reminder of how badly Africa's leaders have failed their people, of the failure of institutions and above all of how governments have never learned that the best thing they can do for African prosperity is to get out of the way.*"[99]

Whether it is China, the United States, Scandinavian countries, Japan, or Europe, outsiders have to deal with corrupt African governments; and they are corrupt to their

---

97. Anshan, "China's New Policy toward Africa," 37.
98. Moyo, "Beijing, a Boon for Africa," A27.
99. French, *China's Second Continent*, 181; emphasis added.

core. Unless these corrupt leaders "get out of the way" there is no amount of money, commerce, or development projects that can change Africa's misery. "The fact that so many African governments can stay in power by relying on foreign aid that has few strings attached, instead of revenues from their own populations, allows corrupt politicians to remain in charge."[100] That is what we are analyzing in the following chapter.

In a world of radical Islamists and terror, it would be wise for the U.S. and China to work closely together for the security of the global community and the development of Africans. If the economic and social problems of Africa are not properly addressed on time, the continent may turn into an incubator of anarchists of all kinds including more groups like Boko Haram and Al Shabab. "In the fractured world of Iran, Iraq and Afghanistan, Africa's fragile and impoverished states are a natural haven for global terrorists. Porous borders, weak law enforcement and security institutions, plentiful and portable natural resources, disaffected populations, and conflict zones make perfect breeding grounds for all sorts of global terrorist organizations."[101] I have already shown how Al Qaida and Hezbollah are engaged in the diamond business. If the concerns above are not addressed, terrorist groups can be multiplied in the continent of Africa and can reap havoc on the investments of the West and China.

The most important area that China is not ready to engage with and will inevitably encounter is the religious life of Africans. With the growth of Christianity and Islam and the worldview of Africans who usually embrace spiritual phenomena, what the dragon has tried to suppress at home will meet him in the public arena of the African continent. Huang observes: "Future Chinese engagement in Africa will need to take into greater account the exceptional religiosity of African societies and develop an official approach, which largely has been absent, of engaging religious leaders. Religious organizations, Muslim and Christian, provide a broad and widening range of social counter parts outside Africa are the fastest growing in membership and participation. Africa's 300 million Muslims constitute highly complex, and variegated communities."[102] Plus, "Seventy per cent of the Arab people and 65 per cent of the Arab lands are now in Africa."[103] If Western foreign policy with Africa doesn't change for the well-being of the African people, and anti-Western sentiment in the Middle East continues to cause havoc, radical

---

100. Ibid.

101. Moyo, *Dead Aid*, 151.

102. Huang, "China's Renewal Partnership with Africa," 302.

103. Mazrui, *African Condition*, 144. "The Arab conquest of North Africa in the seventh and eighth centuries initiated two processes—Arabisation (through language) and Islamisation (through religion). The spread of Arabic as a native language created new Semites, the Arabs of north Africa. The diffusion of Islam created new monotheists but not necessarily new Semites . . . The process by which the majority north Africans became Arabised was partly biological and partly cultural. The biological process involved intermarriage and considerably facilitated by the upward lineage system of the Arabs . . . The number of people in the Middle East who called themselves Arabs expanded dramatically in a relatively short period. This was partly because of the exuberance of the new religion, partly because of the rising prestige of the Arabic language and partly due to the rewards of belonging to a conquering civilization. Religious, political, and psychological factors transformed Arabism into an expansionist culture which absorbed the conquered into the body politics of the conquerors. In the beginning there was an 'island' or a peninsula called 'Arabia.' But in time there were far more Arabs outside of Arabia than within" (Mazrui, *Africans*, 90, 92).

Muslims like Boko Haram and al-Shabab can mushroom in Africa. "The fight against the Islamist terrorists of Boko Haram in Nigeria's north-eastern corner has reached its bloodiest point so far. Once again the army is being criticized as much as the terrorists. On March 14th a military counter-attack after an attempted jail break by suspected member of Boko Haram left around 500 people dead, according to hospital sources, mostly at the hands of soldiers. It was the worst day of casualties since the sect terrorist campaign began in 2009."[104] Boko Haram is a cause for the displacement of millions of Nigerians. "No one is certain how many people have been uprooted. The Internal Displacement Monitoring Center (IDMC), a Swiss-based, Norwegian-backed group, reckons that 3.3m Nigerians have fled their homes not just because of Boko Haram. Intercommunal fighting and floods have added to the toll of families forced to flee. If this figure is correct, Nigeria now has the world' third-highest number of displaced people, after Syria and Columbia."[105]

The piracy off the coast of Somalia has already been a huge headache for the West. There is another group in West Africa that is seldom mentioned but equally dangerous. *The Economist* states:

> The MV City of Xiamen, container ship flagged in Antigua and Barbuda, was about 160km (100 miles) off the Nigerian coast in the evening of April 25th when 14 pirates, armed to the teeth, boarded her and broke into the ship's safe room. They made off with an undisclosed sum of cash and five crew members, who were freed on May 13th, probably after a ransom had been paid.
>
> The incident is typical of piracy in west Africa's Gulf of Guinea: it was violent, quick and almost entirely Nigerian. In the 1990s a peaceful movement protesting against the iniquities of government in the Niger delta decayed into a violent and criminal insurgency. Armed gangs preyed on the fishing boats and stole oil from pipelines. Oil companies responded by more of their operations offshore. The gangs followed during the height of insurgency in 2006–09, they extended their reach beyond Nigerian waters. Since then, ships across the length of the gulf—from Gabon in the south to Liberia in the west—have been targeted.
>
> Figures compiled by the International Maritime Bureau, which tracks piracy worldwide, indicate that the frequency of attacks in the region has waxed and wanted. But security experts say piracy off west Africa is getting worse. Reported incidents jumped from 44 in 2011 to 62 in 2012. This year, with 28 incidents so far, could be the worst ever. Ten of the 2012 assaults on ships in the gulf were hijackings, more than a third of the world's total. Most disconcerting is the pirate's increasing sophistication.[106]

Porous borders and jobless youth in Africa can be prone to be recruiting targets of radical Muslim terrorist groups. "Gloomy youths . . . sound ambivalent towards Boko Haram. Most would rather have jobs than become religious marauders, but given the chance they may be tempted a group that is evidently successful. 'No many other winners here' says one . . . Their parent . . . worry that their children will be receptive to

---

104. "Worse and Worse."
105. "A Rising Tide of Misery."
106. "Gulf of Guinea."

recruitment drives by Boko Haram. They also report an increase in the night-time traffic, which they blame on insurgent movements."[107]

As I have indicated in this book, the dynamic of Christian growth and its influence on the continent is not something that China can afford to ignore either. For the West, improving the economy, freedom, and security of African Christians and facilitating the development of leaders with global vision and integrity in Africa would be a huge contribution to the security of their countries and the global community. The decisive battles during the Second World War were fought in Africa before Normandy. Whoever dominates the future trends of Africa will undoubtedly be the dominating superpower of the world. In the recent "economic war" between China and the West, and their battle for influence in Africa, without a doubt China is way ahead of the game.

> Not so long ago, slow-growing economies with high inflation were the norm in sub-Saharan Africa. Average GDP growth across the continent during the 1990s was only 2.2%, dismal for such a poor region. Average inflation was 27%. Now this has all changed. Since 2001 Africa's GDP has expanded more quickly each year than the global average. In the past decade, only the bloc of developing Asian economies, led by China, has grown faster than Africa . . .
>
> Africa's fortune has been helped by increased trade with China, now the continent's main export market. As China's economy evolves so will Africa's. China's leaders want their economy to expand at a more moderate pace than in the past decade and for growth to be led by consumer spending rather than resource-intensive investment . . . IMF predicts that four of the world's six fates-growing economies in 2014 will be in sub-Saharan Africa. And for the first time in living memory inflation will dip below the GDP growth rate.[108]

107. "African's Jihadists."
108. O'Sullivan, "Digging Deeper," 73.

Chapter 8

Leadership Crisis in Africa

There is nothing basically wrong with the Nigerian character. There is nothing wrong with the Nigerian land or climate or water or air or anything else. The Nigerian problem is the unwillingness or inability of fits leaders to rise to the responsibility. . .of true leadership.[1]

The works of peace cannot flourish in a country governed by intoxicated Despot . . . Now commerce, manufactures, agriculture, and all the peaceful arts, are of the nature of virtues or intellectual powers; they cannot be given; they cannot be stuck in here and there; they must spring up; they must grow of themselves; they may be encouraged; they thrive better with encouragement and delight in it; but . . . they are delicate, proud, and independent . . . But a Tyrant has no joy in anything which is endued with such excellence: he sickens at the sight of it; he turns away from it, as an insult to his own attributes.[2]

Run to and fro through the street of Jerusalem [Africa]
Look and take note!
Search her squares to see
If you can find a man,
One who does justice; . . .
And seek truth; . . .
But they all alike had broken the yoke,
They had burst the bonds . . .
From the least to the greatest of them,
Everyone is greed for unjust gain;

1. Achebe, *Trouble with Nigeria*, 1.
2. Wordsworth, *William Wordsworth's Convention of Cintra*, 208.

And from the prophet to priest,
Everyone deals falsely . . .
There is nothing but oppression within her.
(Jer 5:1, 5; 6:13; 6:6; 8:10)

IT IS IMPOSSIBLE TO cover all the internal factors that contributed to the crisis of Africa that made life unbearable to millions of destitute, to refugees, to those inflicted by civil war, made to languish in prison, to suffer from hunger, and to live in the dark world of the illiterate. Hoping that the reader will gain a broader understanding of the continent through further reading and research in the scholarly writings of other people, in this chapter I focus on the following topics: the leadership crisis, corruption, military rulers, and coup d'état.

Sham Independence

Most African political systems have exhibited the "Big Man" patrimonial rule. Three distinct types of leadership surfaced in the postcolonial era. The first type was the charismatic, associated with such leaders as Nkrumah, Nyerere, Toure, Kaunda, and Mugabe. Their support was based largely on popular appeal of their message and their role in the decolonization struggle . . . The second type of political leadership was the patriarchal, exemplified in such leaders as Jomo Kenyatta, Leopold Senghor, Felix Houphouet-Boigny, Julius Nyerere and Kenneth Kaunda. They acted as the "father of the nation," and their style was that of adjudicator, conciliator, instigator and peacemaker. As father figures, they expected to be revered . . . the third type, revolutionary or populist prophetic, emerged, in the 1980s and near-perfect clones of the earlier-day charismatic leaders: Flight Lieutenant John Jerry Rawlings of Ghana, Yoweri Museveni of Uganda, and the late Captain Thomas Sankara of Burkina Faso. They were impatient and angry at the appalling social misery, economic mismanagement and flagrant injustice in their countries.[3]

Since the 1960s, researchers have examined whether there is a relationship between the basic agreed-on factors that make up personality and leadership. The Big Five personality factors are conscientiousness, agreeableness, neuroticism, openness, and extraversion, which some researchers have labeled the CANOE personality model as an easy aid to remember each factor. Conscientiousness is defined as an individual's tendency to be organized, thorough, controlled, decisive, and dependable. Of the Big Five factors, it is the personality factor that has been related to leadership most strongly (second only to extraversion) in previous research. Agreeableness, or an individual's tendency to be trusting, nurturing, conforming, and accepting, has been only weakly associated with leadership. Neuroticism, or the tendency to be anxious, hostile, depressed, vulnerable, and insecure, has been moderately and negatively related to leadership, suggesting that

---

3. Ayittey, *Africa in Chaos*, 158.

most leaders tend to be low in neuroticism. Openness, sometimes referred to as openness to experience, refers to an individual's tendency to be curious, creative, insightful, and informed. Openness has been moderately related to leadership, suggesting that leaders tend to be somewhat higher in openness than non-leaders. Finally, extraversion is the personality factor that has been the most strongly associated with leadership. Defined as the tendency to be sociable (discussed in greater detail below), assertive, and to have positive energy, extraversion has been described as the most important personality trait of effective leaders. Although research on the Big Five personality factors has found some relationships between these overall personality factors and leadership, focusing on more specific traits has led to more consistent findings between effective leadership and the following five traits: intelligence, self-confidence, determination, sociability, and integrity.[4] There is no scientific leadership study on the personality of African leaders that I know of. However, their love for power, authoritarian style of ruling, corruption, lack of transparency, and accountability and longevity of leadership makes them look like branches of the same tree. Kofi Annan summed up African leadership this way:

> The 1885 Congress of Berlin saw the colonial divide up Africa into territorial units that made no sense on the ground—partitioning kingdoms, states and communities from one another, arbitrarily melding others. Furthermore, the colonial system introduced laws and strength of the colonial authority, rather than attempts to bridge these divides.
>
> It was these arbitrary boundaries and these divisive institutions and systems of law that most newly independent African countries inherited in the 1960s. The resulting challenge of creating genuine national identities within the colonial-created boundaries gave too much opportunity for the new African leaders to assert the value of their personalities in papering over these divisions. In the absence of any organic unity, some African countries turned to the authority of individual rulers instead of attempting to cultivate political pluralism. The colonial state had not encouraged representation or participation, and neither did the leaders who followed.[5]

If we start from the northern part of Africa, "Abdelaziz Bouteflika, Algeria's head of state is a man of diminutive stature and legendary staying power. The 76-year-old secured his first ministerial post in 1962, served as foreign minister for 16 years and has occupied the presidential palace since 1999."[6] The only son of an illiterate Bedouin herder, Muammar Gaddafi assumed the leadership of Libya in 1969 after participating, along with several other officers, in a bloodless coup against King Idris, the nation's first independent head of state. Only twenty-seven years old, he was promoted to the rank of colonel, the highest position in the Libyan army. He declared himself the commander-in-chief of the armed forces and the de facto head of the Libyan state. He ruled Libya with an iron fist and extreme brutality for forty-two years.[7]

---

4. Michelle C. Bligh, 639. For an in-depth understanding see "Personality Theories of Leadership": *Encyclopedia of Group Process and Intergroup Relations*, 2001

5. Annan, *Interventions*, 171.

6. "Dead Live Longer," *Economist*, September 21, 2013, p. 51.

7. See Pargeter, *Rise and Fall of Qaddafi*.

Mubarak took office in 1981, after his predecessor, Anwar Sadat, was assassinated by Islamic militants during a military parade. Mubarak, Sadat's vice-president, escaped with a minor hand injury. In 1981, Mubarak implemented emergency laws as part of his battle against militants and expanded police powers. In one of his first moves, Mubarak said Egypt would stick to the 1979 peace treaty with Israel, the first by any Arab nation with the Jewish state. Mubarak became a major mediator in the Arab-Israeli peace process, remaining a consistent US ally bolstered by billions of dollars in American aid.

During the 1990s, militants launched an uprising aimed at setting up an Islamic state. Gunmen attacked police, assassinated politicians and targeted foreign tourists, a key source of revenue. In 1995, militants attempted to assassinate Mubarak as he visited Ethiopia. Mubarak responded by arresting thousands, crushing the movement by 1997. Mubarak's government subsidized goods such as bread, cooking oil, and gasoline. When bread riots turned violent in 2008, he fired up military ovens to help quell discontent.

Mubarak engineered constitutional amendments that, according to critics, guaranteed ruling-party victories in elections. One banned religious political parties, blocking the Muslim Brotherhood from officially participating in political life. Mubarak was re-elected three times in staged, one-man referendums in which he routinely won more than 90 percent approval.

In 2005, Mubarak allowed the first ever multi-candidate presidential election, which he won easily over ten other candidates amid charges of voter fraud and intimidation. The 2010 parliamentary elections were widely deplored as rigged, and the Brotherhood responded by withdrawing its candidates, who ran as independents, from a second round of voting. On 25 January 2011, thousands of anti-government protesters clashed with police in Cairo during a Tunisia-inspired demonstration to demand Mubarak's removal. The day marked the start of the Arab Spring in Egypt. After three weeks of massive protests against his rule, Mubarak resigned on 11 February 2011, handing power to the military.

On 13 April, authorities detained Mubarak and his two sons in an investigation into corruption, abuse of power, and the killing of protesters. A month later, Mubarak was ordered to stand trial on charges of corruption and conspiracy in the deadly shooting of protesters. Mubarak's trial opened in Cairo on 3 August 2011. From the defendant's cage, Mubarak denied all charges against him.

On 22 February 2012, Mubarak, who had rarely spoken during the trial, turned down his last chance to address the court during the defense's final arguments. On 2 June 2012, the 84-year-old was sentenced to life in prison and was ferried by helicopter from the police academy where the trial was held to the Torah prison in Cairo where his sons and members of his regime had been either serving prison sentences or held pending trials over a variety of corruption charges.

After Mubarak, Mohammed Morsi from the Muslim Brotherhood was democratically elected. However, before too long, he was overthrown by the military. And Egypt entered a new phase of uncertainty. After security forces drove out supporters of President Mohammed Morsi from two sprawling encampments where they had been camped out for six weeks demanding the Islamist leader's reinstatement. The move, which left dozens of protesters dead and saw the arrest of several leaders of Morsi's

Muslim Brotherhood, has left the fundamentalist movement dangerously isolated. It also prompted Vice President Mohamed ElBaradei, a Nobel Peace Prize laureate and pro-reform leader in the interim government, to resign in protest over the violent crackdown as the military-backed leadership imposed a month-long state of emergency and nighttime curfew.[8] The U.S. was giving 1.5 billion annually to Mubarak's regime. He ruled Egypt for thirty years.

While misinformation is rife in the Horn of Africa, at least two of Eritrea's neighbors, Ethiopia and Djibouti, have accused Afewerki of "exporting chaos" by funding armed insurgent groups within their countries. Human Rights Watch writes of Eritrea: "Arbitrary arrests, torture, and forced labor are rampant. Rule by fiat is the norm. The Eritrean government refuses to implement a constitution approved in 1997 containing civil and human rights provisions." Afewerki is also blamed for starting a "pointless" war with Ethiopia in 1998 that led to at least 70,000 deaths on both sides and cost two of the world's poorest countries hundreds of millions of dollars. Perhaps as a result of that war, and Afewerki's apparent penchant for needling his neighbors, military service in Eritrea is mandatory for all men, and there is no time limit on the length of their service, which is often done under the cruelest of conditions. This has contributed in part to the refugee crisis in the country, UNHCR reports.[9] Afeworki has been in power for twenty-one years.

Museveni of Uganda, an ex-army officer, led his National Resistance Army into Kampala in January 1986 to seize power. Since then he managed to win four elections on his own terms of democracy. Despite this, oppositions disputed the results and recently he clamped down on demonstrators that are not happy because of corruption on his government and high living costs in country. He has been president of Uganda for the last twenty-eight years.

In November 1982, Cameroon's first post-independence leader, Ahmadou Ahidjo, formally resigned due to ill health, and handed the presidency to his Prime Minister, Paul Biya. Cameroon's president, Paul Biya, described as running government finances "like a petty cash fund," booked himself and his entourage a $1.2m three week holiday by chartered jet to the French resort of La Baule. They took forty-three rooms in two luxury hotels costing $60,000 a night, went on shopping sprees and splashed cash on casino nights," reported the US embassy in Cameroon. "When Biya traveled to the United Nations general assembly in September 2008, a member of his entourage was caught as he tried to escape from Biya's Geneva hotel with a bag filled with 3.4m Swiss francs (about $6.8 million) in cash." State security forces have been accused of a host of heinous acts, including the killing of as many as 100 protesters in 2009 and the use of violence, arbitrary arrests, and unlawful detentions to prevent opposition political activists from holding meetings. In 2008, Biya had the constitution changed so he is immune from prosecution once leaving office. His ruling party had parliament remove the ability of

---

8. For further reading on Mubarak, see Osman, *Egypt on the Brink*; Gardner, *Five Minds for the Future*.

9. Hurmuzlu, "Detained Eritrean Deserters Leave Yemen for a New Life in Sweden."

the electoral body to announce election results, making it even easier for funny business in the upcoming presidential election. He has been in power for twenty-nine years.[10]

The world cheered when, after leading a long guerrilla war, Robert Mugabe led his Zanu party to victory at the elections in February of 1980, after Zimbabwe had won its independence from Britain. But he is no longer a global favorite and the opposition accuses him of destroying his country in a bid to stay in power. When Mugabe took power,

> He was particularly keen to win the trust of white commercial farmers. One of the most privileged groups in the country, numbering no more than 6,000 in all, they owned nearly 40 per cent of all agricultural land and two-thirds of the best land. Their role was regarded as crucial to the economic welfare of Zimbabwe. They accounted for three-quarters of the output of the agricultural industry and produced a multitude of crops and commodities using sophisticated techniques and equipment. They grew 90 per cent of marketed maize, the main staple; 90 per cent of cotton, the main industrial crop; and virtually all tobacco and other export crops, including wheat, coffee, tea and sugar, accounting in all for one-third of total exports. They employed about one-third of the wage-earning labour force—some 271, 000 people in 1980.[11]

However, "Land shortage and land degradation were deeply entrenched problems, left unresolved over decades of white rule and mounting inexorably as a result of population growth."[12] This led to the eviction of the white farmers from their land. The action caused huge economic crisis, which was heightened by a three-year drought that particularly impacted 400,000 people in Matabeleland.

The general economic, social, educational, and cultural conditions of Zimbabwe in the 90s became very gloom and unpromising:

> By the end of the 1990s Zimbabwe was in dire straits. The unemployment rate had risen to more than 50 per cent. Only one-tenth of the number of pupils leaving school were able to find formal employment. Inflation had reached 60 per cent. The value of wages in real terms had fallen over ten years by 22 per cent. On average, the population of 13 million was 10 per cent poorer at the end of the 1990s than at the beginning. More than 70 per cent lived in abject poverty. Hospitals were short of drugs and equipment; government schools were starved of funds; state corporations were bankrupt; the public transport system was decrepit; fuel supplies were erratic; scores of businesses have closed. Harare, once renowned as one of the cleanest cities in Africa, was noted now for debris on the pavements, cracked cement pavements, broken street lights, potholes, uncollected refuse and burst pipelines. Street crime was endemic.[13]

The Mugabe administration has been criticized around the world for corruption, suppression of political opposition, mishandling of land reform, economic mismanagement, and the deteriorating human-rights situation in Zimbabwe. He is now sharing

---

10. Tchouteu-Chando and Chando, *Paul Biya*.
11. Meredith, *Fate of Africa*, 618.
12. Ibid., 619.
13. Ibid., 634–35.

power, but remains president. He was a student at University of Fort Hare, University of South Africa, University of London, University of Oxford, and Kutama College.

He qualified as a teacher, but left to study at Fort Hare in South Africa, graduating in 1951, while meeting contemporaries such as Julius Nyerere, Herbert Chitepo, Robert Sobukwe, and Kenneth Kaunda. He then studied at Salisbury (1953), Gwelo (1954), and Tanzania (1955–1957). Originally graduating with a Bachelor of Arts degree from the University of Fort Hare in 1951, Mugabe subsequently earned six further degrees through distance learning including a Bachelor of Administration and Bachelor of Education from the University of South Africa and a Bachelor of Science, Bachelor of Laws, Master of Science, and Master of Laws, all from the University of London External Program. The two law degrees were earned while he was in prison, the Master of Science degree earned during his premiership of Zimbabwe.[14] His accumulation of degrees from the Western education curriculum can make him a demonstrable case of the unintelligent intellectual African who cannot relate his studies to his situation. In addition, his education has not spared him from being one of the many corrupt African leaders. He has been in power for twenty-seven years.

President José Eduardo Dos Santos of Angola, nick-named the "quiet dictator," came to power in September 1979. He assumed power on the death of Angola's first president, Agostinho Neto. Dos Santos has been accused of leading one of the most corrupt regimes in Africa by ignoring the economic and social needs of Angola while focusing his efforts on amassing wealth for his family and silencing his opposition. In Angola, nearly 70% of the population lives on less than $2 a day and yet he and his family have amassed a massive sum of wealth, with stakes in international corporations as well as the leading businesses of the nation. But for much of the time after he came to power, he ruled only over half the country, as his MPLA fought a civil war against The National Union for the Total Independence of Angola (UNITA). Now, with the war over, and UNITA crushed at the parliamentary elections of 1992, he is being called on to hold an election for the presidency. No firm date has yet been set. Since then, he has been manipulating the weak opposition. He has been in power for thirty-five years.[15] During Santos's time in power he has watched his people struggling economically living on $2 a day:

> A large portion of Angola's oil wealth was siphoned off for private purposes. Oil production rose six fold after 1983. Between 1997 and 2002 the oil sector generated $17.8 billion. Yet what happened to the income was shrouded in secrecy. An International Monetary Fund report in 2002 showed that 22 per cent of government expenditure between 1996 and 2001 was "unexplained"; a further 16 per cent was listed as "extra-budgetary." Using IMF figures, a Human Rights Watch report published in 2004 calculated that between 1997 and 2002 an amount of $4.2 billion went "unaccounted for"—an average of $700 million a year, nearly 10 per cent of gross domestic product, roughly equivalent to the total sum spent on education, health and social services over the same period. What

---

14. See Chan, *Robert Mugabe*; Arnold, *Robert Mugabe's Zimbabwe*.

15. See *Angola President José Eduardo dos Santos Handbook* (World Strategic and Business Information Library).

had occurred said the report, was gross mismanagement and corruption on the part of Angola's rulers.[16]

President Teodoro Obiang Nguema came to power in Equatorial Guinea in August 3, 1979, and deposed his uncle, Francisco Macias Nguema, in a violent coup d'état, supported by 600 mercenaries licensed from Hassan II of Morocco.[17] Francisco fled but was later captured and executed. Despite its new-found oil wealth, 60 percent of the people of Equatorial Guinea live on less than a dollar a day. The local media said the voters clearly all love President Nguema, as he won 97 percent of the vote at the last election in 2002. He's now the longest serving President in Africa.

Equatorial Guinea is a small country of West Africa, which has recently struck oil and which is now being cited as a textbook case of the resource curse—or the paradox of plenty. Since the mid-1990s the former Spanish colony has become one of sub-Sahara's biggest oil producers and in 2004 was said to have the world's fastest-growing economy.

The country has exasperated a variety of rights organizations that have described the two post-independence leaders as among the worst of human rights abusers in Africa. Francisco Macias Nguema's reign of terror—from the country's independence in 1968 until his overthrow in 1979—prompted a third of the population to flee. Apart from allegedly committing genocide against the Bubi ethnic minority, he ordered the death of thousands of suspected opponents, closed down churches, and presided over the economy's collapse.

His successor—Teodoro Obiang Nguema Mbasogo—took over in a coup and has shown little tolerance for opposition during the three decades of his rule. While the country is nominally a multiparty democracy, elections have generally been considered a sham.

Equatorial Guinea has emerged as one of Africa's largest oil producers, skyrocketing to its current position as the wealthiest per-capita country in Africa. Despite those statistics, World Bank estimates that some 78 percent of Guineans live beneath the national poverty line. Few people have benefited from the oil riches and the country ranks near the bottom of the UN human development index. The UN says that less than half the population has access to clean drinking water and that 20 percent of children die before reaching five years of age. Equatorial Guinea is oil rich, but its people are poor.[18] This is not the unusual paradox of *most* African countries.

"United States policy towards Teodoro Nguema Obiang Mbasogo, the dictator/president of Spanish-speaking Equatorial Guinea, is a perfect case study in the hypocrisy of Western leaders when it comes to African strongmen. Even as Hillary Clinton wraps up her five country African tour promoting democracy and good governance, as representatives of her government and international development organizations continue to

---

16. Meredith, *Fate of Africa*, 613–14.

17. "Equatorial Guinea enjoyed only 145 days of independence before it was pitched into a nightmare of brutality and coercion that lasted for eleven years." For detailed information on Francisco Marcias Nguema, read ibid., 238–41.

18. BBC: Equatorial Guinea profile, 21 March 2014.

ignore many corrupt practices in oil-rich, democracy-poor Equatorial Guinea."[19] Teodoro Nguema Obiang Mbasogo has been in power for nearly thirty-six years.

Jean-Bedel Bokassa's career as a dictator of Central African Republic (CAR) combined not only extreme greed and personal violence but delusions of grandeur unsurpassed by any other African leader. His excesses included having seventeen wives, a score of mistresses and an official brood of fifty-five children. He was prone to towering rages as well as outbursts of sentimentality; and he also gained a reputation for cannibalism. He liked to describe himself as an "absolute monarch" and forbade mention of the words democracy and election. He promoted himself first to the rank of general and then to marshal, for "supreme services to the State." For public appearance he insisted on wearing so many medals and awards that special uniforms had to be designed for him to accommodate them. He delighted in naming after himself a host of schools, hospitals, clinics, roads, and development projects as well as Bangui's new university. The front page of every school exercise book in the entire country was adorned with his picture. He adored the ceremony of state visit and toured the world a number of times taking with him large retinues of assistants and distributing gifts of diamonds to his hosts. His every whim became government policy. He himself held twelve ministerial portfolios and interfered in all the others. He controlled all of the decision-making, administering every promotion or demotion, reward or punishment.[20]

Bokassa's brutal fourteen-year rule, including two years as his country's self-proclaimed emperor, ended in 1979 when French paratroopers overthrew his government while he was on an official trip to Libya. While he was in power, "the French, keen to ensure that the Central African Republic remained within the French orbit, continued to underwrite Bokassa's regime with financial and military support,"[21] until they overthrow him. When he exited Bokassa left a ravaged, impoverished, and failed state.

> One illiterate, savage and unprincipled militant after the other has been causing death and horror to the citizens of CAR, particularly to those who live in major cities like Bangui. Françoise Korako describes how uniformed fighters of Sêlêka crushed her husband's head with rifle butts. His limp body was left bleeding outside her home in Dekoa, a farming village 260 kilometers (162 miles) north of Bangui, the capital, as a warning to anyone else who might challenge them. Sêlêka, meaning "alliance" in Sango, one of the languages of the Central African Republic (CAR), has ruled the country with exemplary brutality since it ousted Françoise Bozizé in March 2013, when he fled for his life to neighboring Cameroon. This followed a three-month advance from Sêlêka's stronghold in the north to Bangui and in the south. On their way, the rebels raped and pillaged unhindered.
>
> Now ensconced as the government, they are far from reposing a modicum of law and order, let alone democracy. At least ten people were killed in clashes that started on August 20th and spread across Bangui, between supporters of the former president and Sêlêka fighters trying to disarm pro- Bozizé people in

---

19. *Morningside Post*, August 7, 2012.
20. See Meredith, *Fate of Africa*, 224–31.
21. Ibid., 227.

their Boy-Rabe stronghold in the capital. The CAR is on its way to becoming a failed state.[22]

Mezayev adds:

> The Central African Republic contains troops from a whole number of countries (Chad, Cameroon, Congo, Gabon and the RSA) which should assist the authorities in restoring legitimate authority. However, since the army has switched over to side with the coupists, the situation has changed. A couple of other "helpers" in overthrowing the government should also be mentioned—France (who sent in nearly 600 servicemen) and the USA (who sent in more than one hundred military advisers).
>
> The Central African Republic directly, borders several "problem" regions in Africa. Firstly, the north of the country is under the control of Chadian rebel groups; secondly, the east borders the Sudan province of Darfur and, finally, to the south of the country is the Democratic Republic of Congo and its rebels. To the southeast of the Central African Republic, the notorious Ugandan "Lord's Liberation Army" is in operation (whose leaders are being hunted by both the Ugandan government and the International Criminal Court). All of this compounds the situation considerably.
>
> The Central African Republic is a real storehouse of natural resources. One of its main treasures is diamonds, deposits of which are present in 40 percent of the country. The country also has reserves of gold. France has been removing gold from the Central African Republic since 1930. However, while more than a tonne per year was being extracted in the 1960s, these days reserves have virtually been exhausted (2–10kg are extracted per year). There are also large deposits of copper and tin but, most importantly, the resource that remains virtually untouched in the Central African Republic is uranium. Known reserves of uranium amount to nearly 15,000 tonnes of ore. France is planning to build a uranium plant with an output of 1,000 tonnes of uranium concentrate. That is quite serious grounds for interfering in the restoration of constitutional order...
> The new head of state's first step was to appeal to France, the USA and the EU for financial help and promise to revise the agreements that François Bozizé had entered into with China.[23]

Time and again, what one encounters in Africa is not lack of natural resources that could have been turned into industry and capital. The wealth has great potential to be used enormously to improve the living standard of Africans, the quality and structure of education, and the salaries of teachers, soldiers, and civil service workers. It could also be used to enhance the value and availability of technological development, health care, transportation, and communication. The continent is lacking leaders who see emerging African intellectuals as a great asset for the effectiveness of their leadership and for the growth and development of African countries rather than a lethal threat to them and the society. As you have seen so far, Africans are suffering and dying sitting on all kinds of minerals and energy resources. What Africa lacks are astute, far-sighted, visionary, accountable, and empowering leaders.

---

22. "Central African Republic."
23. Mezayev, "Central African Republic."

> Swaziland, which is about 85 percent the size of New Jersey, is surrounded by South Africa and Mozambique. The country is largely mountainous. "The geology of Swaziland is complex and diverse and minerals of economic importance include asbestos, iron, gold, diamonds, coal, green chert and various others which have been mined in the past. Currently there are several viable mining options— in particular the national coal reserve is reported to be substantial development of which may lead to increased pressure on the environment through impacts on landscapes and ecosystems, waste accumulation, surface and ground water contamination, life rehabilitation and environmental health."[24] King Mswati III of Swaziland runs his country in free-spending ways. "His vast household includes his 14 wives and their children, as well as countless courtiers. Public spending is rising, much of it going on to upkeep of 13 royal palaces and the security services. Tax receipts depend heavily on the sugar industry but its output is falling . . . At least 31% of adults in the 1.2 million populations have HIV, the highest infection rate in the world. More than a quarter of the workforces is jobless. Corruption is rife; courts are unreliable.[25]

This is what the leadership scenario of African countries looks like. It is impossible to cover all African leaders of the postcolonial era and the social havoc and economic crisis they brought to a continent that enriches the world and impoverishes her own children. In Africa there is no lack of intrigue, bloodshed, coups, zeal, and energy to take the top leadership post of a country. "In the first two decades of independence, there were some forty successful coups and countless attempted coups."[26]

Calderisi writes,

> In the mid-1990s, a tide of political liberties finally seemed to rise across Africa; but hope quickly faded, even among sympathetic observers. The new leaders simply picked up where the old one left off. In early 1998, when Bill Clinton made the first trip of a US president to Africa in 20 years, a fresh generation of politicians was being hailed as precursors of the "African Renaissance." They were Yoweri Museveni (Uganda), Paul Kagame (Rwanda), Meles Zenawi (Ethiopia), Isaias Afewerki (Eretria), and Thabo Mbeki (South Africa). They were an odd group. While modern in some respects, all but Mbeki had risen to power through the barrel of a gun. Within a year of Clinton's visit Museveni and Kagame had invaded the eastern Congo, ostensibly to chase down former members of the extremist Hutu militia responsible for the 1994 genocide of 800,000 Rwandans, but also to plunder gold and other resources suddenly available for the taking. Within two years, Ethiopia and Eritrea were warring over a piece of barren land along their borders. Ten thousand young Ethiopians were sent to their deaths in a single battle, rushing the Eritrean front lines.[27]

Commenting on both the first- and second-generation African leaders, Ayittey writes, "These leaders turned the office of the presidency into their own personal

---

24. Commission of the European Communities (CEC), "Swaziland Country Environment Profile (Draft Report),," June 2006, http://www.eeas.europa.eu/delegations/swaziland/documents/eu_swaziland/swaziland_country_environment_profile_june_2006.pdf.

25. "Swaziland's Election."

26. Meredith, *Fate of Africa*, 218.

27. Calderisi, *Trouble with Africa*, 59.

property. Any attempt to remove them from power for incompetence was derided as 'an imperialist/neocolonial plot.' Ask these leaders about the causes of Africa's problems and they will wax eloquent on colonialism, American imperialism, the pernicious effects of slavery, the unjust international economic system, and exploitation by multinational corporations. Of course, they will never mention their own incompetence and pursuance of wrong-headed policies. Obviously, without a proper diagnosis black African problems cannot be solved."[28]

There are plenty who come to power through "the barrel of a gun" are plenty in Africa. But there are none who write an enduring, functional, and democratic constitution that protects the rights and freedom of Africans. Undemocratic leadership that lacks civility, integrity, and intellectual, emotional, and simple common sense cannot create a society that can conquer poverty, ignorance, hatred, conflict, despair, and self-doubt. Confucius was right when he said, "In ruling a country of a thousand chariots, there should be scrupulous attention to business, honesty, economy, charity, and employment of the people at the proper season. A virtuous ruler is like a pole-star, which keeps its place while all the other stars do homage to it. People despotically governed and kept in order by punishments may avoid infraction of the law, but they will lose their moral sense. People virtuously governed and kept in order by the inner law of self-control will retain their moral sense, and moreover become good...Conduct yourself towards them with dignity, and you will earn their respect; be a good son and a kind prince, and you will find them loyal; promote the deserving and instruct those who fall short, and they will be encouraged to follow the path of virtue."[29] "Africans should begin to study the causes of civilian survival with as much earnestness as any have studied the causes of civilian collapse," said Mazrui.[30] He adds, "Each African country has also to be fair to its citizens, providing a healthier climate of freedom and opportunity for them. Only such congenial conditions at home in Africa could reduce the volume and scale of the second Bantu migration, set in our own time."[31] African leaders do the opposite and the result of their leadership has been to spread greed, misery, poverty, anarchy, and chaos. It has marred the global image of the continent and the African people.

Corruption

"A report prepared for the African Union in 2002 estimated that corruption costs Africa $148 billion annually—more than a quarter of the continent's entire gross domestic product."[32] John Emerich Edward Dalberg-Acton is famous for his remark, "Power tends to corrupt, and absolute power corrupts absolutely. Great men are almost always bad men."[33] This statement is a living truth in the history of Africans leadership. In

28. Ayittey, *Africa Betrayed*, 23.
29. Quoted in G. Garret, *Analectics of Confucius*, 1.
30. Mazrui, *Africans*, 184.
31. Mazrui, *African Condition*, 17.
32. Meredith, *Fate of Africa*, 687.
33. Gary Martin, "Power Corrupts; absolute power corrupts absolutely," Phrase Finder, 1996–2015, http://www.phrases.org.uk/meanings/absolute-power-corrupts-absolutely.html.

all corners of African countries the "Big Men" are bad and corrupt. Based on facts, I have made my best attempt to show the seemingly incurable societal cancer in Africa: corruption. It has killed more Africans than slavery and colonialism combined. It has caused diaspora and tilted the balance of justice within the continent. In the absence of moral value and ethics African leaders are turned into a stumbling block for progress and a nemesis to the people they lead. "Africa is in crisis. Governments are unstable, economies are under strain, infrastructures are decaying . . . The present generation of Africans has worked out a compact with the twentieth century—but a compact which is essentially dishonourable and disloyal to the principle of indigenous authenticity. The result has been Westernisation without modernisation. Africa has Western-style armies which are staging military coups. Western-style police forces which are failing in law enforcement. Western-style bureaucracies which are increasingly *corrupt*, and Western-style agricultural plans which are deficient and unproductive . . . Africa is bleeding; the continent is starving."[34]

Among all African social malaises corruption is the most epidemic and it is engrained in the personalities of those who have positions to serve and are expected to bring positive and lasting changes. "Africa is widely considered among the world's most corrupt places, a factor seen as contributing to the stunted development and impoverishment of many African states. Of the ten countries considered most corrupt in the world, six are in sub-Saharan Africa, according to Transparency International, a leading global watchdog on corruption . . . To compare, developed countries gave $22.5 billion in aid to sub-Saharan Africa in 2008, according to the Organization for Economic Cooperation and Development."[35] Is corruption in Africa unique? Is it isolated from the global context? Is corruption Africa's problem only? It is very important to answer these questions first, in order to fairly and intelligently analyze the corruption within the continent that paralyzed various developments and impoverished Africans.

Laurence Cockcroft, in his book *Global Corruption: Money, Power and Ethics in the Modern World*, explored the nature of corruption across the world, the forces that drive it forward, and the roadblocks to combating it. Many of the issues discussed in his book are common to a range of countries. He particularly focused on five key drivers. The first is the size of the "unrecorded economy"—in many countries from Russia to Nigeria unrecorded transactions amount to at least 40 percent of GDP, constituting a vast reservoir from which corrupt payments can be made without trace. The second is the system of "political finance," by which huge sums of money, often gained corruptly, are invested in the political process with the expectation of a corruptly gained reward once power is secured or resecured. This is easily discernible in most political systems from the U.S. to India. The third is the role of organized crime in securing political support and cover for trading operations ranging from drugs to counterfeit pharmaceuticals—a recognized practice from Italy to Thailand. The fourth is the role of national and international companies in the "mispricing" of products that enable a large chunk of profits to be moved to havens where tax is low or non-existent—a common phenomenon from Russia to Peru. The last is the system by which illegally and corruptly gained products—such as

---

34. Mazrui, *Africans*, 201; emphasis added.
35. Hansen, "Corruption in Sub-Saharan Africa."

oil, timber, and rare minerals—transit from the illegal sector to the legal sector, such as timber from Cambodia or counterfeit drugs in south East Asia.

By these criteria, corruption in Africa is very much part of an international pattern. Some of the illegal diamond trade operated by the African and international companies that we looked at previously concur with Cockcroft's observation.

> A colorful trafficking has spread across north Africa since the Arab awakening two years ago. Smuggling of eggs from Tunisia is now such a big business that some Tunisians fear they will run out at home. A brisk trade in European cars via Libyan ports enables many people to doge import duties. A fifth of Egypt's subsidized fuel is now sold on by smugglers.
>
> The region's government has become especially annoyed by the growing drug trade. Algeria seized 50 tonnes of cannabis in the first half of the year and 79 tonnes last year—almost twice as much as in 2008. That is partly a crackdown by authorities, but drug networks have proliferated through the country and trades have refined their methods thanks to closer collaboration with international criminals.[36]

In a telling case in 2008, for example, German multinational Siemens was found to have had a slush fund totaling more than €1.3 billion ($1.7 billion) to help win overseas contracts from 2001 to 2007. The company was investigated for bribe-paying, corruption, and falsifying corporate books and, after much plea bargaining and negotiating, was fined a record $800 million.

This kind of corruption can sometimes also be part and parcel of African corruption in that such companies are on the lesser-examined supply side of bribes while African governments are on the demand side. In 2010, for instance, BAE[37] Systems, one of the world's largest defense contractors, pled guilty to criminal charges regarding contracts won from countries including Tanzania and South Africa. BAE was investigated by the UK's Serious Fraud Office in a long-running case and ended up paying £286 million ($460 million) in fines.[38] Corruption in Africa has a multidimensional face. Its external scope encompasses almost all the regions of the world. The internal involves the Arab, white, Chinese, Indian, and more as well as black Africans.

Equatorial Guinea as we looked at earlier is rich with natural resources, particularly oil. However, the revenue that the country generates is enriching the long-time president instead of the citizens.

> Obiang's personal fortune is estimated to be about $600 million, largely from oil wealth. There have been multiple U.S. investigations of corruption and abuses against the Obiang regime and against members of his family. In 2011, the United States' Department of Justice made moves to seize more than $70 million in assets from President Obiang's son, Teodorin Nguema Obiang Mangue. Justice Department lawyers alleged Nguema used his position as a minister in Equatorial Guinea to amass more than $100 million through corruption and money laundering, on top of his official government salary of $100,000. The complaints

---

36. "Trafficking in North Africa."
37. British Aerospace Electronic Systems
38. Lewis, "Corruption in Africa."

stated Nguema possessed among his assets a $30 million dollar mansion in Malibu, California, a $38.5 million Gulfstream jet, and more than $2 million in Michael Jackson memorabilia. U.S. Assistant Attorney General Lanny Breuer stated that "While his people struggled, he [Nguema] lived the high life.... we are sending the message loud and clear: the United States will not be a hiding place for the ill-gotten riches of the world's corrupt leaders."

Just last week, agents of the French government seized Nguema's $124 million Paris villa. French authorities have issued an international search warrant for Obiang, on allegations that he, his father, and other African leaders are using illicit state assets to buy property in France.[39]

Paul Biya, in power in Cameroon for thirty years, is partly sustained by the export of illegally felled logs from Cameroon's vast forest reserves. Key politicians in Guinea-Conakry and Guinea-Bissau have become active partners with Colombian drug cartels in the trans-shipment of cocaine to Europe. In Nigeria, oil "bunkering" from the Delta enriches both local and national players in the government and the army—a classic case of illegally acquired products entering the world's legal trade through the Rotterdam market. The price at which Tanzania's booming mineral exports—notably gold, platinum, and uranium—enter the world market is controversial and secret. In Zimbabwe, Robert Mugabe has been maintained in power by an elite group with strong ties to the military. This group once extended its tentacles to the DRC and does so now in the domestic diamond mining industry, the output of which goes largely unrecorded.

Bokassa, who likes to be described as "absolute monarch," was an absolutely corrupt leader.

Using government funds at will and fortunes he made from diamond and ivory deals, Bokassa acquired a whole string of valuable properties in Europe, including four chateaux in France, a fifty-room mansion in Paris, houses in Nice Toulouse and a villa in Berne. He built a huge "ancestral home" at Berengo, fifty miles from Bangui, and ordered a motorway to be built to it. The presidential estate there included private houses and apartments for foreign visitors furnished with reproduction antique furniture and gilt mirrors . . . Bokassa declared the Central African Republic an empire and himself emperor of its 2 million subjects and made elaborate arrangements for his coronation, using a model the ceremony in which Napoleon had crowned himself emperor of France in 1804. From France he ordered all the trappings of a monarchy: a crown of diamonds; an imperial throne, shaped like a golden eagle; an antique coach; thoroughbred horses; coronation robes; brass helmets and breastplates for the Imperial Guard; tons of food, wine, fireworks and flowers for the festivities and sixty Mercedes-Benz cars for the guests . . . the spectacle of Bokassa's lavish coronation, costing $22 million, in a country with few government services, huge infant mortality, widespread illiteracy, only 260 miles of paved roads and in serious economic difficulty, aroused universal criticism.[40]

Kenya boasts to have an eighty percent Christian population. On Sundays, it is not uncommon to see former president Moi attending different churches, seated at the front

---

39. *Morningside Post*, August 7, 2012.
40. Meredith, *Fate of Africa*, 226, 228.

row. However, under his rule, before or after, Kenya is one of the most corrupt African countries in the Horn of Africa. Like the faith of the colonial powers, his Christianity hardly shows in his style of leadership, ethics, and fair treatment of human beings. "I would like minsters, assistant ministers and others to sing like a parrot after me. That is how we can progress," he said in 1984. "He curtailed the autonomy of judges, and the auditor-general, eliminating their security of tenure; he harassed and imprisoned dissidents, condoning the use of torture; he obliterated press freedoms, muzzled trade unions and turned the civil service into a party machine."[41]

> One of the pledges that the National Rainbow Coalition (NRC) government made when it came to power at the end of 2002 was to fight corruption in every way possible. It was with this in mind that President Mwai Kibaki appointed the Goldenberg Commission of Inquiry on Feb. 24, 2003.
>
> The commission was charged with fully investigating the Goldenberg export compensation scandal, which cost Kenya billions of shillings in the early 1990s. According to witnesses at the commission's hearings, as much as 60 billion Kenyan shillings (US$850 million)—a fifth of Kenya's gross domestic product—was looted from the country's Central Bank through billionaire Kamlesh Pattni's Exchange Bank in 1991.
>
> Pattni, it emerged, exploited a government scheme designed to revitalize Kenya's faltering economy in the years surrounding the first Gulf War. In 1990, hoping to persuade exporters to repatriate their hard currency earnings, the government promised a 20-percent premium on foreign currency deposited in Kenya's Central Bank. Claiming that his company, Goldenberg International, was processing gold and diamonds for export, Pattni was able to manipulate loopholes in the system with the help of government officials. He made an agreement allowing the company to earn up to 35 percent compensation for the export of minerals that did not exist.[42]

The Anglo Leasing Scandal, also known as Anglo-fleecing, is the popular name for a corruption scandal in Kenya. The scandal is alleged to have started when the Kenyan government wanted to replace its passport printing system, in the year 2002. A sophisticated passport equipment system was sourced from France and forensic science laboratories for the police were sourced from Britain. The transaction was originally quoted at €6 million from a French firm, but was awarded to a British firm, Anglo Leasing Finance, at €30 million, who would have sub-contracted the same French firm to do the work. The tender was not publicly advertised, and its details were leaked to the media by a junior civil servant. The Anglo-Leasing sales agent was Sudha Ruparell, a forty-eight-year-old woman who is the daughter of Chamanlal Kamani and sister of Rashmikant Chamanlal Kamani and Deepak Kamani. The Kamani family has been involved in various security supplies scandals in the past. In January 2006, the Anglo Leasing Scandal was given fresh impetus through the publication of John Githongo's report. The new revelations indicate that Anglo Leasing Finance was just one of a plethora of phantom entities, including some UK companies, used to perpetrate fraud on the Kenyan taxpayer through non-delivery of goods and services and massive overpricing.

41. Ibid., 385.
42. Karanja, "Corruption Scandal."

The then-British envoy to Kenya, Sir Edward Clay, publicly raised the issue of Anglo Leasing at a dinner in Nairobi. He subsequently came under pressure from Kenyan politicians to make public his evidence, and was reported to have provided the President, Mwai Kibaki, with a dossier containing details of corruption in the government. However, no one was punished and the case slipped from the public eye.

Kenya's minister in charge of the project, Chris Murungaru, was later banned by the UK government from travelling to Britain, on the grounds that it would not be in the public good. It was widely reported that the ban was due to corruption by Mr. Murungaru involving, among others, the Anglo-Leasing scam.

On January 22, 2006, John Githongo named Vice-President Moody Awori as one of four top politicians (with Kiraitu Murungi, former justice minister and later energy minister; finance minister David Mwiraria; and former transport minister Chris Murungaru) as being involved. Public sympathy for Githongo reached its peak when he released audio recordings of an incriminating conversation with David Mwiraria on the internet. One of the tapes is still available (in Nairobi). He also claimed that President Mwai Kibaki was complicit in the affair. Githongo claimed that the money raised would have funded the then-government's forthcoming 2005 Constitutional Referendum and 2007 Election campaign.[43]

The economic consequence of a scandal of such magnitude on the citizens is enormous and unbearable:

> Taxpayers are set to lose in excess of Sh1.6 billion in awards and penalties in Anglo Leasing scandal related suit, which was concluded in two European courts last year, a top official at the National Treasury has said. The suit, which the Kenyan Government lost in London and Swiss courts on December 20, has attracted $7.6 million and $10.6 million in awards respectively. In addition, the Government will pay cumulative penalties of Sh276, 000 ($3,065) in interest per day for its failure to settle these cash awards. The penalties include Sh150, 000 ($1,665) per day on the outstanding $7.6 million award and Sh126, 000 ($1,400) per day on the unpaid $10.6 million award. . .Kenyan assets in the international markets run the risk of being attached including the proceeds of the planned $1.5 million sovereign bond.[44]

As if the Goldenberg and Anglo-leasing scandal were not enough for Kenyans, there were two other major scandals that caught the attention of Kenyans and Africans as well as the international community. They were the maize and education scandals:

> A flurry of activities surrounding the maize scandal—believed to have cost the taxpayer an estimated US$26.1 million (Sh2 billion)—since the Kenyan Prime Minister, Raila Odinga received the final forensic audit report on the saga, have pushed him to call for public patience to allow for its evaluation before he states his official position. Before the PM met journalists on the progress of the scandal which came to the public limelight only last year, on Monday internationally acknowledged auditors, PriceWaterhouse Coopers handed him a 366-page document which he received and assured he will make his position known. The

---

43. For a detailed understanding of this scandal, see Wrong, *It's Our Time to Eat*.
44. Anyanzwa, "Integrated Capital Markets Plan Hits New Headwinds."

following day, on Tuesday, the contents of the audit report were made public and Kenyan Agriculture Minister, William Ruto was named as the main culprit.

The scam was reported in 2008 when the government initiated the subsidized maize scheme to mitigate hunger that had ravaged over 10 million Kenyans. However the program was dogged with corruption allegations and inefficiencies. PWC's report shows evidence of briefcase traders who acted as go between with millers and raked millions of shillings. The Premier turned the heat on private companies that are mentioned to have bribed their way into the allocations and others who participated in 'trading' maize allocations that they too would be pursued.[45]

The Education Minister, Professor Sam Ongeri, has been accused of being involved in the funds scandals involving 4.2 billion shillings meant for free primary education. The embezzlement of these funds was revealed through a recent government audit. Professor Ongeri stated that it was he who had started the forensic audit but in this entire politically-motivated episode, he has been reduced from a "hunter to the one who is hunted."[46]

In Africa in general and Kenya in particular, tribalism has become a reverse apartheid. *It's Our Turn to Eat* refers to a tribal group who are in power because of president Kibaki who is from the Kikuyu tribe. The presidents dole out ministerial and key government positions to those they think are in a "group." "During the Kenyatta era, the Kikuyu who accounted for 20.8 per cent of the population, claimed between 28.6 and 31.6 percent of cabinet seats—far more than their fair share—while the Kalenjin, accounting 11.5 percent of the population, claimed, held only between 4.8 and 9.6 per cent. With Moi's arrival, the Kikuyu share of cabinet posts fell to just 4 percent, while the Kalenjin's share soared to 22 per cent. It was a similar story with permanent secretaries, where the Kikuyu went from 37.5 per cent under Kenyatta to 8.7 per cent under Moi, while the Kalenjin went from 4.3 per cent to 34.8 per cent."[47] Meredith also observed:

> A tribalist at heart, coming from a subgroup of the minority Kalenjin, a language family, Moi handed out key posts to Kalenjin members and promoted Kalenjin interests at every opportunity, using state power to undermine the patronage networks of the old Kikuyu elite established during Kenyatta's regime and to cripple the business interest of his opponents. The business empire he constructed for himself and his sons included assets in transport, oil distribution, banking, engineering, and land. His inner circle known as the "Karbanet Syndicate" after his home town, became exceedingly rich, obtaining loans from banks and pension funds that they never intended to repay and huge kickbacks from government contracts. Foreign business men regularly complained of the bribes that Moi's regime demanded to enable them to start up business or to win contracts. A Nairobi business magazine Financial Review, which published reports in 1989 of political corruption in the coffee and tea industries, was swiftly

---

45. Kebaso, "Raila Odinga Embroiled in $26.1 Million Maize Scandal in Kenya." *Newstime Africa*, March 6, 2013.

46. "Kenya's Education Minister Caught in Allegations Related to Education Scandal," *VoxAfrica*, June 29, 2011, p. 43..

47. Wrong, *It's Our Time to Eat*, 52.

banned. A fake report scheme set up by Moi's cronies in 1991 cost the exchequer an estimated $600 million.[48]

Stephanie Hansen adds, "The experience of Kenya demonstrates how corruption can tip a seemingly stable country into political crisis. Kenyan analysts widely agree that the violence following the December 2007 elections, in which President Mwai Kibaki claimed victory over opposition candidate Raila Odinga, was in large part caused by the zero-sum nature of Kenyan politics: Unless one's ethnic group was in office, there were no possibilities for economic or political advancement."[49]

The great majority of those in positions of power trickles down to the development, educational opportunities, health care, etc., to benefit the political support base, which is the tribe of the ruling power. The growing divide between rich and poor in cosmopolitan cities of Kenya takes an ethnic line. "A Kikuyu in habitant in Nyeri, just north of Kibaki's constituency, could expect to live 23.4 years longer, on average, than his Luo counterpart in Raila's hometown of Kisumu. If 46 per cent of the population in Central Province had only limited access to a qualified doctor, the problem was nearly twice as bad—88 per cent in remote North-Eastern Province. Adult illiteracy, just 16.7 per cent in largely Kikuyu Thika, was 78.1 per cent in Bomet, a heavily Kalenjin Rift Valley town. And so it went on."[50] *The Economist* gives us a real and recent socioeconomic picture of Nairobi:

> Barely a mile away from the Capital Club, the arid fumes of charcoal fires in Kibera, a notorious slum, mingle with the stench of sewage running down the muddy alleys where perhaps 800,000 Nairobians live in a hugger-mugger squalor . . . Manual workers lucky enough to have a job in the metropolis can earn 200–300 shillings ($2–3) a day. Domestic and gang violence are rife. Armed police have a station at the entrance of Kibera, but generally keep out of the slum. Visitors are warned to watch out for robbers and "flying toilet"—bags of excrement chucked out of houses at night . . . These two Kenyans (the rich and the poor) exist cheek by jowl, both of them, in their way, equally dynamic. Half a century after independence from Britain, rich and poor are both locked into a system of patronage and tribe, all competing for advancement, whether for modest jobs in the civil service or for huge bribes to fix contracts for grand infrastructure projects. In the aftermath of a disputed election in 2007, Kibera, whose district are unofficially divided along the tribal lines, was affected as bloodily as anywhere.[51]

The gap between the rich and those who are eking out a living in its teeming slums is a major factor in the high rate of crime, including thievery both at night and in broad daylight. Security in Kenya is a big business. The way the houses are fenced and windows and doors are barred with iron grills demonstrates how residents are insecure in their own compounds and homes. Watchdogs, like Rottweilers and German Shepherds, are in high demand. "The crime rate has undoubtedly been rising. The UN, whose agencies have a large presence in the capital, reckon the number of burglaries in Nairobi doubled

48. Meredith, *Fate of Africa*, 384–85.
49. Hansen, "Corruption in Sub-Saharan Africa."
50. Wrong, *It's Our Time to Eat*, 282.
51. "Kenya: Trotting ahead."

to 300 from the last quarter of this year. Private security companies, who are reckoned to employ more than 100,000 people in Nairobi, are thriving. Evermore cameras' fences and walls are going up, with barbed wire strung along the top. Some robbers dressed as guards, have taken over entire residential compounds and methodically cleaned out all the houses."[52]

"In 2004, the British envoy to Kenya Sir Edward Clay complained about rampant corruption in the country, commenting that Kenya's corrupt ministries were 'eating like gluttons' and vomiting on the shoe of foreign donors. In February 2005 (prodded to make a public apology for his statements given the political maelstrom his earlier comments had made), he apologized—saying he was sorry for the 'moderation' of his language, for underestimating the scale of looting and for failing to speak out earlier."[53] (Moyo 2009:48). Had Edward Clay been John Githongo, he could have been jailed, exiled, or murdered. In Africa truth and justice are crucified. Despite her dismal record in corruption, "Kenya is one of the world leading countries in terms of the funds it get from the United States for combating terrorism. But the government of both countries, disappointed with the results have reduced their level of co-operation."[54]

Corruption in Africa is not limited to the black race as I have tried to indicate. It is also rampant among the Arab-African countries.

> [Algeria] has the world's 13th-biggest foreign-currency reserves. It has vast natural resources mainly of oil and gas. It has a well-educated youth population. But the overwhelming mood for the 38 million people is one of frustration and a woeful lack of development.
>
> The government is spending $286 billion over five years to build new schools, roads and hospitals in an attempt to create jobs by diversifying the economy away from oil and gas, which provide the bulk of state revenues, but the effort is stumbling. The unemployment rate may be as high as 40%. Many of Algeria's 1.5m students will fail—and, when they graduate, have to work in the field for which they have been trained. Algeria imports almost all of its basic goods.
>
> Across the country, Algerians complain about corruption. A scandal involving bribes at Sonatrach, the dominant state owned oil company is particularly aggravating . . . The country is ruled by Le Pouvoir (The Power), a cabal of decision-makers who fought for independence from France in 1962 . . . Abdelaziz Boutefilka, Algeria's president is 76 year old.[55]

Most Africans say their governments are failing in the fight against corruption, and many believe the situation has deteriorated in the last decade, according to the continent's most comprehensive survey of public opinion. John Allen gives us the following details:

> The survey also says nearly one in three Africans say they have paid a bribe in the past year, and almost one in five have paid it to a government official to get an official document or permit. The survey shows that corruption hits those living

52. "Security in Kenya."
53. Moyo, *Dead Aid*, 48.
54. Ibid.
55. "Algeria: Patience Persists."

in poverty the hardest, and police forces are the government institutions most often accused of taking bribes.

These are among the major findings of the latest Afrobarometer survey of public opinion in 34 countries. Afrobarometer is a research project coordinated by independent institutions in Ghana, Benin, Kenya and South Africa, with partners in 31 other countries. It says its surveys are based on nationally representative samples and thus represent the views of about three-quarters of Africans.

The newest report from the survey conducted between 2011 and 2013 was published in Dakar on Wednesday.

It says that 56 percent of the 51,000 people surveyed believe their governments are doing "fairly badly" or "very badly" in the fight against corruption. Only 35 percent say their governments are doing "fairly well" or "very well."

Nigerians and Egyptians are the most dissatisfied—82 percent in each country feel their governments are doing badly—followed by Zimbabweans (81 percent), Ugandans and Sudanese (76 percent), Kenyans (70 percent), Malians (69 percent), Tunisians (67 percent), Togolese, Tanzanians and South Africans (66 percent).

More than half of Liberians (63 percent) and Ghanaians (54 percent) also rated their governments' performances poorly. In Sierra Leone, less than half (44 percent) say their government is doing badly—although the survey also shows that Sierra Leoneans are top of the list in the proportion of citizens who say they have had to pay a bribe in the past year.

Malawians and the Basotho are the least dissatisfied with their governments over corruption, with 28 percent of people rating their governments poorly. In Botswana the figure is 29 percent, in Senegal 32 percent and in Niger 39 percent.

The report says that in the 16 countries surveyed since 2002, those who rate their governments' performances poorly rose from 46 percent to 54 percent of respondents. Perceptions of government performance worsened in 11 of the 16, with Kenya, Zimbabwe, Ghana and Tanzania doing worst.

In Kenya, only 11 percent of people said in 2003 the government was failing, but the figure rose to 70 percent in 2011. Afrobarometer attributed the 2003 figure to "public euphoria" after the 2002 election, in which an incumbent government was removed for the first time.

In Zimbabwe, negative ratings went up by 43 percentage points—from 38 percent in 2002 to 81 percent in 2012—and in Ghana by 31 points and Tanzania 25 points.

The most notable improvement was in Malawi, where those who gave their government negative ratings dropped by 40 percentage points (from 68 percent ratings to 28 percent). There were also improvements in perceptions in Lesotho (18 points), Botswana (11 points) and Senegal (10 points).

Other findings in the report:

- "Police attract the highest ratings of corruption across the 34 countries, with 43 percent of people saying that "most" or "all" of them are involved in corruption. Negative perceptions are highest in Nigeria (78 percent), Kenya (69 percent) and Sierra Leone (69 percent)."
- "Almost one in five people (18 percent) who had gone without enough food to eat one or more times in the past year had paid a bribe to a government official in the past year to obtain medical treatment, compared with just 12 percent among those who never went without food."

- "Almost half the people (46 percent) who go without enough food to eat one or more times a year rate "most" or "all" of police to be corrupt, compared to 39 percent among those who never go without food. And 31 percent of the poorest perceive judges and magistrates to be corrupt, compared to 24 percent among better off citizens."[56]

It is very important that I should not take my reader to another topic before I mention the corruption in South Africa after apartheid, and after Mandela in particular. For centuries, black South Africans' political and economic misery, the illiteracy rate, lack of jobs, bad governance, etc., have been attributed to racism and to the dominance and oppression of the minority whites. As I stated earlier, in large part this is true and that has been the unfortunate history of South Africa. In recent years, however, keen observers are forced to see racism as one facet of the Rainbow Nation. Thamo Beke and Jacob Zuma, the black South African leaders, have not proven to be Moses or Joshua leading the captives in bondage of slavery into the Promise Land. South African black leaders and very few in the black middle class are already in the "Promise Land enjoying the milk and honey," so to speak, "illegally." The majority of black Africans are still in the wilderness of poverty, crime, injustice, joblessness, and illiteracy, languishing in hunger and HIV infection. I say "illegally" because enriching oneself "illegally" does not mean that it is crime in South Africa's socioeconomic and political system. Since the judicial system is equally corrupt, there is no prosecution to face the consequence of financial scandal or abuse of authority. "What the Mandela years witnessed, in fact was a significant widening of the income gap within the black community. The gap had been growing since the late 1970s the black elite-politicians, bureaucrats, entrepreneurs, managers, businessmen—prospered as never before, many acquiring the lifestyle and status symbols so prized in South Africa—executive cars, swimming pools, domestic staff, private-school education, golf handicaps and foreign holidays. Perhaps 5 per cent of the black community reached middle-class status. But for the majority, the same struggle against poverty continued."[57] *The Economist* elaborates the widening economic gap among black South Africans:

> South Africa sits in the middle of international rankings of corruption. It is not Sweden but nor is it Zimbabwe. It has a free and impertinent press. Its constitution gave birth to bodies that check and balance the powers of government, and its judges back their freedoms to poke the executive in the eye.
>
> Indeed, the ruling African National Congress (ANC) has been checked-and-balanced recently rather more than usual. The public protector, a body created by the constitution, published a report last month that chastised the president, Jacob Zuma, as partly responsible for the 246m rand ($24m) lavished on his private home in Nkandla, in KwaZulu-Natal. When the Democratic Alliance, the main opposition party, sent a text message to 1.5m voters saying "the president stole your money," a court upheld its right to do so; the ANC is appealing against the judgment. Another court said Zwelinzima Vavi, a vocal critic of ANC corruption, should be reinstated as boss of the biggest union federation.[58]

56. "Africa: Governments Failing in Corruption Fight," John Allen, 13 November, 2013.
57. Meredith, *Fate of Africa*, 662.
58. "Corruption in South Africa."

The police are leading the record of corruption in South Africa.

> At times South Africa's police force seems rotten to the core—riddled with a corruption, crime, dirty tricks, political machinations and even murder... Last year, 5,869 formal complaints were laid against the police, mainly for assault and attempted murder. Police statistics concede that 556 people, including innocent bystanders, were shot dead or otherwise killed by the police in 2009–10; another 294 died in their custody. In the province of KwaZulu Natal an alleged police squad, known as the "Cato Mannor" unit, disbanded earlier this year after being accused of carrying out scores of assassinations of suspects. Some say the total number of the unit's victims runs into the hundreds. The rate of killing by South Africa's police is among the world's highest.
>
> Corruption is also rampant. In a survey last year by Transparency International, a Berlin-based anti-corruption watchdog, 68% of urban South Africans said the "police were extremely corrupt"; a further 14% called them "quite corrupt." In another survey, more than half of South Africa's motorists claimed traffic police had asked them for a bribe in previous 12 months.[59]

"One out of three South African girls will be raped before she turns 18. Almost three out of four South African women have been sexually abused at least once."[60]

Corruption obviously negatively impacts the GDP and economic growth of a nation.

> As most of Africa begins to prosper, the continents biggest economy is faltering. Figures released on May 28th showed the GDP in South Africa rose at an annualized rate of just 0.9% in the first quarter. A new report from the African Development Bank (ADB) and the OCED,[61] a rich country think-tank, trumpeting Africa's economic prospects, ranks South Africa's a lowly 48th out of 52 countries in terms of economic outlook. Yet South Africa's forecast 2.8% GDP growth for 2003 already looks too optimistic. The sustained 5% rate that the government says is needed to cut unemployment and poverty seems a world away...
>
> Yet there are plenty of hazards at home. South Africa has a current-account deficit of more than 6% of GDP. It relies on foreign capital to bridge the gap between what it spends and what it earns. That makes it vulnerable to shifts in investors' mood. And recent labor unrest has scared many off. Foreigners were net sellers of bonds and stock in the ten days to May 27th, according to the Johannesburg Stock Exchange's figures compiled by Citibank.
>
> Rivalry between unions sparked a recent wild cat strike at Lonmin's platinum mines in Marikana, where dozens of strikers were killed by police last August. Miners there have deserted the National Union of Mineworkers (NUM), whose top brass was seen as to cosy with mine bosses, for the Association of Mineworkers and Construction Union (AMCU), an upstart rival. Now the AMCU want the NUM kicked out of its offices at Lonmin's platinum mine, as it no longer represents most miners there. The fatal shooting of Mawethu Steven, an AMCU organizer, in a tavern on May 12th gave a sinister twist to the union's rivalry.

---

59. "South Africa's Police: Something Very Rotten."
60. Morley, "South Africa."
61. Office of Community & Economic Development.

> The NUM is part of the establishment: it is affiliated to the Congress of South African trade Unions (COSATU), a federation allied to the African National Congress (ANC), which governs South Africa. Yet it now faces a battle for relevance. Its response has been to bid for pay increases of 60% for entry-level workers and 15% for the rest. Other unions have joined in. The National Union of Metal Workers (NUMSA) wants 20% increase for all its members, many of whom work in the car industry. Such steep demands are unlikely to be readily met by employers. If they were, they would offset any cost advantage that exporters would gain from a cheaper rand. So further strikes seem likely . . .
>
> Joblessness is a particular problem for the young. The unemployment rate for those under 25 is 53%. Many are ill-prepared for work. Only 60% pass the matric, the high-school graduation certificate. One legacy of apartheid is that many blacks live far from where the jobs are. Even traveling to a job interview is costly because of poor public transport.[62]

The coming of a black person to power in South Africa, where the whole infrastructure of economy, parliament, constitution, civil service, army, and judicial system were built and run by the minority whites for centuries did not bring the changes and results that black South Africans fought for.

> The legacy of apartheid included a massive disparity in wealth. The average white income was eight times greater than that of the average black. Whites, comprising 13 per cent of the population, earned 61 per cent of total income. Although the black middle class was growing apace, its share of total income was still comparatively small. Barely 2 per cent of all private-sector assets were black-owned. According to calculations published in the United Nations Human Development report for 1994, if white South Africa was treated as a separate country, its standard of living would rank twenty-fourth in the world, just below Spain's; black South Africa on the same basis would rank one hundred twenty-third, below Lesotho and Vietnam. Overall, in terms of human development, South Africa ranked only ninety-third in the world. Out of a population of 40 million, 22, million lacked adequate sanitation, including 7.5 million in urban areas; 12 million lacked clean water supply; 23 million had no access to electricity; and some 2 million children were without schools. Almost half of all households in South Africa lived below the poverty line; a quarter lived on an income of less than half of the poverty-line income; some 8 million were estimated to be "completely destitute." One third of the population was illiterate.[63]

Unless one is blinded by ethnocentrism, racism, lack of information, biased knowledge of human history, or has an oscillating personality that cannot face reality as it is and stand for truth, black Africans can hardly say Africa's problem solely lies with the white atrocities of slave trade, colonialism, and neocolonialism. There is a huge problem of greed, corruption, lawlessness, and injustice within Africa. "South Africa suffered from one of the highest crime rates in the world."[64] That is after apartheid.

---

62. "South Africa's Economy."
63. Meredith, *Fate of Africa*, 648–49.
64. Ibid., 674.

Military Rulers and Coups d'États

The involvement of the military in African politics was gradual. In the first decade of independence, soldiers were barely seen in public, much less in politics. Traditionally, Africans were not used to military institutions. There were generally no standing armies in indigenous Africa, except in the Asante, Dahomey, Zulu, and Muslim states. For the rest of Africans—more than 2,000 tribes—the people constituted the army. In the event of imminent war, self-trained military leaders lead them into battle. After the cessation of hostilities, the "people's army" was disbanded so that it did not act as a drain on the tribal economy. Standing armies were introduced into Africa by the colonialist to enforce their rule and suppress African aspirations for freedom. Armies were thus viewed as agents of imperialism and instruments of oppression. Widespread discriminatory practices also compounded African's distrust and abhorrence of the military. For example, although Ghana had a relatively large educated elite in 1957, only about 10 percent of the army officers were native Ghanaians. In the Belgian Congo in 1960 the *Force Publique* had no African officers to lead its 24,000 recruits. Additionally, many African nationalists, such as Felix Houphouet-Boigny of the Ivory Coast and the Julius Nyerere of Tanzania, opposed an expansion of military establishment.[65]

As independent African countries take the patterns of the Western government system and adopt them in the African continent, the need for building military power has become necessary.

The scar and impact of military conquest on the minds of the Africans and elite leaders is still fresh.

Four causes contributed to the growth of the military and its intervention in the African politics: 1) The increasing recognition of the role of the military in pan-Africanism that was directly attributable to the Kwame Nkrumah of Ghana. He maintained that there was a need to establish an All-African Command Guard, not only to liberate the other colonies, but to fight the forces of imperialism and racism throughout the African continent. 2) The second factor was the self-preservation of the elites in power. The popularity of postcolonial governments began to wane because of human rights abuses and suppression of civil liberties. 3) The third factor that accelerated military intervention in government was the nationalist's generally lackluster and scandalous performance on the economic and political fronts. Virtually all of the nationalists who led the struggle became heads of their respective African states. But in practically every case, they led their countries down the path of economic ruin. 4) The fourth and final factor accounting for increasing military participation in African government was purely selfish—personal ambitions became dominant. Acting like any other politically vocal group, the military sought to increase its own share of government largesse through intimidation, blackmail, and the forcible takeover of the government itself.[66]

Edgerton adds, Military Coups D'états have a long and bloody history. They have occurred in almost every part of the world, including many parts of Europe.

---

65. Ayittey, *Africa Betrayed*, 135–36.
66. Ibid., 136–37.

And although they are most often associated with Latin America—making "junta" a familiar part of the world's lexicon—they have also taken place in staunchly democratic countries. In Greece, for example, there were five successful military takeovers of the government between 1925 and 1936. Another coup by Greek "colonels" led to a military government in 1967 that lasted until 1974. Since independence, African governments have been especially vulnerable to military coups, with over seventy successful military seizures of power taking place since 1957, and there were many others that failed as early as 1968, there were sixty-four attempted coups, twenty-six of them successful, four in Dahomey alone (now known as Benin), and three each in Nigeria and Sierra Leone. From 1963 to 1969, Dahomey had twelve governments and six constitutions. Today only five of the fifty-four countries in sub-Saharan Africa have not had their government seized by a military dictator. Even the Ivory Coast, which had been spared by military coup since its independence in 1960, was briefly ruled by a military junta led by General Robert Guei in 2000.[67]

Ayittey further describe the negative impact of military rulers in Africa: "The second generation of military rulers who assumed control in the 1970s, emerged from the dregs: They were more corrupt, incompetent, and brutal than the civilian administration they replaced. They ruined one African economy after another with brutal efficiency and looted African treasury with military discipline. Africans watched helplessly as they experienced yet another betrayal. These 'military coconutheads,' as Africans call them, came from the bottom of the pit and left wanton destruction and carnage in their wake."[68]

Corrupt military leadership has literally destroyed Somalia.

Although the Somali people speak a single language and are ethnically one people, European colonial forces divided them into five distinct nations: Kenya, Djibouti, and Ethiopia, as well as British and Italian Somaliland. When independence came in 1960, 8–10 million people in the British and Italian territories were joined together as Somalia, a country the size of Texas. Despite their linguistic and ethnic unity, these "Somalis" were sharply divided by their kinship system consisting of six major clans further divided into subclans. Somalia's first president, Ali Shermarke, was a civilian whose government quickly proved incompetent and shamelessly corrupt. On October 15, 1969, Shermarke was assassinated. Six day later, the government was seized by Major General Mohamed Said Barre, who supported by the Soviet Union, quickly expanded the army from 10,000 to 37,000 men. By 1982 it numbered 120,000 and by 1990, over 300,000 men... After Somalia agreed to cut all ties with the Soviet Union, the United States provided substantial military and economic support, as did Italy, Libya, France, Egypt, and China. Chinese aid was particularly extensive. Barre's government was not averse to pocketing large amount of foreign aid. In the late 1980s, for example, Italy gave Barre $70 million to build a fertilizer plant that was never constructed. The $70 million disappeared. Despite the flagrant corruption in Somalia during the 1980s Barre's government was the largest recipient

---

67. Edgerton, *Africa's Armies*, 141.
68. Ayittey, *Africa in Chaos*, 8.

of foreign aid in sub-Saharan Africa. Virtually none of this money reached the people.[69]

Today Somalia is an example of a failed state that bourgeons pirates and al Shabaab, meaning the "youth" or the "youngsters." It is a group of radical Muslims who joined al Qaeda in 2012. Al Shabaab is al Qaeda's affiliate in Somalia and operates primarily out of the country's southern and central regions. The group is fighting an insurgency against the internationally recognized Somali Federal Government, which is based in Somalia's capital, Mogadishu. Al Shabaab has targeted the African Union Mission in Somalia (AMISOM) peacekeepers for their support of the federal government. The group has also repeatedly threatened the United States and the West and has demonstrated the capacity to strike beyond Somalia's borders. On 21 September 2013, unidentified gunmen attacked the upmarket Westgate shopping mall in Nairobi, Kenya. The attack, which lasted until 24 September, resulted in at least sixty-seven deaths, including four attackers. Over 175 people were reportedly wounded in the mass shooting, with all of the gunmen reported killed.

The Islamist group al-Shabaab claimed responsibility for the incident, which it characterized as retribution for the Kenyan military's deployment in Somalia. Many media outlets also suspected the insurgent group's involvement in the attack based on earlier reprisal warnings it had issued in the wake of Operation Linda Nchi from 2011 to 2012.[70]

The Somali pirates also have wreaked havoc on the naval trade and shipments on the Indian Ocean. "Ransom payments to Somali pirates are estimated to have been between $339 million and $413 million in the period 2005–2012, according to a report issued Monday by the International Criminal Police Organization, United Nations Office on Drugs and Crime and the World Bank . . . During the years from 2005 to 2012, 179 ships were hijacked off the coast of Somalia and the Horn of Africa. The average ransom paid was $2.7 million, with ordinary pirates receiving $30,000 to $75,000 each and bonuses paid to those who brought their own weapons or were first to board the ship."[71] Tom Hanks has acted the true story of Captain Richard Phillips and the 2009 hijacking by Somali pirates of the US-flagged MV Maersk Alabama, the first American cargo ship to be hijacked in two hundred years.[72]

When you turn to Ethiopia, in 1974 in the name of the Marxist revolution, the military ended centuries of Ethiopia's monarchy and caused seventeen years of civil war, unprecedented diaspora, death in the millions, imprisonment and torture, and religious and political persecution.

> Mengistu was raised in the army, having become a "boy" at 15. In practice adopted from the British, Ethiopian teenagers used to be placed in the signal corps or non-combatant military services early, and then admitted full rank at age 18.

69. Edgerton, *Africa's Armies*, 143–44.

70. Faith Karimi, Steve Almasy, and Lillian Leposo, "Kenya mall attack: Military says most hostages freed, death toll at 68," CNN, http://www.cnn.com/2013/09/22/world/africa/kenya-mall-attack/index.html.

71. Christopher Harress, "Secret Flow of Somali Piracy Ransoms."

72. *Captain Phillips*, Columbia Pictures, 2013.

> Mengistu attended the Genet Military Training Center and was commissioned as a second lieutenant. He then spent nine months training at the US Army base, Aberdeen military ordnance school. This was in the 1960s, and he was subjected to several racist incidents. Together with the racial prejudice against the non-Amharas that he had experienced at home, this left him with a bitter hatred for the West and the old order in Ethiopia. Mengistu despises the rich, the well off, the educated—he has an obsessive need to be superior to those around him. In the Third Infantry Division (in eastern province of Harar), where he served until the revolution, he had a record of insubordination and was constantly in trouble. He was known as a brawler and was in several barroom fights. One of the reasons he was sent to the Coordinating Committee in 1974 was that the division commander wanted to get rid of him. That same commander, General Hailu Bayekedagne, was one of the 60 people executed by Mengistu in November 1974.
>
> Since Mengistu killed Tefferi Bante in 1977, he has reigned as absolute ruler in Ethiopia. When he was "voted" Chairman of the Military Council he became head of the armed forces, the legislature, the cabinet, and the judiciary. He created a new political structure, COPWE (Commission for the Organization of the Party of the Workers of Ethiopia) separate from the government structures, and became its Chairman. Later, when COPWE became the Workers' Party of Ethiopia (WPE), he made himself President of the Democratic Republic of Ethiopia.
>
> Everything Mengistu has done since 1977 has been with one ultimate goal in mind: to place himself in a position of uncontested power with absolute control over the lives of everyone in Ethiopia. Neither Haile Selassie nor any of the previous Emperors had this insatiable thirst for power. Mengistu has shown time and again that he will do anything to stay in control. At the same time, every decree, every policy, every law, every structure is designed to erect a façade of democracy and legitimacy. The façade is so transparent that it is ludicrous to think anyone is fooled.[73]

It doesn't matter whether the African country is rich with diamond, gold, uranium, oil, copper, etc., like Central African Republic, Congo, or Nigeria. And it doesn't matter whether the African country is getting the biggest foreign aid from the West, like Barre of Somalia and Congo of Mobutu. The military rulers are keen in their mismanagement and amassing of wealth. They eliminate anyone who they think is a threat and surround themselves with cronies who comply with their directives. The sweeping generalization and indictment of the prophet Hosea best apply in African leadership cultural context: "There is no truth, no love, and no knowledge of God in the land; swearing and lying, killing and stealing, and committing adultery, they break all bonds, and blood touches blood" (Hos 4:1–2).

After the Cold War,

> The small West African state of Benin became the first to be caught up in the avalanche of protest. Its military ruler, Mathieu Kêrêkou, and his cronies had looted the state-owned banking system so thoroughly that nothing was left to pay teachers and civil servants, some of whom were owed as much as twelve months' back pay. Three state-owned banks collapsed in 1988 as a result of large unsecured loans awarded to members of Kêrêkou's inner circle and the bogus

---

73. Giorgis, *Red Tears*, 56–57.

companies they had set up, amounting to the sum, according to the World Bank, of $500 million. His closet advisor Mohammed Cissé, a Malian marabout, it was subsequently discovered, had been in the habit of sitting in the manager's office at the Commercial Bank, transferring millions of dollars by telex to his bank accounts in Europe and the United States; in 1988 alone Cissé was estimated to have sent $370 million abroad. With the entire state banking and credit system drained of all liquid funds, normal business activity ground to a halt; companies could not operate, traders could neither sell nor buy.[74]

No matter whether one is a marabout like Mohammed Cissé, or claims to be a devout Christian like Daniel Arap Moi of Kenya, or lists professional degrees from prominent African and European universities like Mugabe, the DNA of African leaders is engrained with corruption and greed. As a person of African origin, it is extremely disturbing and disappointing to me not to be able to mention a good African leader except Mandela. The promising ones like Patrice Lumumba, Tom Boya, and Robert Ouko of Kenya, John P. Garan of South Sudan, Steve Biko of South Africa—to mention the few, articulate, intelligent, educated, and passionately African leaders—prematurely die, causing deep grief and hopelessness to those who love and admire them. The evil ones stay in power until they die or are kicked out by another new and hungry leader of the same feather. "To the crisis of rising expectations that had begun at independence was added the crisis of rising population; within twenty years of independence, states often had half of their population under twenty, and all wanting education and employment, while the infrastructure of postindependnece years crumbled away. Natural disaster—drought, desertification, crop failure—was compounded by human disaster in wars of long duration and high ferocity. The majority of the world's refugees are Africans."[75]

"Nigeria had become one of Africa's most tragic stories, as if a great family franchise had been run into the ground by decadent nephews prematurely handed the reins of management. The callow nephews in the tale were *army generals* and like king Midas in reverse, *the officers who had run the country for the last decade had debased everything they had touched, starting, of course with politics, which they had turned into a contest of self-enrichment*."[76] In Nigeria, "soldiers can be bought with pay increases, subsidized housing, commodities, and faster promotions. In 1993, for example, General Ibrahim Babangida gave nearly 3,000 of his most loyal military chiefs new Peugeot sedans, which cost the equivalent of $21,000 each in Lagos, five times the yearly salary of a senior university professor, who earns about $4000.00 a year. A nurse or mechanic is lucky to bring home more than $1000.00."[77] For six years, 1988–1994, Nigeria's military rulers squandered $12.4 billion in oil revenue, estimated by the Pius Okigbo Commission to be a third of the nations' foreign debt. A Petroleum trust fund set up by former head of state General Ibrahim Babaginda "lost" $600 million. No one was prosecuted. Most Nigerians collapsed into hysterical laughter when they heard that their late head of state, General Sani Abacha, had launched "a war on corruption," because they knew that several of his

---

74. Meredith, *Fate of Africa*, 387–88.
75. Walls, *Cross-Cultural Process*, 109.
76. French, *Continent for the Taking*, 17; emphasis added.
77. Ayittey, *Africa in Chaos*, 165.

cronies, active or retired, are millionaires and no military men involved in the banking scandal [that cost the country $180 million] have been touched. "When the soldiers have eaten enough, he retires them," said a civil rights lawyer.[78]

Kofi Annan rightly observed: "Africa has many challenges—social, economic, geographical and environmental. But in my view, and I see Africa's history bearing this out, leadership is the ultimate cause of the plight of Africa, and the greatest destroyer of leadership and good governance in Africa has been military regimes. The perversion of democratic rule, gross abuses of human rights, and economic mismanagement—the truly great curses of Africa—stem in so many instances from this one infection: the military coup."[79]

Why are so many African countries so coup-prone?

> A major reason is that the technology of destruction in Africa is ahead of the technology of production. And so ultimate power resides not in those who control the means of production, as Marxists would argue, but in those who control the means of destruction.
>
> A related reason why Africa is coup-prone is that most other institutions in Africa (such as labour unions, professional associations, and religious leadership, universities, the judiciary, peasant associations, and even the civil service) are relatively weak. In most cases they are unable to stand up to the military.
>
> A third reason for coups in Africa is the low level of professionalism in the armed forces. Criteria of recruitment and promotion are sometimes ethnic rather than based on merit; methods of professional socialisation are often haphazard; pay is often so low that it encourages corruption. Conditions do vary in different countries, but African soldiers in the streets of African capitals are more likely to display petty arrogance towards civilians than professional pride.
>
> Another reason for military intervention in Africa is boredom in the barracks. Ultimately, what are African armies *for* anyhow? In the majority cases there are no likely wars with foreign powers on the horizon. In most countries there are no major defence needs. Heroism for African soldiers is therefore to be sought not on the battlefield but in the political arena, not in military command against the enemy but in in political command over one's own compatriot. African armies are therefore tempted to proclaim themselves the political and moral custodians of the national interest—rather than the military defenders of the nation's security and sovereignty. It is of such material that coups are made.[80]

Because of the military's bad ruling and their distaste for academics, famous universities, including promising academic colleges, elementary and high schools in Congo, Nigeria, Uganda, and Ethiopia have immensely suffered and lost prominent scholars who can make incredible contributions to their nations and to the continent. Mazrui concurs:

> In the process of decay is Africa's school system. Teachers are becoming less committed. They are often underpaid and in some countries they are not paid at all for months on end. The teachers have to look for moonlighting opportunities

---

78. French, *Continent for the Taking*, 35.
79. Annan, *Interventions*, 175.
80. Mazrui, *Africans*, 182–83.

to give them an additional livelihood. The sense of vocation in education is under severe strain in Africa.

There has been declining support for African universities. In those countries where money has declined in value enormously, professors have to look for additional jobs ranging from taxi-driving to farming, as a method of augmenting their resources...

Africa is quite familiar with schools without walls, classrooms in the open. Teaching can go on without desks, learning can take place without walls, but teaching without teaching materials is a different matter. An entire term had taken place at this school without the basics of writing, without paper, without pens. Someone complained, "why not write the head of state?" Someone else retorted, "Write? With what?"[81]

Lack of food in the grocery stores, medicine in the pharmacies, inadequate or no treatment for the sick, hungry children and teachers in the classrooms, violent treatment—these are the common characteristics of military rule. "The great majority of the military men who carried out coups were dictators who obliterated the media, jailed, tortured, and killed rivals or opponents, and provided themselves with corrupt, greedy, and inept ministers while filling overseas bank accounts with funds stolen from foreign aid or earning from exports. They surrounded themselves with well-paid soldiers and police who they relied on to maintain them in office...Corruption was their trade mark."[82] "What keeps the Africans poor is their powerlessness to rid themselves of predatory governments or force existing ones to adopt the right policies in a peaceful way. More treacherously, those highly educated Africans—the lawyers, professors, and intellectuals—who ought to be the watchdogs have themselves joined the official gangsters and rodents. As a last resort, the people may rise up to overthrow the cabal of looters with destructive consequences. But then again, the next batch of rats will prove no better."[83]

The corrupt political government system in Africa has corrupted the judicial system, which is supposed to be the pillar and foundation of civil society in upholding and promoting justice, equality, and freedom. "A corrupt judicial system is another millstone around Africa's neck. In fact, dishonest judges are as bad as the dictators. Efforts to clean up the judicial system—training judges, computerizing records, strengthening the role of clerks—have borne little fruit because the politicians have found it more convenient to have crooked and malleable judiciary than an independent one. As a result, although numerous judges have gone to France, Canada, and the United States for professional courses, many have returned to their sordid practices once they were back on the bench."[84] Haugen concurs: "Over the last fifty years the affluent nations of the world have been pursuing poverty alleviation programs in countries—without first helping recipient nations to establish a basic platform of law and justice that will allow poor people to hold onto the benefits of these programs. We can give all manner of goods and services to the poor, but if we do not restrain the hands of the bullies from taking it all away, then poor

81. Ibid., 204.

82. Edgerton, *Africa's Armies*, 142. For an in-depth reading on military rule in Africa, see ibid., 141–82; and Meredith, *Fate of Africa*, 387–99.

83. Ayittey, *Africa in Chaos*, 21.

84. Calderisi, *Trouble with Africa*, 89.

simply stay poor. This explains why hundreds of millions of poor people in the world are enslaved, imprisoned, beaten, raped and robbed with ferocious regularity—they simply do not get the protection of basic law enforcement."[85]

> Lagos, a city of about 10 million inhabitants, had no more than 12,000 policemen on its payroll. Underfunded, ill-equipped and poorly trained, the police were no match for criminal gangs. The justice system was chaotic. Prisoners were often locked up without trial for years on end. A government commission investigating overcrowded prisons found that half of the inmates had never been legally sentenced; some had sat in their cells for ten years without ever seeing a judge. Court proceedings were often determined by bribes because they came from prominent families or enjoyed the patronage of powerful politicians. Anyone with sufficient money and influence was able to make use of state institutions to harm opponents, whether in land or business disputes or in personal vendettas.[86]

What you read about Lagos is true of almost all capital cities of African countries. From various prongs of injustice the continent is bleeding. The poor have nowhere to turn; their ultimate and last cry is to the God of justice. As Heschel puts it, "Justice is scarce, injustice exceedingly common. The concern for justice is delegated to the judges, as if it were a matter for professionals or specialists. But to do justice is what God demands of every man: it is the supreme commandment and one that cannot be fulfilled vicariously."[87] Africans should not expect justice only from the courts. Teachers, policemen, and women, parents, religious leaders, businessmen and women, the army, political leaders, husbands, fathers and mothers, etc., can demonstrate justice.

Africans are seeking solace under the wings of the righteous and loving God. Hence, there is a resurgence of Christianity in Africa, unparalleled in Christian history. There are various factors for why Africans are turning to the God of the Bible. In my opinion the major reason is that God seeks out the poor, the oppressed, and the exploited to give them peace and justice. Moltmann describes this phenomenon as follow: "According to Israel's experience of God, YHWH, unlike the other gods, is a God who maintains the cause of the afflicted, and executes justice for the needy' (Ps. 40:12). He 'raises the poor from the dust, and lifts the needy from the ash heap' (Ps. 113:7). He just not lay down what justice and injustices are, like human judges, so as to reward and to punish; he 'creates justice for those who suffer violence' and frees the helpless from the hand of the wicked. And for that reason the book of Job call him 'the hope of the poor' (5:16). So YHWH is not a judge who judges without respect of persons . . . He is quite explicitly the advocate who takes the part of people without rights and puts to rights the unjust."[88]

God gives meaning in the meaningless contexts, hope in hopeless situations, and peace despite life-threatening wars and famines. And he heals wounds of all kinds inflicted on people through acts of injustice. "The Spirit, the Jesus, who makes us live does not merely free the soul from sadness. It also liberates the body from the tensions. It

85. Haugen, *Good News about Injustice*, 23.
86. Meredith, *Fate of Africa*, 581.
87. Heschel, *Prophets*, 261.
88. Moltmann, *Sun of Righteousness Arise!*, 122.

heals not only traumatic memories but psychosomatic illness as well."[89] God knows how to change human disappointment into his appointment and make a redemptive history through individuals or nations. In this process, "Christianity is designed to be the healing beginning of the healed creation in the midst of a disrupted and sick world."[90] It is no wonder, then, that we see stellar Christian growth in the continent of Africa. "In 1900 there were over 390 million Christians in Europe and less than 10 million in the entire continent of Africa. Today there are over 367 million Christians in Africa, comprising one-fifth of the entire Christian church. Throughout the 20th century a net average gain of 16,500 people were coming to Christ every day in Africa. From 1970 to 1985 for example, the church in Africa grew by over six million people. During that same time... 4,300 people per day were leaving the church in Europe and North America."[91] Reflecting on the trend of Christian growth in Africa, Lamin Sanneh writes:

> We should not rejoice because utopia has arrived nor be afraid because Armageddon is threatened, but rather, we should take heart because suffering people have found faith and hope. The people who have lined up, determined to enter the church, have eaten the bread of adversity and tasted the water of affliction, and still they press to come into the church. The church exists to welcome precisely such as these, their personal and material circumstances notwithstanding. There is no entrance fee for membership because the kingdom of God is especially for the least among us. Who are we to begrudge them? I don't want to paint too one sided a picture, or even to suggest that joining the church solves all of the problems of life and society. I'm suggesting that for the new African Christians the church is a good place to work out the problems and challenges of life and society. The norms of faith and forgiveness, undergirded by the practice of the arts of charitable action, community solidarity, trust, and faithfulness, offer a way of the public good, not apart from it.[92]

In Africa, "the poor have nothing left to which they can appeal in order to achieve justice. God is their last hope."[93] While the numerical Christian growth in Africa is exciting, the impact of the church on African society is disappointing. The Ugandan Christian thinker Katongole writes, "Even though in many parts of Africa the church, at least numerically, was strong and powerful institution, it did not make much difference to Africa's social history of violence, corruption, and poverty."[94] He adds, "If Christianity is to be about the business of shaping a new future in Africa, it was becoming clear to me, Christianity itself would have to find a way of overcoming this Western Heritage, to move beyond the narrow of spiritual and pastoral areas to which it is consigned and claim full competence in the social, material, and political realities of life in Africa."[95]

---

89. Ibid., 65.
90. Ibid., 69.
91. Tennent, *Invitation to World Missions*, 34.
92. Sanneh, *Whose Religion Is Christianity?*, 32–33.
93. Moltmann, *Sun of Righteousness Arise!*, 124.
94. Katongole, *Sacrifice of Africa*, 17.
95. Ibid., 19.

In the next three chapters, I make this call more clearly and it is something that is time sensitive, crucial, and very demanding in many ways.

Christian Leadership

The sad and disappointing thing is that quite a number of church leaders are prone to exhibition of power in a domineering way rather than serving the people God assigned them to shepherd.

> Church leaders sometimes show power in a scandalizing manner. This is seen for instance in the way that money is spent on buildings, celebrations, vehicles and liturgical symbols. Here one has to guard against abuses that are sometimes justified in the name of the African culture where people are said to be generous and hospitable . . . It has been noticed that contrary to Christ's and the apostles' warning, some clerical, lay and religious leaders are lording it over the people who are entrusted to them. A pastor should never be oppressive, but a distorted image of power in the Church can lead to terrible abuses. This can be all the more insidious since it is usually hierarchically justified: the one acting wrongly justifies his action from power coming from a superior above.[96]

Along with many other theological tasks the African churches have an enormous responsibility to raise wise leaders whose leadership principle is Christ-centered and culturally relevant.

---

96. Kanyandago, "A Biblical Reflection of Pastoral Authority," 119–20.

Chapter 9

Leading in a Turbulent Cultural Contexts

Over the years, teachers have fashioned ways in which to convey disciplines to young minds. Indeed, in no other way could we continue to have a steady supply of scientists, mathematicians, artists, historians, critics, lawyers, executives, managers, and other kinds of scholars and professionals.[1]

To be Victim Is a Choice

Our culture has a strong influence on our lives and ministry philosophy. For a leadership resource and example, we tend to look for secular books and we take CEOs as our model. We often attempt to be Billy Graham in the suit of Warren Buffet; or, if you are an African, to be Festo Kivengere[2] in a suit of Museveni. Even though we try to integrate the secular and spiritual realities in our minds and have a harmonious worldview, the aspect that we give more attention to dictates our thought and actions. Hence, we function under constant tension between the biblical and secular voice.

If we believe that God still raises leaders and guides, molds, empowers, assigns, and uses them, the Bible has a lot to teach us. From the life of Joseph we can learn valuable principles of leadership. Unlike us, he did not go to a formal business or leadership school. He neither studied law nor political science, yet he excelled to the highest office

---

1. H. Gardner, *Five Minds for the Future*, 30–31.

2. In 1977, Festo Kivengere, an Anglican bishop from Uganda, published a short book entitled *I Love Idi Amin*. Amin was the African dictator routinely referred to as Africa's Hitler. Huge, hulking, alternating between charming buffoon and nightmarish thug, Amin murdered hundreds of thousands of his fellow citizens. In February 1977, he arrested and killed Anglican Archbishop Janani Luwum, simply because the Anglican bishops had dared to speak up against illegal executions.

Kivengere was one of the last people to see Luwum alive. He waited outside the building where Luwum was interrogated until guards forced him to leave at gunpoint. Expecting arrest, Kivengere escaped Uganda on foot. Within the year he had published his book. Stafford, "Costly Love, Radical Forgiveness."

of a then-advanced country, Egypt, and demonstrated leadership skills that saved at least two nations: Egypt and Israel. He did this in a society where the religion, politics, governance, economy, culture, customs, and language were foreign to him. "He never yielded to bitterness and his attitude determined his availability to God . . . A victimizer can injure or even kill, but it takes another's willing participation—and acceptance—to become a victim."[3] However, the African cultural and political environment teaches and promotes the victim mentality: "More than half of Africa's people are under the age of eighteen. Yet, many of their elders, teachers, or governments are trying to persuade them that they are victims, rather than victors in a now-distant struggle for independence. Even Africans who were alive when that struggle was won are still wrestling with their demons."[4] Africans are robbed of their present freedom, privilege, opportunity, and productivity by willingly becoming prisoners of their past. Hence, the current generation is flummoxed by the contradiction of life in Africa—the wealth of natural resources in the continent and the level of poverty are irreconcilable in their minds.

If slavery determines the potential and destiny of a person, Joseph would not have ended up in the palace of the pharaoh, consulting the emperor and saving the lives of many. Additionally, we would not have black American scientists, innovators, and entrepreneurs in the U.S. The fruit of Joseph's leadership in Egypt has long and rich spiritual roots. It is almost impossible not to think of the influence of his spiritual heritage on the later years of Joseph's life. Oral societies pass information to the younger generations verbally. In oral cultures the historical and theological archives of the past are the minds of the living. Then, as well as now, in the words of Alexander Mitscherlich, "family is a social womb."[5] We are born untrained and uninformed, we slowly learn from our family and then from society to be who we are. His great grandfather, Abraham, was called "a friend of God" (2 Chr 20:7); the birth of his grandfather, Isaac, was a fulfillment of God's promise (Gen 18:1–15; 21:1–5); the life of his father, Jacob, was set apart by sovereign election and predestination (Gen 25:23; Rom 9:10–13).

Coming from such a lineage, Joseph knew that he did not come to exist accidentally. Looking at his life in retrospect, at the complete tapestry of his journey, he said to his brothers: "God sent me ahead of you to preserve for you a remnant on earth and to save your lives by a great deliverance. So then, it was not you who sent me here, but God. He made me father to Pharaoh, lord of his entire household and a ruler of all Egypt" (Gen 45:7–8). These statements were not excerpts written for Joseph's theological thesis when he graduated from the finest seminary in Egypt. In fact, for most of his life he lived among a society that worshiped idols, gods, and goddesses.[6] His realization of God's work in his life came out of his deep walk and experience with God. Current Christian families in Africa have the enormous responsibility and duty to raise a generation of Africans who will aspire for a better Africa regardless of outside influence and past history.

Through shame and glory, in the school of loneliness, before a friendly cheering crowd and a hostile one, with and without a family, in childhood, as a teenager,

3. Woodson, *Triumphs of Joseph*, 8.
4. Calderisi, *Trouble with Africa*, 13.
5. Mitscherlich, *Society without the Father*, 18.
6. See Barrett, *Egyptian Gods and Goddesses*.

adolescent, and adult, as a slave and a master, at home and in a foreign land, when the dream seemed so real and bright and the future looked like gloom and doom, Joseph stayed close to God. At the pinnacle of his achievement, he did not need convincing to believe that God has acted in his life and to give full credit to God for the leadership post he was holding in Egypt. That is, he followed God in every aspect of his life—the good and the bad. Against many odds, God made history through the life of Joseph.

The trajectory of Joseph's leadership career, so to speak, began with a dream when he was seventeen years old (Gen 37:5–10). He was the favored son of his father, and as a result his brothers held a grudge against him. When he shared his dream with his brothers and his father, the brothers "hated him all the more" (Gen 37:5), and "his father rebuked him" (Gen 37:10). I'll leave it to psychologists to analyze what kind of leader would come out of a child who was once favored by his father and then rebuked and discouraged from pursuing his dream. He was a child who was "hated by his brothers, stripped of his clothes, thrown into a cistern and sold as a slave to a caravan of Ishmaelite" (Gen 19–25). From a layman's point of view, there is not much hope in the future for one who has drunk a bitter cup of hatred and rejection from the hand of his loved ones. But God's grace and wisdom transcend all circumstances that we might go through to make us better people.

One important quality of a good leader is to be a long-range planner. And some of the qualities of a qualified planner are experience, wisdom, and maturity of judgment, patience, serenity of spirit, and the gift of administration.[7] Joseph had the opportunity to develop these qualities in a most unlikely place—prison (Gen. 39: 22–23). Here is the secret: "While Joseph was there in the prison, the Lord was with him; he showed him kindness and granted him favor in the eyes of the prison warden" (Gen. 39: 21; NIV). GOD WAS WITH JOSEPH IN PRISON—not in a church, not in a temple, or in a synagogue, but in prison. God is Spirit. He transcends our finiteness; he cannot be controlled and manipulated by earthly powers. When God decides to make a leader out of you, there is no authority or place under the sun that can hinder or limit him in accomplishing his objective. The question is do you believe that?

Joseph did. Joseph was not only a man of faith but he was also a man of action. It takes a doer for a dream to become reality. "Long-range planning requires a futuristic commitment, having accurate information, and practical implementation."[8] Joseph possessed those qualities, demonstrated them meticulously, and saved the lives of Egyptians and Israelites. His leadership scope included strategic planning, relational skills, delegation, art and skill of communication, boldness, vision casting, integrity, inspiration, and hope. Christian leadership can be nurtured and developed through various legitimate and constructive means, but nothing can replace the presence of God, his acts of grace and provision, his wonderful counsel, his assuring guidance, and his blessed results in the life of a leader. I hope someday when we reach our milestone, like Joseph, we will be able to say: "the lord brought me here, and he made me a pastor, teacher, missionary, CEO, mother, father, mentor, and a leader."

---

7. Gangel, *Lessons in Leadership from the Bible*, 10.

8. Ibid., 11–14.

Ravi Zacharias wrote, "Is (God's) design for your life pulls together every threads of your existence into a magnificent work or art? Every thread matters and has a specific purpose."[9] Those threads in Joseph's life produced integrity and wisdom from suffering and waiting. Leadership values like humility, forgiveness, and service comfortably suited him and enabled him to lead from a "second chair." The second chair is defined as "a person in a subordinate role whose influence with others adds value throughout the organization."[10]

Unlike many African leaders, Joseph did not fight or cause bloodshed for the first spot in leadership and ruining everything. Launching from where God put him, he made history. As you pursue your leadership career, what lesson can you learn from Joseph? What is the place of dreams in your personal life and theology? Where is God in the journey of your life? What do you make of the various tapestries of your life designed by God? In spite of these many trials, including betrayal and slavery, Joseph demonstrated a positive attitude and hope and faith in God. He did not use leadership for his own sake—he saved many lives, both Jews and gentiles. To be a victim is a choice.

The Bible has many examples of those who suffered under slavery, exile, and foreign domination. Moses inherited 450 years of slavery, suffering, hard labor, and injustice against his people. Daniel and his friends who were taken into exile at a young age saw the destruction of their nation and lived in exile. Paul, who came into the scene of apostolic service under the Roman Empire, lived in a colony, saw the destruction of Israel as a nation, and the dispersion of the Jews. All of these and many others who are heroes of the faith did not have a victim mentality. To the church in Rome, the capital of the empire, after describing the suffering and glorification of creation (Rom 8:20–22), Paul writes, "In all these things we are more than the conquerors through him who loved us" (Rom 8:37). Paul was talking about the travail and redemption of creation and he stated that Christians are not immune to it. "Insecurity is written across all human experience. Christian people are not guaranteed immunity to temptation, tribulation or tragedy, but we are promised victory over them. God's pledge is not that suffering will never afflict us, but that it will never separate us from his love. This is the love of God which was supremely displayed in the cross (Rom. 5:8; 8:32, 37), which has been poured into our hearts by the Holy Spirit (Rom. 5:5), which had drawn out from us through our responsive love (8:28), and which in its essential steadfastness will never let us end (8:35, 39). Our confidence is not in our love for him, which is frail, fickle, and faltering, but in his love for us, which is steadfast, faithful and persevering."[11] Because of God's "steadfast, faithful, and persevering love," Africans should not be defeated twice because of a victim mentality. In the following deep insight of Haugen, Africans should take heed to not yield to hopelessness:

> The battle for justice in the world is not fought where we think it is. The struggle against injustice is not fought on the battlefield of power or truth or even righteousness. There are pitched battles waged on these ramparts, but the war is

---

9. Zacharias, *Grand Weaver*, 17.
10. Bonem and Patterson, *Leading from the Second Chair*, 2.
11. Stott, *Message of Romans*, 259.

> ultimately won or lost on a more forward front. In the end the battle against oppression stands or falls on the battlefield of hope...
>
> The oppressor knows that the primary reason we do nothing is because we have lost any hope of making a difference. It is not that we lack power, compassion, courage or knowledge. Rather we lack a sense of hope that allows us to take what we have into the fray. By sheer inertia, therefore, we lend our own weight to the downward cycle of despair. Our lack of hope keeps us from the front lines of engagement. And our absence only makes the oppressor look stronger, compounding our own despair and that of those who might otherwise be prepared to fight.[12]

Conquering the mind cannot happen unless an individual gives up his/her right by choice. *Man's Search for Meaning,* by Viktor E. Frankl, is a classic bestseller now considered to be one of the most important contributions to psychiatry since the writing of Freud. In it, Frankl gives a moving account of his life amid the horrors of the Nazi death camps, chronicling the harrowing experience that led to the discovery of his theory of logotherapy. A profound revelation born out of Frankl's years as a prisoner in Auschwitz and other concentration camps, logotherapy is a modern and positive approach to the mentally or spiritually disturbed personality. Stressing human freedom to transcend suffering and find a meaning to life regardless of circumstances, it is a theory that, since its conception, has exercised tremendous influence upon the entire field of psychiatry and psychology. Frankl writes, "We who lived in the concentration camps can remember the men who walked through the hurts comforting others, giving away their last piece of bread. They may be few in number, but they offer sufficient proof that everything can be taken from a man but one thing: the last of the human freedoms—*to choose one's attitude in any given set of circumstances, to choose one's own way.*"[13] Chuck Siwndoll was right when he said,

> The longer I live, the more I realize the impact of attitude on life. Attitude, to me, is more important than facts. It is more important than the past, than education, than money, than circumstances, than failures, than successes, than what other people think, say or do. It is more important than appearance, giftedness or skill. It will make or break a company ... a church ... a home. The remarkable thing is we have a choice every day regarding the attitude we embrace for that day. We cannot change our past ... we cannot change the fact that people will act in a certain way. We cannot change the inevitable. The only thing we can do is play the one string we have, and that is our attitude ... *I am convinced that life is 10% what happens to me and 90% how I react to it.* And so it is with you ... we are in charge of our Attitudes.[14]

Despite the hardship Africa has gone through and the unbearable circumstances people still live in, there are lighthearted Africans who serve others by giving them hope to come out of the gloom and doom and the emotionally crippling social and economic conditions. "Africans dance. They dance for joy, and they dance for grief; they dance

---

12. Haugen, *Good News about Injustice,* 81–82.
13. Frankl, *Man's Search for Meaning,* 75; emphasis added.
14. *Improving Your Serve,* 22.

for love and they dance for hate; they dance to bring prosperity and they dance to avert calamity; they dance for religion and they dance to pass the time. They dance with verve, a precision, an ingenuity which no other race can show."[15] Liu, a Chinese entrepreneur in Mozambique, told French, "Chinese people are in a hurry to work, to earn money, to get rich. If they are farmers, the make every day count. Here, it is not the same. Africans like to dance. That is their specialty. They may be poor but they are very happy."[16] Shuai another Chinese entrepreneur in Mali made a relative comment: "Malians [are] among the happiest people in the world. Happier than Americans, and certainly happier than Chinese. If everyone around you is the same. . .you don't have to worry about being poor."[17]

"Jazz is the national treasure of the United States but its root is in Africa." Doug Groothuis writes,

> The roots of jazz are complex and contested, but all grant that jazz sprung from African American slave songs. These songs of lament and hope were tied to rhythms that aided exhausted workers to rally their strength and cheer each other on. This "call-and-response" is intrinsic to jazz–this musical collaboration and cooperation performed without tightly scripted parts. In this tradition, a jazz band performs according to a song structure (or a chart) and solos are taken at the proper places. This requires a deep knowledge of the standards of jazz (the musical canon) and how to play them. (See Ted Gioia, Jazz Standards.) Learning these canonical tunes and mastering one's instrument means spending "time in the woodshed." This is a jazz term for practicing, refining one's skills—also known as "chops," a term coined by Louis Armstrong, one of the seminal jazz pioneers.[18]

Mazrui pertinently captures Africans' broader contributions in the area of music despite the unbearable and humiliating experience they have gone through: "Because of the slave trade there has been a partial Africanisation of the Western world, especially of the Americas. Africa's exported sons and daughters have in part become a transmission belt for African culture and myths, for African music and dance. Jazz, the blues, reggae, rumba, calypso, and even rock 'n' roll have all been rhythms derived from the African experience, and transmitted into world culture through the African Diaspora."[19]

People who dance through joy and sorrow cannot be easily dismissed from the pages of history. "Rejected, unlived, denied life is life that has been missed, and life that is dead."[20] Not so with the African poor. They have maintained the freedom that no one can take from them—to choose to be happy. However, the victims' mentality among African Americans in the U.S. has deterred their social and economic development and has locked them in a vicious circle of poverty and crime. Woodson observes: "Accepting an identity as "victims" has done more damage than years of outright discrimination

---

15. Calderisi, *Trouble with Africa*, 83.
16. French, *China's Second Continent*, 221.
17. Ibid., 157.
18. Groothuis, "How Jazz Can Shape Apologetics."
19. Mazrui, *Africans*, 301–2.
20. Moltmann, *Sun of Righteousness Arise!*, 64.

could accomplish, because it has caused destruction from within. We have fallen prey to an endemic of an entitlement mentality. A victimizer may have knocked us down, but it is up to us to stand up again. The single most devastating of all of the culture of victimhood is the abandonment of the morality, ethics, and personal responsibility which was the glue that once held the black community together."[21]

Indirectly, the current situation of black Americans has prolonged the exploitation and suffering of Africans. While African-Americans could have been a voice for the voiceless, transferring education and technology to Africa, the majority of them are still struggling to survive and have a decent life. The Jews who went through discrimination both in Europe and America are good models of how to overcome adversity and to always remember one's roots. "What made the Israelis military pre-eminent is not the Jewishness of 80 per cent of the total population but the Europeanness of less than half of the Jewish sector. It is the European and Western Jews who have provided the technological foundations of Israel's regional hegemony."[22]

Africans are also very forgiving and generous in sharing what they have, be it personal or national resources. This observation has been made by many Western observers. Dowden writes, "Africa has a reputation: poverty, disease, war. But when outsiders do go they are often surprised by Africa's welcome, entranced rather than frightened. Visitors are welcomed and cared for in Africa. If you go you will find most Africans friendly, gentle and infinitely polite. You will frequently be humbled by African generosity. Africans have in abundance what we call social skills. These are not skills that are formally taught and learned. There is no click-on have-a-nice day smile in Africa. Africans meet, greet and talk, look you in the eye and empathize, hold hands and embrace, share and accept from others without twitchy self-consciousness. All these things are as natural as music in Africa."[23] For example, Portugal had played a major role in the African slave trade, colonization, exploitation, the burning of national archives, and the blood shedding of millions of Africans. Despite this, Africans have openly welcomed Portuguese who have recently run from poverty in the homeland. French observes: "The boom here was also attracting large numbers of Portuguese, Mozambique's colonial masters who were now residents of one of Europe's poorest countries and among the hardest hit by financial crisis. Between 2009 and 2011, the number of Portuguese officially registered with their embassy increased by over 20 percent, with 23,000 of them thought to be living in Mozambique's two biggest cities, Maputo and Beira."[24] Even if Israel is not returning the favor, Africa has been a refuge of the Jewish people who went through multiple tragedies that caused them to leave their homeland:

> North Africa has accommodated clusters of Shepherding Jews, mainly immigrants from Spain and Portugal who entered African in the fifteenth and sixteenth centuries, and Ashkenazic Jews, from northern and eastern Europe who entered Africa in the nineteenth and twentieth centuries. Outside the Republic of South Africa, the numbers of these European Jews in sub-Saharan Africa are

21. Woodson, *Triumphs of Joseph*, 71.
22. Mazrui, *Africans*, 172.
23. Dowden, *Africa*, 1.
24. French, *China's Second Continent*, 213.

modest. But in countries such as Kenya, Jews are often influential and some are exceptionally wealthy.

The biggest number of Jews in the Arab world today is in Morocco. Before the creation of Israel, Morocco had more than a quarter of a million Jews. By 1956 well over 60,000 Jews had emigrated to Israel. Some also left for France. Every Arab-Israeli war created new fears among Moroccan Jews. The number of Jews now remaining there is probably in the region of, at the most, 50,000. Egypt had approximately 100,000 Jews before the Second World War. There are now very few Jews left in Egypt . . . The history of Jews in Algeria goes back 2000 years, but most of them acquired French citizenship through the Cremieux Decree of 1870 . . .

Among the richest of the Jews of the world are those of the Republic of South Africa. What they contribute to the treasury of Israel is next only to the contribution of the Jews of the United States. Indeed, per head of the population, the donation of South Africa's Jewry has in some years been larger than that of American Jews.

Among the white South Africans the Jews have a higher per capita income than the ruling and politically more influential Dutch-speaking Afrikaners . . . South African Jews have been part of white supremacy, a state based on sectional racial supremacy.[25]

By developing an optimistic attitude and cultivating positive African virtues through various arts and theological education, Africans can come out of the economic, social, and political quagmire they have been living in. It takes many wise and godly leaders to achieve that goal. We have a lot to learn from Nelson Mandela. Books written about his life and leadership should be required textbooks for leadership courses in African universities and colleges. "His gestures of good will were manifold. He organized what he called 'a reconciliation lunch,' bringing together wives and widows of former apartheid leaders and leading black activists. He made a special trip to visit a widow of Hendrik Verwoerd, the architect of apartheid, who was living in a small town on the banks of the Orange River which Afrikaner *bittereinders* had preserved as white-only colony. Even more remarkable was the lunch he arranged for Percy Yutar, the prosecutor in the Rivonia trial who had argued for Mandela to be given the death sentence and expressed regret when this did not happen."[26] He adds, "The example he set was profound importance. For if after twenty-seven years in prison, Mandela could emerge insisting on reconciliation, it undermined the demands of those seeking revenge and retribution. His generosity of spirit also had a profound impact on his white adversaries, earning him measures of trust and confidence that laid the foundations for a political settlement."[27] Social capital like trust, love, forgiveness, peace, unity, and mutual respect, are crucial to build nations and peaceful global communities. Instead of importing deadly weapons from Western countries and turning to guerilla warfare to bring about democracy, emerging African leaders need to study the importance of constitutions, civility, dialogue, and open and free speech to build a country. We need to develop a culture that

25. Mazrui, *Africans*, 82, 84–85. The Jews presence in Africa is much more modest than that of the Arabs. Unlike the Jews Arabs primarily came to Africa as traders, conquerors, and propagators of Islam.

26. Meredith, *Fate of Africa*, 652; emphasis original.

27. Ibid., 437.

encourages speaking the truth in love, nurturing our children to have forgiving heart, and empowering them with freedom that allows expression of their good thoughts in a socially, culturally, and biblically acceptable manner.

Small Beginning

As I reflect back on my thirty-seven years of ministry and ponder Scripture and autobiographical books, I am amazed by how often God brings great things out of small beginnings. Contrary to our human ambition, God works with insignificant, despised, poor, unassuming workers to manifest his power, glory, mercy, judgment, and redemptive love. God actively works within human history and the universe. However, this does not mean he is rushing to show results. From what I understand, he is a God of process. Process takes time, the convergence of so many factors, and it demands patience.

Our human nature craves grand results—huge budgets and buildings, large crowds, and sophisticated equipment to put our voice and image on the airwaves. Yes, our desire is to make our Lord known. Undoubtedly, we also love to be known. Many start their call to Christian leadership with mixed and unhealthy spiritual motives, and end up in heartbreaking situations and wrecked families, in both churches and para-church organizations. These kinds of leaders are warning signs for us and they teach us a great deal about how not to do ministry. For positive and enriching examples, let us look at a few models of "small beginnings."

When God wanted to build the nation of Israel, he started with Abraham and Sarah. The possibility of them having children, let alone a nation, was humanly unthinkable. The Scripture rightly describes the impossibility this way: "Against all hope, Abraham in hope believed and so became the father of many nations, just as it had been said to him, 'So shall your offspring be.' Without weakening in faith, he faced the fact that his body was as good as dead—since he was about a hundred years old—and that Sarah's womb was also dead. Yet he did not waver through unbelief regarding the promise of God, but was strengthened in his faith and gave glory to God, being fully persuaded that God had power to do what he had promised" (Rom 4:18–21).

Out of the "dead body and dead womb" the Lord built a nation that has played a significant role in human history. Out of this nation came judges, kings, priests, prophets, apostles, scientists, and poets. Most of all, the savior of the world, Jesus Christ, came out of the nation of Israel. Starting from a humble beginning, Abraham became "the father of us all" (Rom 4:16b). With unwavering faith, tested patience, hope, and endurance, Abraham submitted himself to go through the divine process.

The New Covenant that we are in did not start with glamor, wealth, and power. It began with a baby born in a manger. His nation was a colony. Galilee, the region where he grew up, was stricken with poverty. Jesus grew up seeing his people languishing under Roman taxes and the law of the Pharisees, as well as suffering from disease, hunger, oppression, and injustice. He himself had no home. He didn't establish a university or write a book. He never traveled outside of Israel. Yet, the scope and impact of his life can't be adequately covered in books and songs. By choice and obedience, he accepted a small and humble beginning. Paul writes that Jesus, "being in the form of God, did not consider it robbery to be equal with God, but made himself of no reputation taking the form of a bondservant, and coming in the likeness of men" (Phil 2:6–7). Küng aptly summarizes Jesus' small, unassuming, and yet dynamic engagement with the world:

> *Sakandalon*: a small stone over which one might stumble. Jesus in person, with all that he said and did, had become a stumbling stone, a continual scandal. There was his oddly radical identification of God's cause with man's: to what tremendous consequences in theory and practice this had led. He had been aggressive in all sides, now he was attacked on all sides. He had not played any of the expected roles: for those who supported law and order he turned out to be a provocateur, dangerous to the system. He disappointed the activist revolutionaries by his non-violent love of peace. On the other hand he offended the passive world-forsaking ascetics by his uninhibited worldliness. And for the devout who adapted themselves to the world he was too uncompromising. For the silent majority he was too noisy and for the noisy minority he was too quiet, too gentle for the strict and too strict for the gentle. He was an obvious outsider in a critically dangerous social conflict: in opposition both to the prevailing conditions and to those who opposed them.[28]

Today, for Christian leaders, and, even for some secular leaders who would like to emulate him, Jesus is the epitome of an example.

The biographies of the apostles and prominent pioneering missionaries of our modern times have similar background as their master. The "Upper Room," the first meeting place of the disciples, as opposed to the Temple in Jerusalem, was like a modern shack in Soweto, South Africa or Kibera, in Nairobi. They had no budget, library, or organizational plan. In the eyes of the religious leaders of Israel, the apostles were considered "uneducated." Just read the book of Acts to comprehend what the apostles did in the name of the Lord, starting from a small beginning. William Carey, the father of modern missions was a cobbler. Moffat was a gardener to an English nobleman. Others were artisans, carpenters, and day laborers. Despite their small and humble beginnings, they wrote an exciting chapter in Christian history. In the Gospel of Mark chapter 4, Jesus said "the kingdom of God is like a mustard seed." "The seed is sown in our lives so that it may grow and bring fruit in us. The beginnings are small, but if these beginnings are God's, these effects will be great and marvelous. The seeds of the kingdom are like mustard seed, 'the smallest of all the seeds.' But when they germinate they grow into trees big enough for the birds to nest in. The seed grows automatically all by itself, day and night. Its inner strength develops into a blade, and ear, and the field of wheat. If we don't just concentrate on the transferred sense but look at the original one too, we can see the kingdom of God as the reawakening of nature."[29]

From the latest Christian movement out of Africa, a continent known for its poverty and political and economic turmoil, I would like to cite a good example of a small beginning, which has now captured the attention of scholars, pastors, and seminary students. It is a movement in Kiev, Ukraine, "established in November 1993 as a Bible study group of seven people meeting in Adelaja's [a Nigerian] apartment, the new group

---

28. Küng, *On Being a Christian*, 279; emphasis original.
29. Moltmann, *Jesus Christ for Today's World*, 10.

registered as a church three months later with only forty-nine members. Yet, by 2002, after adopting an outreach strategy that targeted the marginalized group in Ukraine society, the church had grown to twenty thousand. Over one million Ukrainians have reportedly been converted to Christianity as a result of its ministry."[30]

If we stop being influenced by the corporate world and follow the pattern of Scripture, we'll have fewer headaches with paying debts for buildings and have more productive time to enhance the kingdom of God. The fastest growing churches in the world today are based on home fellowships or are meeting in tents and under trees. The converts are baptized in rivers and oceans. Their preachers walk miles to reach the unreached, riding on the backs of mules and horses. I'm not writing this sitting on a professor's lofty chair with no practical experience. I was one of those preachers who walked for ten hours, climbing steep mountains, and crossing valleys and rivers. I'm an eyewitness to small beginnings and astonishing growth. If you are certain of your calling in ministry, trust the Lord, listen to his voice, obey him, be patient, labor diligently, run with a godly motive, and keep your integrity. Both in this world and the one to come, your reward will be a hundredfold. Christ has promised this and his word is infallible. Following Christ's model, the African church has a huge role to play in transforming the society through the power of the gospel. Éla writes, "Christian communities in Africa have no future unless they can trust their own internal dynamics, their ongoing ability to respond to challenges, and their on-going capacity to face all their crises and to make full use of community resources and potential. Ecclesiastical institutions within these communities must undergo radical changes. They are still branded by a form of clerical imperialism that has inhibited their ability to innovate and stunted the growth of the laity. The vision of a Christian community incarnated in the life of a people requires that the community have full autonomy in organizing itself."[31] Lack of innovation and empowerment has made Africans subject to all kinds of suffering.

"Every twelve hours, the same number of people killed at the World Trade Center on September 11, 2001 (3,000), perish from AIDS on the continent. In a single year, 150,000 African mothers-half the number of people drowned or crushed in the 2004 Asian tsunami-die, just giving birth."[32] How long will Africa blame external factors, such as the slave trade, colonization, and globalization for her misery today? No matter how small and insignificant it looks, somewhere, somehow, democracy that gives enough room for constructive development and holistic progress has to start and offer hope and space for each individual's view. Among current African countries, it is difficult to find one country that can be taken be used as a model. Hence, "No region in the world exemplifies the view that migration is 'an irrepressible human urge' more clearly than the African continent . . . African peoples are perpetually on the move, and migration (inter-and intra-continental) represents one of the most conspicuous and recurring themes of Africa's history. Yet, even for this most mobile continents, the last three to four decades have witnessed a phenomenal rise in the volume and scope of migrant movement, as escalating conflicts, brutal regimes, and economic collapse have induced

---

30 Hanciles, *Beyond Christendom*, 120.

31. Éla, *My Faith as an African*, 60–61.

32. Calderisi, *Trouble with Africa*, 2–3.

massive displacements of peoples and population transfer."[33] What hurt Africa the most is the "brain drain" that migration has inflicted on the continent. "At least 70,000 skilled graduates—the very people who could be leading an African Renaissance—abandon the continent every year. Until these gifted and enterprising people can be attracted to return, most of the world's peace-keeping efforts on the continent, and certainly most of its aid, will have little effect."[34] "The post-independence problems of Africa are bigger, their roots deeper, their victims younger."[35] Unless Africa's internal political structure becomes democratic and outside powers' foreign policies favorably change to bring about social stability in Africa, the exit door to exile and the brain-drain will continue. Despite Africa's enormous natural resources, the West is the only green pasture African intelligentsia knows. That said, recently China has started to become another alternative destiny for educated Africans.

On their behalf, and millions of others who are working in various professional field in exile, foreign aid organizations are sending foreign experts as vanguards of industrial development.

> They have become so pervasive that Africa, for example, has more expatriates living in it today than it ever did during the era of colonialism and settlement: there are estimated 80,000 foreign 'experts' working on development projects in the world's poorest continent. To this substantial total must be added the legions of short-stay visitors—agency staff on the project-appraisal missions, VIPs from donor countries, consultants conducting feasibility studies, and, of course, researchers. During the 1970s, when Tanzania's ujiamaa villages were at their most fashionable as examples of successful grassroots development, there were occasions when some villages had more researchers than villagers. Much recently the small and hungry West African country of Burkina Faso hosted no fewer than 340 separate 'missions' from the United Nations agencies in a single year.[36]

It is no wonder more than 80 percent of the money passing through the UN system is lavishly spent on its 50,000 staff. With the same educational degrees and years of experience, UN staff are paid seven to ten times more than experts in the majority world. "Although the world body's pampered staff members cost the host city [New York] $125,000 a month in unpaid parking fines, their generous patronage of restaurants, theatres, bars and department stores pumps at least $800, million a year in the Big Apple's economy. 'Development' UN style has little or nothing to do with meeting the needs of the poor."[37]

For this reason we probed the internal factors that contributed to the demise, poverty, migration, and instability of the African continent. We have looked at some of it already. With honesty and a sense of owning our pitfalls I have presented an in-depth reflection on the greed, brutality, irresponsibility, and lack of vision and integrity in leadership among Africans.

---

33. Hanciles, *Beyond Christendom*, 207.
34. Calderisi, *Trouble with Africa*, 5.
35. Éla, *My Faith as an African*, 137.
36. Hancock, *Lords of Poverty*, 114; emphasis original.
37. Ibid., 102.

Slavery has been as old as human history and it is hard to find a country in this world that has never been colonized by another powerful country. Spain was colonized by the Arabs. France was colonized by Rome for almost one hundred years. Today France hosts over 70 million tourists per year. The United States was colonized by the British and the U.S. is the leading economic, military, and political power in the world. Israel was colonized by Babylonians, Assyrians, Greeks, and Romans and their people have suffered at the hands of many enemies including the experience of the Holocaust. Despite all these setbacks, they bounced back and have established strong nations.

I firmly believe that, in spite of all of the horrifying things that have happened to Africans since the slave trade, the ultimate responsibility for African poverty, migration, underdevelopment, high illiteracy, civil wars, and the current pathetic condition of Africans falls on African leaders and elites. Yes, Africa has enormously and mercilessly suffered because of the brutal actions and greed of the West. Africa is also betrayed and crucified by her own children. The latter have done more damage and are still doing it to the continent. Some have served foreign agencies and were used as tools for causes of untold bloodshed, factions, and fragmentation of their countries. Others have literally looted and siphoned money to deposit it in foreign banks. Soldiers have killed innocent demonstrators and raped many women. Judges have done injustice to the poor by giving them wrong and unfair sentences. If Africa is backward and underdeveloped and her people are languishing in poverty for the last sixty years, it is mainly because of African despots.

The most urgent phenomenon that needs close observation and analysis is the expansion of China; they are amassing the natural resources of Africa, dumping their products, and decongesting their territory to respond to their problem of over population. As I write this book, an estimated one million Chinese are busy making a fortune in the continent of Africa. Whether they succeed legally or illegally, it doesn't seem to matter to the Chinese or the African tyrants. But in many countries, Africans have expressed their disgust, disappointment, and anger at their mistreatment. Let us probe further the role and contribution of Christian leadership in overcoming these issues.

Christ Centered Leadership

When it comes to people who have influenced and impacted our lives, we all have heroes and heroines in our society—sports legends, politicians, scientists, successful business people, missionaries, pastors, theologians, and the like. So long as it is compatible with the teachings of Scripture, there is nothing wrong with drawing principles, values, and ethos from people we would like to emulate. There are many who can be good examples of hard work, dedication, commitment, sacrificial service, focus, time management, and incredible achievements. Christian leaders can use the resources of books, people, and culture to enhance the quality and effectiveness of their leadership. The problem arises when we allow local heroes and heroines to overshadow Christ and we succumb to the values of this world more than the kingdom of God. This can be seen when we preach about eternity and yet are consumed by temporal issues and needs. It is also a problem when we let other works of literature judge Scripture and we embrace the secular message by neglecting the spiritual. When this happens, our leadership cannot be Christ-centered.

If we think of it, both our salvation and our call to ministry are initiated by God and given to us through the grace available to humankind because of the work of Jesus Christ. "For it is by grace you have been saved, it is the gift of God—not by works, so that no one can boast. For we are God's workmanship, created in Christ Jesus to do good works, which God prepared in advance for us to do" (Eph 2:8–10). Who we are in Christ, and what we do in his name, is all by the grace of God, "so that no one can boast." Whether it is we or our legends and heroes, no one can boast and say, "It is me, I did it!" What is there that we haven't received? "For in him we live and move and have our being" (Acts 17:28). If we had to pay a nickel (5 cents) per minute for the oxygen we breathe, how many of us could afford to live in this world? The air we breathe is an extraordinary gift without even beginning to mention the water, sunshine, trees, oceans, and mountains that make the earth a habitable place. Writing about the supremacy of Christ, the apostle Paul said, "For by him all things were created: things in heaven and on earth, visible and invisible, whether thrones, powers or rulers or authorities, all things were created by him and for him. He is before all things and in him all things hold together" (Col 1:16–17). Who else can be the center of our leadership but Jesus Christ? He is the reason for our being, the source of our salvation, a guide during times of uncertainty, a wonderful counselor, and a teacher and a mentor—during our service on earth. He is the one who calls and empowers people for Christian leadership. But what does it mean to make Christ the center of our leadership? Different people with different theological persuasions can have different opinions. For me, it means the following:

1. He is the only man who can claim to be God. We need to believe him and follow his commands with no reservation. We should worship him, not as a god among many gods, but as the God who was there before the creation of the world and as the one who will come to judge the world.

2. He is the only way for eternal salvation. Since Christians believe his claims are true and absolute, we shall continue proclaiming him as the only light for those in the darkness of sin. There is no shortcut, alternative, or human device that can reconcile people with God. In other words, the church cannot be inclusivist: "Salvation is found in no one else, for there is no other name under heaven given to men by which we must be saved" (Acts 4:12).

3. Since he lived an exemplary life while he was on this earth, both in word and deed, as a Christian leader, I uphold him as our ultimate example and our final authority. Like our Savior, a Christian leader is expected to live what he teaches and preaches. Often, we don't fail in articulating a statement of faith but in applying it in real and challenging life situations. In Christ we don't see a contradiction between his words and actions. "Even Jesus' *words* were eminently *deeds*. His word alone demanded total commitment. And it was through his word that decisive event occurred: the *situation* was *fundamentally changed*. Neither people nor institutions, neither the hierarchies nor the norms were ever again the same as they had been before. Both God's cause and man's found expression in his liberating words. He thus opened up

to men completely new possibilities, the possibility of a new life and a new freedom, of a new meaning in life: a life according to God's will for man's well-being, in the freedom of life, outstripping all legalism…Jesus' words therefore did not amount to any sort of pure 'theory': he was, in fact, not particularly interested in theory at all. His proclamation was wholly related, oriented, to practice. His demands required a free response, but imposed new obligations and had consequences."[38]

4. Since Jesus' teachings are true and without error and his values are unquestionable, as the grace of God enables them, Christian leaders need to joyfully embrace, teach, and preach, biblical truth. In his school of leadership, the least are the greatest, servants are masters, poor are rich, last are first, those who give save, those who horde lose. Love, reconciliation, forgiveness, integrity, humility, blameless character, and sacrificial service are marks of his disciples and the leaders who exercise spiritual authority to bring others to Christian maturity. The rules of the game for Christian leaders are different because the one we serve and worship is unique and different. "Jesus called his followers to respond to hunger with food, to nakedness with clothes, to imprisonment with visitation, to beatings with bandages and to injustice with justice Matthew 15:32–38; 25:35–36; Luke 10:34; 11:42."[39]

5. God has given us a mind to think. He expects us to use it to the best of our ability as we lead others. Outlining of thoughts, clear communication, deep teaching, and transformative preaching are expected from Christian leaders. However, reason should not be the prominent and determining factor of our leadership activities. Since the finite can't fully comprehend the infinite, faith should have a significant place for a Christian leader. Without faith we can't please God (Heb 11:6).

6. A leader is a worker in God's vineyard. Therefore, the agendas, goals, objectives, and principles of our leadership should have a spiritual tone and value. Our motives, passion, and actions should reflect that of the Lord's not ours. "Christ isn't merely a person. He is a road too. And the person who believes him takes the same road he took. There is no Christology without christopraxis, no knowledge of Christ without the practice of hearts. We come to understand him through a total, all embracing practice of living; and that means discipleship."[40]

7. A Christian leader is not always popular. There is a cross to bear, a price to pay, and it can be hard to go through rejection, loneliness, suffering, and failure without knowing the one who called us to serve him and completely trust him to heal, provide, and sustain us in the time of difficulty. Paul writes, "I can do everything through him who gives me strength" (Phil 4:13). In the midst of the storms of life, Christ can be a formidable anchor for a leader. "The passionately loving Christ, the persecuted Christ, the lonely Christ, the tortured Christ, the Christ who suffers under God's silence—this is our brother, the friend to whom we can entrust

---

38. Küng, *On Being a Christian*, 265; emphasis original.
39. Haugen, *Good News about Injustice*, 110.
40. Moltmann, *Sun of Righteousness Arise!*, 47.

everything because he knows everything and has suffered everything that can happen to us, and more even than that."[41]

8. To fully enjoy the spiritual blessings of being a Christian leader, one has to seriously consider the spiritual disciplines that draw us to the Lord. These disciplines include prayer, fasting, reading the Scripture, and an open attitude to spiritual gifts.

I could have listed many other points, but for the sake of addressing one final issue, let me turn your attention to Christ. I've tried to explain what I meant by "Christ-centered leadership." Nowadays, it is also important to ask which Christ? Which Christ do we have to put at the center of our leadership? The Christ who promised health and wealth and who always keeps his followers from sickness and poverty? The Christ who Gandhi told Hindus to seriously study and to give him a place in Hinduism? The Christ the Qur'an teaches? The Christ in European Protestant thought that Collin Brown addressed in his book (*Philosophy and the Christian Faith*)? The Christ the humanist portrays and the philosophers describe as an abstract construct dangling in the air? Or, the Christ who is revealed through Scripture that the prophets and the apostles preached? I hope you have sensed my line of thought and conviction by now and my answer should be obvious to you. At the risk of being considered foolish, the Christ the apostles preached should be the center of our leadership (1 Cor 1:18–25). "The word 'Christian' today is more of soporific than a slogan. So much—too much—is Christian."[42] For many, Christ is no longer the chief cornerstone of our faith, but just one of the blocks among many other gods and thinkers who are helping us to build the system of our belief. To be a philanthropist, relevant, modern, enlightened, humanistic, and democratic, the Christ we know in the Gospels is sacrificed on the altar of reason. The popular Christ in the world today is tolerant and inclusive—even the issues contradict his being and teaching. Unequivocally Hans Küng concurs:

> According to the earliest testimony and that of tradition as a whole, the special feature of Christianity again is this Jesus himself who is constantly and freshly known and acknowledged as Christ. Here to there is a countertest: none of the evolutionary or revolutionary humanisms, however much they may occasionally respect as a man even set him up as an example, would regard him as ultimately decisive, definitive and archetypal in all dimensions. The special feature, the most fundamental characteristic of Christianity is that it considers this Jesus as ultimately decisive, definitive, archetypal, for man's relations with God, with his fellowman, with society: in the curtailed human formula, as "Jesus Christ."
>
> From both perspectives the conclusion emerges that, if Christianity seeks to become relevant, freshly relevant, to men in the world religions, to the modern humanists, it will certainly not be simply by saying later what others said first, by doing later what others did first. Such a parrot-like Christianity does not become relevant to the humanisms . . . Christianity can ultimately be and become relevant only by activating—as always, in theory and practice—the memory of

---

41. Ibid., 36.
42. Küng, *On Being a Christian*, 119.

Jesus as ultimately archetypal: of Jesus the Christ and not only as one of the archetypal men.[43]

If you put this Christ at the center of your leadership, your self-image, your concept of success and failure, and your place for the church and the kingdom of God will have a healthy and balanced biblical perspective. Your Christian maturity is guaranteed and the possibility of achieving the goals and dreams God has put in your heart "even if you go through the valley of death" is high.

Developing Wise Leaders

In my reading of many leadership books, I have hardly come across any authors whose focus is to make wise leaders or readers. Topics on motivation, assertiveness, power, organizational culture, human behavior, decision making, vision, strategy, and planning are very common. However, the wisdom that Scripture emphasizes and the teachers of Israel hammered into the hearts and minds of their pupils is hard to come by from the pens and pulpits of Western teachers and pastors. I often wonder whether we have focused on the peripherals and lost the fundamentals of leadership. "Israel's teachers were persistently passionate in their concern to lead their students in the right path. They argued, badgered, reasoned, illustrated, pleaded, and commended in order to make their points. In short, they cared . . . Wisdom for them was a matter of nothing less than life or death. It was a way in which children of the covenant with Yahweh to live. And it was the only course in life that made both present and ultimate sense."[44] Being children of the new covenant, living between the now and the not-yet in creative tension, I argue that our need for wisdom cannot be less than the children of Israel. Leaders especially need a double dose of wisdom in our time, particularly in the African context.

Wisdom is key to survival and success in life. To those who embrace it, wisdom shields them and leads them to victory in the battle of life; it guards the course of the just, saves them from the ways of the wicked, and guards as we try to live by right choices and decisions (Prov 2:1–16). To highlight the importance of wisdom, God described it in military nouns and verbs. To deliver and rescue is wisdom's chief mission. Without having wisdom to shield, guard, protect, and save us, we often take psychological pills to boost our leadership image and self-confidence. When this happens, in the heat of battle, we end up being a Goliath before David.

For those of you who are hungry for wisdom, I encourage you to study the wisdom literature in the Bible, Proverbs in particular. This particular book warns against perverted speech, loose sexuality, ungodly self-reliance, greed, hastiness, lying, laziness, disruptive social behavior, bad company, and many other vices. These ungodly motives and behaviors have been fatal viruses that have ruined the leadership and families of many. Instead of using their God-given intelligence and time for a worthy cause, such as inventing medicine, alleviating the burden of the poor, or giving hope to those who are languishing in hunger and disease, many waste their lives in frivolousness. While

43. Küng, *On Being a Christian*, 123–24.
44. Hubbard, *Communicator's Commentary*, 43.

they could create opportunities for education for many world illiterates, improve the communication and transportation systems in the majority world, or be an ambassador of Christ to spread the good news of salvation and disciple converts into Christ-like maturity, those who hate wisdom waste their life in unproductive, shameful, and regrettable way. Plenty of examples of failed leaders are illustrated in this book. The Bible calls these people fools. The best epitaph we can find for their tombstones, which would fit the description of their lives, would say: "The evil deeds of a wicked man ensnare him; the cords of his sin hold him fast. He will die for lack of discipline, led astray by his own great folly" (Prov 5:22–23). Listen to those who think they have made it in life and enjoy the pleasures of this world but lack of wisdom and end up in addiction, divorce, and insurmountable debt. Watch those whose children have gone into self-destructive lifestyles and make poor decisions because of the bitterness and loneliness they developed as a result of being neglected by their own parents. Spend time with a congregation whose leader committed adultery or embezzled money and listen emphatically to their bitter disappointment and heart-wrenching grief. Then, and only then, can you appreciate the value of wisdom. Wisdom explicitly warns against destructive motives, behaviors, and actions. Wisdom describes her assets this way: "Blessed is the man who listens to me, watching daily at my gates, waiting at the posts of my doors. For whoever finds me finds life, and obtains favor from the Lord; But he who sins against me wrongs his own soul; all those who hate me love death" (Prov 8: 34–36). The book of Proverbs contains not only warnings but also exhorts knowledge, diligence, wisdom, prudence, discretion, learning, listening, hard work, saving, respect for parents and teachers, trusting God, and fearing God.

In contrast to the ABCs of things we learn from home, society, and school, to succeed in life the students of ancient Israel were told, "The fear of the Lord is the beginning of knowledge" (Prov 1:7). In Western culture fear often has a negative connotation. They are groomed "to fear nothing but fear itself." As David Hubbard explained it, "Fear includes worship, it does not end there. It radiates out from our adoration and devotion to our every conduct that sees each moment as the Lord's time, each relationship as the Lord's opportunity, each duty as the Lord's command, and each blessing as Lord's gift. It is a new way of looking at life and seeing what it is meant to be when viewed from God's perspective . . . The point is that obeying God is the ceiling as well as the foundation of life. It should lead to knowledge, and in turn, all knowledge should enhance it."[45] Knowing God, obeying his commands, and willingly applying his teachings to our daily lives and service are "the ceiling as well as the foundation of life." As foolish and as backward as it may sound to a "modern" mind or to African tyrants, the leadership programs in African and Western seminaries need to be anchored in this eternal truth.

Both secular and religious organizations are suffering not because their leaders are lacking degrees, money, and prestige or success stories but because their leaders lack wisdom and are killing the trust put in them to steward the post of influence, power, responsibility, and service. Leaders are entrusted to accomplish their duties with integrity and diligence. Wise leaders avoid perverted speech so that they may not offend their listeners and lose respect in the eyes of their followers. Wise leaders reject ungodly

45. Ibid., 48.

self-reliance that leads to pride and destruction. Unblemished character, integrity, truth, reputable friends, accountability, happy and contented family members—results such as these that edify followers and glorify their God are the ornaments of wise leaders. In setting an exemplary life standard for others in word and deed, wise leaders exhort people saying: "Whatever things are true, whatever things are noble, whatever things are pure, whatever things are lovely, whatever things are of good report, if there is any virtue, and if there is anything praiseworthy—meditate on these. The things which you learned and received and heard and saw in me, these do, and the God of peace will be with you" (Phil 4:8–9). Before he expected the above-mentioned virtues in the lives of Philippian Christians, Paul demonstrated them in his own life while he lived among them. His life was a glass house. With authority and credibility, he told them, "These things which you learned and received and heard and saw in me, these do, and the God of peace will be with you" (Phil 4:9). Hence, wisdom has pedagogical character, Paul taught them. Wisdom is not irresistible; it has to be voluntarily received by its people. Wisdom is observable, and leaders have a primary responsibility to show it. Wisdom is not mere theory; both teachers and students can and should apply it. There are approved and disapproved workers, and the line of separation between the two divides wisdom and folly (2 Tim 2:14–26). Through integrated academic curriculum, contextualized theology, and ministry philosophy, by teaching and modeling, African pastors and scholars have a responsibility to develop and empower wise leaders in all sectors of society. Godly Christian presence and involvement in the judicial, economic, political, academic, and governing aspects of African society are vital if we want Africa to come out of the current political and economic quagmire. In all we do in Christian leadership, our ultimate goal should be to develop leaders who know Christ first before they attempt to make him known. Jesus is the embodiment of wisdom.

Chapter 10

Christ

The Wounded Healer in Africa

Surely he took up our infirmities and carried our sorrows, yet we considered him stricken by God, smitten by him and afflicted. But he was pierced for our transgressions, he was crushed for our iniquities; the punishment that brought us peace was upon him, and *by his wounds we are healed.* We all, like sheep have gone astray, each of us has turned to his own way; and the Lord has laid on him the iniquity of us all. He was oppressed and afflicted, yet he did not open his mouth, he was led like a lamb to the slaughter, and as a sheep her shearers is silent, so he did not open his mouth. By oppression and judgment he was taken away. And he can speak of his descendants? For he was cut off from the land of the living; for the transgression of my people he was stricken. He was assigned a grave with the wicked, and with the rich in his death, though he had done no violence, nor was any deceit in his mouth. Yet it was the Lord's will to crush him and cause him to suffer, and though the Lord makes his life a guilt offering, he will see his offspring and prolong his days, and the will of the Lord will prosper in his hand. After the suffering of his soul, he will see the light of life and be satisfied; by his knowledge my righteous servant will justify many, and he will bear their iniquities. (Isa 53:4–11)

"Jesus, remember me when you come into your kingdom" (Luke 23:42). How could this thief view a beaten, bloodied, and crucified criminal as one who rules over a kingdom?[1]

Suffering as chastisement is man's own responsibility; suffering as redemption is God's responsibility.[2]

1. Treat, *Crucified King*, 25.
2. Heschel, *Prophets*, 193.

During my research, I found Jeremy R. Treat's book *The Crucified King: Atonement and Kingdom in Biblical and Systematic Theology* an oasis in the desert. It quenched my thirst for understanding the African situation from God's redemptive perspective. In his meticulous research and academic work that transcends culture and race, Treat addresses "the problem of the separation of the kingdom and the cross in the church as well as the academy."[3] Being a person of African origin, I found this book to be very enriching to my intellectual pursuits and spiritual life. When Bible scholars make the Scripture speak to your context, it is just like a breath of fresh air.

Treat gives six reasons for the separation of the cross and the kingdom: first, and most important, the wedge driven between kingdom and the cross is largely the result of reactionary debates between those who emphasize the kingdom and those who focus on the cross. Second, the fragmentation of Scripture that has occurred since the Enlightenment has contributed greatly to the severance of the kingdom and cross. If the Bible is not a unified whole, then there is no need to integrate the seemingly incompatible ideas that God reigns and the Son of God dies. Third, the kingdom-cross divide is widened by the "ugly ditch" between biblical studies and systematic theology. Fourth, kingdom and cross have not been integrated because the Gospels (the place in the canon where the kingdom theme is most explicit) have largely been withheld as a source for theology. Fifth, kingdom and cross have been difficult to relate to because of the oversystematization of certain doctrines, such as the states and offices of Christ. Sixth, if one has a mistaken view of the kingdom or the cross respectively, then properly relating the two will be impossible.[4]

While I highly recommend reading the whole of Treat's book, I would like to focus on chapter 2 for its relevance to my topic in this chapter. Treat believes that the Suffering Servant and his kingdom context are not separate episodes that are unrelated to each other. He said, "The rediscovered unity of the book of Isaiah has re-opened the door for scholars to explore the relationship between the Messianic King of Isaiah 1–39 and the servant of Isaiah 40–55, many of them concluding that the two titles refer to one messianic figure."[5] (2014:69). The following points are a summary of Treat's arguments that identify the servant and the king:

1. *The title servant.* The fact that the key figure of Isa 52:13—53:12 is called "my servant" (52:13; 53:11) provides "overwhelming" evidence that he is identifying with the Davidic Messiah.

2. *Anointed for specific tasks.* Both the king and the servant are anointed with the Spirit of Yahweh for the tasks of establishing justice (Isa 9:7 [6]; 42:1–4), bringing light to the nations (9:2; 42:6–7), and opening the eyes of the blind (32:3; 42:7).

3. *Botanical imagery.* The king and the servant are described with botanical imagery, both being called a "root" (Isa 11:10; 53:2).

---

3. Treat, *Crucified King*, 25.
4. Ibid., 26–28.
5. Ibid., 69.

4. *Davidic covenant and kingdom.* The messianic King and the servant are both connected to God's promises to David (Isa 9:7; 55:3).

5. *Royal characteristics.* The promise of victory (Isa 52:12–13), response of the kings (52:14–15; cf. 49:7), and burial with the rich (53:9) suggest a royal interpretation for the servant.

6. *Early Jewish interpretation.* The *Targum of Isaiah* adds "the messiah" after "my servant" in Isa 52:13, showing that early interpreters identified the Suffering Servant with the Messianic King.[6]

More than anything, Treat's book affirms to a Christian reader that humanity is not alone in the tragedy and comedy of life. The God of the Bible is not just transcendent, untouchable, and unreachable, but from the creation to the consummation of human history and the redemption of the cosmos, God is actively engaged in the history of humankind through his redemptive work. With thorough academic research, Treat shows hope in a hopeless world and meaning in a meaningless situations of war, animosity, and hatred.

I don't find any other meaningful and satisfying approach in analyzing the past, present, and future of the continent of Africa than through the suffering of Christ and his kingship. Hence, the following two chapters focus on the crucified Christ and his kingdom in the light of the African context.

What Kind of God?

Even if our knowledge of God primarily derives from the same source (the Bible) through special revelation, it does not mean that all Christians embrace the same understanding of God, or we relate to and comprehend the same kind of God. "It is not enough to say that one believes in God. What is important finally is the kind of God in whom one believes."[7] As we saw earlier, according to the biblical interpretation of some, God is behind the curse of Ham and gave black skin to some and destined them to be slaves to the light skinned race. From that kind of biblical understanding, Westerners perceived themselves to have a greater destiny. Answering the question of who God is, is appropriate for African who desire to know, worship, and serve him within their cultural context and beyond. Africans must also be careful not to fall into the trap of reverse racist theology in the name of liberation. "The question of the kind of God in whom one believes is not only important, it is crucial. It is a question of image. Metaphors matter."[8] Does the God of the Bible relate with human beings with the disclosure of his concern and a concealment of his power, or is he a self-sufficient and good God who is not affected by the tiny particles of his creation as the Greek philosophers say?

According to the Greek thinkers, "God is most commonly thought of as a First Cause that started the world's mechanism working, and which continues to function

---

6. Ibid., 70–71; emphasis original.
7. Fretheim, *Suffering of God*, 1.
8. Ibid., 1.

according to its own inherent laws and processes. It seems inconceivable that the Supreme Being should be involved in the affairs of human existence . . . Since the first condition for happiness is the absence of worry, which can be attained only by *ataraxia*, by living apart from the world, politics and affairs, a concern with which spoils tranquility and peace, it therefore appeared absurd, according to Epicurus, to assume that the gods should concern themselves with the affairs of men."[9] If God is self-sufficient he does not need to engage with human affairs and the world because it is irrelevant to him. There is nothing that human beings add to his excellency, majesty, and power. Human beings are not needed in God's redemptive plan. Because he has set the world like a mechanism, he doesn't and won't interfere in the history of humankind. "In Greek religion, the gods are not regarded as friends of man. Vindictiveness, ill-will, niggardliness on the part of the gods were continually decried by the writers of Hellas."[10] Viewing gods in this way led man to autonomy and self-reliance. "The idea of the self-sufficiency of God became fused with the idea of the self-sufficiency of man. The certainty of man's capacity to find peace, perfection, and the meaning of existence gained increasing momentum with the advancement of technology. Man's fate, it was maintained, depended solely upon the development of his social awareness and the utilization of his own power. The course of history was regarded as perpetual progress in cooperation, an increasing harmonization of interests. Man is too good to be in need of supernatural guidance."[11] However, in spite of what many believe, atheism is not a step forward on the ladder of civilization. "Those who act as if there was no God, no divine order in history, are more foolish than one who would sow and plant, while completely disregarding the nature of the soil or the seasons of the year. They act as if man were alone, as if their deeds were carried out in the dark, as if there were no God Who saw, no God Who knew."[12] The uncaused cause or Greek God, who has nothing to do with human affairs, should not be the God of African intelligentsia who are influenced by Enlightenment academics and philosophers. "A first cause or an idea of the absolute—devoid of life, devoid of freedom—is an issue for science or metaphysics rather than a concern of the soul or the conscience. An affirmation of such a cause or such an idea would be an answer unrelated to our question. *The living soul is not concerned with a dead cause but with a living God*. Our goal is to ascertain the existence of a Being to who we may confess our sins, of a God who loves, of a God who is not above concern with our iniquity and search for Him; a father, not an absolute."[13]

It is not only the philosophers; Eastern religions and Islam also have a different view of God than Christians:

> *Tao*, the ultimate ground from which all things emanate, is a dark abysmal something, nameless and indefinite. *Tao* is the eternal silence, the everlasting calm, and the unchangeable law of cosmic order, immanent in all things. In accordance with *Tao*, freedom from desires is man's supreme virtue. Man must lay

---

9. Heschel, *Prophets*, 299, 300. See also Brown, *Philosophy and the Christian Faith*; and Copleston, *A History of Philosophy*.
10. Ibid., 313.
11. Ibid., 303.
12. Ibid., 87.
13. Heschel, *God in Search of Man*, 125–26; emphasis added.

aside all desires and inclinations, surrender all lusts and passions, and imitate *Tao* in its potent and humble tranquility.[14]

The great Hindu doctrine of karma is the law of consequences by which the amount of pain is precisely equated with the amount of wrongdoing throughout the series of reincarnations. Working by its own efficacy, it operates unequivocally, inexorably, automatically; no god would have any right to come in and confound this beautiful exactitude of adjustment by freeing individual sinners from the consequences of their actions. Karma and its *vipåka*, the act and its fruit, are inextricably interwoven.[15]

Küng adds:

The God of Israel and Jesus is *different from the impersonal divinity of Eastern religions*. *Hinduism* and *Buddhism* also accept a supreme reality. And yet, at least at their higher levels of reflection, they are largely indifferent of a personal creator of the world. The supreme reality—Brahmanic theology, created the world and glories in the fact.

This supreme reality is frequently understood—as in the classical Hindu philosophy of Sankhya—in a strictly monistic way, as an absolute unity of being. While atheism believes only in the world and nothing in God and normal theism in God and the world, so philosophically oriented Hinduism and Buddhism believe—superatheistically—only in God. This absolute, impersonal, one being here too however is by no means nothingness without content, but in fact pure being. And human qualities, even the noblest, are still too feeble and inadequate to serve as a way of describing it. Thus the absolute remains undefinable: it escapes any demarcation in a clearly outlined anthropomorphic concept. That is why there are a great number of truly religious standpoints, of approaches to the absolute, modes of worship. While Jesus then promises entry into the kingdom of God and thus a personal and universal salvation, Hinduism and Buddhism promise entry into nirvana and thus extinction in an eternal repose without desire, without suffering, without consciousness.[16]

The God of the Bible is not only different than that of Eastern religions, he is also different from the God of the Qur'an: "For all the belief in divine mercy, Allah is essentially thought of as unqualified Omnipotence, Whose will is absolute, not conditioned by anything man may do. He acts without regard for the specific situation of man. Since everything is determined by Him, it is a monologue that obtains between Allah and man, rather than a dialogue or mutuality as in the biblical view. Not the relation between Allah and man, but simply Allah himself is central to Islam."[17]

The kind of God one believes in shapes one's perception and pursuits in life, as well as one's understanding of the cosmos and meaning of existence. One's engagement with and interpretation of history and relationship with the world and other human beings can be immensely influenced by the kind of God believed in. The encounters between Moses and the magicians in Egypt, between Elijah and the prophets of Baal, and between

---

14. Heschel, *Prophets*, 303.
15. Ibid., 305.
16. Küng, *On Being a Christian*, 301.
17. Heschel, *Prophets*, 311. See also Küng, *Christianity and World Religions*.

Daniel and the Babylonians, as well as Jesus Christ's encounter in the Greco-Roman world and with the Pharisees are ample evidence for how the kind of God people believe in puts them in worlds apart.

The God of Christians has "a human face." Küng writes:

> God . . . should not be conceived as an abstract idea remote from man, but as concrete reality which is by no means indifferent to him but absolutely involves him and imposes claims on him. He is not a God who remains immovable in (or outside) a moving world, but the God who acts within the scope of human history, makes himself known in human happenings, reveals himself in a human way, makes possible encounter, conversation, association, with himself. He is then not a God who keeps out of everything and remains exalted in a transcendence untouched by the world's suffering, but one who actively takes part and becomes involved in this somber history. He is not a God of solitude, but a God of partnership, of the covenant. He is not an apathetic, unfeeling, impassible, but a sympathetic, compassionate God. In brief, he is a God with a human face.[18]

An aloof and un-relatable God leaves us empty and frustrated by the chasm between him and us. It is a chasm that will keep us restless and frustrated until the loud and empty gap is filled with something. Human beings are not alone. The Bible begins with God addressing, caring for, and empowering humanity. Even after the relationship between God and humanity was affected we see God searching for humanity—"But the Lord God called to the man, where are you?" (Gen 2:8b). The word "but" is important here to understand. It indicates the position of humanity and God toward each other. Adam and Eve were hiding from God while God was searching for them as a woman would search for her lost precious diamond. Adam and Eve were running from God and God was pursuing them. "Sin is not an ultimate, irreducible or independent condition, but rather a disturbance in the relationship between God and man; it is an adverb not a noun, a condition that can be surmounted by man's return and God's forgiveness."[19] He adds, "The predicament of man is the predicament of God Who has a stake in the human situation. Sin, guilt, suffering, cannot be separated from the divine situation. The life of sin is more than a failure of man; it is a frustration to God. Thus, man's alienation from God is not the ultimate fact by which to measure man's situation. The divine pathos, the fact of God's participation in the predicament of man, is the elemental fact."[20] And this God is the same for all humankind and its transgressions—black, white, yellow, rich, poor, educated, or illiterate. It is a sin to create God in our own image and have him endorse our own theological bent to oppress and exploit other human beings and abuse and misuse nature.

Since the Christian faith is founded on the teachings of the apostles and prophets (Eph 2:20), it is important to know the kind of God we believe in. Unlike the Greek gods and the gods of other major world religions, "the God of the prophets is not the Wholly Other, a strange, weird, uncanny Being, shrouded in unfathomable darkness, but the God of the covenant, Whose will they know and are called upon to convey. The God they

---

18. Küng, *On Being a Christian*, 308.
19. Heschel, *Prophets*, 295.
20. Ibid., 291.

proclaim is not the Remote One, but the One Who is involved, near, and concerned. The Silent One may be the antithesis of man, but prophecy is God meeting man."[21] (Heschel 1962:292).

> The modern understanding of God must start out from a coherent understanding of reality: God in this world and this world in God. This is a God who is not merely part of reality, a (supreme) finite alongside the finite, but the infinite in the finite, the absolute in the relative, the hidden-close, the present-hereafter, the transcendent-imminent, ultimate reality in the heart of things, in man and in the history of mankind. He is the God who does not operate merely in some sort of "supernatural" realm or exclusively within the periods of salvation History: in emergencies as a helper in need in history or stopgap in the cosmos: that is, only at the point where man's natural resources fail, where he cannot make further progress. God is the most reality, active in all thing reality: everywhere at all times providing the world and men with a final point of reference, a unity, value and meaning. There is no action of God alongside world history, but only in the history of the world and of man's activity.[22]

Hiebert elaborates on Küng's observation: in the New Testament, the God of the prophets became human—who is "the radiance of God's glory and the exact representation of his being" (Heb. 1:3). "He was with God in the beginning" (John 1:1) and "He was in the world" (John 1:10). "The progressive unfolding of God's self-revelation culminates in the person of Jesus, God became incarnate among us so that we see and hear him. Christ Jesus shows us who God is as far as we can comprehend him. He also shows us what it means to be truly human."[23]

Even if it were a painstaking process, the early church had to come up with a doctrine that defined the kind of God she believed because of the religiously pluralistic world in which she found herself. "The doctrine of one God, the Father and creator, formed the background and indisputable premises of the church's faith. Inherited from Judaism, it was her bulwark against pagan polytheism, Gnostic emanationism and Marcionite dualism. The problem for theology was to integrate with it, intellectually, the fresh data of the specifically Christian revelation. Reduced to simplest these were the convictions that God had made Himself known in the Person of Jesus, the Messiah, raising Him from the dead and offering salvation to men through Him, and that He had poured out His Holy spirit upon the Church."[24] Knowing the kind of God we believe in matters.

The God of the Bible is not only a creator but he is also relationally involved in the affairs of, cares for, and is concerned about humankind. He is righteous in all he does and lover of justice. His wrath and judgment on oppressors and evil-doers is not a reflection of his cruelty. It is a manifestation of his compassion for the poor and his passion for justice. "Justice is not an ancient custom, a human convention, a value, but transcendent demand, freighted with divine concern. It is not only relationship between man and man, it is an *act* involving God, a divine need. Justice is His line, righteousness

---

21. Ibid., 292.
22. Küng, *On Being a Christian*, 295.
23. Hiebert, *Transforming Worldviews*, 266.
24. Kelley, *Early Christian Doctrine*, 87.

His plummet (Isa. 28:17), It is not one of His ways, but in all His ways. Its validity is not only universal, but also eternal, independent of will and experience."[25]

Justice is the central focus of the Old Testament prophets: "Seek justice, undo oppression; defend the fatherless, plead for the widow" (Isa 1:7). "Thus says the Lord: Do justice and righteousness, and deliver from the hand of the oppressor him who has been robbed. Do no wrong or violence to the alien, the fatherless, and the widow, nor shed innocent blood in this place" (Jer 22:3). "Amend your ways and your doings; . . . execute justice one with another; . . . do not oppress the alien, the fatherless or the widow" (Jer 7:5–6). The uncompromised message of the prophets often made them walk a lonely path in life and test the bitter cup of rejection. "The prophets, at the time of the institutionalized kingdom until the fall of the northern and later of southern kingdom, the destruction of the temple and the exile to Babylon. Solitary, powerless not getting a hearing and apparently unsuccessful, these prophets remain without followers and fail to carry with them an enthusiastic movement. The lamentation of the prophets from Elijah to Jeremiah provides abundant evidence of the loneliness, exhaustion, despair of the misunderstood and worn-out messengers of the one God. The tension between their human weakness and the mandate imposed on them, between inability and obligation to speak, threaten to tear them apart."[26] Had it not been for God's compassion and the sacrificial boldness of the prophets, justice might have been an orphan and life could have been a living hell.

The ministry of Christ and the apostles was not indifferent to the misery, plight, and anguish of the poor. Luke in particular gave it special attention in his gospel. Mazamisa comments: "[Luke's] concern is with the social issues he writes about: with the demons and evil forces in first century society which deprived women, men and children of dignity and selfhood, of sight and voice and bread, and sought to control their lives for private gain; with the people's own selfishness and servility; and with the promise and possibilities of the poor and the outcastes."[27]

The first public words of Jesus in Luke's Gospel (Luke 4:18) contain a programmatic statement concerning his mission to reverse the destiny of the poor: "'The Spirit of the Lord is upon me, because he has anointed me to preach good news to the poor. He has sent me to proclaim release to the captives and recovery of sight to the blind; to set at liberty those who are oppressed, to proclaim the acceptable year of the Lord.' These words of from the book of Isaiah become, in Luke's gospel, a sort of manifesto of Jesus . . . [The quote is taken from] Isaiah 61:1f and 58:6 . . . the phrase 'to let the oppressed go free' has a distinctly social profile in Isaiah 58. It stands in the context of prophetic criticism of social discrepancies in Judah, of the exploitation of the poor by the rich. Even on the day of fasting the latter pursue their interest."[28]

Reflecting on Matt 6:21, Craig Blomberg adds, "What one does with one's material possessions will disclose one's ultimate allegiance. Jesus develops this point with an

---

25. Heschel, *Prophets*, 253; emphasis original. See also Heschel, *God in Search of Man*; and Heschel, *Man is not Alone*.

26. Küng, *On Being a Christian*, 299–300.

27. Mazamisa, *Beatific Comradeship*, 99.

28. Bosch, *Transforming Mission*, 100.

analogy from human anatomy as it was understood in the first century. Without modern scientific insight, people naturally assumed that the eyes took light form the outside to fill a person's body with brightness. But if one's eyes were diseased and a person went blind, all they would experience was darkness. Similarly, if one looks on the world and sees only possessions to be acquired and hoarded, it is as if one's eyes are malfunctioning. The spiritual darkness will be great indeed (vv. 22–23; cf. Luke 11:34–36)."[29]

In short, from both the Old and New Testaments, the kind of God we see is a God who communicates with humankind. He speaks to people in their context despite their social, economic, political, or religious status. God deals with people in righteousness and justice irrespective of who they are. God cares and loves. He suffers *for* humanity and *from* humanity's rejection and *with* humanity in its brokenness. Christ demonstrated justice and suffering in creative tension. Treat writes: "While the king is said to have establish 'his kingdom' (Isa 9:7), the servant is described as having 'no . . . majesty that we should look at him' (53:2). The king is called 'Wonderful counselor, mighty God' (Isa 9:6); the servant 'a man of sorrows' (53:3). Of the king Scripture says, 'The government shall be in his shoulder' (Isa 9:6); yet the servant only 'carried our sorrows' (53:4). The king is said to 'strike the earth with the rod of his mouth' (11:4), but the servant 'opened not his mouth' (53:7). The king will rise up to 'kill the wicked' (11:4), but the servant is 'cut off the land of the living' (53:10)."[30]

God dealt with the proud monarchs of Israel, Babylon, Assyria, Persia, and Greece and also had dealt with disobedient people and priests and greedy and oppressive landowners. In this he demonstrated compassion for the poor and mercy and restoration to all sinners who stray from his ways. He hates the injustice, exploitation, and enslavement of people.

In Africa, the plight of the poor is loud; their suffering is long and seems never-ending. It is a continent where life expectancy is low, illiteracy and unemployment are extremely high, and violent war cuts many lives short and forces millions to flee their homes as refugees. Children are malnourished and many die of hunger. In all of this, the God of the Bible should speak to the context of the society. Pastors and theologians, para-church organization leaders, and Christian politicians and educators should not whisper the message of God. Like a mighty river or a lion, they should roar the word of God. The message and life of Christians should pierce the consciences of the greedy, the oppressors, and the exploiters. "The tragedy of this late hour is that we have too many *dead* men in the pulpits, giving too many *dead* sermons to too many *dead* people. . .Preaching without unction kills instead of giving life. The unctionless preacher is a savor of death unto death."[31]

The African church cannot bank solely on the numerical growth of Christianity in Africa. New believers need to know what kind of God the God of the Bible is and how he can relate to them in their cultural contexts—to be precise, in the context of injustice. "It is customary to blame secular science and anti-religious philosophy for the eclipse of religion in modern society. It would be more honest to blame religion for its own defeats.

---

29. Blomberg, *Christians in the Age of Wealth*, 158.
30. Treat, *Crucified King*, 74.
31. Ravenhill, *Why Revival Tarries*, 20; emphasis original.

Religion declined not because it was refuted, but because it became irrelevant, dull, oppressive, and insipid. When faith is completely replaced by creed, worship by discipline, love by habit; when the crisis of today is ignored because of the splendor of the past; when faith becomes an heirloom rather than a living fountain; when religion speaks only in the name of authority rather than with the voice of compassion—its message become meaningless."[32] And I add, this kind of religion does not and cannot represent the God of the Bible or Jesus Christ.

> Jesus turned in word and deed to the weak, sick and neglected. This was a sign not of a weakness, but of strength. He offered a chance of being human to those who were set aside by society's standards at the time: the weak sick inferior, despised. He helped them in body and soul, gave health to many a physically and mentally sick person, gave strength to the many who were weak and hope to all the misfits. All these things were signs of the approaching kingdom of God. He existed for the whole man: not only for the strong, young, healthy, but also for the weak, aged, sick and crippled. In this way Jesus' deeds elucidate his words and his words interpret his deeds. But this one would not have created the amount of scandal which was in fact created. More was involved ... At that time the sick were regarded as responsible for their own misfortune, sickness, was the punishment of sin: the possessed were driven by the devil; lepers, bearing already the mark of death, did not belong to the fellowship of the living. Whether it was fate, sin or simply the prejudices of their time, the reason is not important: they were all social outcasts. But Jesus took up an essentially positive attitude to all of them.[33]

Despite the incredible growth of Christianity in Africa, if the biblical message of the church is irrelevant to the history of the slave trade, colonialism, neocolonialism, to African tyranny, civil wars, ethnic conflicts, and the plethora of ailments in the continent, then it has little meaning. And injustice will remain the norm. If theological and missiological education in Africa are not addressing the social, economic, and cultural exploitation of natural resources, the pros and cons of population growth, and environmental, political, and geopolitical issues on the ground, then Christianity will be irrelevant and will be a dead message by dead people to a dying continent. If Scripture is interpreted correctly and contextually becomes relevant, we will see that Africa is home for the incarnate Christ who was born and raised in a Roman colony, who walked from village to village on the dirty roads of Galilee and lived among the poor as poor, who was homeless, and who experienced hunger and thirst. Hendricks rightly said, "It makes all the difference in the world what you believe, because what you believe determines how you behave. To be sure, you can believe correctly and not behave correctly. But you cannot consistently behave correctly *unless* you believe correctly."[34]

---

32. Heschel, *God in Search of Man*, 3.
33. Küng, *On Being a Christian*, 266.
34. Hendricks, *Teaching to Change Lives*, 92; emphasis original.

Christianity in Africa

The general understanding of the majority of people in the world is that Christianity was introduced to the continent of Africa somewhere around the beginning of the European slave trade and colonialism of Africa. This notion is the result partly of ignorance of the history of Christianity and partly the result of a well-calculated curriculum designed to give a misleading history.

> Africa rarely comes to mind when most people think about the lands of the Bible. The average person may recall Simon of Cyrene who carried Jesus' cross or the Ethiopian eunuch who was baptized by Philip, but for many the Bible is set inland distant to Africa. Until recently, practically all books on biblical themes published in the West portrayed a biblical world that was exclusively European. Randomly leaf through any illustrated biblical book published before the last few decades and you will witness a world where Adam and eve and the heavenly hosts of angels are all depicted as Scandinavian. Africa's exclusion is also evident in the Bible maps that often include all of Italy and just the tip of the modern African continent when they feature the areas that were colonized by Greece or Rome. Whether consciously or unconsciously, those who assumed the responsibility to enhance the biblical message with pictorial aids failed to use all of the colors on the pallet.[35]

Christianity was further whitened through the portrait of Jesus Christ. "On October 12, 1994, the New York Times carried an article concerning Warner Sallman, whom it called the "best-known artist of the century" for his painting of the head of Christ, which has been reproduced more than half a billion times. Our earliest descriptions of the appearance of Jesus come from the Middle Ages. In an alleged report by Lentulus, which dates from the twelfth century, Jesus is described with "wavy hair, rather crisp of the colour of wine, and glittering as it flows down from His shoulders with a parting in the middle of the head after the manner of the Nazarenes . . . He had a beard abundant and of the same hazel-colour as His hair, not long, but forked. His eyes are blue and very bright. This is quite obviously an imaginative Eurocentric portrait of Jesus."[36] Oden concurs: "Some Westerners turn away from even hearing of Africa's ancient Christian heritage because of seated prejudices about assumed unimportance of Africa to world history."[37]

Andrew Walls comments on the strategic timeliness of reviving Africa's place in Christian history and enhancing her contribution to the global church through biblical and authentically African theology. He asserts:

> It is widely recognized that there has occurred with the present century a demographic shift in the center of gravity of the Christian world, which means that more than half of the world's Christians live in Africa, Asia, Latin America, or the Pacific, and that the proportion doing so grows annually. This means that we have to regard African Christianity as potentially *representative* Christianity of

---

35. Burton, *Blessings of Africa*, 17–18.
36. Yamauchi, *Africa and the Bible*, 205.
37. Oden, *African Memory of Mark*, 35.

> the twenty-first century . . . The Christianity typical of the twenty-first century will be shaped by the events and processes that take place in the southern continents, and above all by those that take place in Africa . . . I am not, of course, suggesting that there will not be substantial numbers of Christians outside Africa, or that what they do or what happens to them is of no importance—there have always been plenty of Christians outside the areas of representative Christianity. But the things by which people recognise and judge what Christianity is will (for good or ill) in liturgy, the ethical codes, the social applications of the faith will increasingly be those prominent in Africa. New agendas for theology will appear in Africa. And one of the anvils on which the Christianity of the future will be hammered out will be the question of the nation, the state, the nature of civil society.[38]

In light of the history of the continent and the present realities of various nations in Africa, as well as the findings of his research, Andrew Walls could not have been more accurate. However, African Christian scholars, with rare exception, for various reasons have not yet produced sufficient challenging academic works that desperately needed to guide the rapidly growing church and society as it goes through the process of searching for meaning and asking questions about their past, present, and future. Those who are able to write barely get published unless they are known in the West or have good connections.

Right from its inception biblical Christianity was introduced through Galilean Jews in diverse languages. "Now they were staying in Jerusalem, God-fearing Jews from every nation under heaven. When they heard this sound, a crowed came together in bewilderment, because each one heard them speaking in his own language. Utterly amazed, they asked: "Are not all these men who are speaking Galileans? Then how is it that each of us hears them in his own native language? Parthians, Medes, Elamites, residents of Mesopotamia, Judea and Cappadocia, Pontus and Asia, Phrygia, and Pamphylia, Egypt and the parts of Libya near Cyrene; visitors from Rome (both Jews and those who convert to Judaism); Cretans and Arabs—we hear them declaring the wonders of God in our own tongues! Amazed and perplexed, they asked one another, what does this mean?" (Acts 2:5–12). The answer is obvious. God is a God of diverse kinds of people and Christianity is translatable. There is no nation under the sun who can claim to be the custodian of the gospel and the only preacher and teacher of the Christian faith. Lamin Sanneh accurately asserts, "Christianity was a religion for all seasons, fit for all humanity. Whatever its core was, it was not in any one time, in any one place, or in any one language. The prophets had dreamed and spoken well."[39] He adds,

> At its heart, translation is cultural contingency—each linguistic system operates by its own unique set of rules, making a uniform, universal translation impossible. Because languages are different, translation is an exercise in linguistic particularity and style, and by general consent, such things have an impermanent, ephemeral status in Buddhist thought. For Christianity on the other hand, translation is the warp and woof of religious identity; linguistic difference is not so much an obstacle to be overcome as a necessary boundary of identity and

---

38. Walls, *Cross-Cultural Process*, 85.
39. Sanneh, *Disciples of All Nations*, 14.

adaptation. This fact implicates Christianity in the historical process, not just as a vague, speculative notion, but in the detail and specific sense of vernacular and mother tongue appropriation as an authentic religious process. Christians came upon language not as an obstacle, but as an asset in its own right . . . Without the specific, earthly embodiment of language, Christians would not know themselves or their God.[40]

Furthermore, Sanneh comments, "Giving ourselves freely to God and to one another allows understanding to blossom in all its depth and range."[41]

As global[42] Christianity becomes increasingly made up of people from Asia, Africa, and Latin America, and as these newly emerging indigenous expressions become normative, *the whole structure of our understanding and discourse about Christian history and mission history must also undergo a dramatic change.* In the West our cultural and ecclesiastical tradition flows primarily from the Roman Empire, so what happened in Western Europe dominates our understanding of history. However, after having spent considerable time with Christians from various parts of Asia, I can testify that the Roman Empire does not loom nearly as large in the perspective of people shaped by the Persian, Ashokan, or Han Empires. This background influences how Christian history is understood and told. *Thus the narratives that rehearse mission history needed to be reconceptualized so that they reflect a more global perspective on the church, particularly as African and Asian Christianity become increasingly normative and Western Christianity becomes more ancillary to the larger global movement.*[43]

Lamin Sanneh augments:

World Christianity has such long and diverse roots, so many different and independent actors and manifestations, and such a rich plurality of cultural idioms that it is hard to see a consciously synchronized master plan. Besides, the disenchantment with economic globalization, in which resources of local scale are dwarfed by those of global scale, finds no parallel in the indigenous forces driving religious resurgences. A bottom-up approach is more in tune with the facts on the ground than a top-down approach . . . In its scope range and diversity, world Christianity has now opened a field to us that is unimaginably greater and richer than the old rubrics ever allowed. World Christianity overcame obstacles local and foreign to surge with the primal message of the gospel; as the source of renewal and hope, the movement should challenge us to overcome our cultural shibboleths and bring us to our true ecumenical inheritance. *Christian unity*

---

40. Sanneh, *Summoned from the Margins*, 225.

41. Ibid., 271.

42. Sanneh prefers "World Christianity" instead of global Christianity. He "adopted the term to designate the radical change in the religion's main axis. The term is a way of getting at the expansion of Christianity in a diversity of societies and cultures, with the focus on the local and indigenous roots of the post-colonial resurgence. 'Global Christianity' as alternative designation has also been suggested, in so far as it is an attempt to break free of a parochial view of Christianity, the term is worth discussing. But in the end I reject it, because it evokes too strong a parallel with globalization as economic and technological process orchestrated from financial centers in the West" (ibid., 237).

43. Tennent, *Invitation to World Missions*, 48; emphasis added.

> *now is a matter of intercultural openness more than it is a question doctrinal axe-grinding. The way ahead lies in embracing that reality as a worldwide challenge.*[44]

"The way ahead" cannot be properly and effectively navigated without knowing one's historical root in the Christian faith. Hence, "the whole structure of our understanding and discourse about Christian history and mission history must also undergo a dramatic change."[45] "Perspective is important, and the more diverse the better," said Sanneh.[46] Hence, without being trapped in the anachronistic and paternalistic Western history of Christian mission in Africa, we need to look at the broader picture and genesis of Christianity in the continent.

Thomas C. Oden, in his informative book *The African Memory of Mark: Reassessing Early Church Tradition*, gives us an historical background of African Christianity that goes back to the first century. By deliberately stepping out of the Western academic view of the historical accounts of Mark, Oden has made a significant contribution to African Christianity and also the world. Oden's book about Mark and Mark's foundational contributions to church planting, discipleship, writing of the first gospel, and his martyrdom—all of which have inspired so many African Christians for generations, even to this day—was launched from African memory of Mark. By doing so, Oden confirms that if one has roots in Africa and has contributed significantly to society, the memory of the person will last for centuries.

What does Oden mean by the term African memory? As Oden rightly defines it, "The African memory is the characteristic way of looking at history from within the special experience and outlook of the continent of Africa."[47] Memory, according to Oden's definition, encompasses a two thousand-year-long history, a long-shared tradition of intellectual vitality, extensive literary fruits over many centuries, and an astonishing history of textual output. African memory is not mere oral tradition that cannot be tested within the bar of reason. "It takes into account the full weight of cumulative evidences coming out of the African continent over the length of centuries, including evidences from archaeology, epigraphic and literary sources, as well as oral traditions and stories of the saints."[48] Hence, African memory is not totally divorced from academic rigor; it is just a different approach.

Despite differences in theological persuasion between the Coptic, Catholic, Protestant, and Pentecostal churches in Africa, the memory of Mark is a linchpin that brings unity among African believers. All of them are in basic agreement that Mark was the first apostle to Africa. His birthplace was in Cyrene[49], Pentapolis in Libya, and he was

---

44. Sanneh, *Summoned from the Margins*, 237, 238; emphasis added.

45. Tennent, *Invitation to World Missions*, 48.

46. Sanneh, *Whose Religion Is Christianity?*, 12.

47. Oden, *African Memory of Mark*, 27.

48. Ibid., 29.

49. For further reading on Cyrene, see Yamauchi, *Africa and the Bible*, 191–203. "From the early reign of Nero (A.D. 56) we have an inscription of donors who contributed to the repair of a synagogue in Berenice, near Cyrene. Applebaum suggests that the remains of a building outside of the wall on the southern height of Waldi Bel Gadir may have been a synagogue" (Applebaum, "A Lamp and other Remains," 42).

born somewhere between 5–15 AD. This gives Africans a great sense of identity. The fact that Jesus had the last supper and that the outpouring of the Holy Spirit happened at the house of Mary, the mother of Mark, extends the roots of African Christianity way beyond the nineteenth-century Western missionary endeavor in Africa. If this is the case, why has Western scholarship failed to recognize the historical, missiological, and cultural facts that connect Mark as African and link him to the African church right from its inception?

Oden provides the answer by showing the prejudice and bias of Western scholarship that has failed to recognize not only Mark but also Augustine who grew up in Numidia, Athanasius who was born and bred in Egypt, as well as Tertullian and Cyprian who had African roots. The valuable contribution of these scholars to the early centuries of Christianity is widely recognized in world Christian history. However, their status as genuine Africans is shrouded and still debated in some circles for odd reasons. For Africans, who are concretely relational in their thinking and who learn from the example of Christian icons as much as from theory or theology, the bias of the West has significant implications. The bias means that Africans cannot claim and embrace "their own great heroes and minds and saints, such as Paschomius who contributed so much to the history of prayer and the life of holy living, and Perpetua, the mother with child who set the standard for Christian witness unto death not only in Africa but in the ecumenical community of faith. This bias was wrongly dishonored the Africanness of the Libyan-born Synesius and the Numidian-born Monica."[50]

For Africans, the culture of the Mediterranean world of the first century, the dyadic personality of the people, the honor-shame values, collective mentality, and peasant preindustrial societies are more relevant than the modern and postmodern West. The theology that was built in the first-century African and Mediterranean cultural context is more appealing to them than the theology of Bultman or Karl Barth. "If Christianity wants to reach Africans, to speak to their hearts, and to enter their consciousness and the space where their soul breathes, it must change. To do so, Christianity must do violence to itself and break the chains of Western rationality, which means nothing in the African civilization of the symbol. Without some form of epistemological break with the scholastic universe, Christianity has little chance of reaching Africans."[51]

By viewing Mark as the first apostle to Africa and recognizing his contribution to African Christianity from an African point of view and by identifying all prominent African theologians, church historians, pietists, and church leaders, Oden is uncovering the African intellectual Christian tradition that began in Africa and connects to Jerusalem. Mark and the prominent first-century African intellectuals mentioned above are the bedrock of African Christianity. For the African church and scholars, reaffirming these theological and historical roots, and reinforcing a proper cultural identification, will be one of the most effective medicines for what Oden identified as the "Theological Identity Crisis" of Africans that the late Kwame Bediako addressed in his magnum opus academic work.

---

50. Ibid., 31.
51. Éla, *My Faith as an African*, 41.

Oden is not a lone voice in this daring venture. Early Christian scholars like Clement, Origen, Tertullian, Cyprian, Eusebius, Jerome, and John Chrysostom, guided by the Holy Spirit, have asserted the succession of Apostolic Christianity, the transmission of biblical truth, the planting of the New Testament church in Africa, and all this without any political manipulation of the facts.

In his book, Oden explains that Mark was the most traveled apostle, who covered all of the three well-known continents of the first century. Since Mark had spent most of his youth in Cyrenaic Africa, he would have known the local Punic-Berber dialect as well as Greek. As the son of a displaced Jew from the tribe of Levi, who spent some of his younger life in Jerusalem, he would certainly have learned common Aramaic, as well as Hebrew to expose him to Torah. If he was well educated, he would also have learned some Latin. Tradition holds that Mark was related to the apostle Peter and that he received the gospel truth from the apostle and became an instrument for the conversion of his father Aristopolus and his mother Mary. When Peter was rescued from prison by an angel, he went to Mary's house.

As Oden states, "Mary the mother of Mark was known to be a close relative of Barnabas—depending upon the translation, either his sister or cousin or sister in-law. Thus Mark and Barnabas were bounded by sharing deep bonds of kinship, sharing their family resources together with the disciples, sharing in their faith that Jesus Christ is Lord, and sharing a special calling from God as called and empowered by the Spirit; taking the good news of Jesus to the gentiles (Acts 15:37–39)."[52] The African narrative captured an apparent convergence of biblical texts (Mark 14:14–15; Acts 1:13; 12:12) that Mark's mother lived in the very house where Jesus had a Passover dinner with the disciples, where the outpouring of the Holy Spirit occurred on the day of Pentecost, and where the first Christian church was born. The Messiah, who claimed to have no home in this world, called his disciples for the last supper in the house of a Jewish family who were in diaspora and whose roots went back to Africa. This has a powerful symbolical or typological significance for the African mind: "Just as Africa had given the family of Jesus a home in his childhood in flight from Herod, so now a family in flight from Africa is giving Jesus a home in the last hours before his death."[53] During his infancy and in the last hours of his life, Africa was a historical staging ground for Jesus Christ. As much as African Christianity wanted to connect to this root and develop its history and theology, the opportunities were not there. Oden has opened a path that will challenge most of us to further explore the historical, theological, and archaeological situation of early African Christianity for the enrichment of the global church.

To this end, a group of contemporary scholars are taking a new look at the scholarship and exegesis from the Nile Valley, Libya, Ethiopia, and the Maghreb to investigate why the "African memory" remembered Mark as the native founder of African Christianity, as a son of Libya, as the first Christian martyr in Africa, and as the apostolic father of every believing African Christian then and now. "The evidence is stronger than is generally accredited by the older school of Euro-American historical interpreters and is ripe for a careful review. Many current scholars are now looking at this evidence in a

52. Ibid., 86.
53. Ibid., 92.

different way from that of Harnack, Bauer and company."[54] Even though the conclusive historical datum that could categorically validate the historic truth about Mark's life is not coming soon, contemporary scholars of Mark have definitely raised valid questions on the previous Euro-American interpretation of history on Mark, just like Oden does. Oden believes that the historical truth will be revealed when Alexandria is properly excavated. He thinks that the truth lies in some positions between Western and African views.

John Baur argues that modern Egyptians can trace the origin of their faith to the very origins of Christianity itself. He writes,

> A group of Christian Jews, living in Jewish settlements between AD50–100, constitute the link of the Church in Egypt with the apostles. The unanimous Egyptian tradition venerates St Mark as the founder of the apostolic see of Alexandria having ordained its first bishop Annianus in AD 62. Historians often dismiss this assertion because it is found only in Church History of Eusebius (AD 320), and not in the earlier, extensive though non-historical writings of Clement and Origen. But the authenticity of this tradition is supported by the fact that Mark was the companion of Peter to whom the mission to the Jews had been entrusted. Alexandria was the home of the greatest Jewish diaspora; why should it not have been visited by Peter and his spiritual son? (1 Pet. 5:13). We may therefore with good reason refer to the year AD 62 as the founding date of the first Christian Church in Africa.[55]

According to Ethiopian tradition, Israel's faith was introduced to the kingdom by Menelik I, the legendary son of Solomon and Sheba. However, the Bible is clear that the queen herself came to visit Solomon, because she had heard of his fame (1 Kgs 10:1). She evidenced familiarity with the Israelite God and exhibited a fascination for the prosperous kingdom (1 Kgs 10:9). Judging by the favor she bestowed on Solomon, even in the absence of the Menelik myth, it is clear that she would not have displayed any hostility to any of her subjects who chose to follow Israel's God. In addition, to those who may have taken advantage of the queen's fascination with Israelite faith, some believe that a number of Israelites from the tribe of Dan migrated to Ethiopia during the civil war between Jeroboam and Rehoboam. These, they believe, formed the foundation of the Hebrew believers in Cush.

While none of these explanations have been objectively verified, it is true that by the early Christian centuries there were many in the land of Cush—particularly in Ethiopia—who lived by the precepts of the Bible. The roots in the Israelite faith were so deep in some parts of Ethiopia that, even for Christians, the Tanakh was esteemed over the rest of the Bible. In fact, the Ethiopian Orthodox Church still maintained such practices as seventh-day Sabbath observance, circumcision, and abstention from certain meats. The isolated church also maintained control over its canon, and translated the entire Bible into Ethiopic by the beginning of the sixth century. Longer than the Bible of Catholic and Protestant Christianity, the Ethiopian Bible includes the entire Apocrypha

---

54. Ibid., 230.
55. Baur, *2000 Years of Christianity in Africa*, 21.

and other books deemed psuedepigraphal.[56] "The Ethiopian church's strong Hebraic element gives it a unique role in Christians/Jewish dialogue. It has grown directly from Christianity's Jewish roots, without the admixture of Hellenism."[57] "With Axum begins the long history of Ethiopian Christianity, which over the centuries spread over huge areas by processes we still do not fully understand. Christianity in this part of the world took a distinctive Ethiopian form with some observances apparently unique to it. It found a distant ancestry for itself in an ancient connection with Israel in the days of Solomon—never absolutely cut off from the rest of the Christian world, but generally little touched by it and almost forgotten by it."[58] Aksum was at the height of its power in the middle of the fourth century. Its military intervention in the Nile Valley had already given the tottering kingdom of Meroe the coup de grâce and had brought the former provinces of its old rival under its own sphere of influence. More than a century of direct participation in the local struggle for power among the south Arabian kingdoms had also brought Aksum into its first period of political supremacy in the Arabian Peninsula. Its port of Adulis developed into the most important center of international trade on the African coast of the Red Sea, and with the decline of the land routes of Arabia much of the eastern trade was handled by Roman maritime traders with whom Aksum was on friendly terms.

In Aksum, and other centers of population along the major routes to the coast, former temples were converted into churches, and new places of Christian worship erected. Because of the lack of books in Ethiopic at the time, Greek was probably the major language of the church. Most of the clergy may also have been of foreign provenance.[59] "Christian Ethiopia, like the Coptic community, was not a mission field at all; it was an ancient and thoroughly Africanized church that would have provided most valuable precedents for other African Christians, had they come into contact with it."[60] Andrew Walls accurately observes: "Ethiopia stands for Africa indigenously Christian, Africa *primordially* Christian; for a Christianity that was established in Africa not only before the white people came; for a Christianity that has been continuously in Africa for a far longer than it has in Scotland, and infinitely longer than it has in the United States. African Christians today can assert their right to the *whole* history of Christianity in Africa, stretching back almost to the apostolic age."[61] Philip Jenkins asserts, "By the time the first Anglo-Saxons was converted, Ethiopian Christianity was already in its tenth generation."[62] There is not only need for the works of Ethiopian historians and missiologists but there is also a need for the work of OT and NT Ethiopian scholars to nurture the roots of Christianity in Ethiopia and make the message of the gospel relevant and authoritative in the context of the people.

56. Keith Augusts Burton, *The Blessing of Africa*, 2007:135–136.
57. Isichei, *History of Christianity in Africa*, 49.
58. Walls, *Cross-Cultural Process*, 88.
59. For an in-depth study, see Tamrat, *Church and State in Ethiopia 1270–1527*.
60. Isichei, *History of Christianity in Africa*, 51.
61. Walls, *Cross-Cultural Process*, 91; emphasis original.
62. Jenkins, *Next Christendom*, 19.

Nubia is the biblical Kush ("the South," hence the Swahili "*Kusini*"), which the Septuagint rendered as "Ethiopia" (Land of the Sunburnt Faces). At the time of Isaiah, it ruled over Egypt and sent a military expedition to Palestine (Isa 18:1; 20:3; 37:9). The prophet called them "people tall and bronzed (smooth-skinned)" and the historian Herodotus praised them as the tallest and most beautiful of men.[63] Isichei elaborates, "Nubia was one of the ancient countries in the world that was converted to Christianity without prior experience of the Roman rule; Ethiopia was another. Culturally, its Christianity was greatly influenced by Byzantium. The Nubians used the liturgy of St. Mark, and decorated the walls of their churches with murals that showed their royal dressed in Byzantium style. In 1961, Polish archaeologist excavated what appeared to be a mound of sand, and within found Faras, Cathedral, its wall decorated with 169 magnificent paintings of dark skinned Nubian kings, queens and bishops, and biblical figures and saints."[64] To this Baur adds:

> Almost all available evidence regarding the inner life of the Nubian church is connected with the church buildings. In the early 1200s an Arab visitor spoke of seven dioceses and many monasteries and churches in Makuria. In less developed southern Alodia he mentioned 400 hundred churches, and those in Soba, its capital were decorated with gold. Modern excavation had brought to light at least one hundred church sites and the ruins of few monasteries, some of them containing manuscripts. Most magnificent were the three cathedrals of Faras, Ibrim and Dongola, all constructed of dressed stones, brick walls and granite columns. The excavations in Faras have uncovered the cathedral which was connected with the royal palace; an astonishing number of 169 mural paintings in the Byzantine style; books in Greek, Coptic and Old Nubian—a Nubian lectionary is proof at least a partial translation of the Bible. Some 400 inscriptions contain mostly prayers in the Orthodox tradition. One of them gives the list of the kings, another of the bishops; the latter are 27 in number and, from the year 866, they were called metropolitans. The paintings depict many dark-skinned bishops and rulers, such as the Metropolitan Petros (967–999), whose skull in the tomb is clearly that of a Negro.[65]

Theological School in Alexandria

Like the civilization in Egypt, Alexandrian scholarship is a bone of contention between Eurocentric and Afrocentric scholars. Those who take the Hegelian line of thinking believe that Alexandrian scholars are not Africans and they should never be considered as one. Oden observes:

> It is more accurately described as a specific prejudice of Hegelian idealism to assume that everything of intellectual importance that happened near the Mediterranean is really at heart European and therefore hardly could be imagined to have had an African origin. African origins are prima facie ruled out. Here is

---

63. Baur, *2000 Years of Christianity in Africa*, 31.
64. Isichei, *History of Christianity in Africa*, 31.
65. Baur, *2000 Years of Christianity in Africa*, 32–33.

where Alexandria gets its unjustified reputation as being simply a non-African extension of the European intellect. The generalization too hold that wherever there might have been any modest African influences, they are likely to be views as inferior and backward in relation the unfolding positive development of reason in history that flowed from Europe. The companion premise is that if good ideas appeared in Africa, they must be attributed to Europeans. This bizarre habit consistently viewed the Alexandrian and Egyptian Christians as entirely disconnected from African ways. To deprive Africa of Alexandria is to say that a blossom is unrelated to its climate.[66]

It is also an ethnocentric view of history, human intelligence, culture, and an inadequate way of understanding and describing who Africans are. Africa is a bazar of culture, race, ethnicity, and language. Oden succinctly summarizes the debate as follows:

> The argument for the recovery of early African Christianity cannot easily proceed unless it can be shown that these great intellect were truly Africans, not just in a geographical sense but in spirit and cultural temperament. They were not just temporary trekkers or occupiers, but centuries-rooted African born and bred on this great continent. They were nurtured in families living through untold generations of African life. There is nothing phony or lacking in their African Christian identity. Many were willing to die for that identity.
>
> A debilitating prejudice has invaded the reputation of these great African leaders, as if they were not genuinely Africans, but foreigners in disguise. These is a fairly recent Western intellectual habit that would have seemed odd to worldwide believers of the early Christian centuries. It would be somewhat akin to saying that of English, Irish, Polish of other heritage, whose families had lived in North America for over two centuries, are not real Americans but are (even in the twenty-first century) merely transplanted Europeans. Such Americans would take understandable offense.[67]

Civilization, academic, economic, and other developments in human history resulted from a cross-pollination of the human races from various cultural and geographical backgrounds. Quite a number of astounding American innovations are accomplishments of Americans whose origins are in Asia, Europe, Africa, and Latin America. But all of them are Americans who utilized the conducive technological, economic, and academic situations of the American culture to be innovators and scientists. "North Africa is a part of the Mediterranean world, and it is, in a sense, artificial to analyze the growth of Christianity in isolation from developments in elsewhere. . .Greeks have lived in Egypt from the seventh century BC, and their history there had a great influence on the development of Christianity. In 331 BC, Alexander the Great founded the city that bears his name, and when, after his death, his three generals divided his empire, Egypt fell to Ptolemy, who turned Alexandria into one of the great cities of the ancient world. Its lighthouse was regarded as one of the Seven Wonders of the World, but the title was perhaps more appropriate for the scholars of the Museum, one of whom accurately calculated the circumference of the world."[68] Baur adds, "Alexandria itself became the

---

66. Oden, *How Africa Shaped the Christian Mind*, 58–59.
67. Oden, *African Memory of Mark*, 31.
68. Isichei, *History of Christianity in Africa*, 13.

metropolis of the entire Mediterranean East, a cultural center even more important than Athens. Though the Roman conquered it in 30 BC, it remained a Greek city, and its top philosophical schools extended their influence even to Rome. So it is understandable that *Christian theology in the proper sense of the word started in Alexandria.*"[69] The first historically-known Christian from Alexandria is the Jew Apollos, the famous preacher in Corinth, whose Hellenistic eloquence was a great challenge to Paul. It is presumably in Alexandria that he had been "instructed in the way of the Lord" (Acts 18:24; 1 Cor 3:4–7).[70]

Alexandrian theologians developed their Trinitarian theology and Christology within the context of Middle Platonism, which put insistence on the divine transcendence. A proponent of Middle Platonism was Plutarch of Chaeronea, the author of the celebrated lives of Greek and Roman worthies.

Plutarch aimed at a purer conception of God. He said, "While we are here below, encumbered by bodily affections, we can have no intercourse with God save as in philosophic thought we may faintly touch Him, as in a dream. But when our souls are released, and have passed into the region of the pure, invisible, and changeless, this God will be the guide and the king of those who depend on Him and gaze with insatiable longing on the beauty which may not be spoken of by the lips of man."[71] Among the Middle Platonists are Eudorus of Alexandria, Albinus, Apuleius, Atticus, Celsus, and Maximums of Tyre. While Plutarch's desire for a pure conception of God led him to deny God's authorship of evil, Albinus saw God as unmoved or uncaused cause. Celsus is best known as a determined opponent of Christianity. Maximus speaks of the vision of the transcendent God. The common consensus and concern of all is the gap and bridge between God and humans or God and nature. The connecting link between God and humanity was important to them and the only way the transcendent God could be related to human beings was through intermediaries—angels, demons, spirits, heroes, who were more akin to God; others, in their view, were tainted by the evil of the lower world. Extravagant rites, and barbarous and obscene sacrifices were offered to the evil demons. The good demons were the instruments of providence.[72] As one reads the works of Middle Platonists, their intellectual struggle and concern to find one who could stand between the pure God and the impure humankind is apparent and huge. It was in these philosophers' context that Paul's writing, "For there is one God and one mediator between God and men, the man Christ Jesus, who gave himself as a ransom for all men—and the testimony given at its proper time" (1 Tim 2:5–6), was circulated and read. Therefore, in response to the intellectual quest of their time and the academic and cultural climate of the church, Christology and Trinitarian theology took focus in the minds of early African theologians in Alexandria.

Alexandria produced great theologians like Clement of Alexandria who indeed was the first Christian scholar in full command of the knowledge of his time. "Clement came to Alexandria to learn, and remained to teach. He was immensely learned, and one of

---

69. Baur, *2000 Years of Christianity in Africa*, 21; emphasis added.
70. Ibid., 21.
71. Copleston, *History of Philosophy*, 453.
72. See ibid., 451–56.

his works cites 360 classical texts, many of which do not survive in any other form. Influenced by Philo, he attempted to make Christianity acceptable to those educated in Greek philosophy."[73] For Clement, "God is absolutely transcendent, ineffable, and incomprehensible; He is unity but beyond unity, and transcending the monad, and yet somehow embracing all reality. This is the Father; and He can be known only through His Word, or Son, Who is His image and inseparable from Him, His mind and rationality...He is essential one with Him, since Father is in Him and He in the Father."[74] While he warned his students against the errors of philosophers, he insisted on accepting from the Hellenes "whatever is good, whatever is beautiful."[75]

"To work all the elements of faith and philosophy into a theological system was the glory of Origen. He started with Scripture, establishing a secure text by comparing the various versions and interpreted it, always looking for a deep (often allegorical) meaning of the text. Then he explained the biblical faith further by bringing it into the context of Greek philosophy and presenting it as a systematic unity. Finally he pointed out the ways of perfection to the Christian soul. It is for this reason that he is venerated as the first biblical scholar, theologian, and master of asceticism, a man to whom all later theologians, St. Augustin included, are deeply indebted."[76] "Origen was the first major thinker of the early Church seriously to tackle the intractable problems of Christology."[77] "For Origen the oneness of the Son with the Father is important, but His independence is theologically prior . . . The Son is the Father's image, the reflection of His glory."[78]

Baur gives us the broader theological and ecclesiological climate around Alexandria this way:

> As in Egypt there were three ethnic groups but their reaction to Christianity was quite different. The original population were the *Berbers*, who were poor peasant folks. Then came the *Phoenicians*, the great traders, who in 814 BC founded Carthage, out of which they dominated the Western half of the Mediterranean Sea for centuries. Their Punic language became the lingua franca of North Africa in the same way Swahili is that of modern East Africa. In 146 BC, *the Romans* succeeded in destroying Carthage and began to colonize the country. The settlers were chiefly ex-servicemen, coming from all over the Empire. *Many married Berber women, as did the father of St Augustine. Within this ethnically mixed society, a Latin-speaking cultural upper class developed, composed not only of Roman settlers and officials but also innumerable young African males who went to Rome for higher studies, preferably to become lawyers, as did Tertullian.* It is in garb of the Latin culture that Christianity arrived, blossomed and died in North Africa.
>
> The theological school of Carthage achieved for the Latin West what the school of Alexandria did for the Greek East. Its leaders were *Tertullian* and

---

73. Isichei, *History of Christianity in Africa*, 20.

74. Kelley, *Early Christian Doctrine*, 127.

75. Ibid. Pg. 127

76. Baur, *2000 Years of Christianity in Africa*, 23.

77. Isichei, *History of Christianity in Africa*, 21. For further reading on Gnosticism and monasticism, Donatism, Arianism and monphysitism, the center of systematic theology, Bible and political theology in Carthage, see Burton, *The Blessing of Africa*, 121–34.

78. Kelley, *Early Christian Doctrine*, 129, 130.

Cyprian. Tertullian began to formulate a Latin theology around the year 180, at a time when in Rome the educated Christian thought one could only pray and teach in Greek. In contrast to Alexandrians he avoided philosophical speculations and concentrated on ascetical and moral questions, thus significantly reflecting the more practical Western and African mind. Tertullian was, however, a moral rigorist and believed in a Church of saints. His views being rejected, he joined the enthusiastic sect of Montanists, which came from Asia Minor. One generation later his theology was reworked by St. Cyprian, Bishop of Carthage (248–258). Cyprian sealed his activity not with heresy but with martyrdom; thus he became the undisputed theological authority of the Western church superseded only by St. Augustine.

With St. Augustine, Bishop of Hippo (390–430) *the church of Africa reaches its zenith. Augustine was much more than an African theologian: his work was the culminating point of the whole Western theology. But we should not overlook his deep roots in the African soil, especially through his Berber mother St Monica. From her he inherited much of his African originality and through her incessant prayer and motherly care he was reborn in the Faith. The depth of his own religious personality is autobiographical Confessions*[79] [emphasis added]. In the field of theology he is above all hailed as *Doctor Gratiae*, the Teacher of Grace. He showed the overall importance of the grace of God in the work of salvation against the human asceticism of Pelagius and the moralism of Tertullian.[80]

For Tertullian, "what was believed and preached in the churches was absolutely authoritative because it was the selfsame revelation which they had received from the apostles, the apostles from Christ, and Christ from God . . . He insisted that Christians must not pick and choose doctrines according to their whims; their sole authorities were apostles, who had themselves faithfully transmitted Christ's teaching."[81]

In his book *How Africa Shaped the Christian Mind*, Thomas Oden demonstrates the contribution of African Christianity to the Western Christianity in the following seven ways:

1. How the Western Idea of University was Born in the Crucible of Africa

    The unrivaled library of Alexandria was the model of university libraries all over Europe. It was unsupassed for five centuries.

    The experimental academic model that later became transformed into the Western idea of the university was first an embryo in the community that surrounded that Alexandria library. Is it not proper to say that European university was born in Africa? If not born, at least conceived. The vast learning community of philosophers, scientists, writers, artists and educators that surrounded the Alexandrian library of the third century provided the essential archetype of the University for All of the medieval Europe. The history of the first medieval universities such as Padua (Italy), Paris (France), Salamanca (Spain), and Oxford (England) followed method of text examination, curricular patterns and philosophical imperatives that were refined in second-century African Christianity as early as Pantaenus and Clement of Alexandria. Clement's writings, the *Stomateis*

---

79. Saint Augustine Confessions, 1986.
80. See Baur, *2000 Years of Christianity in Africa*, 26–28.
81. Kelley, *Early Christian Doctrine*, 36.

and *Paedaogus*, reveal much of the method and content of education that became normative in the medieval university . . .

The academic community in Constantinople, still located in the physical residence of the University of Istanbul today, was patterned after academic communities and libraries in Cyrenaica (Libya), Alexandria (Egypt), Carthage (Tunisia), and Hippo (Algeria). African monastic patterns of relating the life of the mind to responsibility in the world became the pattern of study under Alcuin, whose court academy under Charlemagne imprinted the whole of proto-European university education.

Christian Scholarship was born in the leading academic center of the ancient world: Alexandria. The crucible of learning was itself transformed by Christianity and exported to Rome, the Rhone valley, Byzantium and Antioch.

2. How Christian Exegesis of Scripture first Matured in Africa

Basil the Great, Gregory of Nazianzus and Gregory of Nyssa (all of the fourth century C.E.) were crucial in defining early Christian thinking on God the Father, God the Son, and God the Holy Spirit for Orthodox Christianity, both East and West. But it is easy to forget that these Cappadocian fathers were decisively shaped by extensive exegesis of Scripture from Africa. . .

The normative early Greek and Latin Bibles before Jerome (the Septuagint and the Old Latin Bible versions) were both products of Africa.

The editors that produced the twenty-eight volumes of the Ancient Christian Commentary on Scripture at Drew University were astonished to find such a large percentage of texts from Africa or influenced by African writers among the patristic comments on verse after verse of Scripture. Many widely read themes of the widely read homilies of John Chryssostom and Theodore of Cyrrhus and Ambrose followed Origen, Didymus and Cyril of Alexandria in specific details . . . Virtually all Christian exegetes following Origen and Didymus the Blind actively borrowed from their studies in large portions, even while at times resisting or opposing certain aspects of the checkered tradition later called "Origenism."

3. How African Sources Shaped Early Christian Dogma

These African exegetes powerfully affected the dogmatic formulations of the orthodoxy of the East and the West. Dogmatic definitions were working off of textual interpretations hammered out chiefly in Africa, the Maghreb and the Nile Valley . . .

The major battles of heresy were fought out in Africa before they were received ecumenically. Gnosticism, Arianism, Montanism, and Marcionism and Manichaeism were all thoroughly argued as problems of biblical interpretation in Africa before these arguments reached clear definitions in the Rhone and Rhine and Oronets Valleys. What Irenaeus and Hippolytus of Rome learned about Gnosticism was learned largely from African sources (Valentinus, Basilides, the Sethians).

4. How Early Ecumenical Decision Making Followed African Conciliar Patterns

The early African councils provide a practical model for ecumenical debate and resolution. The conciliar movement, which began in Jerusalem (c. 45 C.E.) as reported by Luke, took on formal characteristics in African debates in Carthage, Alexandria, Hippo and Milevis that would gradually come to define the methods for achieving ecumenical consensus elsewhere.

5. How the African Desert Gave Way to Worldwide Monasticism

The suffering of the African martyrs—Mark in Alexandria and Cyprian in the Maghreb—became the pattern for early monasticism in Africa long before it did elsewhere. The African monks' understanding of sacrifice; the daily ordering of the life of prayer, study and work; and radical discipleship were destined to enter into the heart of the whole Christian tradition that would later flower in medieval European Christianity. The matrix in which monasticism was spawned was the Egyptian desert, and soon thereafter Numidia, Libya and Byzacena.

The course of the monastic movement in Africa was well-formed long prior to the time of Benedict of Nursia (480–550), the key figure of European monasticism. After Augustine it would flow into Benedictine and other orders to influence the whole of medieval culture. In due time the African monastic fruits begun by Anthony, Pachomius and Augustine came to flower in Italy and France, and all the way from Ireland and Northumberland to Dalmatia.

6. How Christian Neoplatonism Emerged in Africa

It is seldom mentioned in the philosophical literature that the earliest advocates of Neoplatonism did not reside either in Greece or Rome, but in Africa. It is surprising to Hellenistic chauvinists to be reminded that Philo, Ammonias Saccas and Plotinus—the central players in Neoplatonism—were all Africans. After taking firm root in the Nile Delta, in due time, it would move north to Rome and Athens and Byzantium.

7. How Rhetorical and Dialectical Skills Were Honed in Africa for Europe's Use

Just as Neoplatonism was moving from south to north, and Christian exegesis from Alexandria to Caesarea and Antioch, so also was the advanced dialectical study of rhetoric migrating from Madaurus, Sicca and Carthage to Italy, as it did with many leading Christian figures: Tertullian, Cyprian, Arnobius and Lactantius, all prior to the more famous example of Augustine ... Viewed from Rome or Constantinople, it was Madaura, Sicca, Carthage, Cyrene and Alexandria that were regarded as having the most powerful literary traditions and rhetoricians, more pungent, persuasive and subtly dialectical than those which prevailed elsewhere.[82]

In terms of women disciples, missionaries and martyrs, church leadership and governance, and liturgy and theology, Africa made a significant contribution to world Christianity. "Origen was the first major thinker of the early church seriously to tackle the intractable problems of Christology. Sabellius the Libyan, another thinker from the African continent, attempted to define the Trinity as three modes, or aspects, of one God, so that God has one substance, and three energies. This led to problems—the posing of question like 'Did God the Father died on the cross?' . . . The achievement of Alexandrian catechetical school did not end with Origen. In the fourth century, it was headed by extraordinarily interesting figure Didymus the Blind (313–98). An Alexandrian, Didymus was blind from infancy. Credited with the invention of script for the blind, he was the teacher of Jerome and Gregory of Nazianzus and wrote many books."[83] "Besides being strong in numbers, the church of North Africa produced three of the

---

82. Oden, *How Africa Shaped the Christian Mind*, 42–57.
83. Isichei, Isichei, *History of Christianity in Africa*, 21, 23.

greatest leaders and theologians of the early church: Tertullian, the brilliant defender of the faith, in second century; Cyprian, the energetic builder of the church, in the third century; and Augustine, the greatest theologian since Paul, in the fourth century. Under this great and spiritual giants the church in North Africa, comprising some five hundred dioceses (one-fourth of all Christendom), had a better educated clergy and exercised greater ecclesiastical power than did the churches of Alexandria or Rome."[84]

Despite such a rich theological, ecclesiastical, and historical heritage, it is disheartening often to hear people sarcastically say, "African Christianity is a mile wide and an inch deep." This could be true of the Christianity that came to Africa under the wings of European colonialism, which introduced Christ as an uninvited guest and not a brother who understands suffering and rejection. The task of African theologians today is not only to interpret the Scripture and relate it to the current African context, they also need to redeem the past, because, without it, African Christianity will remain rootless. "In our day there are signs that African theologians are at a similar point in the application of the word about Christ to another vast complex of thought, action, and relationships to that which Greek Christian thinkers reached when they face the problems posed by their cultural identity. *Christian Africa is now having to grapple with the meaning of the African past, and with what God was doing in it. African systems of thought and codes of symbols and nets of kinship are as formidable in this way as the Greco-Roman. The great travail of Christian Africa is over the conversion of the African past. Perhaps no conversion is complete without the conversion of the past.*"[85] This task is enormously challenging and there is no school in the Western hemisphere that can prepare African theologians "to grapple with the meaning of the African past, and with what God was doing in it." What was God doing in the slave trade? What was he doing during European colonialism in Africa? What kind of Christology can make inroads to the hearts and minds of the disinherited, dislocated, oppressed, exploited, and massacred? What does the Scripture say about tyrant rulers, uncontrollable greed, unfair world trade, debilitating loans, and usury? As we try to answer these questions, "the first important point to remember about theology is, since it springs out of practical situations, it is therefore *occasional* and *local* in character . . . The domestic task of Third world theology are going to be so basic, so vital, that there will be little time for barren, sterile, time-wasting by-paths into which so much Western theology and theological research has gone in recent years. Theology in the Third world will be, as theology at all creative times has always been, about *doing* things, about things that deeply affect the lives of numbers of people."[86] Oden adds, "If modern African Christianity had been better grounded in ancient African ecumenical teachings, it would never have felt compelled to be defensive about Hellenistic voices in its own African tradition. For Hellenism in Africa had become profoundly Africanized over the very long period of time of some twenty generations before Origen. Modern African Christians need to get this straight in order to recover their actual historic identity as African. Otherwise Africa needlessly deprives itself of his own heritage."[87]

---

84. Kane, *Concise History of Christian World Mission*, 51.
85. Walls, *Missionary Movement in Christian History*, 53; emphasis added.
86. Ibid., 10; emphasis added.
87. Oden, *How Africa Shaped the Christian Mind*, 67.

Currently, "Black and African theology are confronted with the challenge of integrity in the face of modernism and neo-colonialism. The latter two often operate in tandem with each other and are not always easy to distinguish . . . Black theology was a Christian theological expression of the struggle against apartheid racism, traditional African theology was set on the premise of Africa's cultural unity . . . African theology, in turn, was born out of the need to relate the Christian faith to the religio-cultural traditions of Africa. If racism was the hinge around which Black theology revolved, culture was the focal point of African theology. Reconstruction of Africa's religio-cultural traditions from the past and the relation of these to Christianity in the here and now was the main concern of African theology."[88] "Faith touches on the totality of existence and all of its problems. Thus, when faith seeks to understand itself, to verify itself and to account for itself in Africa, it must begin with the people's struggle to escape from hellish circle in which they risk being permanently imprisoned. We must look at faith, then, at the ground level and clarify the paths faith can take in the structures of daily life. Africans are more and more preoccupied by social problems; the challenges of daily life crowd in on believers."[89] Cognitive theology divorced from the reality of life does not appeal to African Christians. One of the reasons why there is a big disconnect between mass conversion and positive socioeconomic change in Africa is the understanding of biblical salvation as a ticket for the life beyond. When European Christianity came to Africa through the modern missionary movement, the European gospel was almost mute about the present conditions of Africa except on the issue of polygamy.

Western theology as applauded as it is—is not a universal theology. It is local theology and it is occasional. It doesn't matter if you present it in any shape or form, it cannot answer the questions of African Christians. Western theology grapples neither with Africans' past nor present. Western theology does not deal "about issues that deeply affects the lives of [Africans]." Hence, we have "a mile wide and an inch deep Christianity in today's Africa." Christopher Wright observes: "We are all interpreting contextually because all of us interpret in a particular context. Western biblical interpretation has no right to assume that all its insights are 'the standard,' while those from other continents are 'contextualized.' The West is also a context—and not necessarily a better or a worse context for understanding and interpreting the text of the Scriptures than anywhere else on the planet."[90]

Sanneh also comments: "No culture is so advanced and so superior that it can claim exclusive access or advantage to the truth of God, and none so marginal and remote that it can be excluded. All have merit; none is indispensable" (2008:25). "Recognizing this fact has led somewhat to the demise of Western hegemony over exegesis and hermeneutics. We recognize the relativity of hermeneutics the fact that we all need each other. For the Westerners to hear the Bible interpreted, understood, and preached by African, Latin, or Asian brothers [and sisters], in Christ and vice versa, and then to see the perspectives that others are bringing are often very enriching"[91] With the rapid growth

88. Njeza, "Fallacies of the New Afrocentrism," 54–55.
89. Éla, *My Faith as an African*, 67.
90. Wright, "Christ and the Mosaic Pluralism," 82.
91. Ibid.

of Christianity in Africa, scholarly works of African Bible scholars, who can correctly and efficiently relate the message of the prophets and the apostles in African cultural contexts, is in high demand. Without contextual scholarly works and diligent teaching from the Scripture on all spheres of Christian growth, African Christianity will remain prone to syncretism. For the church of Jesus Christ, such a trend will create a dangerous ground where many stray from Christ. If we neglect the importance of theological and biblical education, I am afraid Christ will end up being outside of the African church knocking at her door, asking her permission to go inside, instead of being the head of the Church and giving her vitality and vigor.

The Greeks, the Phoenicians, the Romans, the Arabs, and the Europeans came to Africa to conquer, exploit, and enslave Africans. Asian countries' interest in the continent is also packed with self-interest and greed. But on the other end of the spectrum, Jesus Christ, the creator of the universe and the king of kings, came to Africa with his parents as a refugee. He tasted the bitter cup of colonialism, lived through it, and died under it. "At the time when the New Testament was written the entire civilized world, with the exception of the little-known kingdoms of the Far East, was under the domination of Rome. From the Atlantic Ocean on the west to the Euphrates River, and the Red Sea in the east, and from the Rhone, the Danube, the Black Sea and the Caucasus mountains on the north the Sahara on the south, there stretched one vast empire under the headship and virtual dictatorship of the emperor, called in the New Testament both 'king' (1 Pet. 2:17) and 'Augusts'[92] (Luke 2:1)."[93] As one who left his heavenly glory, he understands what it means to be in exile. He was born and raised in a Roman colony bearing the colonial Roman power and the stamps of Herod's brutality in Jewish society. The Herod who is most prominent in the Gospels is Herod Antipas, the tetrarch of Galilee and Perea. Jesus alluded to him as "that fox" (Luke 13:32), or, more exactly, "that vixen." The epithet was a characterization not only of his slyness, but his craftiness and his vindictiveness as well. Herod Antipas appears in the Gospels as murderer of John the Baptist, and the one before whom Jesus was tried (23:7–12).[94] Destroying the Solomonic dynasty Herod occupied the throne in Jerusalem.

Herod ruled

> in the pride of his power and the reckless cruelty of his ever-watchful tyranny. Everywhere was his mark. Temples to gods and to Caesar, magnificent, and magnificently adorned, outside Palestine and its non-Jewish cities; towns rebuilt or built; *Sebaste* for the ancient Samaria, the splendid city and harbor of *Caesarea* in the west, *Antipatris* (after his father) in the north, *Kypros* and *Phaselis* (after his mother and brother), and *Agreppeion*; unconquerable fortress such as *Essebonitis* and *Machaerus* in Perea, *Alexandreion*, *Herodeion*, *Hyrcania*, and *Masada* in Judea—proclaimed his name and his sway. But in Jerusalem it seemed he had

---

92. Augusts' boast was that he had found Rome brick and he had left it marble. During the forty-one years of his administration he brought order out of chaos. He restored confidence in the government, replenished the treasury, and introduced an efficient public works department, and promoted peace and prosperity (Tenney, *New Testament Survey*, 4).

93. Ibid., 1.

94. Ibid., 37.

gathered up all of his strength. The theater and amphitheater spoke of his Gricianism; Anotnia was a representative fortress; for his religion he had built that glorious temple, and for his residence the noblest of palaces, at the north-west angle of the Upper City, close to where Milo had been in the days of David.[95]

In the environment of imperial expansion, Christianity grew from an obscure Jewish sect to become a world religion. Jesus was born in the reign of Augustus (Luke 2:1); his public ministry and death in the time of Tiberius (3:1); the great period of missionary expansion came in the reign of Claudius (Acts 18:22) and of Nero (25:11, 12). According to tradition, the Apocalypse was written in the reign of Domitian, and its allusion to imperial power and to governmental tyranny may have been reflections of conditions prevalent at that time.[96]

Jesus lived most of his life in Galilee, a region that formed the northern part of the kingdom of Israel. From the eighth to the second century BCE, Galilee was controlled by Assyrians, the Babylonians, the Persians, and the Seleucids; so for centuries the region was dominated by foreign (non-Jewish) influences and was exposed to constant migrant movement. The prophet Isaiah described it as "Galilee of the nations" (Isa 9:1).

In Jesus' day, in fact, Galilee was populated by migrants, the dispossessed, and an abundance of orphans, widows, poor, and unemployed. The enduring impact of foreign influence on the region was such that Galileans could be recognized by their distinctive accent (Matt 26:73). In Galilee there were many more Gentiles than Jews, so it is reasonable to assume that the "large crowds" often said to be traveling with or following Jesus included Gentiles (Matt 4:25; Mark 3:7; Luke 14:25; John 12:20–21).

The Gentiles always approach Jesus—never the reverse. A Roman centurion, a foreigner, is praised for possessing faith that surpassed that of any Israelite (Matt 8:10). Gentile towns (Sodom, Tyre, and Sidon) are favorably compared to Jewish cities that Jesus roundly condemns for rejecting his ministry (Matt 11:20–24). The Queen of Sheba (possibly from modern-day Ethiopia) and the Assyrian city of Nineveh are also upheld as exemplars of responsiveness to the God of Abraham (Luke 11:31, 32). Jesus repeatedly affirmed that God's plan of salvation embraces all peoples. In one instance when he was sought out by Greek delegates, Jesus declares, "and I, when I am lifted up from the earth, will draw all people to myself. *He said this to show the kind of death he is going to die*" (John 12:32).[97]

Unlike Alexander the Great, the Romans, and other conquerors on African soil, Jesus draws Africans toward him through his death on the cross not through the power of the sword. The suffering he went through qualifies him to be a wonderful counselor, a good shepherd, and a wounded healer.

---

95. Edersheim, *Life and Times of Jesus the Messiah*, 19–20.
96. See Tenney *New Testament Survey*, 1–12.
97. See Schnabel, *Early Christian Mission*.

The Suffering Messiah in Africa

N. T. Wright, one of the most brilliant New Testament scholars of our time, engages us with these questions in regard to the suffering and death of Jesus Christ:

> Of all the questions regularly asked about Jesus, the question "Why did Jesus die?" must be among the most frequent. It is certainly the most fascinating—and, as the researcher discovers soon enough the most frustrating. It has the ingredients of all the classic: dense and complex sources; the confluence of two great cultures (Jewish and Roman) in a single, swirling drama, characters who still leap off the page despite the gap of two millennia; tragedies; and tragic ironies, both small and great; gathering storm clouds of philosophy and theology; and, at the entire, a towering but enigmatic figure, who, if the sources are to be believed, had the capacity to evoke anger and admiration in full measure. Small wonder that not only historians and theologians, but also artists and musicians, have returned to the subject times without number. Why did Jesus die . . . Why did the Roman authorities consider it appropriate or desirable to execute Jesus? Why did the Jews authorities consider it right to hand him over to the Romans as deserving of death? And in the middle of it all, what was Jesus' own intention in the matter?[98]

These are fascinating and interesting questions that are pertinent to the African church context, and that need further discussion for their relevance and impact on the minds and hearts of African believers.

Then and now, the crucifixion of Christ was not only enigmatic but it was also considered madness and foolishness. Christians were mocked, degraded, and persecuted because of it.

> The Hellenistic world was familiar with the death and apotheosis of some predominantly barbarian demigods and heroes of primeval times. Attis and Adonis were killed by a wild boar, Osiris was torn pieces by Typhon-Seth and Dionysus-Zagreus by the Titans. Heracles alone of the "Greeks" voluntarily immolated himself on Mount Oeta. However, not only did all this take in the place in the darkest and most dictating past, but it was narrated in questionable myths which had to be interpreted either euhemeristically or at least allegorically. By contrast, to believe that the one pre-existent Son of the one true God, the mediator at creation and the redeemer of the world, had appeared in very recent times in-out-of-the-way Galilee as a member of the obscure people of the Jews, and even worse, had died the death of a common criminal on the cross, could only be regarded as a sign of madness. The real gods of Greece and Rome could be distinguished from mortal men by the very fact they were immortal—they had absolutely nothing in common with the cross as a sign of shame, the infamous stake, the barren, or criminal wood, the terrible cross of the slaves in Plautus, and thus of one who, in the words of Celsus, was bound in the most ignominious fashion and executed in a shameful way.[99]

---

98. N. T. Wright, *Jesus and the Victory of God*, 540.
99. Hengel, *Crucifixion*, 5–7.

Küng adds, "To no one—not a Jew, Greek or Roman—would it have occurred to link a positive, religious meaning with this outlaw's gibbet. The *cross of Jesus was bound to strike an educated Greek as barbaric folly, a Roman citizen as sheer disgrace, and devout Jew as God's curse.*"[100] It was within this worldview and context that Jesus gave up his life as ransom for all humankind. It was a despised and ignominious way of dying for one who claimed to be God and Messiah. Even Thomas doubted the veracity that Jesus was indeed risen from death. Many skeptics of that time, and in our day, have had a hard time accepting it.

> Jesus saw himself, at least, as a prophet like John the Baptist and Jeremiah; their fate, or even worse, would become his. Jesus was welcoming sinners, keeping company with the unclean; their taint was to infect him at last. He took a stand which brought him into inevitable conflict with authorities, but he construed that conflict as being not merely with them but *with the dark power* that, he believed stood behind them. The climax of the story, of the battle for the kingdom, was therefore, inescapably, that Jesus would die, not as an accident, nor as a bizarre quasi-suicide, a manipulated martyrdom, but as the inevitable result of his kingdom-inaugurating career. But this death, as he conceived it, would be the actual victory of the kingdom, by which *the enemy of the people would finally be defeated*. Jesus would act out the role of the revolutionary, at the point at which it could no longer be misunderstood.[101]

Notice the words "the dark power" and "the enemy of the people." As I'll explain later, the real enemy of the Jews or the gentiles as far as Christ was concerned was not the Roman rulers, the Pharisees, or the judicial, economic, or political system. It was Satan. The political and religious leaders were his agents and Jesus "believed [Satan] stood behind them." As African Christian scholars analyze the problem of the continent they cannot omit the real foe of Africans.

The suffering and crucified Christ can relate and appeal to the Congolese and Sierra Leoneans whose hands and legs were amputated. He relates to my Rwandese student who told me that her newborn baby, which she delivered in a refugee camp without the assistance of a nurse or a doctor, died in her hands a few weeks later as she was running away from a raid that was fatal. Many Africans, who were mistreated at the hands of slave traders, slave masters, the colonizer, and African tyrants, can identify with the flogged Christ. Those who belong to the "unjustly hanged" can emphatically categorize themselves with the Christ who was denied justice and was crucified by the Roman colonial powers. "Ever since the slave trade, the history of Africa has been a history of violence, characterized by harassment and by contempt for humanity. In Africa the church cannot hover over the conflict, looking down, and aspiring to a transcendence of the Spirit. It must regain contact with the African soil; not only with the African religions and cultures, but with the humiliations, with the violence of imperialism and political authorities, and with the resistance and struggles of the people."[102] Indeed, Isaiah, rightly called

---

100. Küng, *On Being a Christian*, 397; emphasis original.
101. N. T. Wright, *Jesus and the Victory of God*, 466; emphasis added.
102. Éla, *My Faith as an African*, 154.

Jesus "a man of sorrows" (53:3), who "carried our sorrows" (53:4). Christ understands human suffering.

"God's supreme justice will 'create' justice for the victims of wickedness, will raise them up out of the dust, will heal their wounded lives, and put to rights the lives that have been destroyed. The victims wait for God's creative justice, which will bring them liberty, health and new life. They are waiting for a judgment not based on works but for a *judgment based on the suffering of the sufferers.*"[103] John Stott rightly asserts and expresses my own convictions most exquisitely:

> I could never myself believe in a God, if it were not for the cross. The only God I believe in is the One Nietzsche ridiculed as "God on the cross." In a real world of pain, how could one worship a God who was immune to it? I have entered many Buddhist temples in different Asian countries and stood respectfully before the stature of the Buddha, his legs crossed, arms folded, eyes closed, the ghost of a smile playing around his mouth, a remote look on his face, detached from the agonies of the world. But each time after a while I have had to turn away. And in imagination I have turned instead to that lonely, twisted tortured figure on the cross, nails through hands and feet, back lacerated, limbs wrenched, brow bleeding from thorn pricks, mouth dry and intolerably thirsty, plunged in God-forsaken darkness. That is the God for me! He laid aside his immunity to pain. He entered our world of flesh and blood, tears and death. He suffered for us. Our suffering became more manageable in the light of his. There is still a question mark against human suffering, but over it we boldly stamp another mark, the cross which symbolizes divine suffering. "The cross of Christ . . . is God's only self-justification in a world such as ours."[104]

The cross is not a vaccination that makes us immune to human suffering. "God's love does not protect us *against* all suffering. But it protects us in all suffering. Thus what is admittedly to be completed only in the future does indeed begin in the present: the justification of God in the justification of man, of all men, even of the dead and vanquished, theodicy as anthropodicy. This is the harmony which is not simply given without expiation, but established in the cross. The definitive victory of the love of a God who is not unconcerned, unloving being, whom suffering and injustice cannot move, but who himself has assumed and will assume men's suffering in love. The victory of the love of God as Jesus proclaimed and manifested it, as the final, decisive power: this is the kingdom of God."[105]

When we think of the theology of the cross African thought and its understanding of death is important to comprehend in order to effectively contextualize the message of the cross. To Africans *death is caused by evil*. The African understanding of causation is of relevance here: nothing happens which will not have been *purposefully* caused. To be sure, physical explanations are understood, but the African goes beyond the physical to seek a theological explanation . . . *Death does not end life*. The occurrence of death is not considered to mark the cessation of life . . . *Death does not sever the bond between the*

---

103. Moltmann, *Sun of Righteousness Arise!*, 135; emphasis original.
104. Stott, *Cross of Christ*, 335–36.
105. Küng, *On Being a Christian*, 436; emphasis original.

living and the dead. In most African societies there is great care given to ensure proper burial for the dead so that they arrive safely in the land of the dead. Death rituals may take weeks, or months, or even years . . . *Death is an occasion for seeking more life.* Since death makes people into spirits and thus members of the spirit world, the dead are believed to be in a position to grans blessings. *Death does not negate natural self-expression.* Death does imply loss, but it does not end man's self-expression. Loss may have occurred, but there is on-going life, and this is symbolized in various ways . . . the dancing is a powerful affirmation of life, from the African point of view . . . This affirmation of life is widespread in Africa as part of death rites; it has the effect of saying, very eloquently, that life must go on . . . Death affects the whole community. In African societies death affects a much wider social group than the deceased's immediate family. The ritual in connection with death serves to reaffirm the sense of solidarity of the larger group, and to place the latter's support at the disposal of the bereaved. Relatives, friends, neighbors, and even those who only knew others who had known the deceased—all these would flock around, taking part in wakes, visiting the bereaved and at the appropriate moment making donations to them. Throughout the period of rites there will be a concourse of people, coming and going. There is identification with the family of the deceased. Quite often the number of people present at a funeral is not in direct proportion to the social importance of the deceased when he was alive. Death, whether of the high or low, brings about a great deal of community interaction.[106]

In the light of the African understanding of death, African theologians need to relate the message of the cross to the worldview of Africans. African perception gives a wonderful opportunity to develop the doctrine of human sin as the cause death, and the crucifixion as hope beyond death. The theology of the cross in the African context provides a fertile environment to develop a juxtaposition of shame and glory, death and life, loss and gain, grief and celebration, and defeat and victory within a community of believers and non-believers. In Africa death brings people together with sympathy and empathy to the deceased family with a sense of solidarity instead of alienating the grieved from the community. "Many African cultures will never say that a person has died, but rather that one has departed, one has left us, one is no longer, one has passed on. For the African, death is not the annihilation of a being. Strictly speaking, one is not afraid of death; but what one does fear is dying without leaving children behind. The absence of sons is the worst curse for the black African. This obsession with having children reveals a deep concern—descendants are needed to fulfill the ultimate responsibility of maintaining the cult of the ancestors. It is terrible to die, after having broken the ties of family, clan and community."[107]

To the Corinthians, Paul presented the theology of the cross (the gospel) as a contradiction to wisdom (1 Cor 1:18—2:5).

> The message of the cross is foolishness to those who are perishing, but to us who are being saved it is the power of God. For it is written: "I will destroy the wisdom of the wise the intelligent of the intelligent I will frustrate." Where is the wise man? Where is the expert in the law? Where is the philosopher of this age?

106. Dickson *A Theology in Africa*, 192–95; emphasis original.
107. Éla, *My Faith as an African*, 16.

Has not God made foolish the wisdom of the world? For since in the wisdom of God the world through its wisdom did not know him, God was pleased through the foolishness of what was preached to save those who believe. Jews demand miraculous signs and Greeks look for wisdom, but we preach Christ crucified: a stumbling block to Jews and foolishness to Gentiles, but to those who God has called, both Jews and Greeks, Christ is the power of God and the wisdom of God. For the foolishness of God is wiser than man's wisdom and the weakness of God is stronger than man's strength.

Gordon Fee said that

> This paragraph is crucial not only to the present argument (1:10—4:21) but to the entire letter as well. Indeed, it is one of the truly great moments in the apostle Paul. Here he argues, with OT support, that what God had always intended had foretold in the prophets, he has now accomplished through the crucifixion: He has brought an end to human self-sufficiency as it is evidenced through human wisdom and devices. No, Paul argues with his Corinthian friends, the gospel is not some new *sophia* (wisdom or philosophy), not even a new divine *sophia*. For *sophia* allows for human judgment and evaluations of God's activity. But the gospel stands at the divine antithesis to such judgments. No mere human, in his or her right mind or otherwise, would ever have dreamed up God's scheme of redemption—through a crucified Messiah. It is too preposterous, too humiliating, for a God.[108]

From Paul's argument, it looks like the Corinthians were also ashamed of the cross. Küng asserts:

> On the one side are the progressive, pneumatic *enthusiasts* in the proverbially infamous seaport of *Corinth* who imagine—because they are baptized, have received the Spirit, share in the agape—that they are already in secure possession of salvation even perfect. They regard the wretched earthly Jesus as belonging to the past and prefer to invoke the exalted Lord and victor over the powers of fate. From the fact of possession of the Spirit and from their superior knowledge they deduce a self-assured freedom which permits them to indulge in all kinds of self-glorification, arrogance, uncharitableness, self-opinionatedness, violence, even drinking bouts and intercourse with sacred prostitutes (known as "Corinthianizing"). Paul refers these extravagant, utopian, libertinist, resurrection fantasts, who want to anticipate heaven on earth, to the *Crucified*.[109]

Paul reminds them that "to move beyond the cross is not 'to move on' at all, but to abandon Christ all together. Hence here he argues that the message of the cross is absolute—and fundamental—and as such stands over against the merely human wisdom of their present position."[110] Dickson adds, "No matter what the cultural perspective of the Christian might be, the matter of Christ's death and its significance cannot but be considered most central; Christians everywhere, from whatever cultural background, must react to this central belief . . . the cross underlines the seriousness of sin which

---

108. Fee, *First Epistle to the Corinthians*, 68; emphasis original.
109. Küng, *On Being a Christian*, 399; emphasis original.
110. Fee, *First Epistle to the Corinthians*, 68.

permeates human life and thought."¹¹¹ Treat also comments, "The natural person looks at the cross through the wisdom of the world and sees folly. The spiritual person looks at the cross through the wisdom of God see power."¹¹²

The theology of the cross transcends cultural, racial, economic, and social boundaries. Through the cross, Christ has reconciled humankind with God and with each other. Christ had "destroyed the barrier, the dividing wall of hostility" (Eph 2:14b). "Therefore, if anyone is in Christ, he is a new creation; the old has gone, the new has come! All this is from God, who reconciled us to himself through Christ and gave us the ministry of reconciliation: that God was reconciling the world to himself in Christ, not counting men's sins against them. And he has committed to us the message of reconciliation. We are therefore Christ's ambassadors, as though God was making his appeal through us. We implore you in Christ's behalf: Be reconciled to God" (2 Cor 5:17–20). These were the words of a former Pharisee, a persecutor of the church, who had nothing to do with the Gentiles, and grew up and lived in the colony of Rome. Paul was a person who suffered immensely at the hands of the Jews as well as the Roman rulers. Christianity not only gave him meaning for existence, he found it to be the only truth that can liberate all who are in spiritual, psychological, and physical bondage if they will come to Christ in faith. Hence, preaching the gospel became the mission of his life. He did his task with a sense of obligation—"I am obligated both to Greeks and non-Greeks, both to the wise and the foolish. That is why I am so eager to preach the gospel also to you who are at Rome. I am not ashamed of the gospel, because it is the power of God for the salvation of everyone who believes: first for the Jew, then for the Gentile. In the gospel righteousness from God is revealed, a righteousness that is by faith from first to last" (Rom 1:14–17).

> From the very beginning [Paul] wanted to proclaim the Crucified and him alone. And how could anyone show off his religious talents and powers or boast of his superior wisdom and mighty deeds in view of this Crucified, who died in his weakness for the weak? How could anyone ruthlessly attain his objectives, misuse his freedom, seek to give himself airs before God, in order to set himself above weak men and the weakness of God himself? It is precisely in the weakness and folly of the Crucified—in which the weakness and folly of God himself above weak men and the weakness of God himself seems to be manifested—that God's power to raise the dead and his overwhelming wisdom ultimately prevail. God's weakness, so obvious particularly on the cross, proves to be stronger than the power of men. His folly is shown to be wiser than their wisdom. It is indeed the cross, seen in the light of the new life, which means God's power and wisdom to all who trustingly commit themselves to it. In faith in the Crucified, that is, man becomes capable of using freedom, not as a libertine, but for others: able to apply the individual gifts of the Spirit for the benefit of the community, to proceed in everything boldly by way of active love. This crucified and living Jesus then is for believers the foundation which is already laid and which cannot be replaced by any other. The Crucified as living is the ground of faith. He is the criterion of freedom. He is indeed the center and norm for what is Christian.¹¹³

---

111. Dickson, *Theology in Africa*, 185.
112. Treat, *Crucified King*, 144.
113. Küng, *On Being a Christian*, 399–400.

The reconciliation of God is multidimensional. It reconciles people with God and human beings with each other. This is the good news the church is entrusted to preach— "the message of the cross" that is universal in its scope. "To us who are being saved it is the power of God" (1 Cor 1:18b). "The God of the philosophers is like the Greek *ananké*, unknown and indifferent to man; He thinks, but does not speak; He is conscious of Himself, but oblivious of the world; while the God of Israel is a God who loves, a God who is known to, and concerned with man. He not only rules the world in the majesty of His might and wisdom, *but he react intimately to the events of history*. He does not judge men's deeds impassively and with aloofness; His judgment is imbued with the attitude of One to Whom those actions are of the most intimate and profound concern. God does not stand outside the range of human suffering and sorrow. He is personally involved in, even stirred by, the conduct and fate of man."[114] When we worship and serve a God "who reacts intimately to the events of [our] history" it is important to demonstrate his love, graciousness, kindness, holiness, mercy, righteousness, and justice both in our personal and our communal life. African Christology should be contextual and should encompass all humankind despite the continent's dark history. There has been no moment in all of time when God was absent from the history of Africans. He was and has been suffering with us. "Where there is world there is God; where there is God there is world. There is no God 'left over' in some sphere which is other than world. God, who is other than world, has wholly immersed himself in the world. Thus, whatever may have been the case before the creation of the heavens and the earth, since the creation God has taken up residence within that creation, and thus works from within the world, and not on the world from without."[115] Jeremiah attests to this truth: "Am I only a God nearby, declares the Lord, and not a God far away? Can anyone hide in secret places so that I cannot see him? Declares the Lord. Do not I feel heaven and earth? Declares the Lord" (23:23–24). "To believe today is a matter of faithfulness to the God of hope, who went out from himself to place himself at the side of human beings as they struggle to stand up erect in the image of the Risen One. Such a faith requires a fresh re-reading of revelation."[116]

African Christology

"Christ has been presented as the answer to the questions a white man would ask, the solution to the needs that Western man would feel, the Saviour of the world of the European world-view, the object of the adoration and prayer of historic Christendom. But if Christ were to appear as the answer to the questions that Africans are asking, what would he look like?"[117]

Diane B. Stinton's book, *Jesus of Africa*, reminds me of the christological question above posed by J. V. Taylor. As a Canadian and a woman, Diane has written with good

114. Heschel, *Prophets*, 289; emphasis added.
115. Fretheim, *Suffering of God*, 38.
116. Éla, *My Faith as an African*, 101.
117. Taylor, *Primal Vision*, 16.

insight on an African's Christology. By doing so, she validates that Christ is a universal savior who can be studied without being limited by national boundaries or gender.

Asserting the importance of her research, Stinton stated that, "at the heart of Christian faith is the person of Jesus Christ. Consequently, the very core of Christian theology is Christology."[118] While Stinton admits the critical need to articulate the reality and significance of Jesus Christ in African Christianity, she also demonstrates the centrality of Christ in the African Christian's theology, worship, and praxis. I agree with Stinton that, "in the ongoing development of Christian theology African accounts of Christology warrant careful consideration in view of Africa's prominent place in Christian history at the turn of the millennium."[119] In light of this fact, Stinton's book is a timely contribution to the health of global Christianity because it is good for cross-pollination of christological views and strategic ministry alliance.

Western Christology developed within the cultural influences of the Industrial Revolution, the Enlightenment, and modernity. This Christology has attempted to give meaning to the life, death, and resurrection of Jesus Christ in the lives of Western believers. Through theology, preaching, and hymns, Christ has been understood and worshiped in the West. For the last two centuries, the impact of Christology in the West has been seen in many positive and a few negative ways. Without other alternatives available, the African church and its scholars have been eating the Western Christology with Christians in the West. I wonder if the West is ready to eat African Christology with African Christians.

As Stinton describes, the seed of the gospel is planted in very different but fertile soil in Africa than in the West. African traditional religion, the place of ancestors, "the living dead" (as Mbiti calls them), collective mentality, kinship and marriage, the challenge of sickness and death, poverty, slavery, and colonialism are the cultural context in which Jesus reveals himself to Africans. This is why it is a different soil than the West. Contrary to what many Western theologians and mission experts thought, the primeval African religion and the socioeconomic context, make a fertile soil for the gospel.

In her book, Stinton gives us the portrait of Jesus Christ in an African cultural context. However, as if Christianity began to take root in Africa in the nineteenth century, Stinton's historical and theological contextual research starts from the 1950s. According to her account, "the All African Conference of Churches (AACC), constituted in Kampala in 1963 in hope of achieving selfhood for the African church and inspiring African theology, held an assembly in Abijan in 1969."[120] Even though the concern for African Christology was desired in the form of indigenous liturgies and African expression of doctrine, Christology was not protuberant in the early stages of African theology in the twentieth century.

"On the sociopolitical scene, African theology as an intellectual discipline arose during the 1950s, when the struggle against colonialism led to several newly independent states."[121] Christ began to appear as the answer to the question of Africans in their

118. Stinton, *Jesus of Africa*, 3.
119. Ibid.
120. Ibid., 69.
121. Ibid., 7.

context. He was no longer a messiah of the "pie in the sky" or a stranger who forced himself into Africans' lives. But, as one who genuinely loved them, Africans wanted Christ to intervene in their present subjugation, exploitation, and dehumanizing circumstances under the colonial power.

The cultural revolution that swept the continent in the 60s along with the political winds of change were other factors for the development of African Christology. "To counter the disdain with local cultures had generally been held during colonial times. Africans made intensive efforts to reaffirm their identity and integrity in many spheres of life, including names, dress, music, dance forms, architecture, and indigenous expression affecting church life and practice."[122] In order to be truly Christian, Africans had to have biblical or Western names, dress in Western style, be tuned in to Western music, and churches even had to be built in Western architectural style. The transplanted gospel in Africa produced the Christ of the West who was not embedded in the selfhood of Africans.

The missionaries thought inculcating European values in the minds of Africans under the political shadow of the colonial powers was a good seedbed for Christian faith. The concurrence of colonialism and Western mission in Africa distorted the biblical image of Christ as "a lamb slain for the sin of the world" (Rev 5:9–13), "the good shepherd who gives his life for the sheep" (John 10:14–15), "the wonderful counselor," "the prince of peace" (Isa 9:6), "a brother" (Matt 12:49), etc. In the light of their experience, Africans thought "Christ entered the African scene as a forceful, impatient and unfriendly tyrant. He was presented as invalidating the history and institutions of a people in order to impose his rule upon them."[123] It is no wonder then that Nigerians were thinking of Christ for a long time as "merely a stranger," "an illegal alien," "a refugee, a dissident or a fugitive who in desperation has come to Africa for sanctuary," or as "the most visible and publicized symbol of foreign domination ever."[124] If "African Christianity is a mile wide and an inch deep," one has to look to the root cause of the problem instead of just the current appearance.

As African intellectuals unmercifully began to critique Christianity and missionary domination of the African church, Christology was being developed by Africans in the form of apologetic theology. Priority was given to revitalize local cultures and to indigenizing mission churches within the wider context of African reformation in literature, philosophy, and history. African theologians like John Mbiti, Beyang Kato, Kwame Bediako, and others argued that "Jesus Christ is no stranger to [Africans'] heritage. Jesus is the Universal Savior and thus the Savior of the Africans. Through faith in Christ African believers now share in all promises made to the patriarchs and Israel, and the good news becomes 'our story.'"[125] Through vernacular Scripture, contextualized theology, relevant biblical teaching and preaching, and through indigenized worship, Christ has found home in Africa now. Those who truly know the God of the Bible, both

---

122. Ibid.
123. Ibid., 10.
124. Ibid.
125. Ibid., 11.

Westerners and Africans, have always been "in the pains of childbirth until Christ is formed in [Africans]" (Gal 4:19).

Most African theologians argue that, because Christ is formed in the lives of Africans in diverse places, at different times, and in assorted human situations within the continent, we ought to look at a plurality of Christologies in Africa. The constant dialogue between the biblical text and different contexts in Africa leads to different understandings and interpretations of Christ in the continent. "A widespread methodological presupposition is that genuine Christological reflection cannot be separated from Africa's socio-political, religio-cultural and economic contexts—this is the real and concrete everyday experience within which we Christologize."[126] By intentionally deviating "from the approaches of the dominant theologies of the West, a theology that arises from and is accountable to African people"[127] is developed. This theology does not view Christ as an abstract construct hanging in the air. Christology and Christopraxis are intertwined in order for Christian faith to give meaning to Africans in their various contexts. For the gospel to preserve its vitality and wholeness, theology needs the reflection of the people committed to Christian practice in a particular cultural context. "We must turn away from the beaten paths of traditional theology and explore new directions. Above all we need to imagine new solutions that do not simply copy former models, which are too marked by the historical characteristics of a particular period of Christian life. Truly basic reflection, open to questions from young Christian communities, may show a way out of the current impasses."[128] Orthodoxy should not be divorced from orthopraxis because it demonstrates the Christ who was "powerful in word and deed before God and all the people" (Luke 24:19).

According to Stinton's findings, Christ among Africans is viewed as "life-giver," "mediator," "loved one," and "leader."[129] Stinton's book is not a comprehensive study of African Christology; however, it is an excellent complimentary work to the previous studies of this topic and a good launching pad for further research on African Christology. The Jesus of Africa is the Jesus of the poor and the rejected. By destroying various partitioning walls in Africa he can be a reconciler. In a continent that is prone to chaos, war and bloodshed, he can be a prince of peace. I hope to see further studies on African Christology from African perspective. As an outsider, Stinton has set a noble path.

"After careful reflection," John M. Waliggo stated,, "the single root cause of Africa's suffering is *rejection*, both by powerful outsiders and powerful insiders. From this rejection come all attitudes which continue to oppress Africa and intensify suffering. From rejection there comes failure to seriously think of a lasting solution to the unnecessary suffering on the continent. It is on this theme of *rejection* that my Christological reflections will be constructed."[130] To build up his case for African Christology, he elaborates the degrees and kinds of rejections Africans went through as follows:

---

126. Ibid., 16.
127. Ibid.
128. Éla, *My Faith as an African*, 63.
129. Stinton, *Jesus of Africa*, 250–66.
130. Waliggo, "African Christology in a Situation of Suffering," 101; emphasis original.

> When [European] Christianity came to Africa towards the end of the fifteenth century its theology soon sanctioned Africa's rejection by giving support to the enslavement of Africans. This created a situation which was progressively to sanction rejection of Africans in many other instances.
>
> After almost one thousand years of isolation, when Western mission came in contact with Christian Ethiopia, in the early sixteenth century, they utterly rejected its Christianity as heretical and listed hundreds of errors in it. This closed the door for cooperation between the Ethiopian church and Western Christianity. When the European Christian non-conformists were persecuted at home, they trekked to South Africa during the seventeenth century, and on arrival they rejected the blacks, the owner of the land, as the condemned children of Ham.
>
> The nineteenth century theology of the missionary movement rejected any value in African traditional religions, despised many of the people's cultural values and would not use them as a basis for Christian evangelization.
>
> Throughout the colonial era Christian theology rejected African church leadership. This was even the case with the Anglican Samuel Ajayi Crowther[131] who had been consecrated Bishop in 1864 at the insistence of the far-sighted secretary general of C.M.S., Henry Venn. The rejection of his leadership came in 1890 when many of his African pastors were dismissed without trial on fabricated accusations, and he himself was succeeded by a white missionary bishop in 1891.
>
> When nationalist movements for independence first emerged in Africa from the 1920s and more so after the Second World War, [Western] Christian theology tended to reject them as communistic and Marxist. It remained to the Catholic Portuguese missionaries in Mozambique to outright condemn as evil and sinful the African aspiration for independence as late as 1973. Christian theology, as a whole, tended to support the *status quo* of colonial rule. Once Africans succeeded in their struggle for independence, Christian theology seemed to support the neo-colonialism, the control of Africa from afar.
>
> In the late 1960s when African theologies were emerging, they were rejected by no less a person than the scholarly Jean Cardinal Danielou in a symposium organized in Rome in December 1967. Such theologies were considered as unorthodox and opposed one universal theology for all.
>
> Western Christianity had been equated to Christianity itself. Western Christology had been made equivalent to Christ himself. Even today, the word, *inculturation*, is still rejected in some Western and African circles. Instances of Africans rejection within the history of Christian theology could be multiplied indefinitely.[132]

The rejection that Africans have suffered can be a good context to develop African Christology. Christ experienced rejection by the Jews and the world. "He was in the world, and though the world was made by him, the world did not recognize him. He

---

131. Crowther, though no great scholar or Arabist, developed an approach to Islam in its African setting that reflected the patience and readiness to listen that marked his entire missionary method. He led a mission force consisting entirely of Africans. Sierra Leone, as he and Schön foreseen long ago, was new evangelizing inland Africa. Contemporary mission accounts all praise Crowther's personal integrity, graciousness, and godliness. In the Yoruba mission, blessed with many strong, not to say prickly, personalities, his influence had been irenic. In Britain, he was recognized as a cooperative and effective platform speaker (Walls, *Cross-Cultural Process*, 161–63).

132. Ibid., 101–2; emphasis original.

came to that which was his own, but his own did not receive him" (John 1:10–11). If the gospel is appropriately and effectively communicated, the rejected Christ will find his place, even as he already has in the hearts of millions of Africans.

> What does the gospel bring the poor? Not charitable works. Nor does it make them as rich as the rest. What it does do is to give them new dignity and powerful stimulus. The poor are no longer the suffering objects of oppression and humiliation. They are their own determining subjects, with the dignity of God's first children. Jesus brings the poor the certainty of their indestructible dignity in God's eyes. And with this awareness, people who are poor, slaves, and women who have been sold can get up out of the dust and help themselves. The throw aside the values of the society which daily dins into their ears: "you're failures! You haven't made it! You're good for nothing!" They begin to live with their heads held high, and an upright walk. An inner acceptance of the meritocracy's system of values is always the greatest hindrances to the self-liberation of the poor, because this acceptance endangers self-contempt.[133]

However, because of the past wounds and hurts Africans went through and the concurrence of modern mission and colonialism in Africa, African Christianity should not be perceived as an appendage of Western hegemony. Walls concurs: "Christianity in Africa cannot be treated as a colonial leftover. If it is to reflect its true place in the history of redemption, Africa must be recovered from its place in the margins of Christian thought. If Christianity is indigenous to Africa, if its continuous history in the continent is as long as that of Christianity almost anywhere else in the world, then African Christian thought belongs in the Christian mainstream; and African theology should not be satisfied with a place that reduces it to resolving local difficulties."[134] In other words, African scholarship should not be measured merely by its understanding and analysis of Western theology or its comprehension of the works of Western scholars of all kinds. With a homegrown theology and missiology, backed by academic integrity and sound doctrine, African voices should enter "the Christian mainstream" to interact and dialogue with it and to give and receive from the global hermeneutical community as well as to serve the global church. Interpreting the gospel within our context with freedom and equal rights should lead us to a platform of learning that has level ground with the West. Paternalistic attitudes of the West and the sense of inferiority that has crippled African minds should be a thing of the past. "The way we define a problem will significantly shape its solution. In medicine, a misdiagnosis will not only detract from the remedy but can actually precipitate deadly consequences. So is with theology."[135]

---

133. Moltmann, *Source of Life*, 17–18.
134. Walls, *Cross-Cultural Process*, 91.
135. Treat, *Crucified King*, 194.

Chapter 11

The Hope of Humankind in the Hopeless Continent

And what does the Lord require of you, but to do justice, to love mercy, and to walk humbly with your God? (Mic 6:8)

The Kingdom of God is the redemptive reign of God dynamically active to establish his rule among men, and that his kingdom, which will appear as an apocalyptic act at the end of the age, has already come into human history in the person and mission of Jesus to overcome evil, to deliver men from its power, and to bring them into the blessing of God's reign. The Kingdom of God involves two great moments: fulfillment within history, and consummation at the end of history.[1]

NATURE AND HUMAN-CAUSED PROBLEMS often place us in a precarious, uncertain, and hopeless situation. We often ask ourselves if life is made up of an endless cycle of suffering. From common men to the highest thinkers like Aristotle, Plato, Kant, Hegel, Marx, and Nietzsche, just to mention a few, many have wrestled intellectually with fathoming the beginning and destiny of humanity and the cosmos. Since their search started from a wrong premise, none have achieved the ultimate goal of their pursuit for the meaning and destiny of life. The destiny of humankind is not something that we can take lightly. The tragedies of our time would not allow us to ignore the issue of our being, the history of humankind and where and how it will end. Ladd writes:

> We live in a wonderful and yet a fearful day. It is a wonderful day because of the amazing accomplishments of our modern scientific skills which have provided us with a measure of comfort and prosperity undreamed of a century ago. Great metal birds soar through the air, swallowing up thousands of miles in a few hours. Floating palaces bring to the ocean voyager all the luxuries of the most

---

1. Ladd, *Presence of the Future*, 218.

elegant hotel. The automobile has freed man to explore for himself scenes and slights which to his grandparents were contained only in story-books. Electrical power has brought a score of slaves to serve the humblest housewife. Medical science has conquered the plague, smallpox, and other scourges of physical well-being and is on the threshold of other amazing conquests.

A marvelous age, indeed! Yet happiness and security seems further removed than ever, for we face dangers and hazards of unparalleled dimensions. We have come victoriously through a war in which the foundations of human liberty were threatened; yet the columns of our newspapers are stained with unbelievable stories of the suppression of human freedom, and the fight for freedom goes on. New discoveries in the structure of matter have opened unimaginable vistas of blessing for man's physical well-being; yet these very discoveries hold the potential, in the hands of evil men, of blasting society from the face of the earth.

In a day like this, wonderful yet fearful, men are asking questions. What does it all mean? Where are we going? What is the meaning and the goal of human history? Men are concerned today not only about the individual and the destiny of his soul but also about the meaning of history itself. Does mankind have a destiny? Or do we jerk across the stage of time like wooden puppets, only to have the stage, the actors, and the theatre itself destroyed by fire, leaving only a pile of ashes and the smell of smoke?[2]

Our answers to these questions are crucial for a meaningful existence, to know ourselves and to comprehend human history. They are the beginning, for me, in understanding my being as an African, the African continent and Africans, the West and the East, and in making sense of my existence and my purpose in life. There is nothing under the sun that helped me like knowing the God of the Bible—to be specific, the Christ as reflected by Paul. "At the heart of Paul's thinking is not man (anthropology), nor Church (ecclesiology), nor even salvation history in general, but the crucified and risen Christ (Christology understood as soteriology). This is Christocentrism working out to the advantage of man, based on and culminating in a theocentrism: 'God through Jesus Christ'—'Christ Jesus through God.' As the Holy spirit came to be inserted in such binitarian formulas—as the one in whom God and Jesus Christ are present and active both in the individual and the community—there turned by Paul at this early stage into Trinitarian formulas, the basis for that later development of the doctrine of the Trinity, of the triune God who is Father, Son, and the Holy Spirit."[3]

As I often have done in my last thirty-four years of life in exile, I assume Paul would have wished to see the full restoration of Israel, all those in the diaspora gathered under the same flag living without the bondage of colonial powers. In fact this was the last question of the disciples before Christ's ascension: "Lord, are you at this time going to restore the kingdom to Israel?" (Acts 1:6). Who doesn't want to have a free and prosperous country? Who likes to live under colonial power?

To Paul, it was not only the physical, economic, and political condition of his people that was causing sorrow in his heart and soul. Their dark spiritual condition, their rejection of the king's banquet, their stiff-necked stubbornness, their turning back from the

---

2. Ladd, *Gospel of the Kingdom*, 13–14.
3. Küng, *On Being a Christian*, 403.

God who had hewn them, so to speak, from the dead womb of Sarah was grief beyond description to Paul. Very explicitly, with words that are moving but cannot enable us to fully fathom his agony, Paul writes, "I speak the truth in Christ—I am not lying, my conscience confirms it in the Holy spirit—I have great sorrow and unceasing anguish in my heart, for I could wish that I myself was cursed and cut off from Christ for the sake of my brothers, those of my own race, the people of Israel" (Rom 9:1). One wonders, how can the same person exhort us saying, "Rejoice in the Lord always. I will say it again: Rejoice!" (Phil 4:4). His whole personality and outlook in life must have been anchored on some unshakable foundation to enable him to have a sense of meaning as a Jew who lived under Roman rule and run his race existing between these two extreme poles of reality and feelings. Spiritually, Paul was free in Christ. But politically, he and his people were under Roman oppression. He grieved for the spiritual blindness of the Jews and his rejoices for the conversion of the gentiles. For Paul, "to live is Christ and to die is gain" (Phil 1:21). His christocentric thinking is more evident as expressed in these words: "Whatever was to my profit I now consider loss for the sake of Christ. What is more, I consider everything a loss compared to the surpassing greatness of knowing Christ Jesus my Lord, for whose sake I have lost all things. I consider them rubbish, that I may gain Christ and be found in him" (Phil 3:7–9a). Paul's understanding of life and human history was christocentric. "Each of three chapters [of Romans] (9, 10, and 11) begins with a personal statement by Paul, in which he identifies himself with the people of Israel and expresses his profound concern for them. To him Israel's unbelief is far more than an intellectual problem. He writes of the sorrow and anguish he feels over them (9:1ff.), of prayerful longing for their salvation (10:1), and of conviction that God has not rejected them (1:1f.)."[4]

Paul could have been preoccupied with the news of his day—the political, economic, and social realities of his people. Jerusalem was controlled by legions of Roman army; heathen temples and palaces stood on the promised land of Israel; over three million Jews wandered in diaspora; the Roman and the Pharisees taxes were crushing the poor. The gap between the rich and the poor was wide and the scum of the earth were treated badly not only by the Romans but by their own religious leaders. "Over 90 percent of the population did not have prestigious social connections of financial means. These masses were known as the 'people of the land.' . . . The Pharisees avoided contact with them and refused to eat with them. They were looked down on with contempt, so much so that according to rabbinical law they could not appear as a witness in court nor be appointed as the guardian of an orphan. The Pharisees would not marry them and consider their women as unclean vermin."[5] If he had desired a fertile ground for a civil right or revolutionary movement, Paul had it. Instead of being consumed by the effects of sin, he dealt with the cause and the solution. This is a great lesson that the African or black Christian thinkers and leaders can learn from Paul. Yes, Africa has so many internal and external problems, but what grieves our hearts the most? What are the fundamental questions we wrestle with? What shapes our theological and missiological thinking?

---

4. Stott, *Message of Romans*, 263.
5. Kraybill, *Upside-Down Kingdom*, 83.

> What Paul throughout his life understood by "grace," as the completely unmerited friendliness of God, is based on this living experience of the Crucified who revealed himself to him as the living, the true Lord ... In the light of the whole course of salvation history from creation to consummation, starting out from the universal sinfulness of men, both Jews and Gentiles [black and white], he explains how man's definitive wellbeing, his salvation, can be attained only on the basis of faith in Jesus Christ: on this basis of faith he sketches in a striking way both the new life from the Spirit in freedom and home and God's great plan of salvation for Jews and Gentiles and draws out the most important consequences for a Christian life.[6]

If we are earnest in reconciling people and helping Africans heal from their various kinds of wounds, Paul is a great model both for Western Christian leaders and thinkers and also for Africans. However, one has to know that a christocentric life and engagement with the world is a costly endeavor. To Paul, this meant not only imprisonment, hunger, torture and loneliness; it eventually cost him his life. Africa is a sensitive continent and one cannot avoid discussing, analyzing and critiquing sensitive subjects and issues. Unless a person willingly wants to be an innocuous people pleaser, the way to deal with the injustice in Africa is to speak and act with the indignation of the prophets and their words that are sharper than the two edges of a sword. "The Christian concept of truth is not—like the Greek—contemplative-theoretical, but operative practical. It is a truth which is not merely to be sought and found, but to be pursued, made true, verified and tested in truthfulness. A truth which aims at practice, which calls to the way, which bestows and makes possible a new life."[7] (Küng 1968:410).

Paul's Comprehension of Sin

> The problem of the origin of the evil that is in the world has always been considered as one of the profoundest problems of philosophy and theology. It is a problem that naturally forces itself upon the attention of man since the power of evil is both great and universal, is an ever present blight on life in all its manifestations, and is a matter of daily experience in the life of every man. Philosophers were constrained to face the problem and to seek an answer to the question as to the origin of all the evil, and particularly of the moral evil, that is in the world. To some it seemed to be so much a part of life itself that they sought the solution for it in the natural constitution of things. Others, however, were convinced that it had a voluntary origin, that is, that it originated in the free choice of man, either in the present or in some previous existence. These are much closer to the truth as it is revealed in the Word of God.[8]

Unless we come to grips with the biblical understanding of the origin of evil and deal with it theologically, we cannot solve Africa's problem by using the West or China

---

6. Küng, *On Being a Christian*, 405.
7. Ibid., 410.
8. Berkhof, *Systematic Theology*, 219.

as a scapegoat. Studying Paul's *hamartia*[9] is immensely helpful for understanding the potential of a fallen humanity for destruction.

What strikes me about Paul is not only his deep Christology, Pneumatology, or ecclesiology. His well-defined theological anthropology have saved me from being a racist and encouraged and challenged me to cross my cultural, racial, linguistic, and geographical boundaries to know and appreciate other people. Whether one is a Jew or a gentile, Paul sees humankind under the bondage of sin in need of a redeemer. He writes, "[J]ust as the result of one trespass was condemnation for all men, so also the result of one act of righteousness was justification that brings life for all men. For just as through the disobedience of the one man the many were made sinners, so also through the obedience of the one man the many will be made righteous" (Rom 5:18–19).

> Sin is the term Paul uses for a compulsion or constraint which humans generally experience within themselves or in their social context, a compulsion towards attitudes and actions not always of their own willing or approving. If Paul made anything of its root meaning, *hamartia* would denote that power which draws men and women back from the best and keep causing them to miss the target. In particular, sin is that power which makes human beings forget their humaneness and dependence on God, that power which prevents humankind from recognizing its true nature, which deceives the *adam* into thinking he is godlike and makes him unable to grasp he is but *adamah*. It is that power which turns humankind in upon itself in preoccupation with satisfying and compensating for its own weakness as flesh. It is that power which has caused countless individuals of good will but inadequate resolve to cry out in despair: "I can't help it." "I can't fight it."[10]

The effect of sin is misdirected religion, self-indulgence, breakdown of human relationship, and death. When we look at the ministry of John the Baptist, Jesus, and the Apostles, they did not start or focus on cleaning the outside ritual forms of the Jewish people like their religious rituals, the temple, or dietary and judicial system. Neither did they waste their time and energy in complaining about or attacking the external colonial powers. They addressed the problem of sin, the barrier it created between the people and the merciful and loving God, and its effect on their social, political, and economic life. In fact, when we look at the Scriptures, the cause for Israel's current political and economic conditions was their disobedience to the message of the prophets. Before the Roman conquered the Jews, knowing what was coming Jesus wept for Jerusalem (Luke 13:34–35; 19:41–44; Matt 23:37–39).[11] As Rick Flanders rightly observed, "He was weeping over

---

9. The term hamartia derives from the Greek ἁμαρτία, from ἁμαρτάνειν hamartánein, which means "to miss the mark" or "to err." It is most often associated with Greek tragedy, although it is also used in Christian theology (for a detailed understanding of the theological use, see Ridderbos *Paul*, 91–113).

10. Dunn, *Theology of Paul the Apostle*, 112–13.

11. Jerusalem, the holy city, was built on Abraham's Mount Moriah and David's Mount Zion. Its foundations rested upon the Salem of Melchizedek and the Jebus of the Jebusites. It was made the capital of God's nation during the reign of King David, and served as such until it was destroyed by the Babylonians. Jerusalem was rebuilt by a remnant of the Jews under Zerubbabel, Ezra, and Nehemiah. It had heard the voice and seen the face of the Son of God. One day, the prophets tell us, it will be the capital city of the world and the center of God's kingdom on earth! But as the awful day on which our savior

the tragedy of a lost opportunity. The Israelites that assembled in Jerusalem for the Passover missed the opportunity to be saved from both earthly and eternal destruction. They were visited by their Saviour, but they did not know it. Instead of receiving Him, they killed Him."[12] Even if we are more and more trying to dismiss it from our vocabulary, sin is an issue that Christians need to deal with both from the pulpit and lecture halls. As René Padilla has commented: "Man's problem in the world is not simply that he commits isolated sins or gives in to the temptation of particular vices. It is, rather, that he is imprisoned within a closed system of rebellion against God, a system that conditions him to absolutize the relative and relativize the absolute, a system whose mechanism of self-sufficiency deprives him of eternal life and subjects him to the judgment of God."[13] Both the West and Africa are "imprisoned within a closed system of rebellion against God." A person who is under the bondage of sin neither can emancipate himself/herself or others. "The horizon of the new as of the old people of God is bounded, in the darkness of the present, by the bright hope which is common to both: the coming of salvation for the whole of mankind. The final aim of God's plan of salvation is not the salvation of the Gentiles, nor the salvation of the Jews, but the salvation of all men, the salvation of the one and entire people of God composed of Gentiles and Jews."[14] All people, black and white, are in need of this salvation. There is no race including the Jews that has merit to receive salvation apart from Christ. All have made transgression and all will be saved only by the grace of God and their belief in Jesus Christ.

> The darkest periods of black African history correspond generally to the times when access to God's truth was blocked by everything that tramples and disfigures humanity. Whenever fatalism triumphs and all the mechanisms of poverty and oppression shut the door on hope, God is on trial.
>
> This has been happening in Africa for almost three hundred years. We Africans have been introduced to the Christian God by means of a theology of suffering, which seems to have been created so black people would learn to accept their historical status as a conquered people. That is the message of the curse on Canaan (Gen. 9:25)—a myth used in catechisms, preaching, and prayers to record the genesis of an entire people caught up in a tragedy of identity with outcasts. Yet the true face of God emerges from these shadows. It begins to take form as persons are opened. As the heavy chains of oppression fall from the hands of captives, they raise their heads toward the God who takes their side. For me, this is the logic of the God of our faith.[15]

For Africans, Paul's understanding of sin is liberating in two ways: 1) It helps them to understand that not only the black people but the white people are also sinners like them. This knowledge can give the black people a sense of equality with the whites and a sense of belongingness to all mankind. The "color symbolism underlying the common Christian interpretations of the Black as sinner and as devil and demon" dehumanizes

---

was crucified approached, Jesus wept over the city (Flanders, "Why Did Jesus Weep Over Jerusalem?," 1).

12. Ibid.
13. Padilla, "Evangelism and the World," 120.
14. Küng, *Church*, 196–97.
15. Éla, *My Faith as an African*, 102.

the black race.[16] 2) It gives to the black people a theological ground to forgive all those who treated them wrongfully and heal themselves from their psychological scars or present wounds.[17]

Ridderbos captures Paul's understanding of sin with precise biblical insight this way:

> The unfolding of the Pauline doctrine of salvation demands first of all a deeper insight into the manner in which man and the world have fallen into sin and have need of the redemption revealed in Christ. Further analysis demonstrates that here again the fundamental structure of Paul's preaching is of decisive significance, and that therefore, in approaching the Pauline doctrine of sin, we must not orient ourselves in the first place to the individual and personal, but to the redemptive-historical and collective points of view.
>
> To belong to the world means to be a sinner, to participate in sin and to experience the judgment of sin (1 Cor. 11:32). For Paul, therefore, sin is not in the first place an individual act or condition to be considered by itself, rather the supra-individual mode of existence in which one shares through the single act that one shares in the human life-context and from which one can only be redeemed by being taken up into the new life-context revealed in Christ (Col. 2:13).
>
> Sin must be understood out of the relationship in which God has place man to himself as his creature and in which he has given held out the prospect of life to him. For this reason sin in its essence is rebellion against God, refusal to be subject to him (Rom. 8:7), enmity against God (Rom. 5:10; 8:7; Col. 1:21), disobedience (Rom. 11:32; cf. Gal. 3:22; Eph. 2:2; 5:6, et al.). One can define it as man's willing-to-have-command-of-himself, wanting-to-be-as-God. It is on that account also the violation and corruption of true manhood. As such it can be define as foolishness (Rom. 1:23; 1 Cor. 1:19), worthlessness, vanity, darkness, being alienated from the true life (Eph. 4:18), without God and therefore without hope (Eph. 2:12), being dead (Eph. 2:1, 5; Col. 2:13; Rom. 7:10). For as life and good lie in respect for the right relationship to God, so sin means turning manhood into death (Rom. 7:12ff.).[18]

"*Like Jesus, Paul too starts out from the fact of the sinfulness of man, even the righteous, devout, law-abiding man. But Paul develops this insight theologically, by making use of Old Testament material and especially by the Adam-Christ contrast.*"[19] Like Jesus and Paul, unless we "start out from the fact of the sinfulness of man" in understanding Africa's past and present, we end up in a fruitless blame game, playing the race and reverse-race cards. In African context, there is no doubt that slavery, colonialism, and neocolonialism have ruined Africa. If African Christian thinkers are overly consumed by it, we will prolong the healing and restoration of the continent. Instead of fighting for the past that is already gone, we need to invest our energy and minds to bring about the future. The continent has been playing a catch-up game for the last five hundred years and it has failed, and failed miserably. To continue playing the cards of race, slavery, and

---

16. Goldenberg, *Curse of Ham*, 1.
17. For an excellent read on forgiveness, see Smedes, *Forgive and Forget*.
18. Ridderbos, *Paul*, 91, 93, 105.
19. Küng, *On Being a Christian*, 407; emphasis original.

colonialism is to be on the path of self-deception. Sin, not race or racism, is a defining human problem. We must view sin in its larger scope and with its power to destroy relationships and drive human beings against their will to kill each other. Sin is a power Satan and its legions use to cause havoc, death, war, and destruction. "[S]in is not merely existential separation from God; it is banishment from Eden, exile from the promise land, and ultimately forsakenness Jesus experienced on the cross. Therefore, we need not only reconciliation with God, we need also a new king who will usher in a new kingdom."[20]

The greater problem of Africa right now is from within. To give you a simple example, if you check the textbooks of many courses in African universities, they are outdated, internet connections are extremely poor, exploitation and oppression by Africans is rampant, and many libraries suffer from lack of funding and the cash outflow out of Africa is increasing every year. The health care system is a disaster. The doctor-patient ratio approved by the World Health Organization is 600 patients to a doctor. Malawi and Tanzania has two doctors for 100,000 people. Mozambique, Ethiopia, Burundi, Sierra Leone, and Niger have 3 doctors to 100,000 people. Togo, Benin, and Chad have four doctors for 100,000 people. Hence, Ebola, HIV, and other tropical diseases are ravaging the people in sub-Saharan region.[21] The majority of African countries are more or less in the same category. Explaining the devastation of HIV/Aids, Meredith writes, "The scourge of Aids has inflicted a terrible additional burden. Sub-Saharan Africa is home to just 10 percent of the world's population but bears more than 70 percent of the world's HIV/Aids cases. With the pandemic still in its infancy, by 2004 some 20 million people had died from Aids; 30 million were infected by the HIV virus and their number was rising by an estimated 3 million new case each year."[22] "Although some governments, NGOs and churches have made notable efforts to reduce infection rates and set up infrastructures to cope with the needs of victims, carers and the bereaved, too little has been done. Sadly, the active involvement of most African churches has been poor."[23]

To be at the cutting edge of the global trend one has to have up-to-date information technology, education, transportation, and a health care system. While the West is wrestling with the postmodern issues, Africa is trying to figure out the impact and implication of modernity—that is, among the few privileged Africans. The majority of Africans are in the darkness of illiteracy, are unemployed and unemployable, and are wasting their precious lives without being productive.

Africa is bleeding the most due to African tyrants, selfish and greedy military leaders who use Africans as political pawns and who have no respect for their own people and no heart to care for them. The authoritarian regimes consider themselves as lynchpins of their nations. They allow neither participation nor dissent. They misuse and abuse the natural resources, loot the national banks and treasuries, cause war, recruit young soldiers and watch them as these ill-trained soldiers cause havoc like a plague, including raping women and girls. African dignity, personhood, human rights, and freedom of

20. Treat, *Crucified King*, 195.
21. http://www.ezega.com/news/NewsDetails.aspx?NewsID=1486
22. Meredith, *Fate of Africa*, 685.
23. Johnstone, *Future of the Global Church*, 9.

expression are not trampled or denied by the fading colonial powers in today's Africa. It is by the so-called African leaders. If we cannot see sin as a defining factor of the human problem, we'll continue dealing with the symptoms of Africa's problems rather than their cause.

> Unlucky is the country where indiscipline is seen by ordinary people as the prerogative of the high and mighty. For, by the same token, discipline will be seen as a penalty which the rank and file must pay for their powerlessness. The consequences of such a view on the mental attitudes of a people are too glaring for words. But that is precisely the view of Nigeria elite groups foster in their private and public behavior. The queue is for the little man; the big man has no use of it. Observe the boarding of Nigerian planes, how the VIPs in their suits of feathers walk up to the gangway absolutely oblivious of the waiting line of the ordinary travelers. I don't know any other country where you can find such brazen insensitivity and arrogant selfishness among those who lay claim to leadership and education, or where the ordinary people put up with such arrant nonsense.[24]

Africa has plenty of them. If you want to refresh your memory, all you need to do is revisit chapter 8 of this book. For one who would like to see and describe Africa's problem in ungarnished and uncensored reality, the root cause of Africans' misery is human sin—for the destruction of the continent, the sin of Africans outweighs the sin of the West or China. Haugen draws our attention to this fact:

> Perfectly ordinary human beings are actually capable of being mass murderers. In Rwanda (to nothing of Eastern Europe during the Holocaust) the killing was not performed by specially trained pathological killers but by ordinary people. When all restraints are released, farmers, clerks, school principals, mothers, doctors, mayors and carpenters can pick up machetes and hack to death defenseless women and children. And this happened in a nation where 80 percent of the citizens identified themselves as Christians. Unless we wish to cling to racist theories about Africans or mythologies of education or civilization (as in Germany in 1933), we must face the objective, historical facts of the matter. The person without God (or perhaps worse but claiming "God," "Jesus," "Muhammad," whatever) is a very scary creature.[25]

The Real Enemy of People

Who is the real enemy of Africans? The white people who enslaved and colonized them? The Arabs who started the slave trade? The African tyrants who built castle after castle for their own families and impoverished their people? Before we answer these questions we need to look at Jesus Christ's approach to the complex situation of Israel. How and where did he start to encounter the enemy of Israel? What does the inauguration of his kingdom involve? What does that kingdom of God mean to Africa today?

In first-century Judaism, Jesus was not the only person who fought for the liberty and restoration of the Jewish people. There were many before and after him. Among

---

24. Achebe, *Trouble with Nigeria*, 41–42.
25. Haugen, *Good News about Injustice*, 127.

other things, what makes his mission unique was that he redefined the battle and the enemy of the people and he fought it right on and conquered it. N. T. Wright explains: "Jesus radically redefined the battle that had to be fought. It was because his fundamental agendas collided with those of so many of his contemporaries, particularly Israel's leaders, both *de jure* and self-appointed, that he found himself engaged in controversies as part of *the redefined battle for the kingdom*. Heavy irony swirls in the clouds around this formulation: it was because Jesus found himself fighting, from his point of view, the true battle—against them; or rather, he would have said, against the real enemy, whom he perceived to be operating through them."[26] Who is the real enemy of the people that Jesus fought? Should the battle for humankind be local, global, or cosmic? Should it be merely physical, spiritual, or both? What is the meaning of human existence if God's redemptive plan is not in the present and the present in the future?

As much as Jesus disliked or opposed Caesar's and the High Priest's leadership, as well as the oppressive political religious system of the Roman Empire and the temple, they were not the primary enemies of Israel as far as Christ was concerned. Satan was. Before he started his public ministry and announced the coming of the kingdom of God, he fought with Satan in the outskirts of Jerusalem (Matt 4:1–11). Kraybill calls it a three-legged temptation—political, religious, and economic. Together the three-part temptation fulfilled Jewish hopes for the Messiah who would shuck off oppressing nations, feed the poor, and bask miraculous approval from above.[27] Jesus did not comply with the questions or challenges of Satan. Luke tells us the ending of this confrontation with an interesting caveat: "When the devil had finished all this tempting, he left him *until an opportune time*" (4:13). Even though Satan's plan for Christ in the wilderness was defeated, his scheme was not totally evaporated in the heat of the desert. He left him "until an opportune time." It is in this light that we need to understand the emotionally loaded response of Jesus when Peter rebukes him for talking about suffering. Jesus emphatically declares, "Get behind me Satan" (Mark 8:33). To Jesus Christ Satan is the real enemy of the people who is the cause of destruction, disease, and death who actively works behind the religious and political leaders who are standing in the way of God's plan for humankind. Hence, "Jesus used the language of cosmic warfare to *denote* the specific struggles in which he himself engaged, and to *connote* his belief that the inner dimension for these struggles was a battle, indeed ultimately the battle, against the powers of darkness . . . Jesus believed that he himself had to fight the true battle of the people of YHWH."[28]

Satan was the "strong man" who guards and controls the minds and wills of the people and drives them to rebel against God and to mistreat each other. "When the strong man, fully armed, guards his own house, his possessions are safe. But when someone stronger attacks and overpowers him, he takes away the armor in which the man trusted and divides up the spoils" (Luke 11:21–22), said Jesus to the religious leaders who accused him of casting out the demons by the power of Beelzebub. Matthew describes the episode this way: "Then they brought him a demon possessed man who was

---

26. N. T. Wright, *Jesus and the Victory of God*, 447–48; emphasis original.
27. Kraybill, *Upside-Down Kingdom*, 40–64.
28. N. T. Wright, *Jesus and the Victory of God*, 449; emphasis original.

blind and mute and Jesus healed him so that he could both talk and see. All the people were astonished and said 'Could this be the son of David?' But when the Pharisees heard this, they said it is only by Beelzebub, the prince of demons that this fellow drives out demons. Jesus knew their thoughts and said to them, 'Every kingdom divided against itself will be ruined, and every city or household divided against itself will not stand. If Satan drives out Satan, he is divided against himself. How then can his kingdom stand? And if I drive out demons by Beelzebub, by whom do your people drive them out? So then they will be your judges. But if I drive our demons by the spirit of God, then the kingdom of God is upon you'" (Matt 12:24–29).

There are germs of truth that the Western, Eastern, and African people can learn from this text. First, let us look at the "demon possessed man who was mute and blind." If the predicament of this individual was in the hands of a politician, a psychologist, a social worker, a physician—even a pastor in a conservative church, for that matter—the diagnosis, prognosis, and prescription could have been different. In the first-century Jewish worldview this man was not fully human or an Israelite. Neither the political nor the religious system could restore his dignity, let alone his speech and sight. He was a lost cause, a living dead. "The evidence from Qumran suggests that, in some of Jewish circles at least, a maimed Jew could not be a full member of the community. In addition to the physical burden of being blind, or lame or deaf, or dumb, such a Jew was blemished and unable to be as full Israelite . . . This means that Jesus' healing miracles must be seen clearly as bestowing the gift of *shalom*, wholeness, to those who lacked it, bringing not only physical health but renewed membership in the people of YHWH."[29] Hence, the question of the people, "Could this be the son of David?" In other words, could this be the Messiah that would save Israel and restore the kingdom? Who in the world can deal with the hopeless person as Jesus dealt with him in our world today? How often do we see the predicament of humanity from Jesus' angle? It is only the power of God that can emancipate humankind from the bondage of Satan. Hence, the people asked, "Could this be the son of David?" Treat rightly said, "humans are in bondage to Satan *because* they have rejected God as king; they are in the kingdom of Satan *because* they have been banished from the kingdom of God. Enmity with God—entailing God's wrath on humans and human guilt before God—is therefore the root problem. Bondage to Satan is derivative of the God-human problem, for as soon as distance comes into the relationship, a third party is then able to creep in, which is precisely what Satan did and continues to do."[30]

Jesus didn't put the blame on the Romans or the Pharisees for the blindness and muteness of the demon-possessed person. He put it on the real enemy of the people: the ruler of this world, Satan. In the case of this victim, the war was not between Israel and Rome or Caesar and Christ. It was between the kingdom of God and the kingdom of Satan. As I wrestle with the external and internal problems of Africa intellectually, it is impossible to ignore the power of darkness and the "finger of God" that effectively deals with it. The scene of strife in Africa should not be limited to Africa and the West or Africa and the East; it should be looked at with a deeper meaning and lasting solution for

---

29. Ibid., 91–92; emphasis original.
30. Treat, *Crucified King*, 199; emphasis original.

humankind not only as the black race vs. another race. But as humans history has been influenced both by the power of God and the power of the evil one. People are actors playing the script of the one to whom they are giving their allegiance.

Jesus replied to Satan's temptation, "Man does not live by bread alone" (Matt 4:4). Humanity is free and free indeed when they invite Christ to their lives and allow God's purpose in heaven to be done through and in them on this earth. And this renewed beginning on earth that is ushered in with the presence of the kingdom of God through Jesus Christ is the hope of humankind. As God said through Isaiah: "[T]hose who hope in [him] will not be disappointed" (49:23b). It was this destiny of humankind that was the prime motivator of Paul's mission: "Paul's ultimate aim is not the horizontal reconciliation of Jews and Gentiles, important as that is. Nor is his missionary ambition satisfied why God's saving promises come to fruition among Jews and Gentiles, though he devoted his life to bringing God's saving message to Gentiles. The ultimate goal of Paul's mission was to see God glorified, and this reaches its zenith when Jews and Gentiles together worship and praise God. Such united worship begins on earth and will last forever."[31] To us too, as important as horizontal reconciliation, peace, and prosperity of people are, a vertical relationship with God is critical for a lasting peace and happy ending. If they miss this mark, whether they are white, black, or yellow, as Paul agonized for the Jews so should we agonize for our communities and the world.

In understanding himself, his people, and the world, the dominating factor in Paul's pursuit for the liberating truth was not anthropology, it was theology—not man but God. Dunn writes:

> A systemic study of Paul's theology has to begin with his belief in God. This is not simply because the term "'theology" may be said to have "speech about God" as its primary meaning. It is much more because God is the fundamental presupposition of Paul's theology, the starting point of his theologizing, and the primary subtext of all his writing. The word "God" itself occurs 548 times in Pauline corpus, 153 times in Romans alone. Only two chapters of the extensive Pauline writings lack explicit mention of "God." As a rule in the Pauline letters God is mentioned at once as primary legitimating factor behind Paul's life work—"Paul called to be an apostle . . . through God's will (1 Cor. 1:1). "Paul apostle through God the father" (Gal. 1:1), and the one which becomes stereotypical thereafter, "Paul, apostle of Jesus Christ through God's will" (2 Cor. 11:1; Eph. 1:1; Col. 1:1; 2 Tim. 1:1). The regular greetings of his letters is of "grace to you and peace from God our Father," followed by a thanksgiving to God. In Romans itself the attentive reader cannot but be struck by the steady sequence of genitive phrases which marks the first chapter—"gospel of God," "son of God," "beloved of God," "the will of God," "power of God," "righteousness of God," "wrath of God," "what may be known of God," "the glory of God," "the truth of God," "the judgment of God." Whatever else Paul's theology was it was talk "of God." Nor is it coincidental that the thematic statement of Romans is an affirmation of "God's righteousness" (1:17), that the first main section begins as an assertion of "God's wrath" (1:18), and that the starting point of his indictment is "what may be known of God" (1:19, 21).[32]

---

31. Schreiner, *Paul*, 72.
32. Dunn, *Theology of Paul the Apostle*, 28.

If one thinks Paul's understanding of humanity and the world in the light of God had no impact or that it was a vain effort on his part to bring change to people's life and society—then read history. Like Christ, Paul knew who the real enemy of the people and who the redeemer of all humankind was. That is why he was neither a revolutionary nor a civil rights movement leader or initiator. Such comprehensive biblical understanding of human history and the destiny of humankind doesn't come through mere academic pursuit or accumulation of information or theories on a cognitive level. One has to change from the inside out and go through a radical paradigm shift like Paul did. When the light of the world enlightens us, we can accurately decipher the activities of people in the dark world. The new paradigm gives us a metacultural framework that can emancipate us from the prison of ethnocentrism and parochialism and enable us to treat others equally and justly. Paul resisted the Roman imperial theology nonviolently through Christian theology.

> In Paul's life time *Roman emperors were deemed divine, and first and foremost, Augustus was called Son of God, God, and God of God. He was Lord, Redeemer, and Savior of the World* [emphasis added]. People knew that both verbally from Latin authors like Virgil, Horace, and Ovid and visually from coins, cups, statues, altars, temples, and forums; from ports, roads, bridges, and aqueducts; from landscapes transformed cities established. It was all around them everywhere, just as advertising is all around us today. Without seeing the archaeology of Roman imperial theology, you cannot understand any exegesis of Pauline Christian theology . . . Paul's essential challenge is how to embody communally that radical vision of a *new creation* in a way far beyond even our present best hopes for freedom, democracy, and human rights. The Roman Empire was based on the common principle of *peace through victory* or, more fully on a faith in the sequence of *piety, war, victory*, and *peace*. Paul was a Jewish visionary following in Jesus's footsteps, and they both claimed that the Kingdom of God was already present and operative in this world. He opposed the mantras of Roman normalcy with a *vision of peace through justice* or, more fully with faith in the sequence of *covenant*, nonviolence, justice, and *peace*.[33]

To measure the success of Paul's mission, analyze the impact and scope of Christianity in light of where the Roman Empire is today. He ran his race without the backing of Israel or Rome, with much suffering and endurance, sometimes considering himself the scum of the earth. Africans' economic and political situation cannot be an excuse not to engage in this well-defined and appropriate battle. If we truly love humankind and we would like to see them enjoy authentic freedom and peace, Jesus Christ and Paul have set a model of struggle for us.

The Ruler of this Age

Politicians and historians often see this world's affair in terms of organizational structures, economic systems, and philosophy of governance. Hence we use words like superpowers, cold war, democracy, communism, capitalism, socialism, and the like. If we

---

33. Crossan and Reed, *In Search of Paul*, x–xi; emphasis original.

give a question "Who is the ruler of this world?" to the UN members, one wonders how many correct answers we can get. When a Christian nation like the United States calls itself a superpower, what is the point of hoping Moscow or Beijing to understand who the ruler of this age/world is? During Christ's time Rome was dominating and ruling the majority part of the world. The Babylonian and Athenian Empire had been there before Rome dominating the Mediterranean world. "Of all the cities which have dominated the Mediterranean lands none has exercised such an abiding influence on them, and on others far removed from the Mediterranean, as Rome. Rome's swift rise to power made a deep impression on men's minds in antiquity. A Greek politician named Polybius who was taken to Rome as a hostage in 167 B.C. and had the good fortune to win the friendship of Scipio Aemilianus, the leading Roman general of his day, wrote as historical work (still of exceptional value, in so far as it survives) in order to trace the steps by which the city of Rome in a period of fifty-three years (221–168 B.C.), became mistress of the Mediterranean world—a thing unique in history."[34] Without being overwhelmed by the power of Rome or Caesar like Polybius, Paul tells us who was and is the ruler of this age/world. Ladd observes:

> This Age is dominated by evil, wickedness, and rebellion against the will of God, while The Age to come is the age of the Kingdom of God.
>
> In Galatians 1:4 we read that Christ "gave himself for our sins that he might deliver us from the present evil age." This Age is an evil age; it is characterized by sin and unrighteousness. It is an age from which men need deliverance, a deliverance which can be accomplished only by the death of Christ.
>
> The second chapter of Ephesians gives us an extended discussion of the character of This Age. Paul says, "And you he made alive, when you were dead through the trespasses and sins in which you once walked, following the age of this world" (Eph. 2:1–2). In this verse, both words, "age" and "world" are employed, indicating that while This Age and the world are not synonymous, they are closely related. There is a certain order of human society which characterizes This Age. Paul describes it with the word, "In which you once walked...following the prince of the power of the air, the spirit that is now at work in the sons of disobedience." The character of the age of this world bears the stamp of the Prince of the power of the air, that is, Satan. He is permitted to exercise a terrible influence throughout This Age inducing men and women to walk in a way displeasing to God.[35]

Treat asks, "If Satan is the 'ruler of this world' (John 12:31) and 'the whole world lies in the power of the evil one' (1 John 5:19), what is the nature of this reign and how does he exercise such power?"[36]

Beyond the realm of our political and economic system, biblically speaking, there are two powers that influence individuals and nations: the power of God and the power of Satan. This was the reality of life that both Jesus Christ and the Apostle Paul recognized, lived with, and performed their mission. Modern science and technology has changed so many things in our world since then—both for the better and worse for man.

---

34. Bruce, *Paul Apostle of the Heart Set Free*, 22.
35. Ladd, *Gospel of the Kingdom*, 18–19.
36. Treat, *Crucified King*, 199.

But one thing is constant—this age is ruled by Satan and the age to come, which was inaugurated through Jesus Christ, is ruled by God. The question is who is ruling our lives? Our thoughts and actions, including our destiny, are influenced and determined by the kind of *power* that is ruling our life. If our actions betray our confession like the Jews of Jesus' time who opposed him, then it is clear who we belong to and whose children we are. Jesus said to the religious people who he called wolves in sheeps' clothing, "If God were your Father, you would love me, for I came from God and now I am here. I have not come on my own; but he sent me. Why is my language not clear to you? Because you are unable to hear what I say. You belong to your father the devil, and you want to carry out your father's desire. He was a murder from the beginning, not holding to the truth, for there is no truth in him. When he lies, he speaks his native language, for he is a liar and the father of lies" (John 8:42–44). Referring to John 13:27 and 8:42–44, Mathewson writes, "When the Devil/Satan play a role in the narrative he is a subject of a verb of material process in a primary clause, he enters Judas (13:27). This analysis, then, suggests that the Devil/Satan is not a main character in the Gospel, but rather plays a supporting role within the narrative, inciting or providing the source for the actions of other human actors. He is the ultimate source of the disbelieving and murderous activities of the primary antagonists of Jesus; Judas and the religious leaders."[37]

If one lies on a global platform, or from the palace one leads, deceives the global community or the nations one represents to cover or justify the deaths of innocent children, mothers, and fathers, and goes to war to control natural resources that would inflict pain and suffering to those who have rights over it—as most African tyrants and world leaders do—we can say that this is beyond mere human greed and selfishness. It requires both the human and the spiritual battle. When evil triumphs and destroys millions of lives as in the case of Nazi Germany or King Leopold II in Congo or elsewhere, be it in the name of racial superiority, civilization, religion or politics, "the ultimate cause of murder" according to the Scripture is Satan. The actors are his agents.

In his theology and praxis the Apostle Paul takes the ruler of this age and his authority and influence seriously:

> He explains them further, especially in connection with "this world" and "this aeon," by speaking of the powers of evil, misery, and death that hold sway in this world. What he terms in Gal. 1:4 "this present evil aeon, elsewhere as the of darkness," is set over against the royal dominion of Christ (Col. 1:13); and Eph. 2:2 he further qualifies walking according to "this world-aeon" as following the course of "the prince of the power of the air, the spirit that unity and totality the domain of demonic powers, which he denotes as 'angels,' 'principalities,'" "powers," (Rom. 8:38; 1 Cor. 15:24; Col. 2:14), "the world rulers of this darkness," "the evil spirits in heavenly places" (Eph. 6:12), of which Satan, as the "god of this aeon" (2 Cor. 4:4), is the head (cf. Rom. 16:20; 1 Cor. 5:5, *et al.*).
>
> There is no doubt whatever that this subjection of the world to spiritual demonic powers in Paul does not go back to an original dualism between God and the world, or between God and the powers. For it is true of all that is in heaven and on earth, and in particular of thrones, dominions, principalities, and powers, that they have been created in Christ (Col. 1:16), just as they have been

---

37. Mathewson, "Devil," 124–25.

conquered and reconciled (pacified) in him (Col. 2:15; 1:20); they belong to the creation of God (Rom 8:39), and are even in their activity of enmity against God and tyranny over men, subject to God (2 Cor. 12:7). Similarly, the powers have no original control over the world, but the whole of the groaning creation has been subjected to vanity by God himself (Rom. 8:20). Nevertheless, it is the dominion of these powers that determines Paul's outlook on the present world. It is they who represent the "vanity," the worthlessness and senselessness to which the whole creation, groaning and looking with eager longing for redemption, has been subjected (cf. Rom. 8:19–23 and 8:38, 39). For not only sin, but also suffering, oppression, anxiety, and adversity belong to the dominion of Satan (1 Cor. 5:5; 2 Cor. 12:7; 1 Tim. 1:20; 1 Thess. 2:18). Elsewhere the hunger, want, danger, and sword, are themselves represented as personified powers that attempt still to separate the believer from the love of Christ (Rom. 8:35), just as death is his "last enemy" (1 Cor. 15 26), which employs sin as instrument (1 Cor. 15:56; cf. Rom. 8:38f.).[38]

2 Corinthian 4:4, show how Satan as god of this world, influences individuals and nations—further proof to us that human beings are not acting alone:

> The phrase "god of this world" (or "god of this age") indicates that Satan is the major influence on the ideals, opinions, goals, hopes and views of the majority of people. His influence also encompasses the world's philosophies, education, and commerce. The thoughts, ideas, speculations and false religions of the world are under his control and have sprung from his lies and deceptions.
>
> Satan is also called the "prince of the power of the air" in Ephesians 2:2. He is the "ruler of this world" in John 12:31. These titles and many more signify Satan's capabilities. To say, for example, that Satan is the "prince of the power of the air" is to signify that in some way he rules over the world and the people in it.
>
> This is not to say that he rules the world completely; God is still sovereign. But it does mean that God, in His infinite wisdom, has allowed Satan to operate in this world within the boundaries God has set for him. When the Bible says Satan has power over the world, we must remember that God has given him domain over unbelievers only. Believers are no longer under the rule of Satan (Colossians 1:13). Unbelievers, on the other hand, are caught "in the snare of the devil" (2 Timothy 2:26), lie in the "power of the evil one" (1 John 5:19), and are in bondage to Satan (Ephesians 2:2).[39]

The good thing is that for Christians the ruler of this age is a defeated foe. "Victory over Satan and his demonic agents does not come from some sort of mystical experience, according to Ephesians. Triumph comes through the infusion of the resurrection-life of Christ, which is granted on the basis of the work of Jesus Christ (Eph. 2:4–10). Believers are made alive with Christ, raised with Christ and seated with him."[40] "A fractured relationship between God and humanity results in the shattered *shalom* of creation. The movement of corruption is not from cosmos to community, but from community to cosmos. As humans go, creation goes. The implications for soteriology are

---

38. Ridderbos, *Paul*, 91–92.

39. Read more: "How Is Satan God of This World (2 Corinthians 4:4)?" gotQuestions?.org, http://www.gotquestions.org/Satan-god-world.html#ixzz3EefWNLcd.

40. Schreiner, *Paul*, 233.

immense. Christ's salvation is aimed at both the church and the cosmos, but in proper order. The church is the *focus* of salvation; the comos, the *scope* of salvation."[41] Being free from the bondage of sin and the power of Satan, with effective and relevant biblical teaching, African Christians have the privilege of heralding the good news of the gospel and implementing justice in all sectors of the society they live in.

The Kingdom of God

As Ethiopian-American I have lived both as a citizen under authoritarian rule, sometimes languishing in prison, and in a democratic country that gave me the freedom I was hungry and thirsty for. To the best of my ability I have extensively read about the history of the country of my origin and my adopted country. There is no question that democratic governance is much better than the authoritarian rule. I write this both from experience, and from reading and observation. But being better does not mean being perfect. Where I find most Americans err is in their perception of Western democracy, in their analysis of the role and place of the U.S. in human history. Naively, many have no dividing line between the kingdom of God and the United States. They think we already have reached "the not yet" and they get easily irritated and become defensive when they hear the dark side of the United States of America. From my observation, there are two kinds of "prophets" of America: those who see nothing good but doom and gloom about the U.S., like Noam Chomsky; and there are those who see no evil about the U.S. but glamor and power, like Thomas Freedman. But, the truth about the U.S. exists somewhere between the two extreme views. It is a great country with quite a number of pitfalls to correct. Ignoring the country's weak points, particularly the internal sickness and its foreign policy with African countries, eventually would lead to major crises even to the downfall of the nation, and the consequence would be painful for our children and grandchildren. As Athens, Rome, and Britain had learned, the U.S. will also learn that you could have democracy or empire, but not both. Paul Krugman writes:

> Plunder isn't what it used to be. You can't treat a modern society the way ancient Rome treated a conquered province without destroying the very wealth you're trying to seize. And meanwhile, war or the threat of war, by disrupting trade and financial connections, inflicts large costs over and above the direct expense of maintaining and deploying armies. War makes you poorer and weaker, even if you win.
>
> The exceptions to this dictum actually prove the rule. There are still thugs who wage war for fun and profit, but they invariably do so in places where exploitable raw materials are the only real source of wealth. The gangs tearing the Central African Republic apart are in pursuit of diamonds and poached ivory; the Islamic State may claim that it's bringing the new caliphate, but so far it has mostly been grabbing oil fields.
>
> The point is that what works for a fourth-world warlord is just self-destructive for a nation at America's level—or even Russia's.[42]

41. Treat, *Crucified King*, 198; emphasis original.
42. Krugman, "CONQUEST IS FOR LOSERS."

Had it not been for the kingdom of God at work and for the hope of the glorious coming of Jesus Christ, who is the righteous judge, to reign on this earth and to rule humankind with justice in his everlasting kingdom, life could have been disappointing and purposeless for me as an Ethiopian-American, despite living in the land of plenty. I just cannot deceive myself in the small bubble I live in and be indifferent to the pain and agony of people I see and hear about in the world near and far. And there is no hope for humankind in philosophy or the best economic and political systems. We live in a wonderful and fearful world with perplexity and uncertainty. Where can one go to get solace, meaning for life, and purpose for existence? For a person of African origin who went through the experiences of life that I described in this book, this question is ten times more important.

I live with a sense of victory, rich meaning of life, and assurance of my destiny, not because I am a citizen of a superpower that gives me so many privileges I cannot find in many places in the world, but because I belong to the kingdom of God. This is a gift of God received from him, not by my merit but because of his sheer and abundant grace—Amazing Grace! Pity on me if I cannot understand and interpret human history in the light of the salvation I received in Christ.

> The world does not last forever. Human life and human history have an end. But the message of Jesus tells us that, *at this end*, there is not nothing, there is God. As God is the beginning, so too he is the end. God's cause prevails in any case. The future belongs to God. It is with this future, that we have to reckon: we don't have to calculate days and hours. In the light of this future of God we must shape the present, both of the individual and of society. Here and now. This is not then an empty future, but a future to be revealed and fulfilled . . . It is an *eschaton*, that ultimate reality of the future which is something really different and qualitatively new, which admittedly announces its coming anticipation. We are concerned then, not merely with futurology, but with eschatology. An eschatology without a true, still outstanding, absolute future would be an eschatology without true hope, still to be fulfilled.[43]

What is the historical and theological background of the kingdom of God? Norman Perrin puts the historical background of the kingdom of God this way:

> The roots of the kingdom of God lie in the ancient Near Eastern myth of the kingship of God. This was taken over by the Israelites from the Canaanites, who had received it from the great kingdoms of the Euphrates and Tigris and the Nile, where it had been developed as early as ancient Sumerian times. In this myth the god had acted as king in creating the world, in the course of which he had overcome and slain the primeval monster. Further, the god continued to act as a king by annually renewing the fertility of the earth, and he showed himself to be king of a particular people by sustaining them in their place in the world. This myth is common to all the peoples in the ancient Near East, and elements from one version of the myth were freely used in others. Essentially it is only the name of the god which changes as we move from people to people. In Babylon

---

43. Küng, *On Being a Christian*, 223; emphasis original.

> Marduk is king; in Assyria, Ashur; in Ammon, Malcom; in Tyre, Melkart; in Israel, Yahweh.[44]

Israel was a nation that had gone through various stages of developments. They had the age of the patriarchs, the formative years as a nation after the Exodus and the conquest, then the age under monarchy, marked with a period of national self-determination. This period was followed by the independent Kingdoms of Israel and Judah and ended with crisis and downfall.[45] In all these stages of their progress and downfall as a nation, God seldom left them without a prophet. As Bright rightly said, "We cannot turn from the history of Judah in the late eighth century without some mention of the prophets who exercised their ministry then and ceaselessly addressed themselves to the national emergency. To do so would be to leave history incomplete."[46]

It was the oracle of the prophets in the courts of Israel's kings that brought the kingship of the God of Israel more and more into light. "The monarchy in Judah was given legitimacy, not by the ancient Mosaic covenant, but by Yahweh's eternal covenant with David . . . It was believed and cultically affirmed that Yahweh had chosen Zion his dwelling and promised to David an eternal dynasty; that each king, as Yahweh's anointed 'son' (Ps. 2:7, etc.), would be protected from his foes; that the dynasty would in the end gain a domain greater than David's, with the kings of the earth fawning at its feet (Ps. 2:7–11; 72:8–11; etc.). The state's existence, in short, was not based in the terms of Yahweh's covenant made in the wilderness, but in his unconditional promise to David."[47] God's unconditional Davidic covenant was for the good of the people to prosper and to be ruled justly. The Psalmist writes,

> Endow the king with your justice, O God, the royal son (or the son of the king) with your righteousness. He will judge your people in righteousness, your afflicted ones with justice. The mountains will bring prosperity to the people, the hills the fruit of righteousness. He will defend the afflicted among the people and save the children of the needy; he will crush the oppressor. He will endure as long as the sun, as long as the moon, through all generations. He will be like rain falling on a mown field, like showers watering the earth. In his days the righteous will flourish; prosperity will abound till the moon is no more. He will rule from sea to sea and from the River to the ends of the earth. The desert tribes will bow before him and his enemies will lick the dust. The kings of Tarshish and of distant shores will bring tribute to him; the kings of Sheba and Seba will present him gifts. All kings will bow down to him and all nations will serve him. (Ps 72:1–11)

Even if these verses have messianic reference, all of the kings of Israel and Judah are expected to implement justice, maintain peace, and shepherd the nation from disobeying God. However, the same internal sickness that brought down the Northern Kingdom, even though it was in a reduced scale, brought down Judah.

---

44. Perrin, "Jesus and the Language of the Kingdom of God," 92.
45. For an in-depth reading, see Bright, *A History of Israel*.
46. Ibid., 288.
47. Ibid., 289.

The syncretistic tendencies, followed by Ahaz's recognition of the Assyrian gods, gradually weakened the nation's fundamental structure and negatively contributed to the struggle for existence under the threat of external powers. "With the progressive disintegration of ancestral social patterns, the Siniatic covenant with its *austere religious, moral, and social obligations*, which had been the original basis of Israelite society, had been largely forgotten by many of Judah's citizens, to whom Yahweh had become the national guardian whose function it was, in return for meticulous cultic observance, to give the nation protection and blessing (Isa. 1:10–20)."[48] When the social and moral fabric of a society is disintegrating, things fall apart. Without the social capital of honesty, trust, justice, truth, freedom, etc., hardly any political or economic structure can exist. In Judah's case it was even worse—they abandoned their God who is a prime cause of their existence as a nation. God expressed his grief of rejection in plain and graphic terms: "Hear, O heavens! Listen, O earth! For the Lord has spoken: I reared children and brought them up, but they have rebelled against me. The ox knows his master, the donkey his owner's manger, but Israel does not know, my people do not understand. Ah, sinful nation, a people loaded with guilt, a brood of evil doers, children given to corruption! They have forsaken the Lord; they have spurned the holy one of Israel and turned their backs on him" (Isa 1:2–4). In this kind of a seemingly irreparably-broken relationship between Israel and God, what will happen to the unconditional Davidic covenant? How did the prophets react?

Judah's rebellion against God was foolishness on the side of the people and on the king's side it was almost suicidal. They end up being a tool in the hands of Assyria leading to disillusionment, pain, and suffering. Despite Ahaz's refusal to listen to him,

> Isaiah did not . . . surrender hope. His doctrine of God was far too vast that the nation's dereliction could frustrate the divine purpose and cancel the promises. In spite of his conviction that Ahaz had betrayed his office, perhaps because of it, Isaiah treasured the dynastic ideal as this had been perpetuated in the cult (e.g., Ps. 72) and himself gave classic expression to the expectation of a scion of David's line who would fulfill that ideal (Isa. 9:2–7; 11:1–9), exhibiting justice as Ahaz so notably had not, and bringing the national humiliation forever to an end. Isiah was convinced that his purpose to set up his kingly rule of peace was in control of events, and that his purpose to set up his kingly rule of peace over the nations was sure (chs. 2:2–4; 11:6–9). He therefore viewed the present tragedy as a part of that purpose: a discipline, a purge by which Yahweh would remove the dross in the national character, leaving a chastened and purified people (ch. 1:24–26; cf. ch. 4:2–6) . . . Though repeatedly disappointed, Isaiah never surrendered the hope that God would bring forth from the tragedy a chastened and purified remnant of his people (chs. 28:5f.; 37:30–32).[49]

To the prophet Isaiah "The Lord is Israel's king and Redeemer" (44:6). And God will reign in Zion:

> Terror and pit and snare await you, O people of the earth. Whoever flees at the sound of terror will fall into a pit; whoever climbs out of the pit will be caught in

---

48. Ibid.; emphasis added
49. Ibid., 291–92.

> a snare. The floodgates of the heavens are opened; the foundations of the earth shake. The earth is broken up, the earth is split asunder, and the earth is thoroughly shaken. The earth reels like a drunkard, it sways like a hut in the wind; so heavy upon it is the guilt of its rebellion that it falls—never to rise again. In that day the LORD will punish the powers in the heavens above and the kings on the earth below. They will be herded together like prisoners bound in a dungeon; they will be shut up in prison and be punished after many days. The moon will be abashed, the sun ashamed; for the LORD Almighty will reign on Mount Zion and in Jerusalem, and before its elders, gloriously. (Isa 24:17–23).

"Isaiah's incomparably exalted conception of Yahweh, whose kingly throne (but not whose literal 'dwelling'!) was on Zion, enabled him to interpret the current disaster and the sweep of world events in terms of the national theology with a boldness never before equaled."[50]

Going far beyond Isaiah, Micah pronounced a doom on Judah of total proportion. He said, "Zion will be plowed like a field, Jerusalem will become a heap of rubble the temple hill a mound overgrown with thickets" (3:12). Amazingly, even this destruction did not totally eliminate God's unconditional covenant with David which says: "If his sons forsake my law and do not follow my statues, if they violate my decrees and fail to keep my commands, I will punish their sin with the rod, their iniquity with flogging; but I will not take my love from him, nor will I ever betray my faithfulness" (Ps 89:30–33; 2 Sam 7:14). In spite of his anger over the sin of Judah and harsh oracles against the people, Micah also foretold the coming of Israel's king from Bethlehem: "But you, Bethlehem Ephrata, though you are small among the clans of Judah, out of you will come for me one who will be ruler over Israel, whose origins are from old, and from ancient times . . . He will stand and shepherd his flock in the strength of the Lord, in the majesty of the name of the Lord his God. And they will live securely, for then his greatness will reach to the ends of the earth. And he will be their peace" (5:2, 4).

Zechariah also stated, "Rejoice greatly, O Daughter of Zion! Shout, Daughter of Jerusalem! See, your king comes to you, righteous and having salvation, gentle and riding on a donkey, on a colt, the foal of a donkey. I will take away the chariots from Ephraim and the war-horses from Jerusalem, and the battle bow will be broken. He will proclaim peace to the nations. His rule will extend from sea to sea and from the River to the ends of the earth" (9:9–10).

Another prophetic writing mentions a Son of Man who rules forever over the peoples of the world: "In my vision at night I looked, and there before me was one like a son of man, coming with the clouds of heaven. He approached the Ancient of Days and was led into his presence. He was given authority, glory and sovereign power; all peoples, nations and men of every language worshiped him. His dominion is an everlasting dominion that will not pass away, and his kingdom is one that will never be destroyed" (Dan 7:13–14).

In Psalm 110, the Psalter's Lord is the One who is at Yahweh's right hand and crushes the kings of the earth and judges the nations, which agrees perfectly with what Psalm 2 says about God's Anointed King. Interestingly, verse 5 of Psalm 110 identifies

---

50. Ibid., 296.

this king at God's right hand as *Adonai*, a divine name or title used primarily of Yahweh. This, again, substantiates the fact that the Anointed King is more than a man since he is God as well, which explains why he is able to perform the same functions as Yahweh.

Not surprisingly, the NT applies the language of Psalms 2 and 110 and Isaiah 11 to the Lord Jesus:

> While Jesus was teaching in the temple courts, he asked, "How is it that the teachers of the law say that the Christ is the son of David? David himself, speaking by the Holy Spirit, declared: 'The Lord said to my Lord: "Sit at my right hand until I put your enemies under your feet."' David himself calls him 'Lord.' How then can he be his son?" The large crowd listened to him with delight (Mark 12:35–37).
>
> Which he exerted in Christ when he raised him from the dead and seated him at his right hand in the heavenly realms, far above all rule and authority, power and dominion, and every title that can be given, not only in the present age but also in the one to come (Eph 1:20–21).
>
> And then the lawless one will be revealed, whom the Lord Jesus will overthrow with the breath of his mouth and destroy by the splendor of his coming (2 Thess 2:8).

Isaiah also foretold: "For to us a child is born, to us a son is given, and the government will be on his shoulders. And he will be called Wonderful Counselor, Mighty God, Everlasting Father, and the Prince of Peace. Of the increase of his government and peace there will be no end. He will reign on David's throne and over his kingdom, establishing and upholding it with justice and righteousness from that time on and forever. The zeal of the LORD Almighty will accomplish this" (9:6–7). Isaiah identified the child as the Mighty God, the very name he gave to Yahweh God in the next chapter.

"Why do the nations conspire and the peoples plot in vain? The kings of the earth take their stand and the rulers gather together against the LORD and against his Anointed One (the Messiah). 'Let us break their chains,' they say, 'and throw off their fetters.' The One enthroned in heaven laughs; the Lord scoffs at them. Then he rebukes them in his anger and terrifies them in his wrath, saying, 'I have installed my King on Zion, my holy hill.' I will proclaim the decree of the LORD: He said to me, 'You are my Son; today I have begotten you. Ask of me, and I will make the nations your inheritance, the ends of the earth your possession. You will rule them with an iron scepter; you will dash them to pieces like pottery'" (Ps 2:1–9).

Briefly, with sufficient verses from the Scripture, we've looked at how God wants to be the king of his people and how the Davidic covenant is connected to the coming of Jesus Christ and his inauguration of the kingdom of God. As the prophets and the apostles, particularly Paul, did, we need to understand and interpret the global political and economic trends in the light of the kingdom of God. As we do so, N. T. Wright reminds us, "The most important thing to recognize about the first-century Jewish use of kingdom-language is that it was bound up with the hopes and expectations of Israel. 'Kingdom of god' was not a vague phrase, or a cipher with a general religious aura. It had nothing much, at least in the first instance, to do with what happen to human beings after they died. The reverent periphrasis 'kingdom of heaven,' so long misunderstood by some Christians to mean 'a place, namely heaven, where saved souls go to live after death,' meant nothing of the sort in Jesus' world: it was simply a Jewish way of talking about Israel's god becoming king. And when this god became king, the whole world, the world of space and time, would at last be put to rights. This is the Jewish eschatology."[51]

Many first-century Jews could identify with the phrase "kingdom of God." They eagerly wanted God to send them a leader who would throw off Roman rule and make Judea an independent nation again—a nation of righteousness, glory and blessings, a nation everyone would be attracted to. There was a variety of speculations about how this would be done. The concept was attractive, although it was not very well defined.

In this cultural longing for national restoration, John and Jesus preached the nearness of God's kingdom. Midway through Jesus' earthly ministry, the message continued. He told his disciples to preach, "The kingdom of heaven has come near" and to heal the sick (Matt 10:7; cf. Luke 10:9, 11). But the kingdom most people hoped for did not happen. The Jewish nation was not restored. Even worse, the temple was destroyed and the Jews were scattered. Even now, 2000 years later, the Jewish hopes are still unfulfilled. Was Jesus wrong in his prediction, or was he not predicting a national kingdom?

Philip Yancey summarizes the expectations and disappointment of the Jews people about the kingdom of God Jesus preached:

> Zealots stood at the edge of Jesus' audience, armed and well organized guerillas spoiling for a fight against Rome, but to their consternation the signal for revolt never came. In time Jesus' pattern of behavior disappointed all who sought a leader in the traditional mold. He tended to flee from, rather than cater to, large groups. He insulted the memory of Israel glory days, comparing King Solomon to a common day lily. The one time a crowd tried to crown him king by force, he mysteriously withdrew. When Peter finally did wield a sword on his behalf, Jesus healed the victim's wounds.
>
> To the crowd's dismay, it became clear that Jesus was talking about a strangely different kind of kingdom. The Jews wanted what people have always wanted from a visible kingdom: a chicken in every pot, full employment, a strong army to deter invaders. Jesus announced a kingdom that meant denying yourself, taking up a cross, renouncing wealth, even loving your enemies. As he elaborated the crowds expectation crumbled.[52]

Unlike the expectation of the Jewish people, the kingdom of God Jesus introduced is a present spiritual reality. "For the kingdom of God is not eating and drinking but righteousness and peace and joy in the Holy Spirit" (Rom 14:17). The Scripture also tells us that the kingdom is a realm into which the followers of Christ have entered. Paul writes: "God has delivered us from the dominion of darkness and transferred us to the kingdom of his beloved Son" (Col 1:13).

"Repent, for the kingdom of God is at hand." John the Baptist and Jesus proclaimed the nearness of God's kingdom (Matt 3:2; 4:17; Mark 1:15). A literal translation is "has come near." The long-awaited rule of God was near. This message was called the gospel, the good news. Thousands of people were glad to hear this, and many responded to this message of John and Jesus. Ladd describes the kingdom of God this way:

---

51. N. T. Wright, *Jesus and the Victory of God*, 202–3.

52. Yancey, *Jesus I Never Knew*, 241–42.

> The kingdom of God is here. But there is a mystery—a new revelation about the Kingdom. The Kingdom of God is here; but instead of destroying human sovereignty, it has attacked the sovereignty of Satan. The Kingdom of God is here; instead of making changes in the external, political, order of things, it is making changes in the internal, political order of things, it is making changes in the spiritual order and in the lives of men and women.
>
> This is the mystery of the Kingdom, the truth which God now disclosed for the first time in redemptive history. God's kingdom is to work among men in two different stages. The kingdom is yet to come in the form prophesied by Daniel when every human sovereignty will be displaced by God's sovereignty. The world will yet behold the coming of God's Kingdom with power. God has now come to work among men but in an utterly unexpected way. It is not now destroying human rule; it is not now abolishing human sin from the earth; it is not now bringing the baptism of the fire John had announced. It can work among men but never be recognized by the crowds. In the spiritual realm, the kingdom now offers to men the blessings of God's rule, delivering them from the power of Satan and sin. The Kingdom of God is an offer, a gift which may be accepted or rejected. The Kingdom is now here with persuasion rather than with power.[53]

The African church needs to wrestle with the theology of the kingdom of God in order to get sense and meaning out of the past history of the continent and the present predicament of many African nations. The kingdom of God is a present reality in the lives of believers and it is also a hope for the emancipation of the whole creation. The followers of Christ who are adhering to the kingdom principle are expected to be salt and light in this corrupt world. "In an ambiguous language He instructs us to love our enemies, do good to haters, bless cursers, and forgive up to 490 times. We are instructed to aspire to serve instead of ruling. He demonstrated the way of love . . . the paramount teaching is His own example before the cross. Under the agony of violence He refused to retaliate. With nails searing His flesh He refused to curse—but asked forgiveness . . . We are forced to conclude that Jesus was a revolutionary in violating Sabbath laws, criticizing wealthy hoarders, eating with sinners, and agitating the masses. His message of the kingdom's break-in undercut the power and underscored the temporary character of the other social institutions."[54] N. T. Wright adds, "Evil will be defeated, not by military victory, but by a doubly revolutionary method: turning the other cheek, going the second mile, the deeply subversive wisdom of taking up the cross. The agenda which Jesus mapped out for his followers was the Agenda to which he himself was obedient. This was how the kingdom would come, how the battle would be won . . . The night would get darker and darker and then the dawn would come."[55]

The coming dawn is described by the apostle John this way: "I saw heaven standing open and there before me was a white horse, whose rider is called Faithful and True. With justice he judges and makes war. His eyes are like blazing fire, and on his head are many crowns. He has a name written on him that no one knows but he himself. He is dressed in a robe dipped in blood, and his name is the Word of God. The armies of

---

53. Ladd, *Gospel of the Kingdom*, 55.
54. Kraybill, *Upside-Down Kingdom*, 62–63.
55. N. T. Wright, *Jesus and the Victory of God*, 465.

heaven were following him, riding on white horses and dressed in fine linen, white and clean. Out of his mouth comes a sharp sword with which to strike down the nations. 'He will rule them with an iron scepter.' He treads the winepress of the fury of the wrath of God Almighty. On his robe and on his thigh he has this name written: KING OF KINGS AND LORD OF LORDS" (Rev 19:11–16).

The theology of the kingdom of God is teaching us that God has not created humanity and the cosmos and abandoned human beings to live alone for self-destruction. He has been actively engaged without a break turning his face from neither the tragedies nor the successes of humanity. "God is reconciling humanity to himself—and as a result of this great transaction; he is reconciling all things to himself. He is bringing all things in heaven and earth together in Christ (Col. 1:20; Eph. 1:10) . . . Creation is therefore, the work of God without a rival, who made the world not as warrior digs a trench but as an artist paints a picture."[56] John Stott rightly said, "The ultimate destiny of our body is not death but resurrection."[57] "When the perishable has been clothed with the imperishable and the mortal with immortality, then the saying that is written will come true: 'Death has been swallowed up in victory'" (1 Cor 15:54). This is the hope of all humankind who believe in the God of the Bible. "Those he justified, he also glorified" (Rom 8:30c). "Our destiny is to be given new bodies in a new world, both of which will be transfigured with the glory of God . . . God is pictured as moving irresistibly from stage to stage; from an eternal foreknowledge and predestination, through a historical call and justification, to a final glorification of his people in a future eternity."[58] There is no power under the sun that can deprive the suffering African Christians this final joyful destination. It is in this light that we need to understand and interpret the history of Africa and her present political and economic situation. "Waiting for the new creation is a fundamental component of New Testament spirituality."[59] And this waiting is based in the Old Testament promise of the full ushering of the Kingdom of God through Jesus Christ: "Here is my servant, whom I uphold, my chosen one in whom I delight; I will put my Spirit on him and he will bring justice to the nations. He will not shout or cry out, or raise his voice in the streets. A bruised reed he will not break, and a smoldering wick he will not snuff out. In faithfulness he will bring forth justice; he will not falter or be discouraged till he establishes justice on earth. In his law the islands will put their hope" (Isa 42:1–4). No matter whether our sufferings seem unbearable or our situations get darker than before, Africans should not deviate from this promise and hope. If we do deviate it will be a double jeopardy.

> We shall not be redeemed *from* this earth, so that we could give it up. We shall be redeemed *with* it. We shall not be redeemed *from* the body. We shall be made eternally alive *with* the body. That is why the original hope of the Christians was not turned towards another world in heaven, but looked for the coming of God and his kingdom on this earth. We human beings are earthly creatures, not candidates for angelic status. Nor are we here on a visit to a beautiful star, so as

---

56. Keller, *Generous Justice*, 170–171–72.
57. Stott, *Message of Romans*, 226.
58. Ibid., 253.
59. Wolterstorff, *Journey toward Justice*, 80.

to make our home somewhere else after we die. We remain true to the earth, for on this earth stood Christ's cross. His resurrection from the dead is also a resurrection *with* the dead, and with his blood-soaked earth. In the light of Christ's resurrection we can already trace the contours of the 'new earth' (Rev. 21:1), where "death will be no more, neither shall there be mourning nor crying nor pain any more" (Rev. 21:4).[60]

Küng adds:

The resurrection faith is not an appendage to faith in God, but a radicalizing of faith in God. It is a faith in God which does not stop hallway, but follows the road consistently to the end. It is a faith in which man, without strictly rational proof but certain with completely reasonable trust, rules on the fact that the God of the beginning is also the God of the end, that he is the Creator of the world and man so too he is their Finisher.

The resurrection faith therefore is not to be interpreted merely as existential interiorization or social change, but as a radicalizing of faith in God the Creator. Resurrection means the real conquest of death by God the Creator to whom the believer entrust everything, even the ultimate, even the conquest of death. The end which is also a new beginning. Anyone who begins his creed with faith in "God the almighty Creator" can be content to end with faith in "eternal life." Since God is the Alpha, he is also the Omega. The almighty Creator who calls things from nothingness into being can also call men form death into life.[61]

Knowing and trusting God and his kingdom can make millions of African Christians bear the unbearable, hope against hope, live meaningful and purposeful lives here on earth, and also bring a positive change here and now.

A Call for Justice

The title of this book is *The West and China in Africa: Civilization without Justice*. In the American cultural context, "Justice and rights are the most contested part of our moral vocabulary, contested not only, or even mainly, by philosophers, but within the society generally."[62] One might wonder why I chose this title and ask how civilized nations could lack justice? Most of the chapters in this book can answer this question but here I would like to elaborate more. Nicholas Wolterstorff in his magnum opus, *Justice Rights and Wrongs*, demonstrated that the idea of the natural rights originated neither in the Enlightenment nor in the individualistic philosophy of the late Middle Ages, but has long been present in the Hebrew and Christian Scriptures. So justice is not a human invention—it is humanity's prerogative granted by the one who created humanity in his own image—God. Human rights do not emanate from their race, their culture, or their democratic or authoritarian political system; it is embedded in their being. "One's right

---

60. Moltmann, *Source of Life*, 74; emphasis original.
61. Küng, *On Being a Christian*, 360; emphasis original.
62. Wolterstorff, *Justice*, 1.

are grounded in one's worth, and being treated by one's fellows as befits one's worth is important."[63]

The debate is who is determining one's worth? Before the horrific genocide in Rwanda, the Hutus were calling the Tutsis cockroaches; in the eyes of the Nazis the Jews were vermin; in the eyes of the Jews the Samaritans were worse than pigs; and the examples go on. What right and authority does one human being have to call another human being less of a human and treat him/her as such? Are we not all clay in the hands of a potter? This is where theological anthropology needs to play its best role. Human worth is equally given to all by the one who created them. "The Bible teaches that the sacredness of God has in some ways been imparted to humanity, so that every human life is sacred and every human being has dignity. When God put his image upon us, we became beings of infinite, inestimable value."[64] Despite our racial differences, all human beings are "of one blood" (Acts 17:26). Therefore, "justice is ultimately grounded on inherent rights. Rights are normative social relationships; socially is built into the essence of rights. A right is a right with regard to someone. In the limiting case, that 'someone' is oneself; one is other to oneself. Usually, the other is somebody else than oneself. Rights are toward the other, with regard to somebody else. Rights are toward the other, with regard to the other. And for the most part, those normative bonds oneself to the other are not generated by exercise of will on one's part. The bond is there already, antecedent to one's will on one's part. The bond is there already, antecedent to one's will, binding oneself and the other together. The other comes into my presence already standing in the normative bond to me."[65]

Since rights are inherent and are "normative bonds between oneself and the other," one has a legitimate claim on everyone who initiates communication and relationship with him/her to be treated with dignity. Then, if we agree in our understanding of justice so far, it is a blunt display in the pages of human history that the West by and large and China to a certain extent did not treat Africans with dignity. The omission of justice in their treatment of Africans is the worst thing that the outside powers did to Africans. In this ill treatment of Africans, the African tyrants are full participants and they are equally responsible. Injustice happened to Africans in various forms and for centuries. Keller describes: "Oppression and injustice take . . . virulent forms in many parts of the world. The list includes abusive child labor and sex trafficking, state-sponsored religious persecution, detention without trial or charges, seizure of private land without due process and payment, forced migration, organized violence against ethnic minorities, state, rebel, or paramilitary terrorism, and sponsored torture."[66] African leaders are champions of these human atrocities. As we looked at the situations in Angola, Sudan, Sierra Leone, Central African Republic, Ethiopia, Libya, Egypt, Somalia, to mention the few in this book, these human rights violations are executed with the awareness and funding of either the Western powers or China.

---

63. Wolterstorff, *Journey toward Justice*, 50.
64. Keller, *Generous Justice*, 83.
65. Wolterstorff, *Justice*, 4.
66. Keller, *Generous Justice*, 129.

In such oppressive and depressive social and economic situations in Africa, the church and Christian scholars should be a voice of the voiceless and proclaim the message of justice that is prevalent both in the Old and the New Testament. "The church is an evangelizing and a liberating community. If it is not, it is not Christ's church—nor indeed a church at all."[67] As most African intellectuals did in the past and are still doing, African Christians need to be cautious to advocate neither for the West nor the East's system of political governance. As Africans teach, preach, and write about the justice of God, their focus should be on the transcendental values of the kingdom of God in Africa. "The Biblical understanding of justice is not rooted in any one of these, but in the character and being of God himself. This means that no current political framework can fully convey the comprehensive Biblical vision of justice, and Christians should never identify too closely with a particular political party or philosophy."[68]

> *Wherever inhuman social conditions, political oppression, economic exploitation, social discrimination and violation of elementary human rights prevent man's striving to go beyond himself, he is frustrated in the realization of his being human and reduced to a subhuman state, the condition of a robot.*
>
> *Wherever, finite, intramundane factors—formerly "the nation," "the people," "the true consciousness" of an intellectual elite—are made absolute and regarded as final emancipation, there is no true liberation of man, but totalitarian domination by men over men and thus groups nations, and races and classes: that is, no better society, no justice for all and no freedom for the individual, no true love.*
>
> *On the plane of the linear, horizontal, purely human alone, no truly qualitative ascent to a really different dimension seems possible: without genuine transcendence, there is no genuine transcending.*[69]

"Without genuine transcendence, there is no genuine transcending." When we look at the academic works of both the Afrocentric and the Eurocentric scholars who analyzed and interpreted Africa and Africans, the major thing they lack is a transcending biblical vision for humankind, particularly Africans. A good example is Diop's three books and Mazrui's and Ayittey's works that I read. Without a transcending biblical message, humanity remains in bondage—bondage of sin and demonic powers, bondage of bitterness and hopelessness. Being a slave to sin and the power of spiritual darkness, humanity can neither free itself nor others. Hence, African societies suffer injustice.

Earlier, I asked, "What kind of God do we believe in?" The global church of Jesus Christ, and the African church in particular, need to wrestle with this question if she wants to be relevant to her socioeconomic contexts. The Psalmist said, "The Lord loves righteousness and justice the earth is full of his unfailing love" (33:5). "This is what the Lord says," said Jeremiah: "Let not the wise man boast of his wisdom or the strong man boast of his strength or the rich man boast of his riches, but let him who boast boast about this: that he understands and knows me, that I am the Lord, who exercises kindness, justice and righteousness on earth, for in these I delight, declares the Lord" (Jer 9:23–24). Justice is a very important matter to God and it is nonnegotiable or

---

67. Moltmann, *Jesus Christ for Today's World*, 28.
68. Keller, *Generous Justice*, 163.
69. Küng, *Does God Exist?*, 488; emphasis original.

irreplaceable in any form of religious rituals. "The word for justice is the Hebrew word *mishpat* . . . The word *mishpat* in its various forms occurs more than two hundred times in the Hebrew Old Testament. Its most basic meaning is to treat people equitably."[70] God is "[a] father to the fatherless, a defender of widows" (Ps 68:4–5). All the gods of the ancient societies, as well as the gods of our times for that matter, relate with and benefit the upper echelon of people. They hardly identify with the poor, the oppressed, and the rejected—not so with the God of the Bible. To the evil kings, "This is what the Lord says: Do what is just and right. Rescue from the hand of his oppressor the one who has been robbed. Do no wrong or violence to the alien, the fatherless or the widow, and do not shed innocent blood in this place" (Jer 22:3) was God's message. In Isaiah God is even emphatic: "Is not this the kind of fasting I have chosen: to loose the chain of injustice and untie the cords of the yoke, to set the oppressed free and break every yoke? Is it not to share your food with the hungry and to provide the poor wanderer with shelter—when you see the naked, to clothe him, and not to turn away from your own flesh and blood?" (Isa 58:3, 5–7). We often think the plots and atrocities of corrupt and greedy leaders that are hidden from the public media are also unseen and secret to God. He watches them and is displeased by the indifference of those who were supposed to stand up for truth: "Justice is driven back, and righteousness stands at a distance; truth has stumbled in the streets, honesty cannot enter. Truth is nowhere to be found, and whoever shuns evil becomes a prey. The Lord looked and displeased that there was no justice. He saw that there was no one to intervene" (Isa 59:14–16).

Jesus had strong concern and love for the same kinds of vulnerable and destitute people. When John the Baptist came and asked him if he truly was the Messiah, he said: "Go back and report to John what you hear and see: the blind receive sight and the lame walk, those who have leprosy are cured, the deaf hear and the dead are raised and the good news is preached to the poor" (Matt 11:4–5). Jesus didn't say "Report what you hear," but he said, "Report what you *hear* and *see*." We've much to report in the area of hearing but little to show in the area of justice. The church has so many committees but hardly any committee of justice. During the times of Nazi Germany, South African apartheid, the slave trade, and colonialism, the church gave a blind eye and a deaf ear to the conditions of the victims. "If God's character includes a zeal for justice that leads him to have the tenderest love and closest involvement with the socially weak, then what should God's people be like? They must be people who are likewise passionately concerned for the weak and vulnerable."[71] Jesus Christ is our great model to engage with the situation and issues of the destitute: "Undisturbed by all the talk behind his back, undisturbed by all the open criticism, Jesus got himself involved with the types on the fringe of society, the social outsiders, religious outcasts, the underprivileged and the downgraded. He made common cause with them. He simply accepted them. He not only preached a love open to all men, he also practiced it. Certainly he did not ingratiate himself; he did not by any means share in the activities of disreputable groups. He did not sink down to their level but drew them up to himself. But he did not simply enter

---

70. Keller, *Generous Justice*, 3.
71. Keller, *Generous Justice*, 8.

into discussion with these notoriously bad people, but—quite literally—*sat down with them*. Many were indignant: he was regarded as impossible."[72]

Therefore, the reason we need to engage in human affairs for the cause of justice is not because we love one particular race or group of people over another. It should be because God himself has been passionately involved in human history to defend the poor, the weak, and the vulnerable. Passion for the disinherited does not develop merely in library research and lecture halls. One has to meet the wronged, listen to them, walk with them, and live with them for a while—to feel and see the world from their perspective. "Empathy is what gives the struggle for justice its motivation—not duty, or obligation, or any virtue one might possess, but personal knowledge and understanding of how it feels to be treated unjustly . . . [Empathy] comes to us most powerfully when we are confronted with the faces and the voices of those who are vulnerable and who suffer injustice."[73]

To develop empathy for Africans, one needs to walk in the slums of Africa and go through the stench smell that makes you feel like throwing up, travel across Africa and see the hungry and emaciated bodies of young and old, the sick who have never stepped in a clinic or been treated by a physician, the young illiterate and jobless Africans with no future who are prone to criminal activities, and those who languish in the prisons of authoritarian governments. As Éla said, "We must go and rediscover Christ in the slums, in places of misery and domination, among the majority of the poor and the oppressed people. It is the Third World that allows the church to make salvation in Jesus Christ visible."[74]

Being insulated by our own comfort and security, it is impossible to hear and see the plight of those who suffer injustice in Africa. "Jesus called his followers to respond to hunger with food, to nakedness with clothes, to imprisonment with visitation, to beatings with bandages and to injustice with justice (Matthew 15:32–38; 25:35–36; Luke 10:34; 11:42)."[75] In the name of philanthropy and Christian mission, the Western church and nonprofit organizations have been doing these activities in Africa. Now, it is time to go beyond this modus operandi and deal with the root causes of African poverty, which are sin and greed. "We can say to the entrepreneurs, the trade unionists, the producers, the consumers, and all the people who work to increase the gross national product: forget the profits and forget growth—think of the kingdom of God and its justice and righteousness. Think of justice for the poor in the countries of the Third World and in the shadows of our Western society. Think of justice for the coming generations for who we are working. Think of justice for the nature from which we live. Think in the long term, not the short. Then 'lasting development' shall be added to us all, simply of itself."[76]

---

72. Küng, *On Being a Christian*, 272–73; emphasis original.
73. Wolterstorff, *Journey toward Justice*, x.
74. Éla, *My Faith as an African*, 99.
75. Haugen, *Good News about Injustice*, 110.
76. Moltmann, *Jesus Christ for Today's World*, 29.

Conclusion

As we looked at in the previous chapters, for most of Africa's history, for various reasons, the continent has been a war zone. Hence, African Christians or non-Christians, are "people whose cities and villages have been first plundered, then burned and leveled to the ground, whose daughters and sisters have been raped, whose fathers and brothers have had their throat slit,"[1] or in other instances, killed with a shotgun. The majority of African families have gone through involuntary family splits because of a job search or social unrest and have been hurried to various refugee camps where hunger, malnutrition, disease, and all kinds of abnormal social behavior manifested in their ugliest and most injuring forms. "For how long oh God!" is a question of many Christian African believers. Both Bible scholars and theologians have a lot of work to do in understanding the place of biblical lamentation in a continent where human life is prone to different kinds of suffering.

If Africa is to come out of her paradoxical existence, the major role has to be played by Africans—particularly the leaders. It is obvious that Africa has been losing her natural resources and seldom benefiting from it. On the contrary, natural resources have been causes of war and social and political instability in many African countries. The least-mentioned, but the most devastating, of Africa's losses is the mass exodus of highly educated people. Companies, governments, universities, judicial systems, financial systems, etc., require highly sophisticated systemic thinkers and the use of up-to-date modern technology. Long- and short-term effective planning and implementation is essential for a society to develop and overcome human or nature related challenges and problems. This brain drain has a paralyzing effect in Africa, and tyrant leaders don't seem to care. As we have seen in Uganda and Ethiopia, if university professors sound or look like a threat to the dictators, they will be eliminated or forced into exile. Instead of widening the exit door into exile, African leaders need to be creative to attract African intellectuals in diaspora to go back home and build the infrastructures and improve the educational, economic, and health care sectors. As of now, we've not seen any attempt to do such nation-building efforts from any African leader except Mandela. But they all enjoy and encourage the remittance that is coming from those in diaspora in various parts of the world.

---

1. Blount, *Can I Get a Witness*, 34.

CONCLUSION

Another perpetual damage to Africa is the illegal outflow of money. Unless this huge leakage is decisively and permanently plugged, Africa cannot make economic, social, and technological progress.

> Foreign aid programs continue to pour funds into what seems like Africa's bottomless bucket. Illicit financial flows out of Africa are twice the amount of foreign aid into the region. Between 1970 and 2008, according to a study by Global Financial Integrity (GFI), illicit flows from Africa totaled at least $854 billion, and could reach as high as $1.8 trillion when taking into account missing data from certain countries and other conduits of illicit flows not captured in the study.
>
> Although $1.8 trillion is already an incredible volume of illicit outflows, the actual figure could be higher still. This figure grows if we account for untraceable money generated by smuggling, violations of intellectual property rights, trade in narcotics and other contraband goods, human trafficking, sex trade, and other illegal activities.
>
> Illicit flows have been a consistent and crippling problem in African countries. The GFI study found that illicit funds from the continent continued to ratchet upwards every decade since the 1970s, at an average rate of 12 percent per year. In fact, Africa is a net creditor to the world—it "gives" back to the world through illicit capital flight at least twice, and in some regions thrice, the amount of capital it receives in external assistance. No wonder, then, that this staggering loss of capital seriously hampers Africa's efforts at poverty alleviation and economic development, decade after decade . . .
>
> Development aid to Africa won't be effective as long as these illicit outflows continue to grow. Sub-Saharan African countries experienced the bulk of illicit capital leaving the continent, with the West and Central African region registering the largest outflows. The top five countries with the highest outflows were: Nigeria ($240.7 billion), Egypt ($131.3 billion), South Africa ($76.4 billion), Morocco ($41.0 billion), and Algeria ($35.1 billion). Estimates indicate that Africa lost around $29 billion per year from 1970–2008, of which the sub-Saharan region accounted for $22 billion. On average, countries like Nigeria that export oil lost capital at nearly $10 billion per year, far outstripping the $2.5 billion per year lost by the group of countries exporting non-fuel primary commodities. Indeed, these numbers indicate that much of the wealth generated by oil-exporting African countries does not trickle down sufficiently to benefit the nation's population.[2]

Again, this is not done by Washington, Berlin, London, Moscow, or Beijing, to mention a few. It is done by African leaders and elites who are outrageously plundering the banks and treasuries of their nations. That is why even with the so-called developmental works that China is engaged in Africa in the recent years that *Africans are asking whether China is making their lunch or eating it.* Whether outsiders come in the guise of democracy or communism there is no fundamental change for the African poor. The African context requires the voice of biblical justice. "To understand the preaching of the prophets, we must enter into the whole experience of faith that underlies the Old Testament. When the prophets denounce the injustices of their own time, with a violence that

---

2. Curcio, "Plugging Africa's Leak."

may surprise us, they are simply taking up the cause of the disinherited in the name of God. Exploitation and corruption demand that people speak out (Amos 8:4–8). How are we to remain indifferent in a world of plunder and violence where assassination is the way to power (Zeph. 1:13)?"[3]

The majority of the African countries' constitutions favor the few who hold power rather than the larger society. Those who are governing have the backing of the law, the military, the police, the capital, and the like, which the poor or the common person have no access to and are not privileged by. The oppression and exploitation of the tyrants are systemic and are not easy to change democratically in a civil manner. That is why the continent is in an endless military or dictatorial coup and counter-coup. If Africa needs to heal and reform, the constitutions in many countries need to be rewritten, the civil rights of people have to be upheld, and elections should be done in a transparent and democratic manner and whoever wins needs to have a limited term of service.

Creative writings, democratic speeches, healthy academic climates for innovation, civil debates, journalistic and historical researches of the past and the present, scientific discoveries of the celestial and terrestrial world, medical researches, the contributions of artists, a judicial system that implements the law fairly and across ethnic boundaries and social status, etc., need to be fostered, encouraged, and funded. These activities should operate without the intervention or restrictions of government powers, but with clear accountability to the rule of law and the taxpayers.

In the corrupt African cultural context, the church should remain salt and light. Through word and deed, the church ought to be a beacon of hope to the hopeless, and bring healing to those who are physically, psychologically, and economically sick. "The divine mystery is not just above us in heaven, and not just within us in the ground of our being, but before us, and ahead of us, on our way into the unknown future. That is the God whom Paul calls 'the God of hope' (Rom. 15:13)."[4] It was this hope that enabled Paul to understand the existence of Israel as a colony of the imperial Rome, to accept and live within the Jewish diaspora, the oppression and exploitation of his people, and the injustice that was inflicted on them. It was this hope that gave him meaning for his existence and enabled him to do his apostolic work through torture, chains, and hunger. It was this hope that enabled him to love the Jews and the Gentiles, including the Romans. The African church should not fail to effectively communicate this hope—a hope that promises life beyond the grave and enables us to interpret history accurately—from God's redemptive purpose.

> The resurrection of Christ is without parallel in the history known to us. But it can for this very reason be regarded as a "history-making event" in the light of which all other history is illumined, called in question and transformed. The mode of proclaiming and hopefully remembering this event then must be presented as a mode of historical remembrance which is wholly governed by this event both in content and in procedure. It is not that from the hopeful remembrance of this event we then derive general laws of world history, but in remembering this one, unique event, we remember the hope for the future of

---

3. Éla, *My Faith as an African*, 103–4.
4. Moltmann, *Sun of Righteousness Arise!*, 101.

all world history. Then the resurrection of Christ does not offer itself as analogy to what is come to all. The expectation of what is to come on the ground of the resurrection of Christ, must then turn all reality that can be experienced and all real experience that is provisional and reality that does not yet contain within it what is held in prospect for it. It must therefore contradict all rigid substantio-metaphysical definitions of the common core of similarity in world events, and therefore also the corresponding historical understanding that works with analogy. It must develop a historical understanding which works with eschatological analogy as a foreshadowing and anticipation of the future. The raising of Christ is then to be called "historic," not because it took place in the history to which other categories of some sort provide a key, but it is to be called historic because, by pointing the way for future events, it *makes* history in which we can and must live. It is historic, because it discloses an eschatological future. This assertion must then give proof of itself in conflict with other concepts of history, all of which are ultimately based on other "history-making" events, shocks or revolutions in history.[5]

Theological, historical, and eschatological understandings of human history can give Africans meaning for life in seemingly meaningless life situations. It can provide hope despite many disappointing and discouraging experiences. As the number of Christians grow in Africa, along with deep biblical teachings, mentoring, and discipleship of new believers, an inside-out change with a transcending vision can come. This transcending vision has to manifest the ethics of the kingdom of God, which are forgiveness, loving our enemies, reconciliation, peace, justice, humble service, honesty, transparency, and the like. This cannot happen only through pulpit ministries. Like yeast in dough, Christians should spread or extend the sphere of their influence in the judicial, political, financial, educational, agricultural, and geological aspects of their governments. By speaking the truth in love and demonstrating it in life, the positive change that Africans have been longing for can be achieved in our lifetime. Even then, we will not be at the culmination of history but at a new beginning. A better and perfect world is yet to come. There is no human civilization that can substitute for the full manifestation of the kingdom of God.

5. Moltmann, *Theology of Hope*, 167–68.

Bibliography

Abdulrazak, Shaukat. "Can Africa Go Nuclear? Energy Demands Battle With Safety Concerns Across The Continent." *International Business Times*, June 15, 2014.
Achebe, Chinua. *The Trouble with Nigeria*. Ibadan, Nigeria: Fourth Dimension, 1983.
Adde, Ezbon. "Geology and Mineral Investment Opportunities in South Sudan." Typescript paper. May, 2013.
"African Money Transfer: Let them Remit." *The Economist*, 20 July, 2013, p. 43.
"African's Jihadists, on their Way." *The Economist*, July 26th, 2014, p. 43.
"Algeria: Patience Persists." *The Economist*, 2 November, 2013, pp. 52–53.
Allen, James, et al. *Without Sanctuary: Lynching Photography in America*. Santa Fe, NM: Twin Palm, 2007.
Allen, John. "Africa: Governments Failing in Corruption Fight." *allAfrica*, November, 13, 2013.
Anderson, David. *Histories of the Hanged: Britain's war in Kenya and the end of the Empire*. London: Weidenfeld and Nicolson, 2005.
Annan, Kofi. *Interventions: A Life in War and Peace*. New York: Penguin, 2012.
Anshan, Li. "China's New Policy toward Africa." In *China Into Africa: Trade, Aid, and Influence*, edited by Robert I. Rotberg, 21–49. Washington, DC: Brookings Institution, 2008.
Anyanzwa, James. "Integrated Capital Markets Plan Hits New Headwinds." *Standard*, February 25, 2014.
Applebaum, S. "A Lamp and other Remains of the Jewish Community of Cyrene." *Israel Explorations Journal* 7 (1957) 62–154,.
Arnold, James R. *Robert Mugabe's Zimbabwe*. Minneapolis: First Century, 2008.
"Averting the Sixth Extinction." *The Economist*, September 14, 2013, p.16.
Ayittey, B. N., George. *Africa Betrayed*. New York: St Martin's, 1992.
———. *Africa in Chaos*. New York: St. Martin's Griffin, 1999.
Barnett, Homer. *Innovation: The Basis of Culture Change*. New York: McGraw-Hill, 1953.
Barrett, Clive. *The Egyptian God and Goddesses: The Mythology and Beliefs of Ancient Egypt*. London: Aquarian, 1992.
Baur, John. *2000 Years of Christianity in Africa*. Nairobi: Pauline, 1994.
Bediako, Kwame. *Christianity in Africa: The Renewal of Non-Western Religion*. Edinburgh: Edinburgh University Press, 1995.
———. *Theology and Identity: The Impact of Culture upon Christian Thought in the Second Century and Modern Africa*. Oxford: Regnum, 1999.
Behar, Richard. "Special Report: China Storms Africa." *LEADERSHIP*, June 1, 2008.
Berkhof, Louis. *Systematic Theology*. Edinburgh: Banner of Truth Trust, 1984.
Bernal, Martin. *Black Athena: The Afroasiatic Roots of Classical Civilization*. Vol. 1. New Brunswick, NJ: Rutgers University Press, 1987.
———. *Black Athena: The Afroasiatic Roots of Classical Civilization*. Vol. 2. New Brunswick, NJ: Rutgers University Press, 2002.
———. *Black Athena: The Afroasiatic Roots of Classical Civilization*. Vol. 3. New Brunswick, NJ: Rutgers University Press, 2006.
———. *Black Athena Writes Back: Martin Bernal Responds to His Critics*. Durham, NC: Duke University Press, 2001.
Biko, Steve. *I Write What I Like*: Chicago: University of Chicago Press, 2002.

BIBLIOGRAPHY

———. *Steve Biko: Black Consciousness in South Africa.* New York: Vintage, 1979.
Bligh, C. Michelle. "Personality Theories of Leadership" In *Encyclopedia of Group Process and Intergroup Relations*, edited by John M. Levine and Michael Hogg. 639–43. Thousand Oaks, CA: SAGE, 2001.
Blomberg, L. Craig. *Can We Still Believe the Bible?* Grand Rapids: Brazos, 2014.
———. *Christians in the Age of Wealth: A Biblical Theology of Stewardship.* Grand Rapids: Zondervan, 2013.
Blount, K. Brian. *Can I Get a Witness: Reading Revelation through African American Culture.* Louisville: Westminster John Knox, 2005.
Bonem, Mike, and Roger Patterson. *Leading from the Second Chair.* San Francisco: Jossey Bass, 2005.
Borthwick, Paul. *How to Be a World Class Christian: You Can Be a Part of God's Global Action.* Waynesboro, GA: Authentic Media, 2000.
Bosch, David. *Transforming Mission: Paradigm Shifts in Theology of Mission.* Maryknoll, NY: Orbis, 1991.
Brabazon, James. *My Friend the Mercenary.* New York: Grove, 2010.
Braudel, Fernand. *The Wheels of Commerce: Civilization and Capitalism: 15th–18th Century.* Vol. 2. Berkley: University of California Press, 1992.
Brautigam, Deborah. *The Dragon's Gift: The Real Story of China in Africa.* New York: Oxford University Press, 2009.
Bright, John. *A History of Israel.* 3rd ed. Philadelphia: Westminster, 1981.
Broadman, G. Harry. "Chinese-African Investment: The Vanguard of South-South Commerce in the Twenty-First Century." In *China Into Africa: Trade, Aid, and Influence*, edited by Robert I. Rotberg, 87–108. Washington, DC: Brookings Institution, 2008.
Brodie, James Michael. *Created Equal: The Lives and Ideas of Black American Innovators.* New York: Quill William Morrow, 1993.
Brown, Colin. *Jesus in European Protestant Thought 1778–1860.* Grand Rapids: Baker, 1985.
———. *Philosophy and the Christian Faith.* Downers Grove, IL: InterVarsity, 1968.
Brown, Stephen, and L. Chandra Siriam. "China's Role in Human Rights Abuses in Africa: Clarifying Issues of Culpability." In *China Into Africa: Trade, Aid, and Influence*, edited by Robert I. Rotberg, 250–71. Washington, DC: Brooking Institution, 2008.
Bruce, F. F. *Paul Apostle of the Heart Set Free.* Grand Rapids: Eerdmans, 1991.
Buchanan, Mark. *Spiritual Rhythm: Being with Jesus Every Season of Your Soul.* Grand Rapids: Zondervan, 2010.
Burton, Keith Augustus. *The Blessings of Africa.* Downers Grove, IL: IVP Academic, 2007.
Byrne, Jon, et al. "Evaluating the Potential of Small-Scale Renewable Energy Options to Meet Rural Livelihoods Needs: A GIS- and Lifecycle Cost-Based Assessment of Western China's Options." *Energy Policy* 35 (2007) 4391–4401.
Calderisi, Robert. *The Trouble with Africa: Why Foreign Aid Is Not Working.* New York: Palgrave Macmillan, 2006.
Campbell, Greg. *Blood Diamonds.* New York: Basic, 2004.
Carroll, R., and M. Daniel. *Amos—The Prophet and His Oracles.* Louisville: Westminster John Knox, 2002.
"The Central African Republic: Another Failed State Beckons." *The Economist*, August 31, 2013, p. 39.
Chan, Stephen. *Robert Mugabe: A Life of Power and Violence.* New York: Tauris, 2003.
Chidester, David. *Christianity: A Global History.* New York: HarperCollins, 2000.
Chisholm, A. Clinton. "Afrocentricity Black Consciousness: Challenges for Christianity" Part 1. *Professional Theological Journal For The Caribbean Community* 9 (2005) 1–20.
Church, Leslie, and F. R. Hist, eds. *Mathew Henry's Commentary.* Grand Rapids: Zondervan, 1961.
Clarke, H. John. *Christopher Columbus and the African Holocaust: Slavery and the Rise of Capitalism.* Buffalo, NY: EWORLD, 1998.
Chomsky, Noam. *Hegemony or Survival: America's Quest for Global Dominance.* New York: Metropolitan, 2004.
———. *Profit over People: Neo Liberalism and Global Order.* New York: Seven Stories, 1999.
Cockcroft, Laurence. *Global Corruption: Money, Power and Ethics in the Modern World.* Philadelphia: Pennsylvania University Press, 2012.
Coffey, C. Thomas. *The Lion by the Tail.* New York: Viking, 1974.
Coffin, Pine R. S., trans. *Saint Augustine: Confessions.* New York: Penguin, 1986.
Collingwood, R. G. *The Idea of History.* Oxford: Oxford University Press, 1946.

Copland, Cassie. "South Sudan: A Civil War by Any Other Name." *Africa Report*, no. 217, April, 10, 2014.
Copleston, Fredrick. *A History of Philosophy*. Vol. 1, *Greece and Rome*. New York: Newman, 1971.
"Corruption in South Africa: Nkandla in the Wind." *The Economist*, April 12, 2014, p. 48.
Crossan, D. John, and L. Jonathan Reed. *In Search of Paul*. San Francisco: HarperCollins, 2004.
Curcio, Karly. "Plugging Africa's Leak, Money Is Illegally Flowing out of Africa: Here's How to Fix the Problem." Foreign Policy In Focus (FPIF), May 20, 2010.
Davidson, Basil. *African Civilization Revisited: From Antiquity to Modern Times*. Trenton, NJ: Africa World, 1991.
Davies, Martyn J. "Special Economic Zones: China's Developmental Models Come to Africa." In *China into Africa: Trade, Aid, and Influence*, edited by Robert I. Rotberg, 137–54. Washington, DC: Brookings Institution, 2008.
Davis, D. B. *The Problem of Slavery in Western Culture*. Ithaca, NY: Cornell University, 1966.
"Democratic Republic of Congo: Bigger guns are on their way." *The Economist*, June, 15, 2013, p. 51.
Dickson, Kwesi A. *Theology in Africa*. Maryknoll, NY: Orbis, 1984.
Diop, Anta Cheikh. *The African Origin of Civilization: Myth or Reality*. Chicago: Lawrence Hill, 1974.
———. *Black Africa: The Economic and Cultural Basis for a Federated State*. Chicago: Lawrence Hill, 1978.
———. *Civilization or Barbarism: An Authentic Anthropology*. Chicago: Lawrence Hill, 1991.
Dowden, Richard. *Africa: Altered States, Ordinary Miracles*. New York: Public Affairs, 2009.
Dunn, James D. G. *The Theology of Paul the Apostle*. London: T. & T. Clark, 1998.
Dupuis, Jacques. *Who Do You Say I Am?: Introduction to Christology*. Maryknoll, NY: Orbis, 1994.
Edersheim, Alfred. *The Life and Times of Jesus the Messiah*. Mclean, VA: Macdonald, 1993.
Edgerton, Robert. *Africa's Armies from Honor to Infamy: A History from 1791 to the Present*. Cambridge, MA: Westview, 2002.
Ehret, Christopher. *The Civilizations of Africa: A History to 1800*. Charlottesville: University of Virginia Press, 2002.
Eisenman, Joshua. "China's Political Outreach to Africa." In *China into Africa: Trade, Aid, and Influence*, edited by Robert I. Rotberg, 230–49. Washington, DC: Brookings Institution, 2008.
Éla, Jean-Marc. *My Faith as an African*. Translated by John Pairman Brown and Susan
Perry. Maryknoll, NY: Orbis, 2009.
"Electricity in Africa: Lighting a Dark Continent." *The Economist*, September 27, 2014, p. 46.
Elkins, Caroline. *Britain's Gulag: The Brutal End of Empire in Kenya*. London: Cape, 2005.
Elliot, Michael. "Lighting up Africa: How Electricity Will Transform the Continent." *The Economist*, November 18, 2013, n.p.
Emerson, Michael O., and Christian Smith. *Divided by Faith*. Oxford: Oxford University Press, 2000.
"Energy to South Africa: Fear of the Dark." *The Economist*, November, 30, 2013, p. 48.
"Environmental accountability: Transparency in the haze." *The Economist*, February 8, 2014, p. 44.
"Eritrea and Its Emigrants: Why They leave." *The Economist*, October, 12, 2013, p. 60.
"Ethiopia and Its Press: The Noose Tightens." *The Economist*, August 9, 2014, p. 42.
Fee, Gordon D. *The First Epistle to the Corinthians*. Grand Rapids: Eerdmans, 1991.
Fialka, J. John. *War by Other Means: Economic Espionage in America*. New York: Norton, 1999.
Fink, Steven. *Sticky Fingers: Managing the Global Risk of Economic Espionage*. Lincoln, NE: iUniverse, 2002.
Flanders, Rick "Why Did Jesus Weep Over Jerusalem?" January, 23, 2012. http://ministry127.com/christian-living/why-did-jesus-weep-over-jerusalem.
Frankl, Viktor E. *Man's Search for Meaning: An Introduction to Logotherapy*. New York: Touchstone, 1984.
French, W. Howard. *China's Second Continent: How a Million Migrants Are Building a New Empire in Africa*. New York: Knopf, 2014.
———. *A Continent for the Taking: The Tragedy and Hope of Africa*. New York: Random House, 2005.
———. "Into Africa: China's Wild Rush" *The New York Times*, May 16, 2014.
Fretheim, Terence E. *The Suffering of God*. Philadelphia: Fortress, 1984.
Freud, Sigmund. *Character and Culture*. New York: Crowell-Collier, 1963.
Gangel, O. Kenneth. *Lessons in Leadership from the Bible*. Winona Lake, IN: BMH, 1984.
Garret, E. Henry. "Racial Differences and Witch Hunting," *Science* 135 (1962) 982, 984.
Garret, Gordon B. A. *The Analectics of Confucius*. Norwalk, CT: Eastern, 1933.

Gardner, Howard. *Five Minds for the Future*. Boston: Harvard Business School Press, 2006.
Gardner, Lloyd C. *The Road to Tahrir Square: Egypt and the United States from the Rise of Nasser to the Fall of Mubarak*. New York: New, 2011.
Genovese, E. Fox, and E. D. Genovese. "The Divine Sanction of Social Order: Religious
Foundations of Giles, Leonel Trans. Southern Slaveholders' World View." *Journal of American Academy and Religion* 55 (1987) 211–33, 224.
Giorgis, W. Dawit. *Red Tears: War, Famine and Revolution in Ethiopia*. Township, NJ: Red Sea,1989.
Goldenberg, David. *The Curse of Ham: Race and Slavery in early Judaism, Christianity and Islam*. Princeton: Princeton University Press, 2003.
———. "Early Jewish and Christian Views of Blacks." Paper presented at the Fifth Annual Gilder Lehrman Center International Conference, "Collective Degradation: Slavery and the Construction of Race," Yale University, Nov. 7–8, 2003, 13 typeset pages.
Elisabeth Gouel. "Conflict in South Sudan." Thomson Reuters Foundation, 20 Dec 2013.
Groothuis, Douglas. "How Jazz Can Shape Apologetics." *DEFEND Magazine*. February 19, 2014.
Guinness, Os. *The Case for Civility: Why Our Future Depends on it*. New York: HarperCollins, 2008.
———. *The Dust of Death*. Downers Grove, IL: InterVarsity, 1976.
"The Gulf of Guinea: Another Somalia." *The Economist*, May 25, 2013, p. 48.
Hall, Edward. *Slaves in the Family*. New York: Ballantine, 2001.
Hanciles, J. Jehu. *Beyond Christendom: Globalization, African Migration, and the Transformation of the West*. Maryknoll, NY: Orbis, 2008.
Hancock, Graham. *Lords of Poverty*. London: Macmillan, 1989.
Hankins, Mark. "Why Africa is Missing the Solar Power Boat?" *Renewable Energy World.Com* April 03, 2013. http://www.renewableenergyworld.com/articles/2013/04/why-africa-is-missing-the-solar-electricity-boat.html (accessed Oct. 14, 2015).
Hansen, Stephanie. "Corruption in Sub-Saharan Africa." *Council in Foreign Relation*, August 6, 2009.
Harress, Christopher. "Secret Flow of Somali Piracy Ransoms: 179 Hijacked Ships Generated Some $400M In Payments Since 2005. So where has it all gone?" *International Business Times*, November 4, 2013.
Harris, J. E. *Africans and their History*. New York: New American Library, 1987.
Haugen, A. Gary. *Good News about Injustice: A Witness of Courage in a Hurting World*. Nottingham, UK: InterVarsity, 2009.
Hendricks, Howard. *Teaching to Change Lives*. Colorado Springs: Multnomah, 1987.
Hengel, Martin. *Crucifixion*. Philadelphia: Fortress, 1977.
Herold, J. C. *The Mind of Napoleon*. New York: Columbia University Press, 1955.
Heschel, Abraham J. *God in Search of Man*. New York: Farrar, Straus & Giroux, 1983.
———. *Man is Not Alone*. New York: Farrar, Straus & Giroux, 1979.
———. *The Prophets*. New York: Harper Perennial, 1962.
Hess, R. L. "The Itinerary of Benjamin of Tudela: A Twelfth-Century Jewish Description of North-East Africa." *Journal of African History* 6, no. 1 (1965) 15–24.
Hiebert, Paul G. *Transforming Worldviews: An Anthropological Understanding of How People Change*. Grand Rapids: Baker Academic, 2008.
Hitchens, Peter. "How China Has Created a New Slave Empire in Africa." *Mail Online*, September, 28, 2008.
Hochschild, Adam. *King Leopold's Ghost*. New York: Mariner, 1998.
Hochstein, Manfred P. "Heat Transfer by Hydrothermal Systems in the East African Rifts." Paper presented at the World Geothermal Congress, Antalya, Turkey, April 24–29, 2005.
Huang, Chin-Hao. "China's Renewal Partnership with Africa: Implications for the United States." In *China into Africa: Trade, Aid, and Influence*, edited by Robert I. Rotberg, 296–312. Washington, DC: Brookings Institution, 2008.
Hubbard, David A. *The Communicator's Commentary: Proverbs*. Dallas, TX: Word, 1982.
Huntington, P. Samuel. *The Clash of Civilization and the Remaking of World Order*. New York: Simon and Schuster, 2003.
Hurmuzlu, Cagri. "Detained Eritrean Deserters Leave Yemen for a New Life in Sweden." June 1, 2011. *UNHCR*: The UN Refugee Agency.
Ighobor, Kingsley. "China in the heart of Africa." *Africa Renewal*, January 2013, p. 6.

Isichei, Elizabeth. *A History of Christianity in Africa*. Grand Rapids: Eerdmans, 1995.
Jackson, G. John. *Introduction to African Civilization*. New York: Citadel, 2001.
Jenkins, Philip. *The Next Christendom: The Coming of Global Christianity*. Oxford: Oxford University Press, 2002.
Jiang, Wenran. "China's Emerging Partnership in Africa." In *China into Africa: Trade, Aid, and Influence*, edited by Robert I. Rotberg, 50–64. Washington, DC: Brookings Institution, 2008.
Johnson, H. Douglas. *The Root Causes of Sudan's Civil Wars*. Bloomington: Indiana University Press, 2003.
Joyce, Donovan. *The Jesus Scroll*. Sydney: New American Library, 1972.
Kaiman, Jonathan. "Africa's future leaders benefit from Beijing's desire to win hearts and minds." *The Guardian*, April 29, 2013.
Kamkwamba, William, and Bryan Mealer. *The Boy Who Harnessed the Wind: Creating Currents of Electricity and Hope*. New York: HarperCollins, 2010.
Kane, J. Herbert. *A Concise History of Christian World Mission: A Panoramic View of Mission from Pentecost to the Present*. Grand Rapids: Baker, 1994.
Kanyandago, Peter. "A Biblical Reflection of Pastoral Authority in the African Churches." *Jesus in African Christianity: Experimentation and diversity in African Christology*, edited by J. N. K. Mugambi and Laurent Magessa, 112–13. Nairobi: African, 1998.
Kanza, Thomas. "Zaire's Foreign Policy." In *The Foreign Policy of African States*, edited by Olajide Aluko, 235–43. London: Hodder and Stoughton, 1977.
Karanja, William. "Corruption Scandal." *World Press Review* 50, no. 10 (2003). http://www.worldpress.org/Africa/1499.cfm (accessed September 30, 2015).
Katongole, M. Emmanuel. *The Sacrifice of Africa: A Political Theology for Africa*. Grand Rapids: Eerdmans, 2011.
———. "Violence and Social Imagination: Rethinking Religion and Politics in Africa." In *Religion Conflict and Democracy in Modern Africa: The Role of Civil Society in Political Engagement*, edited by Samuel K. Elolia, 21–50. Eugene, OR: Wipf and Stock, 2012.
Kaufman, Frederick. "The Man Who Stole the Nile: An Ethiopian Billionaire's Outrageous Land Grab." *Harper's Magazine*, July 2014, pp. 1–7.
Kebaso, George. "Raila Odinga embroiled in $26.1 Million maize scandal in Kenya." *Newstime Africa*, March, 6, 2013. http://www.newstimeafrica.com/archives/10833 (accessed Oct. 14, 2015).
Keller, Timothy. *Generous Justice*. New York: Riverhead, 2010.
Kelley, J. N. D. *Early Christian Doctrine*. New York: Harper & Row, 1978.
Kemp, Barry J. *Ancient Egypt: Anatomy of a Civilization*. London: Routledge, 2006.
"Kenya and the International Court: In a Tangle." *The Economist*, October, 19, 2013, p. 54.
"Kenya: Trotting ahead." *The Economist*. March 15, 2014, p. 45.
Koestenbaum, Peter. *Leadership: The Inner Side of Greatness*. San Francisco: Jossey-Bass, 1991.
Konzett, Melanie. "The McMahon Act and Its Effects on Britain's Decision for an Independent Atomic Programme." Paper for "English Literature with History" course, Westminster University, London, 2007. http://www.literra.net/file_download/55/atomicbombpolicy_essay_melanie+konzett.pdf (accessed Oct. 14, 2015).
Krailshemer, A. J. *Pensées*. London: Penguin, 1995.
Kraybill, B. Donald. *The Upside-Down Kingdom*. Harrisonburg, VA: Herald, 2011.
Kritizinger and W. Saayman. *David J. Bosch: Prophetic Integrity, Cruciform Praxis*. Dorpspruit, South Africa: Cluster, 2011.
Krugman, Paul. "CONQUEST IS FOR LOSERS: Putin, Neocons and the Great Illusion." *The New York Times*, Dec. 21, 2004.
Krushelnycky, Askold. "Ukraine: Famine—Survivors Recall The Horrors Of 1933 (Part 2)." *Radio Free Europe*, Wednesday, May 8, 2003.
Küng, Hans. *Christianity and World Religions*. Maryknoll, NY: Orbis, 1993.
———. *The Church*. Colorado Springs: Image, 1976.
———. *Does God Exist?* London: Collins, 1980.
———. *On Being a Christian*. Translated by Edward Quinn. New York: Image, 1968.
Kuo, Lily. "China Promises Africa $1 Trillion in Financing, But the True Sum May Never Be Known." *Quartz*, November 19, 2013.
Ladd, Eldon George. *The Gospel of the Kingdom*. Grand Rapids: Eerdmans, 1959.

---. *The Presence of the Future: The Eschatology of Biblical Realism*. Grand Rapids: Eerdmans, 1974.
Lamb, David. *The Africans*. New York: Random House, 1987.
Lawrence, D. H. *Love among the Haystacks and Other Stories*. New York: Penguin, 1960.
"Leader—Invictus: The Greatness of Nelson Mandela Challenges Everybody—But Especially His Heirs." *The Economist*, December 14, 2013, p. 15.
Lee, Henry, and Dan Shalmon. "Searching for Oil in Africa: China's Oil Strategies in Africa." In *China into Africa: Trade, Aid, and Influence*, edited by Robert I. Rotberg, 109–36. Washington, DC: Brookings Institution, 2008.
Levine, John M., and Michael Hogg. "Personality Theories of Leadership." In *Encyclopedia of Group Process and Intergroup Relations*, edited by John M. Levine and Michael A. Hogg, 639–43. Thousand Oaks, CA: Sage, 2001.
Lewis, B. *Race and Slavery in the Middle East*. New York: Oxford University Press, 1990.
Lewis, Oscar. "The Culture of Poverty." *Scientific American* 215, no. 4 (1966) 19–25.
Lewis, Philippa. "Corruption in Africa: It Takes Two to Tango." *Think Africa Press*, March 1, 2013.
"Liberia: Skin-deep success." *The Economist*, September, 7, 2013, p. 50.
Masters, Kim. "Based on True Events: What Exactly Is "True" about the Last King of Scotland?" HOLLYWOODLAND, Jan. 31, 2007.
Mathewson, L. Dave. "The Devil: Murderer, Liar, and Defeated Foe." *Character Studies in the Fourth Gospel: Narrative Approaches to Seventy Figures in John*, edited by Steven A. Hunt, D. Francois Tolmie, and Ruben Zimmerman, 421–27. Tübingen: Mohr/Siebeck, 2013.
Mazamisa, L. W. *Beatific Comradeship: An Exegetical-Hermeneutical Study on Lk 10:25–37*. Kampen, Netherlands: Kok, 1987.
Mazrui, Ali. *The African Condition*. Cambridge: Cambridge University Press, 1990.
---. *The Africans: A Triple Heritage*. Boston: Little, Brown, 1986.
Mbiti, S. John. *African Philosophy of Religion*. New York: Pager, 1969.
Mead, Margaret, and Martha Wolfenstein, eds. *Childhood in Contemporary Cultures*. Chicago: University of Chicago Press, 1967.
Mekonnen, Alemayehu. *Culture Change in Ethiopia: An Evangelical Perspective*. Oxford: Regnum, 2013.
Meredith, Martin. *The Fate of Africa: From the Hope of Freedom to the Heart of Despair*. New York: Public Affairs, 2005.
Mezayev, Alexander. "Central African Republic: Another Western Backed Coup d'état." *Global Research*, April 5, 2013.
Mintz, W. Sidney. *Sweetness and Power: The Place of Sugar in Modern History*. New York: Penguin, 1985.
Mitscherlich, Alexander. *A Society without the Father: A Contribution to Social Psychology*. New York: Harper Perennial, 1992.
Moltmann, Jürgen. *The Crucified God*. Translated by R. A. Wilson and John Bowden. Minneapolis: Fortress, 1974.
---. *The Church in the Power of the Spirit*. Minneapolis: Fortress, 1977.
---. *God in Creation*. Translated by Margaret Kohl. Minneapolis: Fortress, 1985.
---. *Jesus Christ for Today's World*. Minneapolis: Fortress, 1994.
---. *The Source of Life: The Holy Spirit and the Theology of Life*. London: SCM, 1997.
---. *Sun of Righteousness Arise!: God's Future for Humanity and the Earth*. Minneapolis: Fortress, 2010.
---. *Theology of Hope: On the Ground and the Implications of Christian Theology*. Munich: SCM, 2002.
---. *The Way of Jesus: Christology in Messianic Dimension*. Minneapolis: Fortress, 1990.
Morley, Robert. "South Africa: Where Corruption, Rape and Murder Are Normal." *The Trumpet*, December 2013.
Moyo, Dambisa. "Beijing, a Boon for Africa." *The New York Times*, June 27, 2012.
---. *Dead Aid*. New York: Farrar, Straus and Giroux, 2009.
---. *Winner Take All*. New York: Basic, 2012.
Msoka, A. Gabriel. *Basic Human Rights and the Humanitarian Crises in Sub-Saharan Africa*. Eugene, OR: Pickwick, 2007.
Mukasa, Alli D., et al. "Development of Wind Energy in Africa." *African Development Bank Group*, 2013. Typescript report.

Munene, Macharia. *The Truman Administration and the Decolonization of Sub-Saharan Africa*. Nairobi: Nairobi University Press, 1995.

Mutiga, Murithi. "Africa and the Chinese Way." *The New York Times*, December 15, 2013.

Ndikumana, Lèonce, and K. James Boyce. *Africa's Odious Debts: How African Loans and Capital Flight Bled a Continent*. London: Zed, 2011.

Neill, Stephen. *A History of Christian Missions*. Harmondsworth, UK: Penguin, 1980.

Newbigin, Lesslie. *The Open Secret: An Introduction to the Theology of Mission*. Grand Rapids: Eerdmans, 1995.

Njeza, Malinge. "Fallacies of the New Afrocentrisim." *Journal of Theology for Southern Africa* 99 (1997) 47–57.

Noll, A. Mark. *The New Shape of World Christianity: How American Experience Reflects Global Faith*. Downers Grove, IL: InterVarsity, 2009.

Obama, Barack. *Dreams from My Father*. New York: Three Rivers, 2004.

O'Connor, Kathleen. "The Mystery of Meaning." *Theological Education* 46, no. 1 (2010) 55–66.

Oden, C. Thomas, *The African Memory of Mark: Reassessing Early Church Tradition*. Downers Grove, IL: InterVarsity, 2011.

———. *How Africa Shaped the Christian Mind: Rediscovering the African Seedbed of Western Christianity*. Downers Grove, IL: IVP, 2007.

Orji, Cyril. "Religion, Violence, and Conflict: Ujamaa-therapy as the Dynamic Response to Ethnic Particularities in Africa." In *Religion Conflict and Democracy in Modern Africa: The Role of Civil Society in Political Engagement*, edited by Samuel K. Elolia, 101–30. Eugene, OR: Wipf and Stock, 2012.

Ortiz, Fernando. *Cuban Counterpart*. New York: Knopf, 1947.

Osman, Tarek. *Egypt on the Brink: From Nasser to Mubarak*. New Haven: Yale University Press, 2010.

O'Sullivan, John. "Digging Deeper: Some of the World's Fastest-Growing Economies in 2014 Will Be in Africa." *The Economist*, 2014, p. 73. (This edition has no month).

Padilla, C. Renne. "Evangelism and the World," In *Let the Earth Hear His Voice*, edited by J. D. Douglas, 116–46. Minneapolis: World Wide, 1975.

Pakenham, Thomas. *The Scramble for Africa: White Man's Conquest of the Dark Continent from 1876 to 1912*. New York: HarperCollins, 1991.

"Palm Oil in West Africa: Grow but Cherish Your Environment." *The Economist*, August 16, 2014, p. 38.

Pargeter, Alison. *The Rise and Fall of Qaddafi*. Padstow, UK: TJ, 2012.

"Pentecostalism in Africa: Of prophets and profits." *The Economist*, October 4, 2014, p. 58.

Perkins, John. *The Secret History of the American Empire*. New York: Dutton, 2007.

Perrin, Norman. "Jesus and the Language of the Kingdom." In *The Kingdom of God*, edited by Bruce Chilton, 92–106. Philadelphia: Fortress, 1984.

Peterson, T. V. *Ham and Japheth: The Mythic World of Whites in the Antebellum South*. Metuchen: Scarecrow, 1978.

Philips, Kevin. *America's Theocracy: The Peril and Politics of Radical Religion, Oil, and Borrowed Money in the 21st Century*. New York: Viking, 2006.

Pilger, John. "More than Jihadism or Iran, China's Role in Africa Is Obama's Obsession." *The Guardian*, October 9, 2013.

Pitts, Leonard, Jr. "Let's Talk about Black-on-black Violence." *Miami Herald*, Nov. 29, 2014.

Polgreen, Lydia, Howard W. French. "New Power in Africa: China's Trade in Africa Carries a Price Tag." *The New York Times*, August 21, 2007.

Polstlethwayt, Malchy. *The African Trade, the Great Pillar and Support of the British Plantation Trade in North America*. Charleston, SC: BiblioBazaar, 2012.

Rahner, Karl. *The Trinity*. London: Ebbow Vales, 1997.

Rapley, John. *Underdevelopment: Theory and Practice in the Third World*. 3rd ed. Boulder, CO: Reinner, 2007.

Ravenhill, Leonard. *Why Revival Tarries*. Minneapolis: Bethany House, 1987.

Rice, Xan. "China's Economic Invasion of Africa." *The Guardian*, February 6, 2011.

Ridderbos, Herman. *Paul: An Outline of His Theology*. Grand Rapids: Eerdmans, 1975.

"A Rising Tide of Misery." *The Economist*, June 28th, 2014, p. 42.

Bibliography

Roberts, Janine. *Glitter and Greed: The Secret World of the Diamond Cartel.* New York: Disinformation, 2007.

Robinson, B. A. "Christian Apology for the Crusades: The Reconciliation Walk." Ontario Consultants on Religious Tolerance, Nov. 4, 2005, http://www.religioustolerance.org/chr_cru1.htm.

Rodney, Walter. *How Europe Underdeveloped Africa.* Washington, DC: Howard University Press, 2012.

Rotberg, Robert I., ed. "China's Quest." In *China into Africa: Trade, Aid, and Influence,* edited by Robert I. Rotberg, 1–20. Washington, DC: Brookings Institution, 2008.

Rupp, Stephanie. "Africa and China: Engaging Postcolonial Interdependencies." In *China into Africa: Trade, Aid, and Influence,* edited by Robert I. Rotberg, 65-86. Washington, DC: Brookings Institution, 2008.

Sanders, E. R. "The Hamitic Hypothesis: Its Origin and Functions in Time Perspective." *Journal of African History* 10 (1969) 521.

Sanneh, Lamin. *Disciples of All Nations: Pillars of World Christianity.* Oxford: Oxford University Press, 2008.

———. *Summoned from the Margin: Homecoming of an African.* Grand Rapids: Eerdmans, 2012.

———. *Whose Religion Is Christianity? The Gospel beyond the West.* Grand Rapids: Eerdmans, 2003.

Sasson, Jack M., ed. *Civilization of the Ancient Near East.* Vols. 1 and 2. Peabody, MA: Hendrickson, 1995.

Saunders, J. Trevor, trans. *Plato: The Laws.* New York: Penguin, 1980.

Schnabel, Eckhard J. *Early Christian Mission,* Vol. 1. Downers Groves, IL: InterVarsity, 1989.

Schonfield, Hugh. *The Passover Plot.* New York: Panarm, 1965.

Schraff, Anne. *Dr. Charles Drew: Blood Bank Innovator.* Berkeley Heights, NJ: Enslow, 2003.

Schreiner, R. Thomas. *Paul: Apostle of God's Glory in Christ.* Downers Grove, IL: InterVarsity, 2001.

Schwartz, Matthathias. "Letter from Lampedusa: The Africans Who Risk All to Reach Europe Look to an Exiled Priest as Their Savior." *The New Yorker,* April 21, 2014.

"Science in Africa on the Rise." *The Economist,* August 9, 2014, p. 42.

"Security in Kenya: Little Law, Less Order." *The Economist,* May 10, 2014, p. 47.

Segal, Ronald. *The Race War.* Middlesex, UK: Penguin, 1966.

Senghor, C. Jeggan. *Towards a Dynamic African Economy.* London: Cass, 1989.

Shinn, David H. "Military and Security Relations." In *China into Africa: Trade, Aid, and Influence,* edited by Robert I. Rotberg, 155-88. Washington, DC: Brookings Institution, 2008.

Smedes, B. Lewis. *Forgive and Forget: Healing the Hurt We Don't Deserve.* New York: Pocket, 1984.

Smith, Adam. *The Wealth of Nations.* Blacksburg, VA: Thrifty, 2009.

Sofsky, Wolfgang. *The Order of Terror: The Concentration Camp.* Translated by William Templer. Princeton: Princeton University Press, 1997.

"Somalia Piracy: More Sophisticated Than You Thought." *The Economist,* November, 2, 2013, p. 53.

"South Africa's Economy: Muddle through Will No Longer Do." *The Economist,* June, 1, 2013, p. 49.

"South Africa's Police: Something Very Rotten." *The Economist,* June, 23, 2013, p. 54.

Spindler, Marc. "Meaning and Prospect of Common Witness." *Verbum SVD* 28 (1987) 18-28.

Stafford, Tim. "Costly Love, Radical Forgiveness: What Made African Bishop Festo Kivengere Rejoice in the Face of Monstrous Evil?" *Christianity Today,* April 1, 2007.

Stearns, K. Jason. *Dancing in the Glory of Monsters: The Collapse of the Congo and the Great War of Africa.* New York: Public Affairs, 2012.

Stinton, B. Diane. *Jesus of Africa: Voices of Contemporary African Christology.* Maryknoll, NY: Orbis, 2004.

Stott, John. *The Cross of Christ.* Downers Grove, IL: InterVarsity, 1986.

———. *The Message of Romans.* Downers Grove, IL: InterVarsity, 2003.

"Swaziland's Election: Royal Revelation." *The Economist,* September, 14, 2013, p. 57.

Swindoll, R. Charles. *Improving Your Serve.* Waco: Word, 1981.

Tamrat, Taddesse. *Church and State in Ethiopia 1270-1527.* Oxford: Clarendon, 1972.

Tawney, R. H. *Religion and The Rise of Capitalism.* London: Transaction, 2008.

Taylor, V. John. *The Primal Vision: Christian Presence amid African Religion.* Londong: SCM, 1994.

Tchouteu-Chando, Janvier, and Janvier Cahndo. *Paul Biya Of Cameroon: Three-plus Decades of Misrule under an Anachronistic System.* New York: Tisi, 2014.

Tennent, Timothy C. *Invitation to World Missions: A Trinitarian Missiology for the Twenty-First Century.* Grand Rapids: Kregel, 2010.

Tenney, C. Merrill. *New Testament Survey.* Grand Rapids: Eerdmans, 1978.

Tesema, Teshome. "Tackling Deforestation in Ethiopia through Institutional and Policy Means." Excerpt from a PhD dissertation to be presented at the Alumni conference to be held from April 22–23, 2009, at Bahirdar, Ethiopia.
Thomas, G. P. "Guinea-Bissau: Mining, Minerals and Fuel Resources." *The A to Z of Mining*. Dec. 12, 2013.
Thornton, John. *Africa and Africans in the Making of the Atlantic World, 1400–1800*. New York: Cambridge University Press, 1998.
Thurman, Howard. *Jesus and the Disinherited*. Boston, MA: Beacon, 1996.
"Towards the End of Poverty." *The Economist*, June 1, 2013, p. 11.
"Trafficking in North Africa: Boom." *The Economist*, August 17, 2013, p. 42.
Treat, R. Jeremy. *The Crucified King: Atonement and Kingdom in Biblical and Systematic Theology*. Grand Rapids: Zondervan, 2014.
Twesigye, Emmanuel K. "Church and State Conflicts in Uganda." In *Religion Conflict and Democracy in Modern Africa: The Role of Civil Society in Political Engagement*, edited by Samuel K. Elolia, 148–96. Eugene, OR: Wipf and Stock, 2012.
"Uganda and Its President: A Leader Who Cannot Bear to Retire." *The Economist*, October, 12, 2013, p. 59.
Valentine, Charles A. *Culture and Poverty*. Chicago: University of Chicago Press, 1969.
Velarde, Robert. "Greatness and Wretchedness: The Usefulness of Pascal's Anthropological Argument in Apologetics." *Christian Research Journal* 27, no. 2 (2004) 32–40..
Vidal, John. "Solar Power to the People: Green Energy Could Boost African Development." *The Guardian*, April, 30, 2014.
Vidrovitch, Coquery Catherine. *Africa: Endurance and Change South of the Sahara*. Berkley: University of California Press, 1988.
Waliggo, M. John. "African Christology in a Situation of Suffering." In *Jesus in African Christology: Experimentation and Diversity in African Christology*, edited by J. N. K. Mugabi and Laurenti Magesa, 93–111. Nairobi: Action, 1998.
Walker, Robin. *Blacks and Science*. Vol. 2, *West and East African Contribution to Science and Technology and Intellectual Life and Legacy of Timbuktu*. London: Reklaw, 2013.
Walls, F. Andrew. *The Cross-Cultural Process in Christian History*. New York: Orbis, 2007.
———. *The Missionary Movement in Christian History*. New York: Orbis, 2002.
Wariboko, Nimi. *The Depth and Destiny of Work: An African Theological Interpretation*. Trenton, NJ: Africa World, 2008.
Weber, Max. *The Protestant Ethic and the Spirit of Capitalism*. New York: Scribner's Sons, 1958.
Wessels, Anton. *Europe: Was it Really Christian?* London: SCM, 2012.
Wickins, Peter. *An Economic History of East Africa*. Oxford: Oxford University Press, 1981.
Williams, Chancellor. *The Destruction of Civilization: Great Issues of a Race From 4500 B.C. to 2000 A.D.* Chicago: Third World,1987.
Williams, Eric. *Capitalism and Slavery*. Chapel Hill: University of North Carolina Press, 1994.
Witte, Ludo de. *The Assassination of Lumumba*. London: Verso, 2002.
Wolterstorff, Nicholas. *Journey toward Justice: Personal Encounters in the Global South*. Turning South. Grand Rapids: Baker Academic, 2013.
———. *Justice: Rights and Wrongs*. Princeton: Princeton University Press, 2008.
Wood, William. *A Survey of Trade*. Part III, p. 193. London: 1718.
Woodson, L. Robert, Sr. *The Triumphs of Joseph: How Today's Community Healers Are Reviving Our Streets and Neighbors*. New York: Free, 1998.
Wordsworth, William. *William Wordsworth's Convention of Cintra: A Facsimile of the 1809 Tract*. Provo, UT: Brigham Young University Press, 1983.
"Worse and Worse." *The Economist*, March 29, 2014, p. 49.
Wright, J. H. Christopher. "Christ and the Mosaic Pluralism." In *Global Missiology for the 21st Century*, edited by William D. Taylor, 71–99. Grand Rapids: Baker Academic, 2000.
———. *Old Testament Ethics for the People of God*. Downers Grove, IL: InterVarsity, 2005.
Wright, N. T. *Jesus and the Victory of God*. Vol. 2 of *Christian Origins and the Question of God*. Minneapolis: Fortress, 1996.
Wrong, Michela. *It's Our Time to Eat: The Story of a Kenyan Whistle Blower*. New York: HarperCollins Xun, 2009.

Yamauchi, Edwin M. *Africa and the Bible*. Grand Rapids: Baker Academics, 2004.
Yancey, Philip. *The Jesus I Never Knew*. Grand Rapids: Zondervan, 1995.
Yates, Timothy, ed. *Mission: An Invitation to God's Future*. Sheffield, UK: Cliff College, 2000.
Yergin, Daniel. *The Quest: Energy, Security, and the Remaking of the Modern World*. New York: Penguin, 2011.
Yurco, F. J. "Were the Ancient Egyptian Black or White?" *Biblical Archaeology Review* 15, no. 5 (1989) 24–31.
Zacharias, Ravi. *The Grand Weaver: How God Shapes Us through the Events of Our Lives*. Grand Rapids: Zondervan, 2007.
Zhou, Ed. *The Great Famine in China, 1958–1962*. New Haven: Yale University Press, 2012.

www.ingramcontent.com/pod-product-compliance
Lightning Source LLC
Chambersburg PA
CBHW081146290426
44108CB00018B/2458